CISCO IOS
IN A NUTSHELL

*A Desktop Quick Reference
for IOS on IP Networks*

WITHDRAWN

CISCO IOS
IN A NUTSHELL

A Desktop Quick Reference
for IOS on IP Networks

James Boney

O'REILLY®

Beijing • Cambridge • Farnham • Köln • Paris • Sebastopol • Taipei • Tokyo

Cisco IOS in a Nutshell

by James Boney

Copyright © 2002 O'Reilly & Associates, Inc. All rights reserved.
Printed in the United States of America.

Published by O'Reilly & Associates, Inc., 1005 Gravenstein Highway North,
Sebastopol, CA 95472.

O'Reilly & Associates books may be purchased for educational, business,
or sales promotional use. Online editions are also available for most titles
(*safari.oreilly.com*). For more information contact our corporate/institutional
sales department: 800-998-9938 or *corporate@oreilly.com*.

Editor: Mike Loukides

Production Editor: Emily Quill

Cover Designer: Hanna Dyer

Interior Designer: Melanie Wang

Printing History:

January 2002: First Edition.

ISBN: 1-56592-942-x

[M]

[3/02]

Table of Contents

Preface

This is a book for everybody who has to deal with Cisco's routers.

As you well know, Cisco Systems has created an extremely diverse line of routers and other network products. One unifying thread runs through the product line: virtually all of Cisco's products run the *Internetwork Operating System* (IOS). This is both a great advantage and a great disadvantage. On the one hand, when you're familiar with one Cisco router, you're reasonably familiar with them all. Someone using a small ISDN router in a home office could look at a configuration file for a high-end router at an ISP and not be lost. He might not understand how to configure the more esoteric routing protocols or high-speed network interfaces, but he'd be looking at a language that was recognizably the same.

On the other hand, this uniformity means that just about everything has been crammed into IOS at one time or another. IOS is massive—there's no other way to say it. And it has evolved over many years. The command-line interface isn't graceful, and is often non-uniform: many commands don't do what you think they should, and the same command verbs can mean completely different things in different contexts. This inconsistency is probably a natural result of evolution at an extremely large company with an extremely large number of developers, but it doesn't make life any easier.

So, where do you find out what commands you need to know? There's the almost mythical "green wall" of Cisco documentation, but it's difficult to find what you need in tens of thousands of pages. Of course, even getting to Cisco's online documentation may be impossible if your router doesn't work. And the volume of documentation is imposing. A search for `ip cef traffic-statistics`—not one of the more frequently used commands—yields 163 hits. How do you get to the right one? Beats me. That's why I wrote this book.

This book is primarily a quick reference to the commands that are most frequently needed to configure Cisco routers for standard IP routing tasks. There are plenty of weasel words in there, and they're needed. This is far from a complete quick ref to all of IOS—such a quick ref would probably be well over 2000 pages long, clearly too long to be useful. Therefore, I haven't attempted to cover protocols other than IP (although there is support for everything from AppleTalk to SNA), nor any of the more exotic creatures in the IP space. And even in areas I have covered thoroughly, I was still forced to exclude commands that are useful only in limited cases.

Above all, this is a network administrator's book: it represents practical experience with IP routing on Cisco routers and covers the commands that you're likely to need. No doubt some readers will disagree with the choices I've made—such disagreement is inevitable. But though you occasionally won't find information about a command you need to use, you will far more often find precisely what you need to know at your fingertips.

More than anything else, the goal of this book is to give you information quickly. It aspires not to give you in-depth knowledge of how IP routing works, but to help you remember what arguments you need to give to the snmp-server enable traps command, or to help you scan through the many commands that start with ip to jog your memory about which one configures the forwarding of broadcast packets to selected subnets. If I succeed in doing that, I'm happy.

Organization

This book consists primarily of two parts. The first could be considered a tutorial, but that doesn't quite capture its purpose. I try to teach the basic principles behind configuring the router, but there are many other sources for that information: for example, Scott Ballew's *Managing IP Networks with Cisco Routers*, or Jeff Sedayao's *Cisco IOS Access Lists*, both from O'Reilly. This part of the book breezes quickly through as many examples of different configuration tasks as possible. I provide explanations, but the focus is on the examples. By studying them, you'll see how to accomplish many of the tasks involved in setting up a router.

The bulk of the book is the quick reference. There's nothing fancy here—it's organized alphabetically, and shows the commands that I felt were most useful to someone using a Cisco router in an IP environment.

Conventions

The following conventions are used in this book:

Italic
> Used for filenames and URLs

Constant width
> Used for commands, command keywords, and anything else that has to be typed literally

Constant width italic
> Used for parameters or arguments that must be substituted into commands

Constant width bold
> Used for user input in code

[Keywords and other stuff]
    Used for optional keywords and arguments

{ choice-1 | choice-2 }
    Used to signify either choice-1 or choice-2

    This icon signifies a tip relating to the nearby text.

    This icon signifies a warning relating to the nearby text.

One of the confusing things about working with a Cisco router is the notion of a *command context*. Most commands are legal only in limited situations; all of the quick-reference entries include a command context that indicates how the command is to be used. A context of "command" means that the command is for interactive use and is not entered into the router's configuration; you do not need to enter the configuration mode (configure terminal) to give the command, and you can't include it in a configuration file that you upload. A context of "global" indicates that a command doesn't require any specific context; you can give it as soon as you've entered the configuration mode. A context of "interface" indicates that you must be in the interface configuration submode to give the command; "line" means that you must be in the line configuration submode, and so on.

IOS has no concept of a continuation character for breaking up command lines that are too long. That may be okay for a router, but it's a problem for a book; still, I've decided not to invent a continuation character for the purposes of this book. I've split long commands across lines as it seemed most convenient and clear; just remember that you have to type it all on one line.

We'd Like to Hear from You

Please address comments and questions concerning this book to the publisher:

O'Reilly & Associates, Inc.
1005 Gravenstein Highway North
Sebastopol, CA 95472
(800) 998-9938 (in the United States or Canada)
(707) 829-0515 (international or local)
(707) 829-0104 (fax)

There is a web page for this book, which lists errata and any additional information. You can access this page at:

http://www.oreilly.com/catalog/cisiosnut/

To comment or ask technical questions about this book, send email to:

bookquestions@oreilly.com

For more information about books, conferences, Resource Centers, and the O'Reilly Network, see the O'Reilly web site at:

http://www.oreilly.com

Acknowledgments

This book was a long time in the making. I'd like to thank my editor, Mike Loukides, for giving me the opportunity to write it and for believing that I could bring it to completion. I'd also like to thank my wife, Peggy. Not only did she give me moral support, but she had to listen to me say countless times, "I have to work on the book."

I also want to thank my technical reviewers, who provided invaluable feedback: Terry Slattery, Scott Ballew, Kevin Kelleher, Kennedy Clark, Val Pavlichenko, and Duke Meesuk. Scott provided particularly valuable suggestions on the overall structure of the book, and very detailed suggestions for the quick-reference section.

CHAPTER 1

Getting Started

Introduction

The modern world is networked in a way that could barely be imagined a few decades ago. Today, the Internet reaches into virtually every business and almost every home. Our children and even our grandparents speak of dot-coms, email, and web sites. The Internet is now part of our culture.

Routers are the glue that holds the Internet together. And Cisco is the most prominent router manufacturer, holding the largest share of the market. Their routers come in all sizes, from inexpensive units for homes and small offices to equipment costing well over $100,000 and capable of routing at gigabit speeds. One of the most impressive facts about their product line is its unified operating system. Almost all of their routers, as well as half of their switches—from the smallest to the largest—run the *Internetwork Operating System* (IOS). Therefore, they share the same command set, the same user interface, and the same configuration techniques. While an 800-series home router doesn't have the features or the capacity of a 7500-series router that might be used to connect an ISP to an Internet backbone, you configure them the same way. Both routers use access lists, have similar security mechanisms, support the same set of protocols in the same way, and so on. A home router probably wouldn't have a Frame Relay interface, but if it did, it would be configured just like a Frame Relay interface on a mid-sized corporate router.

IOS is an extremely powerful and complex operating system with an equally complex configuration language. There are many commands, with many options, and if you get something wrong you can easily take your company offline. That's why I've decided to provide a quick-reference guide to IOS. As large a book as this is, though, it's impossible to cover all of IOS. Therefore, I've limited the discussion to IOS configuration for the TCP/IP protocol family. I've included all the commands that you need to work with TCP/IP and the lower-level protocols on which it relies. The trade-off is that I've made no attempt to cover other protocols that IOS supports, and there are many: IPX, AppleTalk, SNA, DecNet, and virtually any other protocol suite that is now or ever has been in widespread use.

1

This book is intended as a quick reference, not as a step-by-step exposition of routing protocols or as an IOS tutorial. I haven't focused on thorough explanation; instead, I've tried to give lots of examples of the things people most frequently need to do when configuring a Cisco router, with just enough explanation to get you by. I'll start with the user interface, then talk about configuring lines and interfaces (Chapters 4, 5, and 6), access lists (Chapter 7), routing protocols (Chapters 8, 9, and 10), and finally, dial-on-demand routing, security, and troubleshooting (Chapters 11, 12, 13, and 14). Chapter 15 is the quick reference. Chances are, by the time the second edition of this book appears, the quick-reference section will be pretty well thumbed and worn out.

At first, the Cisco user interface appears cryptic. But after learning the interface's structure, you'll become much more comfortable with it. Once you have learned some special features, you'll be able to work with the router's configuration easily.

IOS User Modes

There are two primary modes of operation within the IOS: user mode and privileged mode. When you first connect to the router, you are placed in the *user mode*. The Cisco documentation refers to this as the *user exec mode*; I am going to omit "exec" throughout this book. The user mode is indicated by the prompt:

```
Router>
```

 The word "Router" is replaced with your router's hostname if the hostname is already configured.

The show commands in user mode are limited to a few basic levels. You cannot edit or view configurations at this stage; you can only view the router status and other miscellaneous information. To obtain a basic listing of commands, type a question mark:

```
Router>?
```

Editing the router's configuration requires you to be in the *privileged exec mode*, which I simply call "privileged mode." Use the enable command to enter this mode:

```
Router>enable
Password:
Router#          Privileged mode prompt
```

You can always tell whether you are in user mode or privileged mode by looking at the prompt. The user mode prompt has a > at the end; the privileged mode prompt always has a # at the end, regardless of the submode.

If you are familiar with Unix, you can equate privileged mode to "root" access. You could also equate it to the administrator level in NT or the supervisor in NetWare. In this mode, you have permission to access everything inside the router, including configuration commands. However, you can't type configuration commands directly. Before you can change the router's actual configuration, you must enter a submode of the privileged mode by giving the command `configure terminal` (see the following section, "Command-Line Completion," for a shortcut). This command can be entered only when you are in the privileged mode.

```
Router#configure terminal
```
Enter configuration commands, one per line. End with Ctrl-Z
```
Router(config)#          Configuration mode
```

To exit from configuration mode, you can use the command `exit` or type Ctrl-Z. To exit from enable (privileged) mode, you can use the `disable` command. So to exit both configuration and enable mode, use the following sequence of commands:

```
Router(config)#exit
Router#disable
Router>
```

Privileged mode has several submodes in addition to configuration mode; each has its own prompt. To enter these submodes, you must first enter configuration mode by giving the `configure terminal` command. Here's a summary of the most common modes and prompts (there are many others):

Global configuration mode
Prompt: `Router(config)#`

This level allows you to enter commands directly into the router configuration. From this level, you can enter any of the other three levels listed here. Once you are done entering commands into the configuration, use Ctrl-Z, `exit`, or the `end` command to return to the privileged prompt. The device's hostname is a good example of a configuration item you would find in the global configuration mode.

Interface configuration mode
Prompt: `Router(config-if)#`

At this level, you are entering interface-specific commands. To enter this mode from the configuration prompt, use the command `interface` followed by an interface name, such as `ethernet0`, `serial0`, or `serial1`. Interface commands are discussed in Chapter 5. Use the `exit` command to exit from this prompt and return to the configuration prompt.

Line configuration mode
Prompt: `Router(config-line)#`

From this prompt, you can enter line-specific commands. To enter this mode from the configuration prompt, use the command `line`, followed by a line type—such as `vty`, `console`, `tty`, or `async`—and a line number. The line configuration commands are discussed in Chapter 4. Once again, use the `exit` command to exit this mode and return to the configuration prompt.

Router configuration mode
Prompt: `Router(config-router)#`

From this prompt, you can enter only routing commands. To enter this mode from the configuration prompt, use the command `router`, followed by a routing protocol, such as `rip` or `igrp`. These commands differ widely depending on the routing protocol being used. Routing configuration commands are discussed in Chapters 8 through 10. Use the exit command to exit this mode and return to the configuration prompt.

Figure 1-1 is a flow chart that illustrates the transitions between the most common command modes and submodes. (This list is not comprehensive.) The arrows are labeled with the commands that cause the transitions between the modes.

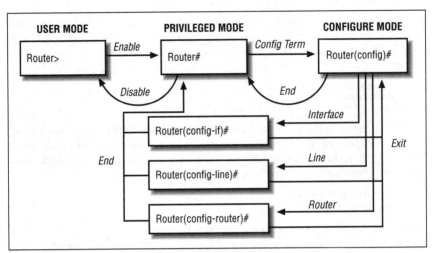

Figure 1-1: Transitions between IOS command modes

Configuration submodes provide a *context* in which certain commands are legal and others disallowed. It's one way that IOS tries to prevent you from making mistakes when configuring a router. In the quick-reference section, I list each command with the context (or mode) in which it can be given. Contexts are clearly important on the command line, where the prompt shows the submode you're in. They are equally important in configuration files, where there are no such hints; you just have to know.

Command-Line Completion

Command-line completion makes the IOS interface much more user-friendly. It saves you extra typing and helps out when you cannot remember a command's syntax. In a previous example, we used the command configure terminal:

Router#**configure terminal**

But you could have saved wear and tear on your hands by typing:

Router#**conf t**

IOS expands the command conf t to configure terminal. Another shortcut is to press Tab after typing "conf"; the router will fill in the best completion, which is "configure". Here is another example:

Router#**show running-config**

This long command can be shortened to:

Router#**sh ru**

The router knows that "show" is what you wanted because show is the only command that begins with "sh"; likewise, the only subcommand of show that begins with "ru" is running-config.

If the router does not understand a command, it repeats the entire command line and places a caret (^) under the point at which it ran into trouble. For example:

```
Router>show itnerface e0
>show itnerface e0
       ^
% Invalid input detected at '^' marker.
```

The caret symbol is pointing to the "t" in "itnerface", which is the command the router does not understand. We can quickly fix that by retyping the command:

```
Router>show interface e0
```

We now get the correct output! Since we also know how to use shortcuts, we can type:

```
Router>sh int e0
```

With this command we get the same result as its lengthy counterpart. Command-line completion saves a lot of typing, and it helps you keep your sanity when you're working with long commands.

Another form of command-line completion is the use of the Tab key. If you start a command by entering the first few characters, you can hit the Tab key. As long as there is only one match, the router will complete the command: for example, if you type "sh" and hit Tab, the router completes the "sh" with "show". If the router does not complete the command, you can enter a few more letters and try again.

Get to Know the Question Mark

Previously, I said that you can get the available commands by typing ? at the prompt. You can also use this trick to find the subcommands of any command. For example, if you know you want to use the copy command but cannot remember which subcommand you need, type:

```
Router#copy ?
  WORD            Copy from flash device - format <dev:>[partition:][filename]
  flash           Copy from system flash
  flh-log         Copy FLH log file to server
  mop             Copy from a MOP server
  rcp             Copy from an rcp server
  running-config  Copy from current system configuration
  startup-config  Copy from startup configuration
  tftp            Copy from a TFTP server
```

Another use of the question mark is to find all commands that match what you have typed so far. For example, if you know the first part of a command, type it and then type a question mark. The router will return a list of all the matching commands. In the following example, we remember that the configure command begins with "co", but that's it. The router gives us the matching commands:

```
Router#co?
configure  connect  copy
```

Note the important difference between these two examples. In the first example, there was a space before the question mark, which gave us the next command that complements copy. Had there not been a space, the router would have tried to complete the word "copy" for us, not given us the next available commands. In the next example, we did not add the space, so the router tried to complete "co" with all the commands it could find that start with "co".

Another important rule to understand is that the router will return only commands that are relevant to the mode you are currently in. For example, if you are in user mode, you will be given only commands that apply to that mode.

Command-Line Editing Keys

IOS provides a number of keyboard shortcuts that let you edit the line you're typing. They should be familiar to any user of Unix or Emacs. Table 1-1 lists the command-line editing keys.

Table 1-1: Command-line editing keys

Keys	Commands
Ctrl-a	Returns the cursor to the beginning of the current line.
Ctrl-b	Moves the cursor back one character. (Equivalent to the left arrow key.)
Ctrl-d	Deletes the character to the left of the cursor.
Ctrl-e	Moves the cursor to the end of the line.
Ctrl-f	Moves the cursor forward one character. (Equivalent to the right arrow key.)
Ctrl-k	Deletes all the characters from the current cursor position to the end of the line.
Ctrl-n	Goes to the next command in the session history. (Equivalent to the down arrow key.)
Ctrl-p	Goes to the previous command in the session history. (Equivalent to the up arrow key.)
Ctrl-t	Switches the current character with the character to the left of the cursor.
Ctrl-r	Redraws or redisplays the current line.
Ctrl-u	Clears the line.
Ctrl-w	Deletes the word to the left of the cursor.
Ctrl-x	Deletes from the cursor position to the beginning of the line.
Ctrl-y	Pastes the most recently deleted characters to the current cursor position.
Ctrl-z	Exits the current configuration mode and returns to the previous configuration mode.
Tab	Tries to finish the current command. (Command completion.)
Up arrow	Moves back through the history of commands.
Down arrow	Moves forward through the history of commands.
Left arrow	Moves the cursor to the left.
Right arrow	Moves the cursor to the right.
Ctrl-^, then x	Aborts the sequence. Breaks out of any executing command.

Pausing Output

Using the terminal command, you can set an important feature of the user interface: the pausing of lengthy output. For example, if you run a command that has more than one page of output, the router will pause after 24 lines with a "—More—" prompt. The value 24 is the default terminal length. Depending on the size of your terminal window, this might not be adequate. You can change the length and width using the terminal command, like this:

```
Router>terminal length 10
Router>terminal width 80
```

These commands set the terminal length to 10 and the width to 80, which means the router will pause after 10 lines of output and that each of these lines will be 80 characters long. You can disable the pausing altogether by setting the terminal length to 0:

```
Router>terminal length 0
```

show Commands

As you work with IOS, you'll become intimately familiar with the show commands. They are among the most useful commands you will ever use; they allow you to view just about any settings within the router. Issuing the command show ? produces output like this:

```
Router>show ?
  clock     Display the system clock
  history   Display the session command history
  hosts     IP domain-name, lookup style, nameservers, and host table
  sessions  Information about Telnet connections
  snmp      snmp statistics
  terminal  Display terminal configuration parameters
  users     Display information about terminal lines
  version   System hardware and software status
```

The show command has many different subcommands. However, notice that we are in user mode. In privileged mode, the show command has a lot more subcommands, which would take up a few pages if we listed them here. The important thing to remember is that show commands often have more than one keyword. For example, the command show ip route works by itself, but there are also many other options that can be applied to it. For example:

```
router#show ip route ?
  Hostname or A.B.C.D  Network to display information about or hostname
  bgp                  Border Gateway Protocol (BGP)
  connected            Connected
  egp                  Exterior Gateway Protocol (EGP)
  eigrp                Enhanced Interior Gateway Routing Protocol (EIGRP)
  igrp                 Interior Gateway Routing Protocol (IGRP)
  isis                 ISO IS-IS
  odr                  On Demand stub Routes
  ospf                 Open Shortest Path First (OSPF)
  rip                  Routing Information Protocol (RIP)
  static               Static routes
  summary              Summary of all routes
  supernets-only       Show supernet entries only
  <cr>
```

I certainly haven't explained routing enough for you to understand the output of this command. However, you can see how to find show keywords with the question mark. The <cr> shown in the previous example indicates that you can hit Return at this point and the command will work. In other words, show ip route is a valid command. The other keywords are optional.

In each section of this book, I emphasize the appropriate show commands for the topic. For the topics covered in this chapter, the following show commands are extremely useful:

- show version
- show history
- show users

The show version command gives a lot more information than just the version of IOS that the router is currently running. You will see this command pop up a few more times later in this book. For now, you can see that it tells us the router type, the IOS image, the system uptime, the current IOS version, all the available interfaces, and the amount of memory on the router:

```
Router#show version
Cisco Internetwork Operating System Software
IOS (tm) 2500 Software (C2500-AJS40-L), Version 11.3(5)T,  RELEASE SOFTWARE (fc1)
Copyright (c) 1986-1998 by cisco Systems, Inc.
Compiled Wed 12-Aug-98 05:53 by ccai
Image text-base: 0x0305770C, data-base: 0x00001000

ROM: System Bootstrap, Version 11.0(10c), SOFTWARE
BOOTFLASH: 3000 Bootstrap Software (IGS-BOOT-R), Version 11.0(10c),
RELEASE SOFTWARE (fc1)

Router1 uptime is 1 week, 2 days, 8 hours, 48 minutes
System restarted by reload
System image file is "flash:c2500-ajs40-l_113-5_T.bin", booted via flash

cisco 2520 (68030) processor (revision M) with 6144K/2048K bytes of memory.
Processor board ID 10353279, with hardware revision 00000003
Bridging software.
X.25 software, Version 3.0.0.
SuperLAT software copyright 1990 by Meridian Technology Corp).
TN3270 Emulation software.
Basic Rate ISDN software, Version 1.1.
1 Ethernet/IEEE 802.3 interface(s)
2 Serial network interface(s)
2 Low-speed serial(sync/async) network interface(s)
1 ISDN Basic Rate interface(s)
32K bytes of non-volatile configuration memory.
16384K bytes of processor board System flash (Read ONLY)

Configuration register is 0x2102
```

The show history command gives a log of the router commands you have used. The length of this history log depends on the size set by the terminal history command. The default is 10 lines.

```
Router#show history
  show history
```

```
show terminal
show users
enable
show version
```

The **show users** command gives a complete listing of all currently connected users:

```
Router#show users
   Line    User     Host(s)                Idle Location
   2 tty 2  steve1   idle
   5 tty 5  john2    Async interface         2
```

CHAPTER 2

IOS Images and Configuration Files

IOS Images

Eventually you will want to upgrade your router's software. Upgrading IOS involves transferring a new IOS image to your router from some kind of server. As we'll see in this chapter, there are several methods for uploading a new IOS image: the most common is to use a TFTP (Trivial File Transfer Protocol) server or an RCP (Remote Copy Protocol) server somewhere on your network. Before we discuss how to transfer a new image, let's define exactly what is meant by an "image file" and how it differs from a configuration file.

IOS image files contain the system code that your router uses to function; that is, the image contains the IOS itself, plus various feature sets (optional features or router-specific features). However, the features are not configured in any way. The router's actual configuration—which features are enabled and how they are used in your particular network environment—is stored in a configuration file written in IOS's configuration language. The commands in this file describe everything from the router's name and the IP address of each interface to the protocols that you're using, address translation, security, and more. The router is useless without a concrete configuration—just like an operating system kernel is useless without the configuration files (for example, the Windows registry, or the files in /etc on a Unix system) that tell the kernel how you want it to operate in a particular situation.

IOS Image File Names

IOS is the software that resides inside the Cisco device. You can think of IOS as the kernel or the actual operating code within your router. The IOS image has a name, which specifies the platform for which the image was built, the features it includes, and where the image is located in memory. To see the name of the image your router is running, give the command show version:

```
Router>show version
Cisco Internetwork Operating System Software IOS (tm)
  3600 Software (C3640-JS-M), Version 12.0(5)T1, RELEASE SOFTWARE (fc1)
```

In this example, C3640-JS-M is the IOS image name. The name has three parts: platform identifier, feature set, and image execution location. In this example, C3640 is the platform identifier, JS is the feature set, and M is the image execution location.

Platform identifier

The *platform identifier* indicates the hardware for which the image was built. Table 2-1 lists the most common platform identifiers. This list is quite extensive and grows as new products are released.

Table 2-1: Common platform identifiers

Identifier	Platforms
as	Access Server 5200 series
ca	Cisco Advantage
cpa	Cisco Pro
cs	Communication Server
c800, c1000, c1005, c1600	Cisco 800, 1003, 1004, 1005, 1600
c2500	2500-series routers
c2600	Cisco 2600
c2800	Catalyst 2800
c2900	Cisco 2910, 2950
c29atm	Cisco 2900 ATM
c3620, c3640, c3800	Cisco 3620, 3640, 3800
c4000,c4500,c4700	4000-series routers
c5fsfc	Catalyst 5000 series
c5rsm	Catalyst 5000 RSP
c5atm	Catalyst ATM
c6400s, c6400r	Cisco 6400 NSP, Cisco 6400 NRP
c6msm	Catalyst
c7000	Cisco 7000, 7010
c7300	Cisco 7200
igs	IGS-, 2500-, 3000-, and 5100-series routers
gs3	AGS and AGS+ gateway routers
gs7	7000-series gateway routers
gsr	Gigabit Switch Router (12000)
ls1010	LightStream 1010
mc8310	Ardent Multiservice Cisco 3810
rpm	MGX 8850
RSP	Cisco 7500 series

Feature set

The *feature set* describes the options that are included in the IOS image. Table 2-2 lists the most popular feature sets. Keep in mind that features are often tied to platforms—any given platform will support only some feature sets. Also, note that the feature set indicators may be combined. For example, the IOS image C3640-JS-M has the feature set JS, which combines the Enterprise Subset feature set (J) with the Source Route Switch feature set (S).

Table 2-2: Common feature sets

Feature set	Contents
A	APPN
A2	ATM
B	AppleTalk
BOOT	Boot image
C	Communications server subset
D	Desktop subset (SNMP, IP, BRIDGING, WAN, Terminal Services, IPX, ATALK, ARAP)
D2	Reduced desktop (SNMP, IP, IPX, ATALK, ARAP)
DIAG	Cisco IOS–based diagnostic image
EBOOT	Ethernet boot image for MC3810
F	FRAD subset
G	ISDN subset
G2	Gatekeeper proxy, voice and video
G3	ISDN subset for c800 (IP, ISDN, Frame Relay)
I	IP subset
I2	IP subset for 3600
I3	Reduced IP subset with BGP/EGP/NHRP removed
J	Enterprise subset (protocol translation)
K	Kitchen sink
K1	Privacy key encryption (11.3 and above)
K3	Triple DES (11.3 and above)
K4	168-bit encryption with SSH
L	IpeXchange IPX, static routing, gateway
M	RMON
N	IPX
O	Firewall
O2	Firewall (3xx0)
O3	Firewall with SSH (36x0, 26x0)
P	Service provider (IP RIP/IGRP/EIGRP/OSPF/BGP CLNS ISIS/IGRP)
R	RSRB (remote source route bridging); this option can be added to other feature sets
S	Source route switch (SNMP, IP, BRIDGING, SRB)
V	VIP and dual RSP support
V2	Voice V2D

Table 2-2: Common feature sets (continued)

Feature set	Contents
V3	Voice feature card
X	X.25 (11.1 and earlier), and on 12.0T on c800 series
X	Frame Relay in 11.2
X	H.323 Gatekeeper/Proxy for 2500, 3620, 3640, MC3810
Y	Reduced IP (SNMP, IP RIP/IGRP/EIGRP, BRIDGING, ISDN, PPP), for low-end routers
Y2	IP variant (SNMP, IP RIP/IGRP/EIGRP, WAN –X.25, OSPF, PIM)
Y3	IP/X.31
Y4	Reduced IP variant (Cable, MIBs, DHCP, EZHTTP)
Y5	Reduced IP variant (Cable, MIBs, DHCP, EZIP) for home office
Y6	Reduced IP variant (c800)

Image execution location

The *image execution location* describes where the image is to be located in the router's memory. For example, given the image name C3640-JS-M, the M indicates that the image can be stored in RAM. Table 2-3 lists the most common execution locations. Keep in mind that some of these can be combined; for example, the location LZ indicates that the image is relocatable and has been compressed.

Table 2-3: Execution locations

Flag	Location
F	Flash
M	RAM
R	ROM
L	Relocatable
C	Flash card (PCMIA)
Z,X,W	Image is compressed

Loading Image Files Through the Network

From time to time you will need to load a new system image, either to upgrade the image that was shipped with your router, to install bug fixes, or to add new feature sets that you've purchased. The most common way to upload an image is to copy it to the router from some other system on your network—after all, the router is a network device, and it's easiest to use the router's networking capabilities. You can also use the console port or an AUX port to upload an image using X-MODEM. In this book, I'll focus on loading image files over the network.

For example, say that you have just purchased a 2501 router and want to upgrade to the latest version of IOS. Assume that you have downloaded the new image from Cisco's web site or that you have it on a floppy disk or some other medium. If you haven't already set the router up, you'll need a serial connection from a terminal (or a PC with a terminal-emulation program) to do some simple configuration before you can install the image: at a minimum, you need to set up an IP address. You'll also need a connection to the network, so the router can access your TFTP server. Once you've set things up, your primitive network will look like Figure 2-1.

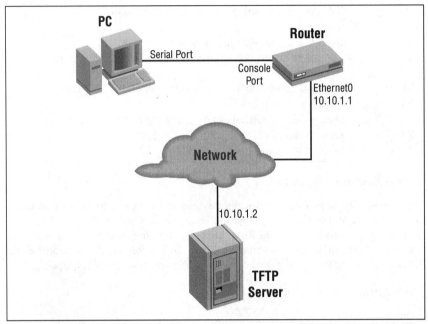

Figure 2-1: Getting an IOS image from a TFTP server

Before you start the upgrade, you must configure the IP address for the router's Ethernet interface (in this case, ethernet0). Let's assume that the address 10.10.1.1 is available for the router and that the TFTP server is 10.10.1.2. Before you load the new image, enter the following commands:

```
Router>enable
Router#config terminal
Router(config)#interface ethernet0
Router(config-if)#ip address 10.10.1.1 255.255.255.0
Router(config-if)#no shutdown
Router(config-if)#exit
Router(config)#exit
Router#ping  10.10.1.2
```

The ping command is a simple sanity check: it proves that the router can actually communicate with the TFTP server. Once you've done this, you're ready to start retrieving the image file. In a sense, TFTP is a blind FTP. There are no user logins and there are no directory listing commands. You cannot ask the server to show you what files are available: the requesting system must know the exact name of the file it wants to download. Because TFTP is so primitive and has no concept of authentication, it is a well-known security risk. We won't discuss how to set up a TFTP server here, but make sure that your server is not accessible from the outside world.

The TFTP server can be another router that is "serving" image and configuration files. To configure a Cisco router as a TFTP server, use the command `tftp-server flash`.

Here is the sequence of steps for upgrading a router from an IOS file called *igs-j-l.110* to *igs-j-l.120*:

1. Ensure there is enough flash memory on your router to load the IOS image you want. Give the **show flash** command and compare the output with the size of the image file on the server.

   ```
   Router#show flash
   System flash directory:
   File  Length   Name/status
     1   6070088  igs-j-l.110
   [6070152 bytes used, 2318456 available, 8388608 total]
   8192K bytes of processor board System flash
   ```

   The router's flash memory has 8192K bytes total with 2318456 bytes available. A directory listing on our TFTP server shows that our new image is the same size as the current one. Therefore, as long as we replace the old image with the new one, we have enough memory for the upgrade.

2. Make a backup of the current IOS image to the network server. This is always a good idea. If the new image does not work or causes problems, you can always load your backup image.

   ```
   Router#copy flash tftp
   System flash directory:
   File  Length   Name/status
     1   6070088  igs-j-l.110
   [6070152 bytes used, 2318456 available, 8388608 total]
   Address or name of remote host [255.255.255.255]? 10.10.1.2
   Source file name? igs-j-l.110
   Destination file name [igs-j-l.110]? igs-j-l.110.bak
   Verifying checksum for 'igs-j-l.110' (file # 1)...  OK
   Copy 'igs-j-l.110' from Flash to server as 'igs-j-l.110.bak? [yes/no]yes
   Writing...
   Done...
   ```

3. Load the new IOS.

   ```
   Router#config terminal
   Router(config)#config-reg 0x2101
   Router(config)#exit
   Router#reload
   ```

   Wait for the router to reboot, then reconnect. Once you're back online, re-enter the enable mode.

   ```
   Router>enable
   Router#copy tftp flash
   Address or name of remote host [255.255.255.255]? 10.10.1.2
   Source file name? igs-j-l.120
   Destination file name [igs-j-l.120]? igs-j-l.120
   Accessing file ' igs-j-l.120' on 172.16.101.101...
   Loading igs-j-l.120 from 10.10.1.2 (via Ethernet0): ! [OK]
   Erase flash device before writing? [confirm] y
   ```

```
Flash contains files. Are you sure you want to erase? [confirm] y
Copy ' igs-j-l.120' from server
  as 'igs-j-l.120' into Flash WITH erase? [yes/no] yes
Erasing device... eeeeeeeeeeeeeeeeeeeeeeeeeeeeeeeee...erased
Loading file1 from 10.10.1.2 (via Ethernet0): !
[OK - 6070088  bytes]
Verifying checksum... OK (0x14x4)
Flash copy took 0:00:31 [hh:mm:ss]
```

Now undo the configuration register.

```
Router#config terminal
Router(config)#config-reg 0x2102
Router(config)#exit
```

To abort TFTP, type Ctrl-Shift-^ then x.

4. Verify your newly loaded image. Even though there are checksums in the image, it is a good idea to verify on your own; you want to be absolutely sure that the new image is not corrupted.

```
Router#verify flash
```

If the verify fails, do *not* move on to Step 5 or reboot your router. Instead, retrieve your backup image with Step 3 by loading the backup copy of the IOS image, which we saved as *igs-j-l.110.bak* in Step 2.

5. Reboot.

```
Router#reload "IOS Upgrade"
```

What you type between the quotes does not matter to the router. It is an information string to tell users and administrators that are currently logged in what caused the router to reboot.

The reload command reboots the router. There is no reboot command. See Chapter 15 for options to the reload command.

Using RCP to download files

RCP uses the Unix remote copy protocol to store and retrieve files. The server on which the file is stored is usually a Unix or Linux system, though some implementations of RCP are available for other platforms. To set up the server, you must create a user account for the router and an *.rhosts* file for that account that gives access to the router. See your Unix manuals for more details.

Why would we want to use RCP? On a slow network, TFTP runs the possibility of timing out because it is UDP-based. RCP uses TCP for the network connection, which provides a more reliable connection in tough network conditions. Because RCP requires an account, you might be tempted to think that it is also more secure than TFTP. It probably is, but the additional security is so minimal that it can hardly be considered an advantage. As with TFTP, you'll want to take steps to ensure that outsiders can't access your RCP server.

To configure the router to use RCP, set the username to be used by the rcp command:

```
Router(config)#ip rcmd remote-username name
```

Replace *name* with the username you have assigned to the router on the RCP server. To upload a new image, use the same five-step process outlined in the previous section, but replace `tftp` with `rcp` in the `copy` commands. For example, in Step 2, use the command:

```
Router#copy flash rcp
```

Be aware that many sites consider the remote shell protocols a security problem and disable them.

You can also run RCP from your Unix workstation. And it's a lot easier to have your routers trust the Unix box than it is to list all of your routers in one *.rhosts* file.

Using the IOS Filesystem for Images

The upgrade procedure described in the previous sections is for a Class B IOS filesystem. Class B filesystems are probably the most common, but they aren't universal—particularly on high-end routers. There are also Class A and Class C filesystems; the filesystem you have depends on the router you're using. Table 2-4 shows which filesystem is used in a number of different routers.

Table 2-4: Flash filesystem types

Filesystem type	Router
Class A	7000 series, C12000, and LightStream 1010
Class B	1003, 1004, 1005, 2500, 3600, 4000, AS5200, 800
Class C	3810

As far as a user is concerned, the filesystems differ primarily in the commands that they support. Table 2-5 lists the filesystem commands and what they do.

Table 2-5: Filesystem commands

Command	Filesystem	Description
cd	All	Changes the working directory.
delete	All	Deletes a file. On Class A filesystems, this command marks the file for deletion; the squeeze command purges deleted files from the filesystem. On Class B filesystems, the files disappear from directory listings (unless you use /all), but there is no way to reclaim the space, short of erasing the entire filesystem. On Class C filesystems, the file is deleted immediately.
dir	All	Displays the directory's contents. The /all option shows deleted and undeleted files.
erase	A, B	Erases the entire filesystem.
format	A, C	Formats the filesystem.
fsck	C	Verifies the filesystem's consistency.
mkdir	C	Makes a new subdirectory.
more	All	Displays a file's contents.
pwd	All	Displays the current directory.
rename	C	Renames a file.
rmdir	C	Deletes a directory.
show file descriptors	All	Shows open file descriptors.

Table 2-5: Filesystem commands (continued)

Command	Filesystem	Description
show file information	All	Shows file size, location, etc.
show file system	All	Shows available filesystems on the device.
squeeze	A	Makes more room by moving files to the beginning of the flash memory, removing deleted files, and removing files with errors.
tftp-server	All	Sets the device to act as a TFTP server.
undelete	A, B	Recovers any deleted files. Erased files cannot be undeleted.
verify	All	Verifies that a file's checksum is correct.

All filesystems use a notation similar to a URL to specify filenames and locations. File specifications look like this:

```
prefix:path/filename
prefix://server-name/path/filename
prefix://username:password@server-name/path/filename
```

The prefix indicates where the file is located; Table 2-6 lists the valid prefixes. The path indicates the directory where the file is found. If the prefix is ftp, rcp, or tftp, the URL refers to a file located on a server; you must supply a server name and, if necessary, a username and a password.

Table 2-6: Valid prefixes

Prefix	File location
bootflash	Boot flash memory.
flash	Flash memory.
ftp	FTP server.
null	Bit bucket; files copied to a null destination are discarded. The null prefix is useful for testing connectivity and determining file size.
nvram	Nonvolatile memory.
rcp	RCP server.
slot0	First PCMCIA flash memory card.
slot1	Second PCMCIA flash memory card.
system	Volatile system memory. Often used for access to the currently running system configuration.
tftp	TFTP server.

You can view and copy files on remote servers using the TFTP, RCP, and FTP protocols, but you cannot delete files from them. For example, the following command uses TFTP to view the file config1 on the server myserver:

```
Router1# more tftp://myserver/config1
!
!
version 12.0
...
```

Upgrading Flash Memory Using the Filesystem Commands

The following example upgrades a 3640 router using flash, slot0 (PCMCIA flash card), and the IOS filesystem. The router is initially running IOS 11.2, which doesn't have the filesystem commands; we will upgrade to a version that does. The new IOS image was shipped to us on a flash card, which we have inserted into slot0 on the router. Now that the card is in, we can see the two images by using the show flash and show slot0 commands:

```
Router#show flash
System flash directory:
File  Length    Name/status
  1   5061960   c3640-ajs40-mz.112-23.P
[5062024 bytes used, 11715192 available, 16777216 total]
16384K bytes of processor board System flash (Read/Write)

Router#show slot0
PCMCIA Slot0 flash directory:
File  Length    Name/status
  1   8611616   c3640-js-mz_120-5_t1.bin
[8611680 bytes used, 8165536 available, 16777216 total]
16384K bytes of processor board PCMCIA Slot0 flash (Read/Write)
```

We have to use the show commands because IOS 11.2 doesn't have commands like dir. The first command shows the contents of the router's flash memory; the second shows the contents of the card we inserted into slot0.

Now we tell the router to load the image in slot0 instead of the image in the flash memory. We use the boot command to tell the router where the image is located; by default, the router loads the first image it finds in flash memory. The boot command modifies the router's running configuration; we copy the running configuration to the startup configuration, then reboot. Upon reboot, the router loads the image from the flash card in slot0:

```
Router#conf terminal
Router(config)#boot system flash slot0:c3640-js-mz_120-5_t1.bin
Router#copy run start
Router#reload
```

After the router reboots, the show version command shows we are running the new image:

```
Router>show version
Cisco Internetwork Operating System Software
IOS (tm) 3600 Software (C3640-JS-M), Version 12.0(5)T1, RELEASE SOFTWARE (fc1)
Copyright (c) 1986-1999 by cisco Systems, Inc.
Compiled Tue 17-Aug-99 22:32 by cmong
Image text-base: 0x600088F0, data-base: 0x60F24000

ROM: System Bootstrap, Version 11.1(20)AA2, EARLY DEPLOYMENT RELEASE SOFTWARE (fc1)

Router uptime is 0 minutes
System returned to ROM by reload
System image file is "slot0:c3640-js-mz_120-5_t1.bin"
```

Now we can use the filesystem commands:

```
Router#dir flash:
Directory of flash:/
   1  -rw-     5061960              <no date>  c3640-ajs40-mz.112-23.P
16777216 bytes total (11715192 bytes free)
```

```
Router#dir slot0:
Directory of slot0:/
   1  -rw-     8611616              <no date>  c3640-js-mz_120-5_t1.bin
16777216 bytes total (8165536 bytes free)
```

Next, we want to copy the image from the PCMCIA card to the router's flash memory—it's not a good idea to rely on booting from the flash card. We can use the filesystem commands to perform this copy:

```
Router#copy slot0:c3640-js-mz_120-5_t1.bin flash:c3640-js-mz_120-5_t1.bin
Destination filename [c3640-js-mz_120-5_t1.bin]?
Erase flash: before copying?[confirm]n
CCCCCCCCCCCCCCCCCCCCCCCCCCCCCCCCCCCCCCCCCCCCCCCCCCCCCCCCCCCCCCCCCCCCCCC
Verifying checksum... OK (0xB648)
8611616 bytes copied in 38.440 secs (226621 bytes/sec)
```

Check the flash contents:

```
Router#dir flash:
Directory of flash:/
   1  -rw-     5061960              <no date>  c3640-ajs40-mz.112-23.P
   2  -rw-     8611616              <no date>  c3640-js-mz_120-5_t1.bin
16777216 bytes total (3103512 bytes free)
```

Now, we can either delete the old 11.2 image or tell the router which image to boot. If we don't use the boot command to specify an image, the router will load the first available image, which will be the old 11.2 image. (Note that this wouldn't have been an issue if we had told the router it could erase flash memory before copying. But that would have left us without a backup image to boot if the new image had failed.) So we issue two more boot commands: the first to tell the router not to boot the image in slot0, and the second to specify the image we want. Then we copy the running configuration into the startup configuration. Finally, we reboot and remove the slot0 memory card.

```
Router#config terminal
Router(config)#no boot system flash slot0:c3640-js-mz_120-5_t1.bin
Router(config)#boot system flash c3640-js-mz_120-5_t1.bin
Router(config)#^Z
Router#copy run start
Router#reload
```

When it reboots, the router loads the correct 12.0 image from its flash memory:

```
Router>show version
Cisco Internetwork Operating System Software
IOS (tm) 3600 Software (C3640-JS-M), Version 12.0(5)T1,  RELEASE SOFTWARE (fc1)
Copyright (c) 1986-1999 by cisco Systems, Inc.
Compiled Tue 17-Aug-99 22:32 by cmong
Image text-base: 0x600088F0, data-base: 0x60F24000

ROM: System Bootstrap, Version 11.1(20)AA2, EARLY DEPLOYMENT RELEASE SOFTWARE (fc1)
ROM: 3600 Software (C3640-AJS40-M), Version 11.2(23)P,  RELEASE SOFTWARE (fc1)
```

```
Router uptime is 0 minutes
System returned to ROM by power-on
System image file is "flash:c3640-js-mz_120-5_t1.bin"
```

Let's delete the old image anyway:

```
Router#delete c3640-ajs40-mz.112-23.P
Delete filename [c3640-ajs40-mz.112-23.P]?
Delete flash:c3640-ajs40-mz.112-23.P? [confirm]y
Router#dir /all flash:
Directory of flash:/

  1  -rw-    5061960              <no date>  [c3640-ajs40-mz.112-23.P]
  2  -rw-    8611616              <no date>  c3640-js-mz_120-5_t1.bin

16777216 bytes total (3103512 bytes free)
```

Notice that our deleted file is still there; it won't be deleted permanently until we give the erase command. On a Class A filesystem, we could use the squeeze command to erase the deleted file. With this filesystem, though, we are stuck with the deleted file until we give the erase command, which erases the entire filesystem. In this case, we would have to reload our new image. Since there's plenty of room in flash, there is no need to clean the filesystem out now. Next time we upgrade this router, though, we will probably answer "yes" to the "Erase flash before copying" question.

The Router's Configuration

Every router has two different configurations to consider:

Running configuration
> The router's active configuration, which is stored in the router's RAM. Every configuration command you give is stored in the running configuration. If you reboot your router, this configuration will be lost. If you make changes that you want to save, you must copy the running configuration to a safe location, such as a network server, or save it as the router's startup configuration.

Startup configuration
> The configuration that is loaded when the router boots. This configuration is stored in the router's nonvolatile memory (NVRAM). You cannot edit a startup configuration directly. All commands you enter are stored in the running configuration, which can be copied into the startup configuration.

In other words, when you boot a router, the startup configuration becomes the initial running configuration. As you modify the configuration, the two diverge: the startup configuration remains the same, while the running configuration reflects the changes you have made. If you want to make your changes permanent, you must copy the running configuration to the startup configuration.

The following command copies the router's current running configuration into the startup configuration:

```
Router#copy running-config startup-config
Building configuration...
```

Similarly, to save the running configuration on a network server using TFTP, you would give the command:

```
Router#copy running-config tftp
```

You'll be prompted for additional information, such as the remote host and the name for the saved file.

The terms "running configuration" and "startup configuration" were added in recent versions of IOS. In earlier versions, you used the command write terminal to display the current router configuration and write memory to store the current configuration. This terminology is outdated; use the copy command.

Loading Configuration Files

Loading and saving configuration files is much simpler than loading a kernel image. This section summarizes the commands that load and save the configuration.

Loading the running-config

Once loaded, the running configuration will immediately be used by the router. Use these commands to load it using either TFTP or RCP:

```
Router#copy tftp running-config      (for TFTP)
Router#copy rcp running-config       (for RCP)
```

Loading the startup-config

The startup configuration is not used until the router is rebooted. Loading the startup configuration can be dangerous, because the router doesn't parse the configuration file and won't give you any warning if the file has errors. The configuration is not parsed until the router is rebooted—and if the configuration is incorrect, the router may not boot properly. Therefore, use the following commands with care:

```
Router#copy tftp startup-config      (for TFTP)
Router#copy rcp startup-config       (for RCP)
```

Saving running-config to startup-config

The following command is the most important of all. If you don't save your running configuration, all your configuration changes will be lost during the next reboot of the device. Once you are satisfied that your current router configuration is correct, copy your configuration to the startup configuration with this command:

```
Router#copy running-config startup-config
```

Viewing a Configuration

The following commands display the startup or the running configuration:

```
Router#show startup-config
Router#show running-config
```

Erasing a Stored Configuration

The following command deletes the startup configuration:

```
Router#erase startup-config
```

Saving a Configuration to a Network Server

The following commands save the running configuration or the startup configuration to a server on the network, using either TFTP or RCP:

```
Router#copy running-config tftp      (for TFTP)
Router#copy running-config rcp       (for RCP)
Router#copy startup-config tftp      (for TFTP)
Router#copy startup-config rcp       (for RCP)
```

CHAPTER 3

Basic Router Configuration

Configuration Soapbox

Managing a handful of routers quickly becomes a large task, and managing thousands of routers is even worse. You can minimize your administrative burden by configuring your routers carefully, completely, and consistently. I strongly recommend that you use every helpful item possible—even if the configuration item is not required. Every moment spent doing configuration groundwork translates into many hours saved when you are troubleshooting or performing maintenance tasks. When you try to solve a network problem at 2 A.M., the importance of properly configured routers becomes painfully clear.

This chapter covers most of the configuration items that make routers more manageable and easier to tame.

Setting the Router Name

The examples in this book use "Router" as the router's name. That's fine for examples, but a bad idea in real life. Eventually, a router should be given a name. To set the router name to "Sphinx", use the hostname command:

```
Router(config)#hostname Sphinx
Sphinx(config)#
```

The router instantly responds by updating the prompt to reflect the new router name. The name can be up to 254 characters long, but don't use a name so long that you can't type it comfortably.

It's a good practice to follow a naming convention for your routers. With a logical, consistent naming scheme, it's easy to remember a router's name, or guess the name if you've forgotten it. For example, let's say that your router names all start with "rtr", followed by the city initials, followed by a number. Then, late one night when you're staring at a blank terminal screen trying to remember the name of the backbone router in New York, you can type *rtr-ny-01* and be reasonably confident that you've guessed correctly.

Don't use underscores (_) in router names. They are hard to type, often lead to confusion, and aren't legal in Domain Name System (DNS) names. Use a hyphen (-) instead. Similarly, avoid mixing upper- and lowercase. Instead of "routerOneNewYork", use "router-one-newyork". The router won't care, but your users will!

Setting the System Prompt

By default, the router uses its hostname as the prompt; the hostname is "Router" if you haven't defined it explicitly. It's often a good idea to put other useful information in the prompt by using the prompt command. For example:

```
Sphinx(config)#prompt %h:%n%p
Sphinx(config)#exit
Sphinx:5#
```

We've used three escape sequences to set the prompt to the hostname (%h), followed by the command number (%n), followed by the appropriate prompt character for the current command mode (%p). The escape sequences for the prompt command are listed in Table 3-1.

Table 3-1: Prompt variables

Escape sequence	Meaning
%%	Percent character
%h	Hostname of the router
%n	TTY number for this EXEC session
%p	Prompt character: either > for user level or # for privileged level
%s	Space character
%t	Tab character

The no prompt command returns the router to the default prompt.

Configuration Comments

It's a good idea to keep your routers' configuration files on a server somewhere. Then you can modify the configuration files using a convenient text editor and upload the files to your routers as necessary. One advantage to this procedure is that you can include comments within your configuration files. A comment is any line beginning with an exclamation point. For example:

```
!
! This is a comment.
!
```

You can also type comments when you are configuring the router from the command line, but comments are never saved as part of the router's configuration. Therefore, when you try to view or save the router's configuration, the comments will be gone.

The Enable Password

The enable password secures the privileged mode, which is required for all commands that change the router's configuration. Configuring the enable password therefore keeps people with general access to your router from changing the router's configuration. It takes only one person with enough knowledge to be dangerous to take down your whole network, so securing the privileged (enable) mode is always the right thing to do.

To set the password, use the enable password command:

```
Router(config)#enable password not2secure
```

The password is now set to "not2secure". Once the password is set, the router will prompt you for the password before it enters privileged mode.

By default, passwords are stored in clear text, which means that anybody who can find your router configuration file or watch you list the configuration on the console can see the enable password. The command service password-encryption (with no arguments) configures the router to store the password in an encrypted form.

Chapter 13 discusses better ways to manage passwords and authentication.

Mapping Hostnames to IP Addresses

Like all network equipment, routers work naturally with numeric IP addresses. However, using IP addresses isn't convenient for humans—including network administrators. It is much more convenient to work with hostnames. Like any other network host, routers implement DNS and can use DNS to look up IP addresses. But the use of DNS presents a problem in a routing environment. If the router can't access the Internet, it can't look up addresses; one reason that the router might not be able to access the Internet could be a routing problem; and if the router is configured to use DNS but can't access the Internet, you will have trouble using the commands you need to diagnose and fix the problem.

There is a good halfway point, however. Like other network hosts, the router can maintain a host table, and you can place any IP addresses that appear in your configuration in the host table. You can then use DNS to look up any hostnames that aren't actually involved in the router's configuration. This will make it easier to understand the output from show commands or to use commands such as ping to check your network connectivity.

IP Host Tables

The ip host command builds and maintains the router's host table. This command takes a hostname followed by one or more IP addresses. You can have up to eight IP addresses per hostname.

```
ip host pyramid 10.10.1.3
ip host sphinx 10.10.1.2 10.10.1.4 10.10.1.5
```

Deleting a host requires you to type the entire hostname and IP address over again!

```
no ip host pyramid 10.10.1.3
no ip host sphinx 10.10.1.2 10.10.14 10.10.1.5
```

Enabling DNS

The Domain Name System (DNS) reduces the need for host entries—although, as I said before, you should have explicit host entries for any IP addresses that appear in your configuration. DNS is enabled by default; to enable it explicitly, use the command ip domain-lookup. To configure DNS, you must specify one or more name servers and the domain name to be used to complete unqualified names (typically, your own domain name). A typical configuration looks like this:

```
! Specify the DNS servers
ip name-server 10.10.9.1
ip name-server 10.10.9.2
!
! Set the name for unqualified hostnames
ip domain-name your-domain.com
```

To disable DNS lookups, use the no form of the command:

```
no ip domain-lookup
```

To re-enable DNS lookups, leave off the no keyword:

```
! Enable DNS lookups
ip domain-lookup
```

Use the show hosts command to view the cached hostnames and the DNS configuration:

```
Router>show hosts
Default domain is your-domain.com
Name/address lookup uses domain service
Name servers are 10.10.9.1 10.10.9.2
```

Host	Flags	Age	Type	Address(es)
Foxtrot	(temp, OK)	18	IP	10.10.1.3
sphinx	(temp, OK)	18	IP	10.10.1.2

Setting the Router's Time

The router's internal clock is set with the clock set command. This command is not a configuration command (i.e., you must be in enable mode to give it, but you don't need to give the configure terminal command) and is not stored in the router's configuration. The time is in military (24-hour) time. For example:

```
Router#clock set 13:00:00 20 jun 1999
```

In addition to setting the time itself, you need to set the time zone using the clock timezone command. This command is part of the router's configuration. For example, a router on the east coast of the United States would have the line:

```
Router(config)#clock timezone EST -5
```

−5 is the UTC (Coordinated Universal Time) offset for the Eastern time zone.

Now that the time and time zone have been set, one final configuration item exists: in most places, you want to observe Daylight Savings Time. The following command tells the router to use Daylight Savings Time in the Eastern time zone:

```
Router(config)#clock summer-time EDT recurring
```

The Calendar Versus the Clock

High-end Cisco routers have a calendar that is separate from the system clock. The calendar runs continuously, even if the router is off. After the calendar has been set, the system clock automatically sets itself every time the router is booted. The following commands set the router's calendar and set the clock's time from the calendar time. The calendar set command simply sets the time, and is not stored in the router's configuration.

```
Router#calendar set 12:10:00 5 September 1999
Router#clock read-calendar
```

Configuring NTP

The Network Time Protocol (NTP) is available in IOS Versions 9.21 and above. This protocol uses an NTP server to synchronize the router's time with other clocks on the network. Configuring NTP is as simple as setting the address of an NTP server. There are several NTP servers on the Internet for your use; your ISP may have its own NTP server.

```
clock timezone EST -5
ntp server 10.10.1.5
```

When you enable NTP, a new command called ntp clock-period appears in the router's configuration. (If you do a show running-config, you will see it in there even if you didn't enter it.) This command is set automatically by the NTP software and it is best to leave it alone.

 Did you allow an NTP server on the gateway router's access list?

On a high-end router, we add a command to the configuration to tell the router to update its internal clock with the NTP time:

```
clock timezone EST -5
clock update-calendar
ntp server 10.10.1.2
```

A high-end router can also be the NTP server for the network. To use the router as an NTP server, add the following commands to the configuration. These commands tell the router to use the internal calendar for NTP time:

```
clock timezone EST -5
clock calendar-valid
ntp master
```

Never use the `ntp master` command on a router that is participating in NTP over the Internet. It will declare the router as a stratum 1 NTP server. Not only will the router no longer change its own time based on NTP information it learns, but it might disturb other NTP hosts on the Internet.

Enabling SNMP

It should be obvious that since you're trying to manage a network, you should be able to use the network to help manage your network equipment. That's the goal of the Simple Network Management Protocol (SNMP). This protocol enables network-management stations to gather information from network nodes. Network nodes can be almost anything, ranging from the simplest bridge to the largest router, and even including software running inside the servers. Virtually all modern network equipment includes an SNMP agent, which is the software that communicates with the management station. Network-management stations can run commercial management software, or they can use homegrown tools.

I will not try to give an introduction to SNMP, nor will I talk about management software.* In this section, I'll briefly describe how to configure the SNMP agent in a Cisco router. If you're not using SNMP, you can skip this section—though you should certainly investigate what SNMP can do for you.

By default, SNMP access is not enabled. To enable SNMP, use the command:

```
snmp-server community name mode access-list
```

The parameters are as follows:

name
> The community string the management station will use to ask for information. This string acts like a password. SNMPv1's implementation is insecure because the string travels across the network in clear text. Anyone snooping on your network will be able to see the community string pass back and forth. To improve security, use the *access-list* option.

mode
> Either RO for read-only access (unprivileged), or RW for read-write access (privileged). RO means that the management station can read information about the router but can't change anything; RW allows the management station to use SNMP to change the router's state. SNMP management stations typically use different community strings for read and write operations.

access-list
> The name or number of a standard access list to control SNMP access. The router responds only to SNMP requests from hosts that pass the access list. Note that you can apply different access lists to different modes. For example, your RW (read-write) access list might allow only a small number of hosts, while your RO (read-only) access list might allow many more hosts. See Chapter 7 for access-list commands.

---

* For an introduction to SNMP, see *Essential SNMP* by Douglas Mauro and Kevin Schmidt (O'Reilly).

It's a good policy to set up different community strings for read-only and read-write access and to give the read-write community string only to a few trusted people. If you enable SNMP, make sure that you change the community strings from their default values, not only on your router but on any other hosts you are monitoring. Almost all vendors configure their SNMP devices to use public as the default community string, so it is the first thing an outsider trying to break into your network will try. You should also use access lists to restrict which hosts can use SNMP to interact with your router.

Here is a simple configuration that allows basic SNMP access:

```
! Set up public access with a community string of "not-public"
snmp-server community not-public RO
!
! Set up privileged access with a community string of "not-secure"
snmp-server community not-secure RW
```

Now, we add some security. We allow public SNMP access only from the 10.10.1.0 network, and allow privileged SNMP access only from host 10.10.1.35:

```
! Enable public access and apply access-list number 1
snmp-server community not-public RO 1
!
! Enable privileged access and apply access-list number 2
snmp-server community highly-secure RW 2
!
! Access-lists (See chapter 7 for syntax and usage)
access-list 1 permit 10.10.1.0 0.0.0.255
access-list 2 permit 10.10.1.35
```

There's one thing left to configure for basic SNMP capabilities. A *trap* is an asynchronous message generated by an SNMP agent and sent to an SNMP management station. SNMP defines a small number of standard traps, but traps can also carry vendor-specific (and even site-specific) information. To use traps, you must define the address of the management station that will receive them, plus a community string that will be sent with the traps; most SNMP management stations ignore traps that don't have an appropriate community string. Here's how to configure a Cisco router to send traps:

```
! Specify what SNMP management station will receive our traps
! Our community string is "little-secure"
snmp-server host 10.10.1.2 little-secure traps
```

The management station, if it is configured properly, will know what to do with the traps when they arrive.

There's a lot more you can do with SNMP configuration, but this is enough to get you started.

Cisco Discovery Protocol

The Cisco Discovery Protocol (CDP) is tremendously helpful when configuring a wide variety of Cisco equipment. It allows you to see what the adjacent routers or switches are, as well as their configured protocols and addresses.

CDP is enabled by default on most available interfaces. (There are a few exceptions, such as ATM interfaces.) This protocol automatically detects neighbor Cisco devices that are directly connected. The following command enables CDP globally:

```
cdp run
```

To disable CDP, use the no form of the command:

```
no cdp run
```

You can disable CDP on particular interfaces by using the no cdp enable command in interface configuration mode.

CDP can display useful information about other routers or switches that are directly connected:

```
Router>show cdp neighbors
Capability Codes: R - Router, T - Trans Bridge, B - Source Route Bridge
                 S - Switch, H - Host, I - IGMP

Device ID      Local Intrfce   Holdtme   Capability  Platform  Port ID
switch1            Eth 0         162         T S        1900     AUI
router2            Eth 0         176          R         4000     Eth 0
```

Disable CDP on any router that is directly connected to the Internet or to another site that you don't trust (e.g., a customer site). CDP can be considered a security risk because it provides information to outside devices. It doesn't provide much information, but there's no reason to give any information away to potential intruders.

System Banners

A router maintains a number of standard messages for communicating with users. These messages are typically associated with the process of logging into the router. For example, a user is typically shown a "message of the day," followed by a login banner, followed by the login prompt itself. After a successful login, the user is usually shown an "exec banner"; in the special case of a reverse telnet connection (see Chapter 4), the user is shown the "incoming banner" rather than the exec banner. In other words, for a typical console session, you would see:

```
This is the message of the day banner.  (motd banner)
This is the login banner.               (login banner)
User access verification

Password:    (not echoed)
This is the exec banner.  (exec banner)
Router>       (user mode prompt)
```

Each banner configuration statement has the same format: *banner-type # message* #. The pound character (#) represents the delimiting character of your choice. It marks the beginning and end of your message. You cannot use your delimiting character inside the message body. For example, the following command sets the message of the day:

```
Router(config)#banner motd #  Router will be rebooted today for maintenance.  #
```

Messages can contain blank lines and line breaks, as in the following example:

```
Router(config)#banner motd $
Enter TEXT message.  End with the character '$'.

Router will be down until tomorrow.

I guess we should have planned it better.
$
Router(config)#
```

Creating Banners

To create a banner of any type, use the banner command followed by the type of banner and the message:

```
Router(config)#banner motd # message #
Router(config)#banner login # message #
Router(config)#banner exec # message #
Router(config)#banner incoming # message #
```

Disabling Banners

Normally, once banners are defined they are displayed. You can't disable a banner; you must delete it with the no form of the banner command:

```
Router(config)#no banner incoming
```

Unlike the other banners, the exec and message-of-the-day banners can be disabled on individual lines by using the no exec-banner and no motd-banner commands:

```
Router(config)#line 5
Router(config-line)#no exec-banner
Router(config-line)#no motd-banner
```

An unusual side effect is that disabling the exec banner also disables the message-of-the-day banner; disabling the message-of-the-day banner has no effect on the exec banner. To re-enable either of these banners, give the exec-banner or motd-banner command.

CHAPTER 4

Line Commands

What Is a Line?

Cisco routers make a fairly basic distinction between the characteristics of a serial line (which you might want to think of as "physical" characteristics) and the characteristics of the protocols running over the line. The physical characteristics of a line are configured by the line command (and various commands that follow it) and include items such as parity and port speed. The high-level protocol characteristics are configured by the interface command (and the commands that follow it); these characteristics include IP addresses and other properties.

The line command can configure:

- The router's console port (CTY)

- The router's asynchronous ports (TTYs), used for dial-in and dial-out modem connections

- The router's auxiliary port (AUX), used for backup modem connections

- Telnet and rlogin connections to the router ("virtual terminals" or VTYs)

The line Command

The line command specifies which line or group of lines you want to configure by entering the line configuration mode. It doesn't actually do the configuration; it is followed by other commands that set up the specific properties you want. Here's the syntax of the line command:

    line [aux | console | tty | vty] starting-line-number ending-line-number

The possible line types are aux, console, tty, and vty. These line types are discussed individually in this chapter. The following example shows how to use the line command to configure some properties of the router's console interface:

    Router>enable   Enter the privileged command mode
    Router#config terminal   Enter configuration mode

```
Router(config)#line console 0                    Select the console line
Router(config-line)#exec-timeout 30 0            Set the timeout to 30 minutes
Router(config-line)#exit                          Exit the line configuration mode
Router(config)#exit                               Exit the configuration mode
Router#
```

If you want to apply line commands to more than one line, you can specify the starting and ending numbers of a group of lines. For example, say you want to apply the command exec-timeout to TTY lines 5 through 10. Instead of typing this command five times, you can configure the entire group with one line command:

```
Router(config)#line tty 5 10
Router(config-line)#exec-timeout 30 0
```

Absolute and Relative Line Numbering

When you're typing the line command, you give it "relative" line numbers: the first TTY is tty0,* the first virtual terminal is vty0, and so on. This numbering scheme is intuitive and convenient. Internally, the router uses an absolute numbering scheme to keep track of the lines. It would be nice if you could ignore the router's internal bookkeeping, but a number of commands use absolute line numbers when reporting information about a line's status.

Absolute line numbers are calculated by their location on the router, in the order of CTY, TTY, AUX, and then VTY. The console port is first; its absolute line number is zero (0). The TTY ports are next, starting at absolute line number 1 and continuing for the number of TTY lines on the router. If you have eight TTY ports, absolute numbers 1 through 8 will be the TTYs on your router. Next is the AUX port, whose absolute line number is the last TTY number plus 1. Finally, the VTYs begin at the AUX port's number plus 1. Table 4-1 clarifies absolute and relative line numbering.

Table 4-1: Absolute and relative line numbers

Line type	Absolute number	Relative number
Console (CTY)	0	0
TTY1	1	1
TTY2	2	2
TTY3	3	3
...	...	...
TTYn	n	n
AUX	n+1	0
VTY0	n+2	0
VTY1	n+3	1
VTY2	n+4	2
VTY3	n+5	3

---

* On some routers, like the 2600, TTY numbering depends on the placement of modules on the router's chassis. On a device such as this, TTY numbers don't necessarily start at 0; depending on how modules are installed, they might start at 32 or some other number. Likewise, the AUX port may be 65, depending on card placement.

To view this table on the router, use the command `show users all`. The first column of the output shows the absolute line number, followed by the line type, followed by the line's relative number:

```
Router>show users all
        Line    User    Host(s)         Idle Location
    0 con 0                              00:00:00
    1 tty 1              incoming         6 10.3.21.229
    2 tty 2              incoming         6 10.3.21.229
    3 tty 3              incoming         6 10.3.21.229
    4 tty 4                              00:00:00
    5 tty 5                              00:00:00
    6 tty 6                              00:00:00
    7 tty 7              incoming        3d13h 10.208.8.103
    8 tty 8              incoming        3d13h 10.208.8.103
    9 tty 9              incoming        3d13h 10.208.8.103
   10 tty 10             incoming        3d08h 10.226.76.6
   11 tty 11             incoming        3d08h 10.226.76.6
   12 tty 12             incoming        3d08h 10.226.76.6
   13 tty 13                             00:00:00
   14 tty 14                             00:00:00
   15 tty 15                             00:00:00
   16 tty 16                             00:00:00
   17 aux 0                              00:00:00
*  18 vty 0              idle             0 10.10.187.204
   19 vty 1                              00:00:00
   20 vty 2                              00:00:00
   21 vty 3                              00:00:00
```

Line Commands

The Console Port

Each router has one console port. This port always has line number 0. You make a connection to the console port by attaching a standard RS232 cable, as shown in Figure 4-1. This cable is often shipped with your router.

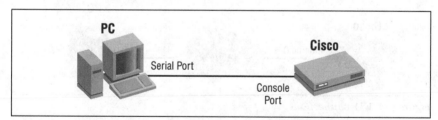

Figure 4-1: Console cable connection

You can use any VT100 terminal-emulation program to talk to the router; just select the correct PC serial interface (the one the console cable is plugged into) and then hit the Return key a few times. The router responds by starting an EXEC session, which is the process within the router that provides the command-line interface. The default settings for the port are 9600 baud, 8 databits, no parity, and 1 stop bit. If you changed any of these defaults on the device, you will have to change the settings on your terminal program to match.

Using the `line` commands, we can define and control access to the console port. Here is a basic configuration:

```
Router#config terminal
Router(config)#service linenumber
Router(config)#line console 0
Router(config-line)#location Building-2A
Router(config-line)#exec-timeout 30 0
```

The `location` command identifies the router's location to the users. The command `service linenumber` displays the location information automatically to the user upon login. This information can be useful when you are administering your routers. Next, we add a basic security measure: a timeout. If the console port is idle for more than 30 minutes, the session automatically closes. You do not want the session active all the time in a real environment. If you forget to log out, someone might come in after you and modify the router's configuration!

A little more security can be achieved by adding a user login:

```
Router(config)#username bob password letmein
Router(config)#line console 0
Router(config-line)#login local
```

These commands provide only minimal security; for more effective security measures, see Chapter 13.

Virtual Terminals (VTYs)

Virtual terminals are logical connections from the network to the router; these are typically telnet or rlogin connections. When a user telnets to a router from the network, as in Figure 4-2, the router starts an EXEC process to handle this connection.

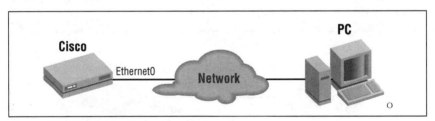

Figure 4-2: VTY connections

Although no physical link is associated with a virtual terminal, VTYs are configured just like normal TTY lines. VTYs are enabled once they are configured. If you do not configure any VTYs, then logical connections, such as telnet, cannot be made to your router from the network. Here is a VTY configuration example:

```
Router(config)#line vty 1
Router(config-line)#exec-timeout 0 30        Set the timeout to 30 minutes
Router(config-line)#password letmeinhere     Set one password for telnet access
Router(config-line)#transport input telnet   Allow only telnet access
Router(config-line)#access-class 10 in       Apply access list 10 to this line
Router(config-line)#exit
Router(config)#access-list 10 permit host 10.10.1.2
```

This example shows a semi-secure configuration for a VTY terminal. We set a timeout for 30 minutes and apply only one password. We then use the `transport input` command to define the protocols that are allowed to use this line; in this case, we are allowing only telnet access. The `access-class` command applies an access list to this interface. We won't explain access lists here; in this example we use a simple access list to permit access from the host at address 10.10.1.2.

  You should configure all your VTYs in the same manner, because there is no way to predict which VTY a user is going to receive when he telnets into the device.

Asynchronous Ports (TTYs)

TTYs are asynchronous connections between the router's async interfaces and serial devices (modems). If you are connecting modems to your router or access server for dial-up or dial-out connections, you will need to configure the TTY ports.

The TTY ports correspond directly to async interfaces. Therefore, whenever you configure a TTY line, you will probably also configure the corresponding interface. If you plugged a modem into async port 1, you would use TTY1 to configure all the hardware aspects of the connection between the router and the modem, and the interface Async1 would configure the protocol. (The interface commands are defined in Chapter 5.) Figure 4-3 demonstrates the possible modem configuration on a router or terminal server.

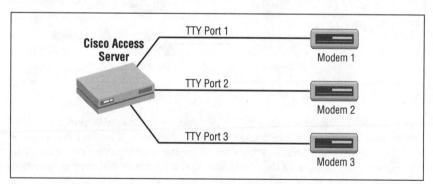

Figure 4-3: TTY connections to modems

Here is an example of a modem configuration on TTY port 3:

```
! Select line 3
line tty 3
  ! Tell the router to use its local username list
  login local
  ! This line is for dial-in access only
  modem dialin
  ! The speed of the serial connection is 115200 bps
```

```
speed 115200
! Use hardware flow control
flowcontrol hardware
! The type of modem is autoconfigured by the router
modem autoconfigure discovery
```

The configuration isn't difficult to read. The router, which is some sort of terminal server, maintains its own list of usernames and passwords (login local); the modem is used only for dial-in; the serial connection between the modem and the router is set to 115200 baud; hardware flow control is used; and the modem is configured by the router.

The Auxiliary (AUX) Port

The router's auxiliary (AUX) port functions as a backup async port. It is most commonly used as a backup console port, but it can also be used as a dial-up port for remote router management and many other functions. It doesn't have the performance of an asynchronous line; its speed is often limited (particularly on older routers), and it does only per-character I/O, which creates a high CPU load if used continuously.

Figure 4-4 shows how you might use the AUX port as a backup for a T1 line. If the T1 connection goes down, Router 1 automatically dials Router 2 using the modem connected to the AUX port. Obviously, the speed of the backup link is not comparable to the T1 connection, but it does provide some level of backup support.

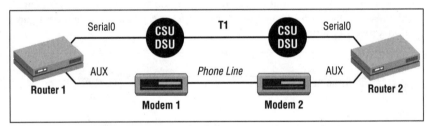

Figure 4-4: Using an AUX port as a backup connection

The following configuration examples show how to use the AUX port as backup connection. This example uses many commands that are well beyond the scope of this chapter; they are included here to make the configuration complete. The comments describe some of the more advanced commands; for more information about PPP and dial-on-demand routing, see Chapter 11.

```
! Configure the primary (T1) interface, with async 4 as a backup.
! See Chapter 5 for info on interface configuration.
! See Chapter 11 for the dialing commands
interface serial0
  ip address 10.10.1.1 255.255.255.0
  backup interface async 4
  backup delay 10 1
!
! The AUX line translates to the async 4 interface.
interface async 4
  ip address 10.10.1.2 255.255.255.0
```

```
    dialer in-band
    dialer string 410-555-5555
    dialer-group 1
    async dynamic routing
!
! Build our dialer lists.
dialer-list 1 protocol ip permit
chat-script script1 " " "atdt 410-555-5555" timeout 60 "connected"
!
! Finally, configure the AUX port using the line commands.
line aux 0
    modem chat-script script1
    modem inout
```

show line

To display the status of a line, use the command show line. This is not a privileged command and can be executed by any user. On an eight-port terminal server, show line gives output like this:

```
Router>show line
  TTY TYP    Tx/Rx      A Modem  Roty AccO AccI  Uses    Noise  Overruns
    0 CTY                -  -      -   -    -     0        0      0/0
    1 TTY  9600/9600     -  -      -   -    -     3        542    0/0
*   2 TTY  9600/9600     -  -      -   -    -     1        0      0/0
    3 TTY 38400/38400    - RIisCD  -   -    -     1        0      0/0
I   4 TTY 38400/38400    - inout   -   -    -     25       0      0/0
I   5 TTY 38400/38400    - inout   -   -    -     3940     0      0/0
I   6 TTY 38400/38400    - inout   -   -    -     1483     0      0/0
I   7 TTY 38400/38400    - inout   -   -    -     364      0      0/0
I   8 TTY 38400/38400    - inout   -   -    -     12       0      0/0
```

Table 4-2 shows what the fields in this report mean.

Table 4-2: Fields in a show line display

Column	Meaning
1st column	I = line is idle; * = line is active.
TTY	Actual line number.
TYP	Type of line: CTY (console), AUX, TTY, VTY, LPT.
TX/RX	Transmit and receive baud rates for this line.
A	Autobaud (automatic baud rate detection) is active.
Modem	Type of modem signal configured for this line (callin, callout, cts-req, dtr-act, inout, RIisCd).
Roty	Rotary group configured for this line.
AccO, AccI	Access lists for this line, both output and input (see access-class in Chapter 15).
Uses	Number of connections made to this line since the router was booted.
Noise	Number of times noise was detected on this line. Can be used to gauge line quality.
Overruns	Number of buffer overruns that have occurred on this line, in the format *hardware/software*. Hardware overruns occur when the hardware receives data from the software faster than it can process it. Software overruns occur when the software receives data from the hardware faster than it can process it. A bad cable could cause overruns.

You can retrieve more detailed information by selecting a single line:

```
Router>show line 5
  Tty Typ     Tx/Rx     A Modem  Roty AccO AccI  Uses   Noise  Overruns
A  5 TTY  38400/38400  - inout    -    -    -    3969      0      0/0

 Line 5, Location: "", Type: ""
 Length: 24 lines, Width: 80 columns
 Baud rate (TX/RX) is 38400/38400, no parity, 1 stopbits, 8 databits
 Status: Ready, Active, No Exit Banner, Async Interface Active
 Capabilities: Hardware Flowcontrol In, Hardware Flowcontrol Out
   Modem Callout, Modem RI is CD, Line usable as async interface
 Modem state: Ready
 Special Chars: Escape  Hold  Stop  Start  Disconnect  Activation
                 ^^x    none   -     -       none
 Timeouts:    Idle EXEC    Idle Session   Modem Answer  Session   Dispatch
              0:00:30        never                        none    not set
 Session limit is not set.
 Time since activation: 2:08:08
 Editing is enabled.
 History is enabled, history size is 10.
 Full user help is disabled
 Allowed transports are lat telnet rlogin mop.  Preferred is lat.
 No output characters are padded
 No special data dispatching characters
 Modem hardware state: CTS DSR  DTR RTS
 Line is running PPP for address 192.101.187.165.
 0 output packets queued, 1 input packets.
  Async Escape map is 000000000000000101000000000000
 Group codes:    0
   Interface Async5: (passive, compression on)
     Rcvd:    5711 total, 4516 compressed, 0 errors
              0 dropped, 0 buffer copies, 0 buffer failures
     Sent:    5085 total, 4032 compressed,
              138729 bytes saved, 3943290 bytes sent
              1.3 efficiency improvement factor
   Connect: 16 rx slots, 16 tx slots, 1275 long searches, 765 misses
            84% hit ratio, five minute miss rate 0 misses/sec, 1 max
```

The first part of this report has the same format given in Table 4-2. However, the rest of the report goes into great detail about the line's characteristics. Table 4-3 shows what these additional fields mean.

Table 4-3: Fields in a show line for a single port

Field	Meaning
Line	TTY line number.
Location	Value of the location keyword set for this line. See location in Chapter 15.
Type	Value specified by the line configuration.
Length	Terminal display length in characters.
Width	Terminal display width in characters.
Baud	Transmit (TX) and receive (RX) baud rates.
Status	State of the line (ready, connected/disconnected, active/inactive, exit banner).
Capabilities	How or for what this line can be used.

Table 4-3: Fields in a show line for a single port (continued)

Field	Meaning
Modem state	Control state of the modem. If not Ready, suspect a modem problem.
Special chars	Settings of characters defined for this line.
Timeouts	Timeouts as specified by the configurations.
Session limit	Maximum number of sessions for this line. Controlled by the session-limit command.
Time since activation	Time elapsed since line activation (i.e., how long the line has been considered active).
Editing	Whether command-line editing is enabled.
History	Length of the command history buffer. Set by the user with the history command.
Full user help	Whether the full-help command has been activated for this line.
Transport methods	Transport mechanisms allowed on this line. See the transport command for more information.
Character padding	See the padding command.
Data dispatching characters	Whether any data-dispatching characters are configured. See dispatch-character for more information.
Line protocol	The protocol and address specified for this line.
Output/input packets	Queued packet counts for this line.
Group codes	AT group codes for this line.

Reverse Telnet

When a user telnets to a router, she is "logged on" directly to the router. Cisco adds a special twist: if you telnet to a special port on the router, the router redirects the incoming telnet connection back out a selected asynchronous line, rather than internally accepting the incoming connection. This is called "reverse telnet." Here are two telnet commands you might give on your Unix or Windows workstation:

```
% telnet router1          Telnet directly into router1
% telnet router1 2001     Telnet to port 2001 on router1
```

The first telnet command connects to the standard telnet port (TCP port 23; remember that we're now talking about TCP ports, not the router's physical ports) and initiates a virtual terminal session with the router. The second command is tricky. It connects to TCP port 2001; the router maps this port to one of its asynchronous lines. The router performs any login requirements, then connects the telnet session to the mapped line. The mapping is simple: just subtract 2000 from the port used for the telnet connection. So in this example, the user would be connected to asynchronous line 1 (tty1). Line 2 (tty2) would be 2002, and so on. If a modem is connected to tty1, the user would be talking directly to the modem.

The only catch to this mapping is the AUX port. The number of the AUX port is the last TTY port, plus 1. So, on a router with 18 TTY ports, the AUX port would be port 2019 (the last TTY, port 2018, plus 1). On a router with no TTY interfaces, the AUX port would be port 2001.

In addition to port 2000, ports 4000 and 6000 can be used. Port 4000 plus the `tty1` gives you a raw TCP port, which is usually for sending data directly to a printer. On port 2000, each carriage return is translated into a carriage return plus a line-feed. Port 6000 is just like port 2000, except it turns off the carriage-return translation.

Reverse telnet requires that the TTY line be configured to allow outbound connections. Here's how you do this:

```
Router(config)#line tty2
Router(config-line)#modem inout
```

The `modem inout` command allows both incoming and outgoing connections. Another way to configure the line is:

```
Router(config)#line tty2
Router(config-line)#modem callout
```

The `modem callout` command allows only outgoing connections.

Another useful command for reverse telnet is `ip alias`. This command lets you assign an IP address to a reverse telnet connection. In other words, the router associates an IP address with a reverse telnet port. If you telnet to this address, the router will connect you directly to the specified port. For example, assume that a router has an Ethernet interface with an address of 10.1.1.1. The following commands configure it to route incoming telnet connections for the addresses 10.1.1.2, 10.1.1.3, and 10.1.1.4 to asynchronous ports 1 through 3:

```
interface ethernet0
 ip address 10.1.1.1 255.255.255.0
 no shutdown
!
! Now configure our reverse telnet IP address
ip alias 10.1.1.2 2001
ip alias 10.1.1.3 2002
ip alias 10.1.1.4 2003
```

Now, when you telnet to 10.1.1.2, you will be connected to the device that is connected to port 1.

Common Configuration Items

This section summarizes the configuration items you are likely to encounter when configuring a line on a router or a terminal server.

Communication parameters

These useful commands set the low-level physical parameters of a line. To set the line speed (baud) you can use the `speed`, `txspeed`, or `rxspeed` commands. For databits, stop bits, and parity, use the commands `databits`, `stopbits`, and `parity`, respectively. For automatic baud rate detection, use the `autobaud` command.

For flow control, use the `flowcontrol` command, which takes as arguments `none`, `software`, or `hardware`. In a modern environment, `hardware` flow control is almost always appropriate.

Transport type

The `transport` command defines which protocols can be used to connect to a line. The default protocol is `none`, which means that no incoming connections are allowed. The command `transport input telnet` specifies that telnet can be used as an incoming protocol, but no other protocols are allowed.

You can also specify the preferred protocol to use after a user has connected to a line. By default, the preferred protocol is `telnet`. Therefore, when users are connected to the router, they can type a hostname, and the router will assume they want to telnet to a device. To disable this behavior, use the command `transport preferred none`.

Session limits and timeouts

IOS provides two ways to limit the number of ongoing sessions. To limit the number of sessions allowed on a line, use the `session-limit` command. To limit a session's idle time, use the `session-timeout` command. If the session is idle longer than the specified time, the router will automatically log the user out. Note that these commands apply to the configuration of lines and not to the router as a whole.

Special characters and key sequences

IOS allows you to specify a number of special characters that control the interaction between a user and the router. The activation character is the character that starts a terminal session when it is typed at a vacant terminal. The default activation character is Return; you can set it to another value using the `activation-character` command. Other special characters are the disconnect character and the hold character, both of which have no defaults. The disconnect character disconnects (terminates) a session, while the hold character pauses a session until any other key is pressed. These characters are set using the `disconnect-character` and `hold-character` commands.

All three of these commands apply to lines; the argument for each command is the ASCII value for the character. For example, to set the disconnect character for line 2 to Ctrl-d (ASCII value 4), use the following commands:

```
Router(config)#line 2
Router(config-line)#disconnect-character 4
```

CHAPTER 5

Interface Commands

Interface configuration is one of the most fundamental aspects of getting a router online. There are many kinds of interfaces, corresponding to different physical media and lower-level protocols; some of the interface types are listed in Table 5-1. For the most part, each media type has its own configuration commands, although a few commands are common to all interfaces. The interface is where much of IP configuration takes place: it's where you set addresses and netmasks and specify how the interface interacts with the routing protocol you have chosen.

Table 5-1: Interface types

Type	Description
async	Async lines are for modem dial-in and dial-out connections. The AUX port is an async line. Terminal servers have numerous async lines for modem connections.
atm	ATM (Asynchronous Transfer Mode) interfaces are used for connections to an ATM switch. This includes DSL connections.
serial	Serial ports are often connected to CSU/DSUs for point-to-point leased lines (56k, T1, etc.).
ethernet	Ethernet ports supporting 10 megabits/second.
fastethernet	Ethernet ports supporting 10 and 100 megabits/second.
bri	BRI (Basic Rate Interface) for ISDN (2B + D service).
tokenring	Token ring network interfaces.
fddi	Fiber Distributed Data Interconnect.
hub	A hub that is built into the router and treated as an interface.
hssi	High-Speed Serial Interface. Supports speeds up to 52 Mbps.
loopback	A virtual interface on the router.
null	Bit bucket interface. Anything sent to this interface is discarded. Used for simple route filtering.
pos	Packet over Sonet interfaces.
vlan	Virtual LAN interfaces.

Naming and Numbering Interfaces

Interfaces are configured by the `interface` command, followed by an interface name, followed by a port number. The space between the interface name and the port number is optional. For example:

```
interface serial 0      Serial port 0
interface serial 1      Serial port 1
interface ethernet 0    Ethernet port 0
interface ethernet 1    Ethernet port 1
```

On high-end routers, the interface cards are in slots; each slot has a series of ports. To specify these interfaces, use the *slot/port* naming scheme. For example, the Ethernet interface on port 5 of the card in slot 4 would be called:

```
interface ethernet 4/5
```

The `interface` command is followed by other commands that perform the actual configuration. If you're entering commands at the console, the `interface` command changes the prompt to `Router(config-if)#`.

VIP2 (Versatile Interface Processor) cards have two Ethernet ports per card. To accommodate these cards, use the syntax *card/slot/port* to specify a particular Ethernet interface. For example, Fast Ethernet card 2 on slot 1 on port 0 would be called:

```
interface fastethernet 2/1/0
```

Subinterfaces

Subinterfaces provide a way to have multiple logical configurations for the same interface; they are most commonly used in Frame Relay, ATM, and Fast Ethernet in switched environments. To specify a subinterface, add a period and the subinterface number to the regular interface name. For example:

```
interface serial 1.1
interface serial 1.2
```

On a high-end router that uses the slot/port notation, append the subinterface number to the port number:

```
interface serial 1/2.1
interface serial 1/2.2
```

Subinterface zero (0) refers to the actual interface; i.e., `serial1` is equal to `serial1.0`.

Here's a simple example that shows how subinterfaces are typically used. Frame Relay permits subinterfaces in both point-to-point and multipoint modes. Each mode can have its own IP address and subnet mask. This multiple–IP address configuration can be accomplished only with the subinterface commands:

```
interface serial 1
   no shutdown
interface serial 1.1 point-to-point
   ip address 10.10.1.2 255.255.255.0
interface serial 1.2 point-to-multipoint
   ip address 10.10.2.2 255.255.255.0
```

In this example, we apply the no shutdown command to serial 1, which includes both subinterfaces. We then assign a different IP address to subinterface 1 and subinterface 2.

Most commands that apply to interfaces can also be applied to subinterfaces. However, there are a few commands that can be applied only to an interface *or* to a subinterface.

Basic Interface Configuration Commands

The following basic commands apply to just about any type of interface.

shutdown

The shutdown command disables an interface. The interface does not transmit packets after it has been shut down; all routing protocols are informed that the interface is unavailable.

```
interface serial0
  shutdown
```

Use the no shutdown command to restart an interface that has been shut down:

```
Router#config terminal
Router(config)#interface serial 0
Router(config-if)#no shutdown
```

There can be side effects to an interface shutdown. The nature of these side effects depends on the interface type. Table 5-2 shows some of the possible side effects.

Table 5-2: Possible side effects of an interface shutdown

Interface	Side effect of a shutdown
Ethernet	Drops link-status indicator to the remote hub or switch
Serial	Drops DTR signal
FDDI	Activates optical bypass switch
Token ring	Removes interface from the token ring

The shutdown command can also be applied to a subinterface. In this case, it stops protocol processing on that subinterface without affecting the other subinterfaces or dropping the entire interface.

Interface Descriptions

An interface's description shows up in the router's configuration and in the output from the show interfaces command. This description is for informational purposes only; it helps you remember the configuration of the interface. For example:

```
interface serial0
  description T1 Connection to Baltimore (Good place to document the circuit id!)
```

Use the no form of this command to remove the description:

```
no description
```

Setting the IP Address and Subnet Mask

Setting the IP address on an interface is fairly simple: use the `ip address` command, followed by the address and the subnet mask. For example:

```
interface ethernet0
    ip address 10.10.1.65 255.255.255.224
```

This command sets the interface IP address to 10.10.1.65 and the subnet mask to 255.255.255.224.

Secondary IP address(es)

The `secondary` keyword allows an interface to have more than one IP address. You can have as many secondary addresses as you like, but keep in mind that each will take processing power and will have an effect on the router. If you are using more than one secondary address, chances are you are doing something wrong with your network configuration.

For example, suppose we had an Ethernet segment with a 255.255.255.224 subnet, which allows 30 hosts per subnet, as in Figure 5-1 (before). Everything is working fine. Then one day your boss comes in and tells you to add 30 more hosts on the segment. The bad news is that there are no more Ethernet ports on your router and you need to add the new machine's addresses today.

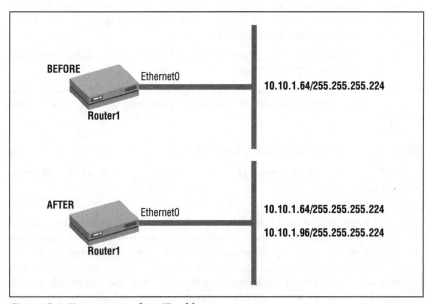

Figure 5-1: Using a secondary IP address

After a few minutes of panic, you weigh your options. One is to resubnet the network. You would then need to change the subnet masks on every machine, which is time-consuming. Even if you are using DHCP, a massive network reorganization is bound to be time-consuming and disruptive for your users.

The second, easier option is to add another subnet to the Ethernet segment by using the **secondary** command. In the old configuration, the original subnet was 10.10.1.64 with 30 hosts. In the new configuration, we add a second subnet, 10.10. 1.96, to the segment:

```
interface ethernet0
    ip address 10.10.1.65 255.255.255.224
    ip address 10.10.1.97 255.255.255.224 secondary
```

Initially, the interface was assigned the address 10.10.1.65; we could assign .66 through .94 to hosts on the segment (.95 is reserved for broadcasts). After adding the .96 subnet, we can assign addresses 10.10.1.98 through 10.10.1.126 as well; .97 is assigned to the **ethernet0** interface as its secondary address. We can go a step further and add yet another subnet, 10.10.1.128, by assigning 10.10.1.129 as an additional secondary address. This gives us a total of three subnets. We can add as many secondary addresses as we want.

```
interface ethernet 0
    ip address 10.10.1.65 255.255.255.224
    ip address 10.10.1.97 255.255.255.224 secondary
    ip address 10.10.1.129 255.255.255.224 secondary
```

Some pitfalls with secondary addresses are:

- Secondary IP addresses are not supported by OSPF.

- Routing updates are not sent out to secondary subnets due to split horizon. For a definition of split horizon and how it relates to routing, see Chapter 8. However, split horizon can be disabled.

- Too many secondary IP addresses often means you are doing something wrong with your network design.

- Host broadcasts may or may not be heard by hosts on the other subnets, depending on the broadcast address used by the host and the hosts' implementations.

Other Common Interface Commands

You will encounter the following commands frequently as you work with interfaces on Cisco routers:

bandwidth

The bandwidth command does not have anything to do with configuring the speed of an interface. Rather, it defines the interface speed for calculating routing metrics and other purposes. You would use this command to tell the router the interface's actual speed if for some reason the default bandwidth was not correct (for example, for a fractional T1 line, the router will use the speed of a full T1 as the default bandwidth), or to "lie" about an interface's bandwidth to influence route metric calculations and steer traffic in a partic- ular direction. Obviously, giving the router incorrect information about an interface's bandwidth is an iffy proposition, but there are times when that's the easiest way to achieve the result you want.

ip directed-broadcasts

A directed broadcast is a broadcast that is sent to a specific network or set of networks. They are frequently used in denial-of-service attacks, in which someone outside your network tries to overwhelm it with illegitimate traffic. To reduce your vulnerability to such attacks, Cisco routers drop directed broadcasts by default. To enable forwarding of directed broadcasts, use the `ip directed-broadcasts` command.

ip proxy-arp

Enabling proxy ARP on an interface allows the router to respond to ARP requests for hosts that it knows about, but that aren't directly reachable by the host making the ARP request. If the router receives an ARP request for a host and the router has a route to that host, the router sends an ARP response with its own data link address to the requestor. The requesting host then sends packets to the router, who in turn forwards them on to the correct destination host.

For example, a host connected via a PPP dial-up link won't be visible to hosts connected to the router via an Ethernet. If a host on an Ethernet sends an ARP request for a host connected via PPP, the router will respond to the ARP request on behalf of the PPP host, listing its own Ethernet address as the destination. The router then takes responsibility for forwarding the packets to the PPP host.

ip source-route

Source routing allows packets to include their own routing information in their headers. This feature is often abused. Source routing is enabled by default but is frequently disabled using the command `no ip source-route`.

ip unreachables

This command enables the generation of ICMP protocol unreachable messages (the default). These messages are generated when the router receives a nonbroadcast message for a protocol it doesn't recognize. This command is usually used in its negative form (`no ip unreachables`) and is often used on the null interface.

Now let's look at some of the specific interface types you're likely to encounter.

The Loopback Interface

The loopback interface is a virtual interface that is always up and available after it has been configured. Note that the loopback interface is not tied to the address 127.0.0.1. It's an interface like any other, and can be assigned its own address. A loopback interface is often used as a termination address for some routing protocols, because it never goes down.

Another common use of a loopback address is to identify a router. For example, say you want to find out whether a particular router is up. You know that the router has an `ethernet0` interface with an IP address of 10.10.1.1. You ping 10.10.1.1 and don't get a response. Does this mean your router is down? It's possible that the router is up and that the ping reached the router on another interface, but you didn't receive a response because ethernet0 is down. To find out unambiguously whether the router is alive, you have to ping another interface. But that interface might be down, causing the same scenario to occur. To avoid this problem, you can configure the router's loopback interface with a unique address. Then, when you want to telnet or ping your router, use the loopback interface's IP address. This method ensures that you will get a response no matter how your packets reach the router.

Here's how to assign an IP address to a loopback interface:

```
interface loopback 0
    ip address 10.10.1.2 255.255.255.255
```

Other ways to use the loopback interface include:

1. Using the unnumbered command on serial links mixed with the loopback interface to eliminate wasted IP addresses on serial links.

2. Various routing protocols, such as OSPF and BGP, make use of a router ID, which should be the address of a link that is always up. The loopback interface is great for this purpose. (OSPF and BGP are discussed in Chapters 9 and 10, respectively.)

3. Use the address of a loopback interface as the IP address for all management software. The management software will test whether the router is alive by pinging the loopback interface's IP address.

The Null Interface

The null interface is the "bit bucket" or "black hole" interface. All traffic sent to this interface is discarded. It is most useful for filtering unwanted traffic, because you can discard traffic simply by routing it to the null interface. You could achieve the same goal using access lists, but access lists require more CPU overhead. If you have fairly simple filtering requirements, it may be more effective to route the offending traffic to the null interface.

There can be only one null interface (null0), and it is always configured. This interface accepts only one configuration command, no ip unreachables. All other commands for this interface are ignored.

```
interface null 0
    no ip unreachables
```

In Figure 5-2, we have networks 10.10.1.0, 10.10.2.0, and 10.10.3.0 (networks 1, 2, and 3). If we do not want users on network 2 (10.10.2.0) to reach network 3 (10.10.3.0), we can add a static route on Router 2 that sends all traffic destined for 10.10.3.0 to the null interface. With this route, any traffic destined for the 10.10.30 network from the 10.10.2.0 network will be automatically discarded. Here's the configuration command that creates the static route:

```
ip route 10.10.3.0 255.255.255.0 null0
```

The null0 interface is often used as part of a security strategy. Pointing unwanted routes to the null0 interface is a good way of stopping undesirable traffic. You can also use null0 to prevent routing loops when using summarized addresses.

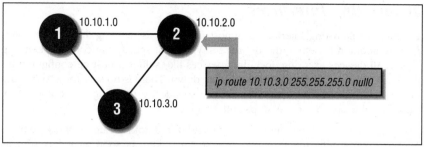

Figure 5-2: Filtering with a null interface

Ethernet and Fast Ethernet Interfaces

Give an Ethernet or Fast Ethernet interface an IP address, and it's ready to go. It's a good idea to give the interface a description, but that's not required. Also, as with all interfaces, don't forget the no shutdown command. For Fast Ethernet interfaces, you can also specify the interface speed and whether it's operating at full or half duplex:

```
interface Ethernet0
  description Internal Office Network
  ip address 10.10.1.1 255.255.255.248
  no shutdown
interface FastEthernet1
  description Fast Network for fileservers
  ip address 10.10.1.17 255.255.255.248
  ! Set the speed to 100 (which is the default)
  speed 100
  ! Set the duplex to full
  duplex full
  no shutdown
```

Ethernet Encapsulation

By default, an Ethernet uses ARPA encapsulation (standard Ethernet Version 2.0). However, you can specify another encapsulation type using the encapsulation command. For example:

```
interface ethernet 0
  encapsulation arpa
  ip address 10.10.1.10 255.255.255.248
```

The possible encapsulation types are shown in Table 5-3.

Table 5-3: Ethernet encapsulation types

Keyword	Encapsulation type
arpa	Standard Ethernet Version 2.0
isol	IEEE 802.3 Encapsulation
snap	IEEE 803.3 Encapsulation per RFC 1042

All the devices connected to an Ethernet must share the same encapsulation type; if they do not, they will not be able to communicate. If you're not sure of the encapsulation type, you're probably using ARPA.

Token Ring Interfaces

Defining a token ring interface is almost as simple as defining an Ethernet interface. In addition to setting the IP address, you must specify the correct token ring speed. All devices in a ring, including devices like sniffers, must be configured for the same speed or the whole ring will shut down. There is no way for a token ring device to autosense ring speed. To set the speed, use the `ring-speed` command. The allowable speeds are 16 Mbps and 4 Mbps.

The other common configuration command for a token ring network, `early-token-release`, tells the router to release the token as soon as it has sent its packet. The default behavior is to wait for acknowledgment after sending packets, then release the token. Here's a simple token ring configuration:

```
interface tokenring0
  ip address 10.10.14.1 255.255.255.0
  ring-speed 16
  early-token-release
```

ISDN Interfaces

ISDN is an important standard for sending digital data over telephone lines. An ISDN link can carry two different kinds of information: the data itself, and control information for the ISDN circuit. Data channels are called B ("bearer") channels and carry either 56 or 64 kilobits/second; the control channels are called D ("data") channels.

ISDN is packaged in two different ways. BRI (Basic Rate Interface) is commonly used over residential phone lines. It provides two B channels plus a D channel, for a maximum B-channel capacity of 128 kbps. PRI (Primary Rate Interface) is more like a T1 connection—in fact, it's really just a repackaged T1 connection. PRI provides 23 B channels and 1 D channel, with a maximum rate of 1.544 Mbps in the U.S. In Europe, on E1 lines you get 30 B channels, for 2.048 Mbps.

BRI is a reasonably common technology for providing home or small-office connectivity. Although it's being displaced by technologies like ADSL and cable modems, there are many places where those technologies are unavailable. ISDN reaches almost anywhere. Let's look briefly at what you need to understand to configure a BRI connection:

- Because ISDN connections are dial-up connections, they rely on DDR (dial-on-demand routing). DDR is discussed in Chapter 11, but we'll look at a simple example in this section.

- It shouldn't be a surprise that PPP is almost always used as an encapsulation protocol for ISDN links. HDLC is also possible, but it's supported only by Cisco equipment. Using PPP guarantees compatibility with other vendors. We will use PPP in all our examples.

- An ISDN configuration requires you to know the type of switch in the telephone office at the other end of your phone line. Table 5-4 shows some basic switch types, but you must consult with your provider about which ISDN switch type it is using.

Table 5-4: Some possible ISDN switch types

Keyword	Switch type
basic-5ess	AT&T 5ess BRI
basic-dms-100	Nortel BRI
basic-ni	National BRI
primary-ni	AT&T National PRI
primary-5ess	AT&T 5ess PRI

 If you change the switch type, reboot the router to be sure that the new switch type is used.

- With most ISDN connections, you receive some number of Service Profile Identifiers (SPIDs), which are essentially phone numbers with a few extra digits. One SPID is assigned to each B channel. Therefore, you normally receive two SPIDs for a BRI line. There are some exceptions: for some AT&T point-to-point services you receive only one SPID, and with some 5ESS connections you don't always need a SPID (this is especially true for connections outside the U.S.). With PRI connections, you never receive a SPID.

- Finally, you can configure an ISDN connection to use one B channel, both B channels, or as many channels as are needed given the bandwidth requirements. The latter option is a good way to reduce the cost of your ISDN link, since most carriers charge on a per-minute basis. However, this type of configuration relies on more advanced methods of dial-on-demand routing. (See Chapter 11 for more information.) In this chapter, we'll stick with a single B channel. You can also configure the B channels to carry 56 kbps or 64 kbps.

A Simple ISDN Configuration

Following are configurations for two routers connected by a dial-up ISDN connection. The connection is activated only on demand; Router 1 dials Router 2 when it has traffic for Router 2's networks, and vice versa. The local network for Router 1 is 192.168.9.0; the local network for Router 2 is 192.168.10.0. The subnet 10.10.1.0 is used for the connection between the two routers. This example uses only one B channel for the ISDN connection, so only one SPID is used for each router.

The configuration for Router 1 looks like this:

```
hostname router1
!
! Define the switch type for the ISDN provider
isdn switch-type basic-dms100
!
! Set up the user for the CHAP authentication
! The username is the hostname of the remote system and MUST match exactly
! Passwords must also be the same on both ends of the connection
username router2 password letmein
```

```
!
! Configure the ISDN line (interface bri0)
interface BRIO
  ip address 10.10.1.10 255.255.255.0
  encapsulation ppp
  ! Configure the bandwidth for routing metric caluclations
  bandwidth 56
  ! Set the Dialer commands
  ! Define the map for the remote site
  dialer map ip 10.10.1.11 name router2 speed 56 broadcast 14105551234
  dialer hold-queue 5
  dialer load-threshold 100
  dialer-group 1
  dialer idle-timeout 300
  !
  ! SPID numbers are provided by your ISDN service provider
  isdn spid1 505555123401 5554321
  !
  ! PPP should authenticate with the CHAP protocol
  ppp authentication chap
  !
  ! Since we used a dialer group of 1 in the BRI configuration,
  ! we need to define the access list (see Chapter 7) to specify
  ! what traffic should cause our ISDN line to activate
  dialer-list 1 list 101
!
! Our access list 101 is going to deny BROADCAST TRAFFIC
! (Not actually deny, but makes broadcast traffic "uninteresting")
! Everything else is permitted
access-list 101 deny ip any 255.255.255.255 0.0.0.0
access-list 101 permit ip any any
!
! Important! Create a static route to the other side of the ISDN link.
ip route 192.168.10.0 255.255.255.0 10.10.1.11
```

Here is the configuration for Router 2. It's similar to Router 1, but without the comments.

```
hostname router2
!
isdn switch-type basic-dms100
!
username router1 password letmein
!
interface BRIO
  ip address 10.10.1.11 255.255.255.0
  encapsulation ppp
  bandwidth 56
  dialer map ip 10.10.1.10 name router1 speed 56 broadcast 15055551234
  dialer hold-queue 5
  dialer load-threshold 100
  dialer-group 1
  dialer idle-timeout 300
  !
  isdn spid1 410555123401 5551234
  !
  ppp authentication chap
  !
  dialer-list 1 list 101
```

```
!
access-list 101 deny ip any 255.255.255.255 0.0.0.0
access-list 101 permit ip any any
!
ip route 192.168.9.0 255.255.255.0 10.10.1.10
```

Serial Interfaces

Serial interfaces are interfaces that connect to a device like a CSU/DSU, which in turn connects to a leased line to complete a point-to-point connection.

Serial Encapsulation

The three primary encapsulation types for a serial interface are PPP, HDLC, and Frame Relay. Other encapsulation types include X.25, SMDS, and ATM DXI. To see which encapsulation is being used on a given interface, use the show interface command. Here are brief descriptions of the different encapsulation types:

PPP

> Point-to-Point Protocol (PPP) encapsulation is initially specified in RFC 1331 and 1332 (and many others). Echo requests are used as keepalives; use no keepalives to disable this feature. PPP is popular and supported by all router vendors. If you are creating a serial link with two different types of routers, you will need to use PPP for the two routers to communicate.

HDLC

> HDLC encapsulation provides synchronous frames and error detection without windowing or retransmission. HDLC is the default encapsulation method for a serial interface, but it is proprietary to Cisco. If you build a serial link with a Cisco router at one end and another type of router at the other end, HDLC is not an option. You will have to use PPP.

> If you can use HDLC, you will find that it is simpler to configure and slightly faster than PPP, because it is less general.

Frame Relay

> In Frame Relay, your packets are handled by a switched network that provides virtual circuits between you and the sites with which you communicate. The switched network is largely invisible to you; it's managed by your Frame Relay provider. Note that Frame Relay really is an encapsulation type, not an interface type; there's no such thing as a "Frame Relay" communications line. Frame Relay communication takes place over some other medium, typically a T1 line. See Chapter 6 for information on Frame Relay.

Serial T1 Connection

Here's a simple configuration for a T1 connection. PPP is used as the encapsulation method. The router at the other end of the connection would have the same configuration, differing only in its IP address.

```
interface Serial1
  description T1 to site xyz
  ip address 10.10.1.1 255.255.255.0
  encapsulation ppp
```

T1 Configuration on a 2524 with a CSU/DSU Card

Routers like the 2524 allow CSU/DSU cards to be inserted into them. These cards eliminate the need for an external CSU/DSU. The `service-module` command is used for configuring these modules. In the following example, the `service-module` command specifies that we have purchased a full T1 from our provider and that we want to use all 24 of the T1's timeslots for this interface:

```
! configuration for a 2524 with a CSU/DSU card
interface Serial0
 description Alternet Link
 no ip address
 encapsulation frame-relay ietf
 bandwidth 1536
 service-module t1 timeslots 1-24
 frame-relay lmi-type ansi
 !
interface Serial0.1 point-to-point
 ip unnumbered Ethernet0
 ip access-group 127 in
 bandwidth 1536
 frame-relay interface-dlci 500 ietf
```

After configuring the service module, we specify Frame Relay encapsulation. We next configure a subinterface of `serial0` for use as a Frame Relay connection. Chapter 6 covers Frame Relay configuration in more detail.

Channelized T1

Some routers have Multi-Channel Interface Processor (MIP) cards. These cards allow a single controller to handle more than one T1 connection by dividing the controller and a single T1 circuit into separate channels. Each of these channels supports a related serial interface. The next example shows a configuration in which a MIP card is in slot 2, port 1 of the router, which we divide into channel 1 and channel 2. We create the two channel groups by assigning some of the T1 connection's time slots to each group. (Note that not all of the time slots are used, which allows us to create more channel groups later if we want.) After that, we configure the serial interfaces for each of the channels at serial slot 2, port 1.

Notice the use of the colon after the serial command (`serial 2/1:2`). The number after the colon refers to the channel group number, not to be confused with a subinterface. (A subinterface is a period followed by a number, e.g., serial 1.1.)

```
! Configure Control Slot 2, Port 1
!
controller t1 2/1
  framing esf
  line code b8zs
  !
  ! Define the first channel group for this MIP card
  ! Use only 2 timeslots (1-2). Allow the speed to default to 56K
  channel-group 1 timeslots 1,2
  !
  ! Define the second channel group for this MIP card
  ! The default speed is 56K, but we want to set it to 64K
  channel-group 2 timeslots 5,7,12-15,20 speed 64
  !
```

```
! Now configure the interface for channel group 1, which is serial 2/1:1
interface serial 2/1:1
   ip address 10.10.1.4 255.255.255.0
   encapsulation hdlc
!
! Now configure the interface for channel group 2, which is serial 2/1:2
interface serial 2/1:2
   ip address 10.10.2.4 255.255.255.0
   encapsulation hdlc
```

Asynchronous Interfaces

Asynchronous interfaces are almost always used to provide dial-in PPP access. The hardware configuration of the asynchronous line (parity, baud rate, etc.) is determined by the corresponding TTY line; for more information about configuring TTY lines, see Chapter 4. When you configure an async interface, you specify logical aspects of the connection. Here is a configuration for an async port with dial-in access. Each command is preceded by a comment describing the command's function.

```
interface Async1
   ! Assign IP address for the router's end of the link
   ! by assigning it the ethernet0 port
   ip unnumbered ethernet0
   ! Set the serial encapsulation to PPP
   encapsulation ppp
   ! Set the interface mode to dedicated since this is a dial-up connection
   async mode dedicated
   ! Assign the IP address for the remote connection
   peer default ip address 10.10.1.20
```

Notice that the asynchronous interface doesn't need its own IP address; it can borrow the IP address of the ethernet0 interface using the unnumbered command. However, we do need to assign an address to the PPP peer that connects through this port. That address is assigned by the peer default ip address command; in this configuration, the peer is given the address 10.10.1.20. It is also worth mentioning that the IP address of the ethernet0 interface should be on the same network as the 10.10.1.20 address.

Using the group-async Command

Here's a basic fact of life: async lines usually occur in large numbers. If you're configuring async interfaces, you're often working with a terminal server that supports many dial-in ports. Therefore, you don't want to configure each interface individually, as we did in the previous example; you want to deal with them in batches.

The group-async command allows you to configure many async interfaces without a lot of repetition. You can apply a list of configuration items to all the interfaces that belong to the group. For example, let's give async ports 1 through 5 the same configuration we set up in the previous example:

```
interface group-async 1
   ! Specify the async interfaces in this group
   group-range 1 5
```

```
! The configuration items to include in all interfaces
ip unnumbered ethernet0
encapsulation ppp
async mode dedicated
! Each interface has a different IP address for the remote end
member 1 peer default ip address 10.10.1.21
member 2 peer default ip address 10.10.1.22
member 3 peer default ip address 10.10.1.23
member 4 peer default ip address 10.10.1.24
member 5 peer default ip address 10.10.1.25
```

In this configuration, async ports 1 through 5 are configured identically. However, we need to assign IP addresses to the remote side of the interface, and these have to be unique. Therefore, we use the member command to assign a different peer IP address to every interface: someone who dials in to async port 1 is assigned the IP address 10.10.1.21, and so on. We've reduced the amount of configuration work, but we still have some configuration left to do for the individual interfaces. We'll see how to go even further in the next example.

Specifying an IP Address Pool

There's an easy alternative to using the member command to assign an IP address to each async interface: we can create an *address pool*. A pool of IP addresses is a group of addresses that can be assigned dynamically to a group of interfaces, as needed. When an IP address is in use, another interface cannot use it.

To create a pool of IP addresses, use the ip local pool command. In this example, we create an address pool named ip-pool1 for the async group we defined earlier. Notice that the pool commands are not interface commands! We use a variation of the peer default ip address command to tell the router that it should assign addresses from the pool to PPP peers that connect to an interface in the async group.

```
! Create an address pool named ip-pool1 for
! addresses 10.10.1.21 through 10.10.1.25
ip address-pool local
ip local pool ip-pool1 10.10.1.21 10.10.1.25
! Now define our async group, this time using the pool
! instead of assigning a separate IP address for every interface
interface group-async 1
  ! Specify the async interfaces in this group
  group-range 1 5
  ! The configuration items to include in all interfaces
  ip unnumbered ethernet0
  encapsulation ppp
  async mode dedicated
  ! Assign the pool for this group to use
peer default ip address pool ip-pool1
```

Using BOOTP Configuration Items for Dial-in Connections

Async interfaces can provide responses to BOOTP requests, making it much simpler for dial-in users to automate their configuration process. The async-bootp command is used to configure the responses the router will send in response to BOOTP requests. In this example, we define the BOOTP options for subnet-mask, default-gateway, dns-server, and lpr-server. They are defined even though some dial-in clients don't support them.

```
async-bootp subnet-mask 255.255.255.0
async-bootp gateway 10.10.18.196
async-bootp dns-server 10.10.18.204
async-bootp lpr-server 10.10.18.200
```

BOOTP can also provide many more aspects of the client's configuration; for more information, see the async-bootp command in Chapter 15. The show async bootp command displays the BOOTP attributes that are currently configured:

```
Router>show async bootp
The following extended data will be sent in BOOTP responses:

subnet-mask 255.255.255.0
gateway 10.10.18.196
dns-server 10.10.18.204
lpr-server 10.10.18.200
```

BOOTP does not accommodate IP pools or understand leases.

Using DHCP for IP Addresses and Dial-in Configuration Items

DHCP represents a significant advance over BOOTP in automating client configuration. It can also be used to assign addresses to PPP peers; when someone dials in, the router requests the peer address from the DHCP server. The client can then request additional configuration information from the router using DHCP, which acts as a proxy and relays the request to the actual DHCP server. The following configuration uses a DHCP server to provide the IP address and other configuration information.

```
! Configure our IP address pool to come from our DHCP server at 10.10.1.2
ip address-pool dhcp-proxy-client
ip dhcp-server   10.10.1.2
! Configure the required BOOTP information, nbns points to our WINS
! server, which in this case happens to be our DHCP and DNS server
async-bootp dns-server 10.10.1.2
async-bootp nbns-server 10.10.1.2
!
! Configure the async interface to use PPP and DHCP
interface Async1
    ip unnumbered ethernet0
    encapsulation ppp
    async mode dedicated
    peer default ip address dhcp
```

You can also use routers as standalone DHCP servers, eliminating the need for a separate server. The proxy configuration shown here is probably more common, however.

Interface show Commands

The router keeps track of lots of information about its interfaces: the number of packets sent, the number of errors, addresses, etc. You can get most of this information by using one of the show commands.

Clearing the show Command Counters

Much of the information the router tracks is numeric: for example, running counts of the number of packets that went out the interface and related items. These counters aren't particularly meaningful unless you know when the counter started counting. To clear the counters that are displayed in the show interface commands, use the clear counters command. This command does not clear the values that are retrieved from SNMP commands, but only the values reported by the show commands discussed in this section. Here are some typical clear counters commands:

```
Router#clear counters ethernet0
Router#clear counters serial0
Router#clear counters
```

The first two commands clear the counters for a specific interface; the last command clears the counters for all the interfaces.

 All counters are unsigned long integers, which means they can go up to about 4 billion before they roll over to 0 (2^32 − 1).

Listing All Interfaces

If you don't know what physical interfaces are available on your router, use the show version command. You'll find a list of interfaces at the end of its output. Here's what happens on a Cisco 2524:

```
Router>show version
...
cisco 2524 (68030) processor (revision J) with 6144K/2048K bytes of memory.
Processor board ID 08291960, with hardware revision 00000000
Bridging software.
X.25 software, Version 2.0, NET2, BFE and GOSIP compliant.
1 Ethernet/IEEE 802.3 interface(s)
2 Serial network interface(s)
FT1 CSU/DSU for Serial Interface 0
No module installed for Serial Interface 1
32K bytes of non-volatile configuration memory.
8192K bytes of processor board System flash (Read ONLY)
```

This router has one Ethernet port, two serial ports, and one built-in CSU/DSU installed on serial interface 0.

Using the show interface Commands

The show interface command displays protocol-specific statistics for the interface. All interfaces report both generic information and media-specific information. For example, here's what you get if you ask for information about an Ethernet segment:

```
Router>show interface ethernet0
Ethernet0 is up, line protocol is up
```

```
Hardware is Lance, address is 0010.7b39.e28e (bia 0010.7b39.e28e)
Description: Office Ethernet segment
Internet address is 10.10.1.1/29
MTU 1500 bytes, BW 10000 Kbit, DLY 1000 usec, rely 255/255, load 1/255
Encapsulation ARPA, loopback not set, keepalive set (10 sec)
ARP type: ARPA, ARP Timeout 04:00:00
Last input 00:00:00, output 00:00:00, output hang never
Last clearing of "show interface" counters never
Queueing strategy: fifo
Output queue 0/40, 0 drops; input queue 0/75, 0 drops
5 minute input rate 2000 bits/sec, 3 packets/sec
5 minute output rate 17000 bits/sec, 3 packets/sec
   11938498 packets input, 4102863937 bytes, 0 no buffer
   Received 60515 broadcasts, 0 runts, 0 giants, 0 throttles
   8 input errors, 0 CRC, 0 frame, 0 overrun, 8 ignored, 0 abort
   0 input packets with dribble condition detected
   12556989 packets output, 1981671402 bytes, 0 underruns
   0 output errors, 11702 collisions, 1 interface resets
   0 babbles, 0 late collision, 20150 deferred
   0 lost carrier, 0 no carrier
   0 output buffer failures, 0 output buffers swapped out
```

Table 5-5 shows how to interpret this information.

Table 5-5: Information from a show interface command

Field	Meaning
Up/down	Whether the interface is up and configured. If the interface is administratively down, the shutdown command has been applied to this interface. If the interface is down, it is not receiving any signal from the attached network cable.
Line protocol	Whether the encapsulation protocol is up or down for this interface. If your interface is up but the line protocol is down, check the encapsulation or see if the line has been unplugged.
Hardware	The type of interface (serial, Ethernet, etc.).
Internet address	The IP address and subnet mask for this interface.
MTU	The Maximum Transmission Unit for this interface (the maximum frame/packet size).
BW	The bit rate in kbps (default is 1544 for serial, 10000 for Ethernet). This value is actually the setting from the interface's bandwidth command, which is used in route metric calculations but has no other impact on the router. In particular, this value has nothing to do with the actual speed at which data is transferred.
DLY	The expected delay for a packet traversing this interface. Like the bandwidth, this parameter is used only for IGRP/EIGRP route metric calculations. Its value can be set with the delay interface command.
Rely	The reliability of this link, as a number between 1 and 255. The value 255/255 indicates that the link is 100% reliable.
Load	The traffic load on the segment, as a number between 1 and 255. The value 255/255 indicates that the link is at 100% of capacity. 1/255 is the lowest value.
Encapsulation	The encapsulation type for this link. For serial links, the encapsulation might be PPP or HDLC. For Ethernet, it might be ARPA.
Loopback	Whether the interface is in the loopback state. If you cannot send packets across your link, you may have loopback set.
Keepalives	Whether keepalives are active on this link.

Table 5-5: Information from a show interface command (continued)

Field	Meaning
Last input/ last output	How long it has been since a packet was received or sent on this interface. This field is not an actual time value, but the number of hours, minutes, and seconds since the packet was received or sent. If the time exceeds 24 hours, the field overflows and asterisks are printed.
Output hang	The time since this interface was last reset because of a transmission that took too long to complete. If the time exceeds 24 hours, the field overflows and asterisks are printed.
Queue	The number of packets in both the input and output queues. The number is in the format "number in queue/max size of queue, number of drops".
5 minute	The five-minute average input and output rate. The rate is given in both bits per second and packets per second over the last five minutes.
Packets input	Number of successful error-free packets this interface has received.
Bytes input	Number of successful error-free bytes this interface has received.
Broadcasts	Number of multicast or broadcast packets this interface has received.
Runts	Number of packets this interface threw away because they were smaller than the minimum packet size.
Giants	Number of packets this interface threw away because they were larger than the maximum packet size.
Input error	Total number of errors encountered by this interface. These errors can include runts, giants, CRC errors, overruns, ignored packets, aborts, buffer overflows, and frame errors.
CRC	The number of checksum failures encountered by this interface. A checksum failure occurs when the calculated checksum does not match the checksum sent by the sending device. Lots of CRC errors mixed with a low number of collisions on an Ethernet interface is an indicator of excessive noise, which points to cable issues.
Frame	The number of frame errors encountered by this interface. These occur when a packet that is malformed or does not contain the correct number of bytes is delivered to the interface.
Overruns	The number of overrun errors within this interface. This occurs when the low-level device driver fails to read a byte before the serialization hardware completes receiving the next byte.
Ignored	The number of packets ignored by this interface. This occurs when the internal buffers are full and the interface ignores incoming packets because it has no place to store them.
Abort	The number of aborts on this interface. Occurs because of a timing problem between the router and serial device.
Packets output	The total number of packets this interface has transmitted.
Bytes output	The total number of bytes this interface has transmitted.
Underruns	The number of underrun errors on this interface. Occurs when the low-level device driver fails to provide the next byte to be serialized before the previous one has been completely transmitted.
Output errors	The number of errors that occurred when this interface tried to transmit.
Collisions	The number of times two hosts sent a packet at the same time; a small number is normal.
Late collisions	This number should always be 0 on a properly configured network. If you see these, suspect a hardware problem.
Restarts	The total number of times this interface reset due to errors. Not shown in the output above.
Carrier transitions	The total number of times this interface has changed state because it lost the carrier signal. Not shown in the output above.

show interface accounting

Another interesting show command is show interface *interfacename* accounting. This command gives you a quick overview of the interfaces and their packet counts:

```
Firewall#show interface ethernet0 accounting
Ethernet0
        Protocol    Pkts In   Chars In    Pkts Out   Chars Out
              IP   10659150   62307981    13906422  3947809402
             ARP     272756   17240212      126066     7563960
             CDP      76294   23585301      186904    57192624
```

This command displays the accounting statistics for the ethernet0 interface. It shows the packets received (Pkts In), characters received (Chars In), packets transmitted (Pkts Out), and characters transmitted (Chars Out) for each protocol. On this router, the protocols in use are IP, ARP (Address Resolution Protocol), and CDP (Cisco Discovery Protocol).

show ip interface

The show ip interface command gives you detailed information about an interface's IP configuration. The related command show ip interface brief provides a summary of the IP configuration for all the router's interfaces. Here's the result of show ip interface ethernet0:

```
Router#show ip interface ethernet0
Ethernet0 is up, line protocol is up
  Internet address is 10.200.212.1/24
  Broadcast address is 255.255.255.255
  Address determined by non-volatile memory
  MTU is 1500 bytes
  Helper address is not set
  Directed broadcast forwarding is disabled
  Multicast reserved groups joined: 224.0.0.10
  Outgoing access list is not set
  Inbound  access list is 145
  Proxy ARP is enabled
  Security level is default
  Split horizon is enabled
  ICMP redirects are always sent
  ICMP unreachables are always sent
  ICMP mask replies are never sent
  IP fast switching is disabled
  IP fast switching on the same interface is disabled
  IP multicast fast switching is disabled
  Router Discovery is disabled
  IP output packet accounting is disabled
  IP access violation accounting is disabled
  TCP/IP header compression is disabled
  Probe proxy name replies are disabled
  Gateway Discovery is disabled
  Policy routing is disabled
  Network address translation is disabled
```

Table 5-6 explains each line in the output.

Table 5-6: Explanation of show ip interface output

Output	Explanation
Internet address is 10.200.212.1/24	Gives the IP address and subnet mask that are currently set for the interface. For this interface, the network mask is /24, which is equivalent to 255.255.255.0.
Broadcast address is 255.255.255.255	Gives the broadcast address for this interface. The default is 255.255.255.255; it can be modified with the `ip broadcast-address` command.
Address determined by non-volatile memory	Specifies the source from which the IP address for the interface was retrieved.
MTU is 1500 bytes	Specifies the Maximum Transmission Unit for this interface. This can be modified with the `ip mtu` command.
Helper address is not set	The `ip helper-address` command sets a destination address for UDP broadcasts. In this example, it is not set. It is normally used to forward BOOTP or other UDP services to a server.
Directed broadcast forwarding is disabled	Specifies whether directed broadcasts are enabled. Directed broadcasts are normally disabled, but can be enabled using the `ip directed broadcasts` command. See the description of directed broadcasts earlier in this chapter.
Multicast reserved groups joined: 224.0.0.10	Lists the multicast group joined by this interface.
Outgoing access list is not set	Shows the outgoing access list for the interface. The `ip access-group number out` command sets the access list.
Inbound access list is 145	Shows the incoming access list for the interface. The `ip access-group number in` command sets the access list.
Proxy ARP is enabled	Gives the status of proxy ARP; either enabled or disabled. See the `ip proxy-arp` description earlier in this chapter.
Security level is default	Gives the IPSO security level for this interface.
Split horizon is enabled	Gives the status of split horizon on this interface; either enabled or disabled. Use the command `ip split-horizon` to enable it. This topic is covered in Chapter 8.
ICMP redirects are always sent	Shows the status of ICMP redirects; either allowed or not. The `ip redirects` command enables them.
ICMP unreachables are always sent	Specifies whether ICMP unreachable messages are sent from this interface. The `ip unreachables` command enables it.
ICMP mask replies are never sent	Specifies whether ICMP mask replies are sent. The `ip mask-reply` command enables it.
IP fast switching is disabled	Specifies whether the fast-switching cache for outgoing packets is enabled. Use `ip route-cache` to enable it.
IP fast switching on the same interface is disabled	Specifies whether the fast-switching cache for packets on the same interface is enabled. Use `ip route-cache` to enable it.
IP multicast fast switching is disabled	Specifies whether the fast-switching cache for outgoing multicast packets is enabled. Use `ip mroute-cache same-interface` to enable it.
Router Discovery is disabled	Specifies whether router discovery is enabled. Use the `ip irdp` command to enable it.
IP output packet accounting is disabled	Specifies whether IP output packet accounting is enabled. If enabled, this line will also describe the accounting threshold. Use the `ip accounting` command to enable it.
IP access violation accounting is disabled	Specifies whether access violation accounting is enabled. Use the `ip accounting access-violations` command to enable it.

Table 5-6: Explanation of show ip interface output (continued)

Output	Explanation
TCP/IP header compression is disabled	Specifies whether TCP header compression is enabled. Use the `ip tcp header-compression` command to enable it.
Probe proxy name replies are disabled	Specifies whether the HP probe proxy is enabled. Use the `ip probe proxy` command to enable it.
Gateway Discovery is disabled	Specifies whether gateway discovery is enabled. Use the `ip gdp` command to enable it.
Policy routing is disabled	Specifies whether policy routing is enabled. The `ip policy` command enables it.
Network address translation is disabled	Specifies whether NAT is enabled on this interface. The `ip nat` command enables address translation. However, it requires some extensive configuration. For more information, see Chapter 12.

Here's the output from **show ip interface brief**. The output is fairly straightforward, except for the meaning of the Method column. This column is the same as the "Address determined" field in Table 5-6.

```
Router#show ip interface brief
Interface      IP-Address      OK? Method Status                 Protocol
Ethernet0      10.200.212.1    YES NVRAM  up                     up
Ethernet1      10.200.210.30   YES NVRAM  up                     up
Serial0        unassigned      YES unset  administratively down  down
Serial1        unassigned      YES unset  administratively down  down
```

Interface
Commands

CHAPTER 6

Frame Relay and ATM

Frame Relay

In the past decade, Frame Relay has become a popular wide-area network (WAN) switching method. Building a WAN by creating virtual circuits inside a provider's Frame Relay network has become a much more attractive option than ordering leased lines between the locations you want to connect. Instead of paying for all those leased lines, you just pay for access to the provider's network. Of course, there is still a leased line to the provider, but it is typically fairly short—much shorter than a leased line between your end locations. It's easy to order the bandwidth you need for each link; furthermore, Frame Relay allows you to reserve a guaranteed minimum bandwidth (called the "committed information rate" or CIR) but lets you use as much bandwidth as is available on the network. In fact, you don't need the same speed circuits at all your sites. For example, your corporate headquarters might use a DS-3 (45-Mbps line), while your regional offices all have T1 lines.

At the physical level, a Frame Relay connection looks just like a serial interface—because it is. A standard leased line (typically a T1 line) connects your site to the Frame Relay provider. Although it's more complex than a simple serial interface, the complexity comes mostly from mapping the IP addresses of the nodes on your network into Data Link Connection Identifiers (DLCIs), which are the Frame Relay equivalent of addresses.

Important Frame Relay Terminology

Before we look at some basic Frame Relay configurations, we need to go over a few important topics and terms. Figure 6-1 shows two routers that connect to each other through a Frame Relay network.

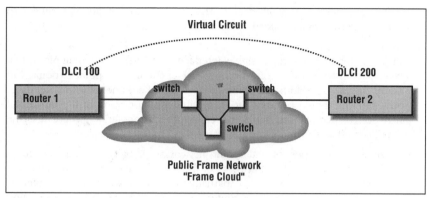

Figure 6-1: A virtual circuit on a Frame Relay network

Here are some terms you'll need to understand when working with Frame Relay:

Frame cloud

When connecting to a public frame network, you only know about your points of entry to the network; the interior of the network (the "cloud") is invisible to you. The network itself is often called a cloud, because you can't see what happens to your packets after they enter it.

Virtual circuit (VC)

A virtual circuit is a logical connection created by the frame provider from Point A to Point B across a frame cloud.

Data Link Connection Identifier (DLCI)

A DLCI is a value assigned by the frame provider to identify a virtual circuit. In other words, it's the Frame Relay equivalent of an address. DLCIs are unique only locally. That is, your router will have a unique DLCI for each virtual circuit it uses from one Frame Relay provider. However, as far as the Frame Relay provider is concerned, DLCIs are just numbers; the provider can reuse DLCIs throughout its network.

The router maps IP addresses to DLCIs so that it can communicate with a remote router by using the appropriate DLCI. There are two ways to map a DLCI to an IP address. First, you can allow the router to discover the DLCI by using inverse ARP, which is enabled by default. Second, you can explicitly map an IP address to a DLCI.

Local Management Interface (LMI)

The LMI is based on the type of Frame Relay switch you are connecting to. Your provider will give you this information. The LMI types are Cisco, Ansi, and q933a; Cisco is the default. Note that the routers at each end of the link may have different LMI settings, because they are connected to different types of switches.

Point-to-point

A point-to-point connection is a single virtual circuit that connects two points. In Figure 6-1, Router 1 connects to Router 2 with a frame network between them. On either side of the frame cloud is a router that knows that there is only one router at the other end. This kind of configuration is similar to connecting two routers directly over a serial line.

Multipoint

In a multipoint network, a single interface is connected to multiple virtual circuits with multiple DLCIs. Each virtual circuit is still point-to-point, but many logical point-to-point connections share the same physical interface. Subinterfaces should be used for each fully-meshed portion of the multipoint network. Remember that subinterfaces use the X.Y notation, where X is the interface and Y is the subinterface.

There are two types of multipoint networks: partially-meshed and fully-meshed. In a fully-meshed network, all the routers have direct connections to each other. In contrast, in a partially-meshed network, each router is connected to at least one other router, but may not have a direct connection to all the routers in the network. For example, you might have three routers, A, B, and C; Routers B and C are connected to Router A, but do not have a direct connection to each other.

Split horizon

Split horizon is a technique commonly used in routing protocols; it means that the router will not send information about a route out the same interface from which it learned the route. Split horizon is normally used to prevent routing loops. However, it can cause problems in a partially-meshed multipoint Frame Relay network. More than one router may be listening at the other end of any interface. Therefore, we don't want to suppress route announcements. For example, assume that we have three routers (i.e., three virtual circuits) connected to our multipoint interface. If a route comes to our interface from any of those points, we want to announce the route to the other two points. If split horizon is enabled, we can't send the route out our interface because that is where the route originated. However, split horizon should be enabled on a fully-meshed multipoint Frame Relay network.

Frame Relay Configuration

Here is the most basic Frame Relay configuration. We don't give the serial interface an IP address; instead, we use the unnumbered command to tell it to "borrow" the address of the ethernet0 interface. To use this command, we must tell the router explicitly that serial2 is a point-to-point interface:

```
interface serial2
  no ip address
  encapsulation frame-relay ietf
  no shutdown
interface serial2.1 point-to-point
  ip unnumbered ethernet0
```

Okay, it will probably never be that easy. So, let's use the network pictured in Figure 6-1, where Router 1 has a DLCI of 100 and Router 2 has a DLCI of 200. Here's the configuration for Router 1:

```
interface serial1
  no ip address
```

```
  encapsulation frame-relay ietf
  frame-relay lmi-type ansi
  no shutdown
!
interface serial1.1 point-to-point
  description connection to baltimore
  ip unnumbered ethernet0
  ! Give the DLCI of the local end of the virtual circuit
  frame-relay interface-dlci 100
```

And here's the configuration for Router 2. The only thing that's different is the DLCI:

```
interface serial1
  no ip address
  encapsulation frame-relay ietf
  frame-relay lmi-type ansi
  no shutdown
!
interface serial1.1 point-to-point
  description connection to new-york
  ip unnumbered ethernet0
  ! Give the DLCI of the local end of the virtual circuit
  frame-relay interface-dlci 200
```

Some notes about this configuration:

- We were forced to break up the configuration into subinterfaces because IOS does not allow us to apply the point-to-point keyword to the main interface.

- There's no IP address for serial1's main interface, since we tie the IP address to the subinterface.

- We used ip unnumbered to establish an IP address for serial1.1. This means that the interface doesn't have its own IP address; it borrows an address from one of the router's other interfaces (in this case, ethernet0). For this to work, we had to specify that the interface is point-to-point and configure both routers appropriately.

- We explicitly defined the DLCIs on each link. We are relying on inverse ARP (enabled by default) to map the IP address of the remote end of the link to the DLCI. The next section discusses how to map addresses to DLCIs in more detail.

Mapping IP Addresses to DLCIs

A key part of Frame Relay configuration is mapping IP addresses to DLCIs. This mapping can take place either explicitly or implicitly. The previous example used an implicit mapping: we simply listed the DLCI for our connection and let the router use inverse ARP to map the DLCI to an IP address. With inverse ARP, the router automatically infers the IP address of the router at the other end of the DLCI. To do so, the router waits for a packet to arrive on the DLCI. The source IP address of the packet is then associated with the remote router's DLCI, allowing the router to build a map of DLCIs and IP addresses.

The primary advantage of an implicit mapping is that you don't have to reconfigure your router if the address of the remote end changes. As your network changes, the router notices the new addresses and adjusts its tables accordingly. All you have to do is list the DLCIs you know about. To clear any maps created by inverse ARP, use the command clear frame-relay-inarp. Inverse ARP is enabled by default.

For an explicit mapping, we would build the map by hand using the frame-relay map ip command. While this method removes the possibility of an error being made by inverse ARP, it is difficult to manage, especially if you have a large network with many virtual circuits.

The next two sections go into more detail about creating an explicit mapping and using implicit mapping in a multipoint configuration.

Explicitly mapping DLCIs

Here's how to create an explicit mapping between IP addresses and DLCIs. In the next section, we will see how to use the multipoint connection with implicit listing of the DLCIs.

```
interface serial1
  encapsulation frame-relay ietf
  frame-relay map ip 192.168.2.1 100
  ! disable inverse mapping because we no longer need it
  no frame-relay inverse-arp
```

With this configuration, DLCI 100 is mapped to IP address 192.168.2.1. We would add additional frame-relay map ip statements for any other addresses we care about. We don't need inverse ARP with an explicit mapping, so we disabled it.

Configuring a multipoint connection

With a multipoint connection, we have one serial interface connected to a Frame Relay network. However, that interface can reach multiple destinations. For example, if we need to communicate with three destinations through the Frame Relay network, as in Figure 6-2, we can create three logical interfaces on a single physical serial interface and then treat each destination as if it has its own interface.

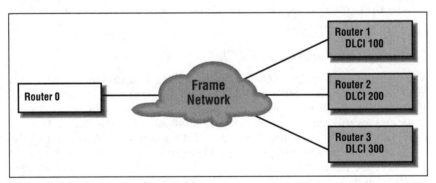

Figure 6-2: Multipoint configuration

There are a couple of ways to configure the router for this network. The simple, laborious way is to list every virtual circuit, giving each one a point-to-point subinterface. Here's the configuration for Router 0:

```
interface serial1
  encapsulation frame-relay ietf
  frame-relay lmi-type ansi
  no shutdown
!
interface serial1.1 point-to-point
  ip address 192.168.1.5 255.255.255.252
  description connection to New York
  frame-relay interface-dlci 100
!
interface serial1.2 point-to-point
  ip address 192.168.2.5 255.255.255.252
  description connection to Texas
  frame-relay interface-dlci 200
!
interface serial1.3 point-to-point
  ip address 192.168.3.5 255.255.255.252
  description connection to Pasadena
  frame-relay interface-dlci 300
```

Let's do it again, this time using the multipoint option so we don't have to configure each virtual circuit separately:

```
interface serial1
  no ip address
  encapsulation frame-relay ietf
  frame-relay lmi-type ansi
  ! disable split-horizon
  no ip split-horizon
  no shutdown
!
interface serial1.1 multipoint
  description connection to New York, Texas, and Pasadena
  ip address 192.168.1.1 255.255.255.0
  ! List all the DLCIs and let the router figure out the mapping
  frame-relay interface-dlci 100
  frame-relay interface-dlci 200
  frame-relay interface-dlci 300
```

Once again, we listed all the DLCIs that are available for this interface. However, we pushed them all into one multipoint subinterface. The router uses inverse ARP to figure out the IP addresses for the remote end of the connection. We could also have used the frame-relay map command to explicitly map each DLCI to an IP address, but that would be much more work in a large network.

Frame Relay show Commands

Table 6-1 lists the show commands that are useful for configuring and troubleshooting Frame Relay connections.

Table 6-1: Useful show commands for Frame Relay

Command	Displays
show interface	DLCI and LMI settings
show frame-relay lmi	LMI statistics
show frame-relay pvc	Frame Relay PVC statistics
show frame-relay map	Current Frame Relay map information
show frame-relay traffic	Traffic statistics and information
show frame-relay route	Configured static routes for Frame Relay
show frame-relay svc	Current SVCs

ATM

ATM stands for Asynchronous Transfer Mode, a cell-switched network technology used for building high-speed backbones. ATM breaks data into fixed-size cells of 53 octets. Five octets are used for the cell header; the remaining 48 are available for data. The fixed size allows an ATM switch to handle the cells quickly and efficiently. An ATM switch is allowed to drop cells as necessary if the switch's capacity is exceeded. There is a mechanism for distinguishing between cells that can be discarded and high-priority cells that should not be discarded (although even high-priority cells can be discarded if there is no alternative).*

Sending IP packets over an ATM network presents some interesting problems. Each packet must be broken into multiple cells, since most IP packets won't fit into 48 octets. If any of the cells are dropped, the packet won't make it through the network undamaged. Therefore, the packet will probably be resent (it will certainly be re-sent if it's a TCP segment). In turn, this means dumping many additional cells into a switch that is already suffering from congestion. This problem is less serious if your ATM network is designed for minimal cell loss.

ATM requires special (and sometimes expensive) hardware to run. Some of the common ATM hardware products provided by Cisco include:

- ATM Network Processor Module (4500/4700-series routers)
- ATM Interface Processor (7500-series routers)
- ATM Port Adapter (7500-series routers)

ATM-DXI allows ATM over a non-ATM interface, such as a serial interface (like HSSI). In this configuration, you typically have an ADSU (ATM CSU/DSU) connected to a high-speed serial port on your router.

---

* An exception to this rule is AAL1 (ATM Adaptation Layer 1). In the case of AAL1, no cells should be discarded. If the switch builds the AAL1 VC, it should pass all the cells. Since this is not a book about ATM, I don't have the time or space to discuss ATM adaptation layers in detail.

ATM Terminology

ATM is a connection-oriented protocol. A separate connection must be established for every device with which a router wants to communicate within the ATM
network. These connections are called virtual circuits (VCs). VCs can be either
permanent (PVCs) or switched (SVCs). PVCs are typically used for WAN connections; SVCs are typically used for LAN connections. The main difference between
PVCs and SVCs is that SVCs can be created and destroyed automatically by the
software. This dynamic creation of circuits makes administration a bit easier. On
the other hand, PVCs are—for a lack of a better word—permanent. It's hard to
imagine a wide-area network in which you wouldn't want permanent circuits
between your nodes. You can think of a PVC as a leased line, while an SVC is
more like a dialed phone call.

A virtual circuit is defined by two numbers, assigned by your ATM provider: a
Virtual Path Identifier (VPI) and a Virtual Channel Identifier (VCI). The VPI identifies a bundle of circuits, while the VCI identifies a circuit within a bundle. It is
easier to think of the VPI/VCI pair as a single parameter, like a DLCI in a Frame
Relay configuration.

Before we examine our first configuration, let's look at ATM encapsulation. Several
types of encapsulation are used for ATM:

aal5snap
> All traffic is on one ATM circuit.

aal5mux
> A dedicated circuit is set up for each protocol (IP, IPX, etc.).

aal5nlpid
> Works with ATM-DXI and encapsulates over Frame Relay.

Another acronym you'll see when working with ATM is LANE, which stands for
LAN Emulation. In this mode, the LANE device emulates a more traditional LAN
technology, such as Ethernet. We'll discuss LANE after we learn how to configure
ATM.

Configuring Permanent Virtual Circuits

When configuring ATM for a WAN connection, you need to:

* Assign an IP address and VPI/VCI to a PVC

* Define the encapsulation method

* Map a remote IP address (the IP address of the router at the other end of the
  circuit) to the PVC

The last step (mapping an IP address to the PVC) is required only for static
mappings. Just as in Frame Relay, there are two ways to manage IP addressing: we
can statically map the IP address of the remote router, or we can let the router
figure out the mapping itself with inverse ARP. I'll show examples of both
configurations.

ATM commands tend to be hardware-specific, partly because ATM is present on products ranging from low-end DSL routers to high-end routers to ATM switches. I've tried to choose examples and commands that work in most environments, but it's important to check the documentation for your router.

Configuring an ATM interface with static IP mapping

Figure 6-3 shows our ATM connection. You will see that we are again using subinterfaces to implement ATM; in more advanced settings, using subinterfaces simplifies the configuration. Here is the configuration for Router 1:

```
interface atm0
  no shutdown
!
interface atm0.1
  ! assign our interface's IP address
  ip address 10.10.1.1 255.255.255.0
  ! Create PVC 20 with a VPI of 0 and a VCI of 60
  atm pvc 20 0 60 aal5snap
  map-group atm-map1
!
map-list atm-map1
ip 10.10.2.1 atm-vc 20 broadcast
```

Figure 6-3: An ATM configuration

This configuration is simple. We have all three steps that we mentioned earlier:

- We assigned a local IP address to our ATM interface.

- We created a PVC with the `atm pvc` command. This command creates PVC 20, which has a VPI of 0 and a VCI of 60, and uses the `aal5snap` encapsulation method. The number we assign to the PVC (20) is used only for referring to the PVC in other parts of the router configuration; it has no other significance.

- We mapped a remote IP address to the PVC with the `map-list` command. The `broadcast` option within the map list is important because it allows routing-protocol updates to propagate to remote hosts. Most routing protocols rely on multicasts or broadcasts, for which ATM has no native support.

Configuring an ATM interface with dynamic IP mapping

Instead of statically mapping an IP address to the PVC, we can use inverse ARP and let the router figure out the mapping itself. Inverse ARP is not the default for

ATM; we need to configure it explicitly. The following configuration is identical to the previous one, except that it uses inverse ARP instead of static mapping. As a result, the configuration is noticeably shorter, even on a simple network. For larger networks, the savings could be significant.

```
interface atm0
  no shutdown
interface atm0.1
  ip address 10.10.1.1 255.255.255.0 inarp 5
  atm pvc 20 0 60 aal5snap
```

The inarp 5 option tells the interface to use inverse ARP for mapping the IP address to the PVC and to set the time period for inverse ARP (the amount of time between inverse ARP requests) to five minutes. The default time period is 15 minutes. Now the system can respond to changes in remote addressing without a change to the ATM configuration; the router will notice any changes on the ATM network the next time it sends an ARP request. Therefore, at most five minutes will elapse before the router notices the change and adjusts its address mappings.

Configuring Switched Virtual Circuits

SVCs are created automatically by software. However, the software that creates and destroys SVCs requires two PVC channels for communication; these must be created explicitly, like any other PVC. One PVC channel uses VPI 0 and VCI 5 for signaling; this channel uses the encapsulation method qsaal. The other required PVC exchanges management information and uses VPI 0 and VCI 16, with ilmi encapsulation. Both of these channels are associated with the "main" ATM interface and not with any subinterfaces.

Another important piece of the SVC picture is the Network Service Access Point (NSAP) address. This address is something like a MAC address for ATM networks. That is, it's a higher-level concept than a physical address (essentially, the VPI/VCI pair) and is persistent: it doesn't change, even though the VPI/VCI to reach any destination will change as the circuit is created and destroyed. The process for creating an SVC operates like this:

1. A device is ready to communicate with another device, so it sends the NSAP address of the destination device to the network signaling channels.

2. The device waits for the circuit to be created.

3. The device can now use the newly created circuit.

NSAP addresses are unique 20-octet hex values.

For an example, consider the network in Figure 6-3. If we were to add a router named Router 3 with an IP address of 10.10.3.1, an SVC configuration for Router 1 might look like this:

```
interface atm1
  ! Configure the two signaling channels that are required for SVC
  atm pvc 1 0 5 qsaal
  atm pvc 2 0 16 ilmi
  !
interface atm1.1
  ! Our interface's IP address
```

```
ip address 10.10.1.1 255.255.255.0
atm nsap-address 22.0011.01.FF1111.00FF.0000.AAAA.1111.1111.1111.11
atm map-group atm-map
!
map-list atm-map
ip 10.10.2.1 atm-nsap 22.0011.01.AAAAAAA.00FF.0000.AAAA.1111.1111.AAAA.11 broadcast
ip 10.10.3.1 atm-nsap 22.0011.01.BBBBBBB.00FF.0000.AAAA.1111.1111.BBBB.11 broadcast
```

With this configuration, circuits to 10.10.2.1 and 10.10.3.1 will be created on demand. There are only a few new concepts here: the signaling channels, the nsap-address for the interface, and the static mapping of the NSAP addresses for the end routers. The configuration for the signaling channels is simple, and is the same on every ATM router that uses SVCs. Similarly, the NSAP addresses are fairly easy to understand, if you can deal with the long hex numbers; your biggest problem will be typing them correctly. That's a big problem, particularly in a large network: we don't want to be typing dozens of 20-byte hex numbers, which may change as the network is reconfigured. What makes the problem even worse is that this map must be replicated on all the routers in your network. The only address excluded from the map is the NSAP address of the router itself. So for a network of 10 routers, you would have to type 90 of these 20-octet NSAP addresses.

It would be great if we didn't need to configure those long NSAP addresses for every IP address on our network. But since ATM isn't a broadcast protocol, there is no way for it to learn about the possible remote NSAP addresses. However, you can do dynamic mapping if your network has an ATM ARP server. This server knows about all the NSAP addresses for your network, which means a router can query the server for NSAP addresses. This is considered Classical IP. If we had an ATM ARP server on our network, our configuration could be reduced to this:

```
interface atm1
  ! Configure the two signaling channels that are required for SVC
  atm pvc 1 0 5 qsaal
  atm pvc 2 0 16 ilmi
interface atm1.1
  ! Our interface's IP address
  ip address 10.10.1.1 255.255.255.0
  atm nsap-address 22.0011.01.FF1111.00FF.0000.AAAA.1111.1111.1111.11
  !
  ! Now just supply the NSAP address of the ARP server
  atm arp-server nsap 22.0011.01.AAAAAAA.00FF.0000.AAAA.1111.1111.AAAA.11
```

Now we have an SVC configuration with dynamic addressing.

ATM ARP server

Since having an ATM ARP server on our network greatly simplified our configuration in the previous example, I'll show you how to configure one. Only one ATM ARP server should exist for each logical IP subnet of an IP network. The configuration of an ATM interface as an ARP server is as simple as this:

```
interface atm0
  ip address 10.10.1.2 255.255.255.0
  atm esi-address 3031.11ba.1181.20
  atm arp-server self
```

We could have used the `atm nsap-address` command instead of the `atm esi-address` command. However, the ESI (End System Identifier) is preferred because it allows the ILMI address registration to work better should a router move within the ATM network.

Configuring with DXI

Using the ATM-DXI mode basically means that you have an ADSU connected to a high-speed serial port on your router. The ADSU in turn connects to the ATM switch and acts like a CSU/DSU. Configuration is not as complicated as having the native ATM interface: we're dealing with a familiar serial interface, and almost all of the ATM-specific complexity is handled by the ADSU. In other words, since we are using outside hardware to communicate via ATM, there is only so much that we can do. Consider the following configuration:

```
interface serial 1
  ip address 10.10.1.1 255.255.255.0
  encapsulation atm-dxi
  ! configure for VPI of 1 and VCI of 2
  dxi pvc 1 2 mux
  ! map the IP 10.10.1.2 to VPI 1 and VCI 2
  dxi map ip 10.10.1.2 1 2 broadcast
```

The line `dxi pvc 1 2 mux` gives us a permanent virtual circuit with a VPI of 1 and a VCI of 2. It also sets the `mux` option, which means that only one protocol is to be used over this PVC. That protocol is defined in the next line, which maps the remote IP address 10.10.1.2 (i.e., the address of the router at the other end of this circuit) to the VPI/VCI pair. The broadcast option allows routing-protocol updates to be sent over this PVC.

ATM show Commands

The `show` commands listed in Table 6-2 are useful for configuring and trouble-shooting ATM.

Table 6-2: Useful show commands for ATM

Command	Displays
show atm map	All configured static ATM maps
show atm vc	Information about ATM virtual connections
show atm interface	ATM-specific information for an interface

LAN Emulation (LANE)

LAN Emulation (LANE) allows an ATM network to emulate legacy LAN types, specifically Ethernet and token ring. In other words, LANE provides the advantages of ATM's larger bandwidth, which allows you to scale your network while keeping already deployed LAN applications. LANE allows you to run any broadcast LAN protocol (IP, IPX, AppleTalk, etc.) across the ATM network without the applications knowing about it. Among other things, LANE provides a way to accommodate broadcast traffic (required for LANs) over ATM, which is not a broadcast technology.

LANE works by encapsulating the LAN packets inside the ATM frames, which results in a smaller MTU because the packets are restricted by the MTU size of the emulated protocol. LANE resolves LAN MAC addresses to ATM addresses through the use of an Emulated LAN (ELAN), which is similar to a virtual LAN (VLAN). Four components are part of every LANE configuration. They are:

LAN Emulation Client (LEC)

The LEC is the ATM client that is participating in the ELAN. A device has one LEC for each ELAN in which it is participating. However, if a device participates in multiple ELANS, it can have multiple LECs (that's plural LEC, not LECS!). Devices that would use the LEC are ATM hosts, LAN switches, and routers. The LEC handles all the communications to the ELAN servers and establishes a mapping to and from LAN MAC addresses and the ATM NSAP addresses. Once the mappings are correct, the LEC opens a private virtual circuit directly to the remote device's LEC.

LAN Emulation Configuration Server (LECS)

The LECS contains the database that lists each client (LEC) and the ELAN to which the client belongs. There is one LECS per ATM network. The clients (LECs) query this server to get the NSAP address (ATM address) of the LES (the server) for their assigned ELAN.

LAN Emulation Server (LES)

The LES maps MAC addresses to NSAP addresses and maintains a database showing which clients are currently active in the ELAN. There is one LES for every ELAN.

Broadcast Unknown Server (BUS)

The BUS forwards unknown, broadcast, and multicast data to the clients in the ELANs. There is one BUS for every ELAN. Because the LES and BUS are so closely related, they are configured as one entity within the router. From this point on, we will refer to the both of them as one object called the LES/ BUS.

LANE configuration notes

The following notes will help you to understand LANE configuration:

- The LECS is configured on the major ATM interface.

- The LES and LEC of the same ELAN can be configured on the same subinterface.

- Clients of different ELANs cannot be configured on the same subinterface.

- Servers of different ELANs cannot be configured on the same subinterface.

- For one client on an ELAN to talk to a client on another ELAN, a router must be present to route between the two ELANs.

- Using automatic NSAP addresses is much easier than supplying a unique NSAP address for every ELAN client. With the command `lane auto-config-atm-address`, the router will automatically generate a unique NSAP address by itself. We use this command throughout the following examples.

Configuring the LECS

Because the LECS needs to know where the LES for each ELAN is located, and because your network may have a large number of ELANs, the LECS configuration can be quite lengthy. All of these examples include the ATM signaling configuration—if ATM isn't working, you're not going to get anywhere with LANE.

In this configuration, we establish two ELANs in the LECS database. The database is called elandatabase1 and the ELANs are elan1 and elan2.

```
! Define the NSAP address of the LES for each and every ELAN
lane database elandatabase1
  name elan1 server-atm-address 47.00918100000000613E5D0301.00603E0DE841.01
  name elan2 server-atm-address 47.00918100000000613E5D0301.008876EF0356.08
  ! We set a default ELAN for LECs that don't know which ELAN they should
  ! join
  default-name elan1
!
! Set up the major ATM interface signaling
interface atm 0
  atm pvc 1 0 5 qsaal
  atm pvc 2 0 16 ilmi
  ! Attach the LANE database that we created to the interface
  lane config elandatabase1
  ! Tell the LECS to use automatic addressing
  lane auto-config-atm-address
```

Configuring the LES/BUS

We could configure the LES/BUS on the same server as the LECS. In this case, we configure it on a separate router. Once again, we are going to configure the signaling for ATM. Then we'll configure the LES/BUS with the lane server-bus command. Finally, we'll configure the interface as a client of the ELAN. If you don't make the LES/BUS a client of the ELAN, the router will function as the LES/BUS but will not be able to do any routing for the ELAN. Making it a client of the ELAN ensures that the router can be the LES/BUS for the ELAN and also route traffic for the ELAN.

```
! Set up the major ATM interface signaling
interface atm 0
  atm pvc 1 0 5 qsaal
  atm pvc 2 0 16 ilmi
  ! Set up LANE default addressing
  lane auth-config-atm-address
!
! Configure the LES/BUS on a separate subinterface
interface atm0.1
  ip address 10.1.1.1 255.255.255.0
  ! Configure this router as LES/BUS
  lane server-bus ethernet elan1
  ! Also make it a client of the ELAN
  lane client ethernet elan1
```

Configuring the LEC

The previous example used the `lane client` command to make the LES/BUS a client of the ELAN. This case is much simpler: we will make the router a LANE client and assume that the LES/BUS is on another device.

```
! Set up the major ATM interface signaling
interface atm 0
  atm pvc 1 0 5 qsaal
  atm pvc 2 0 16 ilmi
  ! Set up lane default addressing
  lane auth-config-atm-address
!
! Configure the LES/BUS on a separate subinterface
interface atm0.1
  ip address 10.2.1.1 255.255.255.0
  lane client ethernet elan2
```

LANE show commands

The commands in Table 6-3 are useful for configuring and troubleshooting LANE.

Table 6-3: Useful show commands for LANE

Command	Displays
show lane default-atm-addresses	The automatically assigned ATM address of each LANE component
show lane client	All LANE information for each LANE client configured on an interface

CHAPTER 7

Lists and Queues

Access Lists

In the most intuitive sense, an access list is a series of rules that instruct the router on how to select or match a route or packet. IOS uses access lists as an extremely general mechanism for controlling many kinds of router behavior, but the best way to understand how they work is to start with the simplest application: controlling the traffic that flows into or out of an interface.

Each rule in a standard access list contains three important parts: a number that identifies the list when you refer to it in other parts of the router's configuration, a deny or permit instruction, and something to identify packets (for example, an address). As incoming or outgoing packets reach an interface that has an access list, the router compares the packets to each rule in the access list and decides whether the traffic should be blocked (denied) or permitted.

For IP traffic, there are two fundamental types of lists: standard and extended. *Standard access lists* filter based on source network addresses. A typical standard access list looks like this:

```
access-list 1 deny 10.10.1.0 0.0.0.255
access-list 1 deny 10.10.2.0 0.0.0.255
access-list 1 permit any
```

This list blocks any traffic from the 10.10.1.0 and 10.10.2.0 subnets, regardless of the packet's destination, and permits anything that makes it past the first two lines. In other words, all traffic is permitted except for the 10.10.1.0 and 10.10.2.0 subnets. Once you have the list, you can apply it to the packets going into or out of a particular interface. To apply this list to the traffic arriving at (i.e., coming into) a particular interface, we would use the ip access-group command:

```
interface ethernet0
  ip access-group 1 in
```

As I mentioned, there are many other contexts in which access lists can be used. You can use them to restrict who can access a particular TTY line, what routes get sent in and out of various routing processes, and to perform many other functions. It's also worth noting that while applying access list 1 to the packets arriving at ethernet0 prevents traffic from subnets 10.10.1.0 and 10.10.2.0 from passing through the router, it doesn't affect traffic arriving at any other interface, nor does it have any effect on protocols other than IP. You have to watch each interface and protocol separately.

Standard access lists perform filtering on the basis of source IP addresses. *Extended access lists* allow you to build much more flexible filters that use source and destination addresses, in addition to higher-layer protocol information. For example, you can build a filter based on ICMP type and code values. For TCP and UDP, you can filter on destination and source ports. Figure 7-1 shows a router with an extended access list applied to ethernet0. This access list blocks incoming TCP traffic for port 23, regardless of the traffic's source or destination address. Since port 23 is the telnet port, this list prevents any hosts on Network A from telneting to hosts on Network B or to the router itself.

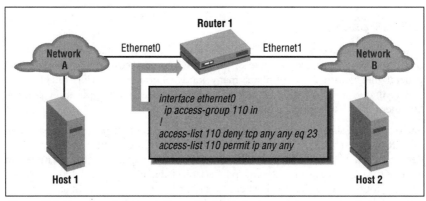

Figure 7-1: An extended access list to block telnet

Access lists can also be applied in the outbound direction. For example, we can create a list that denies traffic on port 80 and apply that list to outbound packets travelling through ethernet0. This will prevent hosts on Network B from accessing web servers on Network A:

```
! Deny traffic on port 80 (www traffic)
ip access-list 111 deny tcp any any eq 80
ip access-list 111 permit ip any any
!
interface ethernet0
  ! Apply access list 111 in the outbound direction
  ip access-group 111 out
```

The access lists we've seen so far have been very simple, but they can be much more complex.

How Packets Match a List Entry

A standard access list is composed of a series of rules. These rules are processed in order and describe which packets should be allowed or denied based on their source addresses. The syntax of an entry in a standard access list is:

```
access-list number action source
```

The parameters are:

number

> A number between 1 and 99, identifying the list for future reference

action

> The keyword **permit** or **deny**, indicating whether to allow or block the packet

source

> The packet's source address

Table 7-1 shows three ways to write the source and destination addresses. In most cases, you'll use address/mask pairs to specify blocks of addresses—if we had to write access lists based on individual IP addresses, they wouldn't be very interesting.

Table 7-1: Specifying addresses in access lists

Syntax	Example	Explanation
address mask	192.168.2.0 0.0.0.255	Describes a block of IP addresses. The mask is used as a wildcard; a one (1) in the mask indicates that we "don't care" about the corresponding bit in the address. A zero (0) in the mask means that the corresponding bit must match exactly. This example specifies addresses from 192.168.2.0 to 192.168.2.255. That is, the wildcard mask says that we ignore the last byte of the address when figuring out whether an address matches.
host address	host 192.168.2.1	The given address must be matched exactly.
any	any	Any IP address will match.

Address/mask pairs (wildcards)

Nearly every user starting out with access lists has a problem understanding wildcard masks. The problem is that wildcard masks look like subnet masks, but they aren't; a wildcard is actually the complement of the corresponding subnet mask. For example, to permit any IP traffic to the 192.168.2.0/24 network (i.e., 192.168.2.0 with a subnet mask of 255.255.255.0), we write an access list entry like this:

```
access-list 10 permit 192.168.2.0 0.0.0.255
```

Now, let's say that a packet comes along with a destination address of 192.168.2.1. How do we tell if a match occurs? The wildcard mask is bitwise ORed with both the actual destination address and the address given in the access list rule. If the two results are equal, a match occurs and the packet is either permitted or denied. To see how this works, let's look at the bits. Table 7-2 shows the relevant addresses and masks in binary.

Table 7-2: Converting addresses to binary

	Decimal form	*Binary*
Wildcard mask	0.0.0.255	00000000.00000000.00000000.11111111
Access list address	192.168.2.0	11000000.10101000.00000010.00000000
Destination IP	192.168.2.1	11000000.10101000.00000010.00000001

Here is the computation:

```
WildCard Mask  = 00000000.00000000.00000000.11111111
Access List    = 11000000.10101000.00000010.00000000
Result One     = 11000000.10101000.00000010.11111111

WildCard Mask    = 00000000.00000000.00000000.11111111
Destination IP   = 11000000.10101000.00000010.00000001
Result Two       = 11000000.10101000.00000010.11111111

Result One = Result Two
```

Because the two results match, the destination address 192.168.2.1 matches the access list. In short, the mask value of 0.0.0.255 means that the last byte of the incoming address can have any value; we don't care about its value. In this case, we match all IP addresses from 192.168.2.0 through 192.168.2.255. Furthermore, since the mask states that we will match any value in the last byte of the incoming address, the last byte of the address in the access list can have any value. That sounds confusing, but all it really means is that 192.168.2.0 0.0.0.255 is the same as 192.168.2.139 0.0.0.255; both address/mask pairs match the same group of addresses (192.168.2.0 through 192.168.2.255).

Computing a wildcard for a given subnet mask

Because the wildcard mask is the complement of the subnet mask, there's a simple formula for computing the correct wildcard mask for any subnet mask. For each byte of the subnet mask, calculate the corresponding byte of the wildcard mask using the formula:

Wildcard = 255 – Subnet

For example, the wildcard mask that corresponds to a subnet mask of 255.255.255. 224 (30 hosts per subnet) is 0.0.0.31 (255 – 224 = 31). Here are two access list entries using this wildcard mask:

```
! For a network of 192.168.2.64 255.255.255.224
access-list 10 permit 192.168.2.64 0.0.0.31
!
! For a network of 192.168.2.96 255.255.225.224
access-list 10 permit 192.168.2.96  0.0.0.31
```

Access list processing

Most of the access lists we have seen so far have consisted of a single rule. But access lists frequently contain many rules. In this case, rules are processed sequentially. The source address of each packet is tested against each rule in the list, starting with the first and ending when a match occurs. Let's take the example in the beginning of this chapter, which permitted everything except traffic from two particular subnets. Here is what the list looked like:

```
access-list 1 deny 10.10.1.0 0.0.0.255
access-list 1 deny 10.10.2.0 0.0.0.255
access-list 1 permit any
```

The router processes each line in order until it finds a match. Therefore, if a packet arrives from 10.10.2.13, it matches the second rule in the list and so is denied. What happens if we change the list, placing the last line first?

```
access-list 1 permit any
access-list 1 deny 10.10.1.0 0.0.0.255
access-list 1 deny 10.10.2.0 0.0.0.255
```

Now all traffic would be permitted through this list. The first line permits all traffic because all incoming packets match it. The second and third lines are never used. For this reason, access lists must be ordered carefully.

Implicit deny

Every time you create an access list, the router adds a line to the end stating, "If nothing matched this list, deny it." If we could see it, this line would look like:

```
access-list 1 deny any
```

All traffic that makes it to the end of an access list is blocked by the implicit deny. This helps us to write more efficient access lists. It would be a pain to write access lists that listed every host (and, for extended lists, every port) you want to permit and every host (and port) you want to deny. Furthermore, the router overhead for processing such large lists would be prohibitive. However, you can take advantage of the implicit deny to write lists that itemize only the traffic you want to permit. Don't bother to list traffic you want to deny—it will be handled by the implicit deny. (But do be careful not to inadvertently permit traffic you want to deny.) A good rule of thumb for designing access lists is to use lots of permit rules and relatively few deny rules.

Access lists are additive

Access lists cannot be freely edited once they have been entered in the router's configuration. If you want to change a single entry in the list, the entire list must be deleted and then re-entered. For example, consider this list:

```
access-list 1 deny host 10.10.1.5
access-list 1 deny host 10.10.1.7
```

After typing this list, you realize there is a mistake: In the first line, the IP address 10.10.1.5 should be 10.10.1.17. Your first attempt to fix the problem is to add another rule by typing:

```
access-list 1 deny host 10.10.1.17
```

This new rule is simply added to access list 1. The result is that you're now denying access by 10.10.1.17—but you are also denying access by 10.10.1.5, which wasn't your original intent. Can you fix this problem by adding a fourth rule that explicitly permits access from 10.10.1.5? No—because rules are processed in order, the first line (denying access) will always be processed before the additional line permitting access. So, can you delete the first line? Trying to do so, you type:

```
no access-list 1 deny host 10.10.1.5
```

This doesn't work either. Instead of deleting just one line, the router sees no access-list 1 and removes the entire list. It is a common mistake to think that a single rule can be deleted from an access list. If you make a mistake in an access list, or want to change it for some reason, your best approach is to delete the entire list and build it again from scratch. Modifying an existing list usually isn't a good idea. In this case, to fix your list you would enter:

```
no access-list 1
access-list 1 deny host 10.10.1.17
access-list 1 deny host 10.10.1.7
```

The best way to edit access lists is to keep an editor open with the access list in it. After you have modified your list, simply paste it into the router. That way, if you make a mistake, you can easily change it within your editor and paste it again.

Outbound access lists are more efficient than inbound

It is much more efficient to filter outgoing packets than to filter incoming packets. This is counterintuitive; at first glance, it seems that filtering incoming packets would save the router from processing all the blocked packets and routing them through to an outbound port. The difference is that an outgoing packet has already been routed (i.e., an outbound interface has been selected for it) before the access list processes it. Incoming packets must be processed by the access list before they arrive, and that's where the problem lies. Processing the access list first means that the router can't use its fast-switching paths and must process-switch the packet. What does this mean? Normally, the router has a cache of routes, which allows it to look up a known route quickly. With an inbound access list, the router· can't use this cache and is forced to select the route another way.

In addition, an outbound access list is often smaller than the corresponding incoming list. For example, if a packet is coming in one interface, you have to write an inbound access list that considers all the possible routes the packet might take. On an outbound list, you already have a lot of information about the packet's destination (e.g., which interface it's going through), which allows you to write shorter, more efficient access lists.

This isn't to say that inbound access lists shouldn't be used. There are plenty of times when you need to use an inbound access list; I'll cover some of these in the next few sections.

Types of Access Lists

There are many different kinds of access lists. The basic concepts I've introduced with standard access lists apply to all of them: for example, they are processed sequentially, new rules are added to old rules rather than overriding old rules, and they permit or deny certain actions (typically, processing of a packet) based on information in the packet's headers.

With a few exceptions, you can tell an access list's type by looking at its number. Each type of access list has been assigned a group of 100 numbers. Table 7-3 summarizes the access list types and their numeric ranges.

Table 7-3: Access list numbers

List type	Numeric range
Standard IP access lists	1–99
Extended IP access lists	100–199
Ethernet type code	200–299
DECnet	300–399
XNS	400–499
Extended XNS	500–599
AppleTalk	600–699
Ethernet address	700–799
Novell	800–899
Extended Novell	900–999
Novell SAP	1000–1099
Additional standard IP access lists	1300–1999
Additional extended IP access lists	2000–2699
Named access lists	None
Reflexive access lists	None
Dynamic access lists	None

In this book, I discuss only standard, extended, named, and reflexive lists. Notice that in recent releases of IOS (11.1(cc) and 12.0), there are additional ranges for both standard and extended access lists.

Extended Access Lists

Extended access lists are a relatively straightforward variation of standard access lists. Standard lists are limited to filtering based on the source and destination addresses of IP packets. Extended lists add the ability to filter based on the protocol and the port specified in the packet. Here's the syntax of an extended access list:

```
access-list number action protocol source s-port destination d-port [optional-args]
```

The action and source address are the same as for standard access lists. The other fields are:

number
: A number identifying the list. For extended access lists, this number must be between 100 and 199.

protocol
: An indication of the protocol to which the rule applies. This must be either ip, tcp, udp, or icmp.

s-port

For TCP or UDP packets, the packet's source port. There are a number of ways to specify ports. This field is optional. If the protocol is IP or ICMP, this field is omitted.

destination

The packet's destination address, specified the same way as the source address. That is, you can have an IP address followed by a wildcard mask, the keyword host followed by the IP address of a specific host, or the keyword any.

d-port

For TCP or UDP packets, the packet's destination port. There are a number of ways to specify ports. This field is optional. If the protocol is IP or ICMP, this field is omitted.

optional-args

An optional keyword that is applicable only if the protocol is TCP. For example, the keyword established is optional.

Specifying ports

When writing extended access lists for TCP or UDP, you can specify source and destination ports along with the source and destination addresses. You can specify either individual ports or a range of ports. By specifying ports you can permit or deny access to specific services, such as SMTP or HTTP. Here are the different ways to specify ports:

lt *n*

All port numbers less than *n*

gt *n*

All port numbers greater than *n*

eq *n*

Port *n*

neq *n*

All ports except for *n*

range *n m*

All ports between *n* and *m*, inclusive

For example, eq 80 refers to the well-known port for a web server; gt 1023 refers to all ports greater than 1023. For most well-known ports, you can use the standard name for the service rather than the actual port number. For example, eq www refers to the well-known HTTP port, which is 80. Likewise, you can use smtp to refer to port 25, and so on. Here are some examples.

The following two rules match (and permit) packets with any source address destined for the SMTP or HTTP ports on the host 10.10.1.5:

```
access-list 110 permit tcp any host 10.10.1.5 eq 25
access-list 110 permit tcp any host 10.10.1.5 eq 80
```

The next rule matches TCP packets with a destination port less than 1024, regardless of the source and destination addresses, and denies access:

```
. access-list 110 deny tcp any any lt 1024
```

This rule matches TCP packets with a destination port between 3000 to 3010, inclusive, and denies access:

```
access-list 110 deny tcp any any range 3000 3010
```

Finally, this rule matches UDP packets with a destination port of 3535, regardless of the source and destination addresses, and permits access:

```
access-list 110 permit udp any any eq 3535
```

Established connections

The established keyword can be added to access rules for TCP. Technically, this keyword matches packets that have the ACK or RST (Reset) bit set. If either the ACK or the RST bit is set, the router assumes that the packet is not the first packet of a session and that a session has already been established.

What does this mean in practice? It gives us a way to distinguish sessions originating inside our network from sessions originating elsewhere. For example, let's say that we want to allow our staff to initiate telnet connections with any site on the Internet but that we don't want people outside our site to be able to establish telnet connections to our systems. An easy way to enforce that policy is to block incoming packets that don't have the ACK or RST bits set by using the established keyword. This means that we allow return traffic for connections that are already established from the inside, and that we don't allow outsiders to establish connections with us. In short, the only people who can establish connections are the users inside our network. Here's how you might create and apply that list:

```
! Inbound access list
access-list 110 permit tcp any any established
access-list 110 deny ip any any
!
! Outbound access list
access-list 111 permit tcp any any eq telnet
access-list 111 deny ip any any
!
interface serial0
  access-group 110 in
  access-group 111 out
```

In practice, it would be a good idea to specify our network's address as the destination for the inbound list, rather than relying on any. The established keyword is almost always used on incoming packet filters, which allows connections to originate "behind" the router but prevents connections from the outside. (It could be used on outgoing access lists, but this would not be particularly useful.) This method of blocking unwanted traffic originating outside the network can be circumvented; it is possible to forge a packet with the appropriate bits set. The later section on reflexive lists covers another way to allow established connections.

ICMP protocol entries

ICMP packets are becoming increasingly important, as they have been used in many recent denial-of-service attacks. We can construct access list rules that permit or deny ICMP packets, allowing us to receive (or block) network error messages and ping packets. Here's a typical ICMP rule:

```
access-list 110 permit icmp any any echo-reply
```

ICMP is a surprisingly complicated protocol with lots of different packet types. It would be nice if you could either block ICMP entirely or allow it into your network without worrying about it. Unfortunately, neither approach is a good idea. You can't just block ICMP, because a number of important mechanisms for controlling traffic flow depend on it. (For example, Path MTU discovery relies on ICMP; if ICMP is blocked, you might find connections that start but die for no apparent reason.) And you can't allow ICMP in unquestioned, because it's the basis for a number of denial-of-service attacks.

Here's a set of access list rules that should be appropriate for most situations. They allow what you need, and block packet types that you don't need or are dangerous:

```
! Allow pings into the network
access-list 110 permit icmp any any echo
! Allow ping responses
access-list 110 permit icmp any any echo-reply
! Allow ICMP source-quench (flow control)
access-list 110 permit icmp any any source-quench
! Allow Path MTU discovery
access-list 110 permit icmp any any packet-too-big
! Allow time-exceeded, which is useful for traceroute
access-list 110 permit icmp any any time-exceeded
! Deny all other ICMP packets
access-list 110 deny icmp any any
```

Applying an Access List to an Interface or Line

We've already used the commands that apply access lists to interfaces fairly liberally, but it's worth looking at them in detail. To apply an access list to an interface, use the access-group command. Here are two examples:

```
interface ethernet0
  ip access-group 110 in
  ip access-group 112 out
```

This code applies access list 110 to inbound packets and access list 112 to outbound packets on the interface ethernet0. Again, packets arriving at an interface and packets leaving the interface are filtered separately. You can apply only one access list per direction to an interface.

To apply a standard access list to a line, use the access-class command. For example:

```
line vty0
  access-class 10 in
```

This means that access list 10 is used to control which hosts can access virtual terminal 0. In effect, this command limits telnet access to the router. You cannot apply an extended access list to a line.

There are many other contexts in which you can use access lists. Unfortunately, each has its own command for applying the list. The commands are more or less similar: you specify an access list number, and usually specify whether the list applies to traffic leaving or entering the router.

Named Access Lists

So far, all the access lists we've seen have been identified by numbers. Numbers have some obvious problems: they're difficult to remember and they're limited— you get only 100 access lists of each type. While this should be plenty, it's strange to have this kind of limitation built into such a critical mechanism. (The most recent versions of IOS have added some additional blocks of numbers for standard and extended IP access lists, but numbers are still awkward, and the more you use, the more inconvenient they are.)

IOS 11.2 and subsequent releases allow you to dispense with numbers and give access lists logical names. To create a simple access list named simplelist, use the command:

```
ip access-list standard simplelist
```

To create an extended list named inboundfilter, use the command:

```
ip access-list extended inboundfilter
```

Follow the `ip access-list` command with the rules that make up the list, omitting everything up to and including the number. For example, here's a standard list named filter1:

```
ip access-list standard filter1
   permit 10.10.1.0 0.0.0.255
   deny 10.10.0.0 0.0.255.255
   permit any
```

If you're typing access lists at the command line, named access lists give you yet another prompt to worry about. Here's how we'd type the preceding list in a console session:

```
Router(config)#ip access-list standard filter1
Router(config-std-nacl)#permit 10.10.1.0 0.0.0.255
Router(config-std-nacl)#deny 10.10.0.0 0.0.255.255
Router(config-std-nacl)#permit any any
```

To apply a named access list to an interface, use the `access-group` command as earlier, but specify the list's name instead of its number:

```
interface serial 1
   ip access-group filter1 in
```

Besides being more descriptive, named access lists have another advantage: you can edit them much more conveniently. That is, you can delete a line from within the access list; you don't have to delete the entire access list and re-enter it, as you do with numbered access lists. The following commands modify the filter1 list defined earlier:

```
Router(config)#ip access-list standard filter1
Router(config-std-nacl)#no permit 10.10.1.0 0.0.0.255
Router(config-std-nacl)#exit
```

```
Router#show access-list filter1
ip access-list standard filter1
   deny 10.10.0.0 0.0.255.255
   permit any any
```

As you can see, the no command didn't erase the entire access list. Instead, it removed only the line we didn't want. However, the editing capabilities aren't perfect. Access lists are still additive; any new rules you add to filter1 will be added to the end. There's no way to modify a rule that's in the list. Therefore, you still must be careful constructing your lists.

 Most commands that require an access list as an argument will take either a numbered or a named list. Some won't. Cisco is gradually fixing this problem by converting all commands to accept either a name or a number.

Reflexive Access Lists

Reflexive access lists are an important tool added to IOS 11.3 and its successors. They allow you to create lists that dynamically change based on what services your users need. Basically, you create an inbound and an outbound access list. The outbound access list creates entries in a temporary access list. This temporary access list is "evaluated" by the inbound access list. To put it another way, packets going out the interface create temporary entries to allow packets of the same session back in. When an outbound session ends, the temporary entries are destroyed, which closes the hole in the inbound access list.

Reflexive lists are similar to extended TCP access lists with the established keyword in that you will usually use reflexive lists to allow communications that have been initiated by your users. As I explained earlier, established connections rely on two bits (ACK and RST) being set in the incoming packet. While the established keyword works, it presents two problems. First, someone attempting to crack your site can exploit the established assumption by illegitimately setting the ACK and RST bits in a packet that doesn't belong to an established session, tricking the router into thinking the packet is legitimate. Second, the system is always open for attacks, even if no outbound sessions are in progress. With reflexive lists, however, we open the entry in the inbound access list only for valid current sessions.

The outbound reflexive list doesn't actually do any filtering, but rather detects attempts to initiate a TCP session. When a new session is started, an entry is automatically entered in the corresponding inbound list, allowing only the traffic belonging to that session. If that session is idle for a certain amount of time (by default, 300 seconds), the automatically generated entry expires, and traffic from the session is no longer allowed.

Creating the outbound reflexive list

The outbound reflexive list doesn't do any filtering; it simply provides a mechanism for generating the corresponding inbound list. The key to the outbound list is the `reflect` command, which watches for attempts to initiate TCP sessions and adds those sessions to the temporary list. Here's a simple list named `outlist`; the temporary list we're building is called `tmplist`:

```
ip access-list extended outlist
  ! Allow everything and add it to the reflexive list called tmplist
  permit tcp any any reflect tmplist
```

All traffic automatically matches this list and is passed through the interface. All outbound traffic will create an entry in the temporary list called `tmplist`.

Creating the inbound reflexive list

Now we need to create an inbound list that evaluates the `tmplist` we've built. To do so, we create a list named `inlist` that uses those temporary entries and add it to our configuration. This list is processed in order, just like any other access list, which means you can use `deny` and `permit` rules as in any other inbound list. In this example, we allow incoming access to our web server, plus any traffic that has been added to `tmplist`. All other traffic is denied.

```
ip access-list extended inlist
  ! allow tcp to our web server
  permit tcp any host 192.168.1.1 eq www
  ! evaluate our temporary reflexive list
  evaluate tmplist
  ! deny everything else
  deny ip any any
```

An entry can be in the `tmplist` only if it corresponds to a session that was initiated from within our internal network.

Applying the inbound and outbound reflexive lists to an interface

To apply the reflexive list to an interface, we just apply the outbound list and the inbound list in the appropriate directions:

```
interface serial0
  description  Internet Gateway interface
  ip access-group inlist in
  ip access-group outlist out
```

Now we do a `show access-list`. The `tmplist` will appear with all the temporary entries that are currently in the list. If there are no temporary entries, the list will be blank.

```
Router1#show access-list
Extended IP access list inlist
    permit tcp any host 192.168.1.1 eq www
    evaluate tmplist
    deny ip any any
Extended IP access list outlist
    permit tcp any any reflect tmplist
Reflexive IP access list tmplist
```

Setting the reflexive timeout

By default, entries in the reflexive list time out after 300 seconds with no traffic; that is, if the session is idle for 300 seconds, the reflexive entry will be removed from the temporary list. If the session was not complete, it will need to be restarted. Five minutes is a long time for a connection to be idle, so let's reduce this to 200 seconds:

```
ip reflexive-list timeout 200
```

Reflexive list notes

Here are a few things you should keep in mind when you use reflexive lists:

- Reflexive lists are designed for use on gateway routers (routers that connect you to the Internet, to a shared backbone, or to another company or organization).

- The `reflect` keyword, which establishes a reflexive list, can be used only on `permit` statements.

- Entries in reflexive lists automatically expire after a certain idle period, even if the session is not complete.

- Entries are removed from the temporary list when the session is complete.

- The outgoing IP addresses/ports and incoming IP addresses/ports will be "swapped" in the temporary lists.

- Reflective lists do not work on protocols such as FTP in which the incoming port does not match the outgoing port. To get FTP to work, perform the steps outlined later in the section "Permitting FTP through an access list."

Specific Topics

Here are a few ideas and tricks that will help you write access lists that are appropriate for your network.

Adding Comments to an Access List

You can add comments to access lists by using the `remark` keyword. Place any descriptive text you want after this keyword. Remarks work in named and numbered access lists.

```
access-list 110 remark Block traffic to 192.168.1.0. They cause trouble
access-list 110 deny ip 192.168.1.0 0.0.0.255 any
access-list 110 remark Worker bob surfs the internet all day, so stop him
access-list 110 deny tcp host 192.168.2.1 any eq www
```

Timed Access Lists

Sometimes, we want to control traffic based on the time of day. For example, we might want to prevent staff members from browsing the Web during work hours. So far, we don't have a way to do that aside from reconfiguring access lists every day at 8 A.M. and 5 P.M. IOS provides an easy solution to this problem. We can use the `time-range` command to establish a time range; then we can apply the time range to access list rules, establishing times when the rule is active.

For example, let's build a time range that includes working hours on weekdays:

```
! This is a global command
time-range block-http
  periodic weekdays 8:00 to 17:00
```

This time range has the name `block-http` and is `periodic`, which means that the time range repeats. (In contrast, an `absolute` time range has a single fixed starting and ending point.) Now, it is just a matter of adding the time range to a rule in an extended access list:

```
! Timed range works only in extended access lists
ip access-list extended list1
  ! block-http is the name of the time range we defined earlier
  deny tcp any any eq www time-range block-http
  permit any any
```

The first rule blocks all HTTP traffic whenever it is in effect; the time range `block-http` defines when the rule is active. The second rule allows all other traffic.

Building a Gateway Router

Figure 7-2 shows a common configuration in which a router serves as a gateway from a local network to the Internet. If a firewall is unavailable, adding an access list on this router can dramatically increase network security.

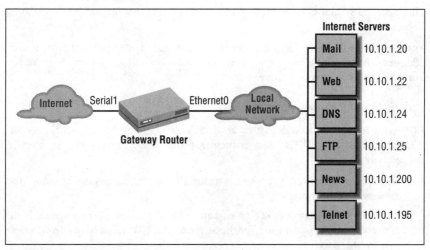

Figure 7-2: A gateway router

 This access list does not provide all the possible security for an Internet connection. Use it with caution!

Before we build the list, we need to review some topics the list will cover.

IP address spoofing

IP spoofing is the act of forging network packets that appear to come from an internal IP address. Because most sites trust their internal hosts more than they trust hosts on the Internet, spoofing allows crackers to evade security restrictions that would otherwise keep them out. For example, packets with a spoofed (internal) IP address might make it through an access list that was designed to prevent access from hosts on the Internet. Once inside your network, these packets may be able to access services that shouldn't be available to the outside world.

Preventing spoofing attacks is relatively easy. Packets originating from our network should never arrive from the Internet or any other external network. Hence, we can easily set up an access list that blocks all IP traffic with our network addresses as the source address, then apply this list to incoming packets on our Internet interface. For example, if our network address is 198.168.10.0/24, the access list for spoofing would be:

```
! List to block spoofing
access-list 111 deny ip 198.168.10.0 0.0.0.255 any
access-list 111 permit ip any any

! Internet interface; to block spoofing, apply 111 to incoming packets
interface serial0
  ip access-group 111 in
```

This access list blocks any traffic with a source address in the 198.168.10.0/24 network.

Another suggestion is to apply an outgoing list that denies packets with source addresses that don't belong to our network. Doing so will keep users from within our network from spoofing to the outside.

Permitting FTP through an access list

FTP has a number of quirks that make it difficult to allow through an access list. "Classic" (non-passive) FTP is a particular problem. A non-passive connection proceeds as follows:

1. The client requests an FTP session to the FTP server using port 21 (ftp), and the server authenticates.

2. The FTP client sends a PORT command to the FTP server. This command tells the server which port to use for the session. The FTP client waits on this new port for the data.

3. The server opens a new connection from port 20 (ftp-data) to the given port on the FTP client.

4. The client and server can now communicate with each other on the new port.

The problem lies in the acceptance of the new port for the FTP session: as it arrives, the access list blocks it because it looks like a new incoming session, not an established one. The new port number for the connection is never known. Therefore, we need to add a line to the access list that allows incoming connections from the ftp-data port to any host on the network:

```
access-list 110 permit tcp any eq ftp-data any gt 1024
```

This line allows incoming FTP connections with two restrictions: the source must be a packet from the ftp-data port on any host, and the destination must be a host on the network with a port greater than 1024.

If you don't add this line to your gateway router's access list, your users will probably complain that they can't FTP to the outside world.

Passive FTP

Passive FTP is an alternative to non-passive FTP that is supported by most clients and servers today. However, it isn't the default; you may need to configure the client to use passive mode when it initiates a connection. With passive FTP, the client sends a PASV command to the server instead of a PORT command. PASV tells the FTP server to communicate with the FTP client on the same port it is using. Thus, the incoming packets look like they belong to an established connection on the FTP port. If you use the established keyword in your access list rule for FTP (or if you have a more general rule that permits all established connections), it will allow the packets from the server back into your network.

The FTP client software must support the passive option for this to work. If you decide to go this route, you must configure all your internal network hosts to use passive FTP, which may prove to be quite a chore.

The actual access list

List 110 implements a simple access policy for our Internet gateway router:

```
! Block spoofing of our IP addresses
access-list 110 deny   ip 10.10.1.0 0.0.0.255 any
!
! Permit any outgoing TCP connections to come back into our network
access-list 110 permit tcp any any established
!
! Allow email (SMTP port 25) to our SMTP server
access-list 110 permit tcp any host 10.10.1.20 eq smtp
!
! Allow web traffic (port 80) to our web server only
access-list 110 permit tcp any host 10.10.1.22 eq www
!
! Allow DNS traffic to our DNS server, both TCP and UDP
access-list 110 permit tcp any host 10.10.1.24 eq domain
access-list 110 permit udp any host 10.10.1.24 eq domain
!
! Allow Internal hosts to access the outside DNS server (192.168.1.100)
access-list 110 permit upd host 192.168.1.100 eq domain any gt 1023
!
! Allow FTP traffic to our FTP server
access-list 110 permit tcp any host 10.10.1.25 eq ftp
access-list 110 permit tcp any host 10.10.1.25 eq ftp-data
!
! Allow news only from legit NNTP servers to our internal NNTP client
access-list 110 permit tcp host 198.168.1.98 host 10.10.1.200 eq nntp
access-list 110 permit tcp host 192.168.1.99 host 10.10.1.200 eq nntp
!
! Allow telnet (port 23) to only one host!
access-list 110 permit tcp any host 10.10.1.195 eq telnet
!
```

```
! Some things we know we want to deny: Xwindows, NFS
access-list 110 deny tcp any any range 6000 6003
access-list 110 deny tcp any any range 2000 2003
access-list 110 deny tcp any any eq 2049
access-list 110 deny udp any any eq 2049
!
! Since we are doing non-passive FTP on our FTP clients, we need the
! following line to allow their FTP sessions back in. If you have an
! FTP server, you have to create a separate entry for it.
access-list 110 permit tcp any eq ftp-data any gt 1024
!
! Allow ICMP into our network
! Warning! ICMP is more than just ping. If you decide to deny it, you
! should explictly deny specific ICMP types (echo, echo-reply, etc.).
! MTU path discovery and source quench rely on ICMP and are very
! important to some links.
! First disallow ICMP redirects broadcasts
access-list 110 deny icmp any any redirect
! Then allow everything else
access-list 110 permit icmp any any
!
! Allow NTP time messages to all our internal machines
access-list 110 permit udp any any eq ntp
!
! Implicit deny
! It is here by default, but we list it so that the show access-list
! command will show the number of packets blocked by the implicit deny.
access-list 110 deny ip any any
```

Apply the list to interface serial1 with the following commands:

```
interface serial1
  ip access-group 110 in
```

Optimizing Your Access Lists

You can list and view all access lists with the show access-list command. If you are interested in only one specific list, use the number of the list at the end of the show command:

```
Router#show access-list 124
Extended IP access list 124
    deny   ip 10.10.1.0 0.0.0.255 any (1855 matches)
    permit tcp any any established (6105063 matches)
    permit tcp any host 10.10.1.20 eq smtp (10246 matches)
    permit tcp any host 10.10.1.21 eq pop3 (11220 matches)
    permit tcp any host 10.10.1.22 eq www (72583 matches)
```

At the end of each line, the router lists the number of times that particular access list rule has been matched. Bear in mind that the numbers are from the last router reboot or counter reset. You must check the number of matches several times over a long period before you get numbers that reflect your actual network traffic. Traffic fluctuates for many reasons, so you're really interested in long-term averages.

The number of matches is useful information, because access lists are processed in order, and processing terminates with the last match. Putting the lines with the most matches at the beginning of the list reduces the load on the router because most matches will occur earlier. In this case, we can move the line allowing WWW

---

connections higher in the list. Note, however, that this line can't become the first line in the list; in order to work effectively, the rule that prevents spoofing attacks must be applied to all incoming packets and therefore must be first in the list. There's a moral here: don't get too excited about optimizing your access lists. Think through the consequences of your changes. Here's how our reordered list would look:

```
! We can't change the first line: it is looking for spoofing and must be
! the first entry.
access-list 124 deny ip 10.10.1.0 0.0.0.255 any
access-list 124 permit tcp any any established
access-list 124 permit tcp any host 10.10.1.22 eq www
access-list 124 permit tcp any host 10.10.1.21 eq pop3
access-list 124 permit tcp any host 10.10.1.20 eq smtp
```

Emulating a Packet Sniffer

You can use some clever access list commands to emulate a simple packet sniffer that logs all traffic arriving at an interface. First, build an access list that catches all IP traffic. Then add a **debug** statement for the list (debugging is discussed in Chapter 14):

```
access-list 110 permit ip any any
debug ip packet list 110
```

Now apply the list to an interface in both directions:

```
interface ethernet0
  ip access-group 110 in
  ip access-group 110 out
```

All traffic traveling across this interface will now be logged by the **debug** command. This example can be taken a few steps further by redirecting the debugging output to a syslog server; the commands for doing so are also covered in Chapter 14. (This can be dangerous: if the route to the syslog server goes through the interface you're trying to debug, you'll create an infinite loop.) When you are done sniffing traffic, turn off logging:

```
no debug ip packet list 110
```

A word of warning: we used an access list here on our **debug ip packet** statement, which kept the output to a minimum. If our access list was too generic or we didn't use one at all, the router would have started displaying every packet. This behavior can effectively render a busy router useless until you issue the **undebug** command. Be careful how and where you use the **debug** command.

Logging Access List Violations

You can log access list violations with IP accounting:

```
ip accounting access-violations
```

You can also use the extended access list keywords **log** and **log-input** to log information about packets that attempt to violate an access list. The **log** keyword causes entries that match that line to be logged:

```
access-list 110 deny tcp any host 10.10.1.22 eq www log
```

The log-input keyword not only logs the packet, but also supplies the packet's source interface.

If you configure the router with the command logging buffered, you will be able to use the show log command to view the stored log entries.

Securely Updating Access Lists

The most secure method for modifying access lists is to shut down the router's interfaces, make your modifications, and then bring the interfaces back up. This method is unpopular for an obvious reason: no traffic is being routed while the lists are being edited. This means that your users will have a broken network while you're doing your work, and that's often unacceptable.

Another way to provide the same security without shutting down the interface is to let the access-group command handle it. At any time, an interface can have only one "in" and one "out" access list. For example:

```
interface ethernet 0
  ip address 10.10.1.1 255.255.255.0
  ip access-group 110 in
  ip access-group 115 out
```

Let's say we want to modify access list 110. To do this, we might shut down the interface, delete list 110, write a new list, and bring the interface back up. Alternatively, we could create a new list, 112, that reflects the changes we want. We can then apply the list to the interface with a single command:

```
interface ethernet 0
  ip access-group 112 in
```

There is no need to do a no access-group 110 in, because the router automatically replaces list 110 with list 112. Since this happens in real time, the change is immediate and there is no need to shut down the interface. List 110 still exists, but it's inactive. You should probably delete it so it won't confuse you later. However, you can now delete it without inconveniencing your users.

The only drawback to this trick is that it can be confusing to network administrators, since your access list numbers change every time you edit the list. However, that's a small price to pay for satisfied users.

Getting the List to a Router with TFTP or RCP

When you need to edit an access list, you can TFTP the router's configuration from the router to the TFTP server, edit the configuration on the server, and then TFTP the access list back to the router. This technique lets you use a familiar editor to modify your access lists, which is much more reliable than trying to type access lists directly into the router's configuration.

Here's an outline of the steps:

1. TFTP or RCP the entire configuration to your server:

   ```
   Router#copy running-config tftp
   ```

2. Edit the configuration file, removing everything except the access lists.

3. Add a `no access-list` command before each access list in the file:

```
no access-list 10
access-list 10 deny 1.2.3.4 1.5.6.7
```

4. Edit the access lists and save the file so you do not have to do Steps 1–3 again in the future.

5. Use TFTP or RCP to copy the file back to your router. This file contains only the access lists, not the entire router configuration. It deletes each access list, then creates a new access list with the desired configuration.

```
Router#copy tftp running-config
```

6. Once you are satisfied that the modified access lists work, save the running configuration:

```
Router#copy running-config startup-config
```

Managing Priorities with Queues

In most cases, you don't need to worry about the details of packet processing. However, when dealing with various kinds of congestion, there are situations in which you need explicit control over how packets flow through the router. IOS gives you three techniques for prioritizing packet delivery: priority lists, custom queue lists, and Weighted Fair Queuing.

Priority Lists

Priority lists allow the router to sort and process incoming packets based on priorities you assign. These lists should be used only on serial WAN links that occasionally become congested; during congested periods, we want to give mission-critical packets top priority. If the serial link is always congested, don't even try using priority lists; more bandwidth is the only solution.

With priority lists, we assign different queue levels to entire protocols or to particular ports. Packets are handled depending on the queue to which they are assigned: `low`, `medium`, `normal`, or `high`. For example, in Figure 7-3 the users on Network 2 access the web server on Network 1 across the WAN link. The web server is the primary application for our users, and it is the interface to the company database. During times of congestion, web traffic should have number-one priority. We give telnet medium priority, which allows our telnet sessions to get through, and give all other traffic normal priority.

The configuration for this priority list is:

```
! Give web access the highest priority
priority-list 1 protocol ip high tcp 80
! Give telnet medium priority
priority-list 1 protocol ip medium tcp 23
! Everything else is default traffic
priority-list 1 default normal
```

To complete the example, we apply the priority list to `serial0` on Router 1 with the following commands:

```
interface serial0
  priority-group 1
```

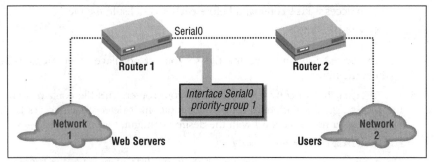

Figure 7-3: Using a priority list

Custom Queue Lists

Queue lists are similar to priority lists in that they allow you to prioritize traffic across a WAN link. However, queue lists create queues of various sizes, then process each queue individually. A round-robin algorithm is used for queue processing. The byte count specifies the amount of data that should be delivered from a queue before moving on to the next queue. Queues in a queue list differ only in the amount of storage space for packets (unlike the queues in a priority list, which differ from each other in the processing time allotted to each packet type).

Setting the queue size

The queue size is the number of packets the queue can hold at any time. Computing the queue size is difficult. If you are calculating IP packet size across a link, you might guess that the maximum packet size is 1500 (the link's MTU). We add 20 to this number to take care of packet headers, which gives us a total of 1520 bytes per packet.

You want to keep the number of packets in the queue relatively small; around 4 or 5 packets. For example, if we want the highest-priority queue to hold 5 packets, we set its size to 7600 bytes (5 × 1520). Likewise, to allow 3 packets in a lower-priority queue, we set its size to 4560 bytes. Here's how to construct a queue list with these two queues:

```
queue-list 1 queue 1 byte-count 7600
queue-list 1 queue 2 byte-count 4560
```

Instead of setting the queue size in bytes, we can set it to a specific number of packets by using the limit keyword. In the following example, we set queue 1 to 10 packets and queue 2 to 5 packets.

```
queue-list 1 queue 1 limit 10
queue-list 1 queue 2 limit 5
```

Applying a queue to an interface

We can apply the queue list to an interface with the command custom-queue-list:

```
interface serial0
  custom-queue-list 1
```

Assigning packets to queues by protocol type

To finish the example off, all we need to do is describe what kinds of packets we want to send into each queue. Let's use the same example we used earlier (in Figure 7-3): high priority for web access, medium priority for telnet access, and some sort of default priority for all other IP traffic. The custom queue list equivalent of the priority list would look like this:

```
queue-list 1 protocol ip 1 tcp 80
queue-list 1 protocol ip 2 tcp 23
queue-list 1 default 3
queue-list 1 queue 1 byte-count 7600
queue-list 1 queue 2 byte-count 4560
queue-list 1 queue 3 byte-count 1520

interface serial0
  custom-queue-list 1
```

Weighted Fair Queuing

To understand the rationale behind Weighted Fair Queuing (WFQ), it's useful to understand the alternatives. In a first-in, first-out (FIFO) queue, the first packet on your interface will be the first packet out your interface. If you have several high-bandwidth connections (such as HTTP or FTP), these connections can hog the queue by filling it up with their packets. When the queue is full and a lower-bandwidth connection such as telnet comes along, the telnet packets will be forced to wait for the other connection's packets. But forcing the later connection to wait just because it is less demanding is unfair.

To solve this problem, WFQ views all incoming packets as part of a "conversation" between two network nodes. It can use the source and destination IP addresses, MAC addresses, ports, or anything else to determine the conversation to which the packets belong. Once it knows which packets belong to which conversations, WFQ can provide equal access to the interface across all conversations.

Figure 7-4 illustrates how the conversations are treated equally. In this diagram, we have three conversations: a telnet session and two HTTP sessions (A and B). Assume that three packets arrive at the interface and are placed in the queue. T1 is forwarded out first, regardless of the number of packets in the queue for HTTP A and HTTP B, because T1 is a telnet packet. We don't want a telnet session to wait for our HTTP traffic. After T1 has gone out, the remaining packets are sent out based on their conversations and timestamps.

WFQ is enabled for all interfaces whose bandwidth is less than or equal to 2.048 Mbps. You can disable it with the following command:

```
interface serial0
  no fair-queue
```

The setting we want to look at is the congestive discard threshold, which is the number of packets (queue size) allowed for each conversation. The default value is 64; it can range from 1 to 512. When this queue size has been reached for a conversation, all incoming packets for that conversation will be discarded.

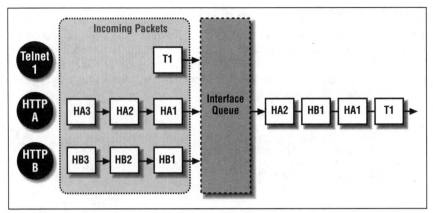

Figure 7-4: Weighted Fair Queuing with three separate conversations

In this example, we set the congestive discard threshold for each queue on the serial0 interface to 200.

```
interface serial0
  fair-queue 200
```

show commands for all queues

Use the show queues command to examine your current queues and their performance. Here we look at the queue for serial0 with the command show queue serial0.

```
Router#show queue serial0
  Input queue: 0/75/0 (size/max/drops); Total output drops: 0
  Queueing strategy: weighted fair
  Output queue: 0/1000/64/0 (size/max total/threshold/drops)
    Conversations  0/1/256 (active/max active/max total)
    Reserved Conversations 0/0 (allocated/max allocated)
```

To show details about custom, fair, or priority-based queues, use the show queuing command followed by the type of queue you want to examine:

```
show queueing custom
show queueing fair
show queueing priority
```

CHAPTER 8

IP Routing Topics

Routing Protocol Topics

To do the job right, a router needs information about how to reach various parts of the network. It can get this information through static routing (i.e., including commands in the configuration that specify explicitly how to reach certain networks) or by exchanging routing information with other routers. To share this information, the router uses a routing protocol such as RIP, IGRP, EIGRP, OSPF, IS-IS, or BGP. In this chapter, we discuss a number of topics that are common to all (or most) of these protocols.

Autonomous System (AS) Numbers

An *autonomous system* is a collection of routers that is under the control of one organization (for example, one corporation's network). Within this one organization, the routers share routing information only among themselves. At a macroscopic level, autonomous systems can be viewed as single entities. An exterior routing protocol, such as BGP, only needs to worry about autonomous systems, and can ignore any structure inside of the autonomous system.

Properly speaking, AS numbers are assigned by ARIN (the American Registry for Internet Numbers) and are used only by BGP. A limited number are available, so they are assigned only to organizations that really need them.* However, IGRP and EIGRP use a unique number to define boundaries between groups of routers that share information. This number can be considered a "locally significant AS" or "local-AS," which means the number is important only to your network. You can configure a router to run multiple routing processes using the same protocol, but

* For more information on AS number assignment, see *http://www.arin.net/regserv/asnguide. htm.*

they won't share routing information because their local-AS numbers differ. Consider the following configuration:

```
router igrp 100
  network 192.168.1.0
router igrp 200
  network 10.0.0.0
```

Here, we have two routing processes running IGRP. However, the two processes don't share information because they have different local-AS numbers (100 and 200). Using local-AS numbers in this way allows you to divide a network into separate domains. A local-AS number is more properly called a *process number* to distinguish it from a true AS number. But you'll see both terms used frequently, and I'll use both in this book.

OSPF uses a unique number called a *process ID* to identify the routing process on the router. These numbers do not partition the network the way a local-AS number does.

RIP does not use AS numbers because it shares routes with any neighboring RIP router that will listen. Therefore, the routing domains are defined by router boundaries. These boundaries can be border routers that are not running RIP, access lists that prohibit the RIP packets from traveling past a certain router, or any router more than 15 hops away, which RIP considers unreachable.

In Figure 8-1, Routers 1, 2, and 3 in Network 1 are running the RIP protocol. Similarly, in Network 2, Routers 4, 5, and 6 share routing information via RIP. Each network distributes routing information to all its routers because RIP communicates with all adjacent routers that are also running RIP. However, RIP routes are not distributed from one network into the other because we are not running RIP on the link between Router 3 and Router 5. Instead, we run EIGRP across the WAN connection with a local-AS number of 98. Since both Routers 3 and 5 use the same local-AS number, they can exchange routing information. However, by default, the EIGRP processes don't know anything about the RIP routes. To make this information available via EIGRP, we need to add route distribution, which is covered later in this chapter.

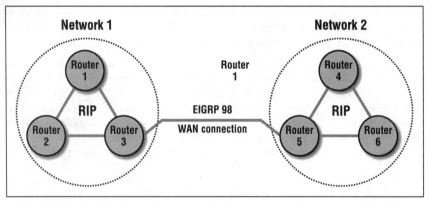

Figure 8-1: The distribution of routing information

When troubleshooting EIGRP and IGRP routing problems you should always make sure that the local-AS numbers agree among routers that are running the same protocol. If they are different, the routers will not share routes.

Interior and Exterior Gateway Protocols

Functionally, routing protocols are divided into two types: interior gateway protocols (IGPs) and exterior gateway protocols (EGPs). *Interior gateway protocols* are used on routers within the same autonomous network, the same administrative domain, or the same intranet. *Exterior gateway protocols* are used to route traffic between routers in different autonomous systems; for example, between Internet service providers (ISPs) or between a single corporate net and two or more ISPs. You might also use an exterior protocol on a single large network that is so widely distributed that it can't be managed as a single unit (for example, a corporate network that spans several continents).

To simplify, internal protocols are intended for routing within an organization, and external protocols are intended for routing between unrelated organizations.

Interior gateway protocols, such as RIP, IGRP, EIGRP, and OSPF, are easier to configure and are designed to handle routing on a smaller scale than exterior gateway protocols. If you have a network with three routers and one connection to the Internet, RIP and a few static routes are all you need. Large networks, or networks with multihomed Internet connections (i.e., more than one ISP) might require a more sophisticated interior protocol, such as EIGRP or OSPF, and may force you to use an exterior protocol for routing to the Internet or between your own autonomous systems.

BGP is the only exterior gateway protocol that is widely used. EGPs are much more complicated than IGPs because they handle more routing information while performing better route summarization. BGP comes at a price in configuration, processing, and the size of the routing table. When configuring BGP for Internet use, you may need a router with sufficient memory to support a full Internet routing table, which contains over 70,000 routes.

Distance-Vector and Link-State Routing Protocols

Interior protocols are further divided into two classes, based on the way they make routing decisions and the kind of information they share: distance-vector protocols and link-state protocols.

Distance-vector protocols

Distance-vector protocols provide two pieces of information for every route: a distance and a vector. These two pieces of information are distributed as part of a network map to all other routers. The distance is some measurement of the route's quality, based on parameters such as bandwidth, delay, or the number of intervening routers; the distance is never related to the actual physical distance

IP Routing

between routers. To avoid confusion, I'll use the term "metric" instead of distance. The vector is simply the IP address of the router to which the packet should be delivered in order to reach its final destination; this is frequently called the "next hop."

Each routing protocol has its own way to calculate the metric. For RIP, the metric is simply the number of hops (i.e., routers) between the current router and the destination. IGRP and EIGRP use a link's bandwidth and delay to calculate a metric value. The router "decides" which path is more cost-effective by using the metric value. A lower metric value means a better route. In RIP, two hops is better than three hops, even if the two hops are slow links and the three hops are fast links. Because IGRP and EIGRP use a more complex metric, they can take into account factors such as link speeds. We'll discuss metrics in more detail when we talk about specific protocols.

Link-state routing protocols

Link-state protocols build snapshots of the network topology on each router. This topology of the surrounding network is then distributed to all other routers, which allows all the routers to build a picture of the entire network. This picture allows each router to compute the best path to any destination at any time.

Once all routers have received the initial flood of network information, they broadcast only changes to the entire network. For example, if a link goes down, the router noticing the problem distributes only that change to the network; it doesn't distribute the entire network table. This link-state information saves network bandwidth by reducing the amount of routing traffic needed for routing updates.

Administrative Distance

The router can learn about routes from many sources: it already knows about any interfaces to which it is directly connected, it can be configured with static routes, and it can learn routes from any number of routing protocols that are running concurrently. The routing protocols, of course, have mechanisms for deciding which routes they prefer. But how does the router decide whether to use a route learned from BGP, a route learned from RIP, or a static default route?

That's where the concept of *administrative distance* comes in. Each route is assigned an administrative distance, based on how the route was learned. The administrative distance tells the router how trustworthy the route is; a lower administrative distance means that a route is more trustworthy and should be used in preference to routes with higher administrative distances. Think of the route's metric as the preference of a route, while the administrative distance is the preference of how the route was discovered. The maximum administrative distance is 255; a route with an administrative distance of 255 is considered to have an unknown source and is unusable. Table 8-1 lists the default administrative distances for all route sources.

Table 8-1: Administrative distances

Routing information source	Administrative distance
Directly connected interface	0
Static route	1
External BGP	20
Internal EIGRP	90
IGRP	100
OSPF	110
IS-IS	115
RIP	120
EGP	140
External EIGRP	170
Internal BGP	200
Unknown	255

Table 8-1 shows that a route learned by a static route is preferred over a route learned by IGRP. And of course, a route to a network attached to a directly connected interface is the most preferred route.

Variable-Length Subnet Masks (VLSM) and Classless Routing

You can also divide interior routing protocols into two groups based on whether they are classful or classless. A *classful* protocol relies on the historical distinction between Class A, B, and C networks to interpret addresses. The router itself can use subnet masks associated with its interfaces, but the routing protocol has no way to tell other routers about the masks. The protocol assumes that the subnet mask is a constant throughout the network. In contrast, a *classless* protocol communicates information about subnet masks explicitly, which allows you to design much more efficient network-addressing schemes.

The biggest drawback of a classful routing protocol is the waste of IP addresses. For example, if you are building a network with a Class C address and a subnet mask of 255.255.255.224, and you need to provide a point-to-point link between two routers, you must assign a whole subnet to that link. This subnet wastes 28 IP addresses: 255.255.255.224 has a total of 32 addresses, of which 2 are not usable (the broadcast address and the subnet address) and 2 are used by the routers at the endpoints of the link; the remaining 28 are not used.

If we use a different subnet mask on this link, the wasted IP addresses can be reclaimed. In this situation, VLSM is the solution. VLSM allows us to assign a smaller subnet mask to the link itself (255.255.255.252). This mask creates an address block that has only four addresses, none of which are wasted.

IP Routing

Another solution for links like this is to use the `ip unnumbered` command. See Chapter 5 for an example of how this command saves you from wasting IP addresses.

VLSM solves most IP-address issues, but it requires a classless routing protocol, i.e., a routing protocol that can explicitly exchange information about subnet masks, rather than inferring the network mask from the address class. The routing protocols that support VLSM (i.e., the classless protocols) are RIP Version 2, OSPF, EIGRP, and IS-IS. (Using static routes is, of course, consistent with VLSM, because it doesn't involve a routing protocol.)

Protocol Comparison

Table 8-2 provides a summary of all the interior routing protocols covered in this book. (BGP isn't included because it's an exterior protocol.)

Table 8-2: Features of common interior routing protocols

	RIP	*RIPv2*	*IGRP*	*EIGRP*	*OSPF*
VLSM support	No	Yes	No	Yes	Yes
Convergence	Slow	Slow	Medium	Fast	Fast
Configuration	Easy	Easy	Medium	Medium	Hard
Bandwidth use	High	High	High	Low	Low
Scalability	Poor	Poor	Good	Good	Good
Interoperability	Yes	Yes	No	No	Yes

Static Routes

Static routes are routes you assign in the router configuration. These routes don't change until you reconfigure them yourself. You might ask, "Why not just use static routes and forget all this routing stuff?" Well, if all you had were static routes and something changed—perhaps you had to add another subnet, or you changed your Internet service provider—you would have to reconfigure every router to conform to the network changes. It would be impossible to react to short-term changes, such as equipment failures, in all but the simplest networks.

Static routes do have their place in a modern network. They are appropriate for default routes, routes to the null interface, routes to stub networks, and other situations in which the possibility of change is minimal.

To define a static route to network 192.168.11.0 via the router 192.168.5.1, you would use the command:

```
ip route 192.168.11.0 255.255.255.0 192.168.5.1
```

Default Static Routes

Static routes are commonly used for the default route. A default route is used when a router does not have a specific route to a certain address. The Internet gateway is always a good default route. For example, if our gateway router's IP address is 192.168.2.1, our default route might look like this:

```
ip route 0.0.0.0 0.0.0.0 192.168.2.1
```

On the gateway router, the static route could point to the interface that is connected to the Internet:

```
ip route 0.0.0.0 0.0.0.0 serial 0
```

The 0.0.0.0 0.0.0.0 route establishes a default only for the current router and the RIP routing protocol. Other routing protocols, such as IGRP and EIGRP, can learn a default route either from another protocol or from an explicit `ip default-network` command. This command tells IGRP and EIGRP to distribute the default route to other routers. To create a default network, use the `ip default-network` command. This route is usually created in tandem with the 0.0.0.0 0.0.0.0 route for completeness, as in this example:

```
! Define the default route for this router
ip route 0.0.0.0 0.0.0.0 192.168.2.1
! Define the default network
ip default-network 192.168.2.0
```

A Static Route to the Null Interface

A static route can be used in conjunction with the null interface to filter unwanted traffic. If we want to drop traffic to the 192.168.3.0 network, we can add a command like this to our router's configuration:

```
ip route 192.168.3.0 255.255.255.0 null0
```

This command defines a route for the 192.168.3.0 network to the null interface. The null interface discards all incoming traffic. This method of disposing unwanted traffic is much more efficient than using an access list.

Backup Static Routes

Static routes are often used to create backup routes that come into effect when a communications link fails. To create backup static routes, you need to use the administrative distance option to the `ip route` command.

Normally, static routes have an administrative distance of 1, which means they are used in preference to routes learned from a routing protocol. (See Table 8-1 for a complete list of administrative distances.) This isn't how we want a backup route to behave—we want it to be used only as a last resort. Therefore, our backup route should have a higher administrative distance than our primary routes.

Let's assume that our routing protocol is RIP, which has an administrative distance of 120. We want to assign the backup route an administrative distance that's higher than the routing protocol's—we'll pick 125. Here is a configuration with a backup static route to 192.168.9.1 being redistributed into RIP:

```
! Define our backup static route with a distance of 125
ip route 192.168.11.0 255.255.255.0 192.168.9.1 125
! Configure the RIP information
router rip
  network 192.168.11.0
  network 192.168.9.0
```

Notice that we are not advertising our backup static route through RIP. (There is no `redistribute` command.) As a general rule, backup static routes should not be advertised; you'll want to use them only when the routes learned from the dynamic routing protocol (RIP, in this case) are unavailable.

For more information on redistributing routing information, see the "Route Redistribution" section later in this chapter.

Split Horizon

Split horizon is designed to stop one of the greatest routing evils, routing loops. Routing loops occur when a loop is formed between two or more routers. For example, say Router 1 has a network route to 192.168.1.0 via Router 2. Router 2 has a route to the same network, but it is back through Router 1. Therefore, Router 1 sends packets for 192.168.1.0 to Router 2, which then sends the packets back to Router 1. This looping continues until the TTL (Time to Live) on the packet expires.

Split horizon helps stop routing loops by telling the router not to advertise routes out the same interface from which the route was originally learned. In other words, if a router learns about a route on a particular interface, it does not broadcast that route information out that interface. Split horizon can't prevent routing loops involving three or more routers, but it's effective at preventing loops between two routers.

Split horizon is enabled by default on most interfaces. It can be disabled with the following command:

```
no ip split-horizon
```

You would want to disable split horizon on a multipoint subinterface. (See Chapter 5 for more information on subinterfaces.) An important note is that routing protocols can often work out routing loops on their own; however, split horizon solves the problem more efficiently because it prevents the loops from developing in the first place.

Passive Interfaces

The `passive-interface` command tells an interface to listen to RIP or IGRP routes but not to advertise them. By disabling routing announcements on an interface, we tell the router to "listen but don't talk." This feature can reduce routing load on the CPU by reducing the number of interfaces on which a protocol needs to communicate. For OSPF and EIGRP, this command completely disables route processing for that interface. Use this command only if you know for sure that the routing protocol doesn't need to talk to anything on the specified interface.

In Figure 8-2, Router 1 and Router 2 can be optimized with the `passive-interface` command. Without getting into the routing protocol specifics, we want to say "Keep the EIGRP routing on the serial links and keep the RIP routing on the Ethernet interfaces." Here's how:

```
router eigrp 300
  network 192.168.10.0
  passive-interface ethernet0
```

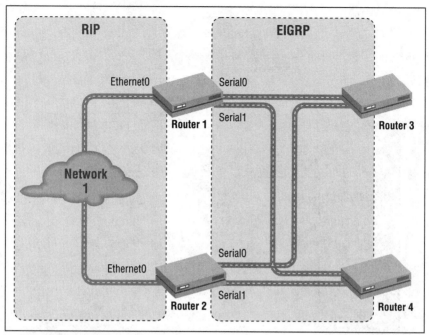

Figure 8-2: Using passive interfaces

```
router rip
  network 192.168.10.0
  passive-interface serial0
  passive-interface serial1
```

This configuration tells Router 1 and Router 2 not to send any EIGRP updates over the Ethernet interface and not to send RIP updates over the serial links. It doesn't solve the problem of getting routing information from our EIGRP process into RIP and vice-versa. We will solve this problem using route redistribution.

EIGRP normally multicasts route information to neighbor routers. But we put EIGRP into passive mode, which turned off all EIGRP processing. If this were IGRP, we could use the `neighbor` command in conjunction with the `passive-interface` command to establish the relationship we wanted. The `neighbor` command tells RIP to send unicast updates to a particular group of routers instead of broadcasting the updates on the link; it allows us to specify which routers should receive updates. (EIGRP ignores the `neighbor` command—it exists only for backward compatibility with IGRP and has no effect.)

The `neighbor` command has greater purposes, which we'll explore in Chapter 10.

Route Redistribution

If a router is running two or more routing processes, the processes don't automatically share their routing information. Route redistribution is a particular issue when different routing protocols are involved, but it also comes up when you have two different processes using the same protocol. Figure 8-3 shows a network that uses both RIP and EIGRP.

IP Routing

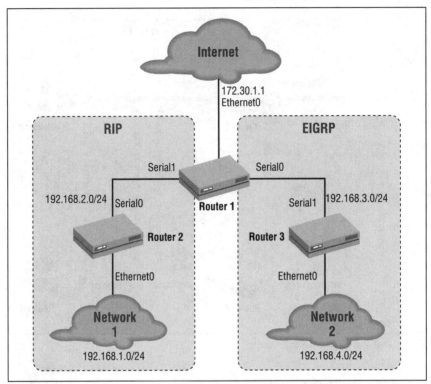

Figure 8-3: Using route redistribution

Table 8-3 shows what the routing table for each router might look like.

Table 8-3: Incomplete routing tables without redistribution

Router 1	Router 2	Router 3
192.168.2.0/24 → serial1	192.168.1.0/24 → ethernet0	192.168.2.0/24 → router1
192.168.3.0/24 → serial0	192.168.2.0/24 → serial0	192.168.3.0/24 → serial1
192.168.1.0/24 → router2	192.168.3.0/24 → router1	192.168.4.0/24 → ethernet0
192.168.4.0/24 → router3		
Default → 172.30.1.2		

Router 1 knows how to get everywhere in our network. However, the other routers don't have enough information to reach all the destinations. There are three problems with these route tables: Router 2 cannot get to Network 2, Router 3 cannot get to Network 1, and neither Router 2 nor Router 3 can get to the Internet.

To look at this correctly, here is the output of show ip route on each router:

```
Router1#show ip route
Codes: C - connected, S - static, I - IGRP, R - RIP, M - mobile, B - BGP
       D - EIGRP, EX - EIGRP external, O - OSPF, IA - OSPF inter area
```

```
Gateway of last resort is not set

       172.168.0.0/24 is subnetted, 1 subnets
C          172.30.1.0 is directly connected, Ethernet0
D      192.168.4.0/24 [90/2195456] via 192.168.3.2, 00:02:00, Serial0
R      192.168.1.0/24 [120/1] via 192.168.2.2, 00:00:08, Serial1
C      192.168.2.0/24 is directly connected, Serial1
C      192.168.3.0/24 is directly connected, Serial0
S*     0.0.0.0/0 [1/0] via 172.30.1.2


Router2#show ip route
Codes: C - connected, S - static, I - IGRP, R - RIP, M - mobile, B - BGP
       D - EIGRP, EX - EIGRP external, O - OSPF, IA - OSPF inter area

Gateway of last resort is not set

C      192.168.1.0/24 is directly connected, Ethernet0
C      192.168.2.0/24 is directly connected, Serial0
R      192.168.3.0/24 [120/1] via 192.168.2.1, 00:00:26, Serial0


Router3#show ip route
Codes: C - connected, S - static, I - IGRP, R - RIP, M - mobile, B - BGP
       D - EIGRP, EX - EIGRP external, O - OSPF, IA - OSPF inter area

Gateway of last resort is not set

C      192.168.4.0/24 is directly connected, Ethernet0
D      192.168.2.0/24 [90/2681856] via 192.168.3.1, 00:09:35, Serial1
C      192.168.3.0/24 is directly connected, Serial1
```

There are a couple of ways to fix our routing problem. One option is to run RIP on the EIGRP side of Router 1 and then set static routes on Router 2 and Router 3 to point to the Internet connection. The drawback is that we are relying on static routes; worse, we have static routes to the same destination on two routers. If our Internet connection changes, we'll have to change the configuration on both Router 2 and Router 3. In this example, changing the static routes wouldn't be too much work. But what if there were 20 routers?

The second option, route redistribution, is a much better solution. To implement route redistribution across all the routing protocols on our network, we change Router 1's configuration to use redistribution between RIP and EIGRP:

```
! Define the static default route for this router and RIP
! We don't use 172.30.1.1 because that is our interface; we want to use
! the IP address of the router at the other end
ip route 0.0.0.0 0.0.0.0 172.30.1.2
!
router rip
 network 192.168.1.0
 network 192.168.2.0
 redistribute static
 redistribute eigrp 100
 passive-interface ethernet0
 default-metric 10
!
router eigrp 100
 network 192.168.3.0
 network 192.168.4.0
```

```
redistribute static
redistribute rip
passive-interface serial0
default-metric 1000 250 255 1 1500
```

With this configuration, all the routes learned on Router 1 are shared among all the routing protocols. This sharing allows Router 2 and Router 3 to learn how to reach each other's networks and the Internet. Table 8-4 shows that our routing tables are complete. The `default-metric` statement tells each routing process how to interpret the routes it is receiving from other sources. For example, the `default-metric` statement for RIP tells it to assign the metric of 10 to routes it receives through redistribution. Since these routes are coming from other protocols, they won't have metrics that make sense to RIP. Likewise, the more complicated `default-metric` statement for EIGRP tells EIGRP how to interpret the routes it is receiving.

Table 8-4: Routing tables completed by redistribution

Router 1	Router 2	Router 3
192.168.2.0/24 → serial1	192.168.1.0/24 → ethernet0	192.168.3.0/24 → serial1
192.168.3.0/24 → serial0	192.168.2.0/24 → serial0	192.168.4.0/24 → ethernet0
192.168.1.0/24 → router2	192.168.3.0/24 → router1	192.168.2.0/24 → router1
192.168.4.0/24 → router3	192.168.4.0/24 → router1	192.168.1.0/24 → router1
Default → 172.30.1.2	Default → 172.30.1.2	Default → 172.30.1.2

The only thing left to do is to configure some filters to prevent routing loops from occurring; we'll do that in the next section.

 The `default-metric` command is required for most redistribution to occur. It tells the other protocols what weight to give the learned routes. Without this command, redistribution occurs only between IGRP and EIGRP processes sharing the same process number (in which case, redistribution is automatic). Also, static routes do not require a `default-metric` in order to redistribute.

Here is the result of **show ip route** for each router, showing the new routing tables:

```
Router1#show ip route
Codes: C - connected, S - static, I - IGRP, R - RIP, M - mobile, B - BGP
       D - EIGRP, EX - EIGRP external, O - OSPF, IA - OSPF inter area
       N1 - OSPF NSSA external type 1, N2 - OSPF NSSA external type 2
       E1 - OSPF external type 1, E2 - OSPF external type 2, E - EGP
       i - IS-IS, L1 - IS-IS level-1, L2 - IS-IS level-2, * - candidate default
       U - per-user static route, o - ODR

Gateway of last resort is 172.30.1.2 to network 0.0.0.0

     172.30.0.0/16 is variably subnetted, 2 subnets, 2 masks
S       172.30.0.0/16 [1/0] via 172.30.1.0
C       172.30.1.0/24 is directly connected, Ethernet0
D    192.168.4.0/24 [90/2195456] via 192.168.3.2, 00:23:26, Serial0
```

```
R    192.168.1.0/24 [120/1] via 192.168.2.2, 00:00:07, Serial1
C    192.168.2.0/24 is directly connected, Serial1
C    192.168.3.0/24 is directly connected, Serial0
S*   0.0.0.0/0 [1/0] via 172.30.1.2

Router2#show ip route
Codes: C - connected, S - static, I - IGRP, R - RIP, M - mobile, B - BGP
       D - EIGRP, EX - EIGRP external, O - OSPF, IA - OSPF inter area
       N1 - OSPF NSSA external type 1, N2 - OSPF NSSA external type 2
       E1 - OSPF external type 1, E2 - OSPF external type 2, E - EGP
       i - IS-IS, L1 - IS-IS level-1, L2 - IS-IS level-2, * - candidate default
       U - per-user static route, o - ODR

Gateway of last resort is 192.168.2.1 to network 0.0.0.0

R    172.30.0.0/16 [120/10] via 192.168.2.1, 00:00:19, Serial0
R    192.168.4.0/24 [120/10] via 192.168.2.1, 00:00:20, Serial0
C    192.168.1.0/24 is directly connected, Ethernet0
C    192.168.2.0/24 is directly connected, Serial0
R    192.168.3.0/24 [120/1] via 192.168.2.1, 00:00:20, Serial0
R*   0.0.0.0/0 [120/10] via 192.168.2.1, 00:00:20, Serial0

Router3#show ip route
Codes: C - connected, S - static, I - IGRP, R - RIP, M - mobile, B - BGP
       D - EIGRP, EX - EIGRP external, O - OSPF, IA - OSPF inter area
       N1 - OSPF NSSA external type 1, N2 - OSPF NSSA external type 2
       E1 - OSPF external type 1, E2 - OSPF external type 2, E - EGP
       i - IS-IS, L1 - IS-IS level-1, L2 - IS-IS level-2, * - candidate default
       U - per-user static route, o - ODR

Gateway of last resort is 192.168.3.1 to network 0.0.0.0

D EX 172.30.0.0/16 [170/3136000] via 192.168.3.1, 00:00:34, Serial1
C    192.168.4.0/24 is directly connected, Ethernet0
D EX 192.168.1.0/24 [170/3136000] via 192.168.3.1, 00:00:34, Serial1
D    192.168.2.0/24 [90/2681856] via 192.168.3.1, 00:22:01, Serial1
C    192.168.3.0/24 is directly connected, Serial1
D*EX 0.0.0.0/0 [170/3136000] via 192.168.3.1, 00:00:34, Serial1
```

Filtering Routes

We can use access lists to get better control over route redistribution. Access lists define filters that control which routes the router will listen to or advertise, depending on the distribute-list command. The distribute-list command specifies the direction (in or out) and the access list to use. The access list is then applied to the route redistribution process. To put it another way, the access list allows us to say "Allow routes from here" and "Don't send routes here."

Filtering incoming routes

To filter incoming routes, the distribute-list command is followed by the in option. In other words, we are filtering routes that the router hears. The following example applies access list 10 to all incoming RIP routes. If the incoming routes do not match access list 10, they are dropped into a bit bucket:

```
access-list 10 permit 192.168.1.0 0.0.0.255
router rip
```

```
network 192.168.1.0
network 192.168.2.0
distribute-list 10 in
```

No matter where the update comes from, any route that does not match network 192.168.1.0 is ignored by RIP. We can take this a step further and say "Any route that arrives via the ethernet0 interface will be checked with access list 10":

```
access-list 10 permit 192.168.1.0 0.0.0.255
router rip
  network 192.168.0.0
  distribute-list 10 in ethernet0
```

Filtering outgoing routes

The distribute-list command can also be applied to information the router sends. Just as distribute-list in controls what the router can hear, distribute-list out controls what the router can announce. In other words, we are filtering outgoing routes. If an outgoing route does not match the access list, it will not be sent. For example:

```
access-list 10 permit 192.168.1.0 0.0.0.255
router rip
  network 192.168.1.0
  network 192.168.2.0
  distribute-list 10 out
```

This configuration globally applies the distribute-list to all outgoing RIP routes. The result is that our router won't tell any other routers about routes that don't match the 192.168.1.0/24 network. And in the same way as before, we can apply the access list to one interface (ethernet0):

```
access-list 10 permit 192.168.1.0 0.0.0.255
router rip
  network 192.168.1.0
  network 192.168.2.0
  distribute-list 10 out ethernet0
```

The addition of ethernet0 says that the router applies access list 10 only to routes announced through the ethernet0 interface. The access list doesn't apply to routes advertised through other interfaces—any other interfaces are allowed to announce any routes that are available.

Filtering updates during redistribution

There is one more thing we can do with the outgoing distribute-list command: control the redistribution of routes from one protocol into another protocol. In the example we have been using, we are redistributing into RIP. Now we add the distribute-list command to ensure that RIP ignores routes from EIGRP that originated from RIP. distribute-list 10 out eigrp 100 means "Apply access list 10 to announced routes that were derived from EIGRP 100."

```
access-list 10 deny 192.168.1.0 0.0.0.255
access-list 10 permit any
!
router rip
```

```
network 192.168.1.0
network 192.168.2.0
default-metric 10
redistribute eigrp 100
distribute-list 10 out eigrp 100
```

Filtering routes that are redistributed from one protocol into another helps to eliminate routing loops by preventing a protocol from learning its own routes from another source.

Revisiting the example

Now let's put all the pieces together. Figure 8-3 shows a network with a routing problem that we solved by redistributing EIGRP into RIP. EIGRP is smart enough to handle the RIP routes and label them as such. RIP is not that smart, so we want to control its redistribution by adding an access list that filters the routes originating from RIP before they are added back into the RIP routing table. Our final configuration adds the necessary filtering to prevent routing loops from forming:

```
! Define the static route for this router and RIP
ip route 0.0.0.0 0.0.0.0 172.30.1.2
!
! Define the RIP process
!
router rip
 network 192.168.1.0
 network 192.168.2.0
 redistribute static
 redistribute eigrp 100
 passive-interface ethernet0
 default-metric 10
 ! Add the distribute-list command with access list 10
 distribute-list 10 out eigrp 100
!
! Define the EIGRP process
!
router eigrp 100
 network 192.168.3.0
 network 192.168.4.0
 redistribute static
 redistribute rip
 passive-interface serial0
 default-metric 1000 250 255 1 150
 distribute-list 11 out rip
!
! Define access list 10
! We want to deny routes from EIGRP that are RIP routes
! but permit everything else
access-list 10 deny 192.168.1.0 0.0.0.255
access-list 10 permit any
! Define access list 10
! We want to permit the RIP routes into EIGRP and
! deny everything else
access-list 11 permit 192.168.1.0 0.0.0.255
access-list 11 deny any
```

Route Maps

Route maps allow you to influence network traffic by changing the attributes of a route based on its characteristics. We can use a route map to modify metrics, the next-hop address, the default interface, and other attributes. This feature becomes increasingly important in BGP and OSPF route redistribution because of the complexity of these protocols.

A route map comprises a list of match criteria, followed by a list of set instructions. The match criteria are similar to access list entries: they describe the incoming routing updates we want to modify. This match can in fact be based on whether a route passes an access list (i.e., matches can be based on an IP address), but it also allows you to select updates based on other criteria, such as route metrics and route tags. The set instructions tell the router what to do with the route once it has a match. In our first example, we change a route's metric based on the source IP address of the packet.

In this example, we define a route map using access list 10. The route map is given the name our-example-map. Route-map names (or *tags*, as they are also called) can be anything you want. After defining the map name, we say that the map uses access list 10 to match a route's destination IP address. (There are many other things we could match. For example, we could match the route's next-hop address, using the command match ip next-hop; or we could match the address of the router from which the route came by using the command match ip route-source. See Chapter 15 for a complete list of match items for route maps.) If any route's destination address matches access list 10, we set the route's metric to 20.

```
! Define the route map named "our-example-map"
route-map our-example-map
  match ip address 10
  set metric 20
!
! Define the access-list that is used in the route-map
access-list 10 permit 192.168.1.0 0.0.0.255
```

In the OSPF section of Chapter 9, route maps are used to control redistribution between RIP and OSPF. In that redistribution, we want to take the external routes from OSPF and redistribute them into RIP. The only way to achieve that granularity of routing control is to use route maps.

Enforcing routing policy with route maps

Route maps allow us to enforce routing policies. We'll start with an example in which we use a route map to control redistribution. We want to give a redistributed RIP route from certain routers a higher metric than a route coming from other routers. In other words, we are going to trust some routers more than others. We may make this decision for political reasons, or we could just know that one router has better routes, for reasons the routing protocol can't determine.

In this example, we will use two additional features of route maps. First, a route map can contain the permit or deny keyword, which gives us finer control over which routes match. Second, a route map can have a sequence number, which lets us build chains of route maps.

Here's how the `permit` and `deny` keywords and sequence numbers are used. If a route map includes the `permit` keyword, the following occurs when a route arrives:

1. The route is tested against the access list. If it does not match, the next route map in the sequence is tried. If there are no more maps in the sequence, the route is not redistributed.

2. If the route does match the access list, the route map's `set` options are applied, and the route is redistributed. No more maps in the sequence are processed.

If the route map includes the `deny` keyword and the route matches the map's access list, the route is not redistributed and no other route maps in the sequence are used.

If a map doesn't contain either `deny` or `permit`, the map is part of a policy. The operation specified by the `set` command is applied if there is a match. In any case, after this map is processed, processing proceeds to the next map in the sequence. No filtering takes place (all routes going through a policy map are eventually redistributed, since no routes are denied), but the route's properties may be changed.

Here is a configuration that redistributes routes from RIP into EIGRP using route maps. The example uses two route maps with the name `rip-to-eigrp`, but with different sequence numbers (10 and 15). The sequence numbers determine the order in which the two maps are processed: first map 10, then map 15.

 It's a good idea to avoid using consecutive sequence numbers when you're first writing a policy. In our example, we used sequence numbers 10 and 15. If we later need to add a map that's processed after 10 and before 15, we can assign it number 12. If we used consecutive sequence numbers, it would be much harder to add a map to the sequence at a later time.

```
! EIGRP configuration
router eigrp 99
   network 10.0.0.0
   default-metric 1000 250 255 1 1500
   ! Set up redistribution of RIP routes into EIGRP using the route-map
   ! named rip-to-eigrp
   redistribute rip route-map rip-to-eigrp
!
! RIP configuration
router rip
 network 10.0.0.0
 !
! Define our route-maps
route-map rip-to-eigrp permit 10
   match ip route-source 2
   set metric 1000 100 250 100 1500
route-map rip-to-eigrp permit 15
   match ip route-source 3
   set metric 500 100 250 100 1500
   !
```

```
! Define the access lists that are used in the route maps
access-list 2 permit 10.11.1.1 0.0.0.0
access-list 3 permit any
```

In this example, routes are first processed by the map named `rip-to-eigrp`, which consists of two submaps, numbered 10 and 15. Map 10 uses access list 2 to select routes that were learned from the router at 10.11.1.1. These routes are given the default metric, which has a bandwidth parameter of 1000. If the route matches, processing ends, and the route is redistributed with the default metric. If the route doesn't match, processing continues with route map 15. This route map uses access list 3, which matches all IP addresses. Therefore, the route map gives all routes that reach it the bandwidth metric of 500, instead of the default; the other parameters are the same. Therefore, we are saying that the 10.11.1.1 router knows about routes that have more bandwidth available than any other routers. Consequently, EIGRP computes a better (lower) metric for them, and uses them in preference to routes learned from other routers.

Enforcing routing policy with the ip policy command

In the previous example, we relied on the `redistribute` command to enforce our redistribution policy. Routing policies can also be enforced on the interface level by using the command `ip policy`, which applies route maps to packets arriving at that interface. The `ip policy` command can be extremely CPU-intensive, so use it with care. Another tool for enforcing routing policies is the command `ip local policy route-map`. Unlike the `ip policy` command, which defines a policy (route map) to be applied to routes coming in an interface, `ip local policy route-map` is a global configuration command that applies the route maps to all routing packets generated by the router.

In this example, we want to assign specific routes based on the packet's destination IP address. The routes are assigned if there are no default routes for the addresses we are matching. We accomplish this by configuring the `serial0` interface to use the route map called `examplemap`. Our route map implements the following rules for packets arriving on `serial0`:

1. Packets to the 172.30.10.0 network are sent to router 172.30.100.1

2. Packets to the 172.30.15.0 network are sent to router 172.30.200.1

3. Rules 1 and 2 apply only if the packets arrive on interface `serial0` and no default route already exists for that destination

4. All other routes coming in `serial0` are passed along as normal

The router configuration would look like this:

```
! Configure the interface serial0
interface serial0
  ip policy route-map examplemap
  ip address 172.30.1.1 255.255.255.0
  !
! Set up the first part of the route map
route-map examplemap permit 10
  match ip address 1
  set ip default next-hop 172.30.100.1
  !
```

```
! Set up the second part of the route map
route-map examplemap permit 15
    match ip address 2
    set ip default next-hop 172.30.200.1
!
! Define the access lists for use in the route maps
access-list 1 permit 172.30.10.0 0.0.0.255
access-list 1 deny any
access-list 2 permit 172.30.15.0 0.0.0.255
access-list 2 deny any
```

Route maps are explored again in Chapters 9 and 10.

Fast Switching and Process Switching

Whether you use fast switching or process switching can affect the way your routes behave. In one project with which I was involved, the administrators wanted to balance traffic across two T1 lines, using EIGRP to perform load balancing. They observed that a daily file transfer was always using a single line, which wasn't what they wanted. The problem was that EIGRP's load balancing is session-based, not packet-based. Therefore, once the file transfer started, it was able to use only one of the lines. The solution was to configure the router for process switching rather than fast switching, because process switching is able to load balance on a per-packet basis.

Before looking at this example further, let's look more closely at the difference between fast switching and process switching and the effect they have on routing.

Fast Switching

When the first packet of a session is going out an interface, a route is selected and placed in a route cache. This route cache entry is used for all packets belonging to this specific destination, which means that all packets belonging to the session take the same route. An entry remains in the route cache until the route cache is flushed, the route changes, or the cache overflows. (When a cache overflows, the entry that was least recently used is removed.)

A session is a communication on a port to a specific host. For example, if Host A is FTPing to Host B, each file is transferred in a single session. Successive file transfers require new sessions—i.e., different connections between the client and the server, using different ports. Looking back at the load-balancing problem we discussed at the beginning of this section, we can see that EIGRP would have been able to perform load balancing across the T1 lines if there were multiple file transfer sessions. Since there was only one file transfer, there was only one session, and there was nothing EIGRP could do. There was no way to put the second line to use.

A route cache eliminates the need for the router to select a new route for each packet of a session. Since selecting a route takes time, the route cache saves processing time and lessens the packet's time inside the router. The first packet of the session determines the route; this route is used for every packet for this destination for as long as the route remains in the route cache.

In Figure 8-4, Router 3 has chosen to send the first packet of a file transfer via Router 1; therefore, this route was added to the route cache. The server, Host B, produces a great deal of traffic for this session, all of which goes across the `serial0` interface (i.e., to Router 1). Load sharing when using fast switching is session-oriented, not packet-oriented, so Router 3 will use `serial0` for the entire file transfer even if there is no traffic on `serial1`.

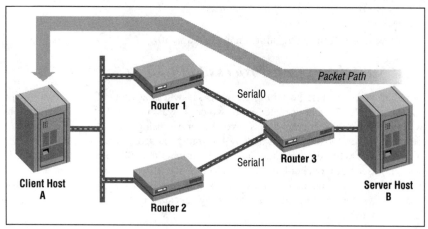

Figure 8-4: Load sharing with fast switching

Process Switching

Process switching is the opposite of fast switching. Every packet that comes into the router is handled independently and can take a different path to its destination. Process switching therefore allows *load sharing* across links that might otherwise not be utilized. Load sharing is not the same as load balancing; load balancing requires more thought on the router's part than simply picking a route for every packet.

Process switching presents two problems: the CPU has to do more work because each packet has to be processed, and sending packets via different routes might cause the packets to arrive at the destination out of sequence. If the packets arrive out of sequence, the destination host needs to do more work to place the packets back together in the correct sequence, which burns up more CPU time and possibly degrades performance.

To enable process switching on an interface, use the `no ip route-cache` command, which disables the route cache on an interface. A new route must be selected for every packet of a session.

For example, let's revisit Figure 8-4. If the main purpose of the remote site were to transfer data every few hours across our T1s, and nothing else, we might want to optimize the router's configuration so that it uses both T1 lines for these file transfer sessions. To do so, we would add the following to Router 3's configuration:

```
! disable route cache on both interfaces
interface serial0
```

```
no ip route-cache
!
interface serial1
 no ip route-cache
```

Now both lines are used to transmit that session's data. Since there is no route cache, load sharing will be handled on a per-packet basis, spreading the load of the file transfer across the two T1s. This feature works well in this example because of the nature of our network and the requirements of our application. In many other environments, disabling the route cache would be a bad idea. For example, a real-time video feed would require a lot of bandwidth and could benefit from load balancing—but the application probably couldn't tolerate packets arriving out of sequence. In other situations, the additional overhead of process switching might degrade the router's performance so much that the actual throughput wouldn't be satisfactory.

Useful show Commands

The most useful show command for IP routing is show ip route, which we used earlier when talking about redistribution. Here is an example of its output:

```
Router1#show ip route
Codes: C - connected, S - static, I - IGRP, R - RIP, M - mobile, B - BGP
       D - EIGRP, EX - EIGRP external, O - OSPF, IA - OSPF inter area
       N1 - OSPF NSSA external type 1, N2 - OSPF NSSA external type 2
       E1 - OSPF external type 1, E2 - OSPF external type 2, E - EGP
       i - IS-IS, L1 - IS-IS level-1, L2 - IS-IS level-2, * - candidate default
       U - per-user static route, o - ODR

Gateway of last resort is 172.30.1.2 to network 0.0.0.0

     172.30.0.0/24 is subnetted, 1 subnets
C       172.30.1.0 is directly connected, Ethernet0
D    192.168.4.0/24 [90/2195456] via 192.168.3.2, 00:00:47, Serial0
R    192.168.1.0/24 [120/1] via 192.168.2.2, 00:00:20, Serial1
C    192.168.2.0/24 is directly connected, Serial1
C    192.168.3.0/24 is directly connected, Serial0
S*   0.0.0.0/0 [1/0] via 172.30.1.2
```

In this example, we have three connected routes, which are listed with a "C". We have one EIGRP route for network 192.168.4.0/24, which is listed with a "D". And finally, the "R" tells us that we have one RIP route for the network 192.168.1.0/24.

We can take this one step further by adding a network to the end of the command to get specific information for that route. For example:

```
Router1#show ip route 172.30.1.0
Routing entry for 172.30.1.0/24
  Known via "connected", distance 0, metric 0 (connected)
  Routing Descriptor Blocks:
  * directly connected, via Ethernet0
      Route metric is 0, traffic share count is 1

Router1#show ip route 192.168.1.0
Routing entry for 192.168.1.0/24
  Known via "rip", distance 120, metric 1
  Redistributing via eigrp 100, rip
  Advertised by eigrp 100
```

IP Routing

```
Last update from 192.168.2.2 on Serial1, 00:00:03 ago
Routing Descriptor Blocks:
* 192.168.2.2, from 192.168.2.2, 00:00:03 ago, via Serial1
    Route metric is 1, traffic share count is 1
```

The last two commands ask for specific route information for the 172.30.1.0 and 192.168.1.0 networks. Given the output, we can see how the router learned the route, which is "connected" in the first example and "rip" the second example. We can see that the 192.168.1.0 network is redistributed into EIGRP, which also advertises it. Finally, we can see when the last routing update occurred.

show ip route summary

A useful option to show ip route is summary. Our router gives us the following output:

```
Router1#show ip route summary
Route Source    Networks    Subnets    Overhead    Memory (bytes)
connected       2           1          156         552
static          1           0          52          184
eigrp 100       1           0          52          184
rip             1           0          52          184
internal        1                                  138
Total           6           1          312         1242
```

This output shows us all the different route sources (connected, internal, static, eigrp, and rip) that are currently configured and running on our router. For each route source, this command shows the total number of networks it has reported and the total number of subnets. The Overhead and Memory columns aren't particularly meaningful. Taken together, they represent the total amount of memory required by these routes. It's not clear what you could do with this information, except possibly to determine that you need to buy memory expansion if your routing table includes a particularly large number of routes.

clear ip route

The clear ip route command allows you to remove entries from the router's routing table. With an IP address as an argument, it clears routes for that particular address. With * as an argument, it clears the entire routing table:

```
Router#clear ip route *
```

show ip protocols

The command show ip protocols gives us a detailed account of each routing protocol that is currently running on the router. Most of the output from this command should look familiar if you're familiar with the routing protocols you're using. Here is the output from a router running EIGRP and RIP:

```
Router1#show ip protocols
Routing Protocol is "eigrp 100"
    Outgoing update filter list for all interfaces is
    Incoming update filter list for all interfaces is
    Default networks flagged in outgoing updates
    Default networks accepted from incoming updates
    EIGRP metric weight K1=1, K2=0, K3=1, K4=0, K5=0
```

```
EIGRP maximum hopcount 100
EIGRP maximum metric variance 1
Default redistribution metric is 1000 250 255 1 1500
Redistributing: static, eigrp 100, rip
Automatic network summarization is in effect
Automatic address summarization:
  192.168.4.0/24 for Serial0
Routing for Networks:
  192.168.3.0
  192.168.4.0
Passive Interface(s):
  Serial1
Routing Information Sources:
  Gateway         Distance      Last Update
  192.168.3.2           90      00:21:33
Distance: internal 90 external 170

Routing Protocol is "rip"
  Sending updates every 30 seconds, next due in 14 seconds
  Invalid after 180 seconds, hold down 180, flushed after 240
  Outgoing update filter list for all interfaces is
  Incoming update filter list for all interfaces is
  Default redistribution metric is 10
  Redistributing: static, eigrp 100, rip
  Default version control: send version 1, receive any version
    Interface      Send Recv  Key-chain
    Serial1          1    1 2
  Routing for Networks:
    192.168.1.0
    192.168.2.0
  Passive Interface(s):
    Serial0
  Routing Information Sources:
    Gateway         Distance      Last Update
    192.168.2.2          120      00:00:06
  Distance: (default is 120)
```

CHAPTER 9

Interior Routing Protocols

RIP

The Routing Information Protocol (RIP) is the oldest routing protocol that is still widely used. It has a large support base and a simple configuration. However, it also has a major drawback: poor route determination. RIP is a distance-vector protocol that looks only at the number of route hops (i.e., the number of routers crossed in traveling from one network to another) in computing the best route. For example, let's say that there are two routes to a destination. The first route crosses two separate 56K links, for a metric of 2; the second route crosses three T1 links, for a metric of 3. RIP always selects the first (two hops) route, even though it is obvious that the second route is better under almost all circumstances. It's possible to use offset lists to force RIP to choose the better route, but that's merely adapting to the problem, not fixing it.

Another problem with RIP is that it can't scale to large networks. There are two scaling issues. First, routers using RIP periodically broadcast the entire routing table to the network. These broadcasts can eat precious bandwidth on lines that often can't afford it. Second, RIP considers any route past 15 hops unreachable. In addition, RIP does not support Variable-Length Subnet Masks (VLSM), an important technique for conserving IP-address space. Nor does it have any mechanism for authenticating other routers; it isn't difficult to trick RIP into believing bogus routing information. And it isn't particularly quick at settling on a new set of routes after the network is disrupted.

RIPv2 tried to solve some of RIP's shortcomings by introducing support for VLSM, bandwidth calculations (a more sophisticated metric for determining the best route), and route authentication. However, it is still limited by the basic scaling problem of its predecessor, the 15-hop limit. Any route that exceeds 15 hops is still considered unreachable.

With all of RIP's drawbacks, which are only partially addressed in Version 2, why would you consider RIP at all? You might find that RIP suits your needs if you have a small network and would like a routing protocol that is easy to manage. It's also supported by just about every piece of network hardware in existence, so you may be forced to use RIP if you have a large installed base that you can't afford to replace. In short, while RIP works well in small environments with only a handful of routers, most networks today require a more sophisticated and scalable routing protocol. Still, despite its drawbacks, RIP will be with us for the foreseeable future.

Basic RIP Configuration

Figure 9-1 shows a network configuration in which we want to enable RIP on Router 1, Router 2, and Router 3.

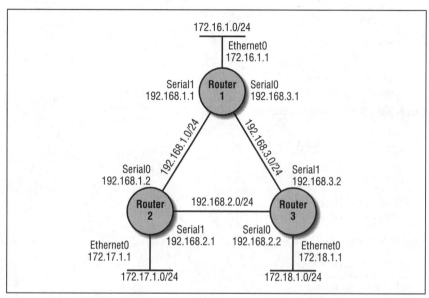

Figure 9-1: A simple network

To enable RIP on the routers, we use the `router rip` command followed by the `network` command, which lists the networks that are directly connected to each router and that are participating in RIP. We don't have to list networks that aren't directly connected—RIP's job is to find out about these. Likewise, we don't need to list networks that aren't running RIP; if there are any (and there aren't in this example), we'll have to handle them through route redistribution.

For Router 1, the configuration looks like this:

```
interface Ethernet0
 ip address 172.16.1.1 255.255.255.0
 !
interface Serial0
 ip address 192.168.3.1 255.255.255.0
 !
interface Serial1
 ip address 192.168.1.1 255.255.255.0
 !
```

```
router rip
 version 2
 network 172.16.0.0
 network 192.168.1.0
 network 192.168.3.0
```

Here's the configuration for Router 2:

```
· interface Ethernet0
 ip address 172.17.1.1 255.255.255.0
 !
interface Serial0
 ip address 192.168.1.2 255.255.255.0
 !
interface Serial1
 ip address 192.168.2.1 255.255.255.0
 !
router rip
 version 2
 network 172.17.0.0
 network 192.168.1.0
 network 192.168.2.0
```

For Router 3, the configuration is:

```
interface Ethernet0
 ip address 172.18.1.1 255.255.255.0
 !
interface Serial0
 ip address 192.168.2.2 255.255.255.0
 !
interface Serial1
 ip address 192.168.3.2 255.255.255.0
 !
router rip
 version 2
 network 172.18.0.0
 network 192.168.2.0
 network 192.168.3.0
```

Remember that RIP (as well as IGRP and EIGRP) is a classful routing protocol. Therefore, we need to be careful about our network statements. For example, on Router 1 we specify 172.16.0.0 (the classful address), not 172.16.1.0.

After the routers are configured, show ip route shows that everything is working nicely:

```
Router1#show ip route
Codes: C - connected, S - static, I - IGRP, R - RIP, M - mobile, B - BGP
       D - EIGRP, EX - EIGRP external, O - OSPF, IA - OSPF inter area
       N1 - OSPF NSSA external type 1, N2 - OSPF NSSA external type 2
       E1 - OSPF external type 1, E2 - OSPF external type 2, E - EGP
       i - IS-IS, L1 - IS-IS level-1, L2 - IS-IS level-2, * - candidate default
       U - per-user static route, o - ODR

Gateway of last resort is not set

R    172.17.0.0/16 [120/1] via 192.168.1.2, 00:00:09, Serial1
     172.16.0.0/24 is subnetted, 1 subnets
C       172.16.1.0 is directly connected, Ethernet0
R    172.18.0.0/16 [120/1] via 192.168.3.2, 00:00:03, Serial0
```

```
C    192.168.1.0/24 is directly connected, Serial1
R    192.168.2.0/24 [120/1] via 192.168.3.2, 00:00:03, Serial0
                    [120/1] via 192.168.1.2, 00:00:10, Serial1
C    192.168.3.0/24 is directly connected, Serial0
```

From this output, we can see that Router 1 knows how to get to the 172.17.0.0/16 network through Serial1. Note that RIP has summarized 172.17.1.0/24 into a classful network boundary. It has done the same for 172.16.0.0/16 and 172.18.0.0/16. Automatic summarization is enabled by default in most protocols. To disable this behavior, use the no auto-summary command. In our little network, summarization works. (If we had subnetted differently, summarization could have been a big problem. See the later section "EIGRP" for a complete example of how auto-summarization can affect a network.) The output from show ip route also shows that Router 1 knows two paths to the 192.168.2.0/24 network.

Now, let's ping to make sure that our network is functional. From Router 1, ping Router 2's Ethernet interface:

```
Router1#ping 172.17.1.1

Type escape sequence to abort.
Sending 5, 100-byte ICMP Echos to 172.17.1.1, timeout is 2 seconds:
!!!!!
Success rate is 100 percent (5/5), round-trip min/avg/max = 28/29/32 ms
```

Now ping Router 3's Ethernet interface:

```
Router1#ping 172.18.1.1

Type escape sequence to abort.
Sending 5, 100-byte ICMP Echos to 172.18.1.1, timeout is 2 seconds:
!!!!!
Success rate is 100 percent (5/5), round-trip min/avg/max = 28/30/32 ms
```

While the pings were successful, this isn't a true test of our routing configuration—it only tests connectivity to the router. Still, ping is an extremely useful tool for showing that your hosts are on the network and reachable.

Enabling RIPv2 on the Network

By default, a Cisco router automatically listens to both Versions 1 and 2 of RIP. However, it sends only Version 1 packets. If you want to use RIPv2, you must enable it by using the version 2 command, as we did in the previous example. To get finer control over which version of RIP you're using, you can use the ip rip command to enable or disable Version 2 at the interface level. This command allows the router to talk Version 2 out one interface and Version 1 out another. See the ip rip command in Chapter 15 for more information.

Redistributing Other Routing Protocols into RIP

Many networks use two or more routing protocols; often, a second protocol is needed at the interface between one network and another. Less often, two protocols will be used within one network, possibly to accommodate older equipment. This raises a problem with metrics: one protocol's route metric might not translate to the metric used by another protocol. We use the default-metric command to assign a default metric value to routes received from other protocols. In the following example, we need to redistribute routes learned from EIGRP into RIP. However, these protocols have incompatible metrics. To solve this problem we assign a default metric of 10, which is given to all routes that don't otherwise have a metric—i.e., routes learned from other protocols (in this case, all routes learned from EIGRP):

```
router rip
  network 10.0.0.0
  default-metric 10
  redistribute eigrp 100
```

In this case, the EIGRP process number is 100. Depending on the routing protocol being redistributed, a process number may or may not be required.

RIPv2 Authentication

RIPv2 authentication provides some basic security to the routing updates. Since RIP automatically listens to anyone on the network who is also using RIP, a malicious user could easily intercept and corrupt the routing tables by injecting false information. RIPv2's authentication provides a password-like mechanism (called a *key*) to authenticate the routes from other machines.

The default authentication method is text, which means the passwords are exchanged in clear text. The keys will appear in every RIPv2 packet, so clear text is not secure. Anyone with a packet-sniffing program (such as *ethereal* or *snoop*) can discover what the passwords are by scanning all the RIP packets on a network. However, the authentication mode can easily be changed to use the MD5 message-digest algorithm, as in the following example. While MD5 is not true encryption, the passwords are no longer exchanged in clear text.

In this example, we configure the key chain and the authentication mode. The key chain is a series of passwords we are willing to accept. The final step is to enable RIPv2 authentication for an interface, which in this case is ethernet1. (For more information on key configuration, see Chapter 15.)

```
interface ethernet1
  ip rip authentication key-chain group1
  ip rip authentication mode md5
!
key chain group1
  key 1
  key-string authme1
  key 2
  key-string authme2
!
router rip
  version 2
  network 10.0.0.0
```

In this configuration, all RIP updates going in and out of ethernet1 are subject to RIPv2 authentication, which requires the key authme1 or authme2.

IGRP

The Interior Gateway Routing Protocol (IGRP) is a distance-vector routing protocol. IGRP has been superseded by Enhanced IGRP (EIGRP), which has many new features and is covered later in this chapter. The two protocols are fundamentally similar, configuration-wise, and this section serves as an introduction for both.

IGRP and EIGRP have a compound metric that takes into account several factors, such as link bandwidth and latency. As such, IGRP is superior to RIP, which takes into account only the hop count, and RIPv2, which uses both hop count and bandwidth. In addition to the compound metric, which allows better route selection, IGRP tends to have better convergence times, meaning that routing stabilizes more quickly after a network disruption. In addition, although it is more difficult to configure than RIP, configuration is still relatively easy.

The biggest drawback of IGRP (and EIGRP) is that it's a proprietary protocol, which means it is implemented only by Cisco routers. If all you have on your network are Cisco devices, using IGRP is not a problem. However, if you have a multivendor environment, you'll be forced to use multiple routing protocols or to agree on a protocol (such as RIP or OSPF) that is supported by all your vendors. Another disadvantage is that IGRP (like RIP) broadcasts the entire routing table, which can consume a lot of network bandwidth. In addition, IGRP does not support VLSM (again, like RIP). If you use VLSM—and you probably should—you need to use EIGRP.

Basic IGRP Configuration

For this example, we will reuse the network diagram in Figure 9-1. We want to enable IGRP on Router 1 and Router 2. We'll add the bandwidth command on the serial interfaces because IGRP uses bandwidth for route metric calculation. The bandwidth command is necessary on the serial interfaces because the router is unable to determine a default bandwidth for them. The Ethernet interface does not need a bandwidth command, as the router will supply a reasonable default.

The IGRP commands for Router 1 look like this:

```
interface Ethernet0
 ip address 172.16.1.1 255.255.255.0
!
interface Serial0
 bandwidth 125
 ip address 192.168.3.1 255.255.255.0
!
interface Serial1
 bandwidth 125
 ip address 192.168.1.1 255.255.255.0
!
router igrp 101
  network 172.16.0.0
  network 192.168.1.0
  network 192.168.3.0
```

For Router 2, they look like this:

```
interface Ethernet0
 ip address 172.17.1.1 255.255.255.0
!
interface Serial0
 bandwidth 125
 ip address 192.168.1.2 255.255.255.0
```

```
!
interface Serial1
 bandwidth 125
 ip address 192.168.2.1 255.255.255.0
!
router igrp 101
  network 172.17.0.0
  network 192.168.1.0
  network 192.168.2.0
```

And for Router 3, they look like this:

```
interface Ethernet0
 ip address 172.18.1.1 255.255.255.0
!
interface Serial0
 bandwidth 125
 ip address 192.168.2.2 255.255.255.0
!
interface Serial1
 bandwidth 125
 ip address 192.168.3.2 255.255.255.0
!
router igrp 101
  network 172.18.0.0
  network 192.168.2.0
  network 192.168.3.0
```

These commands configure IGRP on the proper networks with a local-AS number of 101. The local-AS number is essentially a process number that serves to identify the routers that will exchange routing information. The actual value you pick is immaterial, as long as all the routers running IGRP on the network use the same value. If they do not, they won't share routing information.

Let's do a show ip route and a few pings to make sure everything is running well:

```
Router1#show ip route
Codes: C - connected, S - static, I - IGRP, R - RIP, M - mobile, B - BGP
       D - EIGRP, EX - EIGRP external, O - OSPF, IA - OSPF inter area
       N1 - OSPF NSSA external type 1, N2 - OSPF NSSA external type 2
       E1 - OSPF external type 1, E2 - OSPF external type 2, E - EGP
       i - IS-IS, L1 - IS-IS level-1, L2 - IS-IS level-2, * - candidate default
       U - per-user static route, o - ODR

Gateway of last resort is not set

I    172.17.0.0/16 [100/82100] via 192.168.1.2, 00:01:05, Serial1
     172.16.0.0/24 is subnetted, 1 subnets
C       172.16.1.0 is directly connected, Ethernet0
I    172.18.0.0/16 [100/82100] via 192.168.3.2, 00:00:02, Serial0
C    192.168.1.0/24 is directly connected, Serial1
I    192.168.2.0/24 [100/84000] via 192.168.1.2, 00:01:06, Serial1
                    [100/84000] via 192.168.3.2, 00:00:02, Serial0
C    192.168.3.0/24 is directly connected, Serial0
```

From Router 1, ping Router 2's Ethernet interface:

```
Router1#ping 172.17.1.1

Type escape sequence to abort.
Sending 5, 100-byte ICMP Echos to 172.17.1.1, timeout is 2 seconds:
```

```
!!!!!
Success rate is 100 percent (5/5), round-trip min/avg/max = 28/31/32 ms
```

From Router 1, ping Router 3's Ethernet interface:

```
Router1#ping 172.18.1.1

Type escape sequence to abort.
Sending 5, 100-byte ICMP Echos to 172.18.1.1, timeout is 2 seconds:
!!!!!
Success rate is 100 percent (5/5), round-trip min/avg/max = 28/31/32 ms
```

Once again, the ping shows only that a working path exists between two hosts. It is by no means a complete test of our routing configuration.

IGRP's metric

Previously, we called the metric used by IGRP a *compound* metric, which means it uses more than one value to decide which route to use. The factors IGRP uses to calculate a metric are bandwidth, load, delay, and reliability. Before we examine the formula used to compute the metric, you should understand each of the variables:

Bandwidth
> The speed of the line. The bandwidth of any particular link is a configuration item—it isn't derived from the hardware itself. However, there are defaults for almost all media types except serial links. Ethernet, FDDI, token ring, etc., all have default bandwidth settings. Bandwidth is measured in 1-Kbps units; thus, the bandwidth for an Ethernet link is 10,000.

Delay
> The total delay for the path in 10-microsecond units. To get the delay for the entire route, the delay values for all the route's links are added together and the result is divided by 10.

Load
> A number between 1 and 255, which is a fraction of 255 that reflects the link's usage. A fully loaded link has the value of 255 (which equals 100%); a link with no load is assigned the value 1, which is the lowest possible value. If the loading was at 50%, the load value would be 128 (128/255).

Reliability
> Like load, reliability is a fraction of 255, where 255 represents 100% reliability, and 1 represents the lowest reliability.

In all its gory detail, the metric equation is:

$$Metric = (K1 \times bandwidth) + \frac{(K2 \times bandwidth)}{(256 - load)} + (K3 \times delay)$$

If k5 is greater than 0, you need to apply this second step:

$$Metric = Metric \times \frac{K5}{(reliability + K4)}$$

K1 through K5 are constants used to control the equation behavior. By varying these constants, you can give a higher or lower priority to different variables. By default, K1 and K3 equal 1, and K2, K4, and K5 equal 0. This means that, in effect, the metric calculation is much simpler:

$$Metric = bandwidth + delay$$

As with any distance-vector protocol, the route with the smallest metric (think in terms of weight) is the best route for the packet to travel.

Despite all this talk about a compound metric, it's apparent that IGRP's default metric is really quite simple and depends only on the bandwidth and the delay. What's the use of having a great compound metric if you set up the constants so that most of the interesting features of that metric are discarded? Well, it is possible to adapt the metric for use in special situations. The command for changing the constants is `metric weights` *tos k1 k2 k3 k4 k5*. (The `tos` is a value that is not used; refer to Chapter 15 for an explanation.)

Making intelligent decisions about how to change the constants is beyond the scope of this book. It's easy to make a change that has side effects you don't want. For example, we could tell the router to use the load factor by setting K2 to 1. However, in most networks this change would have a serious side effect. A link's load can increase and decrease fairly quickly. Each change to the load would cause the link's metric to change and a route update to occur. As metrics change, routing updates and broadcasts also change. This can be an important fact when dealing with a state-driven protocol such as EIGRP. For example, using load and reliability might cause unstable routing tables, because they tend to oscillate based on small changes in traffic volume.

There may be situations in which you want this behavior, but on most networks, you don't want to send routing updates more frequently than necessary. Whatever the reasons, changing the K values should be done cautiously, if at all. It's best not to change the metrics.

Packet size

IGRP also keeps track of the Maximum Transmission Unit (MTU) on every path it knows about. The MTU is the largest packet that can be sent without fragmentation. The MTU for an entire route is the smallest MTU of any of the links in that route.

Modifying the range of the network

Like RIP, IGRP also keeps track of hop counts, although they aren't used in computing the routing metric. Hop counts are used to decide when a network has become unreachable. By default, the maximum hop count is 100; you can set it to be as high as 255 using the command `metric maximum hops`:

```
router igrp 101
  metric maximum-hops 200
```

Note that the maximum hop count of IGRP allows it to support much larger networks than RIP, which supports only 15 hops as a maximum.

IGRP's load balancing

IGRP performs either *equal-cost* load balancing or *unequal-cost* load balancing. Load balancing means that IGRP distributes the network traffic load across more than one link. However, IGRP (and EIGRP) do load balancing on a session-oriented basis. Load balancing is not packet-oriented; therefore, once a session has been started with a host somewhere on the network, all packets in that session will be sent through the same interface.

In equal-cost load balancing, a router can have up to four routes to a particular destination, as long as all the routes have the same (equal) metric. For example, let's assume that a route has a metric of 9000, and another route to the same destination comes along. The new route is added to the route table, but it is used for load balancing only if its metric is also 9000. If the metric of the new route is less than 9000, it will be used for all the traffic, and the original route won't be used. On the other hand, if the new route has a metric greater than 9000, the router will know of its existence but won't use it to handle any traffic.

Unequal-cost load balancing requires the use of a metric multiplier, which is called a *variance*. The variance allows other routes to be added to the routing table even if their metrics are not equal. Before any new route is added to the table, however, two rules must be met:

1. The new router's metric to the destination must be less than our router's current metric to the destination. Or more simply, the new router must be closer than our router.

2. The variance multiplied by our router's metric must be equal to or greater than the new route. Or more simply, our route times some number (variance) must be larger than the new route's metric. So we are willing to accept an alternate route if its metric is within some fraction of our current metric.

As with equal-cost load balancing, the router keeps up to four routes to a destination in its routing table. If more than four routes are available, only the best four are used. If you understood the two rules, you realized that equal-cost load balancing is nothing more than unequal-cost load balancing with a variance of 1, which is the default value. So the router performs equal-cost load balancing by default; you can set the variance to another value using the `variance` command. Increasing the variance allows traffic to be distributed over links with unequal metrics. This means that if our primary link is becoming loaded, we can distribute some of the load across the otherwise unused, slower links.

These rules are admittedly confusing; it will help to look at an example. Figure 9-2 shows a simple network with three routers. Our router is Router 1, and we are interested in routes to Router 2. Normally, we would send all our traffic over Route 1, which is a T1 link with a metric of 8000. Of the routes we have available, this route is clearly the best. But let's see what happens with unequal-cost load balancing. Imagine that the variance is 4. Now notice that Router 3 has a route to Router 2 that is also a T1 link with a metric of 8000. So Router 3's route to Router 2 is as good as ours, thus meeting the first of the two criteria. Furthermore, the total metric for a route from Router 1 to Router 2 via Router 3 is 11000. That isn't as good as ours, but it is better than our metric times the variance (11000 is less than 8000 × 4). So if our variance is 4, we will add this second route via Router 3 to our routing table and start using it to carry traffic.

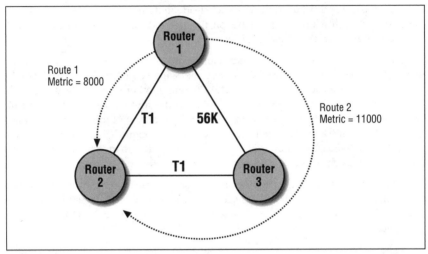

Figure 9-2: An example of unequal-cost load balancing

While we used a variance of 4 to illustrate our example, it's not advisable to use a variance of more than 1.5, because the slower link will have a much larger latency due to transmission time. For example, a 56k link takes .21 seconds to transmit a 1500-byte packet, and a T1 takes .001 seconds.

With unequal-cost load balancing, traffic is distributed across all possible routes in the route table (there are four maximum routes). We can change this behavior so that the best route is used all the time, and extra routes are used only when the best route becomes unavailable. The command that controls this feature is traffic-share, which by default is set to balanced. In the following example, we change traffic sharing to min (minimum), which sends all traffic to the route with the best metric. We also specify a variance of 2:

```
router igrp 100
  network 10.0.0.0
  variance 2
  traffic-share min across-interfaces
```

The advantage of this configuration is that the extra routes are held in the routing table and are immediately available if the primary route goes down, but there is no attempt at load balancing between routes of unequal quality.

You can perform load balancing on a per-packet basis by using process switching, which is discussed in Chapter 8. Process switching is more CPU-intensive, but may be a better solution in some applications.

Redistributing Other Protocols into IGRP

When redistributing RIP into IGRP, you must define a default metric that tells IGRP how to assign metrics for the routes it learns from RIP. The following example uses the redistribute command and the default-metric command:

```
! Define the IGRP routing process
router igrp 100
  network 10.0.0.0
  redistribute rip
  default-metric 10000 100 255 1 1500
! Define the RIP process
router rip
  network 192.168.1.0
```

The default-metric command is required for redistributing most nonstatic routes. In this example, we specify the values that are the input for IGRP's metric computation. The values are bandwidth (10,000, which is 10,000 kbps), delay (in units of tens of microseconds—100 equals a delay of 1 millisecond), reliability (1 to 255), load (1 to 255), and the MTU (1500 bytes). These are all reasonable values for a 10 Mbps Ethernet. A reasonable default metric for a serial link might be:

```
default-metric 1000 100 250 100 1500
```

EIGRP

EIGRP stands for Enhanced IGRP. EIGRP, like IGRP, is a proprietary Cisco protocol; other vendors' routers cannot support EIGRP, but that's about the only disadvantage. EIGRP provides excellent performance, easy configuration, VLSM support, and support for IPX and AppleTalk. It is a distance-vector protocol that also contains the characteristics of a link-state protocol. EIGRP uses the same compound metric as its predecessor, IGRP. And unlike IGRP, which is prone to routing loops, EIGRP is pretty much loop-free. The most unique feature of EIGRP is its dual finite state machine, which provides an extremely fast convergence time. Other features are partial routing table updates (less bandwidth and CPU are used on routing updates), automatic discovery of neighbors, and increased scalability.

Enabling EIGRP on the Network

Here are the EIGRP configurations for Router 1, Router 2, and Router 3 in Figure 9-1. By now, these configurations should look familiar—they're almost identical to the IGRP configurations, except for the name of the protocol.

The configuration for Router 1 is:

```
interface Ethernet0
 ip address 172.16.1.1 255.255.255.0
!
interface Serial0
 bandwidth 125
 ip address 192.168.3.1 255.255.255.0
!
interface Serial1
 bandwidth 125
 ip address 192.168.1.1 255.255.255.0
!
```

```
router eigrp 101
  network 172.16.0.0
  network 192.168.1.0
  network 192.168.3.0
```

For Router 2, the configuration is:

```
interface Ethernet0
 ip address 172.17.1.1 255.255.255.0
!
interface Serial0
 bandwidth 125
 ip address 192.168.1.2 255.255.255.0
!
interface Serial1
 bandwidth 125
 ip address 192.168.2.1 255.255.255.0
!
router eigrp 101
  network 172.17.0.0
  network 192.168.1.0
  network 192.168.2.0
```

And for Router 3, the configuration is:

```
interface Ethernet0
 ip address 172.18.1.1 255.255.255.0
!
interface Serial0
 bandwidth 125
 ip address 192.168.2.2 255.255.255.0
!
interface Serial1
 bandwidth 125
 ip address 192.168.3.2 255.255.255.0
!
router eigrp 101
  network 172.18.0.0
  network 192.168.2.0
  network 192.168.3.0
```

Let's do some simple testing on Router 1 to make sure the routes are good:

```
Router1#show ip route
Codes: C - connected, S - static, I - IGRP, R - RIP, M - mobile, B - BGP
       D - EIGRP, EX - EIGRP external, O - OSPF, IA - OSPF inter area
       N1 - OSPF NSSA external type 1, N2 - OSPF NSSA external type 2
       E1 - OSPF external type 1, E2 - OSPF external type 2, E - EGP
       i - IS-IS, L1 - IS-IS level-1, L2 - IS-IS level-2, * - candidate default
       U - per-user static route, o - ODR

Gateway of last resort is not set

D    172.17.0.0/16 [90/21017600] via 192.168.1.2, 00:00:05, Serial1
     172.16.0.0/16 is variably subnetted, 2 subnets, 2 masks
D       172.16.0.0/16 is a summary, 00:00:03, Null0
C       172.16.1.0/24 is directly connected, Ethernet0
D    172.18.0.0/16 [90/21017600] via 192.168.3.2, 00:00:03, Serial0
C    192.168.1.0/24 is directly connected, Serial1
D    192.168.2.0/24 [90/21504000] via 192.168.1.2, 00:00:05, Serial1
                    [90/21504000] via 192.168.3.2, 00:00:05, Serial0
C    192.168.3.0/24 is directly connected, Serial0
```

From Router 1, ping Router 2's Ethernet interface:

```
Router1#ping 172.17.1.1

Type escape sequence to abort.
Sending 5, 100-byte ICMP Echos to 172.17.1.1, timeout is 2 seconds:
!!!!!
Success rate is 100 percent (5/5), round-trip min/avg/max = 28/28/32 ms
```

From Router 1, ping Router 3's Ethernet interface:

```
Router1#ping 172.18.1.1

Type escape sequence to abort.
Sending 5, 100-byte ICMP Echos to 172.18.1.1, timeout is 2 seconds:
!!!!!
Success rate is 100 percent (5/5), round-trip min/avg/max = 28/30/32 ms
```

From the output, you can see that Router 1's routing table has the expected routes. And the pings establish that Router 1 knows how to get to the Ethernet interfaces on both Router 2 and Router 3.

Comparing the output of show ip route to our previous examples, we see a new summary route for network 172.16.0.0/16 pointing to Null0. EIGRP creates this route by default; it helps to prevent possible black holes when default and summary routes are used. In our network from Figure 9-1, this summarization isn't a problem due to our subnetting design.

EIGRP and Route Summarization

Figure 9-3 shows a network on which we are going to use EIGRP as a routing protocol. It's almost identical to the network in Figure 9-1; it differs primarily in that we are going to conserve some address space by using a /30 subnet on our shared serial links. We've also connected each router to a /24 subnet of the 172.16. 0.0 network, which (to a classful routing protocol) has a 16-bit netmask. This network will allow us to demonstrate how EIGRP can handle classless routing, in addition to showing how it handles automatic route summarization.

Here are the initial configurations for our three routers. The interface commands are included to better illustrate the entire configuration.

Here's the configuration for Router 1:

```
interface Ethernet0
  ip address 172.16.1.1 255.255.255.0
  !
interface Serial0
  bandwidth 125
  ip address 192.168.1.13 255.255.255.252
!
interface Serial1
  bandwidth 125
  ip address 192.168.1.5 255.255.255.252
!
router eigrp 100
  network 172.16.0.0
  network 192.168.1.0
  !
ip classless
```

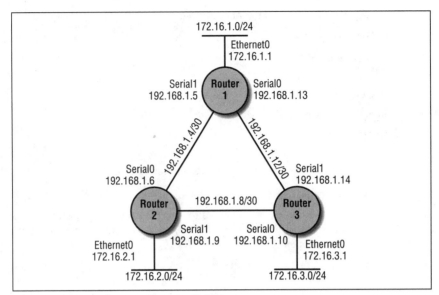

Figure 9-3: A simple network using EIGRP

For Router 2, the configuration is:

```
interface Ethernet0
 ip address 172.16.2.1 255.255.255.0
!
interface Serial0
 bandwidth 125
 ip address 192.168.1.6 255.255.255.252
!
interface Serial1
 bandwidth 125
 ip address 192.168.1.9 255.255.255.252
!
router eigrp 100
 network 172.16.0.0
 network 192.168.1.0
!
ip classless
```

Here's the configuration for Router 3:

```
interface Ethernet0
 ip address 172.16.3.1 255.255.255.0
!
interface Serial0
 ip address 192.168.1.10 255.255.255.252
!
interface Serial1
 ip address 192.168.1.14 255.255.255.252
!
router eigrp 100
 network 172.16.0.0
 network 192.168.1.0
!
ip classless
```

This looks correct. We didn't need to specify classless routing explicitly, because it's the default for EIGRP, but it never hurts to make it clear how you expect your network to behave. However, if we look at the output from show ip route and a few pings, we will see that something is wrong:

```
Router1#show ip route
Codes: C - connected, S - static, I - IGRP, R - RIP, M - mobile, B - BGP
       D - EIGRP, EX - EIGRP external, O - OSPF, IA - OSPF inter area
       N1 - OSPF NSSA external type 1, N2 - OSPF NSSA external type 2
       E1 - OSPF external type 1, E2 - OSPF external type 2, E - EGP
       i - IS-IS, L1 - IS-IS level-1, L2 - IS-IS level-2, * - candidate default
       U - per-user static route, o - ODR

Gateway of last resort is not set

     172.16.0.0/16 is variably subnetted, 2 subnets, 2 masks
D       172.16.0.0/16 is a summary, 00:00:02, Null0
C       172.16.1.0/24 is directly connected, Ethernet0
     192.168.1.0/30 is subnetted, 3 subnets
D       192.168.1.8 [90/21504000] via 192.168.1.14, 00:00:02, Serial0
                    [90/21504000] via 192.168.1.6, 00:00:02, Serial1
C       192.168.1.12 is directly connected, Serial0
C       192.168.1.4 is directly connected, Serial1
```

From Router 1, try to ping Router 2's Ethernet interface:

```
Router1#ping 172.16.2.1

Type escape sequence to abort.
Sending 5, 100-byte ICMP Echos to 172.16.2.1, timeout is 2 seconds:
.....
Success rate is 0 percent (0/5)
```

From Router 1, try to ping Router 3's Ethernet interface:

```
Router1#ping 172.16.3.1

Type escape sequence to abort.
Sending 5, 100-byte ICMP Echos to 172.16.3.1, timeout is 2 seconds:
.....
Success rate is 0 percent (0/5)
```

Our attempts to ping the Ethernet interfaces of the other routers from Router 1 failed. If you look closely at the routing table, you can see why. EIGRP has summarized the entire 172.16.0.0/16 network for us and pointed the route to the null interface:

```
     172.16.0.0/16 is variably subnetted, 2 subnets, 2 masks
D       172.16.0.0/16 is a summary, 00:00:02, Null0
C       172.16.1.0/24 is directly connected, Ethernet0
```

This is actually how EIGRP is supposed to behave, strange as it might seem; the summary route is created because of the way we subnetted 172.16.0.0/16. The same summary route exists on Router 2:

```
Router2#show ip route
...
Gateway of last resort is not set

     172.16.0.0/16 is variably subnetted, 2 subnets, 2 masks
D       172.16.0.0/16 is a summary, 00:05:57, Null0
```

```
C       172.16.2.0/24 is directly connected, Ethernet0
    192.168.1.0/30 is subnetted, 3 subnets
C       192.168.1.8 is directly connected, Serial1
D       192.168.1.12 [90/21504000] via 192.168.1.5, 00:05:57, Serial0
C       192.168.1.4 is directly connected, Serial0
```

And we'd see the same thing on Router 3 if we took the time to look. Although EIGRP can handle classless addresses, it automatically summarizes routes to classful addresses and creates a summary route that points to the Null0 interface. EIGRP points the summary route to Null0 in order to prevent routing loops.

Route summarization occurs only on:

- Routes that are directly connected to this router
- Routes other than the current interface's network

The solution for this network is to disable auto-summary in EIGRP by adding the no auto-summary command to the EIGRP configuration on each router.

For Router 1, the EIGRP configuration now looks like this:

```
router eigrp 100
 network 172.16.0.0
 network 192.168.1.0
 no auto-summary
```

After making this change on every router, we can do a show ip route on Router 1, which should look better. The summary route to Null0 is gone:

```
Router1#show ip route
...

Gateway of last resort is not set

    172.16.0.0/24 is subnetted, 3 subnets
C       172.16.1.0 is directly connected, Ethernet0
D       172.16.2.0 [90/21017600] via 192.168.1.6, 00:00:23, Serial1
D       172.16.3.0 [90/21017600] via 192.168.1.14, 00:00:03, Serial0
    192.168.1.0/30 is subnetted, 3 subnets
D       192.168.1.8 [90/21504000] via 192.168.1.6, 00:00:03, Serial1
                    [90/21504000] via 192.168.1.14, 00:00:03, Serial0
C       192.168.1.12 is directly connected, Serial0
C       192.168.1.4 is directly connected, Serial1
```

Now, we can ping Router 2's Ethernet interface from Router 1:

```
Router1#ping 172.16.2.1

Type escape sequence to abort.
Sending 5, 100-byte ICMP Echos to 172.16.2.1, timeout is 2 seconds:
!!!!!
Success rate is 100 percent (5/5), round-trip min/avg/max = 28/31/32 ms
```

Router 3's Ethernet interface is now also reachable from Router 1:

```
Router1#ping 172.16.3.1

Type escape sequence to abort.
Sending 5, 100-byte ICMP Echos to 172.16.3.1, timeout is 2 seconds:
!!!!!
Success rate is 100 percent (5/5), round-trip min/avg/max = 28/29/32 ms
```

Enabling route summarization on a specific interface

Route summarization can also be controlled at the interface level. On etherneto, we can apply the following command to summarize any route we want:

```
interface etherneto
  ip summary-address eigrp 100 10.101.1.0 255.255.255.0
```

When advertised out etherneto, the 10.101.1.0 summary route is given the administrative distance of 5, which supersedes other EIGRP routes. Consult Chapter 8 for more information on administrative distances.

EIGRP Authentication

EIGRP's authentication prevents unauthorized routers from injecting routes on the network. Here's an example that shows how to enable authentication. First, we create a key chain, which is a series of passwords we are willing to accept. We specify that these passwords have an infinite lifetime—i.e., they will never expire. After the keys are defined, we can enable EIGRP authentication. Here's a configuration that defines a key chain named group1, and then uses this key chain for EIGRP process 100:

```
interface etherneto
  ip authentication mode eigrp 100 md5
  ip authentication key-chain eigrp 100 group1
!
key chain group1
  key 1
  key-string authme1
  accept-lifetime 00:00:00 1 jan 1999 infinite
  key 2
  accept-lifetime 00:00:00 1 jan 1999 infinite
  key-string authme2
!
router eigrp 100
  network 10.10.0.0
```

In this configuration, all EIGRP updates are subject to authentication, which requires the key authme1 or authme2. We used MD5 so the keys won't be transmitted in clear text.

EIGRP Metrics

EIGRP metrics are identical to IGRP metrics, including the K values in the metric equation. The only difference between the two is that EIGRP's metric is multiplied by 256, which makes it a 32-bit integer instead of a 24-bit integer. Consult the previous section "IGRP's metric" for more information on the metric calculation.

Tuning EIGRP

By default, EIGRP allows itself to use at most 50% of a link's maximum bandwidth. In some instances, you might want to change this value; for example, a change might be appropriate if for some reason you told a router that the link's bandwidth was something other than its actual bandwidth. To change the bandwidth usage, use the ip bandwidth-percent eigrp command. In this example, we change the bandwidth EIGRP can use to 65% (100 is the local-AS number, or process number, for the EIGRP process):

```
interface ethernet0
  ip bandwidth-percent eigrp 100 65
```

Hello packets are sent out to discover new EIGRP devices. For most types of links, the default hello interval is five seconds. However, a longer interval might be appropriate for a slower link. To change the hello interval, use the `ip hello-interval eigrp` command:

```
interface ethernet0
  ip hello-interval eigrp 100 10
```

By default, the time an EIGRP route is held is three times the hello interval (i.e., 15 seconds). Increasing the hold time can be beneficial if there is a great deal of latency on a network. However, changing the hold time is not generally recommend as a solution. The following command increases the hold time to 30 seconds:

```
interface ethernet0
  ip hold-time eigrp 100 30
```

EIGRP show Commands

There are several show commands for EIGRP that are not available for other protocols. Here are some of the more useful commands.

show ip eigrp neighbors

This command shows us the EIGRP neighbors that our router knows about. On our network, Router 1 sees Routers 2 and 3. The Interface column shows which interface received the hello from the neighbor. Hold shows the hold time (in seconds) that the router waits to hear from the neighbor before declaring the neighbor down. Uptime is the amount of time elapsed since we first learned of this neighbor. SRTT stands for Smooth Round Trip Time, the number of milliseconds it takes for the router to send an EIGRP packet to the neighbor and for the neighbor to respond. RTO indicates the retransmission timeout, which is the time (in milliseconds) that the router will wait before retransmitting a packet to the neighbor. Q Cnt is the number of queued EIGRP packets that the router is waiting to send. Finally, Seq Num shows the sequence number of the last packet received from the neighbor:

```
Router1#show ip eigrp neighbors
IP-EIGRP neighbors for process 100
H   Address            Interface    Hold Uptime    SRTT  RTO  Q    Seq
                                    (sec)          (ms)       Cnt  Num
1   192.168.1.14       Se0          11 15:40:05    32    1164 0    7
0   192.168.1.6        Se1          10 15:40:22    434   2604 0    9
```

The EIGRP neighbor counters can be cleared with the command:

```
clear ip eigrp neighbors
```

Logging can be enabled with the following command:

```
eigrp log-neighbor-changes
```

Any neighbor changes are written to a log file, which means that you must have a valid syslog configuration if you enable logging.

show ip eigrp topology

This command gives us the router's view of the EIGRP network topology. Each entry in the topology has an associated state, which can be Passive, Active, Update, Query, Reply, or Reply Status. Passive means that no EIGRP computations are being used. Active means that EIGRP is performing calculations for this destination. Update, Query, and Reply simply mean that a packet of the indicated type has been sent to the destination. Reply Status means that a reply packet has been sent and the router is waiting for a reply.

The last piece of information needed to decode this table is FD, which stands for *feasible distance*. This number is used in the feasibility calculation. For each entry, the FD number is followed by a slash (/) and another number. The second number is the reported distance of the neighbor. If the reported distance is greater than the feasible distance, that path becomes the feasible successor for the route.

```
Router1#show ip eigrp topology
IP-EIGRP Topology Table for process 100

Codes: P - Passive, A - Active, U - Update, Q - Query, R - Reply,
       r - Reply status

P 192.168.1.8/30, 2 successors, FD is 21504000
         via 192.168.1.14 (21504000/20992000), Serial0
         via 192.168.1.6 (21504000/20992000), Serial1
P 192.168.1.12/30, 1 successors, FD is 20992000
         via Connected, Serial0
P 192.168.1.4/30, 1 successors, FD is 20992000
         via Connected, Serial1
P 172.16.1.0/24, 1 successors, FD is 281600
         via Connected, Ethernet0
P 172.16.2.0/24, 1 successors, FD is 21017600
         via 192.168.1.6 (21017600/281600), Serial1
P 172.16.3.0/24, 1 successors, FD is 21017600
         via 192.168.1.14 (21017600/281600), Serial0
```

show ip eigrp traffic

This command simply outputs the hellos, updates, queries, replies, and acks that the EIGRP routing process has sent. For each type of packet, the first number is the number sent and the second number is the number received.

```
Router1#show ip eigrp traffic
IP-EIGRP Traffic Statistics for process 100
  Hellos sent/received: 24728/24704
  Updates sent/received: 23/19
  Queries sent/received: 1/1
  Replies sent/received: 1/1
  Acks sent/received: 12/15
```

EIGRP Redistribution

On a multiprotocol network, you need to define default metrics to handle routes redistributed into EIGRP from other protocols.

RIP

Redistributing RIP into EIGRP is as easy as defining the default metric for the incoming RIP routes. Here's an example:

```
! Define the RIP process
router rip
  network 192.168.1.0
! Define the EIGRP process and include the learned RIP routes
router eigrp 100
  network 10.0.0.0
  default-metric 1000 250 255 1 1500
  redistribute rip
```

This is almost identical to the earlier example that showed how to redistribute RIP routes into IGRP. That shouldn't be surprising, since IGRP and EIGRP use the same metric computation. We are redistributing in only one direction in this example—from RIP into EIGRP. You must be careful when redistributing in both directions, in which case you'll want to filter the routers to prevent routing loops. See "Filtering Routes" in Chapter 8 for an example.

IGRP

When mixing IGRP and EIGRP on a router, redistribution is automatic if the process numbers for the RIP and EIGRP routing processes are the same. If they are different, you must use the `redistribute` command. In this example, redistribution occurs automatically because both routing protocols use the same process number (100):

```
! Define the IGRP routing process
router igrp 100
  network 10.0.0.0
! Define the EIGRP with same number as IGRP so the redistribution between
! the two is automatic
router eigrp 100
  network 10.0.0.0
```

In the next example, the routing process numbers differ, so route redistribution is not automatic and we need to use the `redistribute` command. Since both IGRP and EIGRP use the same metrics, the `default-metric` command is not required.

```
! Define the IGRP routing process
router igrp 100
  network 10.0.0.0
! Define the EIGRP process and redistribute the igrp routes
router eigrp 109
  network 10.0.0.0
  redistribute igrp 100
```

Converting an IGRP Network to EIGRP

It's simple to convert a network from IGRP to EIGRP using an incremental approach. In the previous examples, we showed how EIGRP and IGRP share routes automatically if they share the same process numbers. Using this fact, any IGRP network can be converted to EIGRP incrementally, without much downtime.

Figure 9-4 shows a simple network of 10 routers using IGRP. We start the conversion by picking a place to begin. We will start with Router 1, which is the center of the network. We pick this router because as we convert the other networks, it will pull in routes and redistribute them for us.

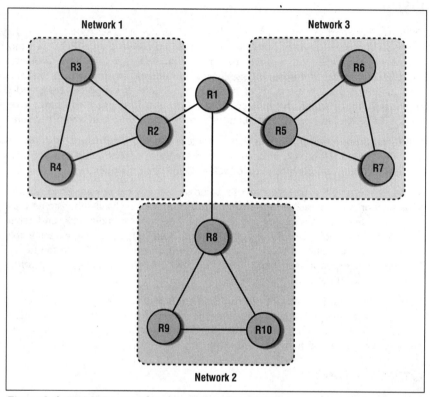

Figure 9-4: An IGRP network to be converted to EIGRP

By enabling IGRP and EIGRP on Router 1, we can slowly migrate Networks 1, 2, and 3 to EIGRP. First we configure Router 1:

```
router igrp 100
  network 10.0.0.0
router eigrp 100
  network 10.0.0.0
```

Now we start with the other networks. Let's start with Network 3, which consists of Routers 5, 6, and 7. We implement the same configuration on each:

```
router igrp 100
  network 10.0.0.0
router eigrp 100
  network 10.0.0.0
```

Once all three routers have this configuration, we remove all IGRP commands. Now Network 3 is using EIGRP exclusively. The process is repeated for Networks 1 and 2. When you have reconfigured all three networks (Routers 2–10), you can remove the IGRP commands from Router 1. At this point, none of the other routers are running IGRP, so running IGRP on Router 1 is only wasting CPU power. We are left with a network that is 100% EIGRP.

OSPF

OSPF (Open Shortest Path First) is a link-state protocol. It's a good choice for networks that need a more sophisticated routing protocol than RIP but are not willing to standardize on a single router vendor, and therefore have problems using EIGRP. It has a number of significant advantages, most of which it shares with EIGRP: it doesn't use a lot of network bandwidth, it supports VLSM, and it converges quickly when the network's state changes. Its biggest advantage over EIGRP is that it is an open standard and is supported by almost all router vendors.

OSPF has a reputation for being very complex, and to some extent, this reputation is deserved. However, in small networks it can be configured quickly. This book does not give a comprehensive look at OSPF or its capabilities.

As you'll see, OSPF forces you to use a certain topological design. OSPF divides your network into areas; area 0 is the "backbone" to which all other areas must connect. While this design fits many (perhaps even most) networks, and while there are some tools for giving you additional flexibility, you might reasonably object to using a routing protocol that limits your network's flexibility in the future. However, some people feel that this aspect of OSPF is an advantage, as it forces the use of decent network-design practices.

One possible disadvantage of OSPF is that it tends to use a lot of CPU time on the router because the OSPF LSA maintenance algorithms are CPU-intensive. This tendency to be a CPU hog can be controlled by restricting the number of routers per area, another good network-design practice.

OSPF Concepts

Before saying anything significant about OSPF, it's important to introduce the basic building blocks. Again, I won't try to explain all the details—just enough of the important concepts to get you started.

Areas

An *area* is a group of routers; a good design should have no more than 50 routers per area (or 100 interfaces). Each area is assigned a number, starting at 0. Area 0 is the backbone area; it must exist in any OSPF network. Figure 9-5 shows how the areas of a network must be ordered in a topological design.

In Figure 9-5, area 0 is the backbone area, with all other areas connecting to it. Areas allow summarization of network addresses, which in turn allows for smaller routing tables. Smaller routing tables mean faster convergence, less routing-protocol bandwidth, and better route determination. However, using a large number of relatively small areas can also mean a more difficult configuration.

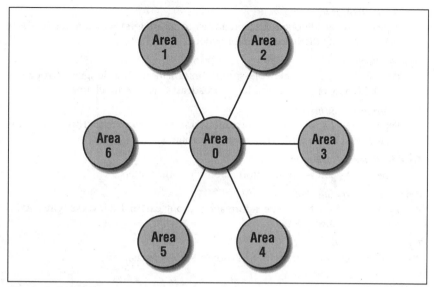

Figure 9-5: OSPF area topology

Router types

An OSPF router can be classified as one of the following types:

ASBR (autonomous system border router)
> A router with one or more interfaces connected to an external network or a network with a different local-AS number.

ABR (area border router)
> A router with one or more interfaces connected to different areas. Information about each area that it is connected to is stored within this router.

Area-internal
> A router whose interfaces are all within the same area.

Backbone
> A router with one or more interfaces connected to the OSPF backbone area. The backbone area is area 0.

Link-state advertisements (LSAs)

Before we discuss the different types of OSPF areas, let's look at how updates are sent between areas. These updates are called *link-state advertisements*, or LSAs. An LSA is an OSPF multicast that describes a routing change or routing update to other routers or areas.

There are six different types of LSAs. An LSA's type defines the type of route that is being advertised and how the announcements are processed. LSAs are sent every 30 minutes or at every link-state change. Following is a list of the different LSA types.

Type 1—Router Link

Type 1 LSAs are flooded (i.e., broadcast to all routers) within an area. These LSAs contain all the link-state information.

Type 2—Network

Type 2 LSAs contain network-specific information. The designated router of the OSPF network (discussed later) broadcasts this LSA to all area routers.

Type 3—Internal Summary

Type 3 LSAs contain route information for internal networks. This information is broadcast by the ABR to all backbone routers.

Type 4—External Summary

Type 4 LSAs contain route information for ASBR routers.

Type 5—Autonomous System

Type 5 LSAs contain route information about external networks. Only ASBR routers send these LSAs.

Type 6—NSSA External LSA

Type 6 LSAs are used by NSSAs (not-so-stubby areas).

Area types

There are several possible area types in an OSPF network:

Backbone

All OSPF designs require a backbone area, which connects multiple areas together. The backbone area is always area 0.

Standard

A standard area connects to the backbone area and accepts both internal and external LSAs.

Stub

A stub area doesn't need all the routes other areas receive; all it needs is a default route and summary LSAs. It doesn't receive external routes. A stub area generally contains at most 50 routers, and its addresses can easily be summarized to areas above it. All areas, except for area 0, can be stubby if they don't contain an ASBR. To create a stub network, use the stub command (for example, area 1 stub).

Totally stubby

A totally stubby area does not accept external or summary LSAs. It's just like a stub area except that it doesn't receive any summary information at all; it receives only a default route. To configure a totally stubby area, add the no-summary command to the area configuration (for example, area 1 stub no-summary).

Not-so-stubby

A not-so-stubby area (NSSA) is like a stub area, but it shares routing information with an external network that is using a different routing protocol. In other words, it is a regular stub area, but it has an ASBR router. The remote network becomes an area of our OSPF network, eliminating the need to implement the different routing protocol within the OSPF network. The ASBR of our NSSA area injects routes redistributed from the other routing protocol and passes them back into the area 0 backbone. To define a network as an NSSA, use the command `area 1 nssa`.

Router ID

Each OSPF router must have a unique router ID to identify it to the OSPF network. By default, the router ID is the address of its loopback interface. If no loopback address is defined, the router ID is the highest IP address of any active interface. Remember that the loopback interface of a Cisco router is an interface that is always up by definition and that has an IP address that is unique on the network (i.e., not 127.0.0.1).

Designated router (DR)

Each network segment needs a *designated router*, known as the DR, before it can exchange routing information. OSPF elects a DR on each multi-access segment. When an OSPF broadcast arrives at the DR, it is the job of the DR to multicast the update to all routers within its area. This keeps OSPF traffic to a minimum, because each router communicates with only the DR to get the routing information. If this didn't happen, the broadcast would have to go to each router, which would in turn broadcast again until every router got the message. In other words, the DR gives us a one-to-many relationship instead of a many-to-many relationship. With DR routers, there is only one place to send an update and one router that updates all the routers within the segment.

A *backup designated router* (BDR) must also be selected. This router becomes the DR if the DR becomes unavailable. If both the DR and BDR are unavailable, new ones are chosen automatically.

Enabling OSPF on the Network

You configure OSPF much like you configure other routing protocols: use the `router` command to establish the protocol and a process number, and use the `network` command to tell the router which networks it's responsible for. It's easy to become confused: with OSPF the `network` command takes a wildcard mask, not a subnet mask. For more information on wildcard masks, see "Access Lists" in Chapter 7. Here's an example:

```
router ospf  99
  network 10.10.1.0 0.0.0.255 area 0
```

Here, we establish an OSPF routing process with the process ID 99. This routing process is responsible for the network 10.10.1.0/24, which belongs to area 0. Therefore, this router is part of the OSPF backbone area. Do not confuse the process ID (99) with the area ID (0).

OSPF will run over all interfaces that match the `network` commands.

Sample OSPF Configurations

Figure 9-6 shows a network in which the backbone consists of one router. There are three other areas, each with a single router. In this configuration, Router 1 is the backbone router, and Router 2, Router 3, and Router 4 are area border routers (ABRs) with interfaces in different areas. One interface for each of these routers connects to the backbone area.

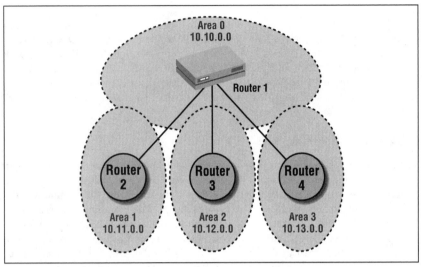

Figure 9-6: An OSPF network with a single backbone router

Router 1 is configured like this:

```
router ospf  99
    network 10.10.0.0 0.0.255.255 area 0
```

The configuration for Router 2 is:

```
router ospf  99
    network 10.10.0.0 0.0.255.255 area 0
    network 10.11.0.0 0.0.255.255 area 1
```

The configuration for Router 3 is:

```
router ospf  99
    network 10.10.0.0 0.0.255.255 area 0
    network 10.12.0.0 0.0.255.255 area 2
```

And here's the configuration for Router 4:

```
router ospf  99
    network 10.10.0.0 0.0.255.255 area 0
    network 10.13.0.0 0.0.255.255 area 3
```

Each router has a network statement for every area in which it participates. Router 1 needs a network statement only for area 0, because it doesn't have interfaces in areas 1, 2, and 3; its only area is the 10.10.0.0 network (area 0). It's important to understand that it's interfaces, not routers, that belong to areas.

The rest of the routers (Router 2, Router 3, and Router 4) are all area border routers, and they need two network statements because they each participate in two areas. Each network statement specifies the subnet that is associated with the area. Therefore, Router 2, Router 3, and Router 4 specify 10.10.0.0 0.0.255.255 for area 0, which is their backbone connection, and they each have an entry for their own areas (1, 2, and 3). Also note that the routers have the same OSPF process ID (99). Unlike local-AS numbers in IGRP and EIGRP, the process ID has no effect outside of the router. If the process IDs were different, routing would still occur.

Now let's look at a variation of this configuration in which we don't have a dedicated backbone router. In Figure 9-7, all three routers share area 0, which makes them all area border routers with no backbone router. The backbone still exists—it just doesn't have its own router. This configuration increases reliability because there's no longer a single point of failure.

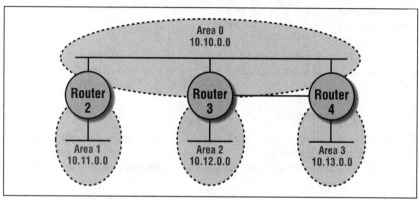

Figure 9-7: An OSPF network with a backbone across three ABRs

Here are the configurations. Not much has changed, except that we have dropped Router 1 from the configuration, and Router 2, Router 3, and Router 4 are all connected on one network segment.

The configuration for Router 2 is:

```
router ospf 99
  network 10.11.0.0 0.0.255.255 area 1
  network 10.10.0.0 0.0.255.255 area 0
```

The configuration for Router 3 is:

```
router ospf 99
  network 10.12.0.0 0.0.255.255 area 2
  network 10.10.0.0 0.0.255.255 area 0
```

And the configuration for Router 4 is:

```
router ospf 99
  network 10.13.0.0 0.0.255.255 area 3
  network 10.10.0.0 0.0.255.255 area 0
```

Route Summarization in OSPF

As with any routing protocol, route summarization helps reduce the routing table size. OSPF distinguishes between two summarization types: inter-area and external.

Inter-area summarization

Inter-area summarization occurs when the ABR summarizes an area's routes. An ABR can summarize routes within its area and beyond, as long as all the subnets are contiguous (bitwise) and summarizable. Just because areas are adjacent doesn't mean their addressing is set up to be summarizable.

To enable inter-area summarization, use the `area range` command. For example, on Router 2 in Figure 9-7, we can summarize the 10.11.0.0 network in the following manner:

```
router ospf 99
  network 10.11.0.0 0.0.255.255 area 1
  network 10.10.0.0 0.0.255.255 area 0
  ! summarize the areas for this router
  area 1 range 10.11.0.0 255.255.0.0
```

We can do this because we know that all the 10.11.0.0 networks are below this router. In an upcoming example, we will use this exact scenario and show the routing tables to prove that they actually get smaller as the router summarizes.

External summarization

External summarization occurs at ASBRs, where the entire network is summarized. We can use external summarization when we are injecting external routes into OSPF. To enable external summarization, use the `summary-address` command. For example:

```
summary-address 10.0.0.0 255.0.0.0
```

We're summarizing the entire network (10.0.0.0/8). Later, in the redistributing example, we will use this command to summarize the EIGRP routes that get redistributed into OSPF.

Virtual Backbone Links

There may be times when it's not possible to have a contiguous backbone, perhaps for political or even design issues. Although OSPF requires a single connected backbone, it includes a mechanism that lets you create a backbone out of two separate areas. Such a backbone is called a *virtual link*.

Figure 9-8 shows a network that requires a virtual link. In OSPF, all areas must be *contiguous*, meaning that they must physically be connected to each other. When two areas are not contiguous, we solve the problem by creating a virtual link.

In this example, we want to make Router 1 and Router 2 part of area 0, even though they are not contiguous. Since they share area 5, we can mend the partitioned area 0 by adding a virtual link to tunnel area 0 (the backbone) across area 5. This tunneling brings the two distant routers together to act as though they are actually connected.

The virtual link affects the configuration of Routers 1 and 2. First, we should define a loopback interface, which we use as an unambiguous identifier for the router. (Remember that a loopback interface is always up, has a unique address,

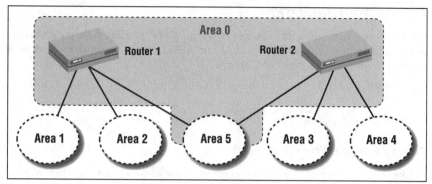

Figure 9-8: An OSPF network with a partitioned Area 0

and is not associated with any hardware.) Then we must create the virtual link with the `area` command.

Here is Router 1's configuration:

```
interface loopback0
    ip address 10.10.7.4 255.255.255.0
router ospf 99
    network 10.10.1.0 0.0.0.255 area 0
    network 10.10.2.0 0.0.0.255 area 1
    network 10.10.3.0 0.0.0.255 area 2
    network 10.10.6.0 0.0.0.255 area 5
    ! Create the virtual link to Router2's ID
    area 5 virtual-link 10.10.7.5
```

And here's the configuration for Router 2, which is very similar:

```
interface loopback0
    ip address 10.10.7.5 255.255.255.0
router ospf 99
    network 10.10.1.0 0.0.0.255 area 0
    network 10.10.4.0 0.0.0.255 area 3
    network 10.10.5.0 0.0.0.255 area 4
    network 10.10.6.0 0.0.0.255 area 5
    ! Create the virtual link to Router1's ID
    area 5 virtual-link 10.10.7.4
```

The major rule to remember is that virtual links cannot cross more than one area.

Interoperability with Other Vendors

Cisco routers use bandwidth as the cost of OSPF links. Other vendors might select another method for calculating the cost value. The `ospf cost` command allows you to define a cost value for OSPF links when talking to another router. A general rule for calculating cost is to take 10^8 (100,000,000) and divide it by the bandwidth. So a T1 link would have a cost of 100,000,000/1,544,000, which is about 64.

```
interface serial0
    ip ospf cost 64
```

Default Routes in OSPF

An ASBR can generate a default route into an OSPF domain with the default-information command. In this example, the ASBR is told to propagate its default route (172.168.10.1) into the OSPF domain:

```
ip route 0.0.0.0 0.0.0.0 172.168.10.1
router ospf 99
   network 10.1.1.0 0.0.0.255 area 0
   default-information originate
```

NSSAs (Not-So-Stubby Areas)

Before NSSAs existed, if a remote site on your network ran another routing protocol, it was difficult to provide full routing and also take advantage of stub areas. But with an NSSA, redistribution within a stub area is possible.

Here's a configuration that uses an NSSA to incorporate a remote network that is using RIP as its routing protocol. Router 2 is an offsite router running RIP; we want to incorporate it into our OSPF network. Router 1 is connected to our OSPF backbone. Area 2 joins Router 1 and Router 2 with an address of 192.168.44.0, and will be our NSSA.

Here's the configuration for Router 1, which is our main office router. It's a simple OSPF configuration, merely specifying that area 2 is an NSSA.

```
router ospf  99
   network 192.168.42.0 0.0.0.255 area 0
   network 192.168.43.0 0.0.0.255 area 1
   network 192.168.44.0 0.0.0.255 area 2
   area 2 nssa
```

Router 2 is the remote office router running RIP:

```
router rip
   network 10.0.0.0
!
! add OSPF and redistribute the RIP routes into it
router ospf  99
   redistribute rip subnets
   network 192.168.44.0 0.0.0.255 area 2
   area 2 nssa
```

This router needs to run both OSPF and RIP, but we have managed to shield Router 1 and the rest of our network from knowing about RIP. The redistribute command brings the RIP information into the OSPF process; we have a simple network command to define area 2; and we specify that area 2 is not so stubby.

OSPF Configuration Example

Figure 9-9 shows an OSPF network consisting of four areas. Area 0 has two ABR routers. Router 1 is the ABR for areas 1 and 2, while Router 4 is the ABR for area 3.

The configuration for Router 1 is:

```
hostname Router1
!
interface Ethernet0
```

```
  ip address 172.16.1.1 255.255.255.0
 !
interface Serial0
  ip address 10.12.1.1 255.255.255.0
 !
interface Serial1
  ip address 10.11.1.1 255.255.255.0
 !
router ospf 100
  network 10.11.0.0 0.0.255.255 area 1
  network 10.12.0.0 0.0.255.255 area 2
  network 172.16.1.0 0.0.0.255 area 0
```

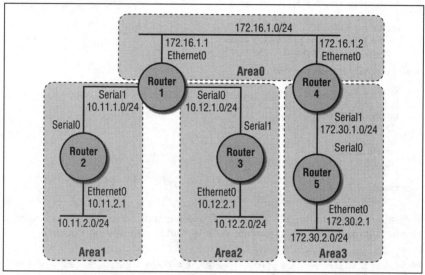

Figure 9-9: An OSPF network

The configuration for Router 2 is:

```
hostname Router2
 !
interface Ethernet0
  ip address 10.11.2.1 255.255.255.0
 !
interface Serial0
  ip address 10.11.1.2 255.255.255.0
 !
router ospf 100
  network 10.11.0.0 0.0.255.255 area 1
```

The configuration for Router 3 is:

```
hostname Router3
 !
interface Ethernet0
  ip address 10.12.2.1 255.255.255.0
 !
interface Serial1
```

```
  ip address 10.12.1.2 255.255.255.0
  !
router ospf 100
  network 10.12.0.0 0.0.255.255 area 2
```

The configuration for Router 4 is:

```
hostname Router4
!
interface Ethernet0
  ip address 172.16.1.2 255.255.255.0
!
interface Serial1
  ip address 172.30.1.1 255.255.255.0
!
router ospf 100
  network 172.16.0.0 0.0.255.255 area 0
  network 172.30.0.0 0.0.255.255 area 3
```

And the configuration for Router 5 is:

```
hostname Router5
!
interface Ethernet0
  ip address 172.30.2.1 255.255.255.0
!
interface Serial0
  ip address 172.30.1.2 255.255.255.0
!
router ospf 100
  network 172.30.0.0 0.0.255.255 area 3
```

To test our configuration, we will run a few commands on Router 1 and Router 4. First, let's look at the output from the show ip route command on Router 1:

```
Router1#show ip route
Codes: C - connected, S - static, I - IGRP, R - RIP, M - mobile, B - BGP
       D - EIGRP, EX - EIGRP external, O - OSPF, IA - OSPF inter area
       N1 - OSPF NSSA external type 1, N2 - OSPF NSSA external type 2
       E1 - OSPF external type 1, E2 - OSPF external type 2, E - EGP
       i - IS-IS, L1 - IS-IS level-1, L2 - IS-IS level-2, * - candidate default
       U - per-user static route, o - ODR

Gateway of last resort is not set

     172.16.0.0/24 is subnetted, 1 subnets
C       172.16.1.0 is directly connected, Ethernet0
     172.30.0.0/24 is subnetted, 2 subnets
O IA    172.30.2.0 [110/84] via 172.16.1.2, 00:03:59, Ethernet0
O IA    172.30.1.0 [110/74] via 172.16.1.2, 00:03:59, Ethernet0
     10.0.0.0/24 is subnetted, 4 subnets
C       10.11.1.0 is directly connected, Serial1
O       10.11.2.0 [110/74] via 10.11.1.2, 00:08:25, Serial1
O       10.12.2.0 [110/74] via 10.12.1.2, 00:08:25, Serial0
C       10.12.1.0 is directly connected, Serial0
```

In this output, we see that we have routes to all networks in our diagram. Routes to networks that are directly connected to Router 1 are noted by a "C" in the left-hand column. All the OSPF routes are noted by an "O". Of course, we have four OSPF routes for the four networks that are not directly connected to Router 1.

Now let's look at the output of show ip ospf neighbor:

```
Router1#show ip ospf neighbor

Neighbor ID   Pri   State       Dead Time   Address      Interface
172.30.1.1     1    FULL/DR     00:00:37    172.16.1.2   Ethernet0
10.12.2.1      1    FULL/ -     00:00:35    10.12.1.2    Serial0
10.11.2.1      1    FULL/ -     00:00:30    10.11.1.2    Serial1
```

Here we have three routers listed: Router 2, Router 3, and Router 4. Router 5 is not in this list because it is not a neighbor of Router 1. Finally, to test connectivity, we will ping the other routers:

```
Router1#ping 10.11.2.1
Type escape sequence to abort.
Sending 5, 100-byte ICMP Echos to 10.11.2.1, timeout is 2 seconds:
!!!!!
Success rate is 100 percent (5/5), round-trip min/avg/max = 28/29/32 ms
Router1#ping 10.12.2.1
Type escape sequence to abort.
Sending 5, 100-byte ICMP Echos to 10.12.2.1, timeout is 2 seconds:
!!!!!
Success rate is 100 percent (5/5), round-trip min/avg/max = 32/32/32 ms
Router1#ping 172.30.2.1
Type escape sequence to abort.
Sending 5, 100-byte ICMP Echos to 172.30.2.1, timeout is 2 seconds:
!!!!!
Success rate is 100 percent (5/5), round-trip min/avg/max = 32/32/36 ms
```

Putting route summarization to use

Everything looks good so far. But now let's look at the output of show ip route on Router 4:

```
Router4#show ip route
Codes: C - connected, S - static, I - IGRP, R - RIP, M - mobile, B - BGP
       D - EIGRP, EX - EIGRP external, O - OSPF, IA - OSPF inter area
       N1 - OSPF NSSA external type 1, N2 - OSPF NSSA external type 2
       E1 - OSPF external type 1, E2 - OSPF external type 2, E - EGP
       i - IS-IS, L1 - IS-IS level-1, L2 - IS-IS level-2, * - candidate default
       U - per-user static route, o - ODR

Gateway of last resort is not set

     172.16.0.0/24 is subnetted, 1 subnets
C       172.16.1.0 is directly connected, Ethernet0
     172.30.0.0/24 is subnetted, 2 subnets
O       172.30.2.0 [110/74] via 172.30.1.2, 00:18:15, Serial1
C       172.30.1.0 is directly connected, Serial1
     10.0.0.0/24 is subnetted, 4 subnets
O IA    10.11.1.0 [110/74] via 172.16.1.1, 00:10:17, Ethernet0
O IA    10.11.2.0 [110/84] via 172.16.1.1, 00:10:17, Ethernet0
O IA    10.12.2.0 [110/84] via 172.16.1.1, 00:10:08, Ethernet0
O IA    10.12.1.0 [110/74] via 172.16.1.1, 00:10:08, Ethernet0
```

While there is nothing wrong with this configuration, you should notice that there are four routes pointing to 172.16.1.1 for the various 10.x.x.x networks. We can simplify the routing table by changing the configuration on Router 1. Let's change

the configuration on Router 1 to use the **area range** command we discussed
earlier in the "Route Summarization in OSPF" section:

```
hostname Router1
!
interface Ethernet0
 ip address 172.16.1.1 255.255.255.0
!
interface Serial0
 ip address 10.12.1.1 255.255.255.0
!
interface Serial1
 ip address 10.11.1.1 255.255.255.0
!
router ospf 100
 network 10.11.0.0 0.0.255.255 area 1
 network 10.12.0.0 0.0.255.255 area 2
 network 172.16.1.0 0.0.0.255 area 0
 ! Add the commands to summarize the 10.11.0.0 and 10.12.0.0 networks
 area 1 range 10.11.0.0 255.255.0.0
 area 2 range 10.12.0.0 255.255.0.0
```

The addition of the two **area range** commands changed the way the areas are
summarized. Running the **show ip route** command on Router 4 proves that the
routing table is smaller:

```
Router4#sh ip route
Codes: C - connected, S - static, I - IGRP, R - RIP, M - mobile, B - BGP
       D - EIGRP, EX - EIGRP external, O - OSPF, IA - OSPF inter area
       N1 - OSPF NSSA external type 1, N2 - OSPF NSSA external type 2
       E1 - OSPF external type 1, E2 - OSPF external type 2, E - EGP
       i - IS-IS, L1 - IS-IS level-1, L2 - IS-IS level-2, * - candidate default
       U - per-user static route, o - ODR

Gateway of last resort is not set

     172.16.0.0/24 is subnetted, 1 subnets
C       172.16.1.0 is directly connected, Ethernet0
     172.30.0.0/24 is subnetted, 2 subnets
O       172.30.2.0 [110/74] via 172.30.1.2, 00:21:41, Serial1
C       172.30.1.0 is directly connected, Serial1
     10.0.0.0/16 is subnetted, 2 subnets
O IA    10.11.0.0 [110/74] via 172.16.1.1, 00:01:22, Ethernet0
O IA    10.12.0.0 [110/74] via 172.16.1.1, 00:01:13, Ethernet0
```

Now you see only two routes for the 10.11.0.0 and 10.12.0.0 networks. In this
example, the savings aren't really significant. But on a real network with much
larger routing tables, simplifying the tables by using summarization can have a
significant impact on your network's performance.

Redistributing Other Protocols into OSPF

Instead of listing how each protocol can be redistributed into OSPF, I'll concen-
trate on one example with more detail. Look at Figure 9-9 and imagine that area 3
is an EIGRP network instead of an OSPF area; i.e., Router 4 runs EIGRP on interface **Serial1**, and Router 5 runs EIGRP exclusively. The challenge is getting

redistribution between OSPF and EIGRP working. Let's start by modifying the configuration on Router 4 to support OSPF and EIGRP with redistribution:

```
hostname Router4
!
interface Ethernet0
 ip address 172.16.1.2 255.255.255.0
!
interface Serial1
 ip address 172.30.1.1 255.255.255.0
!
router eigrp 100
 ! List the EIGRP network
 network 172.30.0.0
 ! Disable EIGRP on the Ethernet0 interface
 passive-interface Ethernet0
 ! Redistribute our static route into EIGRP
 redistribute static
 ! Stop EIGRP from summarizing routes
 no auto-summary
!
!
router ospf 100
 network 172.16.0.0 0.0.255.255 area 0
 ! Use the summary-address command because we are injecting a route into
 ! OSPF (not the area range command, which summarizes OSPF internal
 ! routes)
 summary-address 172.30.0.0 255.255.0.0
 ! Redistribute EIGRP into OSPF
 redistribute eigrp 100 subnets
 default-metric 10
!
 ! Status default route for EIGRP
 ip route 0.0.0.0 0.0.0.0 172.16.1.1
```

Things are much simpler on Router 5. We just need to configure our interfaces and start up EIGRP:

```
hostname Router5
!
interface Ethernet0
 ip address 172.30.2.1 255.255.255.0
!
interface Serial0
 ip address 172.30.1.2 255.255.255.0
!
router eigrp 100
 network 172.30.0.0
```

To verify our configuration, let's look at the route table on Router 1:

```
Router1#show ip route
Codes: C - connected, S - static, I - IGRP, R - RIP, M - mobile, B - BGP
       D - EIGRP, EX - EIGRP external, O - OSPF, IA - OSPF inter area
       N1 - OSPF NSSA external type 1, N2 - OSPF NSSA external type 2
       E1 - OSPF external type 1, E2 - OSPF external type 2, E - EGP
       i - IS-IS, L1 - IS-IS level-1, L2 - IS-IS level-2, * - candidate default
       U - per-user static route, o - ODR
```

```
Gateway of last resort is not set

     172.16.0.0/24 is subnetted, 1 subnets
C        172.16.1.0 is directly connected, Ethernet0
O E2 172.30.0.0/16 [110/10] via 172.16.1.2, 00:07:12, Ethernet0
     10.0.0.0/24 is subnetted, 5 subnets
C        10.11.1.0 is directly connected, Serial1
O        10.11.2.0 [110/74] via 10.11.1.2, 00:07:51, Serial1
O        10.12.2.0 [110/74] via 10.12.1.2, 00:07:51, Serial0
C        10.12.1.0 is directly connected, Serial0
O        10.0.0.0 is a summary, 00:07:45, Null0
Router1#
```

The route to the EIGRP router is there. And since we used the **summary-address**
command, there is only one route to the 172.30.0.0/16 network. To verify connectivity, we ping Router 5:

```
Router1#ping 172.30.2.1

Type escape sequence to abort.
Sending 5, 100-byte ICMP Echos to 172.30.2.1, timeout is 2 seconds:
!!!!!
Success rate is 100 percent (5/5), round-trip min/avg/max = 32/33/36 ms
```

And everything looks good.

OSPF show Commands

The following show commands are particularly useful when you're working with
OSPF. We've already seen some of them in this chapter.

show ip ospf border routers

This command shows the border routers that this router knows about:

```
Router1#show ip ospf border-routers

OSPF Process 100 internal Routing Table

Codes: i - Intra-area route, I - Inter-area route

i 172.30.1.1 [10] via 172.16.1.2, Ethernet0, ABR, Area 0, SPF 28
```

show ip ospf neighbor

This command gives you a list of OSPF neighbors that are directly connected to
the router:

```
Router1#show ip ospf neighbor

Neighbor ID     PRI   State       Dead Time   Address       Interface
172.30.1.1       1    FULL/DR     00:00:37    172.16.1.2    Ethernet0
10.12.2.1        1    FULL/ -     00:00:35    10.12.1.2     Serial0
10.11.2.1        1    FULL/ -     00:00:30    10.11.1.2     Serial1
```

The Neighbor ID is the OSPF router ID for the neighbor. A router's ID is either the
highest IP address of any interface on the router or the IP address of the loopback
interface (if it has been defined). PRI stands for priority. Priorities are used to

establish the DR router; the router with the highest priority is the DR router. The State column reports the state of the connection to the neighbor. The state can be FULL, DOWN, or 2-WAY. FULL means that the routers are fully adjacent. Dead Time is the amount of time the router will wait without hearing a hello from the router before changing the neighbor's state to DOWN. The Address is the IP address of the interface to which the neighbor is connected, and Interface shows the interface through which the neighbor is reached.

show ip ospf database

This command is very verbose, as it displays the entire OSPF database for the router. For each entry, there is a Link ID, ADV Router (short for "advertising router"), Age, Seq#, and Checksum. Some entries have Link and Count information as well.

```
            OSPF Router with ID (172.16.1.1) (Process ID 100)


                Router Link States (Area 0)

    Link ID      ADV Router    Age      Seq#        Checksum Link Count
    10.10.5.2    10.10.5.2     2484     0x8000008D OxAAC3   3
    10.10.5.3    10.10.5.3     2526     0x8000008D OxDE8A   3
    172.16.1.1   172.16.1.1    1617     0x80000002 OxF239   1
    172.30.1.1   172.30.1.1    1549     0x80000002 OxE727   1

                Net Link States (Area 0)

    Link ID      ADV Router    Age      Seq#        Checksum
    172.16.1.2   172.30.1.1    1550     0x80000001 OxEE33

                Summary Net Link States (Area 0)

    Link ID      ADV Router    Age      Seq#        Checksum
    10.11.0.0    172.16.1.1    149      0x80000001 0x65C3
    10.12.0.0    172.16.1.1    140      0x80000001 0x59CE
    172.30.1.0   172.30.1.1    70       0x80000002 OxC0A2
    172.30.2.0   172.30.1.1    70       0x80000002 Ox1A3E
```

This command can be expanded to provide even more information by adding the router, network, or summary keyword.

show ip ospf interface

This command provides a wealth of OSPF information on a per-interface basis:

```
Router1#show ip ospf interface
Ethernet0 is up, line protocol is up
  Internet Address 172.16.1.1/24, Area 0
  Process ID 100, Router ID 172.16.1.1, Network Type BROADCAST, Cost: 10
  Transmit Delay is 1 sec, State BDR, Priority 1
  Designated Router (ID) 172.30.1.1, Interface address 172.16.1.2
  Backup Designated router (ID) 172.16.1.1, Interface address 172.16.1.1
  Timer intervals configured, Hello 10, Dead 40, Wait 40, Retransmit 5
    Hello due in 00:00:00
  Neighbor Count is 1, Adjacent neighbor count is 1
    Adjacent with neighbor 172.30.1.1  (Designated Router)
```

```
  Suppress hello for 0 neighbor(s)
Serial0 is up, line protocol is up
  Internet Address 10.12.1.1/24, Area 2
  Process ID 100, Router ID 172.16.1.1, Network Type POINT_TO_POINT, Cost: 64
  Transmit Delay is 1 sec, State POINT_TO_POINT,
  Timer intervals configured, Hello 10, Dead 40, Wait 40, Retransmit 5
    Hello due in 00:00:00
  Neighbor Count is 1, Adjacent neighbor count is 1
    Adjacent with neighbor 10.12.2.1
  Suppress hello for 0 neighbor(s)
Serial1 is up, line protocol is up
  Internet Address 10.11.1.1/24, Area 1
  Process ID 100, Router ID 172.16.1.1, Network Type POINT_TO_POINT, Cost: 64
  Transmit Delay is 1 sec, State POINT_TO_POINT,
  Timer intervals configured, Hello 10, Dead 40, Wait 40, Retransmit 5
    Hello due in 00:00:09
  Neighbor Count is 1, Adjacent neighbor count is 1
    Adjacent with neighbor 10.11.2.1
  Suppress hello for 0 neighbor(s)
Serial2 is administratively down, line protocol is down
  OSPF not enabled on this interface
Serial3 is administratively down, line protocol is down
  OSPF not enabled on this interface
```

CHAPTER 10

Border Gateway Protocol

Fortunately, this is a Nutshell book, so I don't have to do anything more than give a brief introduction to the Border Gateway Protocol (BGP), one of the most complex topics in network routing. Covering BGP in any detail could easily require hundreds of pages. Unlike the other routing protocols we've discussed, BGP is an exterior routing protocol, which means it routes traffic between different autonomous systems. Its primary use is on the Internet backbone; it shouldn't be used on most networks that are connected to the Internet. However, if you have more than one Internet service provider or your network is multihomed, you must use BGP.

BGP is a successor to EGP, which had many limitations. BGP's main new feature was Classless Interdomain Routing (CIDR), which rescued the almost-exhausted Internet IP address space. The current version of BGP is BGP4; it's unlikely that you'll need to know about earlier versions.

Introduction to BGP

We can run two types of BGP routing on our network:

Internal BGP (iBGP)
> iBGP exchanges BGP information within an autonomous system. Internal BGP sounds counterintuitive, since BGP is supposed to be an "external" routing protocol. The point of internal BGP is to distribute your BGP information between your external BGP routers. Your external routers are usually not close together; iBGP allows them to communicate across your internal network.
>
> iBGP is necessary in networks that have multiple paths to the Internet. It provides a consistent view of routes to and from the Internet.

External BGP (eBGP)
> eBGP distributes your BGP routing information to other autonomous systems. For example, external BGP is used for routing between your local network and two different ISPs.

Many people make BGP out to be the ultimate solution for advanced routing problems. It isn't, and using BGP successfully requires careful planning and design. Therefore, before deciding that you need BGP, you should think carefully about your options and what you're trying to accomplish. Here are some guidelines for when you should avoid BGP:

- If you can accomplish the same thing with a static route, use it; don't use BGP.

- If you have only one connection to the Internet and your network is small, you don't need BGP.

Once you decide that you need BGP, keep in mind that BGP becomes complex quickly. Keeping things as simple as possible is preferable for both operation and troubleshooting. (Isn't that true for all network protocols?) Furthermore, BGP requires (or demands) that routing policies exist for your network. For example, if you have two ISPs, you need to think about which link to prefer. Should you use the closest link? Should you suppress routes from your ISP? If so, which routes? We examine these configuration items later in this chapter.

How BGP Selects Routes

Before we jump into BGP configuration, you should understand the routing metrics it uses. BGP uses more information than other routing protocols to select routes. The most important parameters that go into route selection are:

Weight

Weight is a purely local measure of which route to prefer. A weight is given to a route on a particular router (via a route map, for example) and is used only within that router. The weight is never given to other routers. The higher the weight of a route, the better the route is. Weight is configurable and can be used to select one route over another.

Local preference

Local preference is another measure of which route to prefer. Unlike weight, local preferences are shared among iBGP routers. However, they are not shared with external BGP routers. The default local preference is 100. As with weight, higher numbers indicate better routes.

Multi-exit discriminator (MED)

MED values describe our routes to external routers. Unlike preference and weight, MED actually leaves our network and tells our neighbor routers which link we want them to talk to. And unlike the other metric values, the lower the MED value, the better the route. The default MED value is zero (0).

The name "multi-exit discriminator" is unfortunate and makes the concept unnecessarily confusing. The BGP designers were thinking from the point of view of your ISP: which exit from the ISP's network should be used to reach you? As a result, the MED will make much more sense if you turn it around and think of it as a "multi-entrance discriminator." That is, you use the MED to tell your ISPs which of several entrances to your network they should use.

You should use MED values only if you are multihomed to a single provider.

AS path

BGP routing is based on the list of autonomous systems that are traversed in order to reach a destination. This list is called an AS path. Shorter AS paths are preferred, but there are many ways to filter routes based on their AS paths. AS paths allow BGP to detect routing loops.

BGP selects only one route for a destination; this route is added to the route table and distributed to BGP peers. Here's the process by which a route is selected:

1. Drop the route immediately if its next hop isn't accessible.

2. If there are two routes with different weights, pick the route with the largest (heaviest) weight.

3. If weight values are equal, choose the route with the largest local preference value.

4. If local preference values are equal for multiple routes, choose the route that originated with BGP on this router.

5. If none, or all, of the routes originated on this router, choose the route with the shortest AS path.

6. If all the AS path lengths are the same, choose the path with the lowest origin type. Origin refers to whether the route originated via an internal gateway protocol (IGP) or an external gateway protocol (EGP). Routes that have entered the BGP domain by redistribution are considered incomplete. IGP is lower than EGP, and EGP is lower than incomplete.

7. If all the origin types are the same, choose the path with the lowest MED value.

8. If all the MED values are the same, choose an external route over an internal route.

9. If all the routes are the same, choose the path with the closest IGP neighbor.

10. If the distances to the closest IGP neighbor are the same, choose the path with the lowest BGP router ID. A router's ID is the IP address assigned to the loopback interface or the highest IP address on an active interface at boot time.

Basic Configuration Commands

Basic configuration relies on a number of familiar commands, such as `router`, `network`, and `neighbor`. However, the BGP versions of these commands are a little more complex than for other routing protocols. This section covers the basic configuration items.

The router and network commands

We start our configuration by giving our autonomous system number in the `router bgp` command. Here, 500 is our AS number:

```
router bgp 500
  network 10.0.0.0
```

In other protocols, such as EIGRP and OSPF, we chose the AS numbers pretty much how we pleased—we were required only to be consistent within our own network. In fact, although they are frequently called AS numbers, the numbers associated with EIGRP and OSPF routing processes are really just process IDs. With BGP, you're dealing with true AS numbers, and each AS number must fit into the rest of the global BGP design. This number is given to you by your service provider and must be used accordingly.

In this example, we'll advertise a route to the network 10.10.2.0. This network doesn't have to be directly connected to the router in order for us to advertise it. We don't provide a network mask, as BGP assumes the old classful addressing scheme when a mask isn't provided explicitly. If this is not what you want, you need to add the mask option to specify a classless network. The following network command advertises the network 10.10.2.0/23:

```
router bgp 500
  network 10.10.2.0 mask 255.255.224.0
```

The neighbor command

Next, we need to define our routing peers with the neighbor command. This step also defines whether we are using iBGP or eBGP. If our neighbor router has the same AS number, we are using iBGP. If our neighbor has a different AS number, we are configuring eBGP. In this case, we configured a neighbor with a different AS number, meaning that we are using eBGP. Most configurations will have several neighbor commands.

```
router bgp 500
  neighbor 192.168.1.5 remote-as 400
```

Neighbors don't have to be in an equivalent network statement. For example, we can have the neighbor 192.168.1.5 and not have a network equivalent or subnet of 192.168.1.0/24. Our IGP routing protocol might have the route we need to access that neighbor. We are using the neighbor command only to specify our peers.

When configuring BGP, you often need to list several neighbor commands for each neighboring router. The neighbor command can take a number of optional keywords, including default-originate and next-hop-self, both of which are discussed later.

 If your BGP neighbors aren't communicating, make sure they can actually reach each other. BGP neighbors will not peer if they can't reach each other.

Local-AS numbers

Just as there are private Class C IP addresses (e.g., 10.0.0.0/8 and 192.168.0.0/16), there are private AS numbers to be used for internal networks. This means that it is possible to use BGP for internal routing or routing between you and your ISP even if you're not involved with the Internet backbone. Situations in which you'd want to do this are rare, but you might consider it if you were managing an extremely large network with a number of connections to a single ISP. The AS numbers reserved for local use range from 64512 to 65535. Just as with private IP addresses, your network provider should filter these AS numbers so that they never appear outside of your network.

Synchronization

In BGP, *synchronization* means that a BGP router is not allowed to advertise a route that is learned from another BGP peer until the router knows about the route via an IGP. Synchronization can take time, and in most cases it isn't needed. Disabling synchronization removes this rule. Although disabling synchronization adds the possibility of dropped packets, it can improve convergence time for your routers. To disable synchronization, add the command no synchronization to the BGP configuration.

Synchronization can be disabled safely under either of two conditions: if your network doesn't pass traffic from one AS to another (i.e., other networks do not route their traffic through you), or if all your border routers are running BGP. Disabling synchronization is an absolute must for running iBGP, which is described in the next few sections.

Automatic summary

By default, BGP summarizes routes on class boundaries. There are many situations in which you don't want summarization to follow class boundaries. For example, say you're given the IP address space of 172.30.5.0/24, 172.30.6.0/24, and 172.30.7.0/24. When BGP announces your route, it will try to summarize the route to the classful route 172.30.0.0/16. This behavior is almost certainly not what you want.

If your ISP is worth anything, it will block announcements from you that don't match your network. However, you shouldn't rely on your ISP to prevent you from advertising misleading information. Configuring no auto-summary disables automatic summarization.

default-originate

default-originate (a keyword that can be appended to the neighbor command) causes the BGP router to advertise a default route to other BGP routers, even if it doesn't have a default route defined for itself. (A default route has the address 0.0. 0.0 0.0.0.0.)

next-hop-self

When an iBGP router advertises a route, it advertises the next hop of the route as it learned it. The next-hop-self keyword (used with the neighbor command) tells the router to rewrite the route's next hop as itself. For example, if you have next-hop-self configured from Router 1 to Router 2, Router 1 tells Router 2 that it is the next hop for the routes that it sends to Router 2.

BGP route dampening

Route dampening controls the effect that a flapping route has on the network. Route flapping occurs when a route changes state (up to down, or down to up) repeatedly. This can happen when a router has a bad interface or some other problem exists. Flapping is a problem for any routing protocol, BGP included: when a route changes state, BGP tries to propagate this information to the other routers, consuming a lot of CPU time and network bandwidth in addition to distributing unreliable information.

BGP handles route flapping with the `bgp dampening` command. When this feature is activated, the router tolerates only a certain number of state changes for a route within a certain amount of time. If the state-change threshold (tolerance) is reached, the route is placed in a hold-down (ignored) state for a period. After the hold-down time passes, the route is again allowed into the routing table to see if it behaves. Dampening doesn't stop the route from receiving unstable routes; rather, it prevents the routing from forwarding what it considers to be unstable routes.

You can set the hold-down time and tolerance values with the `dampening` command; if these values are not set, the router uses default values.

iBGP checklist

There are two ways to get iBGP to work correctly. The first is to redistribute all external routes into all of your iBGP routers. This method is not a good idea; the routing table might be large, and some of your routers may not be able to handle it. A much better way to implement iBGP is to:

1. Disable synchronization. Remember that synchronization prevents a router from taking a route that was learned via an iBGP neighbor and entering it into the routing table, unless the route is first learned via an interior routing protocol.

2. Make sure that all of your iBGP routers are fully meshed, i.e., that each iBGP router has a `neighbor` command for every other iBGP router. A full mesh ensures that all routers along the AS path know how to forward packets to the destination router.

3. Make sure that all networks and subnets that connect iBGP routers are known—that is, that a route exists between all of your routers and that your interior routing protocol is doing its job and distributing those routes. If the routers cannot talk to one another, they won't be able to peer.

The example in the next section takes care of all three requirements.

A Simple BGP Configuration

In this section, we'll look at a simple BGP configuration that includes both eBGP and iBGP configurations. A realistic example would be much more complex (particularly for the ISP), but this will help you see how things work. Figure 10-1 shows the sample network. There are two office routers (`office-r1` and `office-r2`); `office-r1` connects to the Internet via an ISP, whose router is named (logically enough) `ISP`.

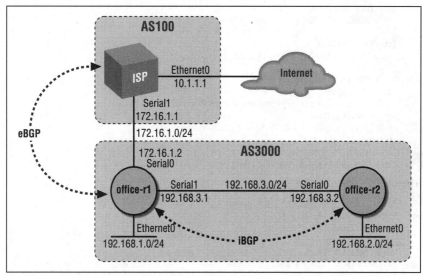

Figure 10-1: A simple BGP network

Here's the configuration for **office-r1**:

```
hostname office-r1
!
interface Ethernet0
 ip address 192.168.1.1 255.255.255.0
!
interface Serial0
 ip address 172.16.1.2 255.255.255.0
!
interface Serial1
 ip address 192.168.3.1 255.255.255.0
!
! Configure BGP for our local-AS 3000
router bgp 3000
 ! We disable synchronization for our iBGP peers
 no synchronization
 ! The networks we want to advertise
 network 192.168.1.0
 network 192.168.3.0
 ! Our EBGP peers
 neighbor 172.16.1.1 remote-as 100
 ! For our IBGP peers, we'll set us as the default-originate
 ! And we'll set us as the next hop using the next-hop-self command
 neighbor 192.168.3.2 remote-as 3000
 neighbor 192.168.3.2 next-hop-self
 neighbor 192.168.3.2 default-originate
 !
 ! Our iBGP peers expect us to be the default route, so we need a local
 ! default route
 ip route 0.0.0.0 0.0.0.0 172.16.1.1
```

The configuration for **office-r2** is:

```
hostname office-r2
!
```

```
interface Ethernet0
 ip address 192.168.2.1 255.255.255.0
!
interface Serial0
 ip address 192.168.3.2 255.255.255.0
!
! Our BGP configuration
router bgp 3000
 ! Once again, no synchronization for iBGP
 no synchronization
 ! Only one network to define
 network 192.168.2.0
 ! Only one neighbor to define
 neighbor 192.168.3.1 remote-as 3000
```

The configuration for ISP is:

```
! If this were a real ISP configuration, we would be fired!
! But it shows the concepts.
hostname ISP1
 !
 interface Loopback0
 ip address 172.16.3.1 255.255.255.0
!
interface Ethernet0
 ip address 10.1.1.1 255.255.255.0
!
interface Serial1
 ip address 172.16.1.1 255.255.255.0
 clockrate 64000
!
router bgp 100
 network 172.16.0.0
 neighbor 10.1.1.2 remote-as 200
 neighbor 172.16.1.2 remote-as 3000
```

To demonstrate some of the BGP show commands, let's look at the office-r2 router. show ip route gives us a quick look at what's going on:

```
office-r2#show ip route
Codes: C - connected, S - static, I - IGRP, R - RIP, M - mobile, B - BGP
       D - EIGRP, EX - EIGRP external, O - OSPF, IA - OSPF inter area
       N1 - OSPF NSSA external type 1, N2 - OSPF NSSA external type 2
       E1 - OSPF external type 1, E2 - OSPF external type 2, E - EGP
       i - IS-IS, L1 - IS-IS level-1, L2 - IS-IS level-2, * - candidate default
       U - per-user static route, o - ODR

Gateway of last resort is 192.168.3.1 to network 0.0.0.0

B    172.16.0.0/16 [200/0] via 192.168.3.1, 00:03:10
B    192.168.1.0/24 [200/0] via 192.168.3.1, 00:03:15
C    192.168.2.0/24 is directly connected, Ethernet0
C    192.168.3.0/24 is directly connected, Serial0
B*   0.0.0.0/0 [200/0] via 192.168.3.1, 00:03:16
```

Everything here should be familiar. The gateway of last resort is set because we have default-originate set on the office-r1 router (192.168.3.1). Note that the route for 172.16.0.0/16 is via 192.168.3.1. This route is set to office-r1's interface because we used the next-hop-self option in one of the neighbor commands for 192.168.3.2 on office-r1. Therefore, office-r1 rewrote the BGP route for 172.16.

0.0, making itself the next hop. If we hadn't put that command in, the route would have looked like this:

```
B    172.16.0.0/16 [200/0] via 172.16.1.1, 00:00:17
```

In this configuration, this route would work as well as the route to 192.168.3.2 because the default route tells our router how to get to that address. If we didn't have the default route, we would have to add an extra network statement, defining 172.16.0.0, to office-r1's configuration. next-hop-self makes the configuration a little easier.

Next, let's look at the output of show ip bgp on office-r2:

```
Office-r2#show ip bgp
BGP table version is 7, local router ID is 192.168.3.2
Status codes: s suppressed, d damped, h history, * valid, > best, i - internal
Origin codes: i - IGP, e - EGP, ? - incomplete

     Network          Next Hop          Metric LocPrf Weight Path
*>i0.0.0.0           192.168.3.1                 100      0 i
*>i172.16.0.0        192.168.3.1            0    100      0 100 i
*>i192.168.1.0       192.168.3.1            0    100      0 i
*>  192.168.2.0      0.0.0.0                0          32768 i
*>i192.168.3.0       192.168.3.1            0    100      0 i
```

The output from this show command gives us a lot of useful information. The left-hand side lists the known networks with different codes (see Table 10-1), indicating the route's status. > indicates the best route to the given network. Then we have the next-hop address, the metric, the local preference (LocPrf), the weight, and finally the AS path.

Table 10-1: Route status codes

Key	Route status
s	Suppressed
d	Damped
*	Valid
h	History
>	Best
i	Internal

The Path column is particularly important. Most of the entries in this column have a path of i, which means that the route was learned through an interior protocol and therefore doesn't cross autonomous system boundaries. The only exception is the 172.16.0.0 network, which is in another autonomous system (AS 100). For this route to reach office-r1, BGP must learn the route from some sort of interior protocol. Therefore, the path for this network is 100 i. AS paths can obviously be much more complex. For a slightly more complex example, imagine that network 172.30.0.0 is attached to the ISP router and has an AS number of 200. The route might look like this:

```
Office-r2#show ip bgp
...
*>i172.30.0.0        192.168.3.1                 100      0 100 200 i
...
```

This path shows that to reach 172.30.0.0, you must cross AS 100, then enter AS 200, which learned the route through an interior protocol such as RIP. Therefore, you don't need to cross any more AS boundaries.

Route Filtering

A big part of working with BGP is filtering routes; that's how you control how your network traffic is carried and how you implement routing policies. You might want to filter routes coming from the outside into your network, or filter routes you advertise to other networks. No matter what your reason for filtering is, there are basically three ways to do it: AS path filtering, community filtering, and aggregate filtering.

AS Path Filters

A lot of what you do with BGP is based on building AS path filters. Filters let you select specific paths (routes) through the network. AS path filters work like access lists, but with a twist: they support regular expression (regex) pattern matching. Here's an example of a simple AS path filter:

```
ip as-path access-list 70 deny ^100_
ip as-path access-list 70 permit .*
```

Like access lists, AS paths have the following rules:

- Each line is a permit or a deny
- The first match wins
- An implicit "deny all" is added to the end of the list

In this case, we want to deny any AS path that starts with AS 100 and permit everything else. We've assigned the filter number 70 (with the command ip as-path access-list 70), which we use when we reference the filter in other parts of the configuration. The last part of each line is the regular expression that determines whether or not a path matches the list. Note that the number assigned to the AS path filter has nothing to do with the numbers assigned to regular IP access lists; there's no concept of regular or extended lists, so you can use any number you want. You can even use the same numbers you used for your IP access lists, although this would probably be confusing.

Table 10-2 shows some of the expressions that can be used in an AS path. A path is nothing more than a list of autonomous systems. The first autonomous system in the path (the AS with which the path originates) is on the right; as the path crosses AS boundaries, new autonomous systems are added on the left. Therefore, the leftmost entry in an AS path is the autonomous system from which we heard the path. An underscore is used to separate AS numbers in the path. ^ matches the start of the path; $ matches the end. * matches any repetition of a character, and . matches any character.[*]

---

[*] For more information about regular expressions, see *Mastering Regular Expressions* by Jeffrey Friedl (O'Reilly).

Table 10-2: AS path regular expressions

Regular expression	Meaning
.*	Matches all (i.e., any AS path).
^$	Matches an empty path. The only routes that can have an empty path are routes that originated within our local AS.
^100$	Specifies a path that consists of the single AS, AS 100. The ^ matches the beginning of the path; the $ matches the end.
^(100|200|300)$	Specifies a path that consists of a single AS, which can be either 100, 200, or 300. The vertical bar (|) means "or"; the parentheses are for grouping.
^100_	All paths that start with AS 100.
_100_	All paths with 100 anywhere in the path.
_100$	All paths that end with 100.

Community Filters

The community attribute allows routing policies to be applied to a destination. They are applied to routes using a set command in a route map. Later, you can use the community strings to perform various kinds of filtering. Three special community strings are defined and cause the router to take some action. Table 10-3 lists the three predefined communities.

Table 10-3: Predefined communities

Community	Action
no-export	Do not advertise to eBGP peers
no-advertise	Do not advertise to any peer
internet	Advertise to the Internet community (all routers belong to it)

In this example, we define a route map named Community1 that matches IP addresses from list 1. This map sets the community string of any matches to the no-advertise community:

```
access-list 1 permit 0.0.0.0 255.255.255.255
!
route-map Community1
  match ip address 1
  set community no-advertise
!
! Now we use the community in the neighbor command
router bgp 500
  neighbor 10.1.1.1 remote-as 200
  neighbor 10.1.1.1 send-community
  neighbor 10.1.1.1 route-map Community1 out
```

By applying the route map in the neighbor command, we use it to check all the route updates we send to neighbor 10.1.1.1. However, the route map matches any route destination (because of access list 1) and sets the route's community string to no-advertise. This means that all routes we send to 10.1.1.1 via BGP will have the no-advertise community. Therefore, when 10.1.1.1 receives a route update from us, it will not advertise any of our routes.

We can assign our own community values to outgoing routes. Our neighbors can then implement filters based on the community values we have set and act appropriately. Consider two routers, Router 1 and Router 2. Router 1 belongs to the 10.1.0.0 network (AS 500), while Router 2 belongs to the 10.2.0.0 network (AS 600). Router 1 sends all routes to Router 2 with a community of 100. Router 2 looks for any routes with a community of 100 and sets the weight to 10.

The configuration for Router 1 is:

```
! Router1 sends all its outgoing routes to neighbor 10.2.0.0 with
! a community value of 100
!
router bgp 500
  network 10.0.0.0
  neighbor 10.2.0.0 remote-as 600
  neighbor 10.2.0.0 send-community
  ! the route-map is set to OUT
  neighbor 10.2.0.0 route-map SET100 out
!
! Define our route map, setting the community to 100
route-map  SET100 permit 10
  match ip address 1
  set community 100
!
! Match all IP addresses
access-list 1 permit 0.0.0.0 255.255.255.255
```

The configuration for Router 2 is:

```
! Router 2 looks for any route with a community of 100 and sets the
! weight to 10
router bgp 600
  network 10.2.0.0
  neighbor 10.1.0.0 remote-as 500
  ! The route map is used to check incoming routes
  neighbor 10.1.0.0 route-map CHECK100 in
!
! Define our route map, looking for community 100
route-map CHECK100 permit 10
  match community 1
  set weight 10
!
! Here is our community-list command. It acts like an access-list. This
! time we are looking for a community of 100
ip community-list 1 permit 100
```

It's easy to get confused by the many layers of indirection. The neighbor statement refers to a route map by name; the match statements inside the route map refer to community lists or access lists by number, and the community list itself finally checks the community.

Note that the predefined communities are mutually exclusive. In contrast, user-defined communities can be made additive by placing the additive keyword on the set community command. A route may therefore belong to several communities.

Aggregate Filters

Aggregate filters allow several different routes to be expressed in one simple (but equivalent) route, thus reducing the size of the routing table. Aggregates can be used only when the routes can be summarized into a single (aggregate) route.

The `aggregate-address` command controls route aggregation and reduces the number of outgoing BGP routes. Let's assume that we own several networks, 192.168.1.0/24 through 192.168.254.0/24. There is no need to advertise all of these networks separately. Instead, we can generate a single route summary for the entire network space:

```
router bgp 600
  network 10.0.0.0
  aggregate-address 192.168.1.0 255.255.0.0 summary-only
```

The `summary-only` keyword tells the router to advertise only the aggregate route. If we leave off `summary-only`, the router will advertise all of our routes plus the aggregate, which is not our intention.

Aggregate routes also allow us to suppress certain addresses from the aggregate list. In this example, we want to advertise our aggregate route and our other routes, but we also want to suppress route 192.168.5.0:

```
router bgp 600
  network 10.1.0.0
  aggregate-address 192.168.1.0 255.255.0.0 suppress-map MAP1
!
! Define our route map
route-map MAP1 permit 1
  match ip address 1
!
! Define our access list to deny 192.168.5.0/24 and permit everything else
access-list 1 deny 192.168.5.0 0.0.0.255
access-list 1 permit 0.0.0.0 255.255.255.255
```

In this case, we use the route map `MAP1` to determine which networks we want to suppress. This route map is based on access list 1.

Now that we've introduced a lot of the concepts, let's look at a complete configuration for a network.

An Advanced BGP Configuration

Figure 10-2 shows a network that consists of two offices connected to two different ISPs. The offices run OSPF between themselves and use BGP to exchange routes with the ISPs. The two offices are part of a single autonomous system, AS 3000. Each ISP has its own AS number (100 and 200). Office 1 has a single router, which takes care of all its needs. Office 2 has two routers: office2-r1 runs OSPF only and is responsible only for interior routing; office2-r2 provides the connection to the outside world through ISP2. On office1-r1, we need to configure eBGP to exchange routes with ISP1. Likewise, we must configure office2-r2 to exchange routes with ISP2. We want to implement a simple routing policy that prevents the ISPs from using our network to send packets to other autonomous networks. That is, we don't want transit traffic flowing through our site—we want only traffic that is destined for our network.

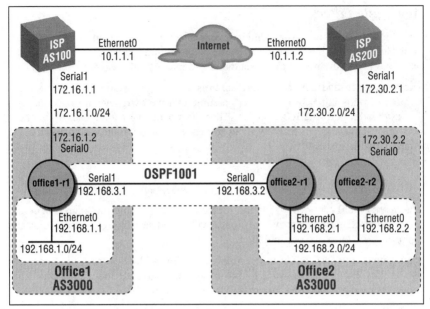

Figure 10-2: BGP network with two service providers

The transit-traffic filtering is accomplished by using AS path filters, which we discussed in a previous section. On both routers, the filtering takes place in AS path access list 1. This is a simple access list: all we need to do is permit routes that originated within our local autonomous system. Our AS number happens to be 3000, but that's not important for writing the filter—we just need to realize that the regular expression ^$ matches routes that originated within our autonomous system, and no others.

Here's the configuration for office1-r1. It runs OSPF (process ID 1001) for communicating with the other office, and it sets up an eBGP connection to AS 100 (ISP1) and an iBGP connection to the office2-r2 router (AS 3000). The filter list that prevents transit traffic is applied to outbound updates destined for ISP1. If we don't tell ISP1 about any routes that don't originate from our own AS, ISP1 will be unable to route transit traffic through our network.

```
hostname office1-r1
!
! Configure our interfaces
interface Ethernet0
 ip address 192.168.1.1 255.255.255.0
!
interface Serial0
 ip address 172.16.1.2 255.255.255.0
!
interface Serial1
 ip address 192.168.3.1 255.255.255.0
 clockrate 64000
!
! We are running OSPF as our IGP
router ospf 1001
```

```
network 192.168.1.0 0.0.0.255 area 1
network 192.168.3.0 0.0.0.255 area 0
! We want to tell other OSPF routers that we are the default router
default-information originate
!
! Our BGP configuration
router bgp 3000
no synchronization
bgp dampening
network 172.16.1.0
! Configuration for ISP1 with an outbound filter list. This list assures
! that we will announce only routes that originated within our AS
neighbor 172.16.1.1 remote-as 100
neighbor 172.16.1.1 filter-list 1 out
! Our neighbor office2-r2
neighbor 192.168.2.2 remote-as 3000
neighbor 192.168.2.2 next-hop-self
no auto-summary
!
! A static route is needed because we are advertising that we are the
! default route for the network, but we need to tell local route traffic
! where the default is for us. (Not required if you have a full routing
! table.)
ip route 0.0.0.0 0.0.0.0 172.16.1.1
!
! The following is a simple AS regular expression. This AS access
! list will permit only routes that originated within our AS
ip as-path access-list 1 permit ^$
```

office2-r1 has a simple OSPF configuration:

```
hostname office2-r1
!
interface Ethernet0
 ip address 192.168.2.1 255.255.255.0
!
interface Serial0
 ip address 192.168.3.2 255.255.255.0
!
! Nothing new here
router ospf 1001
 network 192.168.2.0 0.0.0.255 area 0
 network 192.168.3.0 0.0.0.255 area 0
```

The configuration for office2-r2 is similar to the configuration for office1-r1. Again, this router needs an OSPF process for interior routing. The process number is 1001, which matches the process number on the other routers. For BGP, we set up an eBGP connection to the ISP2 router (AS 200) and an iBGP connection to office1-r1 (AS 3000). The route filtering is identical.

```
hostname office2-r2
!
interface Ethernet0
 ip address 192.168.2.2 255.255.255.0
!
interface Serial0
 ip address 172.30.2.2 255.255.255.0
!
router ospf 1001
 network 192.168.2.0 0.0.0.255 area 0
```

```
    default-information originate
    !
router bgp 3000
 no synchronization
 bgp dampening
 network 172.30.2.0
 neighbor 172.30.2.1 remote-as 200
 neighbor 172.30.2.1 filter-list 1 out
 neighbor 192.168.3.1 remote-as 3000
 neighbor 192.168.3.1 next-hop-self
 no auto-summary
!
ip route 0.0.0.0 0.0.0.0 172.30.2.1
!
ip as-path access-list 1 permit ^$
```

To prove that our configuration works, we can do a show ip bgp from both
office1-r1 and office2-r2. Here are the results:

```
office1-r1#show ip bgp
BGP table version is 50, local router ID is 192.168.3.1
Status codes: s suppressed, d damped, h history, * valid, > best, i - internal
Origin codes: i - IGP, e - EGP, ? - incomplete

   Network          Next Hop         Metric LocPrf Weight Path
*> 172.16.0.0       172.16.1.1            0             0 100 i
*>i172.30.0.0       192.168.2.2           0    100      0 200 I

office2-r2#show ip bgp
BGP table version is 3, local router ID is 192.168.2.2
Status codes: s suppressed, d damped, h history, * valid, > best, i - internal
Origin codes: i - IGP, e - EGP, ? - incomplete

   Network          Next Hop         Metric LocPrf Weight Path
*>i172.16.0.0       192.168.3.1           0    100      0 100 i
*> 172.30.0.0       172.30.2.1            0             0 200 i
```

This output shows that both routers recognize each other via BGP. The output of
show ip route on office2-r2 also shows that the routes are there as expected:

```
office2-r2#sh ip route
Codes: C - connected, S - static, I - IGRP, R - RIP, M - mobile, B - BGP
       D - EIGRP, EX - EIGRP external, O - OSPF, IA - OSPF inter area
       N1 - OSPF NSSA external type 1, N2 - OSPF NSSA external type 2
       E1 - OSPF external type 1, E2 - OSPF external type 2, E - EGP
       i - IS-IS, L1 - IS-IS level-1, L2 - IS-IS level-2, * - candidate default
       U - per-user static route, o - ODR

Gateway of last resort is 172.30.2.1 to network 0.0.0.0

B    172.16.0.0/16 [200/0] via 192.168.3.1, 00:03:15
     172.30.0.0/16 is variably subnetted, 2 subnets, 2 masks
C       172.30.2.0/24 is directly connected, Serial0
B       172.30.0.0/16 [20/0] via 172.30.2.1, 00:03:06
O IA 192.168.1.0/24 [110/84] via 192.168.2.1, 00:49:56, Ethernet0
C    192.168.2.0/24 is directly connected, Ethernet0
O    192.168.3.0/24 [110/74] via 192.168.2.1, 00:49:57, Ethernet0
S*   0.0.0.0/0 [1/0] via 172.30.2.1
```

Finally, to make sure both links work, we can run a quick test on office2-r1.
This test is limited in that it really tests only our OSPF configuration—but it gives

us more confidence that the network as a whole is running. First, show ip route on office2-r1 shows that it prefers office2-r2 as its default router:

```
office2-r1#show ip route
Codes: C - connected, S - static, I - IGRP, R - RIP, M - mobile, B - BGP
       D - EIGRP, EX - EIGRP external, O - OSPF, IA - OSPF inter area
       N1 - OSPF NSSA external type 1, N2 - OSPF NSSA external type 2
       E1 - OSPF external type 1, E2 - OSPF external type 2, E - EGP
       i - IS-IS, L1 - IS-IS level-1, L2 - IS-IS level-2, * - candidate default
       U - per-user static route, o - ODR

Gateway of last resort is 192.168.2.2 to network 0.0.0.0

O IA 192.168.1.0/24 [110/74] via 192.168.3.1, 00:08:06, Serial0
C    192.168.2.0/24 is directly connected, Ethernet0
C    192.168.3.0/24 is directly connected, Serial0
O*E2 0.0.0.0/0 [110/1] via 192.168.2.2, 00:07:20, Ethernet0
```

If we shut down the serial0 link on office2-r2, show ip route on office2-r1 shows that it has recalculated its routes and selected office1-r1 as the default router:

```
office2-r1#show ip route
Codes: C - connected, S - static, I - IGRP, R - RIP, M - mobile, B - BGP
       D - EIGRP, EX - EIGRP external, O - OSPF, IA - OSPF inter area
       N1 - OSPF NSSA external type 1, N2 - OSPF NSSA external type 2
       E1 - OSPF external type 1, E2 - OSPF external type 2, E - EGP
       i - IS-IS, L1 - IS-IS level-1, L2 - IS-IS level-2, * - candidate default
       U - per-user static route, o - ODR

Gateway of last resort is 192.168.3.1 to network 0.0.0.0

O IA 192.168.1.0/24 [110/74] via 192.168.3.1, 00:08:48, Serial0
C    192.168.2.0/24 is directly connected, Ethernet0
C    192.168.3.0/24 is directly connected, Serial0
O*E2 0.0.0.0/0 [110/1] via 192.168.3.1, 00:00:05, Serial0
```

Adding a Preference

Figure 10-2 shows a network with links to two different providers. We've already seen configurations that get the network up and running. Now, we would like to give one provider preference over the other for outbound traffic. Let's assume that ISP1 is more reliable, so whenever possible we want to send our traffic over its network. To do this, we use a route map to modify the local preference metric so that we prefer routes to ISP1. Remember that the local preference metric stays local to our network—that is, we never send the local preference outside of our AS—but is shared among the routers within our AS.

In office2-r2, we add a route map named CHANGE_LOCAL_PREF. This map sets the local preference for routes through ISP2 to 50, making ISP1 more preferable than ISP2. (The default local preference is 100, and higher preferences are better.) The configuration change means that even if we have to traverse our WAN link between the offices, we will use ISP1 rather than ISP2. Here are the changes to the configuration for office2-r2:

```
! While we're at it, we need to make sure OSPF picks the right ISP as
! well, so we'll increase the metric for the default route here
```

```
! to 1000.
router ospf 1001
 network 192.168.2.0 0.0.0.255 area 0
 default-information originate metric 1000
!
! In our BGP configuration, the only change is the addition of the route
! map for neighbor 172.30.2.1. Everything else is the same as it was
! before.
router bgp 3000
 neighbor 172.30.2.1 route-map CHANGE_LOCAL_PREF in
!
! Finally, we create our route map to change the local preference for
! neighbor 172.30.2.1
route-map CHANGE_LOCAL_PREF permit 10
 set local-preference 50
```

show ip bgp on office2-r2 shows that the local preference for the route has indeed changed:

```
office2-r2#show ip bgp
BGP table version is 3, local router ID is 192.168.2.2
Status codes: s suppressed, d damped, h history, * valid, > best, i - internal
Origin codes: i - IGP, e - EGP, ? - incomplete

   Network          Next Hop        Metric LocPrf Weight Path
*>i172.16.0.0       192.168.3.1          0    100      0 100 i
*> 172.30.0.0       172.30.2.1           0     50      0 200 i
```

Finally, let's do a show ip route on office2-r1 and see which default route it prefers:

```
office2-r1>show ip route
Codes: C - connected, S - static, I - IGRP, R - RIP, M - mobile, B - BGP
       D - EIGRP, EX - EIGRP external, O - OSPF, IA - OSPF inter area
       N1 - OSPF NSSA external type 1, N2 - OSPF NSSA external type 2
       E1 - OSPF external type 1, E2 - OSPF external type 2, E - EGP
       i - IS-IS, L1 - IS-IS level-1, L2 - IS-IS level-2, * - candidate default
       U - per-user static route, o - ODR

Gateway of last resort is 192.168.3.1 to network 0.0.0.0

O IA 192.168.1.0/24 [110/74] via 192.168.3.1, 01:51:25, Serial0
C    192.168.2.0/24 is directly connected, Ethernet0
C    192.168.3.0/24 is directly connected, Serial0
O*E2 0.0.0.0/0 [110/1] via 192.168.3.1, 01:40:24, Serial0
```

Neighbor Authentication

As with other protocols, we can force BGP to authenticate other routers with a password. All passwords are scrambled using an MD5 message digest. On the network in Figure 10-1, we can enable password authentication between office-r1 and office-r2 by adding the password command to our BGP configuration. On office-r1, we add the neighbor ... password command after the neighbor ... remote-as command. You must configure the same password on both routers, or they can't communicate with BGP. Here's the configuration for office-r1:

```
router bgp 3000
 neighbor 192.168.3.2 remote-as 3000
 neighbor 192.168.3.2 password letmein
```

The same goes for `office-r2`:

```
router bgp 3000
  neighbor 192.168.3.1 remote-as 3000
  neighbor 192.168.3.1 password letmein
```

Peer Groups

When working with BGP, you will find that many routers require the same `neighbor` statements in their configurations. No matter what kind of routing policy you're implementing and how you're implementing it, if you want the same policy lists applied to a group of neighbors you'll end up giving the same parameters on all the `neighbor` statements. This process can be error-prone and confusing.

Peer groups eliminate redundant configuration lines by allowing you to define a group and then make each neighbor a part of that group. For example, assume that you have a route map that enforces some routing policy. Instead of applying that route map separately on each neighbor, you can add all the neighbors to a peer group and then apply the route map for the group as a whole.

In Figure 10-3, we have a network (AS 500) with three BGP routers. Instead of defining the same route maps for each neighbor in Router 1's configuration, we create a peer group called `policy1`. This peer group defines the non-unique configuration items. We then make Router 2 and Router 3 members of this peer group. Here is the BGP configuration for Router 1:

```
router bgp 500
  ! Define our peer group and apply the configuration items to it
  neighbor policy1 peer-group
  neighbor policy1 remote-as 500
  neighbor policy1 next-hop-self
  neighbor policy1 route-map map1 in
  ! Now define our neighbors as part of peer group policy1
  neighbor 10.10.2.1 peer-group policy1
  neighbor 10.10.3.1 peer-group policy1
```

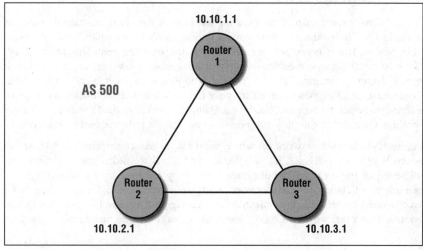

Figure 10-3: iBGP network with peer-group configuration

We can use the same peer-group configuration on Router 2 and Router 3. Unfortunately, we'll still have to type almost identical configurations on each router, but at least we've reduced the amount of duplication on the individual routers. We still have to keep our router configurations in sync, but the peer-group concept makes it easier to keep the configuration uniform within a router.

Route Reflectors

BGP does not advertise a route learned from one iBGP router to another. A route is advertised via iBGP only if it is learned from the iBGP router that first advertised it. For example, assume that Router A advertises a route, and Router B learns about that route. Router B cannot advertise that route to Router C; Router C must learn the route from Router A. In other words, an iBGP router cannot advertise a route it learned from another iBGP router to a third iBGP router. Because of this restriction, if you have multiple routers connected to different AS networks, all of the routers must be fully "meshed."

One solution to this problem is to use *route reflectors*. Route reflectors ease the advertisement restriction by allowing a BGP router to reflect BGP routes it learns about to a third BGP router. Let's assume we don't have a link between Router 2 and Router 3 in Figure 10-3. The following configuration shows how to set up a route reflector on Router 1 that propagates iBGP routes between Router 2 and Router 3:

```
router bgp 500
   neighbor 10.10.2.1 remote-as 500
   neighbor 10.10.2.1 route-reflector-client
   neighbor 10.10.3.1 remote-as 500
   neighbor 10.10.3.1 route-reflector-client
```

With this configuration, Router 1 can advertise Router 2's iBGP routes to Router 3 and Router 3's routes to Router 2.

BGP Confederacies

A *confederacy* is a group of cooperating autonomous systems working together as a single AS. Confederacies allow you to divide an AS into smaller, more manageable pieces. The main reason for doing so is the meshing requirement for iBGP. With 10 to 20 routers, meshing is pretty manageable. However, as your network grows larger, managing all the peer relationships can get very complicated. Confederacies allow you to break up your network into little autonomous systems, making it easier to handle. Inside each little AS, all the iBGP routers are fully meshed. Outside, all the little autonomous systems are fully meshed to each other.

Figure 10-4 shows a network on which we'd like to use confederacies. AS 500 has seven BGP routers: R1, R2, R3, R4, R5, R6, and R7. If we didn't use confederacies, all seven of these routers would have to be fully meshed, or we would have to use route reflectors. In this network, route reflectors would be a problem: we would need more than one reflector, and managing them could easily get out of control. However, we can use confederacies to make a more manageable network.

They are particularly important for large ISPs, but can also be useful for very large corporate networks.

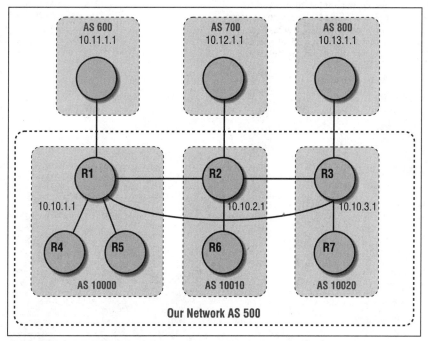

Figure 10-4: BGP confederacies

We can divide AS 500 into three smaller pieces, each of which is connected to a remote AS. Since they are interconnected as neighbors, they will be able to advertise their routes. Now only our three main routers (R1, R2, and R3) are fully meshed with each other, while all our other BGP routers are meshed within their respective confederacies. Although each confederacy has its own AS number, outside networks still see us as AS 500.

Here's how to set up confederacies.

On Router 1:

```
router bgp 10000
  bgp confederation identifier 500
  bgp confederation peers 10010 10020
  neighbor 10.10.2.1 remote-as 10010
  neighbor 10.10.3.1 remote-as 10020
  neighbor 10.11.1.1 remote-as 600
```

On Router 2:

```
router bgp 10010
  bgp confederation identifier 500
  bgp confederation peers 10000 10020
  neighbor 10.10.1.1 remote-as 10000
  neighbor 10.10.3.1 remote-as 10020
  neighbor 10.12.1.1 remote-as 700
```

On Router 3:

```
router bgp 10020
  bgp confederation identifier 500
  bgp confederation peers 10000 10010
  neighbor 10.10.1.1 remote-as 10000
  neighbor 10.10.2.1 remote-as 10010
  neighbor 10.13.1.1 remote-as 800
```

CHAPTER 11

Dial-on-Demand Routing

Dial-on-demand routing (DDR) is useful in applications that don't require a permanent connection between two sites. This is often the case for small offices or home users, who frequently can't justify the expense of a permanent connection. Instead, you want to communicate with some sort of dial-up terminal server using standard telephone service (either analog or ISDN). You want the router to place a call when it has traffic to send and to establish an IP connection using PPP. When the connection is idle, you want the router to hang up automatically.*

DDR is also useful for backup links; a router can establish a dial-up connection if a permanent, leased-line connection fails. It's also useful if you need to make connections to many sites through a limited number of modems or asynchronous ports.

Cisco's IOS support for dial-on-demand routing falls into two categories:

Legacy DDR
> In legacy DDR, all the DDR commands are tied to a specific interface. This includes commands to set up dialer scripts, timeouts, dialer groups ("interesting" traffic), and other DDR information. Legacy DDR is supported from the earliest of IOS versions.

Dialer profiles
> Dialer profiles allow you to create a single profile that contains all the DDR information necessary. The profile can then be applied across many dialer interfaces.

I'll cover both types in this chapter. But first, let's examine the basic DDR commands.

---

* Newer services, such as xDSL and cable modem, could potentially reduce the need for dial-on-demand routing. Both of these services establish permanent connections for low cost. However, dial-up services will be with us for the foreseeable future.

Configuring a Simple DDR Connection

Let's start by configuring a simple dial-up connection to a remote office. The connection will be made only if there is "interesting" traffic for the network at the remote office. For the connection, we'll use an async interface with an analog modem attached to it.

First, we need to define the dialer script (also called a *chat script*) for the modem. Chat scripts define the process by which the router communicates with the modem and logs into the remote site. The script is organized as a sequence of "expect" and "send" strings, that is, strings the router expects to receive and strings the router sends. For example, here's a simple script that dials the number (410) 555-1111 and waits for a connection:

```
chat-script usr-modem "" "atdt 4105551111" TIMEOUT 60 "CONNECT"
```

After the `chat-script` command, we have the name `usr-modem`, which identifies the script in other parts of the configuration. Then we start the expect-send pairs. First, we expect nothing (`""`) and send the familiar modem dialing command, `atdt 4105551111`. We specify a 60-second timeout, during which we expect to receive the string `CONNECT`. The default timeout is 5 seconds.

Next, we'll start configuring the interface. We set up PPP as the encapsulation mode, and specify the authentication procedure (in this case, CHAP) and the username and password to be used for authentication to the remote office. And of course, we need to specify an IP address for this end of the connection. (There are alternatives to providing an explicit IP address—we'll see them later.)

```
! Set up username and password for CHAP authentication on remote router
username office1 password letmein
!
! Async interface
interface async 1
   description DDR link to the remote office
   encapsulation ppp
   ppp authentication chap
   ip address 10.10.3.1 255.255.255.0
```

Now back to setting up DDR. We need to enable DDR on the interface by using the `dialer in-band` command. (This command is not required for BRI interfaces because they are automatically set for dialing.) We specify that the connection should hang up if there is no traffic for 300 seconds (5 minutes). Next, we specify a dialer group. The dialer group corresponds to a dialer list, which in turn points us to an access list that defines the traffic for which the router will establish the connection:

```
! Enable DDR for this interface
dialer in-band
! Extend the idle period to 5 minutes
dialer idle-timeout 300
! This next command specifies that this interface is part of dialer group 2,
! which is defined below with the dialer-list command
dialer-group 2
! Select the correct chat script
dialer map ip 10.10.3.2 modem-script usr-modem
```

Now we need to tell the router when to dial the link by providing a dialer list. The dialer list defines the traffic that we consider interesting. In this case, we use an extended IP access list to state that we're interested in any traffic using the IP protocol. (A dialer list can also specify the allowed protocols directly, without using an access list.) In the following commands, we define dialer list 2, which matches the previous `dialer-group` command. The dialer list points to access list 101:

```
! Define a dialer list for dialer group 2
dialer-list 2 list 101
access-list 101 permit ip any any
```

Access list 101 permits all IP traffic; in this context, it means that IP traffic will cause the router to dial. After the link is established, this access list does nothing to block any traffic traversing the link; it merely controls when the link is dialed.

Finally, we need to create routes to send traffic to the remote office:

```
! Define a static route for the remote-office IP addresses
ip route 10.10.4.0 255.255.255.0 10.10.3.2
ip route 10.10.5.0 255.255.255.0 10.10.3.2
```

Without the static routes, the router would never know the address space of the remote office because no routing protocol can run across a link that is down. With these routes, any traffic bound for the 10.10.4.0 or 10.10.5.0 subnets is routed via the async1 interface. If the interface is down, the connection is automatically dialed. If the connection is idle for more than 300 seconds, the link is disconnected. This example is fairly simple; in most cases the access list needs to be more restrictive to stop unwanted traffic or routing updates from causing our link to come up. Remember that the access list should describe only "interesting" traffic, and most sites using dial-on-demand routing should not consider routing updates interesting—if for no other reason than that routing updates will tend to keep the link up all the time.

Sample Legacy DDR Configurations

One common application for DDR is a dial-up connection to the Internet. Here's a configuration that dials an ISP any time there is traffic that needs to go to the Internet:

```
! Define the chat scripts
chat-script modem1 "" "atz\r" OK "atdt \T" TIMEOUT 30 CONNECT \c
chat-script login1 TIMEOUT 20 login: "bob\r"  password: "mypassword\r"
!
! Set up the dialer interface
interface async1
    ! We are going to let the router negotiate its IP address through PPP
    ip address negotiated
    encapsulation ppp
        ! Enable dialing on this interface
    dialer in-band
        ! Set the idle timeout
    dialer idle-timeout 600
    ! Map our provider's IP address
    dialer map 172.168.1.20 modem-script modem1 system-script login1 14105551212
    dialer-group 2
!
```

```
! Assign the dialer group to an access list
dialer-list 2 list 101
access-list 101 permit ip any any
!
! Set a default route
ip route 0.0.0.0 0.0.0.0 async1
```

In some respects, this is a simpler configuration than the previous one. We use a negotiated IP address (i.e., an address assigned to us by the ISP) rather than specifying the address explicitly. We specify PPP encapsulation, but don't do any special authentication; authentication is handled by a simple login sequence, which we implement in the chat scripts. This is typical of many ISP connections.

This configuration uses a few newer features of IOS. First, we have separated the chat script into two parts, a modem script and a system script, both of which are specified in our dialer map. This separation allows us to divide the parts of the script that configure the modem from the parts that deal with the ISP (i.e., perform a login). These two parts are specified by the dialer map command, which associates an IP address (in this case, the IP address of the ISP's end of the connection) with an actual phone number. The chat scripts also use a number of abbreviations, such as \T, which stands for the phone number. Table 11-1 shows some common abbreviations.

Table 11-1: Common chat script abbreviations

Abbreviation	Meaning
\c	Suppress newline character
\d	Two-second delay
\K	Send a break
\n	Newline character
\p	1/4-second delay
\r	Return character
\s	Space
\t	Tab character
\T	Phone number
\\	Backslash
BREAK	Send a break
EOT	EOT character
" "	Expect a null string

DDR Backup Links

Dial-on-demand is frequently used to provide a backup link for a permanent connection. There are two methods for dial backup: backup interface commands and floating static routes. Backup interface commands are relatively easy to configure, can provide bandwidth on demand, and stay idle until brought online. On the other hand, they are dependent on encapsulation, and they provide only one backup interface per "permanent" interface.

A floating static route is simply a static route whose administrative distance has been raised so that it is less desirable than the primary route. We covered backup static routes and administrative distances in Chapter 8, so this should be familiar. Floating static routes are convenient if you require multiple backup interfaces or backup routes that are encapsulation-independent. But floating static routes are somewhat difficult to configure, require the use of a routing protocol, and require that the "interesting traffic" access list actually cause the backup interface to be dialed.

First let's look at the backup interface commands and what they can do for us. Then we will revisit the example using a floating static route.

Backup interface commands

In this example, the ISDN interface bri0 is defined as a backup to our serial link. If the serial link goes down, the bri0 interface is dialed and the connection is made. Once the serial link has been restored for a period of time, the bri0 link is disconnected. The first number in the backup delay command tells the router to wait 5 seconds before bringing the bri0 interface up after serial1 goes down; the second number tells the router to wait 30 seconds after serial1 comes back online before switching back. These delay values try to ensure that the serial1 link is really up or down before switching over to the backup interface.

```
interface serial1
  description T1 to Baltimore
  ip address 10.10.2.1 255.255.255.0
  ! The backup for this link is bri0. When serial1 goes down, bri0 comes up
  backup interface bri0
  ! Set delay values. Wait 5 seconds before bringing bri0 up
  ! and wait 30 seconds after serial1 comes back up before switching back
  backup delay 5 30
!
interface bri0
  ip address 10.10.3.1 255.255.255.0
  encapsulation ppp
  dialer map ip 10.10.3.2 name baltimore-rtr broadcast 4105552323
  dialer-group 1
!
isdn switch-type basic-5ess
username baltimore-rtr password hello123
!
! Configure the dialer list
dialer-list 1 protocol ip permit
```

DDR bandwidth on demand with backup interface commands

In the previous example, bri0 acts as a backup for serial1. However, the ISDN link is used only as a backup. In this example, we'll take things a bit farther and use bri0 to provide some additional bandwidth, helping out serial1 during periods of congestion. In particular, we will bring up bri0 when the load on serial1 is greater than 70%, using the backup load command. When the load on serial1 drops back to 15%, we drop the bri0 link.

This configuration does not use an explicit access list to specify what traffic is interesting. Instead, it uses a variant of the `dialer list` command that incorporates a simple access list saying "Any IP traffic is permitted." If your requirements are simple, this approach is often clearer and more straightforward than using a separate access list.

```
interface serial1
  description T1 to Baltimore
  ip address 10.10.2.1 255.255.255.0
  ! Set the backup interface to bri0
  backup interface bri0
  ! Use bri0 when load hits 70, take offline when load drops back to 15
  backup load 70 15
!
interface bri0
  ip address 10.10.3.1 255.255.255.0
  encapsulation ppp
  dialer map ip 10.10.3.2 name baltimore-rtr broadcast 4105552323
  dialer-group 1
!
isdn switch-type basic-5ess
username baltimore-rtr password hello123
!
! Configure the dialer list for dialer-group 1
dialer-list 1 protocol ip permit
```

DDR backup with floating static routes

It's easy to write our backup interface example using a floating static route. In order for this example to work properly, we also need to configure a routing protocol—in this case, we'll use EIGRP. So, to get our floating static route to work, we need to set the administrative distance for the static route higher than EIGRP's distance. The default administrative distance for EIGRP routes is 170 (for external routes), so we'll use a distance of 200 for our backup route. The rest is straightforward.

```
! Almost the same serial configuration as before except no backup commands.
interface serial1
  description T1 to Baltimore
  ip address 10.10.2.1 255.255.255.0
  ! We are going to tweak EIGRP so our backup dialer link comes online faster
  ip hello-interval eigrp 1 5
  ip hold-time eigrp 1 15
!
interface bri0
  ip address 10.10.3.1 255.255.255.0
  encapsulation ppp
  dialer map ip 10.10.3.2 name baltimore-rtr broadcast 4105552323
  dialer-group 1
!
isdn switch-type basic-5ess
username baltimore-rtr password hello123
!
! Configure EIGRP
router eigrp 100
  network 10.0.0.0
!
! Configure our floating/backup static route, setting the administrative
```

```
! distance to 200
ip route 10.10.5.0 255.255.255.0 10.10.3.2 200
!
! Configure the dialer list; this time use an access list to block
! EIGRP traffic from bringing up our link
dialer-list 1 protocol ip list 101
!
! Finally, our access list. This list blocks EIGRP and permits everything else.
! REMEMBER: This list is used only to identify interesting traffic. It
! does nothing to block traffic once the link is established.
access-list 101 permit deny eigrp any any
access-list 101 permit ip any any
```

Dialer Maps

Dialer maps allow IP addresses to be mapped directly to phone numbers and dialer scripts. With this feature, one interface can be configured to dial several different sites, or to dial the same site using different phone numbers, based on the IP address.

The most basic form of this command

In the following example, we use the `dialer map` command to configure the two B channels of an ISDN interface `bri0`:

```
interface bri0
  ip address 10.10.3.1 255.255.255.0
  encapsulation ppp
  dialer map ip 10.10.3.2 name ROUTER1 broadcast 4105552323
  dialer map ip 10.10.3.4 name ROUTER2 broadcast 4105552333
  ppp authentication chap
  ppp multilink
  dialer-group 1
!
dialer-list 1 protocol ip permit
```

The `dialer map` commands map the remote device's IP address, its device name (for authentication), and a dial string (phone number). Optionally, we can also set the speed (56 or 64) and whether or not we want to allow broadcasts. The `broadcast` keyword says that we will allow broadcasts, such as routing updates. By default, broadcasts aren't allowed.

Dialer maps are the preferred way to configure dialing of a link. They are used throughout this chapter.

A more complicated use of dialer maps

In this example, we want to set up a router to communicate with two remote offices through a single serial interface. Office 1's local network is 10.10.2.0/24; Office 2's network is 10.10.4.0/24. To create this configuration, we map the IP address 10.10.1.2 and the phone number 555-1111 to the chat script that dials Office 1; we map 10.10.1.4 and 555-1112 to the chat script for Office 2. To do so, we use two `dialer map` commands, plus several `chat-script` commands for setting up the scripts. Both connections are handled by the same interface and the same modem. The static routes set the routes to the proper office network.

In this configuration, it's impossible for both offices to be connected at the same time because we are using a single analog modem. With ISDN, this wouldn't be a problem. BRI interfaces have two B channels, which enable one interface to dial two different locations at once.

Once a connection has been made to either destination, the connection remains up until it has been idle for a certain timeout period. To make this configuration more flexible, we use two different idle timeout periods. The normal timeout, set by the dialer idle-timeout command, is 300 seconds; this timeout is used if there is no traffic waiting for the other office. If there is traffic waiting, the configuration specifies a shorter timeout of 15 seconds, using the dialer fast-idle command.

```
! Set up the chat script for the modem (we have only one type of modem)
chat-script usr ABORT ERROR "" "at z" OK "atdt \T" TIMEOUT 20
!
! Set up the login script for office1
chat-script office1 ABORT invalid TIMEOUT 10 name: frank word: letmein ">"
!
! Set up the login script for office2
chat-script office2 ABORT invalid TIMEOUT 10 name: saul word: letme ">"
!
interface async 3
  description DDR connection to remote offices
  ip address 10.10.1.1 255.255.255.0
  dialer in-band
  ! Create the map for this interface to office1
  dialer map ip 10.10.1.2 modem-script usr system-script office1 555-1111
  ! Create the map for this interface to office2
  dialer map ip 10.10.1.4 modem-script usr system-script office2 555-1112
   ! Set the idle timeouts
  dialer idle-timeout 300
  dialer fast-idle 15
  dialer-group 1
!
! Set a static route to office1
ip route 10.10.2.0 255.255.255.0 10.10.1.2
! Set a static route to office2
ip route 10.10.4.0 255.255.255.0 10.10.1.4
!
! Set up the dialer groups
access-list 110 deny icmp any any
access-list 110 permit ip any any
dialer-list 1 list 110
```

We've made one additional improvement to our earlier configurations: we added a deny rule that blocks ICMP traffic to access list 110. Since this rule is used in a dialer list, it prevents a ping from bringing up the connection. We don't want the line to be dialed every time someone pings the remote site. However, we don't actually block pings—this access list isn't applied to the traffic going into or out of an interface. If the line is up, the ping will succeed.

This configuration assumes that a routing protocol is not in use. A routing protocol would bring up the links each time it sends routing updates to adjacent routers, and this is almost certainly undesirable. If you do use a routing protocol in a configuration like this one, make the DDR interface a passive interface. In the following statements, we start a RIP routing process and specify that the interface async3 is passive:

```
router rip
  network 10.0.0.0
  passive-interface async3
```

Dialer Interfaces (Dialer Profiles)

So far, we have applied all the DDR-specific configuration items directly to a physical interface. This method of configuring DDR is called "legacy DDR." The problem with legacy DDR is that it forces an interface to use the same parameters for all connections, incoming or outgoing. In the previous example, we set up a dialer map that called two different destinations through the same interface; all the other configuration items for the two destinations were the same. With dialer profiles, we can move the DDR information into the virtual dialer interface, which allows us to create rotary groups, dialer pools, or maps to different DDR information on the same physical interface.

The configuration of a dialer interface is no different from any other interface configuration:

```
interface dialer 1
  ip address 10.10.1.5 255.255.255.0
  encapsulation ppp
  dialer string 4105551212
```

Dialer interfaces can be applied to physical interfaces in two ways: via rotary groups or dialer pools.

Rotary Groups

Rotary groups allow a group of interfaces to act as one to make or receive calls. This grouping is accomplished by mapping a single virtual dialer interface to many physical interfaces. Rotary groups are useful when you have one router that needs to call several destinations at the same time. Using a rotary group lets you avoid the most important limitation of our previous configuration: only one of the remote sites could be connected at a time.

In this example, we create a rotary group that supports three remote offices, using three async interfaces:

```
! First, we configure the dialer interface
interface dialer1
  description DDR connection to remote offices
  ip address 10.10.1.1 255.255.255.0
  dialer in-band
  ! Create the map for this interface to office2
  dialer map ip 10.10.1.2 modem-script usr system-script office2 555-1111
  ! Create the map for this interface to office3
  dialer map ip 10.10.1.3 modem-script usr system-script office3 555-1112
  ! Create the map for this interface to office4
  dialer map ip 10.10.1.4 modem-script usr system-script office4 555-1113
  ! Set the idle timeouts
  dialer idle-timeout 300
  dialer-group 1
!
```

```
! Set up the chat script for the modem (we have only one type of modem)
chat-script usr ABORT ERROR "" "at z" OK "atdt \T" TIMEOUT 20
chat-script office2 ABORT invalid TIMEOUT 10 name: frank word: letmein ">"
chat-script office3 ABORT invalid TIMEOUT 10 name: saul  word: letme ">"
chat-script office4 ABORT invalid TIMEOUT 10 name: bob    word: letmeback ">"
!
! Now configure the physical interfaces. Each interface is a member of
! rotary-group 1
! Note that the rotary-group number is the same as our dialer interface
interface async 1
  no ip address
  rotary-group 1
interface async 2
  no ip address
  rotary-group 1
interface async 3
  no ip address
  rotary-group 1
!
! Set a static route to office2
ip route 10.10.2.0 255.255.255.0 10.10.1.2
! Set a static route to office3
ip route 10.10.3.0 255.255.255.0 10.10.1.3
! Set a static route to office4
ip route 10.10.4.0 255.255.255.0 10.10.1.4
!
! Set up the dialer groups
! (Since we left "broadcast" off the dialer maps, denying EIGRP and ICMP
! isn't completely necessary. However, it is here as a reminder.)
access-list 110 deny icmp any any
access-list 110 deny eigrp any any
access-list 110 permit ip any any
dialer-list 1 list 110
```

In this configuration, we use the rotary-group command to collect three async interfaces into rotary group 1. This group is automatically associated with the interface dialer1; the rotary group number *must* match the dialer interface number. The async interfaces don't have their own IP addresses; the IP addresses are assigned to the dialer interface, which eliminates the need to know which interface will call which office.

We also modified access list 110 to prevent EIGRP traffic from bringing up any of the links. Again, this doesn't prevent EIGRP traffic from being sent over the links, provided that they are already up. Denying ICMP and EIGRP explicitly isn't necessary because we didn't use the broadcast keyword in the dialer map command. However, had we added the broadcast keyword, we would need these lines in our access list. It's a good idea to make your assumptions explicit, so the router won't suddenly change behavior if you later decide that you have to allow broadcast traffic.

Dialer Pools

Dialer pools first appeared in IOS 11.2. They are a bit like rotary groups, but they map many physical interfaces to many virtual interfaces. To best illustrate this feature, consider Figure 11-1, which shows four BRI interfaces that are assigned to three pools. Note that we can assign one interface to two or more pools. The physical interfaces are used as needed by the dialer interfaces you create.

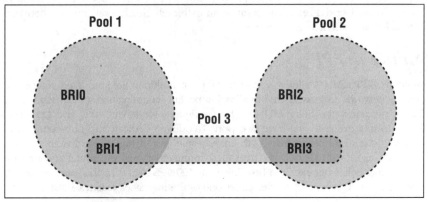

Figure 11-1: Dialer pools

Configuring a dialer pool consists of two steps: assigning a pool number to the dialer interface, and making the physical interfaces pool members. Here's the pool configuration for Figure 11-1:

```
interface dialer1
  ip address 10.10.1.5 255.255.255.0
  encapsulation ppp
  dialer in-band
  dialer pool 1
!
interface dialer2
  ip address 10.10.2.5 255.255.255.0
  encapsulation ppp
  dialer in-band
  dialer pool 2
!
interface dialer3
  ip address 10.10.3.5 255.255.255.0
  encapsulation ppp
  dialer pool 3
!
interface bri0
  encapsulation ppp
  dialer pool-member 1
!
interface bri1
  encapsulation ppp
  dialer pool-member 1
  dialer pool-member 3
!
interface bri2
  encapsulation ppp
  dialer pool-member 2
!
interface bri3
  encapsulation ppp
  dialer pool-member 2
  dialer pool-member 3
```

dialer1 can use any of the interfaces that belong to pool 1; likewise, dialer2 can use any of the interfaces in pool 2, and so on. Note that bri1 and bri3 are both members of two pools, pool 1 and pool 3, so these two interfaces can be used by either dialer1 or dialer3. The result is an extremely flexible relationship between the dialers and the actual interfaces.

Multilink PPP

Multilink PPP (MLP) allows connections over multiple links to have the same remote network address, therefore allowing packet fragmentation and dynamic load balancing across the links. MLP can be configured for async, bri, and pri interfaces. In this example, we have two ports (modems) dedicated to one connection. The traffic is distributed across both links, resulting in a higher-bandwidth connection. We use the dialer load-threshold command to tell the router to bring up the second link whenever the first link is at 100% capacity. In this case, it says to bring up the other link whenever either one of the interfaces reaches 100% capacity:

```
interface async 1
  no ip address
  encapsulation ppp
  dialer rotary-group 1
!
interface async 2
  no ip address
  encapsulation ppp
  dialer rotary-group 1
!
interface dialer 1
  ip unnumber ethernet 0
  encapsulation ppp
  dialer in-band
  dialer load-threshold 100 either
  ppp authentication chap
  ppp multilink
```

Multilink PPP is commonly used to tie the two channels of a BRI ISDN line into a single 128-Kbps connection. Here's what that configuration looks like. We define two ISDN interfaces, one for each B channel; we place those interfaces in the same rotary group; then we configure a dialer interface for the rotary group using PPP encapsulation. The dialer interface has the multilink command, which allows you to use both BRI interfaces simultaneously:

```
interface BRI0
  no ip address
  encapsulation ppp
  dialer idle-timeout 300
  dialer rotary-group 1
  dialer load-threshold 30 either
!
interface BRI1
  no ip address
  encapsulation ppp
  dialer idle-timeout 300
  dialer rotary-group 1
  dialer load-threshold 30 either
!
```

```
! We configure Dialer1 because BRI0 and BRI1 have been
! configured to use rotary group 1 (dialer1)
!
interface Dialer1
  ip address 10.1.1.2 255.255.255.0
 encapsulation ppp
 dialer in-band
 dialer idle-timeout 500
 dialer map ip 10.1.1.1 name baltimore broadcast 55512340101
 dialer load-threshold 30 either
 dialer-group 1
 ppp authentication chap
 ppp multilink
```

Snapshot DDR

In all the previous dial-up examples, we used static routes to define the routing tables for dial-up connections. On small networks, static routes are easily managed, but on larger networks they can quickly get out of hand. However, running a routing protocol in the presence of DDR is a problem, because normal routing protocols would keep DDR links up forever with their constant route updates. In some situations this might be acceptable, but it begs the question of why you're using DDR in the first place.

Snapshot routing was designed to allow the use of routing protocols across DDR connections without keeping the line active constantly. As the name implies, snapshot routing means that the routing protocols are allowed to take a "snapshot" of the network's state at specified intervals rather than sending and receiving constant updates. Therefore, dial-up links come up only at a configurable interval, which saves the headache of static route management and keeps the dial-up link's usage to a minimum. Snapshot routing is compatible with RIP (IP and IPX), EIGRP, IGRP, RTMP (AppleTalk), and RTP (Vines), all of which are distance-vector protocols.

Configuring a link for snapshot routing requires one end to be a snapshot server and the other end to be a snapshot client. In this example, Office 1 has the local network 10.10.0.0 and serves as the snapshot server; Office 2 has the local network 10.11.0.0 and is the snapshot client. There are two dialer maps at each site: one for the normal traffic (map this address to this phone number) and another for the snapshot routing protocol.

Here's the configuration for Office 1:

```
hostname office1
!
interface ethernet0
  ip address 10.10.1.1 255.255.0.0
!
! Set the ISDN switch type
isdn switch-type basic-ni1
!
interface BRI0
  ! Don't need an IP address because we are using the dialer interface
  no ip address
```

```
  encapsulation ppp
  dialer rotary-group 0
  ! Our local SPIDs for our ISDN lines
  isdn spid1 014105551212111 5551212
  isdn spid2 014105551213111 5551213
!
! Configure the dialer interface
interface dialer 0
  ip unnumbered ethernet0
  encapsulation ppp
  dialer in-band
  dialer idle-timeout 300
  dialer map snapshot 1 name office2 speed 56
  ! Map the IPs to the phone numbers at office2
  ! There are two maps, one for each ISDN channel
  ! Broadcast is required here because we are doing routing
  dialer map ip 10.11.1.1 name office2 speed 56 broadcast 14105551312
  dialer map ip 10.11.1.1 name office2 speed 56 broadcast 14105551313
  dialer-group 1
  ! Enable snapshot server, updates every 30 minutes
  snapshot-server 30
  ! Disable CDP for this interface
  no cdp enable
  ! PPP CHAP authentication
  ppp authentication chap
  ! Enable multilink for the PPP (2 channels)
  ppp multilink
!
username office1 password letmein
!
dialer-list 1 protocol ip permit
!
! Enable RIP
router rip
  network 10.0.0.0
  version 2
  no validate-update source
```

Here's the configuration for Office 2:

```
hostname office2
!
interface ethernet0
  ip address 10.11.1.1 255.255.0.0
!
! Set the ISDN switch type
isdn switch-type basic-ni1
!
interface BRI0
  ! Don't need an IP address because we are using the dialer interface
  no ip address
  encapsulation ppp
  dialer rotary-group 0
  ! Our local SPIDs for our ISDN lines
  isdn spid1 014105551312111 5551312
  isdn spid2 014105551313111 5551313
!
! Configure the dialer interface
interface dialer 0
```

```
    ip unnumbered ethernet0
    encapsulation ppp
    dialer in-band
    dialer idle-timeout 300
    dialer map snapshot 1 name office1 speed 56
    ! Map the IPs to the phone numbers at office1
    ! Broadcast is required here because we are doing routing
    dialer map ip 10.10.1.1 name office1 speed 56 broadcast 14105551212
    dialer map ip 10.10.1.1 name office1 speed 56 broadcast 14105551213
    dialer-group 1
    ! Enable snapshot client, updates every 30 minutes
    snapshot client 30 600 suppress-statechange-update dialer
    ! Disable CDP for this interface
    no cdp enable
    ! PPP CHAP authentication
    ppp authentication chap
    ! Enable multilink for the PPP (2 channels)
    ppp multilink
!
username office2 password letmein
!
dialer-list 1 protocol ip permit
!
! Enable RIP
router rip
    network 10.0.0.0
    version 2
```

In this configuration, Office 2 is the snapshot client. Office 2 can exchange routing
information whenever the BRI interfaces come up. If the snapshot timeout expires
(the timeout is set to 30 minutes), the router is allowed to bring the BRI interface
up to exchange routing information even if there is no "interesting" traffic.

Useful show Commands

Here are some show commands that are useful for monitoring DDR on your router.

show dialer

This command can be very verbose. It provides detailed information about all your
DDR interfaces; to limit the output, you can specify the name of a particular dialer
interface.

```
Router1#show dialer
Dialer0 - dialer type = DIALER PROFILE
        Idle timer (120 secs), Fast idle timer (20 secs)
        Wait for carrier (30 secs), Re-enable (15 secs)
        Dialer state is data link layer up


        Dial String      Successes  Failures   Last called  Last status
        5552323                  0         1    00:00:33          failed

BRI0 - dialer type = ISDN

        Dial String      Successes  Failures   Last called  Last status
        0 incoming call(s) have been screened.
        0 incoming call(s) rejected for callback.
```

```
BRIO:1 - dialer type = ISDN
        Idle timer (180 secs), Fast idle timer (20 secs)
        Wait for carrier (30 secs), Re-enable (15 secs)
        Dialer state is data link layer up
        Dial reason: ip (s=192.168.1.1, d=10.1.1.2)
        Interface bound to profile Dialer0
        Time until disconnect 148 secs
        Current call connected 00:00:33
        Connected to 5552323 (Router2)

BRIO:2 - dialer type = ISDN
        Idle timer (120 secs), Fast idle timer (20 secs)
        Wait for carrier (30 secs), Re-enable (15 secs)
        Dialer state is idle
```

The output shows that this router has a Dialer0 interface and a BRIO interface. Table 11-2 describes a few of the more confusing fields in this output.

Table 11-2: Description for values from show dialer

Field	Meaning
Timers (Idle/Fast idle/Wait/Re-enable)	The time, in seconds, for each of the timers. If you didn't set any timers in the configuration, these fields reflect the default values.
Dial string	The dial string (essentially, the phone number) of any logged calls.
Successes/Failures/ Last called/Last status	The number of successful calls; the number of failed calls; the time of the last call; the status of the last call.
Screened/Rejected	The number of incoming calls that have been screened, and the number of calls that have been rejected by the screening process. A dialer profile can be set up to screen incoming calls and handle them in different ways. The most typical way to handle a screened call is to use caller ID callback. If the callback fails, the call is rejected.
Dialer state	data link layer up means that the call connected properly. Any other message means there is a problem with the call.
Dial reason	The source (S) and destination (D) IP addresses for the packet that caused the link to come up.

show dialer map

This command lists all the dialer maps that are defined:

```
Router1#show dialer map
Static dialer map ip 10.1.1.1 name office2 on Dialer1
Static dialer map ip 10.1.1.2 name office3 on Dialer1
```

show isdn active

This command is limited to ISDN interfaces. It provides some valuable information about active ISDN calls:

```
Router1#show isdn active
--------------------------------------------------------------------------------
                                ISDN ACTIVE CALLS
--------------------------------------------------------------------------------
History table has a maximum of 100 entries.
History table data is retained for a maximum of 15 Minutes.
--------------------------------------------------------------------------------
```

Call	Calling or Called	Remote	Seconds	Seconds	Seconds	Recorded Charges
Type	Phone number	Node Name	Used	Left	Idle	Units/Currency
Out	5552323	Router2	88	105	5	0

show snapshot

This command displays information about snapshot routing:

```
Router#show snapshot bri0

Bri0 is up, line protocol is up, snapshot up
Options: dialer support
Length of each activation period: 3 minutes
Period between activations:       30 minutes
Retry period on connect failure:  5
For dialer address 0
 Current queue: active, remaining active time: 1 minutes
 Updates received this cycle: ip
For dialer address 1
 Current queue: client quiet, time until next activation: 27 minutes
```

Everything in this output should be straightforward except for the dialer address. The dialer address number refers to the rotary group number. Therefore, in this example, we're seeing snapshot information for rotary groups 0 and 1.

CHAPTER 12

Special Topics

This chapter covers a number of IP configuration topics that won't find their way into most configurations. However, you should be familiar with them—you never know what features you're going to need the next time you redesign your network. In particular, we cover:

Bridging

So far, we've used routers as routers, which make intelligent decisions about where to send packets based on their IP addresses and information gathered by routing protocols. Cisco routers can also be configured as bridges, which make routing decisions based on the MAC address (e.g., Ethernet address).

Hot standby routing

Cisco's Hot Standby Routing Protocol (HSRP) enables routers to serve as backups for one another.

Network Address Translation (NAT)

Increasingly, the IP addresses visible outside a network are different from the addresses actually in use inside the network. Translating from a small external address space to a much larger internal space conserves addresses (you can have a large network but use a small block of external addresses) and gives you more control over which hosts in your network are visible to the outside world. In these configurations, the router relies on NAT to map your internal addresses to your external addresses.

Tunneling

Tunneling means establishing a TCP/IP connection to another location and then running other protocols through that connection. It can be used as a means of propagating protocols that can't be routed or that don't belong to the TCP/IP family; encrypted tunnels can also be used as part of a security strategy.

Bridging

Bridging is a technique for transferring packets between local networks based on their Layer 2 (MAC) addresses rather than their Layer 3 (IP) addresses. A typical bridge between two Ethernets would notice which Ethernet addresses are in use on each Ethernet and selectively transfer packets from one Ethernet to the other, based on the packets' destination Ethernet addresses. Bridges use their own set of protocols to communicate with each other, preventing the equivalent of routing loops and helping them learn how to handle packets for hosts that aren't connected directly to one of their ports.

Bridging is useful in a number of situations:

- Before routers were commodity products, bridging was a way of extending a network beyond the limits of a single physical medium. In other words, it's a way to connect local networks into a larger network without the complexity of routing.

- Many protocols, such as NetBIOS, can't be routed. If you have to deal with protocols that can't be routed, you may want to consider bridging as a way of propagating those protocols across a larger network. Note, however, that many nonroutable protocols (including NetBios) can be encapsulated within IP, which effectively makes them routable. Encapsulating nonroutable protocols within IP may be a better solution than bridging them.

- Bridging is often used to connect remote networks to an ISP, particularly when using ADSL modem or cable modem. The ADSL or cable modem is often configured as a bridge, which is often less expensive than using a full-fledged router.

Bridging usually does not scale as well as routing, and it takes much more of the router's CPU and memory.

The type of bridging covered in this section is called *transparent bridging*. There is another type of bridging, called *source-routing bridging* (SRB), that has a narrower focus and is not discussed here.

Creating a bridge between two routers is as simple as selecting which spanning-tree bridge protocol to use (almost always `ieee`) and then enabling a bridge group on the interfaces. In this example, Router 1 and Router 2 are connected via their serial interfaces (`serial1`); we create a bridge between the Ethernet interfaces on both routers.

Here's the configuration for Router 1:

```
bridge 1 protocol ieee
!
interface ethernet1
 ip address 10.10.1.1 255.255.255.0
 bridge-group 1
!
interface serial1
 ip address 10.10.2.1 255.255.255.0
 bridge-group 1
```

Here's the configuration for Router 2:

```
bridge 1 protocol ieee
!
interface ethernet1
  ip address 10.10.3.1 255.255.255.0
  bridge-group 1
!
interface serial1
  ip address 10.10.2.2 255.255.255.0
  bridge-group 1
```

Now the two Ethernet segments are bridged via the serial links. The bridge numbers you assign are significant only to the local router—they do not have to match across routers. However, keeping the numbers consistent across routers will keep your configurations simpler.

In this example, the routers will route IP but bridge everything else. By default, IP traffic is routed unless it is explicitly bridged. All other protocols are bridged unless explicitly routed. You must use the global command no ip routing to force IP to be bridged, which is probably not what you want. The first way around this problem is Concurrent Routing and Bridging.

Concurrent Routing and Bridging (CRB)

Concurrent Routing and Bridging (CRB) allows the router to route and bridge the same protocol. However, routing and bridging remain separate islands in the router and aren't allowed to interact. In other words, routing can be enabled on some interfaces, and bridging can be enabled on some other interfaces, but the two groups cannot interact. Each interface can either bridge a protocol or route a protocol, but not both; packets will never be transferred from the bridged interfaces to the routed interfaces. The next section discusses Integrated Routing and Bridging (IRB), which allows more interaction and is usually a better solution.

To configure CRB, we use the global command bridge crb. Once enabled, we list the protocols to bridge with the command bridge 1 route ip, where 1 is the bridge group number and ip is the name of the protocol we want to bridge. Obviously, you can use this command to select other protocols; for example, the command bridge 1 route appletalk bridges the AppleTalk protocol. The following example bridges IP traffic between the Ethernet interfaces ethernet0 and ethernet1 and routes IP traffic between the router's other interfaces, serial1 and serial2:

```
interface ethernet0
  ip address 10.1.1.1 255.255.255.0
  bridge-group 1
!
interface ethernet1
  ip addess 10.1.2.1 255.255.255.0
  bridge-group 1
!
interface serial1
  ip address 10.1.3.1 255.255.255.0
!
interface serial2
  ip address 10.1.4.1 255.255.255.0
```

```
!
bridge crb
bridge 1 route ip
bridge 1 protocol ieee
```

Remember that the routed traffic is isolated to the routed interfaces, while the bridged traffic stays on the bridged interfaces. In other words, a packet can't make its way from `ethernet1` to `serial1`, no matter where it ought to go.

Integrated Routing and Bridging (IRB)

CRB was a nice step toward Integrated Routing and Bridging, which allows routing and bridging to cooperate. IRB allows the router to route and bridge any protocol. In order to do this, we need a special interface called a BVI, which stands for Bridge-Group Virtual Interface. We create a BVI for each bridge group. The BVI is routable and handles all routing tasks for the entire bridge group. Our bridge group interfaces work at Layer 2, while the BVIs work at Layer 3. The router can now happily route and bridge our IP traffic at the same time, in accordance with the bridge-group configurations.

To enable IRB, we use the command `bridge irb`. Once this command has been issued, we can create a bridge group and specify which spanning-tree protocol to use (`ieee`). We specify that this bridge group is supposed to route IP. Then we configure the Ethernet interface without an IP address and place it in our bridge group. Finally, we configure the BVI1 interface, which has an IP address. In a more complex configuration, the BVI would also have commands for packet filtering, address translation, and other Layer 3 tasks. Here is an example of IRB in action.

The configuration for Router 1 looks like this:

```
hostname Router1
!
! Enable Integrated Routing and Bridging
bridge irb
! Allow routing of IP for bridge group 1
bridge 1 protocol ieee
 bridge 1 route ip
 !
interface Ethernet0
 no ip address
 bridge-group 1
 !
! Configure our BVI for bridge group 1
interface BVI1
 ip address 10.1.1.1 255.255.255.0
```

For Router 2, the configuration is:

```
hostname Router2
!
! Enable Integrated Routing and Bridging
bridge irb
bridge 1 protocol ieee
! Allow routing of IP for bridge group 1
 bridge 1 route ip
 !
interface Ethernet0
 no ip address
```

```
  bridge-group 1
!
! Configure our BVI for bridge group 1
interface BVI1
  ip address 10.1.1.2 255.255.255.0
```

Now we can ping Router 1's BVI from Router 2:

```
Router2#ping 10.1.1.1

Type escape sequence to abort.
Sending 5, 100-byte ICMP Echos to 10.1.1.1, timeout is 2 seconds:
!!!!!
Success rate is 100 percent (5/5), round-trip min/avg/max = 4/4/8 ms
```

Bridging show Commands

Depending on how your bridging is configured, most of the following show commands will be useful.

show bridge

This command displays the bridging table for each bridge group. This table includes the MAC addresses of the interfaces in the group, the interfaces associated with the addresses, and some other counters:

```
Router2#show bridge

Total of 300 station blocks, 299 free
Codes: P - permanent, S - self

Bridge Group 1:

    Address      Action   Interface     Age   RX count   TX count
0010.7b3a.f659   forward  Ethernet0      0        16          0
```

show bridge group

This command gives you more detailed information about a particular bridge group.

```
Router2#show bridge group

Bridge Group 1 is running the IEEE compatible Spanning Tree protocol

    Port 2 (Ethernet0) of bridge group 1 is forwarding
```

You can get even more detail by using the verbose option:

```
Router2#show bridge group verbose

Bridge Group 1 is running the IEEE compatible Spanning Tree protocol

    Acquisition of new addresses is enabled
    LAT service filtering is disabled

    Port 2 (Ethernet0) of bridge group 1 is forwarding
        LAT compression is not set
        Input LAT service deny group code list is not set
        Input LAT service permit group code list is not set
```

```
Output LAT service deny group code list is not set
Output LAT service Permit group code list is not set
Access list for input filtering on type is not set
Access list for input filtering for LSAP is not set
Access list for input address filter is not set
Access list for input pattern is not set
Access list for output filtering on type is not set
Access list for LSAP is not set
Access list for output address filter is not set
Access list for output pattern filter is not set
Packets too large for translational bridging: 0 input, 0 output
```

Hot Standby Routing Protocol (HSRP)

In this book, several examples dealt with creating backup links for use in case some other link fails. But routers themselves fail—so how do you implement backup routers? You might think that this shouldn't be a problem: after all, if you have two routers connecting your site to the external world, and one fails, your own routing protocols should eventually route around the failure. However, it's not that simple. If the individual hosts on your network aren't running some sort of routing protocol (such as RIP) or router discovery protocol (such as IRDP), they'll never find out about the failure. And in most cases, you don't want to be running a routing protocol on individual hosts; you want to set up each host with a simple default route and leave it at that. Furthermore, when a router fails, it can take some time for a protocol such as RIP to converge on a new route.

That's the overall picture. More concretely, the top illustration in Figure 12-1 shows a larger network comprising two smaller networks. There are two routers, both connected to the external gateway. Let's assume that you want to configure the hosts on Network 1 and Network 2 with static default routes. To which router should these default routes point? All the hosts on both networks can reach either router, but each host can have only one default route. What happens if the router a particular host is using fails? How does that host find out about the other router, aside from an administrator manually changing its default route?

The elegant solution is Hot Standby Routing Protocol. The second part of Figure 12-1 shows a new router, Router 3. Router 3 is a *virtual router*, meaning that there's no such physical piece of equipment: it's an illusion created by the use of HSRP on Router 1 and Router 2. However, although Router 3 is an illusion, it has a unique IP address and a unique MAC address that is configured between Router 1 and Router 2.

Configuring HSRP is as simple as using the standby command on the appropriate interfaces. In the following configuration, we apply the standby command to the ethernet1 interfaces of both routers. Router 1 has the standby preempt command, which tells the routers that Router 1 should be the active router for the standby group, but only when Router 1 has the higher priority. We ensure it has a higher priority by setting the value explicitly to 120 with the priority command. If Router 1 goes down, Router 2 becomes the standby router and takes over the routing duties for our virtual Router 3. If Router 1 comes back up, it will automatically take over because it has the higher priority and the preempt command. The standby ip command provides the IP address for the virtual router.

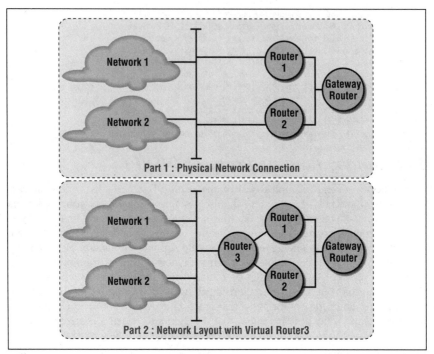

Figure 12-1: HSRP layout

Here's the configuration for Router 1:

```
interface ethernet1
    ! A real IP address is still required for this interface
    ip address 10.10.28.1 255.255.255.0
    standby preempt
    standby priority 120
    ! The IP address for the virtual Router3 is 10.10.28.3
    standby ip 10.10.28.3
```

Here's the configuration for Router 2:

```
interface ethernet1
    ! A real IP address is still required for this interface
    ip address 10.10.28.2 255.255.255.0
    ! The IP address for the virtual Router3 is 10.10.28.3
    standby ip 10.10.28.3
```

With this configuration, all the nodes in Networks 1 and 2 can use 10.10.28.3 as their default gateway address. This is the IP address for the virtual router, Router 3; hosts on the two networks can communicate with Router 3 as if it were a real device. Initially, Router 1 acts as Router 3 and handles packets sent to the virtual router's address. If Router 1 fails, Router 2 takes over immediately. The switchover happens so quickly that the network devices never know that anything has happened; they can continue to use Router 3 as their default router.

It's worth mentioning that the routers adopt a common virtual MAC address as well as a virtual IP address. You don't have to configure the virtual MAC address;

the routers do this for you. A virtual MAC address ensures that the ARP caches remain valid when HSRP switches over to another router.

Multiple-Group Hot Standby Routing

HSRP allows you to create multiple virtual routers, each supported by a number of physical routers, by using the concept of router groups in the standby commands. Multiple standby groups are supported only by newer router models and high-end routers. The 2500-series routers do not support this function (Lance Ethernet chipset).

Our previous example didn't specify a group number, meaning that both routers were in the default group (group 0). In this example, we'll use three physical routers to create three virtual routers, using three router groups. Here's how we'll organize the routers:

Router 1
> Active for group 1 and standby for group 3

Router 2
> Active for group 2 and standby for group 3

Router 3
> Active for group 3 and standby for group 1 and group 2

The virtual router for group 1 has the address 10.10.1.11; group 2 has the address 10.10.1.12; and group 3 has the address 10.10.1.13.

Here's the configuration for Router 1:

```
interface ethernet0
  ip address 10.10.1.1 255.255.255.0
  standby 1 priority 120
  standby 1 preempt
  standby 1 ip 10.10.1.11
  standby 3 ip 10.10.1.13
```

Here's the configuration for Router 2:

```
interface ethernet0
  ip address 10.10.1.2 255.255.255.0
  standby 2 priority 120
  standby 2 preempt
  standby 2 ip 10.10.1.12
  standby 3 ip 10.10.1.13
```

And here's the configuration for Router 3:

```
interface ethernet0
  ip address 10.10.1.3 255.255.255.0
  standby 3 priority 120
  standby 3 preempt
  standby 3 ip 10.10.1.13
  standby 1 ip 10.10.1.11
  standby 2 ip 10.10.1.12
```

HSRP groups help your switches behave reasonably as different routers are enabled. Remember that the router automatically generates a virtual MAC address for each HSRP router. If you have your HSRP routers connected to a single switch (or multiple switches VLANed together), the switch will see the same MAC address on different ports as the HSRP routers become active. With HSRP groups, the routers use a unique MAC address for each HSRP group. So, if you do have your HSRP routers plugged into a single switch, you can use multiple HSRP groups to enforce the use of different MAC addresses on different ports, which keeps switches happy.

Load Sharing with Hot Standby

You can use HSRP for a form of load sharing. Think back to Figure 12-1. In this network, we gave all the hosts a default route to the virtual router (10.10.28.3) and configured Router 1 to act as the virtual router unless it failed. This is clearly inefficient, since most of the time Router 2 was doing nothing: all the traffic flowed through Router 1, and Router 2 just waited for Router 1 to break.

In this example, we configure the networks so that Network 1 uses Router 1 as its default route, and Network 2 uses Router 2. To do so, we create two virtual routers, each with its own IP address. Each physical router is the primary router for one of the virtual routers and the backup for the other. With this configuration, Network 1 can use the virtual Router 1 (10.10.28.3) for its default route, and Network 2 can use the virtual Router 2 (10.10.28.4). This way, they will both carry traffic until one of the routers goes down; then the other router will take over all the traffic.

Here's the configuration for Router 1:

```
interface ethernet1
  ip address 10.10.28.1 255.255.255.0
  standby 1 preempt
  standby 1 priority 120
  standby 1 ip 10.10.28.3
  standby 2 ip 10.10.28.4
```

Here's the configuration for Router 2:

```
interface ethernet 1
  ip address 10.10.28.2 255.255.255.0
  standby 2 preempt
  standby 2 priority 120
  standby 2 ip 10.10.28.4
  standby 1 ip 10.10.28.3
```

Devices within Network 1 use 10.10.28.3 as their default router, and devices within Network 2 use 10.10.28.4 as their default router. This configuration provides a primitive form of load sharing across the two networks. If either router goes down, the other takes over.

HSRP show Commands

The command show standby displays all the HSRP information that the router knows about. In this configuration, we can see that HSRP is configured only on Ethernet0:

```
Router1#show standby
Ethernet0 - Group 0
  Local state is Active, priority 120, may preempt
```

```
Hellotime 3 holdtime 10
Next hello sent in 00:00:02.564
Hot standby IP address is 192.168.1.3 configured
Active router is local
Standby router is unknown expires in 00:00:04
Standby virtual mac address is 0000.0c07.ac00
```

Network Address Translation (NAT)

Network Address Translation provides a method for mapping an internal IP address space to an external IP address space. This mapping is beneficial for making smooth transitions to different ISPs, hiding internal IP address, and conserving IP addresses.

To better understand what NAT does, consider Figure 12-2. NAT is configured on our gateway. The serial0 interface is configured with our global Internet address (from the address space given to our network by our ISP). This is the *outside* portion of NAT. The ethernet0 interface, and any devices that are connected to this Ethernet, have addresses that are invisible to the outside world; this is the *inside* portion of NAT.

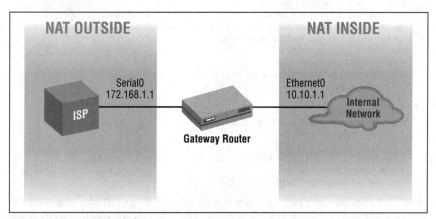

Figure 12-2: NAT example

There are two methods of performing NAT: *static* and *dynamic*. With static translation, each inside address is mapped to a specific outside address. With dynamic translation, possible outside addresses are collected into an address pool and are selected from the pool on an as-needed basis.

Let's look at how to implement the address translation used in Figure 12-2. In this example, the internal network has the address space of 10.10.1.0/24. We need to map these addresses to the external address space, 172.168.1.0/24. First, let's look at the configuration with the static mapping:

```
! Assign IP address for NAT for IP addresses .2 through .10
! (Skip 172.168.1.1 because that is our serial0 interface)
ip nat inside source static 10.10.1.2 172.168.1.2
ip nat inside source static 10.10.1.3 172.168.1.3
ip nat inside source static 10.10.1.4 172.168.1.4
ip nat inside source static 10.10.1.5 172.168.1.5
```

```
ip nat inside source static 10.10.1.6 172.168.1.6
ip nat inside source static 10.10.1.7 172.168.1.7
ip nat inside source static 10.10.1.8 172.168.1.8
ip nat inside source static 10.10.1.9 172.168.1.9
ip nat inside source static 10.10.1.10 172.168.1.10
ip nat inside source static 10.10.1.11 172.168.1.11
!
interface ethernet 0
  ip address 10.10.1.1 255.255.255.0
  ip nat inside
!
interface serial 0
  ip address 172.168.1.1 255.255.255.0
  ip nat outside
```

The static configuration configures only the first 10 IP addresses in our address space, but it's easy to see how to use the rest. Remember that we can't map 172. 168.1.1 because that's the address of the serial0 interface.

Here's the configuration for dynamic NAT. This time, we use our entire global address space, 172.168.1.1 through 172.168.1.254:

```
! Define the IP address pool
! (Leave out 172.168.1.1 because that is our serial 0 interface)
ip nat pool poolone 172.168.1.2 172.168.1.254 netmask 255.255.255.0
ip nat inside source list 20 pool poolone
!
interface ethernet0
  ip address 10.10.1.1 255.255.255.0
  ip nat inside
!
interface serial0
  ip address 172.168.1.1 255.255.255.0
  ip nat outside
!
! Access list for our pool, which is used above to select which IP
! addresses can be translated
access-list 20 permit 10.10.0.0 0.0.255.255
```

Static and dynamic mappings can be combined; just don't include your statically mapped internal addresses in your address pool. This allows you to specify some hosts (such as mail servers) that have a fixed external address but belong to your internal network, while allowing other hosts to be assigned their external address dynamically.

If you're using a bridged configuration, remember that your BVI is the outside interface of your NAT configuration.

Overloading NAT Address Space

If you use the overload command, the pooled NAT address space will be shared among as many internal hosts as possible by multiplexing the ports. In the previous dynamic configuration, changing the third line to the following enables overloading:

```
ip nat inside source list 20 pool poolone overload
```

For example, if an FTP to an Internet host is started from 10.10.1.3, the outbound connection might be mapped to 172.168.1.3. While that connection is going, a telnet connection is started from 10.1.1.4 to another Internet host. This connection might also be mapped to 172.168.1.3. This means that you could have one public IP address shared by hundreds of internal private IP addresses. The router keeps track of what packets belong to what sessions and makes sure that all the packets reach the appropriate destination. This is often called Port Address Translation (PAT), because the router is using the port number to distinguish between different connections using the same address.

In this example, we have one public IP address (172.168.1.2) that is shared by all our hosts on the 10.10.1.0/24 private network:

```
! Define the IP address pool
! (Leave out 172.168.1.1 because that is our serial 0 interface)
ip nat pool poolone 172.168.1.2 172.168.1.2 netmask 255.255.255.0
! Add the overload command
ip nat inside source list 20 pool poolone overload
!
interface ethernet0
  ip address 10.10.1.1 255.255.255.0
  ip nat inside
!
interface serial0
  ip address 172.168.1.1 255.255.255.0
  ip nat outside
!
! Access list for our pool, which is used to select which IP addresses
! should be translated
access-list 20 permit 10.10.0.0 0.0.255.255
```

The previous configuration, which creates an explicit external address pool and then uses it to map inside addresses, is the most common way to set up address translation. But in this case, where you're creating a pool that has only a single IP address, there's a shortcut. You can omit the ip nat pool command and instead tell the ip nat inside command to use the IP address of your serial interface for translations.* The result looks like this:

```
! Define IP address translation (PAT) without using an address pool
ip nat inside source list 20 interface serial0 overload
!
interface ethernet0
  ip address 10.10.1.1 255.255.255.0
  ip nat inside
!
interface serial0
  ip address 172.168.1.1 255.255.255.0
  ip nat outside
!
! Access list for our pool, which is used to select which IP addresses
! should be translated
access-list 20 permit 10.10.0.0 0.0.255.255
```

---

* This version of the ip nat inside command appears to have been added to IOS only recently, so it probably won't work with older versions of IOS.

Mapping incoming ports to different NAT addresses

One of the drawbacks of having all your internal IP addresses mapped to one external address is that you don't have room for adding external services. That is, if you want to run a web server or any other public service, that machine's address must be visible to the outside world. With the kinds of dynamic address translation we've seen so far, that isn't the case—a host isn't visible to the outside world until it initiates a connection, and even then, its address might be shared. If someone from the Internet tries to start a connection to an internal server using a shared address, how will the router know which machine should receive the packets?

Let's take this example a step further. What if you want to run a web server and a mail server? You could put both on the same machine and create one static mapping to a single external address. Or you could put the mail and web servers on different machines and create static mappings to two external addresses. But what if you want the servers on different machines and you want only one external address?

The solution to this problem is static PAT. To do the port-based translation, we use the keyword extendable, which allows us to map UDP and TCP ports to internal addresses. In this example, we have one unique global IP address (172. 168.1.1) mapped to our internal network (10.10.1.0/24) using the overload keyword. We want our incoming email traffic (port 25) to go to 10.10.1.5, and our incoming web traffic (port 80) to go to 10.10.1.4. The following configuration handles this:

```
! Use PAT to overload our internal IP space 10.10.1.0/24 to
! one external IP address 172.168.1.1 (serial0's IP address)
ip nat inside source list 20 interface Serial0 overload
! Map incoming mail (port 25) to device 10.10.1.5
ip nat inside source static tcp 10.10.1.5 23 172.168.1.1 25 extendable
! Map incoming web (port 80) to device 10.10.1.4
ip nat inside source static tcp 10.10.1.4 80 172.168.1.1 80 extendable
!
access-list 20 permit 10.10.0.0 0.0.255.255
```

By changing the port type, you can do translations based on UDP ports as well:

```
ip nat inside source static udp 10.10.1.6 172.168.1.1 69 extendable
```

NAT show Commands

show ip nat statistics and show IP nat translations are the two most helpful show commands for NAT. The statistics show the total number of translations, the interfaces configured for NAT, the hits (the number of times the router looked in the NAT table and found a match), the misses (the number of times the router looked in the NAT table and didn't find an entry), and the number of translations that have expired:

```
Router1#show ip nat statistics
Total translations: 1 (0 static, 1 dynamic; 0 extended)
Outside interfaces: Serial0
Inside interfaces: Ethernet0
Hits: 9  Misses: 1
Expired translations: 0
```

```
Dynamic mappings:
-- Inside Source
access-list 20 pool poolone refcount 1
 pool poolone: netmask 255.255.255.0
         start 172.168.1.2 end 172.168.1.2
         type generic, total addresses 1, allocated 1 (100%), misses 1
```

show ip nat translations simply shows all the NAT translations that are currently occurring.

```
Router1#show ip nat translations
Pro Inside global     Inside local      Outside local     Outside global
--- 172.168.1.2       10.10.1.1         ---               ---
```

This output shows the inside mapping of the local address 10.10.1.1 to the outside global address of 172.168.1.2.

There's one other essential command. It's possible for dynamic address translation to get confused. When this happens, translated traffic stops flowing through the router. There's a simple fix: clear ip nat translations *. The asterisk means to clear all dynamic translations. You can replace it with the address of a particular translation, but that usually isn't worth the effort.

Tunnels

Tunnels take packets from one network, encapsulate them within an IP protocol, and transfer them to another network. This sounds inefficient, and in a sense it is. Why would you want to take perfectly good packets, wrap them up in some other protocol, send them to another location, and unwrap them? For two reasons. First, many protocols can't be routed. If you want to connect two sites using nonroutable protocols, the only way to do so is to wrap the nonroutable protocols within a routable protocol, such as IP. Second, it's increasingly common to use the Internet to connect remote sites to a central office. But this connection has its perils, the most significant of which is security. Do you really want corporate data flowing over the public Internet? To minimize security problems, you can establish a tunnel between the offices and then encrypt all the traffic on the tunnel.

In this section, we'll first look at how to establish a tunnel, then at how to encrypt the traffic traveling over the tunnel. We won't discuss encapsulating nonroutable protocols within IP in any detail. Figure 12-3 shows two offices connected by an ISP. The ISP has assigned two IP addresses for our use: 192.168.1.1 and 192.168.10.2.1. The network numbers used by Offices 1 and 2 are 10.10.1.0/24 and 10.10.2.0/24, respectively.

Here's the configuration for Office 1:

```
hostname Office1
!
! Configure the interface tunnel
interface tunnel1
    ! Use an unnummbered IP address to stay in sync with serial0 and make our
    ! configuration easier
    ip unnumbered serial0
    ! Set up the tunnel's source IP and destination IP, and enable checksums
    tunnel source serial0
```

```
  tunnel destination 198.168.2.1
  tunnel checksum
  ! GRE IP is the default tunnel mode, so this command is optional
  ! GRE IP stands for Generic Route Encapsulation over IP
  tunnel mode gre ip
  no shutdown
!
! Configure the serial interface
interface serial0
  ip address 198.168.1.1 255.255.255.0
  no shutdown
!
! Our ISP is our default route
ip route 0.0.0.0 0.0.0.0 192.168.1.2
! Set up a static route to the other side of the tunnel
ip route 10.10.2.0 255.255.255.0 tunnel1
```

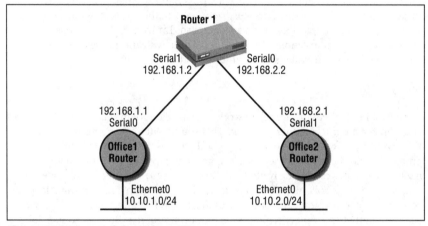

Figure 12-3: A tunnel through an ISP

The trickiest part of the configuration is the routing. We set up a static default route, and then set up a more specific static route that sends any traffic destined for 10.10.2.0 through the tunnel.

Here's the configuration for Office 2; it's very similar to that for Office 1:

```
hostname Office2
!
! Configure the interface tunnel
! We used a different name here (tunnel2) just to show that they
! don't have to match.
interface tunnel2
  ! Use an unnummbered IP address to stay in sync with serial0 and make our
  ! configuration easier
  ip unnumbered serial1
  ! Set up the tunnel's source IP and destination IP, and enable checksums
  tunnel source serial1
  tunnel destination 198.168.1.1
  tunnel checksum
  ! GRE IP is the default tunnel mode, so this command is optional
  ! GRE IP stands for Generic Route Encapsulation over IP
  tunnel mode gre ip
```

```
    no shutdown
!
! Configure the serial interface
interface serial1
    ip address 198.168.2.1 255.255.255.0
!
! Default route
ip route 0.0.0.0 0.0.0.0 192.168.2.2
! Set up a static route to the other side of the tunnel
ip route 10.10.1.0 255.255.255.255 tunnel1
```

We can ping Office 2 from Office 1 using the tunnel:

```
Office1#ping 10.10.2.1

Type escape sequence to abort.
Sending 5, 100-byte ICMP Echos to 10.10.2.1, timeout is 2 seconds:
!!!!!
Success rate is 100 percent (5/5), round-trip min/avg/max = 68/68/68 ms
```

show Commands for Tunnels

The most useful show commands for tunnels are two that we've already seen: show ip route and show interface. This makes sense—tunnels are really just special interfaces, and the most difficult problem with creating tunnels is getting the routing to work correctly.

The command show ip route shows that we have an active route for the 10.10.2.0 network through the tunnel1 interface:

```
office1#show ip route
Codes: C - connected, S - static, I - IGRP, R - RIP, M - mobile, B - BGP
       D - EIGRP, EX - EIGRP external, O - OSPF, IA - OSPF inter area
       N1 - OSPF NSSA external type 1, N2 - OSPF NSSA external type 2
       E1 - OSPF external type 1, E2 - OSPF external type 2, E - EGP
       i - IS-IS, L1 - IS-IS level-1, L2 - IS-IS level-2, * - candidate default
       U - per-user static route, o - ODR

Gateway of last resort is 192.168.1.2 to network 0.0.0.0

     10.0.0.0/24 is subnetted, 2 subnets
C       10.10.1.0 is directly connected, Ethernet0
S       10.10.2.0 is directly connected, Tunnel1
C    192.168.1.0/24 is directly connected, Serial0
S*   0.0.0.0/0 [1/0] via 192.168.1.2
```

The command show interface tunnel1 gives results like any other show interface command. We see that the interface is up, the hardware associated with the interface is Tunnel (i.e., this is a virtual interface rather than a specific hardware interface), the encapsulation is TUNNEL, and the source and destination ports are properly set.

```
office1#show interface tunnel 1
Tunnel1 is up, line protocol is up
  Hardware is Tunnel
  Interface is unnumbered.  Using address of Serial0 (192.168.1.1)
  MTU 1514 bytes, BW 9 Kbit, DLY 500000 usec, rely 255/255, load 1/255
  Encapsulation TUNNEL, loopback not set, keepalive set (10 sec)
  Tunnel source 192.168.1.1 (Serial0), destination 192.168.2.1
```

```
Tunnel protocol/transport GRE/IP, key disabled, sequencing disabled
Checksumming of packets enabled,  fast tunneling enabled
Last input never, output never, output hang never
Last clearing of "show interface" counters never
Queueing strategy: fifo
Output queue 0/0, 0 drops; input queue 0/75, 0 drops
5 minute input rate 0 bits/sec, 0 packets/sec
5 minute output rate 0 bits/sec, 0 packets/sec
   0 packets input, 0 bytes, 0 no buffer
   Received 0 broadcasts, 0 runts, 0 giants, 0 throttles
   0 input errors, 0 CRC, 0 frame, 0 overrun, 0 ignored, 0 abort
   0 packets output, 0 bytes, 0 underruns
   0 output errors, 0 collisions, 0 interface resets
   0 output buffer failures, 0 output buffers swapped out
```

Encrypted Tunnels

In the previous example, we created a tunnel that could carry traffic between routers, but we didn't do anything to secure that traffic: the traffic went through the tunnel without any sort of encryption, so anyone with a packet sniffer and access to our network could see what was traveling through the tunnel. Since one of the biggest applications for tunneling is increased security, cryptography is essential. In this section, we'll explore two ways to encrypt the traffic flowing through the tunnel. First, we will use DSS and DES on a router running Version 11.3 of IOS. Depending on the feature set of your IOS, this form of encryption might be all that's available. (If other encryption methods, such as RSA, are available on your router, the configuration should be the same.) Next, we will look at encryption using IPSec, which is a security protocol that belongs to the TCP/IP protocol suite. The IPSec examples assume that you are using IOS Version 12.0 (or greater).

Tunnel Encryption with DSS and DES

Regardless of the type of encryption you use, an encrypted tunnel requires the generation of public and private keys, some form of authentication and key exchange (each end of the tunnel has to prove that it is who it says it is), and something to encrypt the actual traffic. In this example, we will use DSS (the Digital Signature Standard) for authentication and key exchange. Each host must generate private and public keys, and the hosts must exchange their public keys before traffic can flow. We use DES (the Digital Encryption Standard) for encryption. DES is now considered a relatively weak form of encryption, but it's still useful if your security needs aren't that great.

Generating keys

DSS requires us to generate public and private keys on each router. The routers at each end of the tunnel must share their public keys, which are used to encrypt and decrypt the messages sent across the tunnel. The private keys, of course, are never sent anywhere.

To generate a key pair, you must first use the zeroize command to erase any keys that are currently in the router's memory. (zeroize breaks any encryption that has already been configured. If you already have a key pair, skip this process and use the show command to display your public key.) Then use the command `crypto key generate` to generate the key pair:

```
office1(config)#crypto key zeroize dss
Warning! Zeroize will remove your DSS signature keys.
Do you want to continue? [yes/no]: yes
% Keys to be removed are named office1.
Do you really want to remove these keys? [yes/no]: yes
% Zeroize done.
office1(config)#crypto key generate dss office1
Generating DSS keys ....
  [OK]
```

Now use the command `show crypto key mypubkey dss` to display the key:

```
office1#show crypto key mypubkey dss
Key name: office1
 Serial number: 10609455
 Usage: Signature Key
 Key Data:
  E3F9ECB2 73841C55 42DBFFF4 10245836 0291EC42 8F97FF5E FA2B0314 AF29E520
  407004D5 70AA888C 88B25313 FACD03B6 6608D9EB F0F7C4D0 A679F408 F7E90C5F
```

You must generate a key for each router that will be using this encryption method. Before going any further, save your keys by doing a `copy running-config startup-config`. If you don't, you will lose your keys the next time you reboot.

Configuring encryption on the tunnel

To encrypt our tunnel, we need a crypto map. Defining the map is relatively simple. We give it a name, an encryption method, and an access list. The name allows us to apply the map to the desired interfaces, the encryption method specifies how we want to perform encryption, and the access list ensures that we encrypt only traffic headed to the destination. In this example, we don't want to encrypt all the traffic that goes out the serial interface; we want to encrypt only traffic for the remote office.

The trickiest part of this configuration is to remember that you have to apply the crypto map both to the physical interface the tunnel uses and to the tunnel interface itself.

Here is the configuration for Office 1, with encryption enabled:

```
hostname office1
!
! Define office2's public key using the pubkey-chain command. Older versions of
! the IOS use only the crypto public-key command.
crypto key pubkey-chain dss
 named-key office2 signature
  serial-number 06897848
  key-string
   91A48507 2AC44FB3 C0EDBA3C B87C8F14 E2729110 6734DE5F 509C4476 1117E427
   B157882D B240CD84 2105C0FA 7F00C6B8 2493C4A7 A5C036A8 9E408D91 D5B73870
  quit
!
! Define our crypto map. We named it tunnelmap. The 5 is just a sequence number.
crypto map tunnelmap 5
 set peer office2
 ! Encrypt with 40-bit DES, our only choice on this router's IOS version
```

```
   set algorithm 40-bit-des
   ! Only encrypt traffic for the tunnel with access list 101
   match address 101
   !
 interface Tunnel1
   ip unnumbered Serial0
   tunnel source Serial0
   tunnel destination 192.168.2.1
   tunnel checksum
   ! Apply the crypto map to the tunnel
   crypto map tunnelmap
   !
 interface Ethernet0
   ip address 10.10.1.1 255.255.255.0
   !
 interface Serial0
   ip address 192.168.1.1 255.255.255.0
   ! Don't forget to apply the crypto map here
   crypto map tunnelmap
   !
 ! Static route to our provider
 ip route 0.0.0.0 0.0.0.0 192.168.1.2
 ! Route all tunnel traffic through the tunnel
 ip route 10.10.2.0 255.255.255.0 Tunnel1
 !
 ! Our access list is only one line long. Optionally, we could have used the
 ! keyword "ip" instead of "gre". This access list says encrypt tunnel traffic
 ! from our host to the destination
 access-list 101 permit gre host 192.168.1.1 host 192.168.2.1
```

And here is the configuration for Office 2:

```
 hostname office2
 !
 ! Define office1's public key using the pubkey-chain command. Older versions of
 ! the IOS use only the crypto public-key command.
 crypto key pubkey-chain dss
   named-key office1 signature
     serial-number 10609455
     key-string
     9FFA2039 F4642B77 21A6FBA7 5179E1D8 211DD211 DA96699C 2045730D AB033253
     8A101977 B6580054 FEDBA12E 97F6B1BE 0D40EFB1 6F62ABBC 952F6DAF BB87BE60
     quit
 !
 ! Define our crypto map. We named it tunnelmap. The 5 is just a sequence number.
 crypto map tunnelmap 5
   set peer office1
   ! Encrypt with 40-bit DES, our only choice on this router's IOS version.
   set algorithm 40-bit-des
   ! Only encrypt traffic for the tunnel with access list 101
   match address 101
   !
 interface Tunnel1
   ip unnumbered Serial1
   tunnel source Serial1
   tunnel destination 192.168.1.1
   ! Apply the crypto map to the tunnel
   crypto map tunnelmap
   !
 interface Ethernet0
```

```
ip address 10.10.2.1 255.255.255.0
!
interface Serial1
 ip address 192.168.2.1 255.255.255.0
 clockrate 64000
 ! Don't forget to apply the crypto map to this interface
 crypto map tunnelmap
!
! Static route to our provider
ip route 0.0.0.0 0.0.0.0 192.168.2.2
!
! Route all tunnel traffic through the tunnel
ip route 10.10.1.0 255.255.255.0 Tunnel1
!
! Our access list is only one line long. Optionally, we could have used the
! keyword "ip" instead of "gre". This access list says encrypt tunnel traffic
! from our host to the destination
access-list 101 permit gre host 192.168.2.1 host 192.168.1.1
```

This configuration requires you to create the keys, and then cut and paste them into your router's configuration. That's clearly an awkward, error-prone process. It's possible to perform the key exchange automatically. Take the following steps:

1. On one router, start the key exchange in passive mode. After you press Enter to confirm, the router will wait for another router to initiate a key exchange connection:

   ```
   office1(config)#crypto key exchange dss passive
   Enter escape character to abort if connection does not complete.
   Wait for connection from peer[confirm]
   Waiting....
   ```

2. On the other router, start the key exchange in active mode, supplying the IP address of the first router and the name of the key you want to send to the other router. This is the name given to the key when it was created. After sending the key, the router asks you whether it should wait for a key from the first (passive) router; press Enter to confirm. In the following example, we initiate a key exchange to 192.168.1.1 and send the key named office2:

   ```
   office2(config)#crypto key exchange dss 192.168.1.1 office2
   Public key for office2:
   Serial Number 06897848
   Fingerprint   91A4 8507 2AC4 4FB3

   Wait for peer to send a key[confirm]
   Waiting ....
   ```

3. The first (passive) router receives the key sent by the active router, then asks whether you want to send a key in return. If you have more than one key configured on this router, it will ask you to select which key to send. In this example, we send the key office1 back to the active router:

   ```
   Send peer a key in return[confirm]<Return>
   Which one?
        some-other-key? [yes]: n
        office1? [yes]:<Return>
        Public key for office1:
   Serial Number 06897848
   Fingerprint   91A4 8507 2AC4 4FB3
   ```

4. The second (active) router confirms that it has received the key from the first router.

```
Public key for office1:
Serial Number 10609455
Fingerprint   E3F9 ECB2 7384 1C55
Add this public key to the configuration? [yes/no]: y
```

Now you have configured the keys on each of your routers without having to cut and paste the long key values.

DES Tunnel show Commands

When you're working with DES tunnels, a few show commands are particularly useful.

show crypto engine connections active

This command shows all active encrypted connections:

```
office2#show crypto engine connections active
ID   Interface     IP-Address     State   Algorithm     Encrypt Decrypt
13   Serial1       192.168.2.1    set     DES_40_CFB64    10      0
```

The ID is useful for the clear crypto connection command, which allows you to remove a connection from the map. Clearing a connection is sometimes useful when you suspect that things aren't working when you are first configuring encryption. After you issue a clear, the connection is re-established, which causes the key exchange to occur again.

show crypto engine configuration

This command summarizes the currently running encryption:

```
office2#show crypto engine configuration
crypto engine name:    office2
crypto engine type:    software
serial number:         06897848
crypto engine state:   dss key generated
crypto lib version:    10.0.0

platform:              rp crypto engine

Encryption Process Info:
input queue top:    103
input queue bot:    103
input queue count:  0
```

IPSec Tunneling

IPSec has significant advantages over the other available tunneling methods. Some of these advantages are:

- Multivendor support

- Automatic key management, which makes it much more scalable

- Compression before encryption

IPSec consists of four components. You really don't need to understand all of these pieces, but it is good to know what they mean when you see them in the configuration. The components are:

AH (Authentication Headers)
Provides strong cryptographic checksums for packets

ESP (Encapsulating Security Payload)
Guarantees that your packet wasn't intercepted in transit

IPcomp (IP Compression)
Compresses packets prior to encryption

IKE (Internet Key Exchange)
Manages the keys

In this section, we configure IPSec tunneling for the network in Figure 12-3. Although it looks more complex, this configuration is really quite similar to the configuration of the previous section. Some new items are configuring the IKE policy, setting the key, and setting the transform set.

To configure the IKE policy, we use the command `crypto isakmp policy`. The argument to this command is a priority value; the lower the number, the higher the policy's priority. In this example, the priority isn't important, but it is conceivable that a router will have several policies to choose from (possibly because it creates tunnels to different destinations). In this case, the router will use the highest-priority policy that both ends of the tunnel can agree on. The policy itself does two things: it sets the authentication hash algorithm to MD5, and it sets the authentication method to pre-share. The default hashing algorithm is SHA (Secure Hash Algorithm), but it doesn't matter which hash algorithm you use as long as both ends of the tunnel agree. Pre-share tells the router that it should use pre-shared keys.

To configure pre-shared keys, we use the command `crypto isakmp key`. This command is simple; we provide a name for the key (`officekey`, in this case) followed by the peer's IP address (the address of `office2`). Remember that this key must be the same on both routers.

To configure the transform set, we use the command `crypto ipsec transform-set`. This command defines the protocols used in the set. In this example, we use the transform set `esp-des esp-md5-hmac`, which specifies DES for ESP and MD5 for the authentication algorithm. Other protocol combinations that can be used are `ah-md5-hmac`, `esp-des`, `esp-3des`, `esp-md5-hmac`, `ah-sha-hmac`, `aesp-des`, and `comp-lzs`. Again, the crucial thing isn't the actual protocols you use, but that the protocols on either end of the tunnel agree. The transform set is assigned a name, which in this case is `office1-to-office2`. In our example, we used the same name for the transform set on each router—this will help you to preserve your sanity.

Finally, we create a crypto map, which specifies the `ipsec-isakmp` protocol, the peer address, the transform set, and the access list. Then we create a tunnel interface, to which we apply the crypto map.

Here's the configuration for Office 1:

```
hostname office1
!
! First we define the IKE policy. We are going to use MD5 and a pre-shared
! key that will be defined on both routers.
crypto isakmp policy 25
 hash md5
 authentication pre-share
!
! This command defines the pre-shared key we mentioned.
! This key must be the same on both routers. The IP address is
! that of the peer (office2, in this case).
crypto isakmp key officekey address 192.168.2.1
!
! This command sets the transform set we are going to use. The name can be
! different on each router, but the protocol list must be the same.
crypto ipsec transform-set office1-to-office2 esp-des esp-md5-hmac
 mode transport
!
! Define the crypto map. Since we are using IKE, this map is fairly simple
crypto map tunnelmap 10 ipsec-isakmp
 set peer 192.168.2.1
 ! Point to the transform set we configured earlier
 set transform-set office1-to-office2
 match address 101
!
interface Tunnel1
 ip unnumbered Serial0
 tunnel source Serial0
 tunnel destination 192.168.2.1
 tunnel checksum
 crypto map tunnelmap
!
interface Ethernet0
 ip address 10.10.1.1 255.255.255.0
!
interface Serial0
 ip address 192.168.1.1 255.255.255.0
 clockrate 64000
 crypto map tunnelmap
!
ip route 0.0.0.0 0.0.0.0 192.168.1.2
ip route 10.10.2.0 255.255.255.0 Tunnel1
!
access-list 101 permit gre host 192.168.1.1 host 192.168.2.1
```

Here's the configuration for Office 2:

```
hostname Office2
!
! First we define the IKE policy. We are going to use MD5 and a pre-shared
! key that will be defined on both routers.
crypto isakmp policy 25
 hash md5
 authentication pre-share
!
! This command defines the pre-shared key we mentioned above.
! This key must be the same on both routers. The IP address is
! that of the peer (office1, in this case).
```

```
crypto isakmp key officekey address 192.168.1.1
!
! This command sets the transform set we are going to use. The name can be
! different on each router, but the protocol list must be the same.
crypto ipsec transform-set office1-to-office2 esp-des esp-md5-hmac
 mode transport
!
!
! Define the crypto map. Since we are using IKE, this map is fairly simple
crypto map tunnelmap 10 ipsec-isakmp
 set peer 192.168.1.1
 set transform-set office1-to-office2
 match address 101
!
interface Tunnel1
 ip unnumbered Serial1
 tunnel source Serial1
 tunnel destination 192.168.1.1
 tunnel checksum
 crypto map tunnelmap
!
interface Ethernet0
 ip address 10.10.2.1 255.255.255.0
!
interface Serial1
 ip address 192.168.2.1 255.255.255.0
 crypto map tunnelmap
!
ip route 0.0.0.0 0.0.0.0 192.168.2.2
!
ip route 10.10.1.0 255.255.255.0 Tunnel1
!
access-list 101 permit gre host 192.168.2.1 host 192.168.1.1
```

To show that our IPSec configuration is working, we use the show crypto engine command:

```
office2#show crypto engine connections active

    ID Interface      IP-Address      State  Algorithm            Encrypt  Decrypt
    22 Serial1        192.168.2.1     set    HMAC_MD5+DES_56_CB        10        0
```

In this output, we can see the encrypted connection and the algorithm used to do the encryption.

CHAPTER 13

Router Security

Before deploying a router, you should secure it: that is, you should do everything you can to prevent the router from being misused, either by people within your own organization or by intruders from the outside. This chapter describes the first simple steps you can take toward router security; however, it's not a complete discussion by any means. I don't do anything more than point you in the right direction.

The enable Password

The enable password grants the user access to your complete router configuration. Therefore, it should be guarded carefully. In previous chapters, I showed how to set your enable password:

```
enable password mypassword
```

The problem with setting the password this way is that mypassword is your actual password; anyone looking over your configuration files can see the password, and at that point, it's no longer a secret. Generally speaking, the accepted wisdom for managing passwords is that they should never be written down in clear text—not even in a configuration file that you think no one has access to. Obviously, there are plenty of ways for a clear-text password to leak out: for example, you might print the configuration file so you can take it home to think through some arcane route-redistribution problem and forget that the password is clearly visible to anyone hanging around the printer.

The solution to this problem is to use some sort of encryption. The simplest way to enable encryption is to use the command service password-encryption:

```
service password-encryption
enable password some-password
```

Now when you do a **show configuration**, your password is no longer visible in clear text:

```
Router#show configuration
version 11.3
service password-encryption
!
hostname Router1
!
enable password 7 095F41041C480713181F13253920
```

Now your password isn't clearly visible to anyone casually looking over your shoulder. However, you haven't accomplished as much as you might have hoped. The 7 in the **enable password** command, as it appears in the configuration file, indicates that the password has been encrypted with type 7 encryption, which is very weak. Type 7 encryption uses a simple exclusive-OR algorithm that protects the password from casual observers but does nothing to stop a determined attacker.

To use a stronger form of encryption, give the following command:

```
enable secret some-password
```

Now, when we look at the configuration, we see a slightly different take on our **enable** password:

```
enable secret 5 $1$TbpU$nvCOm4OInOhvguatfNq5mO
```

The encrypted form of the password looks equally inscrutable. But this time, the password is encrypted using an MD5 hash (indicated by the number 5 in the configuration). This algorithm should be resistant even to determined intruders. However, don't relax. It's possible to crack the encryption used here with a brute-force dictionary attack. It's still a good idea to prevent others from seeing the encrypted password. So, for example, if you're trying to solve a problem by asking a question in a newsgroup or mailing list and you want to include your configuration, it's a good idea to remove the hashed password.

Privilege Levels

Privilege levels allow certain users to have access to certain **exec** commands. Allowing users to have access to certain commands, without giving them access to everything, is often useful: for example, you can allow some users to clear a line that is hung, without giving them the ability to trash the entire configuration.

To set up a privilege level, first create an **enable** password with a privilege level assigned to it:

```
enable secret password level 10 ourpassword
```

This command assigns the password **ourpassword** to privilege level 10. Next, assign commands for this level with the **privilege** command:

```
privilege exec level 10 clear line
privilege exec level 10 show running
```

Now users can enter privilege level 10 by giving the following command, followed by the correct password when they are prompted:

```
Router>enable 10
```

After entering the password, a user can give the commands clear line and show running, but not other privileged-mode commands.

Features to Disable on Your Gateway Routers

Your gateway router is the most vulnerable to attacks, especially if it sits outside of your firewall. Table 13-1 lists a number of services that should be disabled to heighten security. The Level column shows whether the command is part of the global configuration or needs to be applied to specific interfaces.

Table 13-1: Features to disable on the router for heightened security

Command	Level	Resulting action
no ip proxy-arp	Interface	Ignores incoming ARP requests for hosts within the network.
no ip directed-broadcast	Interface	Disables translations of directed broadcasts to physical broadcasts.
no ip unreachables	Interface	Disables ICMP unreachable messages on an interface.
no ip redirects	Interface	Disables redirect messages. A redirect message is generated to another device when a datagram is sent out over the same interface through which it was received. The redirect message tells the sending host that it should have been able to get to the destination without going through the router. Redirects have played a role in a number of attacks, so it's safest to disable them.
no ip source-route	Global	Causes the router to discard any packet with source-route information. Presumably, we don't want hosts telling our router how to route the traffic.
no service finger	Global	Disables the finger daemon on the router. Finger has always been a problem source; it lets attackers know who is logged in and provides the user's real user-name. Now all they need is a password!
no service udp-small-servers no service tcp-small-servers	Global	Disables all small UDP and TCP services on your router (*echo*, *chargen*, and some others). These are services that outsiders shouldn't see anyway.

Use a Warning Banner

To properly secure a machine, you need to supply a warning banner. The banner doesn't actually do anything to protect the router, but it does warn people who are connecting to the router that unauthorized access is taken seriously. That way, they can't use the excuse that they didn't know. It's a good idea to ask for legal help in crafting an appropriate message.

The following commands create a warning banner:

```
! Apply a warning banner.
! Seek legal advice to craft a banner to properly protect your network
banner login ^C
        #### WARNING ####
        Authorized Access ONLY!
```

```
All connections are logged and monitored. Any unauthorized
use will be prosecuted to the fullest extent of the law. If
you do not agree to these conditions, disconnect now.
^C
```

Protect VTYs with an Access List

When you telnet to your router, you connect to a VTY (virtual terminal). This terminal lets you configure your router over the network, without a physical connection to the console port. This capability is extremely useful, but also dangerous: if you can configure your router over the network, so can anyone else with the appropriate passwords. One way to make the router more secure is to apply an access list to the VTY ports. This list should allow connections only from certain hosts. The following commands restrict telnet access to the 192.168.1.5 machine. We also apply an exec-timeout, which disconnects idle connections:

```
! Define the access list
access-list 5 permit 192.168.1.5 0.0.0.0
!
line vty 0 4
  ! Only allow telnet
  tranport input telnet
  ! Apply our access list for incoming connections
  access-class 5 in
  ! Finally, apply an exec-timeout, which will disconnect an idle connection
  ! The timeout is 10 minutes and 0 seconds
  exec-timeout 10 0
   Users and Authentication
```

Usernames are optional: many routers have a single password, which is given to everyone who needs access to the router. However, doing without usernames has obvious problems: you can never tell who is logged in, who just rebooted the router, or who is responsible for the configuration changes that broke your Internet connection. Usernames and passwords make it possible to trace who has done what; they add a sense of accountability and allow more fine-grained control over what individuals are allowed to do.

There are several methods for adding users; the more advanced methods allow accounting (tracking what a particular user actually did) as well as authorization (merely verifying that a user has permission to do something). First, let's look at the easiest way to add users to a router's configuration.

The Easy, Unscalable Way

Throughout this book, we have added username and password pairs to the router configuration itself. For example, we can add the users Patty and Pete to the router's configuration with the username command:

```
! First, enable password encryption to "hide" the
! clear-text passwords in the configuration
service password-encryption
! Now define the passwords
username patty password patty1
username pete password pete2
```

Patty's password is now `patty1`, and Pete's password is `pete2`. When we display the router's configuration, we see the passwords in their encrypted form:

```
username pete password 7 0831495A0C4B
```

Now that the passwords are in the configuration, Patty and Pete can log in when they connect to the router. That was certainly simple. But this method doesn't scale—it's not manageable if you need to work with more than a few users and one or two routers. What if you're managing a worldwide corporate network with hundreds of routers and dozens of administrators? What if you're managing an ISP with thousands of dial-up users? In either case, you have a long list of usernames and passwords that needs to be maintained on several different machines. How do you keep the lists in sync? How would you even keep them up to date?

There is a better way. Make a central authentication repository using an authentication protocol, and configure the router to use the authentication server. There are several different protocols that you can use, but the most popular are XTACACS, Radius, and TACACS+. TACACS+ uses the AAA protocol and is supported by the CiscoSecure product.

TACACS and Extended TACACS (XTACACS)

The Terminal Access Controller Access Control System (TACACS) is the oldest of the authentication protocols commonly used on Cisco routers. Its features are limited, and it has largely been replaced by extended TACACS (XTACACS) or by an even newer variant, TACACS+. TACACS was originally an open standard, but its descendants are proprietary Cisco protocols; they aren't supported by other router vendors. Of these three protocols, TACACS+ is the only one that uses encryption. The examples in this section use XTACACS.

Before we can run any of these authentication protocols, we need to set up an authentication server. In the past, XTACACS was available for download from *http://www.cisco.com*. However, this software is unsupported, hard to find, and doesn't compile easily on new operating systems. If you are able to obtain a copy of the XTACACS server and configure it, you can then configure your routers to use it. The following configuration sets up our router to use an XTACACS server at address 10.10.2.1:

```
! our XTACACS server's IP address
tacacs-server host 10.10.2.1
! if the TACACS server isn't available, use the enable password as a last-ditch
! method for gaining access.
tacacs-server last-resort password
! we are using XTACACS
tacacs-server extended
! notify the TACACS server of connections
tacacs-server notify connections
! notifty the TACACS server of enable mode
tacacs-server notify enable
! notify the TACACS server when someone logs out
tacacs-server notify logout
```

That's the basic setup. Next, we need to tell the router's login commands to use XTACACS for usernames and passwords:

```
line 1 8
 ! Timeout of 30 minutes
 exec-timeout 30 0
 login tacacs
 transport input all
```

And that's it. Getting the server going is a pain, but configuring your routers is relatively simple.

AAA (TACACS+)

The authentication, authorization, and accounting model (AAA) is a framework for providing authentication and accounting services across a network. It requires the support of another protocol—typically, Radius or TACACS+. Radius is an open standard (though not yet a full Internet standard) that is supported by a wide range of devices and vendors. Both Radius and TACACS+ encrypt sensitive data.

In this example, we will use Radius to handle authentication for incoming PPP connections. AAA lets us provide PPP authentication, authorization, and accounting (i.e., logging PPP sessions). As with XTACACS, we'll need to set up a server. In this case, though, finding server software isn't hard. You can download software from several sources, including *http://www.livingston.com:80/marketing/products/radius. html, http://www.freeradius.org*, and *http://www.funk.com/RADIUS/*. After you've set up the server and populated its database with usernames and passwords, you're ready to configure the router:

```
! This is required for access to use the AAA method
aaa new-model
!
! Configure the Radius server
radius-server host 10.10.1.2
radius-server key somepassword
!
! Now configure AAA for authentication/authorization/accounting
aaa authentication ppp dialins radius
aaa authorization network radius local
aaa accounting network start-stop radius
```

Note that the router has its own key (essentially a password) for communication with the Radius server. As with XTACACS, after telling the router how to communicate with the server, we need to configure our async lines and interfaces so that they will get their login information from the Radius server:

```
line 1 8
  autoselect ppp
  autoselect during-login
  modem dialin
!
interface group-async 1
  group-range 1 8
  encapsulation ppp
  async mode interactive
  ppp authentication chap dialins
```

For more information on what can be done with the AAA protocol, refer to Chapter 15.

CHAPTER 14

Troubleshooting and Logging

This chapter covers a grab bag of techniques for troubleshooting and monitoring your router. The two tasks are closely related: it's impossible to figure out what's going wrong if you don't have good logs that show what the router was trying (or failing) to do. We'll start with *ping* and *trace*, two tools that are available on virtually any computer that can connect to a network.

ping

ping tests network connectivity by sending an ICMP echo-request message to the remote machine. The remote machine must respond with an ICMP reply message. The ping command takes a single argument: the address or hostname of the remote system. It prints various statistics about the responses it receives:

```
Router>ping 10.10.1.2
Type escape sequence to abort
Sending 5, 100-byte ICMP Echos to 10.10.1.2, timeout is 2 seconds:
!!!!!
Success rate is 100 percent (5/5), round-trip min/avg/max = 1/2/4 ms
Router>
```

Each exclamation point indicates that the router has successfully received a response from the remote host. On a local network, you would expect a success rate very close to 100%. Across the Internet, you would tolerate some failures, but they should still be relatively rare. Many sites configure their routers to block ICMP traffic because it has been used in a number of denial-of-service attacks. Therefore, you can't count on the ability to ping an arbitrary host on the Internet.

 If *ping* locks up, you can abort by typing Ctrl+^ then x. See the "Command-Line Editing Keys" section in Chapter 1 for more information on the abort key sequence.

If you don't give the hostname on the command line, the router prompts you for it, and for other information. You can specify the number of packets to send, the number of seconds to wait for a response before assuming that the ping has failed, the amount of data to include in the packet, and more:

```
Router>ping
  Protocol [ip]: ip              We are doing IP only
  Target IP address: 10.10.1.2   The host we want to ping
  Repeat count [5]: 10           Number of pings to be sent to the destination
  Datagram size [100]:           The actual size of the packet in bytes
  Timeout in seconds [2]:        Timeout value
  Extended commands [n]:         See the Privileged Ping Commands
  Sweep range of sizes [n]:      Changes the packet size as it pings

Type escape sequence to abort.
Sending 10, 100-byte ICMP Echos to 10.10.1.2, timeout is 2 seconds:
!!!!!!!!!!
Success rate is 100 percent (10/10), round-trip min/avg/max = 1/3/4 ms
```

Here we changed the repeat count to 10, which sent 10 ping packets to our destination.

Ping the Broadcast Address

If you want to discover what hosts are active on your subnet, you can ping the network's broadcast address. All nodes on the subnet should respond. Since this tool can be used for malicious purposes, it is available only from the privileged level. For example, if our ethernet0 interface were on the 192.168.1.0/24 subnet, we could ping the broadcast address of that network:

```
Router#ping 192.168.1.255
```

The output will show the responses from all the hosts on the subnet. Another way to find out which hosts the router knows about is to display its ARP table:

```
Router#show ip arp
```

This command lists all the machines from which the router has seen packets in the last 30 minutes.

Extended ping

Extended ping provides more options than the basic ping command. These options can be used to better diagnose a network connectivity problem. To enter the extended ping mode, type the ping command; when it asks for "Extended commands", type "y" for yes:

```
Extended commands [n]: y
Source address or interface: 192.168.1.1
Type of service [0]:
Set DF bit in IP header? [no]:
Validate reply data? [no]:
Data pattern [0xABCD]:
Loose, Strict, Record, Timestamp, Verbose[none]:
Sweep range of sizes [n]:
Type escape sequence to abort.
Sending 5, 100-byte ICMP Echos to 192.168.1.1, timeout is 2 seconds:
!!!!!
Success rate is 100 percent (5/5), round-trip min/avg/max = 4/4/4 ms
```

The most useful of the extended commands is "Source address or interface". This command lets you specify the source address that will be used in constructing the packet; you can specify either the IP address or the name of the interface from which the IP address will be taken. Normally, the router sets the packet's source IP address to the interface that was used to send the ICMP packet, based on the routing table.

What can we test with the source address?

Setting the source address of the ICMP packet allows you to test network connectivity more thoroughly. The host that receives the ICMP packet must reply to the source address given in the packet. This generally means that the remote host replies to the address of the interface through which the packet was sent. But by setting another source address, we can direct the ICMP reply to another address. Consider Figure 14-1.

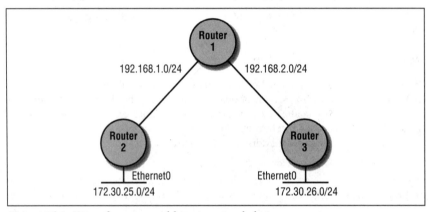

Figure 14-1: Using the source address in extended pings

If Router 2 pings Router 3, the source address of the ICMP packet defaults to the address of the interface closest to Router 3—i.e., the interface on the 192.168.1.0/24 network. If this ping succeeds, we know that Router 3 knows how to get to the 192.168.1.0 network. But what if we want to test whether Router 3 knows how to get to the 172.30.25.0/24 subnet? To execute this test, we perform an extended ping on Router 2 while using the source address on ethernet0:

```
Router#ping
Protocol [ip]:
Target IP address: 172.30.26.1
Repeat count [5]:
Datagram size [100]:
Timeout in seconds [2]:
Extended commands [n]: y
Source address or interface: ethernet0
Type of service [0]:
Set DF bit in IP header? [no]:
Validate reply data? [no]:
Data pattern [0xABCD]:
```

```
Loose, Strict, Record, Timestamp, Verbose[none]:
Sweep range of sizes [n]:
Type escape sequence to abort.
Sending 5, 100-byte ICMP Echos to 172.30.26.1, timeout is 2 seconds:
!!!!!
Success rate is 100 percent (5/5), round-trip min/avg/max = 4/4/4 ms
```

This successful ping proves two things. First, the pings obviously made it to 172. 30.26.1. This shows that routing is working on Router 2, at least to a minimal extent. If routing were not working, Router 2 wouldn't know how to send a packet to 172.30.26.1, to which it doesn't have a direct connection. Second, the pings also made it back to Router 2's ethernet0 interface, which is on the 172.30. 25.0/24 subnet. This proves that some form of routing is working on Router 3— otherwise, it wouldn't know how to get to the 172.30.25.0/24 subnet. If this test failed, it would indicate that either Router 2 did not know how to get to Router 3's network, or Router 3 did not know how to get to Router 2's network.

While this test is useful, it isn't perfect. Even if the packet returns, we really don't know how it made it back. In a more complex network, there may be many ways for a packet to make it from Router 3 back to Router 2. Using the source address doesn't actually prove that a certain network is up or down, but it's helpful as a quick test.

trace

trace (also known as *traceroute* on Unix systems or *tracert* on Windows systems) tries to discover the actual path a packet takes to a selected destination. On Unix, it accomplishes this by using the TTL (Time to Live) field of a UDP packet. On Microsoft platforms, ICMP is used instead of UDP. The TTL is the number of hops a packet is allowed to take before the network gives up the delivery attempt and returns an error message to the sender. Each hop through a router decrements the TTL counter until the TTL hits 0, at which time the router returns the packet to the originator with a "TTL expired" error. Three packets are sent for each TTL, because there's no guarantee that all will make the journey.

trace starts by sending a packet to a UDP port on the destination with a TTL of 1. The UDP port is unimportant as long as it's not being used by the destination. Cisco routers pick a default port of 33434. When the packet hits the first router, it is returned. The host from which the packet was returned (the source address of the returned packet) is the first gateway between your router and the destination. *trace* then sends out a second packet with a TTL of 2. This packet will make it to the second router along the path to the destination, which then returns it. This router is the second gateway in our trace. This process is repeated until the destination is reached and a "port unreachable" message is returned. Figure 14-2 shows this process.

Here's what the output from a trace command looks like:

```
Router#trace sphinx
Tracing the route to sphinx (10.10.3.1)
  1 rtr1 (10.10.1.1) 8msec 8msec 4msec
  2 rtr2 (10.10.2.1) 8msec 8msec 4msec
  3 sphinx (10.10.3.1) 10msec 10msec 10msec
```

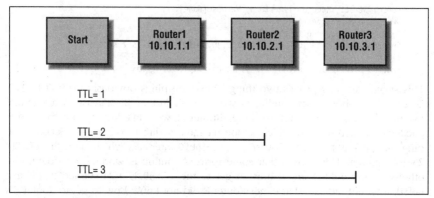

Figure 14-2: Using TTLs to trace the route to a destination

Debugging

Almost every aspect of the router's configuration can have debugging enabled. For example, we could say:

```
debug chat
```

With debugging on, any chat script activity is logged to the router's console (or to the syslog server, if configured). To disable logging, use the undebug command:

```
undebug chat
```

If you forget what debugging you turned on, use the undebug all command to turn all debugging off:

```
undebug all
```

There is a debug all command, but—unless you have major problems—there is rarely a good need for it. When it is executed, all debug information possible is flooded to your screen. You'll be overwhelmed with data, even if logging is enabled. The best practice is to activate debugging only for the items in which you're interested.

Using Debugging in Practice

The debug command is an extremely powerful troubleshooting tool. Assume that you have a serial interface on a router named Baltimore. At the other end of this interface is a router named New-York with an IP address of 10.1.2.55. You are having trouble communicating with the New-York router. One strategy for analyzing the problem is to enable IP-packet debugging on the Baltimore router to see if packets from New-York are arriving. To do so, use the command debug ip packet:

```
baltimore#debug ip packet
IP packet debugging is on
baltimore#
IP: s=10.1.2.55 (Serial0), d=255.255.255.255, len 72, rcvd 2
IP: s=10.1.2.29 (Serial1), d=255.255.255.255, len 72, rcvd 2
IP: s=10.1.2.97 (local), d=255.255.255.255 (Ethernet0), len 72, sending broad/
multicast
```

```
IP: s=10.1.2.66 (local), d=255.255.255.255 (Serial0), len 72, sending broad/
multicast
IP: s=10.1.2.93 (local), d=255.255.255.255 (Serial1), len 72, sending broad/
multicast
IP: s=10.1.2.55 (Serial0), d=255.255.255.255, len 72, rcvd 2
IP: s=10.1.2.29 (Serial1), d=255.255.255.255, len 72, rcvd 2
baltimore#undebug ip packet
```

 This command is very dangerous: it produces a great deal of output and might render a busy router useless. The problem arises because logging debug messages takes priority in IOS. To get around this problem, we could use an access list to limit which packets get displayed. We will cover that trick in a moment.

The s field in the output indicates the source of the packets. This short transcript shows that we've received packets from a number of hosts, including two packets from the New-York router's IP address. Therefore, we are capable of receiving from the other end. Now that we have confirmed that we have communication between the two sites, we can troubleshoot other items, such as our routing configuration.

A safer way to use this command—one that doesn't risk overwhelming the router with its logging duties—is to combine the debug command with an access list that limits which packets get displayed. In the following example, we set up an access list that controls which packets get logged:

```
baltimore(config)#access-list 1 permit 10.1.2.0 0.0.0.255
baltimore(config)#end
baltimore#debug ip packet 1
IP packet debugging is on for access list 1
```

This command is still somewhat dangerous, because you still don't know how much traffic will make it through the access list. But it's significantly less likely to cause problems than enabling packet debugging without some form of access control. Other debug commands aren't as dangerous; we can enable them with some level of confidence that the router won't be overworked. For example, let's debug RIP packets:

```
baltimore#debug ip rip
RIP protocol debugging is on
1d07h: RIP: sending v1 update to 255.255.255.255 via Ethernet0 (10.1.2.97)
1d07h:       subnet  10.1.2.192, metric 1
1d07h:       subnet  10.1.2.64, metric 1
1d07h: RIP: sending v1 update to 255.255.255.255 via Serial0 (10.1.2.66)
1d07h:       subnet  10.1.2.192, metric 1
1d07h:       subnet  10.1.2.96, metric 1
1d07h: RIP: sending v1 update to 255.255.255.255 via Serial1 (10.1.2.93)
1d07h:       subnet  10.1.2.96, metric 1
1d07h:       subnet  10.1.2.64, metric 1
baltimore#undebug ip rip
RIP protocol debugging is off
```

This output shows that we are sending RIP updates from each of our active interfaces. The next step is to see whether the end routers are receiving the updates.

To check, you can turn on debugging on the remote routers, continuing until you have discovered the problem.

There are debug commands for just about everything within the router. When you need help, use the debug ? command to get you started. If you forget what you enabled, always remember that undebug all disables all debug output.

The debug list command

The command debug list allows us to apply an access list or interface to a specific debug command. It's an effective way to control the load debugging places on your router and to limit the amount of debugging output you have to look through. This command takes an access list number or an interface name as an argument; it applies to the next debug statement. For example, assume that we're using EIGRP for routing and we're having problems communicating with the router at 10.1.1.1. We could use the command debug ip eigrp, but that would bombard us with output for all the EIGRP routers. Instead, we first create an access list that permits traffic from 10.1.1.1. Then we use the debug list command to apply the access list to the following debug statement. Finally, we can give the command debug ip eigrp:

```
router1#undebug all
router1#config terminal
router1(config)#access-list 10 permit host 10.1.1.1
router1(config)#exit
router1#debug list 10
router1#debug ip eigrp
IP-EIGRP Route Events debugging is on
        for access list: 10
```

The router responds by saying that EIGRP route event debugging is enabled for access list 10.

The debug list command can also apply to specific interfaces. In the next example, we limit the output from the debug ip eigrp command to EIGRP traffic through ethernet0:

```
router1#undebug all
router1#debug list ethernet0
router1#debug ip packet
IP-EIGRP Route Events debugging is on
        for interface: ethernet0
```

You can apply a debug list to just about any debugging command.

Logging

The router can display logging messages on the terminal, store them in a buffer on the router, or send them to a log server using syslog (syslog is standard on Unix systems, and available for Windows*). You can control how much logging

---

* Two sources for syslog for Windows NT are Syslog for NT (available from *http://www. primenet.com/~buyensj/sysadmin.html#Event*) and SyslogD for NT (available from *http:// www.wgws.com*).

information is collected by using severity levels. For example, you can say that all messages should be sent to the log server regardless of severity, but that only critical messages should be displayed on a console.

Configuring Logging

By default, logging is disabled. If you want to log the router's activity, you must start by enabling logging:

```
logging on
```

We can now configure the syslog server. On a Unix system, you configure syslog by editing the */etc/syslog.conf* file. On Windows, the configuration process depends on the software you use. No matter what operating system you run it on, each log file is associated with a facility and a severity. For example, the *syslog.conf* file might contain the following entry:

```
local5.debug        /var/adm/local5.log
```

This means that messages coming from the user-defined facility local5, with a severity debug (or greater), should be saved in the file */var/adm/local5.log*. Since debug is the lowest possible severity, this statement means that we will log all messages from the local5 facility. On the router, the following commands start logging:

```
! Enable timestamps for all log messages and debug with a time and date stamp.
! The localtime keyword lists the time in local time instead of UTC
service timestamps log datetime localtime
service timestamps debug datetime localtime
! Set the syslog server's IP address
logging 10.10.1.2
! Limit the log messages to informational and higher
logging trap informational
! Set the facility name on the syslog server
logging facility local5
```

The final two commands are the most important. The logging trap command says that we're interested in messages with a severity of informational or higher. The logging facility command says that, when the router generates a message, it should be tagged with the facility local5. The facility name you use must match one of the facilities configured on the server.

Severity Levels

Syslog keeps track of messages using eight severity levels, listed in Table 14-1. If you set logging to any particular level, all messages at that level and above will be logged.

Table 14-1: Severity levels

Level	Name	Level	Name
0	Emergencies	4	Warnings
1	Alerts	5	Notifications
2	Critical	6	Informational
3	Errors	7	Debugging

Buffering Logging and Debug Output

Some other logging commands provide control over how log messages are handled. The first one we will look at is logging buffered, which gives us some control over chatty debug output. For example, if you enable debugging for EIGRP with the command debug ip eigrp, you're in for a lot of logging in the console window. However, you can disable console logging and enable buffered logging with the following commands:

```
router#config terminal
router(config)#no logging console
router(config)#logging buffered
```

Now, when you enable debugging, all the log messages will be stored in the logging buffer instead of scrolling past on the screen. The default size of the logging buffer is platform-specific, but you can change the size by adding a byte count to the end of the logging buffered command. The buffer size can be from 4096 to 4294967295 bytes, but sizes toward the upper end of this range are obviously impractical.

To view the buffer, use the show logging command:

```
router#show logging
Syslog logging: enabled (0 messages dropped, 0 flushes, 0 overruns)
    Console logging: disabled
    Monitor logging: level debugging, 0 messages logged
    Buffer logging: level debugging, 65356 messages logged
    Trap logging: level informational, 86 message lines logged

Log Buffer (4096 bytes):
1w5d: IP: s=10.1.5.1 (local), d=224.0.0.10 (BRIO), len 60, sending broad/multicast
1w5d: IP: s=10.1.5.1 (local), d=224.0.0.10 (BRIO), len 60, encapsulation failed
1w5d: IP: s=10.1.3.1 (Serial0), d=224.0.0.10, len 60, rcvd 2
```

If the log buffer fills up with too much junk, you can clear it with the command clear logging:

```
router#clear logging
```

This command clears the buffer, which allows you to start over.

CHAPTER 15

Quick Reference

---

aaa accounting   global

```
aaa accounting level type server-type
no aaa accounting level type server-type
```

Configures   AAA Accounting

Default   Disabled

Description

This command enables accounting, which can be used for billing and security purposes.

level

> The accounting level is specified using one of the following keywords: system includes all systemwide commands; network includes all networking commands, like ppp. exec includes all EXEC-level commands; and command *level* includes all commands at a specific privilege level.

type

> The type of accounting can be set to one of the following: start-stop creates an accounting entry at the start and end of the command; wait-start makes an entry at the start and end of the command and causes the command to wait until the accounting message has been received by the server; and stop-only sends an accounting entry only when the command has completed execution.

server-type

> Specifies which protocol to use for accounting; either tacacs+ or radius.

Example

The following configuration statements enable AAA accounting for commands at level 5. An accounting entry is generated when the command is initiated and when it is terminated; the command doesn't execute until the server has received the message and the TACACS+ protocol is used to send the entries to the accounting server.

```
aaa new-model
aaa accounting command 5 wait-start tacacs+
```

aaa authentication enable default   global

```
aaa authentication enable default method ... method
no aaa authentication enable default method ... method
```

Configures   Authentication for privileged command level

Default   None

Description

This command configures the router to use AAA to determine whether a user can access the privileged command set. The *method* parameter can be any of the following: enable, line, none, tacacs+, or radius. Each method describes where to get the password for authentication. If more than one method is listed, the methods are tried in order until one succeeds or all fail. This command does not work with TACACS or extended TACACS.

aaa authentication local-override   global

```
aaa authentication local-override
no aaa authentication local-override
```

Configures   The use of local usernames and passwords

Default   Disabled

Description

This command tells the router to check its own username and password database for a match before using any other authentication methods. It is useful if you have a small set of administrators who need access to the router even when the AAA server is down.

aaa authentication login   global

```
aaa authentication login {default | listname} method ... method
no aaa authentication login
```

Configures   AAA authentication method for login

Default   local

Description

This command defines a named list of authentication methods that can be used when a user logs into the device. The *listname* parameter specifies the name of the list; the login authentication command is used to apply a list. default is a special list name; the default list specifies the authentication methods to be used by default (i.e., in the absence of explicit login authentication commands). *method* describes where to get the password for authentication. If more than one method is listed, the methods are tried in order until one succeeds or all have failed. The valid *method*s are: enable, krb5, line, local, none, radius, tacacs+, and krb5-telnet.

Example

The following command defines the default list of login authentication methods. Because this is the default list, it applies to all users, even if there is no login authentication command. The router first attempts to use the tacacs+ method for authentication, then the enable method. Therefore, the enable password is used to authenticate users if the device cannot contact the TACACS+ server.

```
! Set authentication for login
aaa authentication login default tacacs+ enable none
```

---

aaa authentication password-prompt   global

```
aaa authentication password-prompt string
no aaa authentication password-prompt
```

Configures   Password prompt for logins

Default   Password:

Description

This command sets the text displayed for a user's password prompt to *string*.

Example

```
aaa authentication password-prompt "What is your password?"
```

---

aaa authentication ppp   global

```
aaa authentication ppp {default | listname} method ... method
no aaa authentication ppp
```

Configures   AAA authentication method for PPP

Default   local

Description

This command defines a named list of authentication methods that can be used when a user starts a PPP session. The *listname* parameter specifies the name of the list; the login authentication command is used to apply a list. default is a

---

special list name; the default list specifies the authentication methods to be used by default (i.e., in the absence of explicit login authentication commands). *method* describes where to get the password for authentication. If more than one method is listed, they are tried in order until one succeeds or all fail. The valid *method*s are enable, krb5, line, local, none, radius, tacacs+, and krb5-telnet.

Example

The following command defines the default list of authentication methods for PPP users. Because this is the default list, it applies to all PPP users, even if there is no login authentication command. The router attempts to use the tacacs+ method for authentication; if the device cannot contact the TACACS+ server, no other authentication is attempted, and the connection is rejected.

```
! Set authentication for ppp
aaa authentication ppp default tacacs+ none
```

---

aaa authentication username-prompt global

```
aaa authentication username-prompt string
no aaa authentication username-prompt string
```

Configures   Username prompt for AAA authentication

Default   Username:

Description

Like the password-prompt command, this command sets the text used to prompt for a username when using AAA authentication. The prompt is set to *string*.

---

aaa authorization global

```
aaa authorization {network | exec | command level} method ... method
no aaa authorization {network | exec | command level}
```

Configures   Authorization for actions

Default   Disabled

Description

This command sets the authorization method for different command sets.

network
> Sets the authorization method used for network commands.

exec
> Sets the authorization method for any EXEC-level command.

command *level*
> Sets the authorization method for commands at the given privilege level. Privilege levels range from 0 to 15, inclusive.

method ... method

Specifies where the device looks up the authorization information for a user. *method* describes where to get the password for authentication. If more than one method is listed, the methods are tried in order until one succeeds or all have failed. The valid method types are `tacacs+`, `if-authenticated`, `none`, `local`, `radius`, and `krb5-instance`.

Example

The following commands require TACACS+ authentication for users giving commands at level 8.

```
aaa new-model
aaa authorization command 8 tacacs+ none
```

---

aaa authorization config-commands   global

```
aaa authorization config-commands
no aaa authorization config-commands
```

Configures   Authorization for config level access

Default

Disabled, unless the `aaa authorization` command has been given, in which case all config-commands require authorization

Description

This command enables authorization of config-commands (i.e., any command that requires you to give the `conf terminal` command to enter configuration mode). Here's a scenario in which you might use it: if you give the `aaa authorization` command, AAA authorization will be required for all commands. To disable authorization of config-commands, you can give the command `no aaa authorization config-commands`.

Example

```
aaa new-model
aaa authorization command 8 tacacs+ none
no aaa authorization config-commands
```

---

aaa authorization reverse-access   global

```
aaa authorization reverse-access {tacacs+ | radius}
no aaa authorization reverse-access
```

Configures   Authorization for reverse telnet access

Default   Disabled (no authorization for reverse telnet)

Description

This command enables authorization for a user who is requesting reverse telnet access. If specified, `tacacs+` or `radius` is used for authentication.

---

aaa new-model   global

```
aaa new-model
no aaa new-model
```

Configures   Enables AAA access control

Default   Disabled

Description

By default, the AAA model is not enabled, and you cannot use the AAA configuration commands. This command enables AAA and allows you to configure it.

---

absolute-timeout   line

```
absolute-timeout number-of-minutes
no absolute-timeout
```

Configures   Amount of time a connection can be open

Default   None

Description

This command sets the interval before closing a connection to *number-of-minutes*.
Unlike the other timeouts, this command sets a hard limit for the connection time;
it is not an idle timeout. The connection will be closed at this time even if the
connection is not idle. Use the no form of the command to disable the timeout.

---

access-class   line

```
access-class access-list [in | out]
no access-class access-list
```

Configures   Applies an access list to a line

Default   None

Description

This command specifies which access list to apply to this line (*access list*), and
in what direction the list should be applied (in or out). For more information on
creating access lists, see Chapter 7.

Example

The following commands apply access list 10 to outgoing traffic on virtual terminals 0–4.

```
access-list 10 permit host 10.10.1.2
! Apply the access-list to the virtual lines 0-4
line vty 0 4
  access-class 10 out
```

access-enable

access-enable [host] [timeout *minutes*]

Configures   Creates an entry in a dynamic access list

Default   None

Description

This command enables the Lock and Key feature. It allows an entry to be made in a dynamic access list for the current session. The host keyword is optional; it tells the access list to allow access only from the host that initiated the session. The timeout option specifies the time in *minutes* after which the access list entry is deleted if no traffic matching the entry is seen. In other words, if the connection is idle for the given time, the entry in the access list is deleted and the user must re-authenticate.

access-enable is often used with autocommand to create a dynamic access list for an incoming telnet session.

Example

This example creates a dynamic access list for the host that made the connection. The access list times out after five minutes.

    autocommand access-enable host timeout 5

To make use of this entry, there must be an extended access list like the following:

    access-list 110 dynamic incoming-user timeout 5 permit ip any any

This list must be applied to any interfaces that support dial-in users. The permit part of the statement controls the incoming user's access to network resources. The timeout in the access-list command is absolute; the temporary entry exists only for the given number of minutes. It overrides the timeout in the access-enable command.

---

access-list   global

Standard:

access-list *number* {permit | deny} *src-address-spec*

Extended:

access-list *number* {permit | deny} *protocol src-address-spec* [*operator port*]
    dest-address-spec [*operator port*] [established] [precedence *value*]
    [tos *value*] [log]

Named:

ip access-list {standard | extended} *name*

All access list types:

no access-list *number*

Configures An access list

Default None

Description

Access lists are an extremely general method for controlling access to the router, the traffic flowing in and out of the router, and even the routes accepted by the router. This command defines an entry in an access list.

number
>   A number that identifies the list and list type. Table 15-1 shows the ranges assigned to each list type. This book covers only standard and extended IP access lists, plus named and reflexive access lists.

Table 15-1: Access list numbers

List type	Numeric range
Standard IP access lists	1–99
Extended IP access lists	100–199
Ethernet type code	200–299
DECnet	300–399
XNS	400–499
Extended XNS	500–599
AppleTalk	600–699
Ethernet address	700–799
Novell	800–899
Extended Novell	900–999
Novell SAP	1000–1099
Additional standard IP access lists	1300–1999
Additional extended IP access lists	2000–2699
Named access lists	None
Reflexive access lists	None

permit|deny
>   Specifies if the line is to permit or deny matched traffic.

protocol
>   Specifies the protocol to which the access list entry applies. For IP access lists, this option can be ip, tcp, udp, igmp, or icmp.

src-address-spec dest-address-spec
>   The source and destination addresses or networks can be expressed in a number of ways: any, a single host address, or an entire network address, as follows:

>   any
>>   Matches any address. This command is shorthand for the IP address and wildcard mask of 0.0.0.0 255.255.255.255. (See Chapter 7 for more information.)

host *ip-address*
> Matches a single host, identified by its IP address.

ip-address wildcard-mask
> Matches any address in the set specified by the IP address and the wild-card mask. For example, 10.10.1.0 0.0.0.255 matches the address range 10.10.1.0 through 10.10.1.255. Wildcards are covered in Chapter 7.

operator port
> These options, *operator* and *port*, allow you to specify services or groups of services. The operator must be one of the following:

lt   Less than

gt   Greater than

eq   Equal

neq   Not equal

range   The range between two port numbers

> Ports can be specified either by number or by the name of a service (smtp, telnet, www, ftp, etc.).

> If a port expression follows the source address in an access list, packets must have a source port that matches the expression in order to pass the access list. Likewise, if a port expression follows the destination address, packets must have a destination port that matches the expression to pass the access list.

precedence *value*
> Optional. This command allows packets to be filtered on IP precedence level. The value can be 0 to 7.

tos *value*
> Optional. TOS stands for Type of Service. Packets can be filtered by the IP Type of Service, with a value of 0 to 15.

log
> This keyword causes the router to write a log message to the console for packets that match this line. It logs the first packet that matches the line and then repeats only every few minutes, which prevents a flood of log messages. Console logging must be enabled before messages appear.

established
> This keyword matches TCP packets that have ACK or RST bits set, i.e., packets that belonged to an established connection. It is used to prevent hosts from outside the local network from starting connections to hosts within the network, while allowing packets from an established connection back into the network.

icmp-type *value*
> ICMP packets can be filtered based on their type, which is a value from 0 to 255.

igmp-type *value*
> IGMP packets can be filtered based on their type, which is a value from 0 to 15.

Many different kinds of statements are used to apply an access list. The most common are `ip access-group,` which applies an access list to incoming or outgoing traffic on an interface, and `access-class`, which applies an access list to incoming or outgoing traffic on a line.

Note that the `no` form of this command deletes the entire access list, *not* just a single entry.

Named Access Lists (IOS 11.0 and greater)

IOS 11.0 introduced a new method of creating and editing IP access lists, called *named access lists.* As the name implies, named access lists are assigned a string-based name, rather than a number. Otherwise, they are essentially identical to standard and extended IP access lists but with the added ability to do some basic editing.

To create a named access list, start with the `ip access list` command:

```
ip access-list {standard | extended} name
```

The keyword `standard` indicates that this is a standard IP access list; `extended` indicates that this is an extended IP access list. *name* is the name of the list; it must be a unique alphanumeric string. You may then enter a series of `permit` and `deny` commands. For standard access lists, these commands have the following syntax:

```
{permit | deny} src-address-spec
```

For an extended list, the syntax is:

```
{permit | deny} protocol src-address-spec [operator port] dest-address-spec
[operator port] [established] [precedence value] [tos value] [log]
```

The parameters for the `permit` and `deny` commands in named access lists are the same as for extended access lists.

Named access lists cannot always be used in the same places that numbered access lists can, though this is slowly being corrected as IOS evolves.

Example

Here are examples of several types of access list elements. We assume that these access lists are used to restrict incoming traffic on an interface. First, a standard IP access list that permits traffic from the network 10.0.1.0:

```
access-list 5 permit 10.0.1.0 0.0.0.255
```

This access list element permits HTTP traffic from any source to reach the server at 10.1.2.3:

```
access-list 105 permit tcp any host 10.1.2.3 eq http
```

And this element permits TCP traffic to enter the router from any destination, provided that the session was initiated by a host "behind" the router:

```
access-list 105 permit tcp any any established
```

Remember that all access lists end with an "implicit deny," which rejects all traffic not permitted by a statement in the access list.

access-list rate-limit

```
access-list rate-limit access-list {precedence | mac-address |
    mask precedence-mask}
no access-list rate-limit access-list
```

Configures   An access list for Committed Access Rate (CAR)

Default   None

Description

This command selects packets for CAR policies based on IP precedence or MAC addresses. There can only be one command per access list. If you need to assign more than one precedence level to a single access list, use the mask keyword.

precedence
> The IP precedence level to apply to the access list.

mac-address
> The MAC address to apply to the access list.

mask *precedence-mask*
> The precedence mask to apply to the access list. To calculate the mask, convert the precedence value to an eight-bit mask. A precedence of 0 is encoded as 000000001; a precedence of 1 is 00000010. Then AND all the bit values together to get a single mask. For example, the mask that covers a precedence of 1 through 3 would be 00001110. When you have the binary mask, convert it to a two-digit hexadecimal number; for this example, the mask would be 0E.

Example
```
! This command assigns a CAR access-list of 10 to packets with an IP
! precedence of 1 through 3.
access-list rate-limit 10 mask 0E
```

access-template

```
access-template [access-list] [temp-list] [source] [destination]
    [timeout minutes]
```

Configures   An entry in a temporary access list

Default   None

Description

This command creates an entry in a temporary access list on the router to which you are connected.

access-list
> The name or number of the dynamic access list.

temp-list
> The name of the temporary list within the access list.

source

> The usual source address specification (the host and any keywords are allowed).

destination

> The usual destination address specification (the host and any keywords are allowed).

timeout *minutes*

> The maximum time, in *minutes*, that the entry will remain in the list.

For more information about how source and destination addresses are specified, see the description of the access-list command and Chapter 7.

---

activation-character line

```
activation-character ascii-number
no activation-character
```

Configures   The activation character for an idle terminal session

Default   Return character (13)

Description

This command specifies which key initiates a session at an idle terminal. *ascii-number* is the decimal value of the activation character you wish to set. To disable this command and return to the default, use the no form.

Example

These commands set the activation character for a terminal connected to line 2 to ASCII character 13 (Return or Enter):

```
Router(config)# line 2
Router(config-line)# activation-character 13
```

---

aggregate-address router, BGP

```
aggregate-address address mask [as-set] [summary-only] [suppress-map map]
    [advertise-map map] [attribute-map map]
no aggregate-address address mask [as-set] [summary-only] [suppress-map map]
    [advertise-map map] [attribute-map map]
```

Configures   BGP route aggregation

Default   Disabled

Description

This command configures route aggregation when using BGP. An aggregate route is generated by combining several different routes. The new route covers all the smaller routes with a single route, making the routing table smaller and easier to manage.

---

address

The IP address of the destination network for the aggregate route.

mask

The network mask for the aggregate route.

`as-set`

Optional. Generates AS-SET path information.

`summary-only`

Optional. This keyword causes routes that are more specific than the aggregate address to be suppressed.

`suppress-map` *map*

Optional. The map to use to select routes to be suppressed.

`advertise-map` *map*

Optional. The map to use to select routes to create AS-SET origin communities.

`attribute-map` *map*

Optional. The map to use to set the attributes of the aggregate route.

Example

Say that we're configuring a router for the network 10.10.0.0. Instead of advertising all the routes within this network that we know about (10.10.1.0, 10.10.2.0, etc.), we want to advertise an aggregrate address for the whole 10.10.0.0 network:

```
! BGP configuration
router bgp 100
  neighbor 10.1.1.1 remote-as 100
  neighbor 10.2.2.2 remote-as 200
  network 10.10.0.0
  ! Without the summary-only keyword, the router would continue to advertise
  ! the component networks of this summary route.
  aggregrate-address 10.10.0.0 255.255.0.0 summary-only
```

---

alias   global

`alias` *mode alias-name command*

Configures   Command aliases

Default   None

Description

This command allows you to configure an alias, or abbreviation, for any IOS command.

mode

The mode to which the alias and the command that you are aliasing belong. It can be any of the configuration modes: `configuration` (for global commands), `user`, `exec`, `hub`, `interface`, `line`, `map-class`, `map-list`, `route-map`, `router`, etc.

alias-name
    The name to be assigned to the alias.

command
    The IOS command represented by the alias.

Example

To assign the shorthand t1 to the command telnet 10.1.1.1 2001, use the
following command:

    alias exec t1 telnet 10.1.1.1 2001

---

area authentication   router, OSPF

area *area-id* authentication [message-digest]
no area *area-id* authentication

Configures   OSPF authentication

Default   No authentication

Description

This command enables simple password authentication for an OSPF network. All
routers within the OSPF area must be configured to use the same password. The
authentication password is set by the ip ospf authentication-key command.

area-id
    The area to which this command applies.

message-digest
    Enables MD5 authentication for the area.

Example

The following configuration starts an OSPF process using authentication for area 0.
The authentication key is letmein.

    ! Set the OSPF key on interface serial 0 to letmein
    interface serial 0
      ip address 10.100.1.1 255.255.2255.0
      ip ospf authentication-key letmein
    !
    router ospf 99
      network 10.0.0.0 0.255.255.255 area 0
      area 0 authentication

---

area default-cost   router, OSPF

area *area-id* default-cost *cost*
no area *area-id* default-cost

Configures   The OSPF cost for a default summary route

Default   1

Description

This command is used only for an Area Border Router (ABR) to a stub area.

area-id
> The area to which the default-cost applies.

cost
> The value of the cost. Any 24-bit number can be used.

---

area nssa router, OSPF

```
area area-id nssa [no-redistribution] [default-information-originate]
no area area-id nssa
```

Configures   An OSPF NSSA

Default   None

Description

A Not-So-Stubby Area (NSSA) is just like a stub area, but shares routing information with an external network that is using a different routing protocol. In other words, it is a stub area with an ASBR router. The remote network becomes an area to your OSPF network, eliminating the need to implement the different routing protocol within the OSPF network. See the OSPF section in Chapter 9 for more information.

area-id
> The area to which this command applies.

no-redistribution
> Optional. Disables redistribution of normal area routes into the NSSA.

default-information-originate
> Optional. Generates type-7 default routes into the NSSA.

---

area-password router, IS-IS

```
area-password password
no area-password
```

Configures   IS-IS area authentication password

Default   No password authentication

Description

> This command enables password authentication for an IS-IS area. The *password* is transmitted in clear text; it thus provides very little security but may help prevent misconfiguration.

area range   router, OSPF

```
area area-id range address mask
no area area-id range address mask
```

Configures   OSPF route summarization

Default   None

Description

This command tells the OSPF routing process to summarize selected routes for an area. A single route to the given address is generated, instead of separate routes for the individual networks.

area-id
   The area to be summarized.

address
   The IP address of the network to summarize.

mask
   The mask for the IP address, showing which routes to include in the summary.

Example

The following OSPF configuration summarizes all routes for area 2 into a single route for network 10.0.0.0/8:

```
router ospf 99
  network 10.0.0.0 0.255.255.255 area 2
  area 2 range 10.0.0.0 255.0.0.0
```

---

area stub   router, OSPF

```
area area-id stub [no-summary]
no area area-id stub
```

Configures   An OSPF stub area

Default   None

Description

This command defines an area to be a stub area. A stub area receives a default summary route from the ABR for destinations outside the autonomous system. The no-summary option makes the area a Totally Stubby network, which restricts LSA Type 3 packets (intra-area summaries) from entering the stubby area.

area-id
   The area to define as a stub.

no-summary
   Prevents summary link advertisements from entering the stub area.

---

area virtual-link

```
area area-id virtual-link router-id [hello-interval seconds]
   [retransmit-interval seconds] [transmit-delay seconds]
   [dead-interval seconds] [authentication-key key]
   [message-digest-key keyid md5 key]
no area area-id virtual-link router-id
```

Configures   An OSPF virtual link

Default   None

Description

This command establishes a virtual link that connects a broken OSPF backbone; in OSPF, the backbone must be contiguous. It is useful when a contiguous backbone is not possible. Virtual links can also be used to create an area that does not have a direct link to the backbone (area 0).

area-id
> The ID of the area being crossed by the virtual link.

router-id
> The ID of the router at the other end of the virtual link.

hello-interval *seconds*
> Optional. The time in seconds between transmission of hello messages by the router over the virtual link. The default is 10 seconds. All routers participating in the same area must have the same hello interval.

retransmit-interval *seconds*
> Optional. The time in seconds that a router waits before retransmitting a link-state announcement (LSA). The default is 5 seconds. When setting this value, you need to ensure that the time includes the entire round trip of the packet.

transmit-delay *seconds*
> Optional. This is the estimated time in seconds that the interface will take to transmit the packet. An LSA's age is decremented by this value before transmission. The default is 1 second.

dead-interval *seconds*
> Optional. A router is considered down if a hello packet isn't received from it within this interval. All routers participating in the area must have the same dead-interval. The default is 40 seconds.

authentication-key *key*
> Optional. This is the authentication password used for OSPF routing if authentication is enabled. The key can be up to 8 bytes long. If you want to use authentication, all routers in the OSPF network must have authentication enabled, and all neighbor routers must use the same key.

message-digest-key *keyid* md5 *key*
> Optional. This is the authentication key and password to be used by neighboring OSPF routers. The *keyid* is a number between 1 and 255, and is used

to identify this key in subsequent commands. The *key* is essentially a password; it is a string up to 16 characters long. All neighbor routers must use the same *keyid* and *key*.

---

arp   global

```
arp ip-address mac-address type [alias]
no arp ip-address mac-address type [alias]
```

Configures   Adds a static entry to the ARP table

Default   No static ARP entries are made

Description

This command allows you to place a static entry in the ARP table, which is a dynamic table that maps IP addresses to the corresponding MAC (hardware) addresses. The *ip-address* and *mac-address* are simply the IP address and the hardware address for the entry you wish to create. The *type* argument is the encapsulation type (arpa for Ethernet, smds for SMDS, snap for FDDI and token ring, etc.). The optional alias keyword tells the router to respond to ARP requests as if it were the requested device itself; i.e., the router responds to an ARP request for an aliased device with its own IP address.

---

arp   interface

```
arp {arpa | frame-relay | probe | snap}
no arp {arpa | frame-relay | probe | snap}
```

Configures   Interface-specific handling of ARP requests

Default   ARPA (Ethernet)

Description

This command allows you to specify the type of encapsulation to use for ARP packets on this interface. The types are arpa (Ethernet, the default), frame-relay (ARP over Frame Relay encapsulation), probe (HP Probe protocol), and snap (RFC 1042).

---

arp timeout   interface

```
arp timeout seconds
no arp timeout seconds
```

Configures   The lifetime of an ARP entry in the ARP table

Default   14400 seconds

Description

This command allows you to set the time that an entry will remain in the ARP table. The default is 4 hours.

---

async-bootp

```
async-bootp keyword [:hostname] value
no async-bootp keyword [:hostname] value
```

Configures   BOOTP parameters for async dial-up lines

Default   Disabled

Description

This command assigns a *value* to a given BOOTP *keyword*. Table 15-2 shows the
BOOTP parameters and their values. Normally, all BOOTP parameters are sent to
dial-up hosts requesting BOOTP information. Adding *:hostname* to a keyword
applies the BOOTP variable to a specific requesting host. Other hosts that request
BOOTP parameters will not be sent this keyword.

Table 15-2: BOOTP keywords and values

Keyword	Value	Meaning
bootfile	*filename*	Server boot file to be downloaded
subnet-mask	*mask*	The subnet mask to be used
time-offset	*offset*	The offset time in seconds from the Coordinated Universal Time (UTC)
gateway	*address*	The IP address of the default gateway
time-server	*address*	The IP address of the time server
nbns-server	*address*	The IP address of the Windows NT server
dns-server	*address*	The IP address of the DNS server
log-server	*address*	The IP address of the MIT-LCS log server
quote-server	*address*	The IP address of the QOTD (quote of the day) server
lpr-server	*address*	The IP address of the LPR print server
bootfile-size	*size*	The size of the bootfile in terms of 512-byte blocks

Example

The following commands define the DNS server, subnet mask, and NBNS server to
be sent to hosts requesting BOOTP information:

```
! Configure our bootp items
async-bootp subnet-mask 255.255.255.0
async-bootp dns-server 10.1.1.1
async-bootp nbns-server 10.1.1.2
```

async default ip address

```
async default ip address address
no async default ip address address
```

Configures   The IP address used by the connecting (remote) system

Default   None

Description

This command is defunct. Use `peer default ip address` instead.

---

async default routing   interface

```
async default routing
no async default routing
```

Configures   Routing on async interfaces

Default   Disabled

Description

By default, routing protocols like RIP, IGRP, EIGRP, and OSPF are not enabled on asynchronous interfaces. This command allows all the routing protocols to be enabled on these interfaces. It can be used to route between offices that are linked by traditional analog modems. Use the no form to disable routing on this interface.

Example

The following commands set up default routing for a dedicated async line:

```
interface async  2
  encapsulation ppp
  async mode dedicated
  async default routing
```

---

async dynamic address   interface

```
async dynamic address
no async dynamic address
```

Configures   Dynamic IP addresses on async interfaces

Default   Disabled

Description

Dynamic addressing means that a user connecting to the router for a PPP or SLIP session is allowed to select the interface's IP address using the EXEC mode commands. This feature can be used only when the async mode is interactive.

---

async dynamic routing   interface

```
async dynamic routing
no async dynamic routing
```

Configures   Dynamic routing on an async interface

Default   Disabled

Description

Dynamic routing means that remote users who connect to this asynchronous interface can enable routing over their PPP or SLIP connections. By default, no dynamic routing is done on an asynchronous interface.

Example

```
interface async 5
  ip tcp header-compression passive
  async dynamic routing
  async dynamic address
```

---

async mode

interface

```
async mode {dedicated | interactive}
no async mode {dedicated | interactive}
```

Configures   The mode the user receives when connecting to an async interface

Default   Disabled

Description

The mode can either be dedicated or interactive.

dedicated

> The interface is reserved for PPP and SLIP connections. No user prompt ever appears on a dedicated line when a user connects. Instead, the connection parameters are negotiated automatically.

interactive

> Users are given a prompt when they connect to this interface. It is up to the user to start PPP or SLIP, or to interact directly with the router from the command prompt. The autoselect command can be used to detect PPP packets on an interactive async line and start PPP automatically. autoselect is not needed on dedicated mode async lines.

Example

On the first interface (async1), we set up a dedicated interface, which means that an IOS prompt doesn't appear when a user connects to the router through this interface. We make the second interface interactive, allowing the user to enter IOS commands and requiring her to start PPP or SLIP manually.

```
interface async1
  peer default ip address 10.10.1.1
  async mode dedicated
  encapsulation ppp
!
interface async2
  peer default ip address 10.10.1.2
  async mode interactive
```

atm address
global

```
atm address address
no atm address
```

Configures   An ATM address

Default   An automatically generated ATM address is assigned

Description

This command assigns a full (20-byte) ATM address or a partial (13-byte) address. Multiple ATM addresses are allowed. The first address in the list is the active address.

atm arp-server
interface

```
atm arp-server {self [timeout minutes] | nsap nsap-address}
no atm arp-server {self [timeout minutes] | nsap nsap-address}
```

Configures   An ARP server for the network

Default   No ATM ARP server

Description

This command assigns an ARP server for the ATM network. The `self` keyword identifies the current device as the ARP server. The `timeout minutes` option specifies the amount of time that an ARP entry is listed before the server tries to verify the entry; the default timeout value is 20 minutes. The `nsap nsap-address` parameter specifies the NSAP address of the ATM ARP server if the current device isn't acting as the server.

atm esi-address
interface

```
atm esi-address esi.selector
no atm esi-address
```

Configures   End station ID and selector fields of the ATM NSAP address

Default   None

Description

This command specifies the end station ID (ESI) and the selector byte fields of an ATM address. The ESI is 12 hexadecimal characters; the selector byte field is 2 hexadecimal characters.

atm lecs-address

```
atm lecs-address lecs-address [sequence-number]
no atm lecs-address
```

Configures   The LECS address to be advertised

Default   None

Description

This command configures the address of the LAN Emulation Configuration Server (LECS) for the current interface. If this command isn't in the interface's configuration, the LECS defaults to the server given by `atm lecs-address-default`. The *lecs-address* is the NSAP address of the server. The *sequence-number* provides the position in the address in the LECS table.

atm lecs-address-default

```
atm lecs-address-default lecs-address [sequence-number]
no atm lecs-address-default lecs-address
```

Configures   The LECS address to be advertised

Default   None

Description

This command configures the address of the LECS. It is a global command; the server specified here is overridden by the interface-specific `atm lecs-address` command. The *lecs-address* is the NSAP address of the server. The *sequence-number* provides the position in the address in the LECS table.

atm nsap-address

```
atm nsap-address address
no atm nsap-address
```

Configures   The NSAP ATM end-system address of the interface

Default   None

Description

This command sets the NSAP address of the interface, which consists of 40 hexadecimal characters.

atm pvc

```
atm pvc vcd vpi vci encap [peak avg [burst]] [inarp [minutes]]
    [oam [seconds]] [compress]
no atm pvc vcd vpi vci encap [peak avg [burst]] [inarp [minutes]]
    [oam [seconds]] [compress]
```

Configures   Creates an ATM PVC

Default   None

Description

This command creates an ATM Permanent Virtual Circuit (PVC). On recent versions of IOS, it's preferable to use the pvc command, if available. ATM commands are highly hardware-dependent, so the commands available on any particular router vary. For more information on creating PVCs, consult Chapter 6.

vcd
> A Virtual Circuit Descriptor, which is a unique number used to identify this particular VPI/VCI pair on the router.

vpi
> The Virtual Path Identifier of the PVC. This identifier is unique only to the interface. The value can be from 0 to 255.

vci
> The Virtual Channel Identifier of the PVC, which is a value from 0 to 1023. 0 to 31 are typically reserved for specific kinds of management traffic. *vpi* and *vci* may not both be 0.

encap
> The type of encapsulation used on the line. The encapsulation may be aal5mux (a MUX-type virtual connection), aal5snap (the only encapsulation supported for Inverse ARP), aal1 (used for streaming video), aal5voice (used for voice traffic), ilmi, and qsaal.

peak
> Optional, but required for voice circuits. The maximum capacity of the virtual circuit in kbps. *peak* ranges from 56 to 10000. The default is the link's maximum capacity.

avg
> Optional, but required for voice circuits. The average rate at which data is sent over the virtual circuit. Legal values are hardware-dependent. The default is the link's maximum capacity.

burst
> Optional, but required for voice circuits. The maximum number of ATM cells that the circuit can transmit at its peak rate.

inarp *minutes*
> Optional. This option generates inverse ARP packets on this virtual circuit. *minutes* specifies the interval between inverse ARP packets, and ranges from 1 to 60; if omitted, *minutes* defaults to 15.

oam *seconds*
> Optional. This option generates OAM cells on this virtual circuit. *seconds* specifies the interval at which OAM cells are generated, and ranges from 1 to 600; if omitted, *seconds* defaults to 10.

compress
> Optional. This option compresses traffic over the circuit; hardware compression is used if it's available.

Example

The following commands set up a permanent virtual circuit on an ATM interface.

```
interface atm0.1
  ! assign our interface's IP address
  ip address 10.10.1.1 255.255.255.0
  ! Create pvc 20 with a VPI of 0 and a VCI of 60
  atm pvc 20 0 60 aal5snap
```

atm-vc   map-list

ip *address* atm-vc *vci* [class *class-name*] [broadcast] [aal5mux]
no ip *address* atm-vc *vci* [class *class-name*] [broadcast] [aal5mux]

Configures   An ATM PVC

Default   None

Description

This command creates an ATM PVC. The map-list command places you in the map list configuration mode; you must be in this mode to use the atm-vc command.

Note that it is rather bizarre to call this command atm-vc; by normal notions of command naming, it should be called ip. We're following Cisco's usage; in its defense, there are many commands whose names start with ip and that have nothing to do with ATM configuration.

address
   The destination IP address being mapped to this PVC.

vci
   The Virtual Channel Identifier (VCI).

class *class-name*
   Optional. *class-name* is the name of a table that contains encapsulation-specific parameters.

broadcast
   Optional. This specifies that this entry should be used when broadcast packets need to be sent.

aal5mux
   Optional. This specifies AAL5 multiplexing encapsulation. The default is snap encapsulation.

Example

The following commands create an ATM map named atm-map1. It establishes a virtual channel with a VCI of 20, which is mapped to the IP address 10.10.2.1; this virtual channel can be used for broadcast.

```
map-list atm-map1
  ip 10.10.2.1 atm-vc 20 broadcast
```

autobaud

```
autobaud [fast]
no autobaud
```

Configures   Automatic baud rate detection

Default   Disabled

Description

The autobaud command configures a line to select the incoming baud rate automatically. The baud rate must be between 300 and 115200. There are two limitations to this command:

- Autobaud cannot be used on a connection at rates higher than 19,200 baud when the parity bit is set.
- This command cannot be used on outgoing connections.

The optional fast keyword detects the baud rate with exactly three carriage returns.

Many routers do not support the higher baud rates.

Example

The following commands enable automatic baud rate detection on line 3:

```
Router(config)#line 3
Router(config-line)#autobaud
```

To disable autobaud and to return to the default, use the no form of this command:

```
Router(config)#line 3
Router(config-line)#no autobaud
```

---

autocommand

```
autocommand command-string
no autocommand
```

Configures   Automatic execution of a command upon connection

Default   Disabled

Description

This command forces a specified line command, given by *command-string*, to be executed automatically when a login session is started. The command string can be any valid command. Use the no form to delete the selected autocommand.

Example

The following code starts PPP automatically after a successful login on line 5:

```
Router(config)#line tty 5
Router(config-line)#autocommand ppp
```

autodetect encapsulation

```
autodetect encapsulation {lapb-ta | ppp | v120}
no autodetect encapsulation
```

Configures   Automatic detection of encapsulation types

Default   No autodetect

Description

This command enables automatic detection of the encapsulation type for ISDN or point-to-point serial links. The interface changes its encapsulation type if it detects that the remote system is using a different configuration. The valid types are lapb-ta (Link Access Procedure Balanced for ISDN), ppp, and v120 (for V.120 on ISDN B channels).

autohangup

```
autohangup
no autohangup
```

Configures   Automatic line disconnect

Default   Disabled

Description

This command tells the router to hang up the line automatically after the session is closed.

autoselect

```
autoselect {arap | ppp | slip| during-login}
no autoselect
```

Configures   Automatic selection of session type

Default   ARAP sessions

Description

This command configures a line to start the selected session type automatically. The sessions allowed are arap (AppleTalk remote access), ppp, and slip. during-login means that the username and password prompt are presented without a carriage return, and the user must log in normally before autoselection takes place.

Example

The following commands configure the router to start a PPP session automatically on line 10, but only after the user has successfully logged in:

```
line 10
    autoselect ppp
    autoselect during-login
```

auto-summary   router

```
auto-summary
no auto-summary
```

Configures   RIP (Version 2), EIGRP, BGP route summarization

Default   Enabled

Description

By default, subnet routes are summarized to "classful" network routes. If you need to advertise subnets across networks, auto-summary must be disabled. To disable auto-summary, use the no form of this command. For more information, consult Chapter 8.

Example

The following configuration disables auto-summary for an EIGRP routing process:

```
router eigrp 110
    network 10.0.0.0
    no auto-summary
```

backup   interface

```
backup interface interface
no backup interface interface

backup delay {enable-time | never} {disable-time | never}
no backup delay {enable-time | never} {disable-time | never}

backup load {enable-load | never} {disable-load | never}
no backup load {enable-load | never} {disable-load | never}
```

Configures   A backup interface

Default   None

Description

This family of commands configures a backup interface for the current interface. The first command, backup interface, specifies the *interface* to be used as the backup. The backup interface is activated when the primary interface goes down or reaches the load specified by the backup load command.

The backup delay command specifies how long the router should wait before activating (*enable-time*) or deactivating (*disable-time*) the backup interface. Both *enable-time* and *disable-time* are in seconds. Use of the backup delay command allows you to prevent routing instability if you have an intermittent interface. The keyword never, when used for the *enable-time* parameter, prevents the backup interface from being activated; when used for the *disable-time* parameter, it prevents the backup interface from being deactivated once it has been activated.

The `backup load` command specifies the load on the primary interface at which the backup interface should be activated (*enable-load*) or deactivated (*disable-load*). The load is expressed as a percentage of the primary interface's maximum capacity. The keyword **never**, when used for the *enable-load* parameter, prevents the backup interface from being activated; when used for the *disable-load* parameter, it prevents the backup interface from being deactivated once it has been activated.

Example

This example configures `serial1` as a backup interface for `serial0`. If `serial0` goes down for more than 5 seconds, or if the load on `serial0` reaches 70%, the backup interface is activated.

```
interface serial0
  backup interface serial 1
  backup delay 5 20
  backup load 70 20
```

---

bandwidth   interface

```
bandwidth rate
no bandwidth rate
```

Configures   The bandwidth value to be used in computing routing metrics

Default   Depends on the interface

Description

This command describes the bandwidth value to the routing protocols that use the bandwidth in computing routing metrics. It does *not* actually set the bit-rate on the interface itself. It does not affect the speed at which data is transmitted over the link, but does affect how the router selects routes and, therefore, how the link is used.

Example

A T1 connection would be:

```
bandwidth 1536
```

A 56K connection would be:

```
bandwidth 56
```

---

banner exec   global

```
banner exec delimiter message delimiter
no banner exec
```

Configures   The banner that is displayed to the user upon successful login

Default   None

Description

This command specifies the *message* that is displayed after the user has logged in to the router. It is not displayed for reverse-telnet connections. This command defines only the banner message; use the exec-banner command to enable or disable the message. The *delimiter* marks the beginning and the end of the message; it may be any character that isn't used in the message.

Example

Here's an example of a banner:

```
Router(config)# banner exec # Welcome to Pyramid #
```

You can also do multiple lines:

```
Router(config)# banner exec #
Enter TEXT message.  End with the character '#'.
Welcome to Pyramid
    Enjoy your stay
#
```

To delete the banner:

```
Router(config)#no banner exec
```

By default, this banner is automatically active; disabling the banner requires the use of no exec-banner:

```
Router(config)#no exec-banner
```

Note that disabling the exec-banner also disables the motd-banner.

---

banner incoming   global

```
banner incoming delimiter message delimiter
no banner incoming
```

Configures   The banner message for all incoming reverse telnet connections

Default   None

Description

This command specifies the *message* that is displayed to all incoming reverse telnet connections (instead of the exec banner). If you want to disable the message, delete the banner with the no form of this command. The *delimiter* marks the beginning and the end of the message; it may be any character that isn't used in the message.

Example

Here's how to set a banner:

```
Router(config)#banner incoming # Welcome to Pyramid #
```

You can also do multiple lines:

```
Router(config)#banner incoming #
Enter TEXT message.  End with the character '#'.
```

```
Welcome to Pyramid
    Enjoy your stay
 #
```

To disable the message, delete it with the following command:

```
Router(config)#no banner incoming
```

banner login

```
banner login delimiter message delimiter
no banner login
```

Configures   The login banner message

Default   None

Description

This command specifies the *message* that is displayed prior to the login prompt for all connections. This message cannot be disabled. If you do not want it displayed, delete it with the no form of this command. The *delimiter* marks the beginning and the end of the message; it may be any character that isn't used in the message.

Example

Here's an example of a login banner:

```
Router(config)#banner login # Restricted Access #
```

To disable this message, delete it with the following command:

```
Router(config)#no banner login
```

banner motd

```
banner motd delimiter message delimiter
no banner motd
```

Configures   The banner that is displayed before the login prompt

Default   None

Description

This command specifies the *message* that is displayed as the Message Of The Day, the very first message displayed to an incoming connection. This command defines only the message; the motd-banner command enables or disables the display. The *delimiter* marks the beginning and the end of the message; it may be any character that isn't used in the message.

Example

The following commands create a message-of-the-day banner and enable its display:

```
Router(config)# banner motd  # All routers will be rebooted at Sunday 10AM #
Router(config)# motd-banner
```

The `motd-banner` command isn't strictly necessary, since the display is enabled by default. To disable the display, use the `no motd-banner` command:

```
Router(config)#no banner motd
```

bgp always-compare-med   router, BGP

```
bgp always-compare-med
no bgp always-compare-med
```

Configures   BGP route selection

Default   Disabled

Description

This command allows the comparison of the multi-exit discriminator (MED) for paths, regardless of which autonomous system the path comes from.

bgp bestpath as-path ignore   router, BGP

```
bgp bestpath as-path ignore
no bgp bestpath as-path ignore
```

Configures   BGP route selection

Default   Disabled

Description

This command prevents the router from considering the autonomous system path (`as-path`) when selecting routes.

bgp bestpath med-confed   router, BGP

```
bpg bestpath med-confed
no bgp bestpath med-confed
```

Configures   BGP route selection

Default   Disabled

Description

This command enables MED comparison among paths from confederation peers.

bgp bestpath missing-as-worst   router, BGP

```
bgp bestpath missing-as-worst
no bgp bestpath missing-as-worst
```

Configures   BGP route selection

Default   Disabled

Description

By default, routers give a route with a missing MED a value of 1, which causes that route to be considered the best path. This command causes the router to assign a value of infinity to the missing MED, which makes the route the least desirable of all the routes. For more information on MED values, consult Chapter 10.

---

bgp client-to-client reflection   router, BGP

```
bgp client-to-client reflection
no bgp client-to-client reflection
```

Configures   Route reflection

Default   Enabled

Description

A route reflector automatically reflects routes from one BGP client to another. The no form of this command disables route reflection. Route reflection isn't needed if the clients already have fully-meshed IBGP connections, because the clients will learn their routes directly from each other.

---

bgp cluster-id   router, BGP

```
bgp cluster-id id
no bgp cluster-id id
```

Configures   Cluster ID of a route reflector

Default   Router ID

Description

This command specifies the cluster ID (*id*) for a BGP router. When you have one route reflector, its cluster ID is normally its router ID. If there is more than one route reflector in a cluster, they must all have the same cluster ID. In this case, you would use the bgp cluster-id command to specify the ID explicitly. A cluster ID is four bytes long.

Example

The following BGP configuration creates a BGP process for autonomous system 10. This router is designated as a route reflector. We set its cluster ID explicitly, because there is presumably more than one route reflector in the cluster.

```
router bgp 10
    network 10.200.200.1 route-reflector
    bgp cluster-id 10000
```

bgp confederation identifier   router, BGP

```
bgp confederation identifier as
no bgp confederation identifier as
```

Configures   AS number of the confederation

Default   None

Description

This command specifies the autonomous system (AS) number for a confederation. A confederation is a group of small autonomous systems that appear to the world as a single large autonomous system. The autonomous system number for the confederation is set to *as*.

bgp confederation peers   router, BGP

```
bgp confederation peers as [as]
np bgp confederation peers as [as]
```

Configures   A BGP confederation

Default   None

Description

This command lets you list the AS numbers that belong to the confederation.

Example

```
router bgp 1000
    bgp conferation peers 1001 1002 1003 1004
```

bgp dampening   global

```
bgp dampening [half-life reuse suppress max-suppress-time] [route-map map]
no bgp dampening [half-life reuse suppress max-suppress-time] [route-map map]
```

Configures   BGP dampening settings

Defaults

half-life, 15 min; reuse, 750; suppress, 2000; max-suppress-time, 60 min

Description

This command allows you to specify the route dampening values for BGP. Dampening allows you to control "route flap," which is routing instability that results from a route making repeated transitions.

half-life
    The time in minutes after which a penalty is decreased by half.

reuse
    If the penalty for a flapping route increases to this value, the route can be reused.

suppress
>   When the penalty exceeds this limit, the route is suppressed.

max-suppress-time
>   The maximum amount of time a route can be suppressed; this should be about four times the half-life.

route-map *map*
>   A route map that controls which routes are selected for route dampening.

---

bgp default local-preference   router, BGP

```
bgp default local-preference value
no bgp default local-preference value
```

Configures   BGP local preference

Default   100

Description

This command allows you to set the local preference to *value*. The higher the preference, the better the path. Acceptable values range from 0 to 4,294,967,295.

---

bgp deterministic med   router, BGP

```
bgp deterministic med
no bgp deterministic med
```

Configures   BGP route selection

Default   Disabled

Description

By default, the router does not compare the MED values for paths learned from different autonomous systems within the same confederation. This command allows you to enable MED comparison for routes learned from different autonomous systems within the same confederation.

---

bgp fast-external-fallover   router, BGP

```
bgp fast-external-fallover
no bgp fast-external-fallover
```

Configures   BGP fast fallover

Default   Enabled

Description

This command enables the router to reset the BGP sessions of any direct peers immediately if the link that connects the router to the peer goes down.

---

bgp log-neighbor-changes

```
bgp log-neighbor-changes
no bgp log-neighbor-changes
```

Configures   BGP logging

Default   Disabled prior to IOS 12.1

Description

This command allows you to log changes in the status of BGP neighbors.

bgp-policy

```
bgp-policy {source | destination} {ip-prec-map | ip-qos-map}
no bgp-policy {source | destination} {ip-prec-map | ip-qos-map}
```

Configures   Propagation of policy information via BGP

Default   Disabled

Description

This command allows the propagation of policy information that is based on the IP precedence setting via BGP. To enable this properly, you must also configure a route map to set the IP precedence or QoS (Quality of Service) group ID by using the set ip precedence or set ip qos-group commands.

source
>   Use the precedence or QoS bit from the source address.

destination
>   Use the precedence or QoS bit from the destination address.

ip-prec-map
>   Use IP precedence as the QoS policy.

ip-qos-map
>   Use the QoS group ID as the QoS policy.

bridge acquire

```
bridge bridge-group acquire
no bridge bridge-group acquire
```

Configures   Bridge forwarding

Default   Enabled

Description

By default, the router forwards frames from dynamically learned hosts. The no form of this command allows you to change this behavior so that the router only forwards frames from statically configured stations. To create static bridge hosts, use the bridge address command.

bridge address

global

```
bridge bridge-group address mac {forward | discard} [interface]
no bridge bridge-group address mac
```

Configures   Static bridge hosts

Default   None

Description

This command allows a bridge group to filter packets based on the MAC address.

bridge-group

The bridge group to which this command applies. A bridge group can have a value of 1 to 63. On larger routers, the value can be from 1 to 255.

mac

The MAC address to be filtered.

forward

This keyword tells the router to forward frames from the given MAC address to other interfaces in the bridge group.

discard

This keyword tells the router to discard frames from the given MAC address.

interface

Optional. The interface on which the MAC address can be found.

bridge cmf

global

```
bridge cmf
no bridge cmf
```

Configures   Constrained Multicast Flooding (CMF)

Default   Disabled

Description

This command enables CMF for all configured bridge groups.

bridge crb

global

```
bridge crb
no bridge crb
```

Configures   Concurrent Routing and Bridging

Default   Disabled

Description

CRB stands for Concurrent Routing and Bridging. This command allows the router to route and bridge a protocol at the same time but on different interfaces. Unlike

Integrated Routing and Bridging (IRB), the routed and bridged interfaces cannot communicate with each other.

bridge forward-time
global

```
bridge bridge-group forward-time seconds
no bridge bridge-group forward-time seconds
```

Configures The forward delay interval

Default 30 seconds

Description

This command sets the bridge forwarding delay interval for the interface to *seconds*. The value of *seconds* can be from 10 to 200. (Note: Catalysts use 6-40 seconds.)

bridge-group
interface

```
bridge-group bridge-group
no bridge-group bridge-group
```

Configures Makes an interface part of a bridge group

Default None

Description

This command makes the interface a member of the given bridge group. Use the no form of this command to remove the bridge group from the interface.

bridge-group aging-time
global

```
bridge-group bridge-group aging-time seconds
no bridge-group bridge-group aging-time
```

Configures The time that a dynamic entry remains in the bridge table

Default 300 seconds

Description

This command sets the amount of time in *seconds* that a dynamic entry can remain in the bridge table. If the entry is updated, the counter starts over. The value can range from 0 to 1,000,000 seconds.

bridge-group circuit-group
interface

```
bridge-group bridge-group circuit-group circuit-group
no bridge-group bridge-group circuit-group circuit-group
```

Configures   Assigns a circuit group to a bridge group for the interface

Default   None

Description

This command assigns a circuit group for a bridge group. It is used only for HDLC encapsulated interfaces.

bridge-group input-address-list

interface

```
bridge-group bridge-group input-address-list access-list
no bridge-group bridge-group input-address-list access-list
```

Configures   Allows an interface to filter based on an access list

Default   None

Description

This command applies an access list to an interface for a bridge group. This access list must filter based on MAC addresses, which means that the access list must be an Ethernet access list with a number between 700 and 799. By applying an access list, you can permit or deny bridging to hosts based on the MAC addresses.

bridge-group input-lsap-list

interface

```
bridge-group bridge-group input-lsap-list access-list
no bridge-group bridge-group input-lsap-list access-list
```

Configures   An access list for filtering IEEE 802.2 packets

Default   Disabled

Description

This command applies an access list to all IEEE 802.2 packets received on the interface.

bridge-group input-pattern

interface

```
bridge-group bridge-group input-pattern access-list
no bridge-group bridge-group input-pattern access-list
```

Configures   An access list for a bridge group

Default   None

Description

This command applies an access list to incoming packets on an interface for a specific bridge group.

bridge-group input-type-list

interface

```
bridge-group bridge-group input-type-list access-list
no bridge-group bridge-group input-type-list access-list
```

Configures   An access list for a bridge group

Default   None

Description

This command applies an access list to all incoming Ethernet and SNAP frames on an interface for a specific bridge group.

bridge-group output-address-list

interface

```
bridge-group bridge-group output-address-list access-list
no bridge-group bridge-group output-address-list access-list
```

Configures   Filtering based on an access list

Default   None

Description

This command allows you to apply an access list to an interface for a bridge group. This access list can filter based on MAC addresses, which means the access list must be an Ethernet access list numbered 700 through 799. With this command, you can permit or deny bridging to hosts based on the MAC addresses.

bridge-group output-lsap-list

interface

```
bridge-group bridge-group output-lsap-list access-list
no bridge-group bridge-group output-lsap-list access-list
```

Configures   An access list for outgoing IEEE 802.2

Default   Disabled

Description

This command applies an access list to all IEEE 802.2 packets leaving the interface.

bridge-group output-pattern

interface

```
bridge-group bridge-group output-pattern access-list
no bridge-group bridge-group output-pattern access-list
```

Configures   An access list for a bridge group

Default   None

Description

This command applies an access list to outgoing packets on an interface for a specific bridge group.

---

bridge-group output-type-list   interface

```
bridge-group bridge-group output-type-list access-list
no bridge-group bridge-group output-type-list access-list
```

Configures   An access list for a bridge group

Default   None

Description

This command applies an access list to all outgoing Ethernet and SNAP frames on an interface for a specific bridge group.

---

bridge-group path-cost   interface

```
bridge-group bridge-group path-cost value
no bridge-group bridge-group path-cost value
```

Configures   Changes a bridge group's path cost for an interface

Default   Based on the interface's bandwidth setting

Description

This command changes the path cost for an interface, which is usually calculated as 10000 ÷ bandwidth, where the bandwidth is the value set by the bandwidth command or the default bandwidth for the interface. The *value* can be from 1 to 65535. The higher the value, the higher the cost.

---

bridge-group priority   interface

```
bridge-group bridge-group priority value
no bridge-group bridge-group priority value
```

Configures   Assigns a priority to a bridge group

Default

32768 for bridges using the IEEE protocol; 128 for bridges using the Digital spanning-tree protocol

Description

This command assigns a priority to an interface within the given *bridge-group*. *value* specifies the interface's priority; this must be between 0 and 65535. A higher priority increases the chance that the interface will be selected as the root bridge.

bridge-group spanning-disabled interface

```
bridge-group bridge-group spanning-disabled
no bridge-group bridge-group spanning-disabled
```

Configures   Use of the spanning-tree algorithm

Default   Enabled

Description

This command disables the spanning-tree algorithm for the given *bridge-group*. The spanning algorithm can be disabled safely for bridge groups that have no possible loop paths at layer 2.

Example

```
interface ethernet 1
  bridge-group 1
  bridge-group 1 spanning-disabled
```

bridge hello-time global

```
bridge bridge-group hello-time seconds
no bridge bridge-group hello-time seconds
```

Configures   The interval between hello packets

Default   2 seconds

Description

This command sets the hello interval for the given *bridge-group* to *seconds*. The value of *seconds* can be from 1 to 10.

bridge irb global

```
bridge irb
no bridge irb
```

Configures   Integrated Routing and Bridging

Default   Disabled

Description

IRB stands for Integrated Routing and Bridging. Like CRB (Concurrent Routing and Bridging), IRB allows a router to both route and bridge a single protocol. However, unlike CRB, IRB allows the routed and bridged interfaces to communicate with each other. See also interface bvi.

bridge max-age

```
bridge bridge-group max-age seconds
no bridge bridge-group max-age seconds
```

Configures   The time to save Bridge Protocol Data Units (BPDUs)

Default   15 seconds

Description

This command sets the maximum time that the router will wait to hear from the root bridge for the given *bridge-group*. If the router does not hear from the root bridge within this interval, the spanning tree is recomputed. The value of *seconds* can be from 6 to 200. (Note: Catalysts use 6–40 seconds.)

bridge multicast-source

```
bridge bridge-group multicast-source
no bridge bridge-group multicast-source
```

Configures   Bridging to support the forwarding of multicast packets

Default   Disabled

Description

This command permits the given *bridge-group* to forward multicast packets.

bridge priority

```
bridge bridge-group priority value
no bridge bridge-group priority value
```

Configures   The priority of an individual bridge

Default

32768 for bridges using the IEEE protocol; 128 for bridges using the Digital spanning-tree protocol

Description

This command assigns a priority to an individual bridge within the given *bridge-group*. *value* specifies the interface's priority; *value* must be between 0 and 65535. A higher priority increases the chance that an interface will be selected as the root bridge. To set an interface to a specific priority, use the `bridge-group priority` command.

bridge protocol

```
bridge bridge-group protocol {ieee | dec}
no bridge bridge-group protocol {ieee | dec}
```

Configures   The spanning-tree protocol

Default   None

Description

This command selects the spanning-tree protocol to use for the *bridge-group*. Possible values are dec, for the Digital spanning-tree protocol, and ieee, for the IEEE spanning-tree protocol. IEEE is the recommend protocol.

bridge route

```
bridge bridge-group route protocol {apollo | appletalk | clns | decnet | ip
    | ipx | vines | xns}
no bridge bridge-group route protocol {apollo | appletalk | clns | decnet | ip
    | ipx | vines | xns}
```

Configures   Routing of a protocol in a bridge group

Default   None

Description

This command enables routing of the given *protocol* on a specific bridge group. The protocol parameter may be apollo, appletalk, clns, decnet, ip, ipx, vines, or xns.

Example

This example enables routing of both IP and IPX in a CRB environment:

```
bridge crb
bridge 5 protocol ieee
bridge 5 route ip
bridge 5 ipx
```

busy-message

```
busy-message hostname delimiter message delimiter
no busy-message
```

Configures   The message displayed when a connection fails

Default   None

Description

This command sets the message that is displayed when a telnet connection to a specific host (given by the *hostname* parameter) fails. The new *message* replaces the generic "host failed" message. To disable this message, delete it with the no form of this command. This banner is useful when you want to give the user information about the connection failure. The *delimiter* marks the beginning and end of the message; it may be any character that is not used in the message.

Example

```
Router(config)#busy-message sunserver2 # server2 is down,
please contact sysadmin at 555-1234 #
```

---

calendar set   command

```
calendar set hh:mm:ss day month year
```

Configures   The system calendar

Description

The calendar is available only on high-end routers. It is an internal clock that continues to run even when the router is powered off. This command allows you to set the calendar to a new time. The *month* must be a name, for example, june. The *year* must be a complete four-digit value, for example, 2000.

---

callback forced-wait   global

```
callback forced-wait seconds
no callback forced-wait seconds
```

Configures   The time the router waits before a callback

Default   None

Description

This command specifies the amount of time in *seconds* that the router waits before initiating a callback to a remote modem.

---

cd   command

```
cd [URL]
```

Description

This command changes the current working directory within the router's filesystem. The URL is optional; if not provided, the system defaults to the *flash:* directory. See the copy command for other valid filesystem URLs.

---

cdp advertise-v2   global

```
cdp advertise-v2
no cdp advertise-v2
```

Configures   Cisco Discovery Protocol (CDP)

Default   Enabled

Description

This command enables Version 2 of CDP, which provides added information. CDP is available only on Cisco routers.

---

cdp enable

interface

```
cdp enable
no cpd enable
```

Configures   Cisco Discovery Protocol (CDP)

Default   Enabled

Description

This command enables Cisco Discovery Protocol (CDP) on a specific interface. CDP provides information about neighboring Cisco routers. It is a proprietary protocol, and therefore isn't implemented by other router vendors. Use show cdp neighbors to see the output.

Example

```
interface ethernet0
    cdp enable
```

---

cdp holdtime

global

```
cdp holdtime seconds
no cdp holdtime seconds
```

Configures   CDP holdtime

Default   180 seconds

Description

This command sets the amount of time, in *seconds*, that the router holds CDP packets before discarding them.

---

cdp run

global

```
cdp run
no cdp run
```

Configures   Globally enables/disables CDP

Default   Enabled

Description

This command enables CDP on all interfaces.

Example

```
Router(config)#cdp run
```

---

cdp timer

```
cdp timer seconds
no cdp timer seconds
```

Configures   CDP update broadcast interval

Default   60 seconds

Description

This command sets the interval, in *seconds*, at which the router transmits CDP updates to its neighbors.

channel-group

```
channel-group channel-number timeslots range [speed kbps]
no channel-group channel-number timeslots range [speed kbps]
```

Configures   T1 or E1 timeslots

Default   None

Description

This command defines the channel timeslots for a fractional T1 or E1 line. Your service provider determines the timeslots for your lines.

channel-number
> A number identifying the communication channel you are defining. For T1 lines, the channel number can be from 0 to 23; for E1 lines, 0 to 30.

timeslots range
> A list of timeslots that make up this communication channel. The list can be a series of comma-separated timeslot numbers, or a pair of timeslots separated by a dash to indicate a range. Timeslot numbers range from 1 to 24 on a T1 line; 1 to 31 for E1. A timeslot cannot belong to more than one channel group.

speed kbps
> The speed of a single timeslot in kbps. Allowable values are 48, 56, and 64. 56 is the default for T1; 64 is the default for E1.

Example

When defining the timeslots range, the value can be a single number or a group of ranges separated by commas and hyphens. For example, the following ranges are all valid:

```
channel-group 3 timeslots 4
channel-group 5 timeslots 4,6-15,24
channel-group 8 timeslots 4-10
```

channel-group

```
channel-group channel-number
no channel-group channel-number
```

Configures   A Fast EtherChannel group

Default   None

Description

This command allows a Fast Ethernet interface to be part of a Fast EtherChannel group. A Fast EtherChannel group allows multiple point-to-point Fast Ethernet interfaces to act as one logical interface. At most, four Fast Ethernet interfaces can belong to a channel group.

chat-script

```
chat-script name script-string
no chat-script name script-string
```

Configures   A chat script for placing a call over a modem

Default   None

Description

The chat-script command defines the script to use for modem communication when dialing to a remote device. *name* identifies the chat script for use in other commands; *script-string* specifies the script itself. The *script-string* contains a series of expect/send characters that communicate with the modem. Table 15-3 shows special characters and escape codes that can be used in chat scripts. Chat scripts are allowed only on asynchronous interfaces like ASYNC and BRI.

Table 15-3: Special values and escape codes for chat scripts

Character or code	Meaning
" "	Null string
ABORT string	The string following the ABORT indicates why the script failed
TIMEOUT timeout	Set the timeout to wait for a response; default is 5 seconds
EOT	End of transmission character
BREAK	Send a BREAK character
\c	Suppress newline at end of string
\d	Cause a two-second delay
\n	Send a newline
\p	Pause for one-fourth of a second
\r	Send a return character
\s	Send a space character
\t	Send a tab character
\\	Send a backslash character
\T	Replaced with phone number

class

```
class name
no class name
```

Configures   Associates a map class with a DLCI

Default   None

Description

This command associates the map class given by *name* with a Data Link Connection Identifier (DLCI).

clear

```
clear command
```

Description

A clear command erases counters for various statistics or performs a reset action. For example, clear line clears an asynchronous line and drops the connection, while clear cdp counters resets the Cisco Discovery Protocol statistics. Table 15-4 summarizes the many clear commands.

Table 15-4: Clear commands

Command	Subcommand	Action
clear access-list	counters	Clears access list statistical information
clear access-template		Clears the access template
clear arp-cache		Clears the entire ARP cache
clear bridge		Resets bridge forwarding cache
	multicast	Resets multicast group state
clear bstun		Clears counters displayed in show bstun
clear cdp		Resets CDP information
	counters	Clears CDP counters
	table	Clears the CDP table
clear counters	*interface*	Clears counters on one or all interfaces
clear controller		
clear crypto		Resets encryption subsystem
clear dialer	*interface*	Clears dialer statistics
clear frame-relay-inarp		Clears inverse ARP entries from the map table
clear host	*	Deletes all host table entries
	name	Deletes the given host table entry
clear hub	ethernet *n*	Clears (resets) a hub
	counters	Clears hub statistics
clear interface		Clears the hardware logic on an interface
clear ip access-list counters		Clears access list statistical information

Table 15-4: Clear commands (continued)

Command	Subcommand	Action
clear ip access-template		Clears the IP access template
clear ip accounting		Clears the IP accounting database
clear ip bgp		Clears BGP connections (resets all connections)
	*	Clears all BGP connections
	as number	Clears the peer AS number
	ip address	Clears the IP address of peer
	dampening	Clears route-dampening information
	flap-statistics	Clears route-flap statistics
	peer-group	Clears connections of a BGP peer group
clear ip cache		Deletes cache table entries
clear ip cgmp	*interface*	Resets the Cisco Group Management Protocol (CGMP); if no interface is specified, resets all interfaces
clear ip drp		Clears director responder counters
clear ip dvmrp		Clears DVMRP counters
clear ip eigrp		Clears IP-EIGRP (resets all connections)
	as number	
	neighbors	
clear ip igmp group		Clears IGMP group cache entries
clear ip mroute		Deletes multicast route table entries
	*	Deletes all entries
	IP-address or *name*	Deletes entries for the group name or IP address
clear ip mtag		Clears multicast Tag Information Base (TIB) entries (resets all connections)
clear ip nat		Clears NAT
	statistics	
	translation	
clear ip nhrp		Clears the NHRP cache
clear ip ospf redistribution		Clears OSPF redistribution counters
clear ip pim	auto-rp	Clears the auto-rp table
	interface	Clears the PIM packet count for that interface
clear ip prefix-list		Clears the prefix list
clear ip redirect		Clears the redirect cache
clear ip route	*	Deletes all route table entries
	IP-address	Deletes route to IP addresses
clear ip rsvp		Clears RSVP
	reservation	
	sender	
clear ip rtp header-compression		Clears RTP/UDP/IP header compression statistics

Table 15-4: Clear commands (continued)

Command	Subcommand	Action
clear ip sdr	group-ip	Clears the Session Directory (SDPv2) cache
clear ip trigger-authentication		Clears trigger-authentication host table
clear isis		Clears all IS-IS data structures
clear kerberos creds		Clears Kerberos credentials
clear line		Resets a terminal line
clear logging		Clears logging buffer
clear rif-cache		Clears the entire RIF cache
clear smrp		Clears Simple Multicast Routing Protocol (SMRP) statistics
clear snapshot		Clears Snapshot timers
clear source-bridge		Clears counters displayed in show source-bridge
clear tarp		Resets TID Address Resolution Protocol (TARP) information
clear tcp		Clears a TCP connection or statistics
	line	Clears TTY line
	local	Clears local host
	statistics	Clears TCP protocol statistics
clear vpdn		Clears a VPDN entity
clear x25		Resets X.25 circuits

client-atm-address name   LANE database

```
client-atm-address atm-address name elan-name
no client-atm-address atm-address
```

Configures   Adds a LANE client address to the database

Default   None

Description

This command adds a LANE client address to the LAN emulation configuration server's database.

atm-address
> Either a complete ATM address or a template that specifies matching ATM addresses. You can create a template by using wildcard characters: an asterisk (*) to match a single character, or an ellipsis (...) to match any number of leading, middle, or trailing characters. A full address is 20 bytes (40 hex characters) long, and is similar to (though not the same as) an NSAP address.

name *elan-name*
> The name of the emulated LAN. The maximum length of a name is 32 characters.

If you use a template, any name that matches the template is associated with the ELAN. If the given address or template matches addresses that are already in the database, the command has no effect; the database is not changed.

clock calendar-valid global

```
clock calendar-valid
no clock calendar-valid
```

Configures   Network Time Protocol (NTP)

Default   Disabled

Description

This command tells the router to consider the RTC calendar in hardware to be a valid source of time. This command is valid only on high-end routers (5000, 6000, 7500, 8500, etc.).

clock rate interface

```
clock rate bps
no clock rate
```

Configures   Clock rate for serial devices

Default   None

Description

By default, no clock rate is configured for any serial devices. This command specifies the bit rate for DCE serial devices in bps. Possible values for *bps* are 1200, 2400, 4800, 9600, 19200, 38400, 56000, 64000, 72000, 125000, 148000, 500000, 800000, 1000000, 1300000, 2000000, and 4000000.

This command is most useful for connecting routers back-to-back in a lab setting. In this case, the command is required only on the DCE end of the link. You usually don't need this command when connecting to a WAN service because the network provider provides the clockings.

clock read-calendar command

```
clock read-calendar
```

Configures   Calendar time

Description

This command manually updates the calendar time into the router's system clock. It is not a configuration command and is not stored in the router's configuration. Normally, the system clock is updated from the calendar during system boot-up. This command is available only on high-end routers (5000, 6000, 7500, 8500, etc.).

clock set
command

```
clock set hh:mm:ss day month year
```

Description

This command manually sets the router's internal clock. It is not stored in the router's configuration. The time is specified in terms of a 24-hour clock; the year must be a full four digits (for example, 2001).

clock summer-time
global

```
clock summer-time zone recurring [sweek sday smonth shh:mm eweek eday emonth
    ehh:mm][offset]
clock summer-time zone date sday smonth syear shh:mm eday emonth eyear ehh:mm
    [offset]
no clock summer-time
```

Configures   Daylight Savings Time behavior

Default   No Daylight Savings Time

Description

This command tells the router to update for Daylight Savings Time. The recurring form of the command specifies that Daylight Savings Time should be observed at the given time every year. The date form of the command specifies a specific start date and end date for Daylight Savings Time. Use the no form of the command to return to the default, in which Daylight Savings Time is not observed.

zone
> The time zone (EDT, CDT, etc.).

sweek, eweek
> The week of the month (1, 2, 3, 4, 5, last) on which Daylight Savings Time begins (sweek) or ends (eweek). (This is only used in the recurring form of the command.)

sday, eday
> The day on which Daylight Savings Time starts (sday) or ends (eday). For the recurring form of the command, use the actual name of the day (Monday, Tuesday, etc.) For the date form of the command, use a numeric date (1-31).

smonth, emonth
> The month in which Daylight Savings Time starts (smonth) or ends (emonth). Use the actual name of the month (September, October, etc.).

syear, eyear
> All four digits of the year. syear is the year in which Daylight Savings Time starts; eyear is the year in which it ends (used only in the date form of the command).

shh:mm, ehh:mm
> The time in hours and minutes at which Daylight Savings Time starts or ends.

offset
>   The number of minutes to add for Daylight Savings Time (optional; the default is 60).

Example

The following command sets the time zone to use U.S. rules in the Eastern time zone:

```
clock summer-time EDT recurring
```

---

clock timezone   global

```
clock timezone zone hours [minutes]
no clock timezone
```

Configures   The router's time zone

Default   Coordinated Universal Time (UTC)

Description

This command sets the router's time zone and the number of hours from the UTC. *minutes* is optional and is also an offset from the UTC.

zone
>   The time zone (PST, EST, etc.).

hours
>   The offset from the UTC (a positive or negative integer).

minutes
>   Optional. The offset from the UTC in minutes (a positive or negative integer).

---

clock update-calendar   command

```
clock update-calendar
```

Configures   Updates the calendar

Description

This command manually updates the calendar from the router's system clock. The calendar is a separate internal clock that continuously runs even if the router is powered off. This command is available only on high-end routers (5000, 6000, 7500, 8500, etc.).

---

compress   interface

```
compress {predictor | stac}
no compress {predictor | stac}
```

Configures   Type of compression used across an interface

Default   None

Description

This command enables compression for the selected interface. Compression can be enabled only for PPP or HDLC encapsulation. Two types of compression are supported:

predictor
> Can be used on PPP connections; consumes more of the router's CPU and memory, but less bandwidth.

stac
> Can be used on HDLC or PPP connections; consumes more bandwidth, but requires less CPU power.

Compression should not be activated on lines where link speeds are very high or most of the data is already compressed. If the data is already compressed, the router spends valuable CPU cycles for no reason.

When using compression, monitor the router's CPU usage. If the CPU usage is consistently high (65%), compression might be hindering the router.

The same type of compression must be enabled on both ends of the link.

Example

The following commands enable stac compression for the serial1 interface, which uses HDLC encapsulation.

```
interface serial1
  encapsulation hdlc
  compress stac
```

---

config-register   global

config-register *value*

Configures   Sets the configuration register

Default   Depends on the product

Description

This command allows the user to change the configuration register. Setting the configuration register is useful for recovering lost passwords and remedying other situations.

value
> The value to set in the configuration register. The register is 16 bits wide, so legal values range from 0x0 to 0xFFFF in hexadecimal (0 to 65535 decimal). Table 15-5 shows the significance of the bits in the configuration register. (There are some differences in bit assignments on different products; check your documentation.)

Table 15-5: Configuration register settings

Value	Action
0x0000	Remains at the system bootstrap prompt.
0x0001	Boots system image on EPROM.
0x0002 – 0x000f	Specifies a Netboot filename, where the filename is in the form cisco-processor_name. The *n* in the filename is taken from the hexadecimal value of these bits.
0x0040	Ignores NVRAM contents.
0x0080	Enables OEM bit.
0x0100	Breaks Disabled. If you enable this bit, the break key can cause the router to go to boot ROM at any time. During the first 60 seconds of bootup, the break key is enabled no matter what this bit field is set to.
0x0400	Sets the IP broadcast address to all zeros.
0x0800 – 0x1000	Sets the console line speed.
0x2000	Boots default ROM software if network boot fails.
0x4000	IP broadcasts do not have network numbers.
0x8000	Enables diagnostic messages.

---

configure   command

```
configure {terminal | memory | network | overwrite-network}
```

Configures   Enters global configuration mode

Description

The conf terminal command places you in configuration mode. conf memory executes the commands stored in memory (essentially a reload of the startup config). Note that the commands conf network and conf overwrite-network have been deprecated; it is now preferable to use copy tftp running-config.

Example

The following command places you in configuration mode; from there, you can enter global configuration commands.

```
Router#configure terminal
Router(config)# ! I can now enter configuration commands!
```

---

controller   global

```
controller {t1 | e1} slot/port
controller {t1 | e1} number
```

Configures   T1 or E1 controllers

Default   None

Description

This command places you in the controller mode, allowing you to configure a controller for a T1 or E1 line. *slot/port* and *number* identify the controller that you are configuring.

---

copy

copy *source* [*destination*]

Description

This command allows you to copy system images and configuration files. You can copy files within the router's memory (for example, copy running-config startup-config), or you can copy files to or from a TFTP server or an RCP server. Table 15-6 shows possible values for the *source* and *destination* parameters. If you omit the destination, the router will prompt you for it.

Table 15-6: Sources and destinations for the copy command

Sources and destinations	Meaning
running-config	The currently running configuration
startup-config	The configuration that will be loaded when the router boots
tftp	An external TFTP server
rcp	An external RCP server
ftp	An external FTP server
flash	The router's flash filesystem
slot0: slot1:	The router's PCMCIA flash memory cards
disk0: disk1:	The router's internal drives (high-end routers)
bootflash	The internal bootstrap flash memory; only on some devices (4500)

Newer versions of IOS also permit the use of URLs. The syntax of a URL can look like this:

```
tftp:[[//hostname]/path]/filename
ftp:[[//[username[:password]@]hostname]/path]/filename
rcp:[[//[username@]hostname]/path]/filename
```

In each of these URLs, the *hostname* is simply the hostname or IP address of the end device. TFTP doesn't require a username or password. FTP and RCP can have an optional username and password, which depends on the server configuration.

To use the URL, simply provide the correct hostname and path in the source or destination.

Example

Here are some accepted uses of the copy command:

```
copy running-config startup-config
copy startup-config tftp
copy running-config tftp
```

```
copy flash tftp
copy startup-config rcp
copy running-config rcp
copy flash rcp
copy tftp running-config
copy tftp://ourserver/newconfig running-config
copy ftp://bob:letmein@oursever/newconfig running-config
```

crc   interface

```
crc length
no crc
```

Configures   The length of the CRC checksum

Default   16 bits

Description

This command sets the *length* (in bits) of the CRC (Cyclic Redundancy Check) on
FSIP (Fast Serial Interface Processor) and HIP (HSSI Interface Processor) interfaces. These interfaces are found only on the 7500 series routers. The length must
be 16 or 32 bits.

custom-queue-list   interface

```
custom-queue-list list-number
no custom-queue-list list-number
```

Configures   Applies a custom queue list to an interface

Default   None

Description

This command applies a custom queue to the current interface. The *list-number*
must be between 1 and 16. Custom queue lists are used to implement priority-
based queueing; they allow you to configure the bandwidth used by a particular
type of traffic. To create a queue list, use the `queue-list` command. If you're
configuring a Frame Relay interface, see the `frame-relay custom-queue-list`
command. Queue lists are discussed in Chapter 7.

databits   line

```
databits {5 | 6 | 7 | 8}
```

Configures   Databits per character

Default   8

Description

This command defines the number of databits per character that are interpreted
and generated by the hardware. Possible values are 5, 6, 7, and 8.

Example

The following commands configure TTY 3 for seven databits per character:

```
Router(config)#line tty3
Router(config-line)#databits 7
```

---

data-character-bits   line

```
data-character-bits {7 | 8}
```

Configures   Software databits per character

Default   8

Description

This command defines the number of databits per character that are interpreted
and generated by the software. Possible values are 7 and 8.

---

dce-terminal-timing enable   interface

```
dce-terminal-timing enable
no dce-terminal-timing enable
```

Configures   Interface timing

Default   Off (the DCE provides its own clock)

Description

This command prevents phase-shifting of data on high-speed data lines that span
long distances. Phase-shifting is prevented by taking the clock from the DTE to
provide timing for the DCE. (The DTE's timing is called SCTE.)

---

debug   global

```
debug level
undebug level
undebug all
```

Configures   System debugging

Default   Disabled

Description

This command enables debugging at the specified *level*. Just about every configuration item within the IOS has a debug level associated with it. The debug ?
command gives you an extensive list that allows you to find the debug level that
meets your needs.

Be careful in selecting your debug level; you can easily crash a busy router with
the incorrect selection. For example, debug ip packet might render a busy router
useless until debugging is disabled. See Chapter 14 for more information on using

debug correctly. If you get in trouble, issue the command undebug all, which disables all debug output.

Example

Here is the output from debug ip ?:

```
Router#debug ip ?
  bgp        BGP information
  cache      IP cache operations
  cgmp       CGMP protocol activity
  dvmrp      DVMRP protocol activity
  egp        EGP information
  eigrp      IP-EIGRP information
  error      IP error debugging
  ftp        FTP dialogue
  http       HTTP connections
  icmp       ICMP transactions
  igmp       IGMP protocol activity
  igrp       IGRP information
  mcache     IP multicast cache operations
  mobile     Mobility protocols
  mpacket    IP multicast packet debugging
  mrouting   IP multicast routing table activity
  ospf       OSPF information
  packet     General IP debugging and IPSO security transactions
  peer       IP peer address activity
  pim        PIM protocol activity
  policy     Policy routing
  rip        RIP protocol transactions
  routing    Routing table events
  rsvp       RSVP protocol activity
  sd         Session Directory (SD)
  security   IP security options
  tcp        TCP information
  udp        UDP based transactions
```

Though there is a debug all command, using it is not recommended. It produces so much output that it will overwhelm you and the router. Use it only as a last resort.

The undebug all command disables all debugging that is currently enabled.

---

default-information   router, EIGRP, IGRP

```
default-information {in | out} access-list
no default-information {in | out}
```

Configures   Default routing information

Default

EIGRP announces the candidate default route in both incoming and outgoing updates

Description

When redistributing EIGRP into IGRP, you can use this command to allow (or suppress, using the no form of the command) the redistribution of the default

---

routes or exterior routes from EIGRP. By default, all exterior routes (including default routes) are passed between IGRP and EIGRP.

in
> Allows the protocol to receive the default route via redistribution.

out
> Allows the protocol to propagate the default route via redistribution.

access-list
> The number or name of a simple access list that permits or denies the default routes you want to propagate.

Example

The following commands prevent IGRP from receiving exterior or default routes via redistribution from EIGRP.

```
router igrp 109
  network 10.0.0.0
  redistribute eigrp 100
  no default-information in
```

To disable the default routes in outgoing updates, use the no form of the command.

```
router eigrp 100
  network 10.0.0.0
  no default-information out
```

---

default-information originate router, BGP, OSPF

```
default-information originate [route-map map]
no default information originate
```

BGP:
```
default-information originate
no default-information originate
```

OSPF:
```
default-information originate [always] [metric metric-value] [metric-type type]
    [route-map map]
no default-information originate [always] [metric metric-value] [metric-type
    type] [route-map map]
```

Configures   Redistribution of the default route

Default   Disabled

Description

This command allows the protocol to propagate the default route (0.0.0.0). The use of a route map, *map*, tells the router to inject the default route if the route map's conditions are met.

For OSPF, this command tells an Autonomous System Border Router (ASBR) to inject a default route into the OSPF domain. When used with OSPF, this command has the following additional parameters.

---

always
> Optional. Specifies to advertise the route even if the software does not have a default route.

metric *metric-value*
> Optional. The metric value of the default route. The default metric is 10.

metric-type *metric-type*
> Optional. Defines the link type associated with the default route. Possible values are 1 (Type 1 external route) and 2 (Type 2 external route; the default).

route-map *map*
> Optional. Defines the route map to use for the default route. The route is advertised only if the route map is successful. This option can be used to set a different default metric depending on the host to which the route is sent.

Example

```
! BGP
router bgp 150
  default-information orginate
!
! Ospf
router ospf 110
  default-information originate metric 100 metric-type 1
```

default-metric   router

BGP:

```
default-metric number
no default-metric number
```

RIP:

```
default-metric number
no default-metric
```

IGRP/EIGRP:

```
default-metric bandwidth delay reliability loading mtu
no default metric bandwidth delay reliability loading mtu
```

OSPF:

```
default-metric number
no default-metric number
```

Configures   Default metric for routes learned from a different routing protocol

Default   Depends on the protocol

Description

When redistributing routes from one routing protocol to another, the metrics used by the different protocols are not compatible. This command allows you to set the metric values for routes learned from other protocols.

For RIP and OSPF, this command simply sets the metric value to *number*.

For BGP, this command sets the value for the multi-exit discriminator (MED) metric to *number*.

For IGRP and EIGRP, this command sets the default metric for redistributing other protocols into EIGRP. (Note that IGRP and EIGRP have compatible metrics, so the default metric set by this command is not required when distributing routes between these two protocols.) The default metric is computed using the following parameters:

bandwidth
> The route bandwidth measured in kilobits per second.

delay
> The route delay in microseconds.

reliability
> An estimate of the reliability of packet transmission on this link. It must be a value between 0 and 255; 255 indicates 100% reliability and 0 indicates that the link is completely unreliable (no packets are transferred correctly).

loading
> The effective bandwidth of a route as a fraction of the bandwidth's capacity. This value must be between 0 and 255; 255 indicates 100% loading.

mtu
> The maximum transmission unit for this route in octets.

Example

The following commands assign metric 10 to all routes redistributed from OSPF into RIP:

```
router rip
    network 192.168.1.0
    default-metric 10
    redistribute ospf 110
```

The following commands provide various parameters for computing an EIGRP metric to be used when redistributing routes from RIP into EIGRP:

```
router eigrp 101
  network 10.0.0.0
  redistribute rip
  default-metric 1000 100 250 100 1500
```

---

default-name   LANE database

```
default-name elan-name
no default-name
```

Configures   A default ELAN for clients

Default   None

Description

This command sets the default name for the ELAN (Emulated LAN) in the configuration server's database. This name is used for clients who do not have an explicit name set. The name can be up to 32 characters in length and must already be in the configuration server's database. To put a name in the LANE emulation server database, use the commands `lane database` and `name server-atm-address`.

delay   interface

```
delay tens-of-milliseconds
no delay
```

Configures   Link delay

Default   Depends on the interface type

Description

This command is used to specify the latency of an interface in *tens-of-milliseconds*. The value is used as input to route metric calculations; it does not set anything on the interface itself.

delete   command

```
delete URL
```

Description

This command marks a file as deleted in the flash filesystem. The actual behavior of this command depends on the type of filesystem implemented for your router. In a Class A filesystem, deleted files are only marked for deletion, and can be recovered with the `undelete` command; the `squeeze` command permanently deletes the marked files. In a Class B filesystem, files are deleted immediately, but the space they occupied can't be recovered without erasing the entire filesystem. In a Class C filesystem, files are deleted immediately, and their space is recovered immediately. Filesystems are described in more detail in Chapter 2.

description   interface

```
description text
no description
```

Configures   A description for the interface

Default   None

Description

This command provides a description for the interface, letting you build some documentation into your IOS configuration. The description is for informational purposes and does not affect the interface's behavior. The description you give appears in the output of some `show` commands.

Example

```
interface serial0
  description T1 Connection to Baltimore
```

dialer aaa
interface

```
dialer aaa
no dialer aaa
```

Configures   AAA for dial-on-demand routing (DDR)

Default   Disabled

Description

This command enables AAA for a dialer interface.

dialer callback-secure
interface

```
dialer callback-secure
no dialer callback-secure
```

Configures   Callback security

Default   Disabled

Description

This command enables secure callback dialing on the interface.

dialer callback-server
interface

```
dialer callback-server [username] [dialstring]
no dialer callback-server
```

Configures   An interface to return calls

Default   Disabled

Description

This command enables an interface to return calls. The username keyword tells the router to identify the caller by looking up the authenticated hostname in the dialer map command; this is the default behavior for this command. The dialstring keyword tells the router to identify the caller during callback negotiation.

dialer caller
interface

```
dialer caller number [callback]
no dialer caller number [callback]
```

Configures   Caller ID screening

Default   Disabled

Description

This command configures a dialer interface to reject calls that do not match the given *number*. The *number* can be any phone number; the character x can be used as a wildcard. The callback keyword enables Caller ID callback; in this case, the incoming call is refused, and the router initiates a call to the Caller ID number. This may help you to manage your telephone charges.

This feature is available only on certain routers with special dialer interfaces. A switch that supports Caller ID is also required for this operation. If you enable this feature and do not have the required hardware for Caller ID, all calls are denied.

Example

The following command allows any number from 4105554290 through 4105554299:

```
dialer caller 410555429x
```

---

dialer dtr   interface

```
dialer dtr
no dialer dtr
```

Configures

Enables DDR and specifies that the modem handles only DTR signaling

Default   None

Description

Configures interfaces that are connected to modems that require DTR (Data Terminal Ready), and enables DDR (dial-on-demand routing). Interfaces configured with this command cannot receive calls; they can only make them.

---

dialer enable-timeout   interface

```
dialer enable-timeout seconds
no dialer enable-timeout
```

Configures   The amount of time the interface remains down

Default   15 seconds

Description

Sets the time in *seconds* that an interface remains down between calls or failed connections.

dialer fast-idle

```
dialer fast-idle seconds
no dialer fast-idle
```

Configures   The amount of idle time when there is contention for the line

Default   20 seconds

Description

This command can apply to interfaces or map-class configurations. When used on an interface or a map class, it defines the number of *seconds* that must pass before a line is disconnected when there is contention for the interface, i.e., when there is traffic waiting for a different destination other than the current connection.

When used for a map class, this command defines the number of seconds to wait before placing another call, and defaults to the fast-idle setting for the interface.

For regular idle-timeouts for a DDR interface, see the `dialer idle-timeout` command.

Example

Interface configuration:

```
interface async 5
    dialer fast-idle 55
```

Map-class configuration:

```
map-class dialer office
    dialer fast-idle 55
```

dialer-group

```
dialer-group number
no dialer-group number
```

Configures   Associates an interface with a dialer group

Default   None

Description

This command adds the interface to the dialer group specified by *number*. An interface can have only one dialer group associated with it. Each dialer group has an associated access list that defines "interesting" traffic for this interface. If the traffic is permitted by the access list, a call is initiated for the interface if the interface is not already connected.

Example

The following commands add the `async1` interface to `dialer-group 1`. `access-list 110` specifies the traffic that causes this interface to initiate a call; in this case, ICMP traffic doesn't bring up the connection, but any other IP traffic does. Note that this access list does not block ICMP traffic once the link is up; it just prevents ICMP traffic from bringing it up in the first place.

```
! Set the interface as part of the dialer group
interface async 1
  dialer-group 1
!
! Set the dialer group to use access-list 110
dialer-list 1 list 110
!
! Configure the access-list for the dialer group
access-list 110 deny icmp any any
access-list 110 permit ip any any
```

dialer hold-queue   interface

```
dialer hold-queue packets timeout seconds
no dialer hold-queue packets timeout seconds
```

Configures   A queue that holds packets until a dial-up connection is established

Default   Disabled

Description

Instructs the interface to queue traffic until the dial-up connection is completed. By default, queueing is not enabled and packets are dropped until the connection is established.

packets
> The number of packets to hold in the queue, waiting for the connection. The value can be set from 0 to 100.

timeout *seconds*
> The period of time after which the connection attempt is determined to have failed, and the waiting packets discarded.

dialer idle-timeout   interface, map-class

```
dialer idle-timeout seconds
no dialer idle-timeout seconds
```

Configures   The amount of idle time before a connection is disconnected

Default   120 seconds

Description

This command can apply to interfaces or map-class configurations. When used on an interface or a map class, it defines the number of *seconds* an interface must be idle (no traffic) before the connection is closed. When there is contention for a dialer (i.e., traffic for a destination different from the one to which the interface is currently connected), then the fast idle timeout is used. (See dialer fast-idle.)

Example

Interface configuration:

```
interface async 4
    dialer idle-timeout 300
```

Map-class configuration:

```
map-class dialer office
    dialer idle-timeout 300
```

dialer in-band interface

```
dialer in-band [no-parity | odd-parity]
no dialer in-band
```

Configures   Dial-on-demand routing (DDR)

Default

Disabled; no-parity is the default when the command is issued with no options

Description

This command configures an interface to support DDR.

no-parity
: Optional. Chat scripts to the modem have no parity.

odd-parity
: Optional. Chat scripts to the modem have odd parity.

This is not required on BRI interfaces.

dialer isdn map-class, dialer

```
dialer isdn [speed value] [spc]
no dialer isdn [speed value] [spc]
```

Configures   Bit rate used on the B channel

Default   64

Description

This command is for map-class configurations only. It defines the bit rate for the B channel of an ISDN connection and sets up semipermanent connections for the map class.

speed *value*
: Optional. Defines the bit rate in kbps for the B channel; either 56 or 64. Default is 64.

spc
: Optional. Requires the use of ISDN semipermanent connections for this map class (Germany only).

Example

```
map-class dialer office
    dialer isdn speed 64
```

---

dialer-list   global

```
dialer-list group list access-list
dialer-list group protocol protocol {permit | deny | list} access-list
no dialer-list group
```

Configures   Assigns an access list to a dialer group

Default   None

Description

The first version of this command specifies a group number and applies the given access list to that group. The access list defines "interesting" traffic for the dialer group. If traffic matches the access list, it is deemed interesting, and the DDR interface establishes a connection (if one hasn't been already established).

group
> The dialer group number.

list *access-list*
> The access list that defines interesting traffic for this group.

The second version of this command allows you to specify the traffic that brings up the connection without using an external access list. Its parameters are:

group
> The dialer group number.

protocol *protocol*
> The protocol to allow (or reject): **ip**, **ipx**, etc.

permit
> Permits traffic using this protocol.

deny
> Denies the entire protocol.

list *access-list*
> Applies an access list to the protocol. Used to single out ports within the protocol.

Examples

The following commands define a dialer group, assign an interface to that dialer group, and specify that the interface should be brought up if traffic matching access list 110 appears on the interface.

```
interface async 5
    dialer-group 10
    !
    ! Define the access-list for group 10
    dialer-list 10 list 110
    !
```

```
! Define the list ( all IP traffic to 10.10.1.0 network)
access-list 110 permit ip any 10.10.1.0 0.0.0.255
```

The following commands define a dialer group, assign an interface to that dialer group, and specify that the interface should be brought up for any IP traffic. No access list is used.

```
interface async 5
  dialer-group 10
  !
  ! Define all ip traffic as interesting
  dialer-list 10 protocol ip permit
```

---

dialer load-threshold interface

```
dialer load-threshold load [{outbound | inbound | either}]
no dialer load-threshold
```

Configures   The threshold for opening an additional connection

Default   None

Description

This command defines the threshold at which the router opens an additional connection to obtain more bandwidth. Another connection can be made only if this interface is part of a rotary group. This command can be used only if the interface belongs to a rotary group.

load
> The utilization at which another connection to the destination is established. The number can be from 1 to 255 (255 = 100% utilization).

outbound
> Optional. Load is considered only for outbound traffic.

inbound
> Optional. Load is considered only for inbound traffic.

either
> Optional. Default. A new connection is established if the utilization exceeds the given load in either the outbound or inbound direction.

---

dialer map interface

```
dialer map protocol destination [name hostname] [class name] [broadcast]
  [spc] [speed {56|64}] [modem-script script-name] [system-script
  script-name] [dial-string]
no dialer map protocol destination [name hostname] [class name] [broadcast]
  [spc] [speed {56|64}] [modem-script script-name] [system-script
  script-name] [dial-string]
```

Configures   Any non-DTR dialer interface for PPP callback

Default   None

Description

The dialer map command allows an interface to call one or more different sites by mapping a destination address to connection-specific dial strings and connection scripts.

protocol
> Names the protocol to use for the connection. Valid values are ip, appletalk, bridge, decnet, ipx, novell, snapshot, vines, and xns.

destination
> The destination address to use for this map. The next-hop address of a packet is the destination address in map configurations.

name *hostname*
> Optional. The name of the remote system for the DDR connection.

class *name*
> Optional. Names a map class to use for this mapping. A map class is defined with the map-class command.

broadcast
> Optional. Allows broadcast packets to be forwarded over this connection.

spc
> Optional. ISDN only; Germany only. Configures a semipermanent connection between the ISDN device and the exchange.

speed *speed*
> Optional. ISDN only. Defines the speed of an ISDN B channel in kbps. Valid values are 56 and 64. The default value is 64.

modem-script *script-name*
> Optional. Names the modem script to use for dialing the connection. Required only if no dialer string is defined for the interface used.

system-script *script-name*
> Optional. Names the system script to use for logging into the remote system.

dial-string
> Optional. This option must be the last entry on the command line. It defines the telephone number to be sent to the dialing device. For multipoint ISDN connections, you can append the subaddress to the dial string (separated by a colon).

---

dialer map snapshot   interface

```
dialer map snapshot seq-number dial-string
no dialer map snapshot seq-number
```

Configures   Snapshot routing

Default   None

Description

This command configures client snapshot routing on a DDR interface.

---

seq-number
Identifies the dialer map. This number can range from 1 to 254.

dial-string
The telephone number to dial for this snapshot connection.

---

dialer max-link

```
dialer max-link number
no dialer max-link
```

Configures

The maximum number of open links that a dialer profile can have to a destination

Default   255

Description

This command sets the maximum number of links that a dialer profile can have open to a single destination at any time. This command can be used only on dialer interfaces. *number* can be from 1 to 255.

---

dialer pool

```
dialer pool pool-number
no dialer pool pool-number
```

Configures   The dialing pool to use to connect to a specific network

Default   None

Description

Specifies the dialer pool to which a dialer interface belongs. Pool numbers range from 1 to 255. For more information on dialer pools, consult Chapter 11.

Example

The following code configures a dialer interface with an IP address and PPP encapsulation, and assigns the interface to dialer pool 5.

```
interface dialer1
  ip address 10.10.1.0 255.255.255.0
  encapsulation ppp
  dialer pool 5
```

---

dialer pool-member

```
dialer pool-member pool-number [priority value] [min-link value]
  [max-link value]
no dialer pool-member pool-number
```

Configures   Assigns a physical interface to a dialer pool

Default   Disabled

Description

Any interface can belong to a dialer pool. Dialer pools are configured using the `dialer` interface. This command assigns an interface to a pool.

pool-number
> The pool to which the interface is assigned.

priority *value*
> Optional. This value is the interface's priority within the pool. The interface with the highest priority is selected first for dialing out. This value can be from 0 to 255; the default is 0.

min-link *value*
> Optional. This is for ISDN lines; it specifies the minimum number of B channels that are reserved on this interface. The value can be from 0 to 255; the default is 0.

max-link *value*
> Optional. This is for ISDN lines; it specifies the maximum number of B channels that are reserved on this interface. The value can be from 0 to 255; the default is 0.

Example

The following commands assign the ISDN interface BRI1 to dialer pool 1:

```
interface BRI1
  encapsulation ppp
  dialer pool-member 1 priority 50
```

---

dialer priority   interface

dialer priority *value*
no dialer priority *value*

Configures   The priority of an interface in a rotary group

Default   0

Description

This command sets the priority of the interface within a rotary group. *value* can be from 0 to 255. The highest-priority interface is selected first for dialing.

---

dialer remote-name   interface

dialer remote-name *username*
no dialer remote-name *username*

Configures   The authentication name for the remote router

Default   None

Description

This command sets the username to use when connecting to a remote system with CHAP or PAP authentication.

---

dialer rotary-group   interface

```
dialer rotary-group group-number
no dialer rotary-group group-number
```

Configures   Includes the interface as part of a dialer rotary group

Default   None

Description

This command sets the rotary group for an interface to *group-number*. The number of the rotary group must match the number of the dialer interface for which the rotary group is defined. The group number can range from 0 to 255.

---

dialer rotor   interface

```
dialer rotor {priority | best}
no dialer rotor {priority | best}
```

Configures   The method for selecting the next interface to use to dial out

Default   Disabled

Description

For rotary groups, this command tells the router whether to select the interface with the highest priority (`priority`) or the interface with the most recent connection success (`best`).

---

dialer string   interface

```
dialer string string [class dialer-map-name]
no dialer string
```

Configures   Legacy DDR phone numbers

Default   None

Description

Specifies the dial string for the interface's modem. Table 15-7 shows the codes that can be used in the dialer string. This command is used only for legacy dial-on-demand routing (DDR); on modern routers, it's more flexible to use dialer pools or dialer map statements, which allow more than one destination to be called.

The `class` option names the dialer map associated with this dialer string.

Table 15-7: Codes for use in legacy DDR

Code	Meaning
T	Use tone dialing
P	Use pulse dialing
&	Flash
:	Wait tone
= ,	Separators 3 and 4 (for international use)

dialer wait-for-carrier-time
interface, map-class

```
dialer wait-for-carrier-time seconds
no dialer wait-for-carrier-time
```

Configures   The amount of time the interface waits for a carrier

Default   30 seconds

Description

This command sets the maximum amount of time in *seconds* that the router waits for a carrier when bringing up a dialer interface. It can be used on an interface or map-class configuration.

dialer watch-disable
interface

```
dialer watch-disable seconds
no dialer watch-disable
```

Configures   Delay time for the backup interface

Default   Disabled

Description

This command configures the time in *seconds* to keep the backup link up after the primary link recovers, if the backup link has been brought up by a dialer watch group.

dialer watch-group
interface

```
dialer watch-group group-number
no dialer watch-group group-number
```

Configures   Enables backup DDR for an interface

Default   Disabled

Description

This command is used to configure an interface as a backup DDR link using a watch list. The *group-number* identifies the watch list that triggers calls on this interface; the interface is brought up if the router doesn't have any routes to the networks listed in the watch list. A watch list is created by the `dialer watch-list` command; the interface must have a dialer map that corresponds exactly to the networks listed in that command.

dialer watch-list global

```
dialer watch-list group-number ip address mask
no dialer watch-list group-number ip address mask
```

Configures   A watch group number assigned to an IP address range

Default   None

Description

This command allows you to define a group of routes based on IP address and mask, and assign that group to a *group-number*. If no routes to these networks are in the routing table, the router dials a backup connection. Note that this connection is dialed regardless of whether there is any traffic for these destinations; dialing depends only on the existence of a route. This command is used in conjunction with `dialer watch-group`, `dialer watch-disable`, and `dialer map`. Valid group numbers are from 1 to 255.

dir command

```
dir [/all] [filesystem:]
```

Description

This command displays the files in the router's filesystem. If you supply a directory as an argument, the command lists the files in that directory; otherwise, it lists the current working directory. Use the `/all` keyword to list all files, including those marked for deletion.

disable command

```
disable [level]
```

Description

This command exits privileged mode and returns the user to user mode. The optional *level* parameter value ranges from 0 through 15. 0 is the normal user mode; 15 is the privileged user mode. If no level is specified, the user is returned to level 0 (user mode). See the `privilege` command for more information on setting the level values.

Example

```
Router# disable
Router
```

disconnect

command

disconnect

Description

This command terminates a background telnet session.

---

disconnect-character

line

disconnect-character *ascii-number*
no disconnect-character

Configures The character to use to disconnect a session

Default None

Description

This command defines the character that a user types to end an interactive session. As with the `activation-character` command, the *ascii-number* is the decimal value of the desired character.

Example

In this example, we set the disconnect character to `control-D`, which is ASCII number 4, and we inform the users with a banner message.

```
Router(config)# line 2
Router(config-line)# activation-character 13
Router(config-line)# disconnect-character 4
Router(config-line)# vacant-message #
Router(config-line)#          ***** Welcome to Sphinx *****
Router(config-line)#     Press the return key to start the connection
Router(config-line)#     Disconnect with a control-D key
Router(config-line)# #
```

---

dispatch-character

line

dispatch-character *ascii-number*
no dispatch-character

Configures The character that causes a packet to be sent

Default None

Description

This command defines the character that causes a packet to be sent. Setting the dispatch character causes the router to buffer a group of characters into a packet before sending them to the remote host. *ascii-number* is the decimal value of the desired character.

Example

The following example sets the Return key (ascii 13) as the dispatch character for virtual terminals 1 through 4.

```
line vty 1 4
  dispatch-character 13
```

---

distance   router

```
distance distance [address mask] [access-list]
no distance distance [address mask] [access-list]
```

Configures   Administrative distance

Default   Depends on the protocol

Description

The distance command allows you to change the trustworthiness of a route's source relative to other routing protocols. The lower the distance, the more the route's source is trusted. Routes with a distance of 255 are not added to the route table. Chapter 8 discusses how routing protocols use administrative distances and lists the default value for each protocol.

distance
> The administrative distance to be assigned to this protocol (or to routes selected by the other arguments to this command). Administrative distance must be a value from 1 to 255.

address mask
> Optional. If these arguments are present, the administrative distance applies only to routes whose destinations match this address/mask pair.

access-list
> Optional. If this argument is present, the administrative distance applies only to routes that match the given access list.

---

distance bgp   router, BGP

```
distance bgp external-distance internal-distance local-distance
no distance bgp
```

Configures   Administrative distance for BGP

Default   External distance, 20; internal distance, 200; local distance, 200

Description

The distance bgp command allows you to change the trustworthiness of a route's source relative to other routing protocols. The lower the distance, the more the route's source is trusted. Routes with a distance of 255 are not added to the route table. *external-distance* applies to external BGP routes (routes learned from a peer outside your AS); *internal-distance* applies to internal BGP routes (routes learned from a peer within your AS); *local-distance* applies to routes added with the network command. It's usually not a good idea to change BGP's routing distances.

Example

The distance bgp command is often used to change the internal distance so that its value is equal to the external distance, as in the following example:

```
router bgp 101
  distance bgp 20 20 200
```

---

distance eigrp   router, EIGRP

```
distance eigrp internal-distance external-distance
no distance eigrp
```

Configures   Administrative distance for EIGRP

Default   External distance, 170; internal distance, 90

Description

This command sets the internal and external administrative distances for the EIGRP protocol. The administrative distance reflects the trustworthiness of a route's source relative to other routing protocols. The *internal-distance* applies to internal routes, which are routes learned from the current EIGRP routing process (commonly called "autonomous system"). The *external-distance* applies to routes learned from other EIGRP routing processes. *internal-distance* and *external-distance* must be in the range of 1 to 255. Chapter 8 discusses the use of administrative distance and shows the default distances for the different routing protocols.

---

distribute-list in   router

```
distribute-list access-list in [interface]
no distribute-list access-list in [interface]
```

Configures   An access list to filter incoming routing updates

Default   None

Description

This command allows you to apply an access list to incoming route updates to a routing protocol. If no interface is specified, the access list is applied to all incoming route updates. If an interface is specified, the access list is applied only to route updates received on that interface. The access list should be a standard access list.

Example

The following distribute list applies access list 1 to incoming routes:

```
route rip
  network 10.0.0.0
```

```
    distribute-list 1 in
  !
  ! Deny network 10.1.1.0
  access-list 1 deny 10.1.1.0
  ! Permit everything else
  access-list 1 permit 0.0.0.0 255.255.255.255
```

distribute-list out router

```
distribute-list access-list out [interface | routing-process]
no distribute-list access-list out [interface | routing-process]
```

Configures   A filter list to be applied to outbound routing updates

Default   None

Description

This command applies the given access list to outbound routing updates. The access list must be a standard IP access list; it defines which networks will be denied or permitted. The *interface* name applies the list to routing updates going out a specific interface. (This does not apply to OSPF.) The *routing-process* applies the access list to routes going to another routing process. The connected and static keywords may be used to specify a routing process.

Example

```
route rip
  network 10.0.0.0
  distribute-list 1 out
!
! Deny network 10.1.1.0
access-list 1 deny 10.1.1.0
! Permit everything else
access-list 1 permit 0.0.0.0 255.255.255.255
```

domain-password router, IS-IS

```
domain-password password
no domain-password
```

Configures   Password for IS-IS routing

Default   Disabled

Description

This command assigns a *password* for exchanging L2 routing information for IS-IS. Like the area-password command, this password is transmitted in clear text and provides very little security.

downward-compatible-config

global

```
downward-compatible-config version
no downward-compatible-config
```

Configures   Configuration

Default   Disabled

Description

This command generates a configuration that is compatible with an earlier IOS *version*. The version number must be 10.2 or later.

---

down-when-looped

interface

```
down-when-looped
no down-when-looped
```

Configures   Loopback detection

Default   Disabled

Description

This command tells the interface to go down when a loopback is detected. The default behavior is for the interface to remain up when the device is placed in loopback, so you can place a DCE device such as a CSU/DSU in loopback and ping the interface. This allows you to test the cable between the router and the DCE device.

Use the no form of this command to disable this behavior. If this command is given, the interface shuts down when the DCE device (CSU/DSU) is placed in loopback mode.

---

dte-invert-txc

interface

```
dte-invert-txc
no dte-invert-txc
```

Configures   Inverts TXC clock signal

Default   Disabled

Description

This command inverts the TXC clock signal when the interface is operating as the DTE.

early-token-release

```
early-token-release
no early-token-release
```

Configures   Token ring interfaces

Default   Disabled

Description

This command tells the interface to immediately release the token back to the ring after transmitting a packet. Normally, a token ring interface waits for a transmitted packet to return before releasing the token. This command is used only on 16-Mb rings where all devices support it.

---

editing

```
editing
no editing
```

Configures   Enhanced editing mode

Default   Enabled

Description

The no form of this command disables the enhanced editing mode for a line: i.e., the support for control keys such as Ctrl-w, which erases a word. The command-line editing keys are discussed in Chapter 1; they should be familiar to users of Unix and Unix-like operating systems.

---

eigrp log-neighbor-changes

```
eigrp log-neighbor-changes
no eigrp log-neighbor-changes
```

Configures   Logging for EIGRP neighbor states

Default   Disabled

Description

This command enables logging of changes in the status of EIGRP neighbors. Logging provides information to help you detect routing or connectivity problems.

---

enable

```
enable [level]
```

Description

With no arguments, this command takes an interactive session from user EXEC mode to privileged EXEC mode. If the *level* argument is present, it can be used to enter any of 16 levels, 0 through 15. Level 0 is the normal user mode (user EXEC mode) and 15 is the privileged user mode (privileged EXEC mode). See the privilege command in Chapter 4 for more information on setting the level values.

---

enable last-resort global

```
enable last-resort {password | succeed}
no enable last-resort {password | succeed}
```

Configures   The action to take if the TACACS servers do not respond

Default   Disabled

Description

This command tells the router what to do if the TACACS server times out, and you are using TACACS for the enable password. The password keyword tells the router to prompt for the enable password that is in the configuration. The succeed keyword tells the router to go to enable mode without further action. The latter behavior is very insecure.

---

enable password global

```
enable password [level level] password
no enable password
```

Configures   The password for the enable mode

Default   None

Description

This command sets the password for the enable mode. It can also be used to establish passwords for other levels. In the router's configuration, the password is stored in the clear and can be viewed by using show running-config and other commands.

You can encrypt this password as well as other passwords with the command service password-encryption. However, because this encryption uses a very simple XOR algorithm, it is easily cracked.

---

enable secret global

```
enable secret [level level] password
no enable secret
```

Configures   The password for the enable mode

Default   None

Description

This command set the password for the enable mode. It can also be used to establish passwords for other levels. In the router's configuration, the password is stored in an encrypted form and is never displayed in the clear.

---

enable use-tacacs global

```
enable use-tacacs
no enable use-tacacs
```

Configures   TACACS authentication for the privileged (enable) command level

Default   Disabled

Description

This command requires the use of TACACS for the enable password. If you use this command, be sure that you also use the `tacacs-server authenticate enable` command.

---

encapsulation interface

```
encapsulation type
no encapsulation
```

Configures   Encapsulation method used by the interface

Default   Usually `hdlc`

Description

This command sets the encapsulation method for this interface. Possible values for the encapsulation type are `atm-dxi`, `bstun` (block serial tunnel), `dot1q`, `frame-relay` (see Chapter 6), `hdlc`, `isl`, `lapb`, `ppp`, `sde`, `dlc`, and `smds`.

For Frame Relay interfaces, the options are `cisco` and `ietf`. The default is `cisco`, which is Cisco's proprietary encapsulation method. `ietf` sets the encapsulation method to the IETF standard, which is used when connecting to another vendor's Frame Relay router or switch.

Example

The following code uses `hdlc` encapsulation on a serial line:

```
interface serial0
  encapsulation hdlc
```

This uses PPP on an ISDN line:

```
interface bri0
  encapsulation ppp
```

end

any configuration mode

```
end
```

Description

This command exits the current configuration mode and must be used to mark the end of any configuration file.

Example

```
! lengthy configuration file omitted
! some commands here
! end of configuration file
end
```

---

erase

command

```
erase [startup-config] [flash]
```

Description

This command erases the stored configuration (startup-config) or the flash memory (flash) on the router. Flash memory stores the IOS operating system image; obviously, this command is dangerous.

Example

This command erases your stored configuration:

```
Router# erase startup-config
```

This one erases your IOS image:

```
Router# erase flash
```

---

escape-character

line

```
escape-character ascii-number
no escape-character
```

Configures
The system escape character

Default
Ctrl-∧

Description

This command defines the character that terminates a running command. The default, as specified in the hot-key listing, is Ctrl-∧ (Control+Shift+6 on most keyboards). *ascii-number* must be the decimal value of the character you want to use. The Break key cannot be used as an escape character.

The no form of the instruction returns the escape character to the default.

Example

The following commands set the disconnect character to Ctrl-C, which has a decimal value of 3:

```
Router(config)# line 2
Router(config-line)# escape-characer 3
Router(config-line)# vacant-message #
Router(config-line)#          ***** Welcome to Sphinx *****
Router(config-line)#          Escape key is Ctrl-C
Router(config-line)# #
```

exception core-file   global

```
exception core-file name
no exception core-file name
```

Configures   A core dump filename

Default   *routername-core*

Description

This command sets the *name* of the core file that is generated when a router crashes. Use the exception protocol command to set the protocol that the router uses to transmit the core file.

exception dump   global

```
exception dump ip
no exception dump
```

Configures   The exception dump server IP address

Default   None

Description

This command sets the IP address of the server to which the router sends a core dump when the router crashes.

exception memory   global

```
exception memory {fragment size | minimum size}
no exception memory
```

Configures   Memory parameters that cause a core dump

Default   Disabled

Description

This command causes a core dump if certain memory parameters are exceeded. The fragment size is the minimum contiguous block of memory in the free pool in bytes; the minimum size is the lowest allowable size of the free memory pool in bytes. If these parameters are exceeded, a core dump is generated. For example, if you set the minimum size to 100000 and the memory goes below 100,000 bytes, a core file is generated.

---

exception protocol   global

```
exception protocol {ftp | rcp | tftp}
no exception protocol
```

Configures   Protocol to transmit a core file to a server

Default   tftp

Description

This command sets the protocol to use for transmitting a core file to a server. The protocol can be ftp, rcp, or tftp. Use the exception dump command to set the IP address of the server.

Example

```
exception protocol tftp
exception dump 192.168.1.1
```

---

exception spurious-interrupt   global

```
exception spurious-interrupt [number]
no exception spurious-interrupt
```

Configures   The number of spurious interrupts that generate a core dump

Default   Disabled

Description

This command sets the number of spurious interrupts that will cause the router to generate a core file and reboot. *number* can be from 1 to 4294967295.

---

exec   line

```
exec
no exec
```

Configures   Access to the router command interface

Default   Enabled

Description

The no form of this command disables EXEC processes, which are enabled by default. Disabling EXEC processes is useful for lines on which you do not want users to access (log in) to the router. For example, you might want to disallow login access on a dial-in line.

---

exec-timeout

```
exec-timeout minutes [seconds]
no exec-timeout
```

Configures   The time an EXEC session can be idle

Default   10 minutes

Description

This command sets the amount of time a session waits for user input before timing out and closing the session. *minutes* specifies the number of minutes in the timeout period; *seconds* specifies the number of seconds.

Don't set the EXEC timeout to be extremely short; for example, don't give a command like `exec-timeout 0 1`. You may never get back into your router without doing a configuration recovery.

Example

The following command sets the timeout period to 4 minutes and 59 seconds:

```
exec-timeout 4 59
```

exit

```
exit
```

Description

This command closes your current connection if you are in user EXEC mode or privileged EXEC mode. If you are in a subconfiguration mode such as the interface or routing configuration mode, this command takes you to the next higher level (e.g., back to EXEC mode from interface configuration mode).

Example

```
Routerexit
Connection Closed

Routerenable
Router#conf t
Enter configuration commands, one per line.  End with CNTL/Z.
Router(config)#interface serial0
Router(config-if)#exit
Router(config)#
```

fair-queue

```
fair-queue [congestive [dynamic [reservable]]]
no fair-queue [congestive [dynamic [reservable]]]
```

Configures   Weighted Fair Queueing

Default

Enabled for interfaces with bandwidth less than or equal to 2 Mbps; default values are congestive 64, dynamic 256, reservable 0

Description

This command enables Weighted Fair Queueing on an interface.

congestive
> Optional. The number of messages allowed in each queue past which traffic is discarded. The value can range from 1 to 512.

dynamic
> Optional. The number of queues for best-effort conversations. Valid values are 16, 32, 64, 128, 256, 512, 1024, 2048, and 4096.

reservable
> Optional. The number of queues for reserved conversations. The value can be from 0 to 1000.

---

fair-queue aggregate-limit   interface

```
fair-queue aggregate-limit packets
no fair-queue aggregate-limit
```

Configures   Maximum number of packets for DWFQ

Default   Based on buffer space in the Versatile Interface Processor (VIP)

Description

This command sets the total number of buffered packets allowed before packets are dropped. This is the sum of all packets in buffers for Distributed Weighted Fair Queuing (DWFQ). If the buffered packets stay below this limit, no packets are dropped.

---

fair-queue individual-limit   interface

```
fair-queue individual-limit packets
no fair-queue individual-limit
```

Configures   Maximum queue depth for an individual queue

Default   Half of the aggregate queue limit

Description

This command sets the maximum number of *packets* allowed in an individual queue during periods of congestion.

fair-queue limit

```
fair-queue {qos-group group | tos number} limit class-packet-size
no fair-queue {qos-group group | tos number} limit class-packet-size
```

Configures   Maximum queue depth for a specific DWFQ class

Default

Half the aggregate limit size unless the individual limit is set, in which case that is the default

Description

This command sets the queue size for a specific DWFQ. The `qos-group` number can be from 1 to 99; it is used to match the value set by the Committed Access Rate (CAR) or the BGP policy propagation. The `tos` value is used to match the two low-order IP precedence bits in the ToS (Type of Service) field. The *class-packet-size* is the maximum number of packets allowed in the queue during periods of congestion.

---

fair-queue qos-group

```
fair-queue qos-group
no fair-queue qos-group
```

Configures   DWFQ based on QoS (Quality of Service) group numbers

Default   Disabled

Description

This command enables DWFQ based on QoS group numbers. The QoS group numbers, which are taken from the CAR or BGP policy propagation, are used to sort traffic into queues. The `fair-queue weight` and `fair-queue limit` commands set up the appropriate queues.

---

fair-queue tos

```
fair-queue tos
no fair-queue tos
```

Configures   DWFQ based on ToS (Type of Service) values

Default   Disabled

Description

This command enables DWFQ based on ToS values. The ToS fields in the packet provide two low-order IP precedence bits, which are used to sort packets into queues. The `fair-queue weight` and `fair-queue limit` commands set up the appropriate queues.

fair-queue weight

```
fair-queue {qos-group group | tos number} weight value
no fair-queue {qos-group group | tos number} weight value
```

Configures   Assigns a specific weight for DWFQ

Default

For qos-group, unallocated bandwidth defaults to group 0; for tos, the default class/weight values are 0/10, 1/20, 2/30, and 3/40

Description

This command allocates a specific weight (percentage of the bandwidth) to each QoS group or ToS type. *value* must be between 0 and 100.

fddi burst-count

```
fddi burst-count size
no fddi burst-count
```

Configures   Buffers to allocate to handle extra FDDI traffic

Default   3

Description

This command enables an FDDI interface to allocate extra buffers ahead of time. These buffers are used to handle possible traffic bursts. The buffer *size* can be from 1 to 10; the default is 3.

fddi c-min

```
fddi c-min microseconds
no fddi c-min
```

Configures   The C-Min timer

Default   1600 microseconds

Description

This command sets the C-Min timer on the interface to *microseconds*.

fddi cmt-signal-bits

```
fddi cmt-signal-bits signal-bits [phy-a | phy-b]
no fddi cmt-signal-bits signal-bits [phy-a | phy-b]
```

Configures   CMT transmission bits

Default   None

Description

This command sets the bits to be transmitted during the signal phase of CMT. Changing these values is not recommended and should be done only to debug specific CMT problems. *signal-bits* is the hexadecimal value of the bit fields you wish to set. phy-a and phy-b select the physical sublayer, either a or b. Table 15-8 describes the bit fields.

Table 15-8: Bit values for CMT signals

Bit position	Meaning
0	Escape bit
1–2	Physical type
3	Physical compatibility
4–5	Link confidence test duration
6	MAC for link confidence test
7	Link confidence test failed
8	MAC for local loop
9	MAC on physical output

---

fddi duplicate-address-check   interface

```
fddi duplicate-address-check
no fddi duplicate-address-check
```

Configures   Duplicate address checking during ring initialization

Default   Disabled

Description

This command enables an FDDI interface to detect duplicate addresses on the ring.

---

fddi encapsulate   interface

```
fddi encapsulate
no fddi encapsulate
```

Configures   Encapsulation mode

Default   Enabled (SNAP)

Description

This command enables the bridge encapsulating mode for this interface, which is used to interface the CSC-FCIT with other FDDI modules. The CSC-FCIT has bridging enabled by default. no fddi encapsulate disables bridging for this interface.

---

fddi frames-per-token   interface

```
fddi frames-per-token number
no fddi frames-per-token
```

Configures   Number of frames that an interface transmits per token capture

Default   3 frames

Description

This command sets the number of frames that an interface transmits during a token capture. *number* can be from 1 to 10.

---

fddi smt-frames   interface

```
fddi smt-frames
no fddi smt-frames
```

Configures   Enables SMT frame processing

Default   Enabled

Description

This command enables the interface to process and generate SMT (FDDI Station Management) frames.

---

fddi tb-min   interface

```
fddi tb-min milliseconds
no fddi tb-min
```

Configures   TB-min timer

Default   100 milliseconds

Description

This command sets the TB-min timer in the Physical Connection Management (PCM) for this interface.

---

fddi tl-min-time   interface

```
fddi tl-min-time microseconds
no fddi tl-min-time microseconds
```

Configures   Minimum time to transmit a physical line state

Default   30 microseconds

Description

This command sets the minimum time to transmit a physical line state before transitioning to the PCM state for this interface. Changing this field is not recommended.

---

fddi token-rotation-time interface

```
fddi token-rotation-time microseconds
no fddi token-rotation-time microseconds
```

Configures   Ring scheduling

Default   5000 microseconds

Description

This command sets the time in *microseconds* for the ring to recover from ring errors. The range can be from 4000 to 165000 microseconds.

fddi t-out interface

```
fddi t-out milliseconds
no fddi t-out
```

Configures   The t-out timer

Default   100 ms

Description

This command sets the t-out timer for the PCM.

fddi valid-transmission-time interface

```
fddi valid-transmission-time microseconds
no fddi valid-transmission-time microseconds
```

Configures   Time to recover from a transient ring error

Default   2500 microseconds

Description

This command sets the transmission time for the interface. The range can be from 40 to 1342200 microseconds.

flowcontrol line

```
flowcontrol {none | software [lock] [in | out] | hardware [in | out]}
no flowcontrol {none | software [lock] [in | out] | hardware [in | out]}
```

Configures   Flow control for a line

Default   No flow control

Description

This command defines the serial flow control between the router and the device connected to a serial line.

> No flow control.

software
> Sets to software flow control.

lock
> Makes it impossible to turn off flow control.

hardware
> Sets to hardware flow control.

If neither in nor out are specified, flow control is assumed to be in both directions, i.e., the router accepts and sends flow control.

---

format command

Class C filesystem:

format *filesystem*:

Class A filesystem:

format [spare *number*]*filesystem*:

Configures A Class C or Class A filesystem

Description

This command formats a flash filesystem. Each filesystem name must be followed by a colon; for example, format slot0:.

The spare option is valid only for Class A filesystems, which allow you to reserve a number of spare sectors. *number* can be from 0 to 16. The default is 0.

---

frame-relay adaptive-shaping map-class

frame-relay adaptive-shaping {becn | foresight}
no frame-relay adaptive-shaping

Configures The type of backward notification

Default Disabled

Description

This command selects the type of backward notification to which the Frame Relay interface should respond. It can be set to becn (backwards explicit congestion notification) or foresight.

---

frame-relay [bc | be] map-class

frame-relay {bc | be} {in | out} *bits*
no frame-relay {bc | be} {in | out} *bits*

Configures The committed and excess burst sizes

Default   7000 bits for both bc and be

Description

This command specifies the incoming (in) or outgoing (out) committed burst size (bc) and the excess burst size (be) for a Frame Relay virtual circuit. The burst size is given in *bits*.

---

frame-relay becn-response-enable

```
frame-relay becn-response-enable
no frame-relay becn-response-enable
```

Configures   The use of BECNs to regulate output traffic

Default   Enabled when frame traffic shaping is in use

Description

This command is enabled when traffic shaping is in use. The use of BECNs (backwards explicit congestion notifications) regulates output traffic. You won't see this command in the configuration when you do a show. Use the no form to disable traffic shaping.

---

frame-relay broadcast-queue

```
frame-relay broadcast-queue size byte-rate packet-rate
no frame-relay broadcast-queue
```

Configures   Queues for broadcast traffic

Default   Size, 64; byte rate, 256000 bps; packet rate, 36 packets per second

Description

This command sets the broadcast queue parameters for a Frame Relay interface. A broadcast queue is used for any broadcast packets that have to be replicated for multiple DLCIs on the interface.

size
   The number of packets to hold in the queue. Normally, you want at least 20 for each DLCI on the interface.

byte-rate
   The maximum number of bytes to be transmitted per second. This value should be less than:

   — 1/4 the local access rate (in bytes per second)

   — N/4 times the minimum remote access rate, where N is the number of DLCIs to which the broadcast should be replicated

packet-rate
   The maximum number of packets to be transmitted per second.

frame-relay cir

map-class

```
frame-relay cir {in | out} bps
no frame-relay cir {in | out} bps
```

Configures   Incoming or outgoing CIR

Default   56000 bps

Description

This command sets the Committed Information Rate (CIR) for a Switched Virtual Circuit (SVC) to *bps* (bits per second). The CIR is the guaranteed available bandwidth for the circuit, and may be 0. The in and out keywords specify the direction to which the CIR applies.

frame-relay class

interface

```
frame-relay class name
no frame-relay class name
```

Configures   Associates a map class with an interface

Default   None

Description

This command applies the map class given by *name* to a Frame Relay interface. The map class may be built from Frame Relay commands used in the map-class context.

Example

In this example, we assign a map class called MAP1 to interface serial1.1:

```
interface serial1.1
    frame-relay class MAP1
!
! Now make the map-class
map-class frame-relay MAP1
    frame-relay cir in 56000
    no frame-relay becn-response-enable
```

frame-relay custom-queue-list

map-class

```
frame-relay custom-queue-list list
no frame-relay custom-queue-list list
```

Configures   The custom queue list to be used for the interface

Default   None (FIFO)

Description

See the queue-list command for information about creating a custom queue list.

frame-relay de-group

```
frame-relay de-group group-number dlci
no frame-relay de-group
```

Configures Discard Eligibility (DE)

Default None

Description

This command applies a DE group to a DLCI. *group-number* can be from 1 to 10. DE groups are defined with the command `frame-relay de-list`; they identify traffic that may be discarded if the traffic on the interface exceeds the committed information rate and the Frame Relay switch is congested.

---

frame-relay de-list

```
frame-relay de-list list-number {protocol type | interface type number}
    characteristic
no frame-relay de-list list-number {protocol type | interface type number}
    characteristic
```

Configures Discard Eligibility (DE)

Default None

Description

This command defines packets that are eligible for discard during times of congestion on a Frame Relay switch. Packets matched by this list have the "discard eligible" bit set in the Frame Relay header.

list-number
> An identifying number. This number identifies the list when it is referenced by other commands, particularly `frame-relay de-group`. A DE list may be defined by several `frame-relay de-list` statements with the same number.

protocol type
> Specifies the protocol of the packets to be selected by this list. Possible values are `arp`, `apollo`, `appletalk`, `bridge`, `clns`, `clns_es`, `clns_is`, `compressedtcp`, `decnet`, `ip`, `ipx`, `vines`, and `xns`.

interface type number
> Specifies the interface of packets to be selected for the list; that is, you can specify that all traffic coming through a certain interface should be marked as discard-eligible. The interface must be a serial interface, an Ethernet interface, or the null interface.

characteristic
> Specifies the characteristics of the packets that are eligible for discard. It must be one of the following: `fragments` (fragmented packets eligible for discard), `tcp port` (TCP traffic on the specified port), `udp port` (UDP traffic on the specified port), `list access-list` (traffic matched by the given access list), `gt`

---

bytes (packets larger than the given size; make sure to include all headers), or lt *bytes* (packets less than the given size; again, include all headers).

frame-relay idle-timer

map-class

```
frame-relay idle-timer seconds
no frame-relay idle-timer seconds
```

Configures   Idle timeout for an SVC

Default   120 seconds

Description

This command sets the idle timeout for a Switched Virtual Circuit (SVC) to *seconds*.

frame-relay interface-dlci

interface

```
frame-relay interface-dlci dlci [broadcast] [ietf | cisco]
no frame-relay interface-dlci dlci [broadcast] [ietf | cisco]
```

Configures   DLCI for a Frame Relay subinterface

Default   No DLCI is set as default

Description

Assigns a Data Link Connection Identifier (DLCI) to a Frame Relay subinterface.

dlci
    The DLCI number to be used on the current subinterface.

broadcast
    Allows broadcast packets on this connection.

ietf
    Specifies IETF encapsulation for this connection.

cisco
    Specifies CISCO encapsulation for this connection.

frame-relay intf-type

interface

```
frame-relay intf-type [dce | dte | nni]
no frame-relay intf-type
```

Configures   Frame Relay switch type

Default   dte

Description

This command sets the Frame Relay switch type. It is valid only if Frame Relay switching has been enabled with the global frame-relay switching command. The keyword dce causes the router to function as a switch connected to another router; dte is used when the router is connected to a

---

Frame Relay network; nni (Network-to-Network Interface) is used when the router connects to another switch.

frame-relay inverse-arp

```
frame-relay inverse-arp [protocol] [dlci]
no frame-relay inverse-arp [protocol] [dlci]
```

Configures   Inverse ARP for Frame Relay

Default   Enabled

Description

This command configures the use of inverse ARP for associating an IP address with a Frame Relay interface. This command is useful if inverse ARP was globally disabled on the router, but you want to enable inverse ARP for a particular interface or subinterface. To enable or disable inverse ARP for a specific protocol and DLCI pair, use both arguments (*protocol* and *dlci*); for all protocols on a DLCI, use only the *dlci* argument; for all DLCIs, use only the *protocol* argument.

protocol

The protocol to support on this interface. Supported protocols include appletalk, decnet, ip, ipx, vines, and xns.

dlci

One of the DLCI numbers for this interface. The value can be from 16 to 1007.

frame-relay ip rtp header-compression

```
frame-relay ip rtp header-compression [active | passive]
no frame-relay ip rtp header-compression
```

Configures   RTP header compression on the interface

Default   Disabled

Description

This command enables RTP header compression on the interface. The active keyword tells the device to compress all headers; the passive keyword tells it to compress headers only if the incoming packet had its headers compressed. The default is active.

frame-relay ip tcp header-compression

```
frame-relay ip tcp header-compression [passive]
no frame-relay ip tcp header-compression
```

Configures   Compression of TCP/IP packet headers

Default   Enabled

Description

This command configures an interface so that its PVCs compress IP headers.

passive
> Optional. Performs compression only if the incoming packets are compressed.

---

frame-relay lmi-type   interface

```
frame-relay lmi-type {ansi | cisco | q933a}
no frame-relay lmi-type {ansi | cisco | q933a]
```

Configures   The LMI

Default   Autosense

Description

This command allows you to set the Local Management Type (LMI) of the Frame Relay switch the router is talking to. Setting the LMI type explicitly deactivates autosensing. Use the keepalive command with this command.

Example

```
interface serial0
    encapulation frame-relay
    frame-relay lmi-type cisco
    keepalive 20
```

---

frame-relay local-dlci   interface

```
frame-relay local-dlci number
no frame-relay local-dlci
```

Configures   The local DLCI

Default   None

Description

This command sets the local DLCI. It is rarely needed because LMI is normally used to set the local DLCI. If you don't use LMI, this command allows you to set the local DLCI explicitly.

---

frame-relay map   interface

```
frame-relay map protocol protocol-address dlci [broadcast] [ietf | cisco]
    [payload-compress {packet-by-packet | frf9 stac [hardware-options]}]
no frame-relay map protocol protocol-address
```

Configures   Frame Relay connection parameters

Default   None

Description

This command defines a mapping between a protocol-specific destination address and the DLCI to use for connections to that destination.

protocol
> One of appletalk, decnet, dlsw, ip, ipx, llc2, rsrb, vines, or xns.

protocol-address
> The destination address.

dlci
> The DLCI to use.

broadcast
> Optional. Activates forwarding of broadcasts to this address when multicast is not enabled.

ietf
> Optional. Use IETF encapsulation on this interface.

cisco
> Optional. Use Cisco's encapsulation method on this interface. If neither ietf nor cisco is specified, the interface uses the encapsulation specified by the encapsulation frame-relay command.

payload-compress packet-by-packet
> Optional. Activates packet-by-packet compression using the Stacker method. Packet-by-packet compression is a proprietary Cisco feature and won't interoperate with other vendors' equipment.

payload-compress frf9 stac
> Optional. Activates FRF.9 compression using the Stacker method.

hardware-options
> Optional. Can be distributed, software, or csa. distributed causes compression to be performed in a VIP2; software causes compression to occur in the IOS software on the main processor; csa *csa-number* specifies the CSA to use for a particular interface (available only on 7200 series routers).

---

frame-relay map bridge   interface

```
frame-relay map bridge dlci [broadcast] [ietf]
no frame-relay map bridge dlci [broadcast] [ietf]
```

Configures   Broadcast forwarding

Default   None

Description

This command specifies that broadcasts are to be forwarded.

dlci
> The DLCI to use for bridging on this interface.

broadcast
> Optional. Forwards broadcasts when multicast is not enabled.

ietf
> Optional. Forces the use of IETF encapsulation, which is used when talking to a non-Cisco device.

---

frame-relay map clns interface

```
frame-relay map clns dlci [broadcast]
no frame-relay map clns dlci [broadcast]
```

Configures   Broadcast forwarding for ISO CLNS routing

Default   None

Description

This command causes broadcasts to be forwarded when ISO CLNS is used for routing.

dlci
> The DLCI to use for CLNS broadcast forwarding.

broadcast
> Optional. Causes broadcasts to be forwarded when multicast is not enabled.

---

frame-relay map ip compress interface

```
frame-relay map ip address dlci [broadcast] compress
no frame-relay map ip address dlci [broadcast] compress
```

Configures   Compression for both RTP and TCP headers

Default   Disabled

Description

This command enables compression for both RTP and TCP packet headers.

address
> The IP address of the destination or next hop.

dlci
> The DLCI number.

broadcast
> Optional. Forwards broadcasts to the specified IP address.

frame-relay map ip rtp header-compression   interface

```
frame-relay map ip rtp address dlci rtp header-compression [active | passive]
no frame-relay map ip rtp address dlci rtp header-compression
    [active | passive]
```

Configures   Compression for RTP headers per DLCI

Default   Disabled

Description

This command enables RTP compression for a specific *dlci* on a link. The active
keyword means that the router should always compress the RTP headers (this is
the default). The passive keyword specifies that the router should compress
packets only when the incoming packet was compressed.

frame-relay map ip tcp header-compression   interface

```
frame-relay map ip address dlci [broadcast] [cisco| ietf] [no compress] tcp
    header-compression {active | passive}
no frame-relay map ip address dlci [broadcast] [cisco| ietf] [no compress] tcp
    header-compression {active | passive}
```

Configures   Compression methods for a map

Default   None

Description

This command maps a Frame Relay DLCI to an IP address, enabling TCP header
compression for this connection. It's useful if header compression isn't the default
for the interface.

`address`
> The IP address.

`dlci`
> The DLCI to use.

`broadcast`
> Optional. Causes broadcasts to be forwarded.

`cisco`
> Optional. Uses Cisco's encapsulation method.

`ietf`
> Optional. Uses RFC 1490 encapsulation.

`no compress`
> Optional. Disables compression.

`active`
> Causes every TCP/IP packet header to be compressed.

`passive`
> Compresses packet headers only if the incoming packet was compressed.

frame-relay mincir

interface

```
frame-relay mincir {in | out} bps
no frame-relay mincir {in | out} bps
```

Configures   The CIR

Default   56000 bps

Description

This command sets the minimum incoming (in) or outgoing (out) Committed Information Rate (CIR) that you are willing to accept, in bits per second (*bps*).

frame-relay multicast-dlci

interface

```
frame-relay multicast-dlci dlci
no frame-relay multicast-dlci
```

Configures   The DLCI to be used for multicasts

Default   None

Description

This command defines a *dlci* for multicasts. This command is used for testing Frame Relay configurations and is not required in a production configuration.

frame-relay payload-compress packet-by-packet

interface

```
frame-relay payload-compress packet-by-packet
no frame-relay payload-compress packet-by-packet
```

Configures   Payload compression

Default   Disabled

Description

This command enables compression on the link, using a proprietary compression protocol that will not work with other vendors' equipment.

frame-relay priority-dlci-group

interface

```
frame-relay priority-dlci-group group-number high-dlci medium-dlci normal-dlci
    low-dlci
```

Configures   Assigns a priority to different DLCIs

Default   Disabled

Description

This command sets the priority levels for DLCIs in the group specified by *group-number*. Within a group, there are four priority levels (high, medium, normal, and low); one DLCI is assigned to each priority level (*high-dlci* to the high priority level, etc.). If fewer than four DLCIs are given, the last DLCI is assigned to the remaining priority levels.

---

frame-relay priority-group   interface

```
frame-relay priority-group list-number
no frame-relay priority-group list-number
```

Configures   Applies a priority list to a Frame Relay virtual circuit

Description

This command is similar to the `priority-group` command for the interface, except that it applies the priority list to a Frame Relay virtual circuit.

list-number
> The priority list number. Priority lists are defined with the `priority-list` command.

Example

The following example applies `priority-list 1` to the Frame Relay configuration:

```
interface serial 0
    encapsulation frame-relay
    frame-relay interface-dlci 200
    frame-relay priority-group 1
!
priority-list 1 protocol ip high
```

---

frame-relay route   interface

```
frame-relay route in-dlci out-interface out-dlci
no frame-relay route in-dlci out-interface out-dlci
```

Configures   Static routes for PVC switching

Default   None

Description

This command allows you to assign a static route based on DLCIs.

Example

In the following configuration, packets from DLCI 100 received by the `serial0` interface are routed out through DLCI 200 on `serial1`. Likewise, packets received from DLCI 101 on `serial0` are routed out through DLCI 201 on `serial1`.

```
interface serial0
    frame-relay route 100 interface Serial1 200
    frame-relay route 101 interface Serial1 201
```

---

frame-relay svc

```
frame-relay svc
no frame-relay svc
```

Configures   SVC operation on the interface

Default   Disabled

Description

This command enables Switched Virtual Circuit (SVC) processing on the interface and all its subinterfaces.

frame-relay switching

```
frame-relay switching
no frame-relay switching
```

Configures   Enables PVC switching

Default   Disabled

Description

This command enables Permanent Virtual Circuit (PVC) switching on the router.

frame-relay traffic-rate

```
frame-relay traffic-rate average [peak]
no frame-relay traffic-rate average [peak]
```

Configures   Traffic shaping for a virtual circuit

Default   The bandwidth of the line

Description

This command allows you to configure traffic shaping for a virtual circuit. It doesn't provide the granularity of other commands that configure traffic shaping; it lets you specify only average and peak traffic rates.

average
> The average rate in bits per second, which is the same as the contracted CIR.

peak
> Optional. The peak rate expected for this interface in bits per second. If this option is omitted, the default value is the line rate calculated from the bandwidth command.

frame-relay traffic-shaping

interface

```
frame-relay traffic-shaping
no frame-relay traffic-shaping
```

Configures   Traffic shaping

Default   Disabled

Description

This command enables traffic shaping for the interface.

---

fsck

command

```
fsck [/nocrc] filesystem:
```

Configures   Checks and repairs a Class C filesystem

Description

This command checks the given *filesystem*, which must be a Class C filesystem, and repairs any problems it finds. The /nocrc option forces fsck to skip CRC checks. The filesystem name must be followed by a colon.

---

ftp-server enable

global

```
ftp-server enable
no ftp-server enable
```

Configures   Enables FTP server

Default   Disabled

Description

This command enables FTP services on the router; the router runs an FTP server that can be used to upload and download files in the router's filesystem. To use this feature, you must also configure the ftp-server topdir command.

---

ftp-server topdir

global

```
ftp-server topdir directory
no ftp-server topdir
```

Configures   The directory to which FTP clients have read/write access

Default   None (all read and write operations are denied)

Description

This command sets the *directory* in the router's filesystem that FTP clients are allowed to access. Access is also allowed to subdirectories of this directory. If this command has not been given or if `no ftp-server topdir` has been given, no access is allowed via FTP.

Example

The following commands enable the router's FTP server and allow it to access the directory *disk1:/logs* and all its subdirectories.

```
ftp-server enable
ftp-server topdir disk1:/logs
```

---

full-duplex   interface

```
full-duplex
no full-duplex
```

Configures   Full-duplex mode

Default   Half-duplex

Description

This command enables full-duplex mode on interfaces that support it.

---

full-help   line configuration

```
full-help
no full-help
```

Configures   Full help for a line

Default   Disabled

Description

This command enables full help on a line configuration.

---

group-range   interface

```
group-range start end
no group-range start end
```

Configures   An interface group

Default   None

Description

This command specifies a range of interfaces that are treated as a group for the purposes of configuration. It is used in conjunction with the `interface group-async` command. `start` and `end` are the beginning and ending numbers of the interfaces that are configured as a group.

Example

The following commands group the async interfaces 1 through 7. Once a group has been defined, specific interfaces can be singled out for special treatment with the member command: for example, specific IP addresses can be applied to each interface.

```
interface group-async 0
  group-range 1 7
  ip unnumbered ethernet0
  async mode interactive
  member 1 peer default ip 10.10.1.1
  member 2 peer default ip 10.10.1.2
  member 3 peer default ip 10.10.1.3
  member 4 peer default ip 10.10.1.4
  member 5 peer default ip 10.10.1.5
  member 6 peer default ip 10.10.1.6
  member 7 peer default ip 10.10.1.7
```

half-duplex   interface

```
half-duplex
no half-duplex
```

Configures   An SDLC interface for half-duplex

Default   Disabled

Description

This command configures an SDLC interface for half-duplex mode.

half-duplex controlled-carrier   interface

```
half-duplex controlled-carrier
no half-duplex controlled-carrier
```

Configures   Controlled carrier mode versus constant carrier mode

Default   Constant carrier mode

Description

Low speed serial interfaces use constant carrier mode by default. This command places the interface in controlled carrier mode; it can be used only on interfaces that have been configured for half-duplex.

help   command

```
help
```

Description

Displays a brief listing of user-level commands. To get more verbose help, use the full-help command.

history   global

```
history [number-of-lines]
no history
```

Configures   History buffer size

Default   10 lines

Description

This command enables the user interface's history mechanism. A history is a listing of commands that have been executed in the current session. This command is stored in the router's configuration and applies to all user sessions. *number-of-lines* is the size of the history buffer and must be in the range of 0–256. If omitted, the buffer size is set to the default value.

Use the no version of this command to disable the history mechanism; use the show history command to view the current history buffer. If you want to activate a history buffer only for your current session, use the command terminal history.

Example

```
Router# history 255
Router# no history
Router# show history
```

---

hold-character   line

```
hold-character ascii-number
no hold-character
```

Configures   The character that suspends output

Default   None

Description

This command sets the character that suspends output to a terminal screen. *ascii-number* is the value of the character in decimal. Having a pause key benefits users who need to scroll through a lot of text; pressing any character resumes output to the screen.

Example

```
Router(config)# line 2
Router(config-line)# hold-character 19
Router(config-line)# vacant-message #
Router(config-line)#                 ***** Welcome to Sphinx *****
Router(config-line)#        Press the return key to start the connection
Router(config-line)#                 Suspend with Ctrl-S
Router(config-line)# #
```

hold-queue

```
hold-queue packets {in | out}
no hold-queue packets {in | out}
```

Configures   Size of the hold queue

Default   Input queue, 75 packets; output queue, 40 packets

Description

This command specifies the length of the input queue (in) or the output queue (out) in *packets*. Slower links require smaller queue sizes than faster links.

Example

```
interface Async4
    ip unnumbered Ethernet0
    hold-queue 20 out
    async default ip address 192.101.187.164
    async mode interactive
```

hostname

```
hostname name-string
no hostname
```

Configures   The hostname of the router

Default   Factory-assigned "Router"

Description

This command sets the hostname of the router.

hssi external-loop-request

```
hssi external-loop-request
no hssi external-loop-request
```

Configures   Support for CSU/DSU

Default   Disabled

Description

This command enables support for CSU/DSUs that provide the LC signal. The LC signal allows the CSU/DSU to request loopback from the router.

hssi internal-clock

```
hssi internal-clock
no hssi internal-clock
```

Configures   Use of the internal clock

Default   Disabled

Description

This command configures an HSSI interface to provide a 45 Mhz master clock. It is used when two HSSI interfaces are connected via a null modem cable; one of the two interfaces must provide a clock signal on the link. Both interfaces cannot provide clocks, so use this command only on one side of the link.

---

hub   global

hub ethernet *hub-number* *first-port* [*last-port*]

Configures   Hub configuration mode

Default   None

Description

The hub command enters hub configuration mode, in which you can enter commands that configure a hub. It is applicable only to routers that are equipped with hub interfaces. *hub-number* is the number of the hub that you are configuring. *first-port* is the beginning of a range of consecutive ports to be configured as part of the hub; *last-port* is the last port in the range. If you omit *last-port*, this command adds a single port to the hub.

Example

To configure one port of a hub:

```
hub ethernet 0 1
    source-address 00:00:0c:ff:d0:04
```

To configure all ports of a hub:

```
hub ethernet 0 1 7
    no link-test
    auto-polarity
```

---

ignore-dcd   interface

ignore-dcd
no ignore-dcd

Configures   Determination of a link's status

Default   A DTE serial interface monitors the DCD signal

Description

This command tells the interface to ignore the DCD signal and use the DSR signal to determine whether the link is up or down. By default, all DTE serial interfaces monitor the DCD signal for the link's status.

---

interface global

interface *interface.subinterface* [{point-to-point | multipoint}]

Configures   Allows configuration of a given interface

Default   None

Description

This command enters the interface configuration mode for the given *interface* and *subinterface*. The interface most commonly consists of an interface type followed by the number of the particular interface (for example, ethernet0). A space is allowed (and commonly used) between the interface type and the number. Table 15-9 shows the most common interface types. On more complex routers, the interface number can be specified in a number of different ways: as a *slot/port* combination, as a *slot/adapter/port* combination, or as a *slot/ port:channel-group* combination. The appropriate form depends on the hardware you're dealing with. The interface specification can include a subinterface number; subinterfaces are most common when using protocols like Frame Relay or ATM, which can package a number of communications channels on a single physical connection. The point-to-point keyword indicates that a subinterface is logically connected to a single remote node; multipoint indicates that it is logically connected to a number of remote nodes. multipoint and point-to-point are most commonly used on Frame Relay and ATM interfaces.

Table 15-9: Common interface types

Type	Description
async	An asynchronous interface (a standard terminal or modem line)
atm	ATM
bri	ISDN BRI (2 B channels)
dialer	Dial-on-demand interface (see the interface dialer command)
ethernet	Ethernet
fastethernet	100-Mbps Ethernet
fddi	FDDI
gigabitethernet	Gigabit Ethernet
group-async	A logical grouping of asynchronous interfaces to which all configuration commands apply (See the interface group-async command)
hssi	High-speed serial interface
lex	Lan extender
loopback	The internal software virtual interface
null	Null interface; packets sent to this interface are discarded
pos	OC-3/SONET
serial	Serial interface (used for leased line, T1, and T3)
tokenring	Token ring
tunnel	A virtual interface for a tunnel configuration

interface 359

interface bvi

global

```
interface bvi bridge-group-number
no interface bvi bridge-group-number
```

Configures   Bridging

Default   None

Description

The Bridge-Group Virtual Interface (BVI) becomes available on routers when the `bridge irb` command has been given. This interface allows the router to route and bridge the same protocol over the same interface. The `bridge group-number` must match the bridge group defined for the bridge.

Example

In this configuration, `serial0` and `serial1` are bridged, and traffic is routed through those interfaces out through `ethernet0`:

```
bridge irb
bridge 1 protocol ieee
!
interface serial0
 bridge-group 1
!
interface serial1
  bridge-group 1
!
interface ethernet 0
  ip address 10.11.1.1 255.255.255.0
!
! Configure the virtual bvi interface with a bridge group number of 1
interface bvi 1
  ip address 10.10.3.1 255.255.255.0
!
! Now configure the routing for the bridge
bridge 1 route ip
```

interface dialer

global

```
interface dialer number
no interface dialer number
```

Configures   A dialer configuration

Default   None

Description

This command allows you to define a virtual dialer configuration that can be applied to a set of physical interfaces. Once you configure this interface, you can make other interfaces use this configuration by using the `dialer rotary-group` command. `number` is the virtual interface number, and can be a value from 0 to 9.

Example

```
interface dialer 0
  encapsulation ppp
  dialer in-band
  dialer map ip 10.1.1.1 name bob 5551111
  !
interface async 1
  dialer rotary-group 0
```

interface group-async   global

```
interface group-async number
no interface group-async number
```

Configures   A group of interfaces that can share configuration parameters

Default   None

Description

This command allows you to create a group of async interfaces to which you can apply commands. Actual interfaces that belong to the group inherit the settings you apply to this virtual interface. The **group-range** command defines which physical async interfaces are included in the group. A physical interface can belong only to one group.

Example

The following commands define a group-async interface that includes async interfaces 1 through 7. The **ip unnumbered** and **async mode** commands apply to all the interfaces in the group.

```
interface group-async 0
  group-range 1 7
  ip unnumbered ethernet0
  async mode interactive
```

ip access-group   interface

```
ip access-group access-list [in | out]
no ip access-group access-list [in | out]
```

Configures   Assigns an access list to an interface

Default   No access lists defined

Description

This command applies the given access list to the interface in the direction specified (**in** or **out**). Access-list commands are discussed in Chapter 7. Each interface can support only one access list in either direction.

Example

The following commands apply access list 110 to filter incoming packets on the **serial1** interface, and access list 111 to filter outgoing packets:

```
interface serial1
  ip access-group 110 in
  ip access-group 111 out
```

To remove an access list from an interface, use the no form of this command:

```
interface serial1
  no ip access-group 111 out
```

If you use the no access-list command, your access list will be deleted. Be sure to use no ip access-group when removing lists from interfaces.

---

ip access-list
global

```
ip access-list {standard | extended} name
```

Configures   Named access lists

Default   None

Description

This command allows you to create a named access list. A named access list is really no different from a numbered access list as defined by the access-list command, except that it is identified by a logical name. A named access list may be either standard or extended. This command is followed by permit and deny commands that specify the access-list rules. For more about access lists, see Chapter 7 and the discussion of the access-list command.

Example

The following commands define a named access list that allows HTTP traffic from any host to the server at 10.1.2.3 and permits all other TCP traffic that has the SYN flag set. Remember that all access lists end with an implicit deny, which rejects all traffic not permitted by a statement in the access list.

```
ip access-list extended bogus-firewall
  permit tcp any host 10.1.2.3 eq http
  permit tcp any any established
```

---

ip accounting
interface

```
ip accounting [access-violations]
no ip accounting [access-violations]
```

Configures   IP accounting for an interface

Default   Disabled

Description

This command enables IP accounting based on the source and destination IP addresses that are passing through this router. Traffic that terminates at the router is not logged. The access-violations option enables logging based on access lists. For an access list to log information, the log keyword must be specified at the end of the access-list command.

Example

The following interface has IP accounting enabled and logs access-list violations:

```
interface serial 1
  ip address 10.10.2.3 255.255.255.0
  ip access-group 110 in
  ip accounting access-violations
! Deny telnet to the outside and log it when someone tries
access-list 110 deny tcp 10.10.2.0 0.0.0.255 any eq 23 log
access-list 110 permit ip any any
```

---

ip accounting-list   global

```
ip accounting-list address mask
no ip accounting-list address mask
```

Configures   An accounting filter

Default   None

Description

This command defines an IP *address* and wildcard *mask* for use as an accounting filter. Once a filter has been created, traffic is logged only if it matches the filter. If an IP address fails to match this filter, it is considered a transit IP packet and is logged to a separate table. See `ip accounting-transits`.

Example

The following command logs traffic to and from the 10.10.0.0 network:

```
ip accounting-list 10.10.0.0 0.0.255.255
```

---

ip accounting-threshold   global

```
ip accounting-threshold log-size
no ip accounting-threshold log-size
```

Configures   The IP accounting log table

Default   512 entries

Description

This command sets the size of the IP accounting table to *log-size* bytes. Each entry takes up to 26 bytes. Therefore, an accounting table defined at 100 entries could consume up to 2600 bytes of memory. This calculation should be kept in mind when defining new thresholds, as memory usage has adverse affects on the router.

Example

To double the accounting buffer:

```
ip accounting-threshold 1024
```

---

ip accounting-transits global

```
ip accounting-transits number
no ip accounting-transits
```

Configures   The table used for logging transit IP addresses

Default   None

Description

This command sets the size of the table for transit IP accounting to *number* entries. A transit IP packet is any packet with a source or destination that does not match the filter defined in the `ip accounting-list` command. If no accounting filters are defined, there are no transit IP packets.

Example

To set the transit table to 200 entries:

```
ip accounting-transits 200
```

---

ip address interface

```
ip address address subnet-mask [secondary]
no ip address address subnet-mask [secondary]
```

Configures   The IP address for an interface

Default   No IP address

Description

This command sets the IP address for the interface to *address*; the network mask used on the network is *subnet-mask*. The `secondary` keyword is used to apply a second (or third, or fourth...) address to an interface. It is allowed only if the interface allows multiple IP addresses.

Example

This command sets the IP address of the `ethernet0` interface to 10.10.1.1 and the subnet mask to 255.255.255.0:

```
interface ethernet0
   ip address 10.10.1.1 255.255.255.0
```

The following commands use the `secondary` keyword to add a second IP address to the `ethernet0` interface:

```
interface ethernet0
   ip address 10.10.1.1 255.255.255.0
   ip address 10.10.2.1 255.255.255.0 secondary
```

This interface will now answer and provide routing for both the 10.10.1.0/24 and 10.10.2.0/24 subnets.

ip address negotiated

```
ip address negotiated
no ip address negotiated
```

Configures   PPP address negotiation

Default   Disabled

Description

This command configures an interface to obtain its IP address via PPP.

---

ip address-pool

```
ip address-pool [dhcp-proxy-client | local]
no ip address-pool
```

Configures   Default address pooling

Default   Disabled

Description

This command provides an IP address pool to be used on dial-in or ISDN interfaces.

dhcp-proxy-client
    Optional. The router works as a proxy between the dial-in peers and the DHCP server to provide the address pool.

local
    Optional. Tells the router to use the local address pool.

---

ip alias

```
ip alias ip-address port
no ip alias ip-address
```

Configures   IP address mapping for reverse telnet

Default   None

Description

This command allows you to provide aliases in the form of IP addresses for various ports on the router. This feature is helpful if you are configuring a communication server with reverse telnet.

ip-address
    The IP address of the port for which you want to establish an alias.

port
    The port that you want to use as an alias for the IP address.

Example

Say we have a communication server (router) with three ports to which we allow reverse telnet access: 2001, 2002, and 2003. Instead of requiring users to type the router's IP address and the port every time, we assign (alias) an available IP address to each of our ports. The following commands create three IP address aliases (172.30.1.1, 172.30.1.2, and 172.30.1.3):

```
ip alias 172.30.1.1 2001
ip alias 172.30.1.2 2002
ip alias 172.30.1.3 2003
```

ip as-path access-list   global

```
ip as-path access-list access-list {permit | deny} as-regex
no ip as-path access-list access-list {permit | deny} as-regex
```

Configures   A BGP access list

Default   None

Description

This command allows you to build an access list for BGP autonomous system (AS) paths. These lists can be applied to a neighbor with the filter-list option to the neighbor command. *access-list* is a number that identifies the list; *as-regex* is a regular expression that matches AS paths. For more information on valid regular expressions for BGP, see Chapter 10.

Example

The following commands create an AS-path access list that denies (blocks) routes that include AS 111. This access list is then applied to routes that are sent to the BGP neighbor 11.1.1.1.

```
ip as-path access-list 1 deny _111_

router bgp 120
  network 10.1.0.0
  neighbor 11.1.1.1 remote-as 200
  neighbor 11.1.1.1 filter-list 1 out
```

ip authentication   interface

```
ip authentication key-chain eigrp as-number key-chain
no ip authentication key-chain eigrp as-number key-chain

ip authentication mode eigrp as-number md5
no ip authentication mode eigrp as-number md5
```

Configures   Authentication of EIGRP packets

Default   None

Description

The `ip authentication key-chain` command defines the key chain to be used for authenticating EIGRP packets. It is used with the `ip authentication mode eigrp` command, which applies the key chain to the correct EIGRP process. Key chains are defined with the global `key chain` command.

as-number
> The EIGRP process to which this key applies.

key-chain
> The name of an EIGRP key chain.

Example

```
interface ethernet0
  ip authentication key-chain eigrp 100 key1
  ip authentication mode eigrp 100 md5
```

---

ip bandwidth-percent eigrp   interface, EIGRP

`ip bandwidth-percent eigrp` *as-number percent-value*

Configures   The bandwidth that EIGRP is allowed to use

Default   50 percent

Description

This command sets the bandwidth percentage that EIGRP is allowed to consume on a link. It is particularly useful if the link's bandwidth has been set to a fake value for some reason (such as metrics).

as-number
> The EIGRP process whose bandwidth is being limited.

percent-value
> The percentage of the interface's total bandwidth that can be used by EIGRP. The interface's bandwidth is defined by the `bandwidth` command and may not be the same as the actual bandwidth available on the link. Note that *percent-value* may be greater than 100; this is useful if the bandwidth has been set to an artificially low value and doesn't reflect the actual capacity of the link.

---

ip bgp-community new-format   global

`ip bgp-community new-format`
`no ip bgp-community new-format`

Configures   Display of the BGP communities

Default   Disabled

Description

This command changes the display of BGP communities from NN:AA to AA:NN.

---

ip bootp server

```
ip bootp server
no ip bootp server
```

Configures   Use of a BOOTP server from the network

Default   Enabled

Description

This command enables or disables the router's BOOTP server. Disabling this feature prevents hosts from accessing the BOOTP service on the router; that is, the router won't act as a BOOTP server.

ip broadcast-address

```
ip broadcast-address address
no ip broadcast-address address
```

Configures   A broadcast address for an interface

Default   Depends on the settings in the config-register

Description

This command specifies the interface's broadcast address. All hosts on the network to which the interface is connected must use the same broadcast address. Broadcast addresses are usually formed by setting the "host address" portion of the IP address to 1, which is the default for the router and virtually all modern computer systems. Some very old systems may form the broadcast address by setting the host portion to 0, and may be incapable of using the "1" form. In this case, you must explicitly set the broadcast address of the router interface (and all other hosts on the network) to use the older form.

Example

The following code changes the broadcast IP address for **serial 0** to 10.10.10.255:

```
interface serial 0
    ip broadcast-address 10.10.10.255
```

ip cef

```
ip cef [distributed]
no ip cef
```

Configures   Cisco Express Forwarding (CEF)

Default

Depends on the hardware: disabled on the 7000 and 7200; enabled on the 7500 and 12000

Description

This command enables CEF on the router. CEF is a Layer 3 switching technology that increases network performance for certain types of network traffic. The optional distributed keyword enables distributed CEF (dCEF), which distributes CEF information to line cards on the router.

---

ip cef traffic-statistics global

```
ip cef traffic-statistics [load-interval seconds] [update-rate seconds]
no ip cef traffic-statistics
```

Configures Time intervals that control when NHRP creates or destroys an SVC

Default load-interval is 30 seconds; update-rate is 10 seconds

Description

This command sets the intervals that NHRP uses when building or tearing down an SVC. The load-interval is used in conjunction with the ip nhrp trigger-svc command; its value can range from 30 to 300 seconds. The update-rate is the frequency, in seconds, at which the port adapter sends statistics to the route processor (RP). When using NHRP in distributed CEF switching mode, the update rate must be set to 5 seconds.

---

ip classless global

```
ip classless
no ip classless
```

Configures IP classless routing for the router

Default Depends on the IOS version

Description

This command enables routing based on "classless" addresses. With classless routing, packets can be routed if the router knows a route for a supernet of the addressee. Without classless addressing, the packet is discarded if it arrives at the router and there is no network route for its destination. Assume that a packet arrives with the destination of 10.10.1.5, but we have routes only for 10.10.2.0/24, 10.10.3.0/24, and 10.10.0.0/16. With IP classless routing enabled, the router forwards the packet to the 10.10.0.0/16 network because 10.10.0.0/16 is the best matching supernet of 10.10.1.5.

---

ip community-list global

```
ip community-list number {permit | deny} community
no ip community-list number
```

Configures A community list for BGP

Default None

Description

This command defines a community list, which is basically an access list for a BGP community. A community list can be used with the `match community` command in a route-map configuration.

number
> A value identifying the community list that this command belongs to. Values can be 1 to 99.

`permit | deny`
> Permits or denies the given community.

community
> The community to permit or deny. This parameter may be a community number between 1 and 99, or one of the default community names (`internet`, `no-export`, `no-advertise`).

Example

```
ip community-list 1 permit internet
```

---

ip default-gateway   global

```
ip default-gateway address
no default-gateway address
```

Configures   The default gateway for the router

Default   None

Description

This command establishes *address* as the router's default gateway, which is the gateway to which nonlocal packets are forwarded in the absence of a better route. It is useful if the `no ip routing` command has been issued or if you are running from boot mode, in which IP routing is disabled. This command allows you to forward traffic to the default gateway when routing is disabled. Use the `no` form of this command to remove the entry from the router's configuration.

---

ip default-network   global

```
ip default-network network
no ip default-network network
```

Configures   Gateway of last resort

Default   None

Description

This command defines a gateway of last resort. The *network* argument is a network address; any route to the network becomes the default route. For RIP, this is the 0.0.0.0 route; for OSPF, it is an external route.

ip dhcp-server

global

```
ip dhcp-server address
no ip dhcp-server address
```

Configures   The DHCP server for the router

Default   None

Description

Specifies the *address* of the DHCP server for this router. You can provide the hostname of the DHCP server instead of its IP address. This DHCP server is then used for creating address pools with the `ip address-pool` command.

ip directed-broadcast

interface

```
ip directed-broadcast [access-list]
no ip directed-broadcast
```

Configures   Broadcast forwarding

Default   Enabled (disabled for IOS 12.0 and later)

Description

By default, the router automatically translates directed broadcasts to physical broadcasts within your network. In other words, Layer 3 broadcasts to the IP broadcast address (10.10.1.255 for the subnet 10.10.1.0/24) are translated into Layer 2 broadcasts with an address appropriate for the interface (e.g., `ff:ff:ff:ff:ff:ff` for an Ethernet interface).

While this can be useful, an interface that is configured to the outside world could allow a potential hacker to flood your network by pinging the broadcast address on your interface. It is recommended that `directed-broadcast` is disabled on your external interfaces to prevent this attack from occurring. Directed broadcast is also the primary mechanism used for the "smurf" attack. It is recommended that you disable directed broadcast on all your interfaces unless you have a very good reason to use it.

Example

To disable directed broadcasts:

```
interface serial 0
    no ip directed-broadcast
```

ip domain-list

global

```
ip domain-list domain
no ip domain-list domain
```

Configures   Domain name completion

Default   None

Description

This command allows you to define a series of domain names to be used (in turn) to complete an unqualified domain name. It behaves just like the `domain-name` command except that it allows you to list a series of domains.

Example

These commands set the domain list to `mydomain.com`, `com.com`, and `mycom.com`:

```
ip domain-list mydomain.com
ip domain-list com.com
ip domain list mycom.com
```

Use the `no` form of the command to delete an entry:

```
no ip domain-list com.com
```

---

ip domain-lookup global

```
ip domain-lookup
no ip domain-lookup
```

Configures DNS lookups for hostnames

Default Enabled

Description

This command enables the DNS lookup feature. To disable DNS, use the `no` form of this command. Disabling this feature is useful because you don't usually want the router trying to perform a DNS lookup on every word that you type at the command prompt. (You can accomplish the same thing by enabling `transport preferred none` on all lines.) Furthermore, if you are having network problems, you may not be able to reach any DNS servers to perform lookups.

Example

To disable DNS lookups:

```
no ip domain-lookup
```

---

ip domain-name global

```
ip domain-name domain
no ip domain-name domain
```

Configures Domain name completion

Default None

Description

This command sets the domain name that the router will use to complete any unqualified domain names. See also `ip domain-list`.

Example

Here, all unqualified hostnames are taken to be in the `mydomain.com` domain:

```
ip domain-name mydomain.com
```

ip dvmrp accept-filter interface

```
ip dvmrp accept-filter access-list [distance] [neighbor-list access-list]
no dvmrp accept-filter access-list
```

Configures   Incoming filter for DVMRP reports

Default   All reports are accepted with a distance of 0

Description

This command applies an access list to incoming DVMRP reports. The lower the distance, the higher the precedence of the route when computing the Reverse Path Forwarding value.

`access-list`
> The number of a standard IP access list (0–99). Routes matching the access list are assigned the given administrative distance. If the access list number is 0 (which is not a legal access list number), all reports are accepted with the given administrative distance.

`distance`
> Optional. The administrative distance to be assigned to routes matching the filter. Default is 0.

`neighbor-list list`
> Optional. The number of a standard IP access list (1–99). DVMRP reports are accepted only from neighbors who match this access list.

ip dvmrp auto-summary interface

```
ip dvmrp auto-summary
no ip dvmrp auto-summary
```

Configures   DVMRP auto summarization

Default   Enabled

Description

Auto summarization occurs when a route is summarized into a classful network route. Use the `no` form of this command to disable it, which you will want to do if you are using the `ip dvmrp summary-address` command.

ip dvmrp default-information   interface

```
ip dvmrp default-information {originate | only}
no dvmrp default-information
```

Configures   Advertises a default route to DVMRP neighbors

Default   Disabled

Description

This command causes the default route (0.0.0.0) to be advertised to DVMRP neighbors.

originate
     Routes more specific than 0.0.0.0 can be advertised.

only
     Only the default route is advertised.

---

ip dvmrp metric   interface

```
ip dvmrp metric metric [list access-list] [[protocol process-id] | [dvmrp]
no ip dvmrp metric
```

Configures   Metrics for DVMRP

Default   1

Description

This command lets you specify a metric to be used with the DVMRP routing protocol. The specified metric is assigned to multicast destinations that match the access list.

metric
     The metric associated with DVMRP reports; it can range from 0 to 32. 0 means the route is not advertised; 32 means that the route's destination is unreachable.

list access-list
     Optional. If used, this metric is assigned only to multicast destinations that match the access list.

protocol
     Optional. bgp, eigrp, igrp, isis, ospf, rip, static, or dvmrp.

process-id
     Optional. The process ID of the routing protocol, if required.

dvmrp
     Optional. Allows routes from the DVMRP routing table to be advertised with the configured metric route map.

ip dvmrp metric-offset
interface

```
ip dvmrp metric-offset [in | out] value
no ip dvmrp metric-offset
```

Configures   Metrics of advertised DVMRP routes

Default   in; the default value for in is 1, for out is 0

Description

This command allows you to increment the metric for DVMRP routes. The given *value* is added to either metrics received (in) or metrics sent (out) by the router.

ip dvmrp output-report-delay
interface

```
ip dvmrp output-report-delay milliseconds [burst-packets]
no ip dvmrp output-report-delay
```

Configures   Interpacket delay of a DVMRP report

Default   100 milliseconds; 2 burst packets

Description

This command sets the number of milliseconds that elapse between packets of a DVMRP report.

milliseconds
   Number of milliseconds between transmission of packets.

burst-packets
   Optional. The number of packets in the set being transmitted.

ip dvmrp reject-non-pruners
interface

```
ip dvmrp reject-non-pruners
no ip dvmrp reject-non-pruners
```

Configures   Peering with DVMRP non-pruners

Default   Disabled

Description

When enabled, this feature tells the interface not to peer with DVMRP hosts that do not support pruning. By default, the router will peer with all DVMRP neighbors.

ip dvmrp routehog-notification
global

```
ip dvmrp routehog-notification route-count
no ip dvmrp routehog-notification
```

Configures   Number of routes accepted before a syslog message is generated

Default   10,000

Description

This command sets the number of DVMRP routes that can be accepted within one minute to *route-count*. If more than this number of routes is accepted within a minute, the router generates a syslog message. This usually helps capture any router that is misconfigured and injecting too many routes.

ip dvmrp route-limit
global

```
ip dvmrp route-limit count
no ip dvmrp route-limit count
```

Configures   Number of advertised DVMRP routes

Default   7000

Description

This command sets the limit on the number of DVMRP routes that can be advertised over an interface to *count*.

ip dvmrp summary-address
interface

```
ip dvmrp summary-address address mask [metric value]
no ip dvmrp summary-address address mask
```

Configures   A summary DVMRP route

Default   None

Description

This command configures a summary DVMRP route to be advertised over an interface.

address
    The IP address of the summary route.

mask
    The network mask of the summary route.

metric *value*
    Optional. The metric to be assigned to the summary address. Default is 1.

ip dvmrp unicast-routing

```
ip dvmrp unicast-routing
no dvmrp unicast-routing
```

Configures   DVMRP unicast routing

Default   Disabled

Description

This command enables DVMRP unicast routing on the interface.

---

ip forward-protocol

```
ip forward-protocol {udp [port] | any-local-broadcast | spanning-tree |
    turbo-flood}
no ip forward-protocol
```

Configures   Forwarding of broadcast packets for certain services

Default   Enabled with the ip helper-address command

Description

When the ip helper-address command is configured for an interface, the router "helps" hosts find certain UDP services by forwarding the packets. These services are BOOTP (DHCP), DNS, TFTP, TACACS, TIME, and NetBIOS name and datagram servers. This command allows you to define additional UDP ports that you want forwarded automatically to the helper IP address.

port
> Optional. Without this parameter, all the default UDP ports listed here are forwarded. This keyword allows you to forward a specific port. You can disable a default port with the no version of this command.

any-local-broadcast
> Forwards any broadcasts including local subnet broadcasts.

spanning-tree
> Forwards IP broadcasts that meet the following criteria: First, it must be a MAC level broadcast; second, it must be an IP level broadcast; and third, it must be TFTP, DNS, NetBIOS, ND, TIME, BOOTP, or any other UDP packet specified by an ip forward-protocol udp command.

turbo-flood
> Speeds up the flooding of UDP datagrams when using the spanning-tree algorithm. This command should be used in conjunction with the ip forward-protocol spanning-tree command.

Example

To forward port 21000 for a specific application:

```
ip forward-protocol udp 21000
```

ip ftp passive global

```
ip ftp passive
no ip ftp passive
```

Configures   Passive FTP mode

Default   Disabled (normal FTP)

Description

This command configures the router to use passive FTP. Passive FTP is often used when connecting through firewalls or access lists that block normal FTP connections. With passive FTP, the file transfer occurs on the same port as the initial connection. You may need to use passive FTP when copying a file or image to an FTP server.

ip ftp password global

```
ip ftp password [encryption-level] password
no ftp password
```

Configures   The FTP password

Default   *username@routername.domain*

Description

This command sets the password to be used for FTP connections. The default password is appropriate for anonymous FTP connections. If you do not use anonymous FTP, you must use this command to provide an appropriate secret password. The *encryption-level* allows you to encrypt the password within the router's configuration, so people who have access to the configuration file won't learn it. The *encryption-level* may be 0 or 7; 0 does not encrypt the password, while 7 uses a proprietary (but not particularly strong) encryption scheme.

ip ftp source-interface global

```
ip ftp source-interface interface
no ip ftp source-interface
```

Configures   The FTP source address

Default   The IP address of the interface closest to the destination

Description

This command sets the source address for FTP connections to the IP address of the given *interface*.

ip ftp username

```
ip ftp username username
no ip ftp username
```

Configures   The FTP username

Default   anonymous

Description

This command sets the username for FTP connections. If no username is supplied, the router attempts an anonymous FTP file transfer.

Example

The following commands configure the router to use passive FTP with the username saul and the password pleaseletmein.

```
ip ftp passive
ip ftp username saul
ip ftp password pleaseletmein
```

ip hello-interval eigrp

interface

```
ip hello-interval eigrp as-number seconds
no ip hello-interval eigrp as-number seconds
```

Configures   Hello interval for EIGRP

Default   5 seconds

Description

This command sets the interval at which EIGRP hello discovery packets are sent out on a link. The default value for the hello interval is 5 seconds. On links where latency is high, changing this value to a higher number can be advantageous.

as-number
    The EIGRP process number (frequently called an AS number).

seconds
    The interval between hello discovery packets.

ip helper-address

interface

```
ip helper-address address
no ip helper-address address
```

Configures   IP address to which certain broadcast UDP packets are forwarded

Default   Disabled

Description

This command sets the helper address to *address*. The helper address should be the address of a host that can answer UDP requests from other hosts. The router sees these requests broadcast on a LAN interface and forwards them to the helper address (generally a unicast address) if one is defined. A helper is particularly useful for DHCP requests; without some kind of forwarding, DHCP requires you to have a separate server on every subnet. By itself, this command forwards packets for the BOOTP (DHCP), DNS, TFTP, TACACS, TIME, and NetBIOS name and datagram services. The `ip forward-protocol` command can be used to forward additional UDP services.

Example

To configure interface `ethernet0` to have a helper address:

```
interface ethernet0
    ip address 10.10.1.2 255.255.255.0
    ip helper address 10.10.2.5
```

---

ip hold-time eigrp   interface

```
ip hold-time eigrp as-number seconds
no ip hold-time eigrp as-number seconds
```

Configures   Hold time for EIGRP networks

Default   15 seconds

Description

This command defines the number of seconds that a route is held before hearing from a neighbor router. If the router doesn't hear from a neighbor within this time, the routes from that neighbor are considered invalid. The default holdtime is three times the hello interval, which is 15 seconds on most links. Slower links might have a holdtime of 180 seconds and a hello interval of 60 seconds.

as-number
> The EIGRP process number (frequently called an AS number).

seconds
> The holdtime for this EIGRP process.

---

ip host   global

```
ip host name [tcp-port] address [address]
no ip host name address
```

Configures   A static hostname that maps to one or more IP addresses

Default   None

Description

This command allows you to define an IP address for a hostname. Each hostname can have up to eight IP addresses associated with it. This is similar to a host file on a workstation (for example, the */etc/hosts* file on Unix).

name
> The name of a host.

tcp-port
> Optional. The port to connect to on the host when using the telnet command.

address
> The address assigned to the host.

Example

The following commands define two IP hosts; the second one has two IP addresses:

```
ip host gateway1 10.10.1.1
ip host gateway2 10.10.1.2 10.10.1.3
```

---

ip http   global

```
ip http server
no ip http server

ip http access-class access-list
no ip http access-class access-list

ip http authentication method
no ip http authentication method

ip http port port
no ip http port port
```

Configures   Web IOS interface

Default   Disabled; when enabled, listens on port 80

Description

This command configures support for the Web IOS interface software. This feature enables an HTTP server on the router and allows you to configure the router by pointing any web browser at this server. The access-class option lets you specify an access list that limits access to the HTTP server. The port option lets you specify the port on which the server listens.

The acceptable authentication methods are enable, local, tacacs, and aaa.

Example

The following commands enable the web browser interface and specify a non-default port:

```
ip http server
ip http port 8008
```

---

ip identd

```
ip identd
no ip identd
```

Configures   Identification support

Default   Disabled

Description

This command enables the IDENTD identification protocol. To disable IDENTD, use the no form of the command.

ip igmp access-group

```
ip igmp access-group access-list version
no ip igmp access-group access-list version
```

Configures   Controls multicast groups

Default   All groups are enabled; default version is 2

Description

This command allows you to set an *access-list* that controls which groups are available on the interface for hosts to join. If a host is in the access list, it will be allowed to join multicast groups. The *version* parameter changes the IGMP version.

ip igmp helper-address

```
ip igmp helper-address ip-address
no ip igmp helper-address ip-address
```

Configures   Forwards IGMP messages to another IP address

Default   Disabled

Description

This command causes all IGMP Host Reports and Leave messages to be sent to the host specified by the *ip-address* parameter.

ip igmp join-group

```
ip igmp join-group group-address
no ip igmp join-group group-address
```

Configures   Has the router join a multicast group

Default   None

Description

This command causes the router to join the multicast group specified by the IP group address on the interface.

---

ip igmp query-interval   interface

```
ip igmp query-interval seconds
no ip igmp query-interval seconds
```

Configures   Query message interval

Default   60 seconds

Description

This command configures the router to send IGMP host-query messages at the specified interval. Changing this value may affect multicast forwarding.

---

ip igmp query-max-response-time   interface

```
ip igmp query-max-response-time seconds
no ip igmp query-max-response-time seconds
```

Configures   Response time advertised in IGMP query packets

Default   10 seconds

Description

This command sets the time in *seconds* that the responder has to respond to a query before the router deletes the group. This command works only with IGMP Version 2.

---

ip igmp query-timeout   interface

```
ip igmp query-timeout seconds
no ip igmp query-timeout seconds
```

Configures   Query timeout

Default   2 times the query interval

Description

This command sets the query timeout period in *seconds*. This is the time that the router waits after the last querier stops querying, and takes over as the querier.

---

ip igmp static-group   interface

```
ip igmp static-group group-address
no ip igmp static-group group-address
```

Configures   A static *igmp* group for the router

Default   Disabled

Description

This command enrolls the router in the multicast group specified by the *group-address*. Unlike the ip igmp join-group command, this command allows packets to the group to be fast-switched out the interface.

---

ip igmp version   interface

```
ip igmp version {1 | 2}
no ip igmp version
```

Configures   The IGMP version type

Default   2

Description

This command sets the version number of IGMP supported by the router (1 or 2). Make sure that your hosts support the same version. Version 3 is planned for later releases of the IOS.

---

ip irdp   interface

```
ip irdp [multicast | holdtime seconds | maxadvertinterval seconds |
    minadvertinterval seconds | preference value | address ip-address
    [preference]]
no ip irdp
```

Configures   IRDP

Default   Disabled

Description

This command enables ICMP Router Discovery Protocol (IRDP) on an interface. Other hosts on the network can use this protocol to negotiate a default router based on the preference parameter.

This command has many options. Instead of writing a single long command, it's often more convenient to issue a number of shorter commands, each setting one option.

multicast
> Optional. Tells the router to use the multicast address instead of the broadcast address for IRDP.

holdtime seconds
> Optional. The time in seconds that advertisements are held. By default, this value is three times the maxadvertinterval.

maxadvertinterval seconds
> Optional. Sets the maximum interval in seconds between advertisements. The default is 600 seconds.

minadvertinterval *seconds*

> Optional. Sets the minimum interval in *seconds* between advertisements. The default is the maximum interval.

preference *value*

> Optional. Sets the preference *value* for this router, which is used by the routers running IRDP to select the default gateway. The default preference is 0. The higher the preference, the more preferred this router is to hosts.

address *ip-address* [*preference*]

> Optional. Tells the router to generate proxy advertisements for the given *ip-address*. If you specify a *preference*, it is associated with the given *ip-address*. This allows routers that do not run IRDP to participate in router discovery.

Example

```
interface ethernet0
  ! Enable IRDP on this interface
  ip irdp
  ! make this router preferred
  ip irdp preference 10
```

---

ip load-sharing

interface

```
ip load-sharing [per-packet] [per-destination]
no ip load-sharing [per-packet] [per-destination]
```

Configures   Cisco Express Forwarding (CEF)

Default   per-destination

Description

This command enables load sharing for Cisco Express Forwarding (CEF). By default, CEF uses per-destination load sharing, in which all traffic for a given destination is sent through the same interface. The per-packet keyword changes the behavior of CEF so that packets for the same destination may be sent through different interfaces. This approach makes load sharing more effective because it increases the effective bandwidth between the router and the destination. However, packets might arrive at the destination out of order, requiring the destination host to reassemble them.

---

ip local policy route-map

global

```
ip local policy route-map map
no ip local policy route-map map
```

Configures   Policy routing

Default   None

Description

This command enables local policy routing. In brief, policy routing means using criteria other than the shortest path to the destination (as computed by a routing protocol) for route selection. The *map* parameter is the name of a route map that specifies the routing policy. Unlike the `ip policy` command, which applies a routing policy to a single interface, this command applies the policy to traffic originating on the router.

Example

In this example, a route map named `map1` states that any traffic that matching access list 101 will be routed to the 10.1.1.1 router. Access list 101 matches all IP traffic destined for network 10.1.5.0/24. The `ip local policy` command is used to apply this route map, effectively routing all traffic for 10.1.5.0 through 10.1.1.1 regardless of what the routing protocols might tell the router to do. There are many possible reasons for this policy—for example, the traffic for 10.1.5.0 might be highly confidential, and we want to make sure that it passes only through trusted routers.

```
access-list 101 permit ip 10.1.5.0 0.0.0.255 any
!
ip local policy route-map map1
!
route-map map1
  match ip address 101
  set ip next-hop 10.1.1.1
```

ip local pool   global

```
ip local pool {default | poolname} low-ip-address [high-ip-address]
no ip local pool {default | poolname}
```

Configures   A pool of IP addresses

Default   None

Description

This command allows you to create a pool of IP addresses that are used when a remote system connects to one of your interfaces. The default pool is the one used if no name is given on the interface.

`default`
> Default pool configuration.

`poolname`
> The name of the pool you are configuring.

`low-ip-address`
> The starting (lowest) IP address in the address pool.

`high-ip-address`
> The ending (highest) IP address in the pool. This is optional. If omitted, the only IP address in the pool is the `low-ip-address`.

Example

```
! Assign a pool called dialins1 that goes from 172.30.25.10 to 172.30.25.100
ip local pool dialins1 172.30.25.10 172.30.25.100
```

ip mask-reply

```
ip mask-reply
no mask-reply
```

Configures   Responses to ICMP mask request messages

Default   Disabled

Description

By default, the router does not respond to ICMP mask requests. This command enables responses through the interface.

Example

```
interface ethernet 1
  ip mask-reply
```

---

ip mroute

```
ip mroute source mask [protocol as-number] {rpf-address | interface} [distance]
no ip mroute source mask [protocol as-number] {rpf-address | interface}
    [distance]
```

Configures   A multicast static route

Default   None

Description

This command adds a static multicast route.

source
> The source IP address.

mask
> Network mask for the source address.

protocol as-number
> Optional. The unicast routing protocol you are using, followed by the protocol's process number or autonomous system number, if applicable.

rpf-address
> The address of the incoming interface for the multicast route. This address can be a host address or a network address.

interface
> The incoming interface for the route (e.g., serial0).

distance
> Optional. This value is used to decide if a unicast, DVMRP, or static route should be used for RPF lookup.

ip mroute-cache   interface

```
ip mroute-cache
no ip mroute-cache
```

Configures   IP multicast fast switching

Default   Enabled

Description

This command enables fast switching for multicast routing, which is analogous to the route cache for unicast routing. If disabled with the no form of the command, every packet is switched at the process level.

---

ip mtu   interface

```
ip mtu bytes
no ip mtu bytes
```

Configures   Maximum Transmission Unit (MTU) for the interface

Default   Depends on the interface's media type

Description

This command sets the MTU for the interface to *bytes*. The MTU is the largest packet size that can be sent over the interface. The default MTU depends on the media type; Table 15-10 shows default MTU values for some common media. This command allows you to modify the MTU for any interface. Larger MTU values are more efficient with highly reliable networks; lower MTU values can help if an interface is unreliable, or in situations where protocols do not support fragmentation.

Table 15-10: Default MTU values

Interface type	Default MTU
Ethernet/Serial	1500
HSSI/ATM/FDDI	4470

Example

```
interface ethernet 0
  ip mtu 1250
```

---

ip multicast boundary   interface

```
ip multicast boundary access-list
no ip multicast boundary
```

Configures   A multicast boundary

Default   None

Description

The *access-list* defines the multicast boundary, which is used to keep multicast packets from being forwarded out the interface.

---

ip multicast cache-headers   global

```
ip multicast cache-headers
no ip multicast cache-headers
```

Configures   Buffers multicast packet headers

Default   Disabled

Description

This command enables the router to cache IP multicast packet headers. These headers can be viewed with the show ip mpacket command.

---

ip multicast helper-map   interface

```
ip multicast helper-map group-address broadcast-address access-list
no ip multicast helper-map group-address broadcast-address access-list

ip multicast helper-map broadcast multicast-address access-list
no ip multicast helper-map broadcast multicast-address access-list
```

Configures   Multicast tunneling

Default   None

Description

Use this command to send broadcast packets through a multicast network that connects two or more broadcast-capable networks. At one multicast network, you convert the multicast packets to broadcast packets and send them through the broadcast network, which converts them back to multicast packets at the other end.

group-address
 Multicast group whose traffic is to be converted to broadcast traffic.

broadcast
 Specifies that the traffic is going to be converted from broadcast to multicast.

broadcast-address
 When using the *group-address* parameter, this parameter specifies the IP address to which to send the broadcast traffic.

multicast-address
 When using the broadcast option, this variable specifies the multicast address to which converted traffic is sent.

access-list
 An extended access list that uses the UDP port number to control which broadcast packets will be converted.

Example

The following configuration converts multicast traffic for the multicast group 224.1.
1.2 to broadcast traffic using the broadcast address 10.1.1.255 and UDP port 5000:

```
interface ethernet 0
  ip multicast helper-map 224.1.1.2 10.1.1.255 101
  ip pim dense-mode
!
! Convert to UDP port 5000
access-list 101 permit any any udp 5000
access-list 101 deny any any udp
!
! Forward UDP port 5000
ip forward-protocol udp 5000
```

The next configuration is the other end of the tunnel. It converts broadcast traffic
on UDP port 5000 to multicast traffic:

```
interface ethernet 0
  ip multicast helper-map broadcast 224.1.1.2 101
  ip pim dense-mode
!
! Use access list to convert traffic to UDP
! port 5000
access-list 101 permit any any udp 5000
access-list 101 deny any any udp
!
! Forward udp port 5000
ip forward-protocol udp 5000
```

---

ip multicast rate-limit   interface

```
ip multicast rate-limit {in | out} [video | whiteboard]
    [group-list access-list] [source-list access-list] kbps
no ip multicast rate-limit {in | out} [video | whiteboard]
    [group-list access-list] [source-list access-list] kbps
```

Configures   The rate at which a sender can send to a multicast group

Default   No rate limit

Description

This command controls the rate at which hosts matching a source list can send
multicast packets to a multicast group.

in
> The limit applies only to incoming packets.

out
> The limit applies only to outgoing packets.

video
> Optional. Rate limit applies only to video traffic.

whiteboard
> Optional. Rate limit applies only to whiteboard traffic.

group-list *access-list*
> Optional. The rate limit applies only to multicast groups that match the access list.

source-list *access-list*
> Optional. The rate limit applies only to hosts sending multicast traffic that match the access list.

kbps
> The total bandwidth, in *kbps*, that is used for multicast traffic that matches the preceding parameters. Traffic in excess of this rate is discarded. If the rate is set to 0, no traffic is permitted.

---

ip multicast-routing   global

```
ip multicast-routing
no ip multicast-routing
```

Configures   IP multicast routing

Default   Disabled

Description

By default, the router does not forward multicast packets. This command enables multicast routing.

---

ip multicast ttl-threshold   interface

```
ip multicast ttl-threshold ttl
no ip multicast ttl-threshold
```

Configures   TTL threshold of forwarded packets

Default   0

Description

This command configures the TTL threshold for packets that are being forwarded out the interface. Only packets with TTL values greater than the threshold are forwarded. The default value is 0, which means all packets are forwarded. The value of *ttl* can be from 0 to 255.

---

ip name-server   global

```
ip name-server address [address]
no ip name-server address
```

Configures   DNS server name

Default   None

Description

This command sets the name servers that the router uses for DNS queries. You can specify the *address*es of up to 6 different DNS servers on one command line. Because you are configuring domain name service, be sure to use an IP address and *not* a hostname for the server!

Example

The first line configures one name server; the second line configures six name servers:

```
ip name-server 10.10.2.5
ip name-server 10.10.1.5 10.10.2.5 10.10.3.5 10.10.4.5 10.10.5.5 10.10.6.5
```

---

ip nat   interface

```
ip nat {inside | outside}
no ip nat {inside | outside}
```

Configures   IP Network Address Translation (NAT)

Default   Disabled

Description

This command configures an interface for NAT. The translation can occur for inside or outside addresses.

Example

In the following configuration, ethernet0 is our internal network with the internal IP address; serial0 is our external interface to the Internet. The NAT translation should be inside on ethernet0 and outside on serial0.

```
interface ethernet0
   ip address 10.10.1.1 255.255.255.0
   ip nat inside
interface serial0
   ip address 192.168.1.1 255.255.255.0
   ip nat outside
```

---

ip nat inside destination   global

```
ip nat inside destination [list access-list] pool pool-name
no ip nat inside destination [list access-list] pool pool-name

ip nat inside destination [list access-list] static global-ip local-ip
no ip nat inside destination [list access-list] static global-ip local-ip
```

Configures   Enables NAT for inside destination IP addresses

Default   Disabled

Description

This command enables the mapping of internal (inside) destination addresses to global destination addresses.

list *access-list*
> Optional. Defines an access list for the translation. If an address is not blocked by the access list, it is translated.

pool *pool-name*
> The name of the address pool for allocating global IP addresses.

static *global-ip local-ip*
> A static mapping of a global IP address to a local IP address.

---

ip nat inside source global

```
ip nat inside source [list access-list] pool pool-name [overload]
no ip inside source [list access-list] pool pool-name [overload]

ip nat inside source [list access-list] static local-ip global-ip
no ip nat inside source [list access-list] static local-ip global-ip
```

Configures   Enables NAT for inside source IP addresses

Default   None

Description

This command enables the mapping of internal (inside) source addresses to global addresses.

list *access-list*
> Optional. Defines an access list for the translation. If an address is not blocked by the access list, it is translated.

pool *pool-name*
> The name of an address pool to be used for selecting global IP addresses.

overload
> Optional. Allows many local IP addresses to share a few global IP addresses by multiplexing the ports.

static *local-ip global-ip*
> A static mapping of a local IP address to a global IP address.

---

ip nat outside source global

```
ip nat outside source [list access-list] pool pool-name
no ip nat outside source [list access-list] pool pool-name

ip nat outside source [list access-list] static global-ip local-ip
no ip nat outside source [list access-list] static global-ip local-ip
```

Configures   Enables NAT for outside source IP addresses

Default   None

Description

This command enables the mapping of external (outside) source addresses to internal addresses.

list *access-list*
> Optional. Defines an access list for the translation. If an address is not blocked by the access list, it is translated.

pool *pool-name*
> The name of the address pool for allocating global IP addresses.

static *global-ip local-ip*
> A static mapping of a global IP address to a local IP address.

---

ip nat pool   global

ip nat pool *name starting-address ending-address* [netmask *value* |
    prefix-length *length*] [type rotary]
no ip nat pool *name starting-address ending-address* [netmask *value* |
    prefix-length *length*] [type rotary]

Configures   The IP address pool to be used in the NAT configuration

Default   None

Description

This command defines a sequential range of IP addresses to use with NAT configurations.

name
> Name of the address pool.

starting-address
> The beginning of the pool's IP address range.

ending-address
> The last IP address in the pool.

netmask *value*
> Specifies the netmask for the pool address range.

prefix-length *length*
> Specifies the number of ones in the bitmask.

type rotary
> Optional. Specifies that the range of IP addresses corresponds to real hosts for which load distribution should occur. This means that the pool is defined as a round-robin set of address for load balancing. As new TCP connections are made, a new address is selected from the pool. Non-TCP traffic passes through without translation.

ip nat translation global

```
ip nat translation {timeout | udp-timeout | dns-timeout | tcp-timeout |
    finrst-timeout} seconds
no ip nat translation {timeout | udp-timeout | dns-timeout | tcp-timeout |
    finrst-timeout} seconds
```

Configures   None

Default   See description

Description

This command specifies different timeouts for NAT translations.

timeout *seconds*
> The timeout on all translations except overloads. Default is 86400 seconds.

udp-timeout *seconds*
> The timeout on UDP port translations. Default is 300 seconds.

dns-timeout *seconds*
> The timeout on DNS (Domain Name Service). Default is 60 seconds.

tcp-timeout *seconds*
> The timeout on TCP ports. Default is 86400 seconds.

finrst-timeout *seconds*
> The timeout on Finish and Reset TCP packets. Default is 60 seconds.

---

ip netmask-format line

```
ip netmask-format [bitcount | decimal | hexadecimal]
no ip netmask-format [bitcount | decimal | hexadecimal]
```

Configures   How subnets are displayed by the show command

Default   Decimal format (255.255.255.0)

Description

This command determines the format that the show commands use for displaying subnet masks. Table 15-11 shows the possibilities.

Table 15-11: Netmask formats

Format name	Example
decimal	255.255.255.0
bitcount	10.10.1.0/24
hexadecimal	0xffffff00

ip nhrp authentication
interface

```
ip nhrp authentication string
no ip nhrp authentication
```

Configures   Authentication for NHRP

Default   Disabled

Description

This command sets an authentication `string` for Next-Hop Resolution Protocol
(NHRP). By default, no authentication is performed. The string can be up to eight
characters in length. All routers within the NBMA (Non-Broadcast Multi-Access)
must use the same authentication string.

---

ip nhrp holdtime
interface

```
ip nhrp holdtime seconds
no ip nhrp holdtime
```

Configures   NHRP holdtime

Default   7200 seconds

Description

This command sets the number of `seconds` to advertise to other routers that they
should keep NHRP information.

---

ip nhrp interest
interface

```
ip nhrp interest access-list
no ip nhrp interest
```

Configures   Which packets should trigger NHRP requests

Default   All non-NHRP packets trigger NHRP requests

Description

This command specifies an `access-list` that the router uses to select which
packets should generate NHRP traffic.

---

ip nhrp map
interface

```
ip nhrp map ip-address nbma-address
no ip nhrp map ip-address nbma-address
```

Configures   A static NBMA-to-IP address mapping

Default   None

Description

This command allows you to define a static *ip-address* to *nbma-address* mapping. The NBMA address can be a MAC address for Ethernet or an NSAP address for ATM. For NHRP, you usually need to configure one static mapping to get to the next-hop server.

---

ip nhrp map multicast   interface

```
ip nhrp map multicast
no ip nhrp map multicast
```

Configures   An NBMA address for broadcast or multicast packets

Default   None

Description

This command defines a Non-Broadcast Multi-Access (NBMA) address to which to send broadcast or multicast traffic. An NBMA address is a MAC address for Ethernet networks or an NSAP address for ATM networks. A configuration may include several of these commands, each defining another NBMA address. This command allows you to send multicast traffic through a tunnel that crosses networks that do not support IP multicasting. It may be used only on tunnel interfaces.

---

ip nhrp max-send   interface

```
ip nhrp max-send packet-count every interval
no ip nhrp max-send
```

Configures   Frequency of NHRP packets

Default   packet-count is 5; interval is 10 seconds

Description

This command controls the rate at which NHRP packets can be sent. At most, *packet-count* packets can be sent every *interval* seconds. *packet-count* can be from 1 to 65535; *interval* can be from 10 to 65535. NHRP traffic cannot exceed this rate. Both locally generated and forwarded traffic count toward the total.

---

ip nhrp network-id   interface

```
ip nhrp network-id id
no ip nhrp network-id id
```

Configures   Enables NHRP

Default   Disabled

Description

This command enables NHRP on an interface by assigning a unique identifier for the network. All hosts participating in NHRP on a logical NBMA network must use the same network ID. *id* can be from 1 to 4294967295.

---

ip nhrp nhs   interface

```
ip nhrp nhs ip-address [network mask]
no ip nhrp nhs ip-address [network mask]
```

Configures   The NHS address

Default   None

Description

This command configures the *ip-address* of the Next-Hop Server (NHS). Optionally, you can provide a *network* address and *mask* that specify the network that the NHS serves. To specify multiple networks for a single NHS, enter this command multiple times with different *network* and *mask* parameters.

When NHS servers are configured, they override the normal NHRP forwarding table.

---

ip nhrp record   interface

```
ip nhrp record
no ip nhrp record
```

Configures   The use of forward and reverse record options in NHRP packets

Default   Enabled

Description

The no form of this command disables the forward and reverse record options in NHRP request and reply packets. These options provide loop detection.

---

ip nhrp responder   interface

```
ip nhrp responder interface
no ip nhrp responder interface
```

Configures   The IP address to use as the source of NHRP reply packets

Default   The IP address of the interface that received the NHRP request

Description

This command specifies the *interface* whose IP address is used as the source for NHRP reply packets. Normally, the IP address of the interface that received the NHRP packet is used. This command is useful on next-hop servers because it allows a form of loop detection: the server can look for its own unique IP address.

---

ip nhrp server-only interface

```
ip nhrp server-only [non-caching]
no ip nhrp server-only
```

Configures   NHRP on an interface acting in server mode only

Default   Disabled

Description

This command enables NHRP on an interface in server mode only. In server mode, an interface does not originate NHRP requests. The optional `non-caching` keyword disables the cache of NHRP information.

ip nhrp trigger-svc interface

```
ip nhrp trigger-svc trigger-threshold teardown-threshold
no ip nhrp trigger-svc
```

Configures   The thresholds for building an SVC based on traffic rates

Default   Trigger threshold, 1 kbps; teardown threshold, 0 kbps

Description

This command sets the thresholds for traffic rates that define when an SVC is built or destroyed. The `trigger-threshold` is the average traffic rate at (or above) which NHRP will create an SVC for a destination. The `teardown-threshold` is the traffic rate at (or below) which NHRP will tear down an SVC. Both parameters are in kbps; they are calculated during the load interval. The load interval is the length of time over which the router calculates the interface's throughput for comparison with the trigger and teardown thresholds. It is always a multiple of 30 seconds and is set by the `ip cef traffic-statistics` command.

ip nhrp use interface

```
ip nhrp use count
no ip nhrp use
```

Configures

A usage count that defers NHRP requests for some number of packets

Default   1

Description

By default, when the router has a packet that is eligible for NHRP address resolution, the router sends the NHRP request immediately. This command allows you to defer the NHRP request until `count` packets have been sent to the destination. The packet count can be from 1 to 65535.

The packet count is destination-based. If the count was set to 3 and the router received five packets, two for destination 1 and three for destination 2, the router would generate an NHRP request only for destination 2.

---

ip ospf authentication
interface

```
ip ospf authentication [message-digest | null]
no ip ospf authentication
```

Configures   OSPF authentication

Default   No authentication

Description

This command enables OSPF authentication for an interface, to be used if the area authentication command is not enabled. If you enable this command with no options, specify the password with the ip ospf authentiation-key command. If you use the message-digest option, specify the password with the ip ospf message-digest-key command.

The null option can be used to disable authentication for this interface if authentication of the entire area has already been configured.

---

ip ospf authentication-key
interface

```
ip ospf authentication-key password
no ip ospf authentication-key
```

Configures   A password to authenticate OSPF neighbors

Default   None

Description

This command assigns a *password* for communicating with neighboring routers to this interface. All adjacent routers should be configured with the same authentication key. The password can be from 1 to 8 bytes in length.

---

ip ospf cost
interface

```
ip ospf cost value
no ip ospf cost value
```

Configures   A default OSPF cost for packets sent out on this interface

Default 10^8 / bandwidth

Description

This command sets the cost of sending an OSPF packet on an interface to *value*. By default, Cisco routers use the bandwidth to determine the link's cost; high-speed links have a lower cost and are therefore more preferred. Other vendors might have an alternative method for cost calculation. This command can be used

---

as needed to set the cost appropriately in a multivendor environment, or to change the preference of two links of the same type. By default, OSPF attempts load balancing across links of the same type; this command changes that behavior by modifying the cost associated with each link.

Example

In this example, there are two FDDI links. The second link has a higher cost, causing the router to prefer the first.

```
interface fddi0
    ip ospf cost 2
interface fddi1
    ip ospf cost 5
```

---

ip ospf dead-interval   interface

```
ip ospf dead-interval seconds
no ip ospf dead-interval
```

Configures   The interval that can pass between hello packets

Default   4 times the hello interval

Description

This command specifies the length of time in *seconds* that must pass before receiving a hello packet. If the time passes without a hello packet from a neighbor router, the router is marked down.

---

ip ospf demand-circuit   interface

```
ip ospf demand-circuit
no ip ospf demand-circuit
```

Configures   Dial-on-demand behavior

Default   Disabled

Description

This command tells OSPF that this interface is a demand circuit (i.e., an interface configured for dial-on-demand routing). OSPF will suppress verbose traffic (such as periodic hello packets), thus preventing the circuit from being kept up all the time.

Example

This example configures an ISDN interface as a DDR link for OSPF:

```
interface bri0
    ip address 10.12.1.5 255.255.255.0
    encapsulation ppp
    ip ospf demand-circuit
```

ip ospf hello-interval

interface

```
ip ospf hello-interval seconds
no ip ospf hello-interval
```

Configures   The interval between hello packets

Default   10 seconds

Description

This command sets the number of *seconds* between hello packets on a given interface. All nodes on a network must have the same hello interval. If you change the interval on one router, you must change it on all routers within the area.

ip ospf message-digest-key

interface

```
ip ospf message-digest-key keyid md5 key
no ip ospf message-digest-key keyid md5 key
```

Configures   MD5 authentication

Default   Disabled

Description

This command enables MD5 password authentication for the interface. The *keyid* can be from 1 to 255; the *key* can be up to 16 bytes in length.

ip ospf name-lookup

interface

```
ip ospf name-lookup
no ip ospf name-lookup
```

Configures   DNS lookups for OSPF show commands

Default   Disabled

Description

This command enables DNS name lookups for all OSPF show commands. By default, show commands display IP addresses in numeric form.

ip ospf network

interface

```
ip ospf network {broadcast | non-broadcast | point-to-multipoint}
no ip ospf network
```

Configures   The type of OSPF network

Default   Depends on the interface type

Description

Given the interface's type, the OSPF process selects a default network type. This command allows the default network type to be changed.

broadcast

> The interface is connected to a broadcast network.

non-broadcast

> The interface is connected to a nonbroadcast network, i.e., a network with no effective way of dealing with broadcast packets. One example is a point-to-point network.

point-to-multipoint

> The interface is connected to a point-to-multipoint network.

Example

By default, a serial interface is point-to-point. The following commands configure a serial subinterface as part of a broadcast network:

```
interface serial0.1
    ip ospf network broadcast
```

---

ip ospf priority   interface

```
ip ospf priority priority
no ip ospf priority priority
```

Configures   OSPF priority

Default   1

Description

This command sets the priority for the router within the OSPF area to which the interface is connected. The priority determines which routers are selected as the area's DR and BDR, and can range from 0 to 255. Routers with a priority of 0 are excluded from the selection process; the router with the highest priority is selected.

Example

```
interface serial0
    ip ospf priority 10
```

---

ip ospf retransmit-interval   interface

```
ip ospf retransmit-interval seconds
no ip ospf retransmit-interval seconds
```

Configures   The interval between LSAs

Default   5 seconds

Description

This command sets the interval (in *seconds*) at which link-state advertisements (LSAs) are sent to adjacent routers via the interface. The interval can range from 1 to 65535 seconds.

Example

```
interface serial0
    ip ospf retransmit-interface 3
```

---

ip ospf transmit-delay   interface

```
ip ospf transmit-delay seconds
no ip ospf transmit-delay seconds
```

Configures   Estimated time to send a link update on the interface

Default   1 second

Description

This command lets you estimate the number of *seconds* required to transmit a link-state advertisement through this interface. It's most useful on slow interfaces where it may take a significant amount of time to transmit the announcement. The estimate is used in computing the packet's age; its value can range from 1 to 65535 seconds.

Example

```
interface serial0
    ip ospf transmit-delay 3
```

---

ip pim   interface

```
ip pim {sparse-mode | dense-mode | sparse-dense-mode}
no ip pim
```

Configures   IP multicast routing on the interface

Default   Disabled

Description

This command enables PIM (Protocol-Independent Multicast) and IGMP on the interface.

sparse-mode

In this mode, the router forwards multicast packets only if it has received a join message from a downstream router or if it has group members directly connected to this interface.

dense-mode

In this mode, the router forwards multicast packets until it can determine whether there are group members or downstream routers. Unlike sparse-mode, it doesn't wait for a join message to begin sending multicast packets.

sparse-dense-mode
> This mode allows the router to operate in both sparse-mode and dense-mode, depending on what the other routers in the multicast group are using.

ip pim accept-rp

ip pim accept-rp {*address* | auto-rp} [*access-list*]
no ip pim accept-rp {*address* | auto-rp} [*access-list*]

Configures   Processing of multicast join and prune messages

Default   Disabled

Description

By default, all join and prune messages are processed. This command lets you tell the router to process join and prune messages destined for a specific Rendezvous Point (RP) or a specific list of groups.

address
> The RP allowed to send messages to the multicast groups specified by the group access list.

auto-rp
> Accepts only messages from RPs in the auto-rp cache.

access-list
> Optional. An access list that defines the multicast groups for which we want to process join and accept messages.

ip pim message-interval

ip pim message-interval *seconds*
no ip pim message-interval *seconds*

Configures   Interval for join/prune messages

Default   60 seconds

Description

In sparse-mode operation, this command allows you to control the interval in *seconds* for sending join and prune PIM messages. A router is pruned if it is not heard from in three times this interval. The interval's value can be from 1 to 65535 seconds.

ip pim minimum-vc-rate

ip pim minimum-vc-rate *packets-per-second*
no ip pim minimum-vc-rate

Configures   Which VCs are eligible for idling

Default   0 (all VCs)

Description

This command sets the packet rate at which ATM virtual circuits (VCs) can be idled. A VC is idled if its traffic rate falls below *packets-per-second*, which can range from 0 to 4294967295. This command applies only to ATM interfaces in PIM sparse mode.

---

ip pim multipoint-signalling interface

```
ip pim multipoint-signalling
no ip pim multipoint-signalling
```

Configures   PIM's ability to open ATM SVCs for multicast groups

Default   Disabled

Description

This command enables an ATM interface to open multipoint SVCs for each PIM multicast group that it joins.

---

ip pim nbma-mode interface

```
ip pim nbma-mode
no ip pim nbma-mode
```

Configures   NBMA mode

Default   Disabled

Description

This command sets the interface for Non-Broadcast Multi-Access (NBMA) mode and is used on non-multicast interfaces such as Frame Relay and ATM. Use this command only with `ip pim sparse-mode`.

---

ip pim neighbor-filter interface

```
ip pim neighbor-filter access-list
no ip pim neighbor-filter access-list
```

Configures   A method to filter (deny) PIM packets from other routers

Default   None

Description

This command allows you to specify a standard IP *access-list* to control which routers receive PIM packets. The standard access list denies PIM packets from the source, preventing the router from joining PIM.

ip pim query-interval

```
ip pim query-interval seconds
no ip pim query-interval
```

Configures   The frequency of PIM query messages

Default   30 seconds

Description

This command sets the query interval to *seconds*. The query message is used to determine which router on the subnet will be the designated router. The designated router sends IGMP messages to the rest of the routers on the LAN; it also sends messages to the rendezvous point when operating in sparse-mode. The query interval defaults to 30 seconds and can be set to a value between 1 and 65535 seconds.

---

ip pim rp-address

```
ip pim rp-address ip-address [group-access-list] [override]
no ip pim rp-address ip-address
```

Configures   Defines the RP for a group

Default   None

Description

This command specifies the Rendezvous Point (RP) for a particular multicast group.

ip-address
    IP address of the PIM rendezvous point.

group-access-list
    Optional. Defines the multicast groups for which this RP address should be used. If there is no access list, the RP address is used for all groups.

override
    Optional. If the rendezvous point address defined by this command conflicts with the rp-cache, the override option causes this command to override the auto-rp cache.

---

ip pim rp-announce-filter

```
ip pim rp-announce-filter rp-list access-list group-list access-list
no ip pim rp-announce-filter rp-list access-list group-list access-list
```

Configures   A filter for incoming RP announcements

Default   All announcements are accepted

Description

RP routers periodically send out auto-rp announcement messages. This command controls which of these messages are accepted.

rp-list *access-list*
> A standard access list that defines the list of allowable RP addresses for the group list.

group-list *access-list*
> A standard access list that defines the multicast groups that the RPs serve.

---

ip pim send-rp-announce global

```
ip pim send-rp-announce interface scope ttl group-list access-list
no ip pim send-rp-announce interface scope ttl group-list access-list
```

Configures   The auto-rp cache

Default   Disabled

Description

This command tells the router to use the auto-rp cache to define the multicast groups for which the router is willing to become the RP. You normally use this command in the router that you wish to become the RP.

interface
> The interface that identifies the RP address.

scope *ttl*
> Time-to-Live value for announcements. TTL is roughly equivalent to a hop count.

group-list *access-list*
> An access list that defines the groups for which this router should be the RP.

---

ip pim send-rp-discovery global

```
ip pim send-rp-discovery scope ttl
no ip pim send-rp-discovery scope ttl
```

Configures   The router to be the RP mapping agent

Default   Disabled

Description

This command configures the router to be the RP mapping agent for the PIM domain. The Time-to-Live value (*ttl*) should be large enough to cover the entire domain.

ip pim vc-count

```
ip pim vc-count number
no ip pim vc-count
```

Configures   The number of VCs that PIM can open

Default   200 VCs per ATM interface or subinterface

Description

This command sets the maximum *number* of virtual circuits (VCs) that PIM can open. *number* must be between 1 and 65535.

ip pim version

```
ip pim version {1 | 2}
no ip pim version
```

Configures   PIM version to use on an interface

Default   2

Description

This command sets the PIM version to use for an interface. The version can be 1 or 2.

ip policy route-map

```
ip policy route-map map
no ip policy route-map map
```

Configures   Policy routing

Default   None

Description

This command enables policy routing for an interface. In brief, policy routing means using criteria other than the shortest path (as computed by a routing protocol) for route selection. The *map* parameter is the name of a route map that specifies the routing policy. The map applies only to traffic arriving on the interface.

Example

The following configuration applies the route map map1 to packets arriving on the serial1 interface. This route map selects packets that match access list 101 and sends them to the router at 10.1.1.1 for further routing, regardless of other information in the routing table.

```
access-list 101 permit ip 10.1.5.0 0.0.0.255 any
!
```

```
interface serial 1
  ip policy route-map map1
!
route-map map1
  match ip address 101
  set ip next-hop 10.1.1.1
```

ip proxy-arp   interface

```
ip proxy-arp
no ip proxy-arp
```

Configures   The proxy-arp feature for an interface

Default   Enabled

Description

ARP allows machines to find hardware addresses (MAC addresses) using the corresponding IP addresses. The router's proxy-arp feature helps the machines find each other across subnets. When a host sends an ARP packet requesting information about a host that can't receive the ARP broadcast, the router helps out by responding to the ARP packet on behalf of the requested host.

While proxy-arp is often useful, it can be a burden on the router in large networks. Disabling proxy-arp and relying on proper subnetting is a better solution than relying on proxy-arp to solve subnetting problems.

Example

The following commands disable proxy-arp on ethernet0. All hosts on this subnet must have the proper subnet mask because proxy-arp isn't there to help them.

```
interface ethernet0
  ip address 10.10.1.64 255.255.255.224
  no ip proxy-arp
```

ip rarp-server   interface

```
ip rarp-server address
no ip rarp-server address
```

Configures   RARP

Default   Disabled

Description

This command enables a router's interface to act as a Reverse Address Resolution Protocol (RARP) server. The *address* parameter is the address to be used in responses to RARP queries.

ip rcmd rcp-enable   global

```
ip rcmd rcp-enable
no ip rcmd rcp-enable
```

Configures   RCP to the router

Default   Disabled

Description

This command allows remote users to use the Remote Copy Protocol (RCP) to transfer files to and from the router, and RSH to access the router. For security reasons, RCP is disabled by default.

---

ip rcmd remote-host   global

```
ip rcmd remote-host local-username {ip-address | hostname} remote-username
    [enable [level]]
no ip rcmd remote-host local-username {ip-address | hostname} remote-username
    [enable [level]]
```

Configures   Which users can access the router via RSH and RCP

Default   None

Description

This command defines a local and remote username pair that allows remote users to perform remote shell tasks (RSH and RCP).

local-username
> A locally defined username or the router's hostname. The user must provide a local username to perform an operation via RSH or RCP.

ip-address or *hostname*
> The remote host from which the router accepts remote shell commands.

remote-username
> The username on the remote host from which the router accepts remote shell commands.

enable *level*
> Optional. Provides the remote user the ability to execute privileged commands via the remote shell. *level* specifies a privilege level; the user may execute commands up to and including that level. For more information about privilege levels, see Chapter 4 and the privilege level command.

---

ip rcmd remote-username   global

```
ip rcmd remote-username username
no ip rcmd remote-username username
```

Configures   The username to use when performing remote copy commands

---

Default   The username for the session or the router's hostname

Description

This command sets the *username* that the router uses when connecting to remote hosts to execute remote copy commands. By default, the router uses the username of the current session. If that username isn't valid, the router uses the router's hostname.

---

ip rcmd rsh-enable   global

```
ip rcmd rsh-enable
no ip rcmd rsh-enable
```

Configures   Remote shell access by remote users

Default   Disabled

Description

This command enables remote shell access to the router via the rsh command. For security reasons, remote shell access is disabled by default.

---

ip redirects   interface

```
ip redirects
no ip redirects
```

Configures   ICMP redirects for interfaces

Default   Enabled

Description

An ICMP redirect packet is generated by a router to inform a host of a better route to some specific destination. The recipient of an ICMP redirect overrides its route table with the information given in the redirect packet. This command configures the sending of ICMP redirects for an interface. The router never processes received ICMP redirects while IP routing is enabled.

Redirects are enabled by default on all interfaces unless Hot Standby Routing Protocol (HSRP) is configured.

Example

To avoid sending ICMP redirect packets out the ethernet0 interface:

```
interface ethernet 0
  no ip redirects
```

ip rip authentication

```
ip rip authentication key-chain name
no ip rip authentication key-chain name

ip rip authentication mode {md5 | text}
no ip rip authentication mode {md5 | text}
```

Configures   RIP route authentication

Default   Default mode is clear text

Description

This command specifies a key chain to be used for authentication of RIP routing updates. *name* is the name of the key chain to be used. Once the key chain is applied, the interface expects to authenticate any incoming RIPv2 routes. The key chain must be defined separately with the key command.

The mode version of this command specifies the authentication mode for an interface: either text (clear text) or md5.

Example

The following commands specify that RIP routes should be authenticated using MD5 encryption with the key chain defined in group1:

```
interface ethernet 1
  ip rip authentication key-chain group1
  ip rip authentication mode md5
!
key chain group1
  key 1
  key-string authme1
  key 2
  key-string authme2
```

---

ip rip receive version

```
ip rip receive version {1| 2 | 1 2}
no ip rip receive version
```

Configures   Version of RIP to receive on an interface

Default   The version in the router configuration

Description

This command tells an interface which RIP version to listen for. This version can be 1, 2, or both (1 2). By default, the router listens for the version specified by the version command in the router configuration.

Example

This configuration accepts only Version 2 packets on ethernet0:

```
interface ethernet0
 ip rip receive version 2
```

---

ip rip send version interface

```
ip rip send version {1| 2 | 1 2}
no ip rip send version
```

Configures   The version of RIP to send

Default   The version in the router configuration, or 1 if no version specified

Description

This command tells an interface which RIP version to use when sending RIP packets. This version can be 1, 2, or both (1 2). By default, the router uses the version specified by the version command in the router configuration.

Example

This configuration sends only Version 2 packets on ethernet0:

```
interface ethernet0
  ip rip send version 2
```

---

ip route global

```
ip route network mask next-hop-address [distance] [permanent]
no ip route network mask next-hop-address [distance] [permanent]
```

Configures   A static route for a network

Default   None

Description

This command defines a static route to the destination network specified by its *network* address and *mask*. *next-hop-address* is the IP address of the router to which traffic for this destination network should be sent. *distance* is an optional administrative distance that allows you change the way the static route behaves. If the distance is high enough, it can be overwritten by dynamic protocols. See Chapter 8 for more information about administrative distances. The permanent keyword tells the router to keep the route in the route table even if the interface goes down. The router normally removes static routes that are invalid because the interface is down.

Example

The following commands create two static routes. The first route sends traffic for the 192.168.1.0/24 network to 10.1.1.1; the second route sends traffic for the 192. 168.2.0/24 network to 10.2.2.2.

```
ip route 192.168.1.0 255.255.255.0 10.1.1.1
ip route 192.168.2.0 255.255.255.0 10.2.2.2
```

ip route-cache   interface

```
ip route-cache [cbus] [flow] [same-interface] [cef] [distributed]
no ip route-cache
```

Configures   The route cache for an interface

Default   Enabled for most interfaces

Description

A route cache stores a route in a temporary table for the duration of a network session. When the session is completed or the session times out, the routing entry is removed from the route cache. The no form of this command disables the route cache, which causes the router to look up the route for each packet of the network session. In some applications, this can be the desired behavior; see "Fast Switching and Process Switching" in Chapter 8.

cbus
> Optional. Enables fast switching and autonomous switching.

flow
> Optional. Enables the RSP to perform flow switching.

same-interface
> Optional. Enables fast switching packets back out the interface on which they arrived.

cef
> Optional. Enables Cisco Express Forwarding on an interface after it has been disabled globally.

distributed
> Optional. Enables VIP distributed switching.

Example

The route cache can be disabled with the no form of this command.

```
interface serial 0
  no ip route-cache
```

---

ip router isis   interface

```
ip router isis [tag]
no ip router isis [tag]
```

Configures   An interface for IS-IS routing

Default   Disabled

Description

This command identifies an interface to be used for IS-IS routing. The optional *tag* allows you to identify the IS-IS routing process if the process has a tag.

Example

```
interface ethernet 0
ip router isis
```

---

ip routing {style=global}

ip routing global

```
ip routing
no ip routing
```

Configures   IP routing

Default   Enabled

Description

This command enables or disables routing.

---

ip source-route {style=global}

ip source-route global

```
ip source-route
no ip source-route
```

Configures   Routing of source-routed packets

Default   Enabled

Description

This command allows the router to route packets that contain source-routing options. (Source routing is an IP option that allows the packet to specify the route it should take to its destination.) Source routing is a potential security problem, so it is best to disable this feature unless required.

Example

To disable IP source routing:

```
no ip source-route
```

---

ip split-horizon {style=interface}

ip split-horizon interface

```
ip split-horizon
no ip split-horizon
```

Configures   Split horizon for the interface

Default   Varies with the interface type; usually enabled

Description

When split horizon is enabled, any route learned from an interface is not advertised back out the same interface. This rule is intended to stop routing loops with distance-vector protocols. With most interfaces, split horizon is enabled. However, with multipoint interfaces—such as a multipoint Frame Relay interface—split horizon is disabled. See Chapter 8 for more information on split horizon.

---

ip subnet-zero
global

```
ip subnet-zero
no ip subnet-zero
```

Configures   The zero subnet

Default   Enabled in recent versions of IOS (12.X)

Description

When subnetting a network, the 0 subnet (the subnet whose subnet bits are all 0) is normally not allowed because of potential confusion between the subnet address and the network address. In practice, this confusion is rarely an issue. This command allows the router to use the all-zeros subnet.

Example

The following command enables the zero subnet:

```
ip subnet-zero
```

ip summary-address eigrp
interface

```
ip summary-address eigrp  as-number address mask
no ip summary-address eigrp as-number address mask
```

Configures   A summary aggregate for a specific interface

Default   None

Description

This command lets you specify a summary address for routes advertised through a specific interface by EIGRP. This command must be applied only to interfaces. It is beneficial if auto-summary has been disabled for EIGRP, as this allows you to define a specific summary address. This address receives an administrative distance of 5, which is more preferred than regular EIGRP routes.

as-number
   The number of the EIGRP routing process.

address
   The IP address for the summarized route.

mask
   The net mask for the summarized route.

ip tcp chunk-size
global

```
ip tcp chunk-size size
no ip tcp chunk-size
```

Configures   The number of bytes that a telnet or rlogin session can read at once

Default   0 (the largest size possible)

Description

This command sets the maximum number of bytes (*size*) that a telnet or rlogin session can read at the same time. A value of 0 means the largest size possible for that connection.

---

ip tcp compression-connections   interface

```
ip tcp compression-connections number
no ip tcp compress-connections number
```

Configures

The maximum number of TCP connections that can use header compression

Default   16

Description

This command sets the number of connections through an interface that can use TCP header compression. The *number* of connections can be from 3 to 256. A buffer is allocated for each connection that can be compressed. Both sides of a serial link must have the same number of buffers defined.

---

ip tcp header-compression   interface

```
ip tcp header-compression [passive]
no ip tcp header-compression [passive]
```

Configures   TCP header compression for an interface

Default   Disabled

Description

This command enables TCP header compression on the interface. The `passive` keyword tells the interface to compress headers only when the incoming packets are compressed.

Example

```
interface serial 0
  ip tcp header-compression passive
```

---

ip tcp mtu-path-discovery   interface

```
ip tcp mtu-path-discovery [age-timer minutes] [infinite]
no ip tcp mtu-path discovery
```

Configures   Path MTU discovery

Default   Disabled for most interfaces; special interfaces use 10 minutes

Description

This command enables or disables path MTU discovery on new TCP connections.

---

age-timer `minutes`

Optional. *minutes* specifies the interval after which the router recalculates the MTU; its value must be between 1 and 30.

infinite

Disables the age timer.

---

ip tcp queuemax global

```
ip tcp queuemax packets
no ip tcp queuemax packets
```

Configures   The queue for outgoing TCP packets

Default   5 for TTY (async and console) interfaces; 20 for others

Description

This command sets the size of the outgoing TCP queue to *packets*. The queue is maintained per-connection; i.e., every connection has its own queue.

Example

```
interface serial 0
  ip tcp queuemax 15
```

---

ip tcp synwait-time global

```
ip tcp synwait-time seconds
no ip tcp synwait-time seconds
```

Configures   The time the router waits for a TCP connection to open

Default   30 seconds

Description

This command sets the number of *seconds* that the router waits for a TCP connection to open, before it times out. The value must be between 3 to 300. A longer synwait-time can be useful for dial-on-demand connections where you have to wait for the line to be dialed before a connection can open. This setting applies only to traffic originating within the router, not traffic coming through the router.

Example

If you are telneting from the router to a remote site through a DDR connection, you might want to increase the synwait-time to more reasonable level so that telnet does not time out:

```
ip tcp synwait-time 100
```

ip tcp window-size

global

```
ip tcp window-size bytes
no ip tcp window-size bytes
```

Configures   The window size of a TCP connection

Default   2144 bytes

Description

This command sets the size of the TCP window to *bytes*. Changing the size of the TCP window modifies the size and number of packets that can fit within that window. With the default window of 2144 bytes, you could buffer two 1000-byte packets, or 21 100-byte packets. Regardless of the window's size, the number of packets within the window is restricted to the values set by the ip tcp queuemax command; they default to 5 for TTY interfaces (async and console interfaces) and 20 for other interfaces. The maximum size of the window is 65536 bytes.

Example

```
ip tcp window-size 4000
```

ip telnet source-interface

global

```
ip telnet source-interface interface
no ip telnet source-interface
```

Configures   The source address for telnet connections

Default   None

Description

This command sets the address used as the source address for outgoing telnet connections to the address of the given *interface*.

ip tftp source-interface

global

```
ip tftp source-interface interface
no ip tftp source-interface
```

Configures   The source IP address for TFTP traffic

Default   The IP address of the interface closest to the destination

Description

This command sets the interface from which the router takes the source IP address for all TFTP traffic.

ip unnumbered

```
ip unnumbered interface
no ip unnumbered interface
```

Configures   Interface IP address

Default   None

Description

Normally, creating point-to-point links requires dedicating a subnet specifically for the link. This works well if all your equipment supports variable-length subnet masks (VLSM), but can be very wasteful if your equipment doesn't support VLSM. This forces you to assign relatively large subnets to your point-to-point links.

The `ip unnumbered` command tells the router to use the IP address of the selected *interface* as the address for this link. In other words, the router "borrows" the IP address of the named interface and uses that as the link's address.

Example

Assume that older equipment in our network forces us to use a subnet mask of 255.255.255.0. This means that assigning a subnet to a point-to-point link would use 254 addresses, of which only two are actually doing something. Instead of wasting 252 addresses, we can use the `ip unnumbered` command to borrow the address of another interface for use on the serial link:

```
interface serial0
  ip unnumbered ethernet0
  encapsulation ppp
  clockrate 1300000
```

Borrowing the address of the loopback interface for an unnumbered interface is often a good idea because the loopback interface is always up. The following configuration uses the loopback interface to provide the IP address for interface async2:

```
interface loopback 0
    ip address 10.10.1.4 255.255.255.0
interface async2
  ip unnumbered loopback0
```

ip unreachables

```
ip unreachables
no ip unreachables
```

Configures   Sending of ICMP unreachable messages for an interface

Default   Enabled

Description

ICMP unreachable messages are generated when something about an incoming packet is unknown to the router. For example, an "ICMP host unreachable" message is generated if the router cannot deliver a package to its final destination. There are many different types of ICMP unreachable messages, and they all mean that the packet can't be delivered for some reason. Disabling these messages can improve security because the messages can be used to discover information about your network.

Example

The following commands prevent the router from sending IP unreachable messages through the serial0 interface:

```
interface serial0
  no ip unreachables
```

---

isdn answer1, isdn answer2   interface

```
isdn answer1 [called-party-number][:sub-address]
no isdn answer1 [called-party-number][:sub-address]

isdn answer2 [called-party-number][:sub-address]
no isdn answer2 [called-party-number][:sub-address]
```

Configures   Verification of the called party

Default   None

Description

This command configures the interface to verify that the telephone number being called (which is reported by the ISDN switch as part of call setup) matches the telephone number of the router. By default, calls are processed without verification. If this command is configured, the router verifies the incoming *called-party-number* before allowing the connection. Using this command can reduce the potential for confusion when several ISDN devices share the same ISDN local loop. Use isdn answer2 to verify a second called-party number.

To list a *called-party-number* or a *sub-address*, use any number of digits up to 50; an x specifies a wildcard. You must specify either the *called-party-number* or the *sub-address*, but you are not required to specify both. If you specify only one, the other is taken as a wildcard.

---

isdn autodetect   interface

```
isdn autodetect
no isdn autodetect
```

Configures   Automatic detection of ISDN SPIDs and switch types

Default   Disabled

Description

This command enables the automatic detection of ISDN SPIDs and switch types on an interface. It works in North America only.

---

isdn bchan-number-order

```
isdn bchan-number-order {ascending | descending}
no isdn bchan-number-order
```

Configures   ISDN PRI

Default   descending

Description

This command sets the order (ascending or descending) of outgoing B channels. It is for PRI configurations only.

isdn busy

```
isdn busy dsl number b_channel number
no isdn busy dsl number b_channel number
```

Configures   A false busy signal on an ISDN B channel

Default   Disabled

Description

This command sets a false busy signal on an ISDN B channel; that is, the ISDN interface reports to the switch that the channel is busy even if it isn't.

dsl *number*
>   The digital subscriber loop (DSL) number.

b_channel *number*
>   The range of B channels to be set to a busy signal. *number* can range from 0 to 24 on a PRI interface (it isn't clear whether this command applies to BRI interfaces); 0 indicates the entire interface.

isdn caller

```
isdn caller phone-number [callback]
no isdn caller phone-number [callback]
```

Configures   ISDN caller ID screening

Default   Disabled

Description

If your ISDN switch supports caller ID, this command lets you specify a *phone-number* from which incoming connections are allowed. If the inbound call does not originate from this number, it will be rejected. You may use the letter x in the phone number as a wildcard character; for example, 458-xxxx means "any number in the 458 exchange." The callback keyword causes the router to reject the call and initiate a callback to the caller's number; this feature may help you manage phone costs.

isdn call interface

command

```
isdn call interface interface telephone-number [speed {56 | 64}]
```

Description

This command initiates an ISDN call from the IOS command line in privileged EXEC mode. To make the call, supply the *interface* to use, the *telephone-number* to call, and optionally the line speed (56 or 64 kbps). The line speed defaults to 64 kbps.

Example

```
Router# isdn call interface bri0 4105551212
```

isdn calling-number

interface

```
isdn calling-number phone-number
no isdn calling-number phone-number
```

Configures   The phone number of the device making the outgoing call

Default   None

Description

This command sets the *phone-number* of the ISDN device making an outgoing call. The router presents this number to the switch when placing a call.

isdn conference-code

interface

```
isdn conference-code code
no isdn conference-code
```

Configures   Three-way calling

Default   60

Description

This command configures a conference code. Conference codes can be used if you have ordered three-way calling as part of your service.

isdn disconnect interface

command

```
isdn disconnect interface interface channel
```

Configures   Disconnects an ISDN call

Default   None

Description

This command disconnects an ISDN call on the given *interface* without bringing down the interface. The *channel* may be b1 for the first B channel, b2 for the second, or all for both B channels.

isdn fast-rollover-delay

```
isdn fast-rollover-delay seconds
no isdn fast-rollover-delay seconds
```

Configures   Time delay between consecutive dial attempts

Default   Disabled (0 seconds)

Description

If more than one dialer map is provided for an ISDN interface, this command provides the time to wait (in *seconds*) after the first map fails before placing a call using the second map.

isdn incoming-voice

```
isdn incoming-voice {56 | 64}
no isdn incoming-voice {56 | 64}
```

Configures   Accepts calls on the voice lines

Default   Disabled

Description

By default, incoming voice calls on data lines are not answered. This command allows you to use voice lines to transfer data by configuring the router to answer voice calls, which can result in significant savings in some areas. The call speed can be either 56 or 64; if no speed is specified, the speed is set to the incoming call's speed.

isdn leased-line bri 128

```
isdn leased-line bri number 128
no isdn leased-line bri number 128
```

Configures   ISDN interface for leased-line service at 128 kbps

Default   Disabled

Description

This command configures ISDN access over a leased line. There are no phone numbers; both of the line's B channels are combined to provide a single line with a capacity of 128 kbps. *number* is the number of the BRI interface.

isdn not-end-to-end

```
isdn not-end-to-end {56 | 64}
no isdn not-end-to-end {56 | 64}
```

Configures   Overrides the speed the network reported it will use

Default   64 kbps

Description

This command forces the speed of an incoming connection. Sometimes, when ISDN ports don't belong to the same network, incorrect speed selection by the router causes the ISDN connection to fail. This command lets you set the speed manually for incoming connections. Valid speeds are 56 and 64 kbps.

---

isdn nsf-service   interface

```
isdn nsf-service {megacom | sdn}
no isdn nsf-service
```

Configures   Network-specific facilities (NSF)

Default   Disabled

Description

This command enables NSF on an ISDN PRI for outgoing voice calls. megacom is for AT&T Megacom NSF, and sdn is for AT&T SDN NSF.

---

isdn outgoing-voice   interface

```
isdn outgoing-voice {info-transfer-capability {3.1kHz-audio | speech}}
no isdn outgoing-voice
```

Configures   Information transfer capability set for outgoing voice calls

Default   None

Description

This command sets the information transfer capability for outgoing voice calls through an interface. It isn't clear what the optional keywords mean; presumably they request different kinds of signal processing adapted for general audio or speech.

---

isdn overlap-receiving   interface

```
isdn overlap-receiving
no isdn overlap-receiving
```

Configures   ISDN overlap receiving

Default   Disabled

Description

This command enables ISDN overlap receiving for an interface. In this mode, the interface waits for additional information from the switch before establishing the call. This command can be useful when carrying voice traffic through the router.

---

isdn send-alerting

```
isdn send-alerting
no isdn send-alerting
```

Configures   Sending an Alerting message

Default   Disabled

Description

This command enables the sending of an Alerting message before a Connect message when making ISDN calls. Some types of switches want to receive an Alerting message before a Connect message.

isdn sending-complete

```
isdn sending-complete
no isdn sending-complete
```

Configures   The sending of a Sending Complete element in the Setup message

Default   Disabled

Description

This command configures the router to include the Sending Complete element in the Setup message. Some switches require this message, which tells the switch that it has all the information for the call in the Setup message.

isdn service

```
isdn service dsl number b_channel number state value
no isdn service dsl number b_channel number state value
```

Configures   A B channel range to a specified state

Default   Disabled

Description

This command sets a range of B channels or an entire PRI interface to "in service," "maintenance," or "out of service."

dsl *number*
> The digital subscriber loop number.

b_channel *number*
> The B channel or range of B channels to which the command applies. *number* can range from 0–24, where 0 means the entire PRI interface. A range of consecutive channels is indicated by *n-m*, where *n* and *m* can range from 1–24.

state *value*
> The state to which you wish to set the channels. The state is indicated by a number between 0 and 2; 0 is for "in service," 1 is for "maintenance," and 2 is for "out of service."

isdn spid1 (spid2)   interface

```
isdn {spid1 | spid2} spid [local-directory-number]
no isdn {spid1 | spid2} spid [local-directory-number]
```

Configures   ISDN SPIDs

Default   None

Description

This command provides the service profile identifier (SPID) for the B1 channel (spid1) or the B2 channel (spid2). You can also use this command to specify the *local-directory-number* (optional). Your ISDN carrier (i.e., your phone company) provides the SPIDs and the local directory number. Some carriers and switch types do not require SPIDs (for example, if they are not used in Europe).

isdn switch-type   global

```
isdn switch-type type
no isdn switch-type type
```

Configures   ISDN switch type

Default   None

Description

There are many different types of ISDN switches in use. The router must be configured with the appropriate switch *type* in order to interact with the telephone network. While there are exceptions, your geographic location is the best clue to the type of switch in use. Table 15-12 lists common switch types.

Table 15-12: Common ISDN switch types

IOS type	Switch
basic-5ess	AT&T switches (North America)
basic-dms100	Northern Telecom (North America)
basic-ni1	National ISDN-1 (North America)
basic-ts013	Australian
basic-ltr6	German
basic-nwnet3	Net3 switches (Norway)
basic-net3	Net3 switches (Europe/Taiwan)
basic-nznet3	Net3 switches (New Zealand)
vn2	VN2 (French)
vn3	VN3 (French)
ntt	NTT (Japan)

isdn tei
global

```
isdn tei [first-call | powerup]
no isdn tei
```

Configures   ISDN endpoint negotiation

Default   powerup

Description

TEI stands for Terminal Endpoint Identifier. This command enables TEI negotiation on the ISDN interface. TEI negotiation occurs at **powerup** or when it places its first call (first-call).

isdn tei-negotiation
global, interface

```
isdn tei-negotiation {first-call | powerup}
no isdn tei-negotiation
```

Configures   When TEI negotiation occurs

Default   powerup

Description

This command sets when TEI negotiation occurs. By default, negotiation takes place when the router is first turned on (**powerup**). The first-call option states that negotiation should occur when the first ISDN call is placed or received.

isdn transfer-code
interface

```
isdn transfer-code code
no isdn transfer-code
```

Configures   Call transferring

Default   61

Description

This command enables call transferring. This feature is available only if your service provider supports it. *code* is supplied by your service provider.

isdn twait-disable
interface

```
isdn twait-disable
no isdn twait-disable
```

Configures   Time to wait on startup

Default   Enabled

Description

After a power failure, ISDN interfaces wait a random period of time (1 to 300 seconds) before starting up. This command prevents the interfaces from coming back online at the same time when power is restored and the ISDN devices are restarting. This feature can be disabled with the no form of this command.

---

isdn voice-priority   interface

```
isdn voice-priority ISDN-directory-number {in | out} {always | conditional |
    off}
no isdn voice-priority ISDN-directory-number
```

Configures   The priority of data and voice calls

Default   A data call is never bumped

Description

This command allows you to set the priority of a data call relative to a voice call. *ISDN-directory-number* is the directory number assigned by your telephone company. in and out specify whether the command applies to incoming or outgoing voice calls. always means always bump a data call for a voice call. conditional means bump a data call if there is more than one call to the same destination. off means never bump a data call for a voice call.

---

isis circuit-type   interface

```
isis circuit-type {level-1 | level-1-2 | level-2-only}
no isis circuit-type
```

Configures   Type of IS-IS routing on an interface

Default   level-1-2

Description

This command sets the type of IS-IS routing used on an interface. It is rarely used except for border routers (routers that lie between areas).

---

isis csnp-interval   interface

```
isis csnp-interval seconds [{level-1 | level-2}]
no isis csnp-interval
```

Configures   CSNP interval

Default   10 seconds

Description

This command sets the interval (in *seconds*) for CSNP packets on border routers. CSNP packets are broadcast at the specified interval to ensure that the routing database is synchronized. This command can be used only in multiaccess interfaces.

The `level-1` and `level-2` keywords are optional; they specify that the interval applies only to the given level.

---

isis hello-interval
interface

```
isis hello-interval seconds [{level-1 | level-2}]
no isis hello-interval
```

Configures   IS-IS hello interval for an interface

Default   10 seconds

Description

This command sets the hello interval for IS-IS routing to *seconds*. By default, the hello interval is the advertised holdtime multiplied by the hello multiplier, which has a default of 3. The optional `level-1` and `level-2` keywords allow you to apply this command to an individual level; otherwise the interval is applied to both levels.

---

isis hello-multiplier
interface

```
isis hello-multiplier value [{level-1 | level-2}]
no isis hello-multiplier
```

Configures   The holdtime value multiplier

Default   3

Description

For IS-IS, the holdtime is calculated by taking the hello interval and multiplying it by the hello multiplier. This command sets the hello multiplier to *value*. By changing the hello multiplier, you effectively change the holdtime. The optional `level-1` and `level-2` keywords allow you to apply this command to an individual level; otherwise the interval is applied to both levels.

Example

The following commands configure IS-IS routing for the interface `ethernet 1`. The hello interval is set to 5 seconds (for level 1) and the multiplier is set to 5, yielding a holdtime of 25 seconds.

```
interface ethernet 1
  ip router isis
  isis hello-interval 5 level-1
  isis hello-multiplier 5 level-1
```

---

isis lsp-interval
interface

```
isis lsp-interval milliseconds
no isis lsp-interval
```

Configures   Time delay between LSPs for IS-IS routing

Default   33 milliseconds

Description

This command sets the number of *milliseconds* between IS-IS link state packets (LSPs). If a router has many IS-IS interfaces, it might have trouble sending all the LSPs. This command lets you increase the time between the packets, which should reduce the load on the router's CPU.

---

isis metric   interface

```
isis metric value [{level-1 | level-2}]
no isis metric
```

Configures   The default IS-IS metric for the interface

Default   10

Description

This command sets the default metric for the interface to *value*. By using the keywords level-1 or level-2, you can specify a metric for a specific routing level. If no level is specified, level-1 is used.

---

isis password   interface

```
isis password password [{level-1 | level-2}]
no isis password
```

Configures   The authentication password for IS-IS routing

Default   None

Description

This command sets the authentication *password* for IS-IS routing for the interface. All IS-IS communication to other routers through this interface must be authenticated with this password. However, like other password settings for IS-IS, this password is sent out in clear-text, providing little security. The level-1 and level-2 keywords are optional; they allow separate passwords to be applied to each level. If no level is specified, level-1 is used.

---

isis priority   interface

```
isis priority priority [{level-1 | level-2}]
no isis priority
```

Configures   A priority value for the interface for IS-IS routing

Default   64

Description

This command allows you to set the router's *priority* in an IS-IS network. The priority is used to determine which routers become the designated router (DR) and the backup designated router (BDR). The priority can range from 0 to 127; 127 is the highest. The optional keywords level-1 and level-2 allow you to set a different priority for each level; otherwise the priority value applies to both levels.

---

isis retransmit-interval
interface

```
isis retransmit-interval seconds
no isis retransmit-interval
```

Configures   The time between link state packet (LSP) retransmissions

Default   5 seconds

Description

This command sets the time (in *seconds*) between LSP retransmissions. It should be used only on point-to-point links.

---

isis retransmit-throttle-interval
interface

```
isis retransmit-throttle-interval milliseconds
no isis retransmit-throttle-interval
```

Configures   Time between retransmissions of LSPs

Default   Calculated from the isis lsp-interval command

Description

This command sets the interval in *milliseconds* between retransmissions of IS-IS LSPs.

---

is-type
router

```
is-type {level-1 | level-1-2 | level-2-only}
no is-type level-1 | level-1-2 | level-2-only}
```

Configures   The level at which the IS-IS routing protocol will operate

Default   level-1-2

Description

This command sets the level at which the IS-IS routing protocol operates, which also defines the type of IS-IS router it is (station or area). By default, the router operates at both levels, which means it is both a station router and an area router.

level-1
    The router performs only as a station router.

---

level-1-2
> The router performs as both a station and an area router.

level-2-only
> The router performs only as an area router.

Example

```
router isis
  is-type level-2-only
```

---

keepalive

```
keepalive seconds
no keepalive
```

Configures   The keepalive interval

Default   10 seconds

Description

The keepalive command specifies the interval (in *seconds*) that the router waits before sending a message on the interface to test the link and determine whether it is up or down. On Ethernet interfaces, the router sends the message to itself. On serial interfaces, the message is sent to the router on the other end of the link.

Keepalive settings can be very sensitive. If the keepalive interval is too low, the keepalive packets might be delayed by other traffic. If the interval is set too high, the router will take longer to update the interface's status, which slows route convergence.

On Frame Relay interfaces, the keepalive value should match (or be less than) the LMI interval configured on the carrier's switch.

Example

```
interface ethernet 1
    keepalive 5
```

---

key
key chain configuration mode

```
key number
no key number
```

Configures   An identification number of a key on a key chain

Default   None

Description

This command applies an identification *number* to an authentication key on a key chain. ID numbers can range from 0 to 2147483647. See the key chain command for more information.

key chain

```
key chain name
no key chain name
```

Configures   Enters the key chain configuration mode

Default   None

Description

This command enters the key chain configuration mode, which allows you to create authentication keys for routing protocols and other uses. Each key chain must have at least one key defined with the key command. A key chain may have as many as 2147483647 keys.

Example

```
! Create a key chain called "ExampleKeyChain" with two keys
key chain ExampleKeyChain
  key 1
    key-string MyKey1
  key 2
    key-string MyKey2
```

key config-key

```
key config-key 1 string
```

Configures   A private DES key for the router

Default   None

Description

This command defines a private DES key for the router. This key can be used to encrypt various parts of the router's configuration with DES. The key itself does not appear in the configuration. If you lose the key, it can't be recovered. The string can be from 1 to 8 alphanumeric characters long.

key-string

```
key-string string
no key-string string
```

Configures   An authentication string for a key

Default   None

Description

This command sets the actual authentication string for a key. *string* can be from 1 to 80 alphanumeric characters in length; the first character cannot be a number. See the key chain command for more information.

lane auto-config-atm-address

```
lane [config] auto-config-atm-address
no lane [config] auto-config-atm-address
```

Configures   Automatic configuration of the configuration server's ATM address

Default   No ATM address

Description

This command specifies that the configuration server address and the client's address should be automatically computed. When the optional config keyword is used, the command applies only to the LANE Configuration Server (LECS).

lane bus-atm-address

```
lane-bus-atm-address atm-address
no lane-bus-atm-address
```

Configures   The ATM address of the BUS

Default   Automatic ATM address assignment

Description

This command specifies the ATM address of the Broadcast and Unknown Server (BUS). The *atm-address* can be a complete ATM address or an ATM template. A template may use * as a wildcard to represent any single character, or ... to represent any group of consecutive characters.

lane client

```
lane client {ethernet | tokenring} [elan-name]
no lane client {ethernet | tokenring}
```

Configures   Activates a LANE client

Default   None

Description

This command activates a LANE client for the interface. The ethernet and tokenring keywords specify the type of Emulated LAN (ELAN) that the interface is connected to. *elan-name* is optional; it defines which ELAN the client belongs to. If you do not include an *elan-name*, the client contacts the LAN emulation configuration server to find out which ELAN to join.

lane client-atm-address
interface

```
lane client-atm-address atm-address
no lane client-atm-address atm-address
```

Configures   The ATM address for the LANE client on the interface

Default   Automatic ATM address

Description

This command specifies the ATM address for the LANE client on the interface. The *atm-address* can be a complete ATM address or an ATM address template.

---

lane config-atm-address
interface

```
lane [config] config-atm-address atm-address
no lane [config] config-atm-address atm-address
```

Configures   The ATM address for the configuration server

Default   None

Description

This command sets the ATM address for the LANE server and the LANE client. If the optional config keyword is used, the ATM address applies only to the configuration server. The *atm-address* can be a complete ATM address or an ATM address template.

---

lane config database
interface (major only; no subinterface)

```
lane config database name
no lane config database
```

Configures   The LANE database for the LANE configuration server

Default   None

Description

This command specifies the name of the LANE database for the current interface. The database must exist before you give this command. There can be only one LANE database per interface. The LANE database is created with the lane database command.

---

lane database
global

```
lane database name
no lane database name
```

Configures   A named configuration database

Default   None

Description

This command creates a named configuration database (a LANE database) that is associated with a configuration server.

Example

The following commands create a database named `elandatabase1`. The `lane database` command sets up the name and enters the LANE database configuration mode. The remaining commands set up the database by mapping an ELAN name to a LANE emulation server address, and then setting up a default ELAN name.

```
! Define the ELAN database named elandatabase1
lane database elandatabase1
   name elan1 server-atm-address 47.00918100000000613E5D0301.00603E0DE841.01
   ! We set a default lane for LECs that don't know the ELAN they should join
   default-name elan1
```

---

lane fixed-config-atm-address   interface

```
lane [config] fixed-config-atm-address
no lane [config] fixed-config-atm-address
```

Configures   The LECS used by the ATM address assigned by the ATM forum

Default   No address set

Description

This command sets the address of the ATM server to the default address assigned by the ATM Forum. The NSAP address is 47.007900000000000000000000. 00A03E000001.00. The optional `config` keyword specifies that the address applies to the configuration server only.

---

lane global-lecs-address   interface

```
lane global-lecs-address address
no lane global-lecs-address address
```

Configures   A list of LECS addresses to use

Default   None

Description

This command specifies a LECS address to use when the ILMI cannot be used. Normally, the router obtains the LECS address from the ILMI. This command can be used as many times as necessary to create a list of LECS addresses.

lane le-arp

lane le-arp {*mac-address* | route-desc segment *segment-number* bridge
   bridge-number} *atm-address*
no lane le-arp {*mac-address* | route-desc segment *segment-number* bridge
   bridge-number} *atm-address*

Configures   Assigns a static MAC address to an ATM address

Default   None

Description

This command adds a mapping between a static MAC address and an ATM address to the ARP database. You may either specify the MAC address explicitly, or specify a route description using the **route-desc** keyword. In this case, you must specify a *segment-number* (1–4095) and *bridge-number* (1–15) instead. ARP entries created by this command do not expire. To remove them from the table, use the no form of this command.

lane server-atm-address

lane server-atm-address *atm-address*
no lane server-atm-address *atm-address*

Configures   LANE server ATM address

Default   The server's ATM address is provided by the configuration server

Description

This command sets the ATM address of the configuration server, overriding the address provided by the configuration server itself. The *atm-address* can be a complete ATM address or an ATM address template.

lane server-bus

lane server-bus {ethernet | tokenring} *elan-name*
no lane server-bus {ethernet | tokenring} *elan-name*

Configures   Enables a LANE server and a BUS on a subinterface

Default   None

Description

This command enables a LANE server and a BUS on the subinterface. The ethernet and tokenring keywords specify the type of Emulated LAN attached to the interface. The *elan-name* is the name of the ELAN, and can be up to 32 characters in length.

line

global

line [*line-type*] *line-number*[*end-line-number*]

Description

This command enters the line configuration mode. Valid *line-types* are aux, console, tty, or vty. If no *line-type* is given, the *line-number* is treated as an absolute line number. (See the results of a show line to see absolute line numbers.)

The *line-number* is the number of the first line you want to configure. The *end-line-number* is the last line you want to configure. If you want to configure only a single line, omit *end-line-number*.

Example

The following commands set the password on lines 0 through 4, inclusive, and then set the connection speed on line 5.

```
! change the password on vty 0 4 to vtyin
line vty 0 4
  password vtyin
! Change the speed on tty 5
line tty 5
  speed 38400
```

linecode

controller

linecode {ami | b8zs | hdb3}
no linecode {ami | b8zs | hdb3}

Configures The line encoding used on a T1/E1 line

Default ami for T1 lines; hdb3 for E1 lines

Description

This command specifies the line encoding for a T1 or E1 line. ami can be applied to either T1 or E1; b8zs can be used only for T1 lines, and hdb3 only for E1 lines. The encodings used must match at both ends of the line; in practice, this means that the encoding is defined by your carrier.

link-test

interface (hub)

link-test
no link-test

Configures Link-test functionality on a hub interface

Default Enabled

Description

This command is specific to Cisco devices with built-in hub interfaces. It enables the port's link-test function. Use the no form to disable the link test.

Example

```
hub ethernet 0 1
   no link-test
```

---

location

```
location text
no location
```

Configures   The location description for a line

Default   None

Description

This command has no effect on the line's configuration; it simply lets you document the location of the equipment connected to a particular line. This information can be displayed to the user at login by placing the service linenumber command in the configuration.

Example

```
line tty3
   location Router-Room11,port 34
   service linenumber
```

---

logging

```
logging syslog-server
no logging syslog-server
```

Configures   A server for logging messages

Default   None

Description

This command specifies the hostname or IP address of the log server (*syslog-server*) to which the router sends log messages. These messages use the standard Unix/Linux syslog facility; there are implementations of this facility for other operating systems (notably Windows NT and Windows 2000).

For syslog configuration on a Unix box, see the */etc/syslog.conf* file and the *syslogd* manpage.

---

logging buffered

```
logging buffered [size] [level]
no logging buffered
```

Configures   Messages logged to the internal buffer

Default   Depends on the platform; usually enabled

Description

This command enables logging to an internal buffer.

size

> Optional. The size of the internal buffer, in bytes. The default size depends on the platform; you can give a buffer size from 4096 to 4294967295. If you set the buffer size too high, the router will run out of memory for routing tasks.

level

> Optional. A numeric severity level or the name of a severity level. Any message at this severity or higher are logged to the internal buffer. Severity levels are: emergencies (0), alerts (1), critical (2), errors (3), warnings (4), notifications (5), informational (6), and debugging (7). Note that the numeric levels are the opposite of what you'd expect: a lower number indicates a higher severity.

---

logging console global

```
logging console level
no logging console
```

Configures   Logging of messages to the console

Default   Debugging (7)

Description

This command enables logging to the console screen, thus setting the severity level of messages that will be displayed. All messages at the given *level* (either a level name or a level number) are logged. By default, all messages are logged.

---

logging facility global

```
logging facility facility
no logging facility
```

Configures   The syslog facility to which the messages are sent

Default   local7

Description

A syslog server separates messages according to their facility type. This command states the *facility* to which messages generated by the router belong. Valid facilities are auth, cron, daemon, kern, lpr, mail, news, syslog, local0 through local7, sys9 through sys14, user, and uucp.

Example

The following command configures the router to send syslog messages to the local7 facility:

```
logging facility local7
```

The behavior of the syslog server depends on its own configuration. With the following line in *syslog.conf*, the server saves `local7` messages with a debugging severity to the file */var/log/debug-logfile*:

```
local7.debug        /var/log/debug-logfile
```

logging history   global

```
logging history level
no logging history
```

Configures   The severity levels to be logged

Default   Warnings (4)

Description

This command sets the type of syslog messages that are entered into the syslog history table. These messages are also set to an SNMP management station, if one is configured; all messages at the given level or higher are logged.

Example

The following command logs messages with a severity of errors (3) or greater, i.e., critical (2), alerts (1), and emergencies (0):

```
logging history errors
```

logging history size   global

```
logging history size number
no logging history size
```

Configures   The size of the history table

Default   1

Description

This command sets the size of the history table. *number* is the number of messages saved in the table; the value can be from 1 to 500.

logging monitor   global

```
logging monitor level
no logging monitor
```

Configures   Messages logged to terminal lines (monitors)

Default   Debugging (7)

Description

This command controls which messages are sent to the console and other terminal lines. *level* can be either the name of a severity level or a number. Messages at the given level and higher are sent to the terminal lines. The default level sends all messages to the terminal lines because debugging is the lowest severity level.

logging on global

```
logging on
no logging on
```

Configures   Controls all logging

Default   Enabled

Description

This command allows you to enable or disable all logging. Use it with caution, as the router often waits for error messages to be displayed on a console before continuing.

logging source-interface global

```
logging source-interface interface
no logging source-interface
```

Configures   The interface from which syslog packets are sent

Default   The router uses the interface "closest" to the destination

Description

This command sets the interface that the router uses to send syslog packets, and therefore sets the source IP address for syslog packets that originate from the router. Specifying the source interface allows you to control the path that logging packets take from the router to the network management station, which can be an important security consideration. By default, packets originate from the interface closest to the destination.

logging synchronous line

```
logging synchronous [level severity | all] [limit number-of-messages]
no logging synchronous
```

Configures   Display of log messages

Default

Disabled; when enabled, default severity level is 2 and buffer message limit is 20

Description

This command controls the printing of log messages to a user's terminal. By default, messages are printed at any time, possibly disrupting the user's current command. This command tells the router to wait until the user's current command and its output are completed before displaying any logging messages.

level *severity*

> The severity level that this command affects. All messages with a severity at or below (i.e., with a higher number than) the given level are sent synchronously (i.e., after waiting for the user to complete the current command and the router to generate the requested output).

all

> Equivalent to level emergencies; all messages are sent synchronously.

limit *number-of-messages*

> Specifies the number of messages that will be queued waiting for delivery.

Example

The following commands specify that on terminal lines 0 through 8, log messages at levels 6 and 7 (informational and debugging) will be delivered synchronously.

```
line 0 8
  logging synchronous level 6
```

---

logging trap   global

```
logging trap level
no logging trap
```

Configures   Messages sent to syslog servers

Default   Disabled

Description

This command limits the type of messages that are sent to the syslog servers. Only messages of the given severity level and higher are sent to the server.

---

login   line

```
login [local | tacacs]
no login [login | tacacs]
```

Configures   The login authentication method for connections

Default   No authentication

Description

This command tells the line to authenticate the user before allowing access. If you give this command without any arguments, you must use the password command to specify a password for this line. The local keyword tells the router to maintain its own database of users, created using the username command. The tacacs keyword tells the router to authenticate users by contacting a TACACS server.

When using login local, make sure you have at least one username configured before you log out. Otherwise, you will be locked out of the specified lines.

Example

To enable simple authentication using a single password for all access through this line:

```
line vty 0 4
   login
   password letmein
```

These commands enable authentication using a local database of usernames and user-specific passwords; users Bob, Ann, and John are the only ones able to log into this line.

```
username bob password letmein
username ann password letmein2
username john password letmein3
line vty 0 4
   login local
```

---

login authentication   line

```
login authentication {default | list-name}
no login authentication {default | list-name}
```

Configures   TACACS+ authentication for logins

Default   No authentication

Description

This command configures the login authentication method. The methods used to perform authentication can be taken either from the default list or a named list.

default
>   Uses the default list created with the aaa authentication login command.

list-name
>   Specifies a list created with the aaa authentication login command.

---

logout-warning   line

```
logout-warning seconds
no logout-warning
```

Configures   A warning message before an automatic logout

Default   None

Description

This command activates the logout warning message. This message warns users that a forced logout is about to occur. The *seconds* parameter specifies how much warning time is given; that is, the time that will elapse before the session closes after the warning is issued.

```
loopback [options]
no loopback
```

Configures   Loopback mode

Default   Disabled

Description

The `loopback` command sets the equipment at some point between a router interface and the other end of the line to reflect all data back to the router. Loopbacks
are extremely useful for troubleshooting. With no options, `loopback` tests the local
interface: all packets sent to the interface are immediately reflected back to the
router without being sent to the destination. The various *options* and parameters
allow you to place the loopback point farther down the line:

applique
> Sets the internal loopback for an HSSI interface.

dte
> Sets the loopback at the CSU/DSU, which tests the cable between the router
> (the DTE) and the CSU/DSU. The CSU/DSU must support this option.

line [payload]
> Sets the loopback at the "far end" of the CSU/DSU, which sends the packets
> completely through the CSU/DSU and back to the router. The CSU/DSU must
> support this option. On routers with built-in CSU/DSUs (2524 or 2525) you
> can add the payload keyword, which creates the loopback at the DSU.

remote *option*
> Sets the loopback at the remote CSU/DSU, which sends packets all the way to
> the remote end of the connection before reflecting them back to the router.
> This command tests the entire communications link between the router and
> the far end of the line. The remote CSU/DSU must be configured for remote
> loopback. Additional options give you more control over the behavior of
> remote loopback.

The following options are applicable to the `loopback remote` command:

full
> Places the loopback at the remote CSU.

payload
> Places the loopback on the DSU side of the remote device and transmits a
> payload request.

smart-jack
> Places the loopback at the remote smart-jack connection.

0in1
> Transmits an all-zeros test pattern for verifying a B8ZS-encoded line.

1in1
> Transmits an all-ones test pattern.

1in2
> Transmits alternating test patterns of all ones and all zeros.

1in5
> Transmits the standard test pattern for testing lines.

1in8
> Transmits a stress-test pattern for testing repeaters and their timing recovery.

3in24
> Transmits a test pattern for testing AMI lines.

qrw
> Transmits a quasi-random word pattern test to simulate real-world data patterns.

user-pattern *value*
> Transmits a pattern defined by the *value* parameter. This pattern is a binary string and can be as long as 24 bits.

511
> Transmits a random test pattern that repeats every 511 bits.

2047
> Transmits a random test pattern that repeats every 2047 bits.

Example

The following commands place the remote device in loopback mode and send the qrw test pattern:

```
interface serial 0
  loopback remote full qrw
```

In response, the router produces the following output, reporting that it has changed the line's state to down (because it can't be used for data while it is in loopback mode) and has succeeded in placing the remote CSU/DSU in loopback mode:

```
%LINEPROTO-5-UPDOWN: Line protocol on Interface Serial0, changed state to down
%LINK-3-UPDOWN: Interface Serial0, changed state to down
%SERVICE_MODULE-5-LOOPUPREMOTE: Unit 0 - Remote unit placed in loopback
```

---

map-class dialer   global

```
map-class dialer name
no map-class dialer name
```

Configures   A map class for configuring DDR

Default   None

Description

Defines a map class that can be used in dialer map commands. The name of the map class is an alphanumeric string. After you give the map-class command, the router enters the map-class context, in which you can enter commands that configure the map class.

Example

The following code configures a map class named `myclass`. This map class is used within a `dialer` command to specify the properties of the telephone line used for the dial-on-demand connection.

```
! Define the map class and its commands
map-class dialer myclass
  dialer isdn speed 64
!
! Configure ISDN inteface
interface bri 0
  encapsulation ppp
  dialer map ip 10.10.1.5 name office2 class myclass 014105551234001
```

---

map-class frame-relay   global

```
map-class frame-relay name
no map-class frame-relay name
```

Configures   A map class to define QoS attributes for an SVC or PVC

Default   None

Description

This command creates a special kind of map class used to define QoS attributes for a Frame Relay SVC or PVC. The following `frame-relay` commands can be applied to the map class:

`frame-relay custom-queue-list` *list*
Specifies a custom queue list for the map.

`frame-relay priority-group` *list*
Specifies a priority queue for the map.

`frame-relay adaptive-shaping [becn | foresight]`
Enables the type of BECN (backwards explicit congestion notification) information that will throttle the transmission rate.

`frame-relay cir [in | out]` *bps*
The inbound or outbound committed information rate. If neither in nor out is specified, the command applies to both directions.

`frame-relay mincir [in | out]` *bps*
The minimum incoming or outgoing committed information rate. If neither in nor out is specified, the command applies to both directions.

`frame-relay bc [in | out]` *bits*
The incoming or outgoing committed burst size. If neither in nor out is specified, the command applies to both directions.

`frame-relay be [in | out]` *bits*
The incoming or outgoing excess burst size. If neither in nor out is specified, the command applies to both directions.

`frame-relay idle-time` *duration*
The idle timeout interval for the map.

Example

The following code defines a Frame Relay map that specifies an incoming and outgoing committed information rate of 56 kbps:

```
map-class frame-relay map1
  frame-relay cir 56000
```

map-group   interface

```
map-group name
no map-group name
```

Configures   Applies a map list to an interface

Default   None

Description

This command applies a map list to an interface. See the `map-list` command for an example.

map-list   global

```
map-list map-name src-addr {e164 | x121} source-address dest-addr {e164 | x121}
  destination-address
no map-list map-name src-addr {e164 | x121} source-address dest-addr
  {e164 | x121} destination-address
```

Configures   A map list for a Frame Relay SVC

Default   None

Description

Use this command to define a map list for a Frame Relay SVC.

map-name
> The name of the map.

src-addr *{e164 | x121}*
> Type of source address; it may be either e164 of x121.

source-address
> The actual source address.

dest-addr *{e164 | x121}*
> Type of destination address; it may be either e164 of x121.

destination-address
> The actual destination address.

Example

The following commands set up a map list that brings up a Frame Relay SVC in response to IP or AppleTalk traffic. The map list, named map1, is applied to the serial0 interface using a **map-group** command. The map list itself consists of two statements that specify the protocol and address we're interested in, followed by a map class that specifies the quality of service parameters to be used by the circuit.

```
interface serial0
  ip address 172.30.8.1
  encapsulation frame-relay
  map-group map1
!
map-list map1 source-addr E164 112233 dest-addr E164 445566
  ip 10.1.1.1 class some-map-class
  appletalk 2000.2 class some-map-class
!
map-class frame-relay some-map-class
  frame-relay be out 9000
```

match as-path   route-map

```
match as-path path-list-number
no match as-path path-list-number
```

Configures   BGP route filtering

Default   None

Description

This command allows you to require that any route in a route map pass an AS path access list. Routes that are permitted by the list undergo further processing. You might use this command to create a route map that modifies routing metrics or changes the routes in some way, depending on the routes' AS path. These modifications are applied only to routes matching the AS path access list.

Example

The following code filters all routes to be sent to the neighboring router 10.10.1.1 through the AS path list 1. The AS path list is applied in the route map test-as-path, which adds our AS number (300) to all routes that match this list.

```
route-map test-as-path
  match as-path 1
  set as-path prepend 300
!
ip as-path access-list 1 permit .*
!
router bgp 300
  neighbor 10.10.1.1 route-map set-as-path out
```

match community-list   route-map

```
match community-list community-list-number [exact]
no match community-list community-list-number [exact]
```

Configures   BGP route filtering

Default   None

Description

This command lets you build a route map that requires a match to a BGP community list. If the route's community string matches the named list, the set commands of the route map are applied. The exact keyword states that all the communities within the community list must be present for the route. Without the exact keyword, only one match is required.

---

match interface   route-map

```
match interface interface [... interface]
no match interface interface [... interface]
```

Configures   Route filtering

Default   None

Description

This command lets you build a route map that selects routes according to the interfaces they use. For the route to match, its next hop must be through one of the interfaces listed. Routes that match are processed according to the other statements in the route map.

Example

In the following route map, all routes must have a next hop through the serial0 or serial1 interface for the route to match.

```
route-map example1
  match interface serial0 serial1
```

---

match ip address   route-map

```
match ip address access-list
no match ip address access-list
```

Configures   Route filtering

Default   None

Description

This command is used to match the IP address of the route's destination. If the destination matches the specified access list, the route is included in the map and processed according to the other statements in the route map. With this command, you can use extended access lists to implement routing policies.

---

match ip next-hop   route-map

```
match ip next-hop access-list [... access-list]
no match ip next-hop access-list [... access-list]
```

Configures   Route filtering

Default   None

Description

This command lets you specify that a route's next hop IP address must match the specified access list (or lists) to be included in the map. If a route passes any of the access lists, it is processed according to the other statements in the route map.

match ip route-source   route-map

```
match ip route-source access-list [... access-list]
no match ip route-source access-list [... access-list]
```

Configures   Route filtering

Default   None

Description

This command lets you specify that a route's source address (i.e., the router that originally advertised the route) must match the given access lists to be included in the map. If a route passes any of the access lists, it is processed according to the other statements in the route map.

match length   route-map

```
match length min max
no match length min max
```

Configures   Route filtering

Default   None

Description

This command lets you build a route map that selects packets whose size is between *min* and *max*. If a packet's size falls in this range, it is processed according to the other statements in the route map. This command is used with policy routing.

Example

In this example, we want to match packets that are between 10 to 100 bytes long. We then send matching packets out through the serial0 interface.

```
interface ethernet1
  ip policy route-map example1
!
route-map example1
  match length 10 100
  set interface serial0
```

match metric

route-map

```
match metric value
no match metric value
```

Configures   Route filtering

Default   None

Description

This command lets you build a route map that selects routes with a certain metric, given by *value*. The metric value can be from 0 to 4294967295. If a route's metric matches the given value, it is processed according to the other statements in the route map.

match route-type

route-map

```
match route-type {local | internal | external [type-1 | type-2] | level-1 |
    level-2}
no match route-type {local | internal | external [type-1 | type-2] | level-1 |
    level-2}
```

Configures   Route filtering

Default   None

Description

This command lets you build route maps that match routes of a certain type. The types you can match are:

local
   BGP internal routes.

internal
   EIGRP internal routes or OSPF inter-area and intra-area.

external
   EIGRP and OSPF external routes. type-1 and type-2 will only match OSPF type-1 and type-2 routes, respectively.

level-1
   Level 1 IS-IS routes.

level-2
   Level 2 IS-IS routes.

match tag

route-map

```
match tag tag-value [... tag-value]
no match tag tag-value [... tag-value]
```

Configures   BGP route filtering

Default   None

Description

This command lets you build route maps that match routes with certain tag values. If a route has a tag that matches any given *tag-value*, it is processed according to the other statements in the route map. The *tag-value* parameters can have values from 0 to 4294967295.

---

maximum-paths   router

```
maximum-paths number
no maximum-paths number
```

Configures   The maximum number of paths with equal metrics

Default   1 for BGP; 4 for other protocols

Description

This command lets you set the *number* of paths with equal metrics that the router will maintain in its routing table. *number* can range from 1 to 6.

For BGP, the meaning of this command is slightly different, since BGP doesn't have a simple routing metric. For BGP, this command allows you to increase the number of parallel equal-length paths that the router maintains in its tables.

---

metric holddown   router, IGRP

```
metric holddown
no metric holddown
```

Configures   Keeps a route from being used for a given amount of time

Default   Disabled

Description

This command tells IGRP to wait a specific time before implementing new routes. It helps you to avoid routing loops in networks that converge slowly by delaying routing updates. Routing loops are still possible, however, if all routers within the same IGRP domain are not configured the same way. Using this command can result in very slow convergence.

---

metric maximum-hops   router, IGRP, EIGRP

```
metric maximum-hops hops
no metric maximum-hops hops
```

Configures   The maximum number of hops that a route can take

Default   100

Description

This command allows you to change the maximum hop count for EIGRP and IGRP. Routes that exceed the given limit are considered unreachable. The maximum number of hops is 255:

Example

The following commands configure the router to mark routes as unreachable if they require more than 180 hops:

```
router igrp 101
    network 10.10.0.0
    metric maximum-hops 180
```

---

metric weights   router

```
metric weights tos k1 k2 k3 k4 k5
no metric weights
```

Configures   EIGRP and IGRP metric calculation

Default   tos=0; k1=1; k2=0; k3=1; k4=0; k5=0

Description

This command allows you to tune the routing metric for EIGRP and IGRP. The metric is calculated as follows:

$$metric = (k1 \times bandwidth) + \frac{(k2 \times bandwidth)}{(256 - load)} + (k3 \times delay)$$

If k5 greater than zero, the calculation continues:

$$metric = metric \times \frac{k5}{(reliability + k4)}$$

The tos (Type of Service) parameter is currently unused. It should be set to 0 when you use this command.

Example

The following commands modify the values of k4 and k5 and set the other values to their defaults:

```
router igrp 100
    network 10.10.0.0
    metric weights 0 1 0 1 2 2
```

---

media-type   interface

```
media-type type
no media-type type
```

Configures   The type of media for specific interfaces

Default   Depends on the interface type

Description

Certain interface types can be associated with several types of ports. For example, the Ethernet module on a 4000 series or an FEIP (Fast Ethernet interface processor) on a 7000/7500 series can be associated with an AUI, 10BaseT, or 100BaseT port. The type depends on the actual interface you are configuring; the possible types are shown in Table 15-13.

Table 15-13: Media types

Type	Meaning
aui	15-pin AUI port
10baset	10BaseT RJ45 port
100baset	100BaseT RJ45 port
mii	Media-independent interface

Example

```
interface ethernet 0
    media-type 100baset
```

member   interface

```
member number command
no member number command
```

Configures   Applies a configuration to one async interface of a group

Default   None

Description

This command is used in conjunction with the **group-range** command. It allows a certain command to be applied to one specific interface of a given range. The *number* specifies the group member to which the given *command* should be applied. Only two commands can be applied to an interface using the **member** command: **peer default ip** and **description**. For examples, see the **group-range** command.

menu   global

```
menu name [clear-screen | line-mode | single-space | status-line]
no menu name
```

Configures   Menu display options

Default   None

Description

This command displays the menu with the given *name* and allows you to specify menu display options. Menus can be used to provide simple configuration commands for users connecting to the router through telnet or reverse telnet; the menu itself is defined using the menu command. The available options are:

clear-screen
> Forces a clear screen before displaying the menu.

line-mode
> Allows the user to backspace over a selected item and press Return to execute a command.

single-space
> Displays the menu single-spaced instead of double-spaced.

status-line
> Displays a status line about the current user.

Menus are constructed using the commands menu command, menu text, and menu title.

---

menu command
global

menu *name* command *number command*

Configures   Commands for user interface menus

Default   None

Description

This command lets you build arbitrary menus for executing configuration commands. The menus are accessible from the router's command-line prompt.

name
> The name of the menu. Names cannot be more than 20 characters long.

number
> The selection number associated with the menu entry.

command
> The command to be executed when the given number is selected.

---

menu text
global

menu *name* text *number text*

Configures   Descriptive text for menus

Default   None

Description

This command lets you provide descriptive text to associate with menu items. The menus are accessible from the router's command-line prompt using the menu command, followed by the menu name.

name
> The name of the menu. Names cannot be more than 20 characters long.

---

number

> The selection number associated with the menu entry.

text

> The text to be displayed for the given menu selection.

Example

The following commands set up a menu called **incoming** with several selections. If a user types 1, the command **telnet 10.1.1.1** is executed; if she types 2, the command **telnet 10.1.1.2** is executed; if she types 3, the menu exits.

```
menu incoming command 1 telnet 10.1.1.1
menu incoming text 1 Telnet to New York router (10.1.1.1)
menu incoming command 2 telnet 10.1.1.2
menu incoming text 2 Telnet to San Francisco router (10.1.1.2)
menu incoming command 3 menu-exit
menu incoming text 3 Exit
```

---

menu title   global

menu *name* title *delimiter text delimiter*

Configures   A title for a user interface menu

Default   None

Description

This command allows you to assign a title to the user interface menu identified by *name*. The *text* is the menu's title; the *delimiter* can be any character that does not appear within the *text* that serves to mark the beginning and end of the *text*.

---

mkdir   command

mkdir *directory*

Description

This command allows you to create a directory on a Class C filesystem.

---

modem

This family of commands is used to configure modems on TTY lines. The discussion is limited to commands that are available for all routers. Terminal servers with manageable modems, such as the AS5200, AS5300, and CS3600 series products, have additional commands.

modem answer-timeout *time*

> Sets the amount of time the router waits for the carrier signal after answering an incoming RING.

modem autoconfigure discovery

> The router automatically tries to discover the modem type.

```
modem autoconfigure type type
```
Sets the modem to the type known by the router. To view a list of known modems, use the command `modem autoconfigure type ?`.

```
modem callin
```
Enables support of modems that use DTR to control hook-status.

```
modem callout
```
Enables reverse connections. (See "Reverse Telnet" in Chapter 4.)

```
modem chat-script script-name
```
Specifies which chat script to use when the modem is automatically dialing. See Chapter 11 for more information.

```
modem cts-required
```
Configures a line to require the CTS (clear to send) signal.

```
modem dialin
```
Configures a modem to accept incoming calls only.

```
modem dtr-active
```
Configures the modem line to leave the DTR signal low unless there is an active connection.

```
modem inout
```
Allows both incoming and outgoing connections to the modem. This command enables reverse telnet, so be sure this what you want to do.

---

motd-banner   line

```
motd-banner
no motd-banner
```

Configures   Suppresses the message of the day

Default   Enabled

Description

By default, the motd (message-of-the-day) banner is enabled on all lines. This command allows you to suppress the banner on selected lines.

Example

```
! Don't display the motd on lines 5 through 10
line 5 10
  no motd-banner
```

---

mrinfo   command

```
mrinfo [host] [source-interface]
```

Configures   Queries a multicast router

Description

This command allows you to query a multicast router. If you provide no arguments to this command, the router queries itself.

host
> Optional. Specifies the IP address or name of the host to query.

source-interface
> Optional. Specifies the IP address or name of the interface to use as the source of the request.

---

mstat   command

mstat *source* [*destination*] [*group*]

Configures   Displays multicast statistics

Description

This command displays multicast statistics, including the packet rate and the number of packets lost. If you do not provide arguments to this command, the router prompts you for them.

source
> Specifies the IP address or name of the multicast source.

destination
> Optional. Specifies the IP address or name of the destination. If not provided, the router uses itself as the destination.

group
> Optional. Specifies the IP address or name of the group to display. The default is 224.2.0.1.

Reference
K-M

---

mtrace   command

mtrace *source* [*destination*] [*group*]

Description

This command provides a trace from the source to the destination for a multicast distribution tree.

source
> Specifies the IP address or name of the multicast source.

destination
> Optional. Specifies the IP address or name of the destination. If not provided, the router uses itself as the destination.

group
> Optional. Specifies the IP address or name of the group to display. The default is 224.2.0.1.

mtu
interface

```
mtu bytes
no mtu bytes
```

Configures   Maximum transmission unit (MTU)

Default

Depends on media type (defaults for some common media are listed in Table 15-10, under the ip mtu command)

Description

This command allows you to modify the MTU for any interface. The default MTU depends on the media you are using (FDDI, Ethernet, etc.); for example, Ethernet has an MTU of 1500.

Performance considerations may lead you to modify this value; a smaller MTU might give better performance on a lossy or noisy line.

Example
```
interface ethernet0
    mtu 1250
```

---

name elan-id
LANE database configuration (ATM)

```
name name elan-id id
no name name elan-id id
```

Configures   ELAN ID of an ELAN in the LECS database

Default   None

Description

This command sets the *name* and *id* number for an Emulated LAN (ELAN) in the LECS database.

---

name local-seg-id
LANE database

```
name elan-name local-seg-id segment-number
no name elan-name local-seg-id segment-number
```

Configures   The token ring number of an ELAN

Default   None

Description

This command sets the token ring's ring number of an ELAN. The *segment-number* is the number to be assigned, which can be from 1 to 4095.

name preempt

```
name name preempt
no name name preempt
```

Configures   Preempt for the ELAN

Default   Disabled

Description

This command allows you to enable preempting of an ELAN. This is useful when a
LAN Emulation Server (LES) of a higher priority fails and then comes back online;
it allows the higher-priority LES to preempt the lower-priority LES, avoiding
network flapping and instability.

name server-atm-address

LANE database

```
name elan-name server-atm-address atm-address [restricted | un-restricted]
   [index value]
no name elan-name server-atm-address atm-address
```

Configures   The LANE server's ATM address for the ELAN

Default   None

Description

This command sets the ATM address of the LANE server for the ELAN.

`elan-name`
    The name of the ELAN.

`atm-address`
    The LANE server's ATM address.

`restricted | un-restricted`
    Optional. If restricted, only LANE clients defined in the ELAN's configuration
    server can be members of the ELAN.

`index value`
    Optional. This keyword sets a priority for the LANE server. (You can assign
    multiple LANE servers for fault tolerance.) 0 is the highest priority.

neighbor

router

RIP/IGRP/EIGRP:

```
neighbor address
no neighbor address
```

OSPF:

```
neighbor address [priority value] [poll-interval seconds]
no neighbor address [priority value] [poll-interval seconds]
```

Configures   A routing neighbor

Default   No neighbors defined

Description

The behavior and syntax of this command depend on the routing protocol you are using.

For RIP, this command specifies a RIP neighbor. This is useful when you have routers that cannot receive RIP broadcasts. In this situation, use the neighbor command to specify the IP addresses of routers that should receive RIP packets directly. If you use this command, RIP packets are not broadcast; they are sent only to the specified neighbors. The neighbor command is frequently used with the passive-interface command, which specifies that the interface should only listen for routing updates.

For IGRP, the command specifies an IGRP neighbor for the router to communicate with. It is often used with the passive-interface command. As with RIP, you can use the neighbor command together with passive-interface to send updates to one or more routers without sending updates to other routers on the network. Multiple neighbor commands are allowed.

For EIGRP, the neighbor command is accepted by the parser but has no effect on the EIGRP process. It is accepted for backward compatibility with IGRP configurations.

For OSPF, you use the command to define a router's OSPF neighbors explicitly. The OSPF version of this command has the following parameters:

address
    The IP address of the neighbor.

priority *value*
    Optional. The priority of the neighbor, from 0 to 255. The default is 0.

poll-interval *seconds*
    Optional. The frequency at which the neighbor is polled. The default is 120 seconds.

Example

In the following configuration, we have an IGRP routing process that we have told not to advertise (broadcast) IGRP updates out interface ethernet0. We use the neighbor command to explicitly tell the routing process to communicate with the router at 10.10.1.5, which happens to be reachable through the ethernet0 interface. We are thus using the neighbor command to control which routers receive IGRP information:

```
router igrp 100
    network 10.0.0.0
    passive-interface ethernet0
    neighbor 10.10.1.5
```

The following commands set up a similar routing configuration using RIP. As in the previous example, we use passive-interface to suppress routing broadcasts out ethernet0, and the neighbor command to list explicitly the routers with which we want to communicate:

```
router rip
  network 10.0.0.0
  passive-interface ethernet0
  neighbor 10.10.1.5
```

In the following example, we create an OSPF routing process and list a priority 1 neighbor explicitly:

```
! OSPF neighbor with a priority of 1
!
router ospf  99
  neighbor 192.168.1.2 priority 1
```

---

neighbor advertisement-interval   router, BGP

```
neighbor {address | peer-group} advertisement-interval seconds
no neighbor {address | peer-group} advertisement-interval seconds
```

Configures   Minimum interval between BGP routing updates

Default   5 seconds for internal peers; 30 seconds for external peers

Description

This command sets the BGP routing update interval. *seconds* can be from 0 to 600. You must specify either the *address* or *peer-group* of a particular peer.

---

neighbor database-filter   router, OSPF

```
neighbor address database-filter all out
no neighbor address database-filter all out
```

Configures   Filter LSAs to a certain OSPF neighbor

Default   Disabled

Description

Normally, all outgoing LSAs are flooded to all neighbors. This command allows you to disable flooding to a specific neighbor in point-to-multipoint networks. In broadcast, nonbroadcast, and point-to-point networks, you can disable flooding by using the ospf database-filter command.

---

neighbor default-originate   router, BGP

```
neighbor {address | peer-group} default-originate [route-map map]
no neighbor {address | peer-group} default-originate [route-map map]
```

Configures   Sends the default route to a BGP neighbor

Default   Disabled

Description

This command tells the router to send the default route to a neighbor, identified either by *address* or by *peer-group*. By default, no default route is sent. The use of the route map *map* allows you to place conditions on the sending of the route.

---

neighbor description   router, BGP

```
neighbor {address|peer-group} description text
no neighbor {address|peer-group} description
```

Configures   A text description of a BGP neighbor or peer group

Default   None

Description

This command allows you to give a text description for a neighbor, identified either by *address* or by *peer-group*. The text can be up to 80 characters. The description is purely for documentation and doesn't affect the router's behavior.

Example

```
router bgp 200
    neighbor 10.200.200.1 description Peer in the pasadena office
```

---

neighbor distribute-list   router, BGP

```
neighbor {address|peer-group} distribute-list {access-list | prefix-list name}
    {in | out}
no neighbor {address|peer-group} distribute-list {access-list | prefix-list
    name} {in | out}
```

Configures   Applies a distribute list to a neighbor or peer group

Default   None

Description

This command applies an access list or a prefix list to filter incoming (in) or outgoing (out) routes exchanged with the given neighbor (specified by *address* or *peer-group*).

---

neighbor filter-list   router, BGP

```
neighbor {address | peer-group} filter-list access-list {in | out}
no neighbor {address | peer-group} filter-list access-list {in | out}
```

Configures   A filter for BGP

Default   None

Description

This command sets up an AS path access list that filters BGP routes sent to or received from a specific neighbor. Routes that match the access list are discarded.

address or peer-group
> The address or peer group of the neighbor.

`filter-list` *access-list*
> The name of an AS path access list defined by the `ip as-path access-list` command.

`in`
> The filter applies to incoming routes.

`out`
> The filter applies to outgoing routes.

---

neighbor maximum-prefix   router, BGP

`neighbor {`*address|peer-group* `maximum-prefix` *max* `[`*threshold*`]` `[warning-only]`
`no neighbor {`*address|peer-group* `maximum-prefix` *max* `[`*threshold*`]` `[warning-only]`

Configures   The number of prefixes that can be received from a neighbor

Default   No limit

Description

This command allows you to set a limit on the number of prefixes that the router can receive from the neighbor.

address or peer-group
> The address or peer group of the neighbor.

`maximum-prefix` *max*
> The maximum number of prefixes you are willing to accept.

threshold
> Optional. The percentage of the maximum number of prefixes at which the router will start generating warning messages. The default is 75%.

`warning-only`
> Tells the router to generate a warning message about reaching the maximum value, but not to take any other action.

---

neighbor next-hop-self   router, BGP

`neighbor {`*address|peer-group*`}` `next-hop-self`
`no neighbor {`*address|peer-group*`}` `next-hop-self`

Configures   Next-hop processing of the neighbor router

Default   Disabled

Description

This command forces the router to advertise itself as the next hop to the neighbor. The neighbor router is identified by its IP *address* or *peer-group*.

---

neighbor password   router, BGP

```
neighbor {address|peer-group} password word
no neighbor {address|peer-group} password word
```

Configures   MD5 authentication between BGP peers

Default   Disabled

Description

This command requires authentication between BGP peers (identified by *address* or by *peer-group*). The MD5 algorithm is used for authentication. The password, *word*, can be any alphanumeric string up to 80 characters long; spaces are allowed, but the first character cannot be a number.

---

neighbor peer-group   router, BGP

```
neighbor address peer-group  peer-group
no neighbor address peer-group peer-group
```

Configures   Assigns a neighbor to a peer group

Default   None

Description

When configuring BGP, you often want to apply the same set of configuration items to a number of BGP neighbors. Peer groups let you simplify the router configuration by making a neighbor a peer group member. Once you have created a peer group, all configuration items for that group apply to all the members of the group. *address* is the IP address of the neighbor to be added to the peer group; *peer-group* is the name of the peer group.

Example

In this example, we create a peer group called **group1** and place all our neighbors into this peer group (179.69.232.53, 54, and 55). Having created the peer group, we can apply **neighbor filter-list** commands to the group as a whole, rather than to the individual neighbors. We still have to configure the unique features (such as remote AS numbers) of the neighbors individually.

```
router bgp 200
  neighbor group1 peer-group
  neighbor group1 filter-list 100 in
  neighbor group1 filter-list 102 out
  neighbor 171.69.232.53 remote-as 300
  neighbor 171.69.232.53 peer-group group1
  neighbor 171.69.232.54 remote-as 400
  neighbor 171.69.232.54 peer-group group1
```

```
neighbor 171.69.232.55 remote-as 500
neighbor 171.69.232.55 peer-group group1
```

neighbor prefix-list

```
neighbor {address | peer-group} prefix-list prefix-list-name {in | out}
no neighbor {address | peer-group} prefix-list prefix-list-name {in | out}
```

Configures   Assigns a prefix list to a BGP neighbor

Default   None

Description

This command lets you filter BGP routes by assigning a prefix list to a neighbor instead of using an AS path filter.

address or peer-group
> The address or peer group of the neighbor.

prefix-list *prefix-list-name*
> The name of the prefix list defined by the ip as-path access-list command.

in
> The filter applies to incoming routes.

out
> The filter applies to outgoing routes.

neighbor remote-as

```
neighbor {address | peer-group} remote-as as-number
no neighbor {address | peer-group} remote-as as-number
```

Configures   The remote AS number of a BGP neighbor

Default   None

Description

This command specifies a neighbor's AS number. This number is used to determine whether the neighbor is an internal or external BGP router. If the neighbor's AS number is the same as the AS number in the current BGP configuration, the neighbor is an internal BGP router; likewise, if the AS numbers are different, the neighbor is an external BGP router.

address or peer-group
> The address or peer group of the neighbor.

as-number
> The AS number of the neighbor router (or the routers in the peer group).

Example

In this example, the neighbor (10.200.200.3) is an internal BGP router because its AS number is the same as the local AS number:

```
router bgp 100
    neighbor 10.200.200.3 remote-as 100
```

In the following example, the neighbor (10.200.200.4) is an external BGP router:

```
router bgp 100
    neighbor 10.200.200.4 remote-as 200
```

neighbor route-map   router, BGP

```
neighbor {address | peer-group} route-map map {in | out}
no neighbor {address | peer-group} route-map map {in | out}
```

Configures   Assigns a route map to a BGP neighbor

Default   None

Description

This command assigns a route map to a BGP neighbor. The route map is used to filter or otherwise modify routes that are sent to or received from the neighbor.

address or *peer-group*
> The address or peer group of the neighbor.

map
> The number of the map used to filter the routes.

in
> The map is applied only to incoming routes.

out
> The map is applied only to outgoing routes.

neighbor route-reflector-client   router, BGP

```
neighbor address route-reflector-client
no neighbor address route-reflector-client
```

Configures   BGP route reflector

Default   None

Description

This command configures the local router as a route reflector; the neighbor at the specified *address* is a client of the route reflector. Route reflectors allow you to get around the rule that all internal BGP speakers (peers) must be fully meshed. A route reflector passes iBGP routes from one router to another without modification.

neighbor send-community

```
neighbor {address | peer-group} send-community
no neighbor {address | peer-group} send-community
```

Configures   Community attribute

Default   None

Description

This command tells the router to send the COMMUNITIES attribute to BGP neighbors. The neighbors that receive this attribute are identified either by *address* or by *peer group*.

neighbor shutdown

```
neighbor {address | peer-group} shutdown
no neighbor {address | peer-group} shutdown
```

Configures   Removes a BGP neighbor from the BGP configuration

Default   None

Description

This command disables the neighbor (specified by *address* or *peer-group*) so that it no longer takes part in the BGP routing protocol or exchanges BGP routing information and tables. Use the no form to re-enable the BGP neighbor.

neighbor soft-reconfiguration inbound

```
neighbor {address | peer-group} soft-reconfiguration inbound
no neighbor {address | peer-group} soft-reconfiguration inbound
```

Configures   Storage of received updates

Default   None

Description

This command enables the storage of received updates, which is required for an inbound soft reconfiguration.

neighbor timers

```
neighbor {address | peer-group} timers keepalive holdtime
no neighbor {address | peer-group} timers keepalive holdtime
```

Configures   Timer values for BGP routing information

Default   keepalive is 60 seconds; holdtime is 180 seconds

Description

This command allows you to set the timer information for BGP routes. The *keepalive* parameter specifies the frequency (in seconds) that keepalive messages are sent to the specified neighbor (as identified by *address* or *peer-group*). The *holdtime* parameter specifies the interval (in seconds) within which the router expects to hear a keepalive message from the given neighbor or peer group before declaring the peer dead.

---

neighbor update-source
router, BGP

```
neighbor {address|peer-group} update-source interface
no neighbor {address|peer-group} update-source interface
```

Configures   Best interface to reach a neighbor

Default   The closest interface (sometimes called the best local address)

Description

This command tells the router to use a certain interface for a neighbor (as specified by *address* or *peer-group*) rather than the default. Use this command when other routers are peering to your loopback address.

---

neighbor version
router, BGP

```
neighbor {address | peer-group} version value
no neighbor {address | peer-group} version value
```

Configures   The BGP version to use for the neighbor

Default   Version 4

Description

This command lets you specify which BGP version to use when talking to the given neighbor (as specified by *address* or *peer-group*). The version number must be 2, 3, or 4. Although Version 4 is the default, the router should dynamically negotiate down to Version 2 if the neighbor doesn't support Version 4.

---

neighbor weight
router, BGP

```
neighbor {address | peer-group} weight value
no neighbor {address | peer-group} weight value
```

Configures   The weight metric for a BGP neighbor

Default

Routes learned from the local router have a weight of 32768; routes learned from other BGP peers have a weight of 0

Description

This command lets you assign a weight to routes learned from the given neighbor (as specified by *address* or *peer-group*). Routes with a higher weight are chosen first. You can use this command to tell BGP to prefer routes learned from a given neighbor. This is a Cisco proprietary attribute.

Example

In the following configuration, we assign a weight of 100 to routes learned from the neighbor 10.200.200.3. This weighting causes the router to prefer routes learned from 10.200.200.3 to routes learned from other BGP peers.

```
router bgp 200
  neighbor 10.200.200.3 weight 100
```

---

net   router, IS-IS

net *value*
no net *value*

Configures   The NET for an IS-IS routing process

Default   None

Description

In order to configure an IS-IS routing process, you need to define a Network Entity Title (NET). Essentially, a NET serves as the area number and the system ID for the routing process. The NET is an NSAP whose last byte is 0.

Example

Let's assume that we have an IS-IS system ID of 0000.0000.0004 and an area ID of 04.0002. This gives us a NET of 04.0002.0000.0000.0004.00, which is the area ID followed by the system ID followed by the ending zero. The following configuration shows how the net command is used to assign the appropriate value:

```
router isis
  net 04.0002.0000.0000.0004.00
  is-type level-1
!
interface ethernet 0
  ip router isis
  ip address 10.1.1.1 255.255.255.0
```

---

network   router

BGP:

network *network-number* [mask *network-mask*]
no network *network-number* [mask *network-mask*]

IGRP/EIGRP/RIP:

```
network network-address
no network network-address
```

OSPF:

```
network network-address wildcard-mask area area-id
no network network-address wildcard-mask area area-id
```

Configures   The network for which the routing process is responsible

Default   None

Description

The network command provides a way to tell the routing process what networks it is responsible for. With IGRP, EIGRP, RIP, and, to a degree, BGP, all you need to do is list the network addresses (one per line) for the routing process. To remove a network from the routing process, use the no form of the command.

In OSPF, the network command requires three parameters: a *network-address*, a *wildcard-mask*, and an *area-id*. You must include the area ID. The wildcard mask specifies the portion of an IP address that isn't part of the network address; for example, a 24-bit mask subnet would use the wildcard mask 0.0.0.255. An interface can be attached only to a single OSPF area. If the address ranges (i.e., address/mask combinations) of two network commands overlap, the OSPF process takes the first match and ignores the rest.

For BGP, the network address is specified using a subnet mask, not a wildcard mask; for example, an 8-bit subnet would use the subnet mask 255.255.255.0. The mask is optional. If it is omitted, a mask of 255.255.255.0 is assumed.

Example

The following commands define a network for RIP and EIGRP routing processes:

```
router rip
    network 10.0.0.0
!
router eigrp
    network 11.0.0.0
```

The following commands configure OSPF with a process ID of 99 and two areas:

```
router ospf 99
    network 10.10.1.0 0.0.0.255 area 0
    network 10.10.2.0 0.0.0.255 area 1
```

---

network backdoor   router, BGP

```
network address backdoor
no network address backdoor
```

Configures   A backdoor route to a BGP border router

Default   None

Description

This command allows you to give a backdoor route to a BGP router. This route acts like a local network but is not advertised.

---

network weight

router, BGP

```
network address mask weight weight [route-map map]
no network address mask weight weight [route-map map]
```

Configures An absolute weight to a BGP network

Default None

Description

This command sets the weight for routes to the given network, overriding any weight value learned by other means (redistribution, etc.).

address mask
> The address of a network, specified as an IP address followed by a subnet mask.

weight weight
> The weight to be assigned to these routes. It can have any value from 0 to 65535.

route-map map
> A route map to be applied to these routes.

---

nrzi-encoding

interface

```
nrzi-encoding
no nrzi-encoding
```

Configures T1 encoding type

Default Disabled (i.e., B8ZS)

Description

This command enables "Nonreturn to Zero Inverted" encoding on T1 lines. The default encoding for T1 lines is B8ZS.

Example

```
interface serial1
    nrzi-encoding
```

---

ntp access-group

global

```
ntp access-group [condition] access-list
no ntp access-group [condition] access-list
```

Configures Network Time Protocol (NTP) service

Default　　　None

Description

This command applies an access list to the router's NTP service.

`condition`
> Optional. Specifies the type of NTP queries to which the access list applies. Valid values are `query-only`, `serve-only`, `serve`, and `peer`. `query-only` allows NTP control requests only; `serve-only` allows time requests only; `serve` allows time requests and NTP control requests, but does not allow the router to synchronize its time with another NTP peer; `peer` allows time requests, NTP control requests, and time synchronization with other NTP peers. If this keyword is omitted, the access list applies to all queries.

`access-list`
> A standard access list to be applied to NTP connections.

---

ntp authenticate　　　　　　　　　　　　　　　　　　　　global

```
ntp authenticate
no ntp authenticate
```

Configures　　　Network Time Protocol (NTP) service

Default　　　No authentication

Description

This command enables NTP authentication on the router.

---

ntp authentication-key　　　　　　　　　　　　　　　　　global

```
ntp authentication-key number md5 value
no ntp authentication-key number
```

Configures　　　Network Time Protocol (NTP) service

Default　　　None

Description

This command defines the authentication key to be used for NTP. Use the no form of this command to delete this key.

`number`
> A value that identifies this key (1 to 4294967295).

`md5 value`
> The actual key value.

ntp broadcast

```
ntp broadcast
no ntp broadcast
```

Configures   Network Time Protocol (NTP) service

Default   Disabled

Description

This command tells the router to transmit NTP broadcast packets through the interface.

ntp broadcast client

interface

```
ntp broadcast client
no ntp broadcast client
```

Configures   Network Time Protocol (NTP) service

Default   Disabled

Description

This command tells the router to receive NTP broadcast packets through the interface.

ntp broadcastdelay

global

```
ntp broadcastdelay microseconds
no ntp broadcastdelay
```

Configures   Network Time Protocol (NTP) service

Default   None

Description

This command sets the estimated round-trip delay for NTP broadcast packets in microseconds.

ntp disable

interface

```
ntp disable
no ntp disable
```

Configures   Network Time Protocol (NTP) service

Default   Enabled on all interfaces if NTP is configured

Description

This command disables the interface's ability to receive NTP packets.

ntp master   global

```
ntp master stratum
no ntp master stratum
```

Configures   Network Time Protocol (NTP) service

Default   The router is not a master

Description

This command configures the router as the master NTP server from which other
NTP peers can receive their NTP time. (See the ntp peer command for setting peer
values.) This command should be used with extreme caution, as it can declare the
router's clock to be stratum 1 (most accurate) without any safeguards about how
accurate the clock really is.

stratum
> The NTP stratum number for this server. The value can be 1 through 15.

---

ntp peer   global

```
ntp peer address [version value] [key keyid] [source interface] [prefer]
no ntp peer address
```

Configures   Network Time Protocol (NTP) service

Default   None

Description

This command defines the address of an NTP peer. The router synchronizes its
time with the peer's time and attempts to update the peer's time. Notice how a
peer is different from a server. If you specify an NTP server with the ntp server
command, the router gets its time from the server but does not attempt to update
the server's time.

address
> The IP address of the NTP peer.

version value
> The NTP version (1 through 3). The default is 3.

key keyid
> Authentication key to use for this peer. The ntp authentication-key
> command defines the keys and their key IDs.

source interface
> The interface the router should use to communicate with this peer.

prefer
> Makes this peer preferred over others.

Example

The following command sets an NTP peer at 10.11.1.2, which is available via the
ethernet0 interface.

```
ntp peer 10.11.1.2 version 2 source ethernet0
```

ntp server   global

```
ntp server address [version value] [key keyid] [source interface]
no ntp server address
```

Configures   Network Time Protocol (NTP) service

Default   None

Description

This command tells the router which NTP server to use. The router derives its time
from the server but does not try to update the server's time.

address
:   The IP address of the NTP peer.

version value
:   The NTP version (1 through 3). The default is 3.

key keyid
:   Authentication key to use for this peer. The ntp authentication-key
    command defines the keys and their key IDs.

source interface
:   The interface the router should use to communicate with this server.

Example

The following command sets our NTP server to 10.11.1.5:

```
ntp server 10.11.1.5 version 2
```

ntp source   global

```
ntp source interface
no ntp source interface
```

Configures   NTP source interface

Default   The closest interface to the destination

Description

This command allows you to define the interface to be used as the source interface for generating NTP traffic. By default, the router normally uses the interface
closest to the destination as the source interface.

ntp trusted-key

global

```
ntp trusted-key keyid
no ntp trusted-key keyid
```

Configures   Network Time Protocol (NTP) service

Default   None

Description

This command sets the authentication key to use to synchronize with the NTP server.

keyid
> The authentication key to use. The ntp authentication-key command defines the keys and their key IDs.

---

ntp update-calendar

global

```
ntp update-calendar
no ntp update-calendar
```

Configures   Network Time Protocol (NTP) service

Default   Disabled

Description

On high-end routers (7500, 5000, 6000, 1010, 8500, etc.), this command tells the router to update the calendar using NTP. Normally, the calendar is not updated through NTP; only the system clock is updated.

---

offset-list

router

```
offset-list access-list {in | out} value [interface]
no offset-list access-list {in | out} value [interface]
```

Configures   Adds an offset value to incoming or outgoing routing metrics

Default   None

Description

This command allows you to apply an offset to the metric of incoming or outgoing routes.

access-list
> The offset is applied to routes matching this access list (name or number). 0 means all routes.

in *or* out
> The direction in which to apply the metric offset. in applies the offset to incoming routes; out applies the offset to outgoing routes.

value

The amount by which route metrics will be increased. The value must be positive; the acceptable range depends on the routing protocol.

interface

Optional. The offset will be applied only to routes traveling through the given interface.

Example

The following configuration adds an offset of 10 to routes that match access list 1 (i.e., routes with the destination 10.10.1.0) traveling out through the ethernet0 interface:

```
access-list 1 permit 10.10.1.0 0.0.0.255
!
router eigrp 100
  offset-list 1 out 10 ethernet0
  network 10.10.0.0
```

ospf auto-cost reference-bandwidth   router

```
ospf auto-cost reference-bandwidth value
no ospf auto-cost reference-bandwidth value
```

Configures   How OSPF calculates default metrics

Default   100 Mb

Description

The default OSPF metric is calculated by dividing the reference bandwidth by the bandwidth of the interface. The default value of the reference bandwidth is 10^8 or 100000000. Using this formula, the OSPF cost for a T1 is 65 (100000000/1544000). This number is also convenient because it causes the cost of an FDDI link or Fast Ethernet to be 1. This command allows you to modify the reference bandwidth to support interfaces that are faster than 100 Mbps.

ospf log-adj-changes   router

```
ospf log-adj-changes
no ospf log-adj-changes
```

Configures   OSPF state change logging

Default   None

Description

This command enables syslog logging of changes in the state of neighbor routers.

output-delay
router

```
output-delay value
no output-delay value
```

Configures   Delay between packets in a multipacket route update

Default   0 (no delay)

Description

This command modifies the interpacket delay during RIP updates. *value* specifies the delay in milliseconds between consecutive packets in a multipacket update. A delay is useful when a fast router needs to communicate with a slower one, as it allows the slower router to catch up.

Example

This example sets the output delay of multipacket router updates to 5 milliseconds:

```
router rip
  network 10.10.0.0
  output-delay 5
```

---

padding
line

```
padding ascii-number count
no padding ascii-number
```

Configures   Pads a specific character with NULLs

Default   No padding

Description

This command pads a specific output character with NULL characters. It supports older terminals that require padding after certain characters, such as the Return key. Unless you are using a terminal that requires padding, you will never need this command.

`ascii-number`
    The decimal value of the character that needs padding.

`count`
    The number of NULL bytes to send after this character.

---

parity
line

```
parity {none | even | odd | space | mark}
no parity
```

Configures   Parity

Default   None

Description

This command defines the parity bit for an asynchronous serial line. Its value may be none, even, odd, space, or mark.

Example

```
Router(config)#line tty 2
Router(config)#parity none
```

---

passive-interface
router

```
passive-interface interface
no passive-interface interface
```

Configures

Disables a routing protocol on a specific interface either partially (RIP, IGRP) or completely (EIGRP, OSPF, etc.)

Default   None

Description

For RIP and IGRP, this command causes the specified *interface* to listen for routing updates but prevents it from sending them. For OSPF, EIGRP, or other "hello-based" routing protocols, this command effectively disables the protocol on that interface (both sending and receiving). These protocols cannot operate without exchanging hello messages.

Example

```
router igrp 100
  network 10.0.0.0
  ! Suppress routing advertisements on serial 1
  passive-interface serial 1
```

---

password
line

```
password value
no password value
```

Configures   A login password for the line

Default   No password

Description

This command allows you to assign a password to any available line. Most lines must also be configured with the login command.

Example

The following example sets the login password to *cisco* for the console and the five VTY lines.

```
! First the console
line con 0
```

```
password cisco
login
! And the five virtual terminals (for incoming telnets)
line vty 0 5
password cisco
login
```

peer default ip address   interface

```
peer default ip {address address | dhcp | pool pool}
no peer default ip {address address | dhcp | pool pool}
```

Configures   Address assignment for PPP or SLIP peers

Default   pool

Description

This command allows you to assign an IP address to peers that connect to this interface using PPP or SLIP. There are three ways in which an *address* can be assigned: you can specify a single address to be used whenever a peer connects to this interface; you can specify an address *pool* from which an address is taken; or you can specify that the router should obtain an address for the peer through dhcp. This command overrides the global setting for the default IP address selection.

async-bootp can also be used to provided addresses to dial-up clients.

peer neighbor-route   interface

```
peer neighbor-route
no peer neighbor-route
```

Configures   Generation of neighbor routes for incoming PPP connections

Default   Enabled

Description

The generation of a neighbor route for a new PPP connection is enabled by default. The no form of this command disables that behavior.

physical-layer   interface

```
physical-layer {sync | async}
no physical-layer {sync | async}
```

Configures   Whether the interface is synchronous or asynchronous

Default   sync

Description

This command lets you specify whether a serial interface is synchronous or asynchronous. It is available on low-speed serial interfaces.

ping   command

```
ping
ping host
```

Description

The `ping` command sends a sequence of ICMP echo request packets to the specified *host*. It is one of the simplest and most commonly used troubleshooting tools.
If you omit the host from the command line and are in privileged EXEC mode, the
router prompts you for the rest of the information.

Ping prints a special character for each packet indicating whether the router
received the corresponding echo reply. Table 15-14 shows what these special
characters mean. Ping also summarizes the success rate and the round-trip times.

Table 15-14: Ping success codes

Character	Meaning
!	Ping successful
.	Timed out waiting for reply
?	Unknown packet
&	TTL of packet was exceeded
A	Access list denied packet
C	Network congestion
I	User interrupt (if you hit CTRL+^)
U	Destination unreachable

Example

```
Router# ping 10.10.1.2
Type escape sequence to abort.
Sending 5, 100-byte ICMP Echos to 10.10.1.2, timeout is 2 seconds:
!!!!!
Success rate is 100 percent (5/5), round-trip min/avg/max = 1/3/4 ms
```

ppp   command

```
ppp
```

Description

This command is given by a user who wants to establish a PPP session after
connecting to one of the router's interfaces (for example, a dial-up serial interface) and logging in using some kind of terminal emulation. Giving this command
at the user EXEC command prompt establishes the PPP connection.

ppp authentication interface

```
ppp authentication {chap | pap} [if-needed] [list] [callin]
no ppp authentication
```

Configures   Enables CHAP or PAP authentication

Default   No authentication

Description

This command enables CHAP or PAP authentication on interfaces. In addition to the type of authentication, this command may have the following parameters:

if-needed
> Optional. Prevents reauthorization if the user has already been authorized at some other point during the session.

list
> Optional. Provides a list of AAA authorization methods. To set up an authorization list, use the command aaa authentication ppp.

callin
> Optional. Tells the interface to authorize incoming (dial-in) connections only.

---

ppp bridge ip interface

```
ppp bridge ip
no ppp bridge ip
```

Configures   Bridging a PPP connection

Default   Disabled

Description

This command enables half-bridging of IP packets across a serial or ISDN interface.

---

ppp chap interface

```
ppp chap password password
no ppp chap password password
```

Configures   CHAP authentication

Default   Disabled

Description

This command configures a single *password* for PPP authentication using the CHAP protocol.

ppp compress

```
ppp compress {predictor | stac}
no ppp compress {predictor | stac}
```

Configures   Compression

Default   None

Description

This command enables compression for the PPP connection. For compression to work, both ends of the PPP connection must be configured to use the same type of compression.

ppp multilink

```
ppp multilink
no ppp multilink
```

Configures   Multilink PPP (MLP) over multiple interfaces

Default   Disabled

Description

If you have two or more communications links between the router and the destination, you can use multilink PPP to send traffic over several interfaces in parallel to get higher throughput. Asynchronous serial interfaces, ISDN BRI interfaces, and ISDN PRI interfaces can make use of multilink PPP.

Multilink PPP works best on digital lines such as ISDN; it is less effective on low-speed analog connections.

ppp quality

```
ppp quality percentage
no ppp quality percentage
```

Configures   Quality monitoring

Default   Disabled

Description

This command enables link quality monitoring. Once enabled, the PPP link is shut down if the quality degrades below a certain value. The value, commonly thought of as a *percentage*, is expressed as a number between 1 and 100, with 100 indicating the highest quality.

ppp reliable-link   interface

```
ppp reliable-link
no ppp reliable-link
```

Configures   LAPB numbered mode negotiation

Default   Disabled

Description

This command enables LAPB numbered mode negotiation, which means that the router will try to negotiate a reliable link, not necessarily build a reliable link. This command is not available on asynchronous interfaces and doesn't work with multilink.

---

ppp use-tacacs   interface

```
ppp use-tacacs
no ppp use-tacacs
```

Configures   TACACS authentication for PPP

Default   Disabled

Description

This command enables the use of TACACS for PPP authentication.

---

priority-group   interface

```
priority-group list
no priority-group
```

Configures   A priority list for the interface

Default   None

Description

This command applies a priority list to an interface. See the `priority-list` command for information on constructing priority lists.

Example

The following commands apply priority list 1 to the `serial0` interface:

```
interface serial0
  priority-group 1
```

priority-list global

```
priority-list number default level
no priority-list number default level

priority-list number protocol value level port-type port
no priority-list number protocol value level port-type port

priority-list number queue-limit high-limit medium-limit normal-limit low-limit
no priority-list number queue-limit
```

Configures   Priority lists for priority traffic queueing

Default   None

Description

The `priority-list` command is a set of three related commands that are used to construct a list. A priority list is a set of four queues, one for each of four priority *levels*: high, medium, normal, and low. Each queue has its own capacity (in packets); the queue sizes are set using `priority-list queue-limit`, although I recommend that you don't modify the default queue sizes. The `priority-list protocol` version of the command assigns packets to a queue based on their protocols and, optionally, their ports. The `priority-queue default` command assigns a queue to all packets that aren't explicitly assigned to a queue (i.e., all packets not associated with a protocol and port specified with the `priority-list protocol` command).

Once you have created a priority list, use the `priority-group` command to apply a priority list to an interface. The queues in the list are then used for all traffic going out the interface.

The parameters for these commands are:

number
> The number of the priority list you are configuring; it can be a value from 1 to 10.

protocol value
> The protocol to prioritize. In mixed-protocol environments, the protocol can be `ip`, `ipx`, etc. The examples here all use IP.

level
> The queue you are configuring: `low`, `medium`, `normal`, or `high`.

port-type
> Either `tcp` or `udp`.

port
> A port number.

high-limit, medium-limit, normal-limit, low-limit
> When configuring queue sizes, the number of packets in the high, medium, normal, and low priority queues. The default number of packets for each queue is given in Table 15-15.

Table 15-15: Default sizes for queues in a priority list

Queue	Default size
low	80 packets
normal	60 packets
medium	40 packets
high	20 packets

Example

The following example creates priority list 1, which sends all IP packets to the medium priority queue. Next, all telnet packets (TCP packets with a destination port of 23) are assigned to the high priority queue. Finally, all other traffic (non-IP traffic) is assigned to the normal priority queue:

```
priority-list 1 protocol ip medium
priority-list 1 protocol ip high tcp 23
priority-list 1 default normal
```

The next example changes the size of the queues in the priority list:

```
priority-list 1 queue-list 30 20 15 10
```

---

privilege level (line)   line

```
privilege level level
no privilege level
```

Configures   Privilege level information

Default

Level 1 consists of all user EXEC commands; Level 15 consists of all enable commands

Description

This form of the `privilege` command applies a privilege level to a line, and therefore must be used in the context of line configuration. Applying a privilege level to a line means that the given privilege level becomes the default level for the line; anyone who can access the line can run the commands in the default privilege level without giving the enable password. See also `privilege level` (global).

level
  A number from 1 to 15 indicating the level to which you're assigning the command. Each level is a superset of the previous levels; for example, level 13 automatically includes all the commands for levels 1 through 12.

---

privilege level (global)   global

```
privilege mode level level command
no privilege mode level level command
```

Configures   Privilege level information

Default

Level 1 consists of all user EXEC commands; Level 15 consists of all enable commands

Description

The privilege level commands allow you to control access to a set of commands. The first of these commands, where you supply a mode and a command name, is used to set up a privilege level: a group of commands protected by a password. This is a global command—it is used outside of any context. Passwords for privilege levels are defined with the enable password command.

mode
> The configuration mode to which the command belongs. exec is most common; configuration, controller, hub, interface, ipx-router, line, map-class, map-list, route-map, and router are also used.

level
> A number from 1 to 15 indicating the level to which you're assigning the command. Each level is a superset of the previous levels; for example, level 13 automatically includes all the commands for levels 1 through 12.

command
> The command that you are assigning to a level.

Example

The first command in the following configuration assigns the clear command to privilege level 14. The password guessme is assigned to privilege level 14, requiring users to give this password before they can execute any of the clear commands. Since the other enable commands are assigned to level 15, users who know this password are not necessarily allowed to make general changes to the router's configuration; without the enable password, they can give only the clear commands (and any other commands that belong to level 14).

Next, we make privilege level 14 the default privilege level for the aux 0 port. This means that anyone who can access the aux 0 port and knows the password guessme can give the clear command and any other level 14 commands defined.

```
! assign the clear command to level 14
privilege exec level 14 clear
! set the password for level 14 to guessme
enable password level 14 guessme
!
! configure the default level for the aux port
line aux 0
  privilege level 14
```

---

prompt global

prompt *string*
no prompt *string*

Configures   The router prompt

Default   %h

Description

This command sets the prompt to the specified string. The string can have any combination of characters and escape sequences. The special characters are listed in Table 15-16. Use the no form of this command to set the system prompt to the default value.

Table 15-16: Escape sequences for the router prompt

Escape sequence	Meaning
%%	Percent character
%h	Hostname of the router
%n	TTY number for this EXEC session
%p	The prompt character; either > for user level or # for privileged level
%s	Space character
%t	Tab character

pulse-time   interface

```
pulse-time seconds
no pulse-time seconds
```

Configures   The DTR signal pulse intervals

Default   0 seconds

Description

This command sets the interval between the DTR pulsing signals, in *seconds*. When a line goes down, the DTR is held inactive for the duration of the pulse-time.

pvc   interface

```
pvc [name] vpi/vci [encap]
no pvc [name] vpi/vci [encap]
```

Configures   ATM PVC

Default   None

Description

This command configures a Permanent Virtual Circuit (PVC) on an ATM interface. It isn't supported on all ATM hardware; more sophisticated ATM hardware tends to use the atm pvc command.

name
     Optional. A name to be assigned to this PVC.

vpi/vci

The Virtual Path Identifier and the Virtual Channel Identifier, separated by a slash. If you omit the slash and the *vci*, it defaults to 0. If *vci* is 0, *vpi* cannot be 0, and vice versa.

encap

Optional. The type of encapsulation to use on the channel. Possible values are ilmi, qsaal, and smds. ilmi is used to set up a connection for the Integrated Local Management Interface, and is normally used with the VPI/VCI pair 0/16. qsaal sets up a PVC used for setting up and tearing down SVCs (switched virtual circuits), and is normally used with the VPI/VCI pair 0/5. smds is used only for SMDS networks.

---

queue-list global

```
queue-list number protocol value  queue-number [port-type port-number]
queue-list number protocol value  queue-number [list list-number]
queue-list number interface interface  queue-number
queue-list number queue-number byte-count size-in-bytes
queue-list number queue queue-number limit size-in-packets
queue-list number default queue-number
no queue-list number
```

Configures   Custom queueing

Default   None

Description

The queue-list commands define a custom queue list, which is a group of queues that can be used to configure the amount of bandwidth used by specific types of traffic. A custom queue is different from a priority queue in that a priority queue only allows you to set the relative priority of different traffic types. The queue-list byte-count command creates queues within the list and assigns each queue a transmission size. The default transmission size is 1500 bytes. The queue-list queue command specifies the absolute size of a queue, in packets. The queue-list protocol command assigns traffic for a given protocol and port to one of the queues in a queue list; instead of specifying a protocol and port, you can specify an IP access list. The queue-list interface command assigns traffic arriving for a given interface to one of the queues; and the queue-list default command assigns all otherwise unassigned traffic to one of the queues.

To use a queue list, it must be applied to an interface using the custom-queue-list command.

When sending traffic out an interface, the router works through the queues in order, emptying each queue before moving to the next. Therefore, increasing the size of a queue increases the bandwidth that can be used by the traffic assigned to the queue.

When assigning traffic to a queue, the router processes the queue-list statements in order.

number

A number identifying the queue list; it can be from 1 to 10.

`protocol` *value*

Specifies the protocol to be assigned to the queue. Valid protocols are `ip`, `ipx`, `dlsw`, etc.

`interface` *interface*

Used for establishing queuing priorities based on incoming interface for the packet.

queue-number

The queue within this list that is being described.

port-type port-number

A port type (`tcp` or `udp`) and port number; traffic for this port is assigned to a particular queue within the list. You can specify either a port number, or the name of a well-known port.

`list` *list-number*

An access list of an appropriate type for the given protocol. Traffic matching this access list is assigned to the specified queue.

`byte-count` *size-in-bytes*

Specifies the queue's transmission size, in bytes. The router works through the list of queues in order, taking *size-in-bytes* bytes of traffic from each queue before proceeding to the next. Therefore, a larger queue size assigns more bandwidth to the protocols that are routed through this queue.

`limit` *size-in-packets*

An absolute maximum for the number of packets that can be waiting in the queue. Packets in excess of this limit are discarded. The default limit is 20 packets.

Example

The following commands create a custom queue list (list 5) and apply that queue list to the `serial0` interface, where it is used to prioritize the traffic sent out that interface. The queue list consists of four queues with transmission sizes of 1000, 4000, 5000, and 4000 bytes. Therefore, queue 3 within the list is the highest priority and is allocated the most bandwidth; queue 1 is the lowest priority. Traffic is assigned to the queues as follows:

- Telnet traffic is assigned to queue 1 (low priority)
- Traffic that matches access list 10 (not shown) is assigned to queue 2 (moderate priority)
- Traffic arriving on the interface `tunnel1` is assigned to queue 3 (high priority)
- Otherwise-unassigned IP traffic is assigned to queue 4 (moderate priority)
- All remaining traffic (i.e., non-IP traffic) is assigned to queue 4 (moderate priority)

Note that the queue list is processed in order. Therefore, adding another traffic assignment statement after the `queue-list default` statement has no effect.

The effect of this queue is to transmit 1000 bytes from queue 1, then 4000 from queue 2, then 5000 from queue 3, then 4000 from queue 4, and so on, in round-robin fashion. Even though queue 1 has the lowest priority, it is guaranteed some bandwidth during each queue-processing cycle. In this respect, a custom queue is unlike a priority queue, which always sends the highest-priority packets first and may therefore starve low-priority traffic.

```
interface serial0
  ! apply the custom queue list
  custom-queue-list 5
!
! Define the custom queue list
queue-list 5 protocol ip 1 tcp telnet
queue-list 5 protocol ip 2 list 10
queue-list 5 interface tunnel1 3
queue-list 5 protocol ip 4
queue-list 5 default 4
queue-list 5 queue 1 byte-count 1000
queue-list 5 queue 2 byte-count 4000
queue-list 5 queue 3 byte-count 5000
queue-list 5 queue 4 byte-count 4000
```

---

radius-server   global

```
radius-server host {hostname | ip-address}
no radius-server host {hostname | ip-address}
```

```
radius-server key string
no radius-server key string
```

```
radius-server retransmit retries
no radius-server retransmit retries
```

```
radius-server timeout seconds
no radius-server timeout seconds
```

Configures   Radius server

Default   None

Description

This set of commands is used to specify a radius server that the router will use for authentication. The `radius-server host` command allows you to specify which radius server to use, either by hostname or IP address. You can define more than one radius server; the router attempts to contact the servers in the order that you specify.

The `radius-server key` command specifies the encryption string to be used for communication with the radius server. Obviously, this string must match the setting on the radius server. If you use multiple servers, they must all share the same key.

The `retransmit` and `timeout` forms of this command specify the number of times the router searches the list of radius servers before giving up, and the amount of time that it will wait for any given server to reply before retrying.

redistribute router

```
redistribute {protocol | static} [metric value] [metric-type type]
    [route-map map] [weight weight] [subnets]
no redistribute protocol
```

Configures   Redistribution of routes between protocols

Default   Disabled

Description

This command allows you to redistribute routes from one routing protocol to another. It also allows you to redistribute static routes into a routing protocol. Some protocols require you to specify a default metric that will be assigned to external routes. See the default-metric command and Chapters 8 and 9 for more information.

protocol
> This is the protocol from which routes are redistributed. If a process ID or local AS is required for the protocol, you must provide that as well. Possible values are bgp, igrp, eigrp, isis, ospf, and rip. You can also redistribute static routes.

metric *value*
> Optional. This keyword sets the metric value for the redistributed route. If you don't have a value defined here, the router uses the default metric as defined in the default-metric command. For most redistribution, you must define a default metric. Exceptions to this rule are static routes and IGRP to EIGRP redistribution.

metric-type *type*
> Optional. This keyword applies to OSPF and IS-IS only. For OSPF, this allows you to assign two possible metric type values: 1 (Type 1 external route) and 2 (Type 2 external route). The default type for OSPF is Type 2. For IS-IS, the options are internal (the metric is less than 63) and external (the metric is greater than 63 but less than 128). The default metric type for IS-IS is internal.

route-map *map*
> Optional. This keyword allows you to apply a route-map filter to the routes before they are redistributed into the protocol.

weight *weight*
> Optional. This keyword is for BGP only; it allows you to assign a BGP weight to the redistributed route.

subnets
> Optional. Used for redistributing routes into OSPF. When this keyword is used, it causes OSPF to accept all subnet routes. Without this keyword, OSPF only redistributes routes that are not subnets.

Example

The following example shows redistribution into OSPF of both EIGRP and RIP routes. For EIGRP, we are redistributing routes from `eigrp 1001` and assigning a metric of 100. The `subnets` keyword tells OSPF to redistribute all subnet routes. As for RIP, we are assigning a much higher metric of 200 to its routes.

```
router ospf 1000
  redistribute eigrp 1001 metric 100 subnets
  redistribute rip metric 200 subnets
```

When you don't use the `metric` command in the redistribute line, you must have a `default-metric` statement defined (except for static route redistribution).

```
router rip
  redistribute eigrp 1002
  default-metric 10
```

---

refuse-message   line

```
refuse-message delimiter message delimiter
no refuse-message
```

Configures   The message the user receives when a connection is busy.

Default   None

Description

This command defines the `message` that is displayed when the user attempts to connect a line that is already in use. `delimiter` is a character that marks the beginning and end of the message; it must not appear within the message itself.

Example

In this example, the user is told that the line is busy and to try another one:

```
line 1
  refuse-message # This line is currently busy, please try lines 2-8 #
```

To disable this message, delete it with the `no` form of this command:

```
line 1
  no refuse-message
```

---

reload   command

```
reload [in hh:mm] [at hh:mm [month day]] [cancel] [text]
show reload
```

Description

This command causes the router to reload the IOS operating system and reboot. You can specify a time for the reload to occur by using the `in` and `at` options. The `show` version of the command gives you the status of any pending reloads.

text

The reason for the reload; this reason is stored in memory and is used for a show reload command, sending warning messages, or sending messages to syslog servers.

in *hh:mm*

Tells the router to reload some time from now. For example, to start a reload in two hours, enter in 2:00.

at *hh:mm month day*

Tells the router to reload at a specific time (*hh:mm*). Optionally, you can specify a month and a day of the month, but the reboot must occur within 24 days.

cancel

Cancels a scheduled reload.

This command can be helpful when you are configuring a router remotely. One problem with working remotely is that if you make a mistake, you can kill your connection to the router, which may leave the router in a state that doesn't allow you to reconnect. Use this command before executing "dangerous" configuration commands remotely. If you make a mistake and haven't saved the configuration, the router will reboot and return to the previous configuration. If you don't make a mistake and your changes work, you can simply cancel the impending reload.

Example

```
Router#reload in 2:00 "IOS upgrade"
Router#reload cancel
Router#show reload
No reload is scheduled.
```

---

rename   command

```
rename current-name new-name
```

Description

This command allows you to rename a file from *current-name* to *new-name* in a Class C filesystem.

---

ring-speed   interface

```
ring-speed {4 | 16}
no ring-speed {4 | 16}
```

Configures   Token ring interface default speed

Default   16 Mbps

Description

This command sets the speed for a token ring interface to either 4 or 16 Mbps. The default speed is 16 Mbps. Be sure to set the correct speed; specifying an incorrect speed on a token ring interface will cause the ring to go down.

---

rlogin command

`rlogin hostname`

Description

This command allows you to log into the remote machine given by *hostname*. You can specify either a hostname or an IP address. `rlogin` stands for remote login, which follows the remote shell rules. If this command doesn't work, try `telnet`.

---

rmdir command

`rmdir directory`

Description

This command allows you to remove a directory from a Class C filesystem.

---

route-map global

`route-map tag-name [permit | deny] [sequence-number]`
`no route-map tag-name [permit | deny] [sequence-number]`

Configures   A route map for route redistribution or policy routing

Default   None

Description

A route map is a very flexible mechanism for specifying what to do with routes. A route map lets you match certain routes and set various parameters of the matching routes. The `route-map` command merely defines the list; the `match` command specifies which routes the map should match (something like an access list); and a number of `set` commands specify what to do with the matching routes.

A route map is identified by a name (*tag-name*); any number of `route-map` commands can share the same name. `route-map` commands with the same name are processed in the order given by the *sequence-number*. Although most route processing is specified by the `set` commands associated with the map, the `permit` and `deny` keywords can be used to specify some very simple processing. `permit` is the default; it means that normal route processing (as specified by the `set` commands) takes place for all routes that match the map. Processing continues with other route maps that share the same sequence number. The `deny` keyword specifies that if a match occurs, the route is not distributed and no further processing of other route maps takes place.

To delete a route map, use the `no` form of the command. Note that if you omit the *sequence-number*, this command deletes all maps matching the given *tag-name*.

tag-name
>   An identifying name.

permit
>   Optional. Specifies that normal route processing should occur when a route matches the map.

deny
>   Optional. Specifies that routes matching the map should not be propagated and that no further processing should occur.

sequence-number
>   A sequence number that indicates the order in which route maps sharing the same name are processed.

Example

The following commands define a route map named check with a sequence number of 10. The match command selects the routes that match the map; it refers to community list 1, which specifies routes that include community 100. The set command sets the weight of any route matching this community list to 10.

```
route-map check permit 10
  match community 1
  set weight 10

ip community-list 1 permit 100
```

---

router   global

RIP:
```
router rip
no router rip
```

BGP:
```
router bgp as-number
no router bgp as-number
```

EIGRP:
```
router eigrp as-system
no router eigrp as-system
```

IGRP:
```
router igrp as-system
no router igrp as-system
```

IS-IS:
```
router isis [tag]
no router isis [tag]
```

OSPF:
```
router ospf as-system
no router ospf as-system
```

Configures   Enters the routing configuration mode

Default   None

Description

This command starts the configuration of a routing process: it identifies the routing protocol you want to run and other parameters necessary for the routing protocol. The RIP protocol doesn't require additional parameters; BGP requires an AS number; EIGRP, IGRP, and OSPF require process numbers (commonly called AS numbers); and IS-IS can optionally have a tag that defines a name for the routing process.

Example

```
! Configure our rip process
router rip
    network 10.0.0.0
```

---

rsh   command

```
rsh host [/user username] command-to-execute
```

Description

This command executes a command on a remote host via a remote shell.

host
  The hostname of the machine on which to execute the command.

/user username
  The username to use when executing the command.

command-to-execute
  The command to be executed.

Example

The following command executes the command ls on a machine named sun-machine as user bob.

```
rsh sun-machine /user bob ls
```

---

rxspeed   line

```
rxspeed speed
no rxspeed
```

Configures   Receive speed

Default   9600 bps

Description

This command sets the receive speed for this line to *speed*, in bits per second.

send
command

send {*line-number* | * | aux *n* | console *n* | tty *n* | vty *n*} *message*

Description

This command sends a message immediately to one or more terminals. It is not stored in the router's configuration.

line-number
> The line number to which to send the message.

*
> Sends the message to all TTY lines.

aux *n*
> The AUX port to which to send the message.

tty *n*
> The TTY port to which to send the message.

vty *n*
> The VTY port to which to send the message.

console *n*
> The console line to which to send the message.

message
> The message you wish to send. It may span multiple lines, and must be terminated with Ctrl-Z on a line by itself.

Example

The following commands send a message to all TTY lines:

```
Routersend *
Enter message, end with CTRL/Z; abort with CTRL/C:
REBOOTING Router in ten minutes for an emergency repair!
^Z
Send message? [confirm]y
Router

***
***
*** Message from tty19 to all terminals:
***
REBOOTING router in ten minutes for an emergency repair!
```

service
global

service *service*
no service *service*

Configures   Service level items

Default   Depends on the service

Description

The service command disables or enables certain router features. These features range from minor TCP/IP servers to the router's callback behavior. The services controlled by this command are:

config
> Enables autoloading configuration files from a server. This command is required for boot network commands to work.

exec-callback
> Enables the callback feature for clients. A callback tells the router to authenticate a dial-in user, disconnect, and then call the user back at a prearranged number. See Chapter 11 for more information.

exec-wait
> Delays the display of the prompt.

finger
> Allows finger requests to be made to the router (i.e., enables a finger server). For IOS 12.0 and later, this has been superseded by ip finger.

hide-telnet-address
> Hides the IP address of the destination host when a telnet command is issued. When a user executes a telnet command at the EXEC prompt, the IP address of the destination machine is usually displayed with a message like "Trying machinename (10.10.1.4)."

nagle
> Enables the Nagle congestion control algorithm.

password-encryption
> Enables password encryption. By default, password encryption is enabled.

prompt config
> Enables the display of the (config) prompt when in the configuration mode.

tcp-keepalives-in
> Enables TCP keepalives on incoming connections (connections initiated by remote hosts).

tcp-keepalives-out
> Enables TCP keepalives on outgoing connections (connections initiated by the router).

tcp-small-servers
> Enables servers for the so-called "small TCP services" (the *echo, discard, chargen,* and *daytime* protocols). By default, these services are disabled as of IOS 11.2 and later.

telnet-zeroidle
> When enabled, this feature tells the router to set the packet window to zero when a telnet connection is idle.

udp-small-servers
> Enables servers for the small UDP services (*echo, discard,* and *chargen*). By default, these services are disabled as of IOS 11.2 and later.

service compress-config global

```
service compress-config
no service compress-config
```

Configures   Compression of configurations in memory

Default   Disabled

Description

This command lets you compress the configuration file; this feature is available only on high-end routers (5000, 6000, and 7500 series). To disable compression, use the no form of the command.

---

service linenumber line

```
service linenumber
no service linenumber
```

Configures   Line number display

Default   Disabled

Description

This command configures the router to display the line number, line location, and hostname after the incoming banner.

---

service-module 56k interface

```
service-module 56k parameters
no service-module 56k parameters
```

Configures   Internal 56k (DS0) CSU/DSU

Default   Depends on the command

Description

The service-module commands are for routers that have 56k CSU/DSU modules built into them. These commands set various options on the internal CSU/DSU. The parameters that can be configured are:

clock rate *speed*
> Configures the line speed for a four-wire 56k line. The valid speeds are 2.4, 4.8, 9.6, 19.2, 38.4, 56, and 64. The default is 56.

clock source {line | internal}
> By default, the clock source is the line, which is provided by the carrier. This command allows you to switch to the internal clock source on the module.

data-coding {normal | scrambled}

> normal data coding is the default behavior for service modules. scrambled data coding should be used only on lines configured for 64 kbps. Both ends of the link must use the same data coding.

network-type {dds | switched}

> Determines whether the line is configured for DDS (unswitched) or switched service. dds is the default for four-wire service; switched is the default for two-wire service.

remote-loopback

> By default, the service module accepts remote-loopback commands from the remote CSU/DSU. To disable remote loopback, use the no form.

switched-carrier {att | sprint | other}

> The switched-carrier setting must be appropriate for your 56k provider. att is the default on four-wire CSU/DSUs; sprint is the default on two-wire CSU/DSUs. This command can be used only if the network-type is set to switched.

---

service-module t1 interface

service-module t1 *parameters*
no service-module t1 *parameters*

Configures   Internal T1 CSU/DSU

Default   Depends on the command

Description

The service-module commands are for routers that have T1 CSU/DSU modules built into them. These commands set various options on the internal CSU/DSU. The parameters that can be configured are:

clock source {internal | line}

> By default, the clock source for a T1 CSU/DSU is the line, which is provided by the carrier. This command allows you to switch to the internal clock source on the module.

data-coding {inverted | normal}

> By default, the data coding is set to normal. Setting the data coding to inverted instructs the module to convert all 1s to 0s and all 0s to 1s. If the data coding is inverted on one end of the line, the other end must also be inverted or the connection will fail.

framing {esf | sf}

> This command sets the framing type for the T1 module, which can be esf (Extended Superframe) or sf (Superframe). The default framing type for a T1 module is ESF.

lbo {-15 db | -7.5 db | none}

> This command sets the line build-out value. −15 db decreases the outgoing signal by 15 decibels; −7.5 db decreases it by 7.5 decibels. Your provider will know what the build-out should be for your link. The default is no build-out (none) on the outgoing signal.

Reference R-S

```
linecode {ami | b8zs}
```
By default, the line encoding is set to b8zs. It can be changed to ami with this command. Your service carrier provides the T1 linecode type.

```
remote-alarm-enable
```
This command allows the generation and detection of remote alarms on the T1 line. All alarms are disabled by default.

```
remote-loopback {full | payload}
```
By default, the service module accepts full and payload remote-loopback commands from the remote CSU/DSU. The no form of this command allows you to disable this behavior.

```
timeslots {all | range} [speed 56|64]
```
This command defines the timeslots that make up a fractional T1 line. The keyword all includes all the timeslots; to specify a subset of the available timeslots (i.e., fractional T1), use a range of numbers between 1 and 24 (for example, 1-3,7 for timeslots 1, 2, 3, and 7). The optional speed parameter defines the timeslot speed, which can be 56 or 64. The default is all timeslots operating at 64 kbps.

---

service timestamps global

```
service timestamps {log | debug} [uptime]
service timestamps {log | debug} datetime [msec] [localtime] [show-timezone]
no service timestamps {log | debug}
```

Configures   Timestamps on log messages

Default   No timestamps

Description

This command forces timestamps on logging or debugging messages. uptime is the default if no options are specified.

```
log
```
Applies timestamps to logging messages.

```
debug
```
Applies timestamps to debugging messages.

```
uptime
```
Optional. The time is calculated since the router was started.

```
datetime
```
Uses the actual clock time.

```
msec
```
Optional. Displays the millisecond value in the timestamp.

```
localtime
```
Optional. Timestamps are relative to the local time zone.

```
show-timezone
```
Optional. Displays the time zone value in the timestamp.

---

session-limit

```
session-limit number
no session-limit
```

Configures   Maximum sessions per line

Default

Depends on the hardware; show terminal shows you the default for your device

Description

This command sets the maximum number of terminal sessions per line.

session-timeout

```
session-timeout minutes [output]
no session-timeout
```

Configures   Minutes before a session on the line times out

Default   0 (never times out)

Description

This command sets the interval that the router waits for traffic before closing the connection, i.e., the amount of time the line can be idle. The timeout period is specified in *minutes*. The output keyword tells the router to use both input and output traffic to reset the counters. If you omit this keyword, only the input traffic on the line causes a counter reset.

set as-path

```
set as-path {tag | prepend as-path-string}
no set as-path {tag | prepend as-path-srting}
```

Configures   Properties of routes matching a route map

Default   None

Description

Route maps let you select routes based on certain criteria and modify the properties of those routes using one or more set commands. This command allows you to modify the autonomous system path for BGP routes that match the route map's criteria. (To define a route map, use the route-map command; to specify a route map's matching criteria, use the match command.) The set as-path command has the following arguments:

tag

> When redistributing routes into BGP, converts the tag of the route directly into an autonomous system (AS) path.

prepend *as-path-string*
>   Adds the *as-path-string* to the beginning of any AS path.

Example

In this example, we create a route map called **test-as-path**. Inside the map, we match any AS path list with the number 1. We then use the **set as-path** command to prepend our local autonomous system (300) to all routes advertised to our neighbor (10.10.1.1).

```
route-map test-as-path
  match as-path 1
  set as-path prepend 300
!
ip as-path access-list 1 permit .*
!
router bgp 300
  neighbor 10.10.1.1 route-map test-as-path out
```

---

set automatic-tag   route-map

```
set automatic-tag
no set automatic-tag
```

Configures   Properties of routes matching a route map

Default   None

Description

This command causes automatic tag calculation for a learned route that is matched by a route map.

---

set community   route-map

```
set community {community-number [additive]} | none
no set community {community-number [additive]} | none
```

Configures   Properties of routes matching a route map

Default   None

Description

This command sets the BGP community for a route matched by the route map.

community-number
>   The community number to use; its value can be a number from 1 to 4294967200, or the predefined communities of **no-export** or **no-advertise**.

additive
>   Optional. Causes the new community to be added to any communities that the route already belongs to.

none
>   Optional. Removes all community attributes from the route.

---

set default interface

```
set default interface interface [... interface]
no set default interface interface [... interface]
```

Configures   Properties of routes matching a route map

Default   None

Description

This command sets the output interface for destinations that match the criteria in the route map if there is no explicit route to the destination. In other words, if the route is matched by this route map and has no explicit destination, this command can tell it which interface to use as a default route. This allows you to have different default routes for different hosts or networks.

You may list any number of interfaces; if the first interface in the list is down, the next is tried, and so on. This command should be used in conjunction with the `ip policy route-map` command.

Example

The following commands establish a route map named `policy-one` for policy-based routing. This map takes all packets for the destinations matched by access list 1 (i.e., all destinations that match 10.1.0.0/16) and sends them out through interface `serial0`.

```
inteface ethernet0
  ip policy route-map policy-one
  ip address 10.1.1.1 255.255.255.0
!
! this access-list is for the match ip command below
access-list 1 permit 10.1.0.0 0.0.255.255
!
route-map policy-one
  match ip address 1
  set default interface serial0
```

set interface

```
set interface interface [... interface]
no set interface interface [... interface]
```

Configures   Properties of routes matching a route map

Default   None

Description

This command is similar to the `set default interface` command. It differs in that the interface specified in this command is always used regardless of any other routing information: it can't be overridden by an explicit route to the destination. This command should be used in conjunction with the `ip policy route-map` command.

set ip default next-hop

```
set ip default next-hop ip-address [... ip-address]
no set ip default next-hop ip-address [... ip-address]
```

Configures   Properties of routes matching a route map

Default   None

Description

This command sets the next-hop address for an incoming packet if there is no explicit route for the packet already. This command should be used in conjunction with the `ip policy route-map` command. The IP address does not have to be an address that is adjacent to the router.

---

set ip precedence

```
set ip precedence qos
no set ip precedence
```

Configures   The precedence bits in the IP header

Default   Disabled

Description

This command sets the Quality of Service bits in the IP header. The Quality of Service value, qos, can be specified either by number or by name. Table 15-17 lists the valid number and names that can be used.

Table 15-17: QoS numbers and names

QoS number	QoS name
0	routine
1	priority
2	immediate
3	flash
4	flash-override
5	critical
6	internet
7	network

---

set ip next-hop

```
set ip next-hop ip address [... ip address]
no set ip next-hop ip address [... ip address]
```

Configures   Properties of routes matching a route map

Default   None

Description

This command sets the next-hop address for an incoming packet regardless of any explicit route for the packet. It is similar to the set ip default next-hop command except that a next-hop address specified with this command cannot be overridden by an explicit route. This command should be used in conjunction with the ip policy route-map command. The IP address does not have to be an address that is adjacent to the router.

---

set level   route-map

```
set level {level-1 | level-2 | level-1-2 | stub-area | backbone}
no set level {level-1 | level-2 | level-1-2 | stub-area | backbone}
```

Configures   Properties of routes matching a route map

Default   backbone for OSPF; level-2 for IS-IS

Description

This command sets the level into which routes that match the route map are imported.

level-1
    Imports into level-1 area.

level-2
    Imports into level-2 subdomain.

level-1-2
    Imports into both level-1 and level-2.

stub-area
    Imports into the OSPF NSSA area.

backbone
    Imports into the OSPF backbone area.

---

set local-preference   route-map

```
set local-preference value
no set local-preference value
```

Configures   Properties of routes matching a route map

Default   100

Description

This command sets the preference value for routes that match the map. In BGP, the preference influences route selection.

set metric

```
set metric metric-value
no set metric metric-value

set metric bandwidth delay reliability loading mtu
no set metric bandwidth delay reliability loading mtu
```

Configures   Properties of routes matching a route map

Default   The default metric for the routing protocol

Description

This command sets the metric value for a matching route. The first form of the command (with a single *metric-value* parameter) is used for most routing protocols; the metric value must be appropriate for the protocol's routing metric. For IGRP and EIGRP, you must use the second form of the command with five parameters:

bandwidth
    The bandwidth of the route in kilobits per second. The value can be from 0 to 4294967295.

delay
    The route delay in tens of microseconds. The value can be from 0 to 4294967295.

reliability
    A value from 0 to 255. 0 indicates total unreliability; 255 indicates complete reliability.

loading
    A value from 0 to 255. 0 means no load; 255 means 100% loaded.

mtu
    The smallest MTU for any link in the route, in bytes. The value can be from 0 to 4294967295.

---

set metric-type

```
set metric-type {internal | external | type-1 | type-2}
no set metric-type {internal | external | type-1 | type-2}
```

Configures   Properties of routes matching a route map

Default   Disabled

Description

This command sets the metric type used for routes that match the map. The metric type is used by the OSPF and IS-IS protocols.

internal
    IS-IS internal metric.

external
> IS-IS external metric.

type-1
> OSPF external type 1 metric.

type-2
> OSPF external type 2 metric.

---

set metric-type internal
route-map

```
set metric-type internal
no set metric-type internal
```

Configures   Properties of routes matching a route map

Default   Disabled

Description

This command is for BGP routing. It causes the MED value for all advertised routes that match the route map to be set to the corresponding interior routing protocol metric of the next hop.

---

set origin
route-map

```
set origin {igp | egp as-system | incomplete}
no set origin {igp | egp as-system | incomplete}
```

Configures   Properties of routes matching a route map

Default   The default origin value

Description

This command sets the BGP origin code for the matched route. The possible origins are:

igp
> The route was learned from an interior routing protocol.

egp *as-system*
> The route was learned from an exterior routing protocol with the given autonomous system number.

incomplete
> The origin of the route is unknown.

---

set-overload-bit
router, IS-IS

```
set-overload-bit
no set-overload-bit
```

Configures   The overload bit for IS-IS routing

Default   Disabled

Description

This command sets the overload bit, which tells other routers not to use it as the intermediate hop in the Shortest Path First (SPF) calculation.

---

set tag route-map

```
set tag value
no set tag value
```

Configures   Properties of routes matching a route map

Default   The route's tag is passed directly into the new routing protocol

Description

This command sets the matched route's tag value. The value can be from 0 through 4294967295.

---

setup command

```
setup
```

Description

This command places the router in setup configuration mode. In this mode, the router asks a series of questions; the answers allow the router to build a basic configuration. You must be in enable mode to run this command.

Example

Here is the beginning of the system configuration dialog:

```
ROUTER#setup

        --- System Configuration Dialog ---

Continue with configuration dialog? [yes/no]: yes

At any point you may enter a question mark '?' for help.
Use ctrl-c to abort configuration dialog at any prompt.
Default settings are in square brackets '[]'.

First, would you like to see the current interface summary? [yes]: n

Configuring global parameters:

  Enter host name [ROUTER]: myrouter

  The enable secret is a password used to protect access to
  privileged EXEC and configuration modes. This password, after
  entered, becomes encrypted in the configuration.
  Enter enable secret:
```

set weight

route-map

```
set weight value
no set weight value
```

Configures   Properties of routes matching a route map

Default   The default weight value

Description

This command sets the BGP weight value for a matched route. The weight value can be 0 through 65535.

show

command

```
show parameters
```

Description

The show commands are extremely helpful when configuring or debugging a router. Just about anything you want to know about the router's configuration or state can be found with a show command. Table 15-18 summarizes the common show commands.

Table 15-18: Common show commands

Command	Subcommand	Displays
show access-lists [acl]		All access lists. If you give an access list number, this command displays that particular list.
show accounting		All the accounting information on the system
show aliases [mode]		All aliases that have been defined for commands. If you provide the name of a mode, this command only displays the aliases for that mode. Use ? to see the list of acceptable modes. Aliases are created with the alias command.
show arp		The router's ARP table
show async	bootp	BOOTP parameters for an asynchronous interface
	status	Status of the asynchronous interfaces
show atm	accounting	ATM accounting information
	addresses	Active ATM addresses
	arp-server	ATM ARP server table
	connection-traffic-table	ATM connection traffic parameters
	filter-expr	ATM filter expressions
	filter-set	ATM filter sets
	ilmi-configuration	ILMI configuration information
	ilmi-status	ILMI status information
	interface	ATM information relative to an interface

Table 15-18: Common show commands (continued)

Command	Subcommand	Displays
	map	ATM static maps to remote hosts
	qos-defaults	Default ATM QoS configuration
	resource	ATM global resource manager configuration
	rmon	Status of the ATM RMON MIB
	route	ATM routing table
	signalling	ATM signaling information
	snoop	ATM port snooping configuration
	snoop-vc	ATM port snooping configuration per virtual connection
	snoop-vp	ATM port snooping configuration per virtual path
	status	Current ATM status for the router
	traffic	ATM traffic layer information
	vc	Information about ATM virtual connections
	vp	Information about ATM virtual paths
show bridge		Entries in the bridge forwarding database
	circuit-group	Status of the interfaces in a circuit group
	group [verbose]	Status of all bridge groups
	multicast	Transparent bridging multicast state information
	vlan	Virtual LAN subinterfaces
show bootflash:		Information about the router's bootflash
show bootvar		Contents of the bootvar variable
show buffers		Buffers and buffer statistics
show calendar		Calendar hardware setting
show caller		Incoming caller information on access servers
show cdp		Global CDP information
	entry	Information about an entry in the CDP table
	interface	Interfaces for which CDP is enabled
	neighbors [detail]	Information about CDP neighbors
	traffic	Traffic information from the CDP table
show cef		Information about Cisco Express Forwarding
show clock [detail]		Current clock information
show compress		Compression statistics
show configuration		Initial startup configuration. This command has been replaced with show startup-config.
show controllers [controller]		Information about the physical port. By default, you get all the controller information. Use the controller parameter to name a specific controller.
show crypto cisco		Cisco encryption policies
	algorithms	Supported cryptographic algorithms
	connections	Pending and completed encrypted connections

Table 15-18: Common show commands (continued)

Command	Subcommand	Displays
	key-timeout	Timeout values for the router's session keys
	pregen-dh-pairs	Pregenerated pairs
show crypto engine		Information about the cryptographic engine
	configuration	The cryptographic engine's configuration
	connections	Current connection information
show crypto key		Public key information
	mypubkey	The router's public keys
	pubkey-chain	The peer's public keys
show crypto map		All cryptographic maps
	interface	All cryptographic maps for a specific interface
	tag	Maps for a specific tag
show debugging		Type of debugging that is enabled
show dhcp	lease	DHCP information learned from a server
	server	DHCP servers that the router knows about
show diag		Power-on diagnostics for certain types of routers
show dialer		All dialer configuration and state information
	interface	Dialer information for a specific interface
	maps	Dialer map information
show environment		Current temperature and voltage information. Only available on some routers.
show file		Information for a class C filesystem
	descriptors	Open file descriptors
	information *url*	Information about a specific file
	systems	All available filesystems
show flash		The status and contents of flash memory
show frame-relay	ip rtp header-compression	IP/RTP statistics
	ip tcp header-compression	IP/TCP statistics
	lapf	LAPF status
	lmi	LMI statistics
	map	Frame Relay map table
	pvc	PVC statistics
	qos-autosense	qos-autosense information
	route	Frame Relay route
	svc maplist	SVC information
	traffic	Frame Relay protocol statistics
show hardware		Hardware information like IOS image, memory, flash size, interface list, and config-register setting
show history		The commands in the history buffer

Table 15-18: Common show commands (continued)

Command	Subcommand	Displays
show hosts		The host table, which lists hosts whose addresses are explicitly configured in the router
show hub		Information about hub interfaces
show interfaces		Statistics for all interfaces
	interface	Statistics for a specific *interface*
	interface accounting	Interface accounting
	interface crb	Routing and bridging information
	interface irb	Routing and bridging information
	interface type	Virtual LAN types
	fair-queue	Fair-queueing statistics for interface
	ip-brief	A single-line IP status for each interface
	stats	Information about packets handled and switching paths for interfaces
	switch	Details about switching paths for interfaces
show ip access-lists [*list*]		All the current IP access lists. Optionally, you can provide the number of a specific list.
show ip accounting		Information about packets that passed access control and were routed successfully
	access-violations	Information about packets that failed access control and were not routed
	checkpoint	The checkpoint database
	output-packets	Information about successfully routed packets
show ip aliases		The IP addresses that have been mapped to ports for reverse telnet
show ip arp		The ARP cache
show ip bgp		Entries in the BGP routing table
	cidr-only	Routes that have CIDR network masks
	community *community*	Routes that belong to a specific BGP community
	community-list	Routes permitted by a specific BGP community list
	dampened-paths	Information about route dampening
	filter-list list-number	Routes permitted by a specific BGP filter list
	inconsistent-as	Routes with inconsistent originating AS numbers
	neighbors	Statistics about BGP neighbors
	paths	All BGP paths in the BGP database
	peer-group	Statistics about BGP peer groups
	regexp *expression*	All routes that match the given regular expression
	summary	Status of all current BGP connections

Table 15-18: Common show commands (continued)

Command	Subcommand	Displays
show ip cache		The routing table for fast-switched IP traffic
	flow	The flow table for switching cache
show ip cef		Global information about CEF
show ip dvmrp route		Contents of DVMRP routing table
show ip egp		All EGP connections and neighbors
show ip eigrp	interfaces	Interface-specific EIGRP information
	neighbors	Discovered EIGRP neighbors and their hold-time status
	topology	The EIGRP topology table
	traffic	The types of EIGRP packets that were sent and received
show ip flow export		Information about flow export statistics
show ip igmp	groups	Multicast groups learned via IGMP
	interface [*interface*]	Multicast information about all interfaces. If you list a specific interface, this command displays multicast information about that interface.
show ip interface [brief]		Interfaces configured for IP. By default, you get all interfaces; you can specify a single interface. Use the brief command to get a summary.
show ip irdp		The status of the Router Discovery Protocol and which interfaces have it enabled
show ip local policy		The route map used for local policy routing
show ip local pool		The IP address pools
show ip masks		The network masks that are currently used, which helps when doing variable-length subnet mask troubleshooting
show ip mcache		Contents of the IP multicast fast switching cache
show ip mpacket		Contents of the circular cache-header buffer
show ip mroute		Contents of the IP multicast routing table
show ip nat		
	statistics	NAT statistics (total translations, interfaces, hits, misses, and expired translations)
	translations	Active translations
show ip nhrp		The NHRP cache
show ip ospf		General information and statistics about OSPF
	bad-checksum	
	border-routers	The routes to the ABR and ASBR in the internal routing table
	database	The entire OSPF database for the device. Options to this command give you more specific information: asb-summary, router, network, external, summary, and database-summary.
	interface	Interface-specific OSPF information, or information about a given interface

Table 15-18: Common show commands (continued)

Command	Subcommand	Displays
	neighbor	Information about OSPF neighbors on an interface basis
	request-list	All LSA requests by a router
	retransmission-list	All LSA requests waiting to be retransmitted
	statistics	
	virtual-links	Information about configured OSPF virtual links
show ip pim		
	interface	Information about interfaces that are configured for PIM
	neighbor	All PIM neighbors that the router has discovered
	rp	The rendezvous-point routers that are used with sparse-mode multicast
show ip policy		Policy routing information
show ip protocols		The currently configured IP routing protocols and their state information
show ip redirects		Default gateways and the IP addresses from which redirects have been received
show ip route		The route table
	[*routing-protocol*]	Routes for the specified protocol
	summary	Summary of the IP route table
	supernets-only	Only the supernets in the routing table
show ip rpf		Information about reverse path forwarding for multicast routing
show ip sockets		IP sockets that are currently open
show ip tcp header-compression		Statistics about TCP header compression
show ip traffic		General statistics about IP traffic
show isdn		Various ISDN statistics
	active	All current calls
	history	Historic ISDN information
	memory	ISDN memory pool statistics
	status	ISDN interface status; you can list a specific interface to get a status report for that interface
	timers	Layer 2 and Layer 3 timer information
show isis	database	The contents of the IS-IS database
	spf-log	When and how often the router had to perform an IS-IS SPF calculation.
show key chain		All information about authentication key chains
show lane		ATM LANE information for an interface or a complete summary
	bus	ATM LANE information for the BUS

Table 15-18: Common show commands (continued)

Command	Subcommand	Displays
	`client`	Information for LANE clients
	`config`	Information for the LANE configuration server
	`database`	The database of the LANE configuration server
	`default-atm-addresses`	The automatically assigned ATM address for each LANE component
	`le-arp`	The LANE ARP table
	`name`	The LANE ARP server
	`server`	Global information for the LANE server
`show line`		Information about configured serial lines (AUX, TTY, and VTY). On TTY ports, a large number of overruns might signal a bad cable.
`show logging`		The logging that is enabled
`show memory`		Information about the device's memory usage
`show microcode`		The microcode image information for a line card
`show modem`		Statistics for manageable modems. Used for access servers and for routers with managed (internal) modems.
	`at-mode`	Manageable modems that have current AT sessions
	`call-stats`	Call statistics and disconnect reasons
	`configuration`	Current modem configurations
	`connect-speeds`	Connection speed statistics
	`cookie`	Information about the modem cookie
	`csm`	Information about the CSM
	`log`	Modem event history
	`mapping`	All the firmware versions for the modems
	`mica`	Information about MICA modems
	`operational-status`	Performance statistics for modems
	`summary`	A summary report for all managed modems
	`test`	The managed modems test log
	`version`	Modems firmware information
`show modem-pool`		Status and configuration for a modem-pool
`show network clocks`		Information about network clock sources
`show ntp`	`associations`	A table of NTP hosts and their status
	`status`	The status of NTP on the device
`show ppp multilink`		Information about PPP Multilink
`show privilege`		All the privilege levels currently configured for the device
`show processes`		All the processes that are currently running on the device
	`cpu`	CPU utilization for each process
	`memory`	Memory utilization for each process

Table 15-18: Common show commands (continued)

Command	Subcommand	Displays
show protocols		Configured routing protocols and protocol information for each interface
show queue interface		The queue status and queueing strategy for the specified interface
show queueing		All configured queuing methods: custom, fair, priority, random-detect, vc
show registry		Registry ATM information
show reload		When the next reload is scheduled
show rhosts		Which hosts are configured for remote shell usage
show rmon		General RMON statistics
	alarms	The RMON alarms table
	events	The RMON events table
show route-map		Information about all current route maps; if you provide the name of a route map as an argument, displays information about the specified route map
show rsp		Current memory cache policies
show ip rtp header-compression		RTP compression information
show running-config		The configuration that is currently running
show service-module		Performance information for an integrated CSU/DSU
show sessions		Telnet or rlogin connections to the device
show snapshot		Current snapshot routing information
show snmp		Status of SNMP on the device
	mib	The object IDs supported by the currently loaded MIBs
show sscop		SSCOP details for ATM interfaces
show stacks		Stack utilization of internal processes
show standby		Information about HSRP
show startup-config		The stored configuration that will be used when the router boots
show tacacs		Current TACACS+ statistics
show tcp		Status of all TCP connections
	brief	Summarizes the status of TCP connections
show tech-support		Information to be used when calling for technical support
show terminal		The terminal configuration parameters for the current connection
show users [all]		For all users currently logged in, displays the line number, the username, the user's idle time, and the location of the user's terminal. Use the all keyword to show all lines, even if no one is connected to them.
show version		Boot image, memory, interfaces, and config-register settings
show vc		Active virtual circuits

Table 15-18: Common show commands (continued)

Command	Subcommand	Displays
show vpdn		Session and tunnel information for a virtual private dial-up network
	session	Information about L2F or L2TP sessions in a virtual private dial-up network
	tunnel	Information about L2F or L2TP tunnels in a virtual private dial-up network
show whoami		Information about the current user

shutdown   interface

```
shutdown
no shutdown
```

Description

This command shuts down the interface: no packets will be routed to it and all routing protocols will be notified that the interface is unavailable. It is a common mistake for new users to configure the interface and forget to do a no shutdown.

Example

Use the following sequence of commands to reset an interface:

```
Router(config)#interface serial0
Router(config)#shutdown
Router(config)#no shutdown
```

smt-queue-threshold   global

```
smt-queue-threshold number
no smt-queue-threshold number
```

Configures   FDDI queue size

Default   The number of FDDI interfaces on the router

Description

This command sets the queue size for unprocessed FDDI station management frames (SMT) to *number* frames.

snapshot   interface

```
snapshot client active-time quiet-time [suppress-statechange-updates] [dialer]
no snapshot client active-time quiet-time [suppress-statechange-updates]
    [dialer]

snapshot server active-time [dialer]
no snapshot server active-time [dialer]
```

Configures   Snapshot routing

Default   Disabled

Description

Configures a client or a server router for snapshot routing. Snapshot routing is useful for dial-on-demand connections where you don't want routing updates to bring up the link but you still want to use a dynamic routing protocol (as opposed to static routes). When performing snapshot routing, the router alternates between active periods, when it contacts all the route servers and builds a snapshot route table, and quiet periods, when the snapshot route table is used and no route updates are performed.

active-time
>   Time in minutes during which routing updates are exchanged between client and server. The value can be from 5 to 100.

quiet-time
>   Time in minutes for which routing updates are suppressed after an active period.

suppress-statechange-updates
>   Optional. Disables routing updates during interface state changes.

dialer
>   Optional. Tells the router that it needs to dial the remote router.

Example

To configure a client for snapshot routing:

```
interface dialer 1
  snapshot client 2 100 suppress-statechange-updates dialer
```

To configure a server for snapshot routing:

```
interface dialer 1
  snapshot server 2
```

---

snmp-server   command

```
no snmp-server
```

Configures   Disables SNMP

Default   Enabled

Description

This command, which is not part of the router's configuration, disables the router's SNMP agent. It exists only in the negative form.

---

snmp-server chassis-id   global

```
snmp-server chassis-id string
no snmp-server chassis-id
```

Configures   A number to identify the device

Default

Certain high-end routers use their serial number as the default; otherwise, no default

Description

This command sets the value of the router's serial number to *string*. The chassis ID can be obtained via SNMP. This number is assigned by the user, and is not necessarily the serial number of the router.

Example

```
snmp-server chassis-id 123456789
```

---

snmp-server community   global

```
snmp-server community string [view view-name] {ro | rw} [access-list]
no snmp-server community string
```

Configures   SNMP community access strings

Default   Read-only access; community string `public`

Description

This command sets the community string for SNMPv1 protocol access.

string
> The password for the SNMP access.

view *view-name*
> Optional. *view-name* is the name of a view defined with the `snmp-server view` command. `view` defines which SNMP objects can be viewed with this SNMP community string.

ro
> Defines the community string for read-only access.

rw
> Defines the community string for read/write access.

access-list
> Optional. The number of a standard access list. The community string defined with this command is usable only by hosts whose IP addresses match this access list.

Example

The following command defines the community string `mystring`, which allows read-only access from any IP address.

```
snmp-server community mystring RO
```

snmp-server contact   global

```
snmp-server contact text
no snmp-server contact
```

Configures   SNMP agent

Default   None

Description

This command sets the value of the SNMP contact string (`system.sysContact`). It has no effect on the router's behavior. You can provide any text, but by convention, you should include contact information for the person responsible for administering the router.

---

snmp-server enable traps   global

```
snmp-server enable traps [type] [option]
no snmp-server enable traps [type] [option]
```

Configures   SNMP agent; trap behavior

Default   Disabled; with no arguments, this command enables all traps

Description

This command enables SNMP traps. Traps are unsolicited messages from the router to the management stations. Usually, traps notify the management station of an event or error. At least one trap recipient must be defined (using the `snmp-server host` command) before any traps are generated.

type
> Optional. This command allows you to enable or disable a specific trap type. Valid trap types are shown in Table 15-19.

option
> Any options that are valid for the trap type. Most trap types do not have any options; the exceptions are `atm pvc`, `envmon`, `isdn`, and `repeater`.

Table 15-19, the list of trap types, is a puzzle. Cisco's documentation shows similar but different lists of trap types for this command and `snmp-server host`. Since the commands are used together, there's no reason why the two trap lists should be different. It would be easy to write this off as mistaken documentation, but a check on some routers reveals that the built-in help for these commands also shows different trap lists. Table 15-19 lists all the traps, regardless of which command accepts them as arguments; it indicates whether a trap is documented for `snmp-server enable traps`, `snmp-server host`, or both. Use it in good health. Fortunately, the traps for which there is disagreement correspond to fairly exotic features that aren't on all routers.

Table 15-19: Valid trap types

Trap type	Description	enable/host
atm pvc	ATM Permanent Virtual Circuit information. Options are interval *seconds* and fail-interval *seconds*.	enable
bgp	Border Gateway Protocol state change information	both
config	Configuration changes on the router	both
dspu	Downstream Physical Unit notifications	host
entity	Entity MIB modifications	both
envmon	Environment monitor traps (7000 series). Options are voltage, shutdown, fan, supply, temperature.	both
frame-relay	Frame Relay traps	both
hsrp	Hot Standby Routing modifications	both
isdn	ISDN traps. Options are call-information and isdn u-interface.	both
llc2	Logical Link Control, type 2 traps	host
repeater	Ethernet hub repeater traps. Options are health, reset.	both
rsrb	Remote Source Route Bridging traps	host
rsvp	Resource Reservation Protocol notifications	both
rtr	Response Time Reporter notifications	both
sdlc	SDLC traps	host
sdllc	SDLLC traps	host
snmp	SNMP specific traps	both
stun	Serial tunnel traps	host
syslog	Error message traps	both
tty	Cisco Enterprise–specific traps	host
x25	X25-specific traps	host

snmp-server engine-id global

```
snmp-server engine-id local string
no snmp-server engine-id
```

Configures   SNMP Version 3

Default   None

Description

This command sets the ID of the router's SNMP engine to *string*. The engine ID is used by SNMP Version 3 when it computes various cryptographic keys. This book doesn't cover SNMPv3 configuration, so there isn't a lot to say about the engine ID. However, if you have configured SNMPv3, it is important to know that changing the engine ID has many side effects, including invalidating the authentication information for all SNMP users.

The ID string is 24 characters long. If you do not specify the entire 24 characters, it will be padded with zeros on the right.

snmp-server group   global

```
snmp-server group [name access] [mode view] [access access-list]
no snmp-server group
```

Configures   SNMP

Default   No groups defined

Description

This command allows you to associate one or more views (defined by the **snmp-server view** command) in a group for the purpose of controlling access to the data objects included in the view.

name access

> The *name* of the group, followed by the type of *access* allowed to the group. The *name* is any string; possible values for *access* are listed in Table 15-20.

> *Table 15-20: Types of SNMP access*

Access type	Privileges granted
v1	Access allowed to SNMP Version 1 managers (insecure)
v2c	Access allowed to SNMP Version 2 managers (insecure)
v3 auth	Access allowed to SNMP Version 3 managers; cryptographic authentication required; the packets themselves are not encrypted
v3 noauth	Access allowed to SNMP Version 3 managers; no authentication required (insecure)
v3 priv	Access allowed to SNMP Version 3 managers; cryptographic authentication required; the packets are encrypted

mode view

> The mode in which access is granted, followed by the name of the view to which the privileges apply. *mode* may be either **read** (read-only access), **write** (write-only access), or **notify** (access to traps and notifications). Cisco recommends against using the **notify** option; use the **snmp-server host** command to control trap destinations. In one command, you can specify a read view, a write view, and a notify view. If you don't specify any views, the router generates a group that contains a read-only view of the entire Internet (1.3.6.1) object tree.

access access-list

> An access list that controls access to the group.

If you're using SNMPv3, you must also use the **snmp-server user** command to define users and their cryptographic keys.

---

snmp-server host   global

```
snmp-server host hostname [version {1 | 2c}] community [udp-port port]
    trap-type
no snmp-server host hostname
```

Configures   SNMP agent; trap behavior

Default   Disabled

Description

This command defines which host should receive SNMP traps.

hostname
> The hostname or IP address of the host that should receive traps.

version *n*
> The version of SNMP to use (1 or 2c).

community
> The SNMP community string to use when sending traps to this host.

udp-port *port*
> The UDP port to use. Default is 162.

trap-type
> Optional. Specifies which types of traps are sent to this host. If no trap type is specified, all traps are sent to this host. Possible values are listed in Table 15-19, under the command `snmp-server enable traps`.

Example
```
snmp-server enable traps
snmp-server host myhost.xyz.com public
```

---

snmp-server location   global

```
snmp-server location text
no snmp-server location
```

Configures   SNMP agent

Default   None

Description

This command sets the SNMP location string (`system.sysLocation`). It has no effect on the router's behavior. This can be any text, but it should represent the router's physical location.

---

snmp-server packetsize   global

```
snmp-server packetsize size
no snmp-server packetsize size
```

Configures   SNMP agent

Default   1500 bytes

Description

This command controls the maximum packet size for SNMP. The *size* can be 484 to 8192 bytes.

---

snmp-server queue-length global

```
snmp-server queue-length length
no snmp-server queue-length length
```

Configures   SNMP message queue length

Default   10 traps

Description

This command specifies the number of SNMP trap packets that can be held for each trap destination before the queue is cleared.

---

snmp-server system-shutdown global

```
snmp-server system-shutdown
no snmp-server system-shutdown
```

Configures   SNMP agent

Default   Disabled

Description

This command enables or disables the SNMP remote reload feature, which allows a remote host with the SNMP read/write community string to reboot the router. The no form of this command disables this feature.

---

snmp-server tftp-server-list global

```
snmp-server tftp-server-list access-list
no snmp-server tftp-server-list
```

Configures   SNMP agent

Default   Disabled

Description

This command allows an access list to be applied to SNMP TFTP server tasks, which include loading and saving of configuration files.

---

snmp-server trap-source global

```
snmp-server trap-source interface
no snmp-server trap-source
```

Configures   SNMP agent; trap behavior

Default   The router uses the closest interface to the destination

Description

This command specifies the interface (and consequently the IP address) that should be used to send SNMP traps. If you have a separate network for management tasks (a good idea), you can use this command to ensure that traps are sent only over the management network.

Example

The following command tells the router that all SNMP traps should be sent via the ethernet0 interface:

```
snmp-server trap-source ethernet0
```

---

snmp-server trap-timeout   global

```
snmp-server trap-timeout seconds
no snmp-server trap-timeout seconds
```

Configures   Time to keep an SNMP trap in the queue

Default   30 seconds

Description

If the device wants to send a trap to a host that is unavailable, the device puts the trap in a queue. This command states how long the packet will remain in the queue before timing out and being retransmitted.

---

snmp-server user   global

```
snmp-server user name group version [encrypted] [auth hash auth-pwd
    [priv des56 priv-pwd]] [access access-list]
no snmp-server user name
```

Configures   SNMP users

Default   None

Description

This command defines SNMP users, associates them with a group (which in turn defines the information they're allowed to view), and specifies encryption requirements together with the appropriate passwords.

name
> The name of the user you are defining.

group
> The SNMP group the user is associated with.

version
> The version of SNMP that is in use. Possible values are v1, v2c, and v3; v3 is the only version that supports encryption.

encrypted

If this keyword is present, the *auth-pwd* and *priv-pwd* passwords are present as an MD5 hash rather than in plain text.

auth *hash auth-pwd*

SNMPv3 only. Configures an authentication key for the user. *hash* is the name of the hashing algorithm used to create the key; possibilities are md5 and sha. *auth-pwd* is the actual password assigned to the user. The router stores this password in encrypted form.

priv des56 *priv-pwd*

SNMPv3 only. Configures an encryption key for the user, using the des56 algorithm. (Currently, des56 is the only algorithm supported.) *priv-pwd* is the actual password assigned to the user. The router stores this password in encrypted form.

access *access-list*

Optional. An access list that restricts the hosts from which the user can access the group.

The encryption of the password and the authentication key depend on the router's SNMP engine ID. This ID is set with the command snmp-server engineid. Changing the engine ID therefore invalidates all users that are currently defined.

---

snmp-server view   global

```
snmp-server view view-name oid-tree {excluded | included}
no snmp-server view
```

Configures   An SNMP view

Default   None

Description

This command defines an SNMP view that can be used in the snmp-server community command. A view is a list of SNMP object trees. By default, the entire SNMP object tree is available for access. A view restricts access to some subset of the entire tree. Different views can be made available to different SNMP communities.

view *view-name*

A unique name that identifies this SNMP view.

oid-tree

An SNMP object ID (in either numeric or human-readable form). All nodes underneath the given object belong to the tree. Asterisks can be used as wild-cards when specifying the object ID.

excluded *or* included

Specifies whether the given *oid-tree* is included in or excluded from the view.

Example

Say that you want to give some group SNMP access to the ifEntry table for inter-face 2. (Perhaps this group is connected to the router through interface 2. Note that the interface number here is an index into the SNMP interface table, not an IOS interface name.) To achieve this, define a view:

```
snmp-server view subset2 ifEntry.*.2 included
```

Then set the community string for this view:

```
snmp-server community sub2in view subset2 RO
```

Now users can use the community string sub2in to access the ifEntry table for interface 2, but aren't allowed to access other SNMP objects.

---

snmp trap link-status   interface

```
snmp trap link-status
no snmp trap link-status
```

Configures   SNMP agent; trap behavior

Default   Enabled

Description

This command allows you to enable or disable the sending of SNMP traps when an interface goes up and down. This command is useful on interfaces that you expect to change state frequently (for example, dial-on-demand interfaces). You may not want to send an SNMP trap to your network management stations when-ever these interfaces change state.

---

source-address   interface (hub)

```
source-address mac-address
no source-address mac-address
```

Configures   Hub behavior

Default   All addresses are allowed

Description

The source-address command allows you to specify a MAC address that will be the only traffic source for a specific port. In other words, only network traffic from the specified *mac-address* will be allowed on the port. By default, traffic from all MAC addresses is accepted on all hub ports.

Example

The following commands restrict the traffic forwarded to port 0 of hub 4 to traffic with the source Ethernet address of 00:00:0c:ff:d0:04.

```
hub ethernet 0 4
   source-address 0000.0cff.d004
```

---

speed   line

```
speed bits-per-second
no speed
```

Configures   Transmit and receive speeds for a line

Default   9600 bps

Description

This command sets the transmit and receive speeds for this line to *bits-per-second*. Use the no form of this command to remove the command from the configuration and return to the default setting.

---

squeeze   command

```
squeeze filesystem:
```

Description

This command cleans the filesystem by permanently deleting files that have been marked for deletion. It works only for Class A filesystems; it is ignored on other filesystem types.

---

squelch   interface

```
squelch {normal | reduced}
no squelch {normal | reduced}
```

Configures

Allows certain interfaces to extend the 10baseT limit of 100 meter cables

Default   Normal

Description

This command allows a 10baseT segment to exceed the 100-meter cable length limitation. Currently, this option is available only on the Cisco 4000-series router.

normal
    The default setting for a 10baseT Ethernet segment.

reduced
    Allows 10baseT cables beyond the 100-meter length.

---

sscop cc-timer   interface

```
sscop cc-timer seconds
no sscop cc-timer
```

Configures   ATM

Default   10 seconds

Description

This command sets the SSCOP connection control timer value to *seconds*. This value determines the transmission times between SSCOP BGN, END, or RS PDUs.

---

sscop keepalive-timer
interface

```
sscop keepalive-timer seconds
no sscop keepalive-timer
```

Configures   The ATM SSCOP keepalive timer

Default   30 seconds

Description

This command sets the keepalive timer to *seconds*. This value determines the number of seconds between polling PDUs when no other traffic is transmitted.

---

sscop max-cc
interface

```
sscop max-cc retries
no sscop maxcc
```

Configures   Maximum number of transmits of control messages for SSCOP

Default   10 retries

Description

This command sets the maximum number of times that SSCOP sends control messages until an acknowledgment is received. The value of *retries* can range from 1 to 1600.

---

sscop poll-timer
interface

```
sscop poll-timer seconds
no sscop poll-timer
```

Configures   ATM SSCOP poll timer

Default   10 seconds

Description

This command sets the number of *seconds* between SSCOP poll PDUs.

---

sscop rcv-window
interface

```
sscop rcv-window packets
no sscop rcv-window
```

Configures   ATM SSCOP receive window in packets

Default   7 packets

Description

This command sets the size of the receive window in *packets*. This value determines the number of packets the interface receives before sending an acknowledgment. The value of *packets* can range from 1 to 6000.

---

sscop send-window   interface

```
sscop send-window packets
no sscop send-window packets
```

Configures   ATM SSCOP send window in packets

Default   7 packets

Description

This command sets the size of the send window in *packets*. This value determines the number of packets the interface transmits before expecting an acknowledgment. The value of *packets* can range from 1 to 6000.

---

standby authentication   interface

```
standby [group] authentication string
no standby [group] authentication string
```

Configures   HSRP authentication string

Default   Group, 0; authentication string, "cisco"

Description

This command enables authentication for a hot standby group. *group* specifies the hot standby group number, and *string* sets the authentication string (essentially a password). All HSRP routers must use the same authentication string in order to communicate. *string* can be from 1 to 8 characters long.

Example

```
interface serial 0
  ip address 10.1.2.1 255.255.255.0
  standby 1 authentication letmein
```

---

standby ip   interface

```
standby [group] ip address [secondary]
no standby [group] ip address [secondary]
```

Configures   Hot Standby Routing Protocol (HSRP)

Default   None; *group* defaults to 0

Description

This command enables the specified IP *address* to be used as the HSRP address. The optional secondary keyword is useful if the interface has a secondary IP address applied to it. (See Chapter 5 for a discussion of secondary IP addresses.)

---

standby preempt   interface

```
standby [group] preempt
no standby [group] preempt
```

Configures   Hot Standby Routing Protocol (HSRP)

Default   Disabled; *group* defaults to 0

Description

This command instructs the interface to become the active HSRP interface if no other HSRP router within the given *group* has a higher priority. In other words, if this interface becomes active and has the standby preempt command, it interrupts any other HSRP interface and becomes the active HSRP interface. The default group number is 0.

---

standby priority   interface

```
standby [group] priority value
no standby [group] priority value
```

Configures   Hot Standby Routing Protocol (HSRP)

Default   Group, 0; priority value, 100

Description

This command defines the interface's HSRP priority within the given *group*. The priority *value* can be from 0 to 255.

---

standby timers   interface

```
standby [group] timers hello-seconds hold-seconds
no standby [group] timers hello-seconds hold-seconds
```

Configures   Hot Standby Routing Protocol (HSRP)

Default   Group, 0; hello seconds, 1; hold seconds, 3

Description

This command allows you to change the hello and hold intervals for HSRP. If this router doesn't hear from another router in this HSRP *group* for a period of *hello-seconds*, the other router is considered "down." Once a router is declared "down," it is considered down for a period of at least *hold-seconds*.

---

standby track interface

```
standby [group] track interface [interface-priority]
no standby [group] track interface [interface-priority]
```

Configures   Hot Standby Routing Protocol (HSRP)

Default   Group, 0; interface priority, 10

Description

This command configures the HSRP interface to track another *interface*. If the other interface goes down, the HSRP interface's standby priority decreases by the value *interface-priority*. The rationale for this behavior is that if the tracked interface is down, this router is less desirable as a standby router. The standby track command must be used in combination with the preempt command.

Example

In this example, ethernet0 is the HSRP interface tracking interface serial0. If serial0 goes down, ethernet0's priority is decreased by 20. When serial0 comes back up, ethernet0's priority is increased by 20 (i.e., returned to its original value).

```
interface ethernet0
  standby 1 ip 10.10.1.1
  standby 1 preempt
  standby 1 track serial0 20
```

stopbits line

```
stopbits {1 | 1.5 | 2}
no stopbits
```

Configures   The stop bits transmitted per byte

Default   2

Description

This command sets the stop bits transmitted per byte for the specified line. The settings are limited to 1, 1.5, or 2 stop bits.

summary-address router, OSPF, IS-IS, BGP

BGP:

```
summary-address address subnet-mask
no summary-address address subnet-mask
```

OSPF:

```
summary-address address subnet-mask [not-advertise] [tag tag-value]
no summary-address address subnet-mask
```

IS-IS:
```
summary-address address subnet-mask {level-1 | level-2 | level-1-2}
no summary-address address subnet-mask {level-1 | level-2 | level-1-2}
```

Configures Route summarization

Default Disabled

Description

This command allows you to create a single route that covers a set of smaller routes, thus reducing the number of routes in the routing table. Use the no form of the command to return to the default, where the router does not summarize routes.

address
> The destination address for the summarized route.

subnet-mask
> A subnet mask that indicates which addresses should be included in the summarized route.

level-1, level-2, level-1-2
> IS-IS only. The router summarizes only routes that are being redistributed into the given level.

not-advertise
> Optional. OSPF only. Routes are not advertised when translating a type 7 link state announcement from OSPF.

tag *tag-value*
> Optional. OSPF only. Used as a match value for route maps.

Example

Assume that we know routes for 10.10.1.0, 10.10.2.0, 10.10.3.0, and so on. Instead of advertising separate routes, we can summarize by combining these routes into a single route for 10.10.0.0:

```
summary-address 10.10.0.0 255.255.0.0
```

---

synchronization   BGP

```
synchronization
no synchronization
```

Configures Synchronization between a BGP and an IGP protocol

Default Enabled

Description

The no form of this command causes the router to advertise a network route without waiting for the other routing protocol. The rule of synchronization says that an IBGP router cannot advertise a route until the route is known via an IGP routing protocol. See Chapter 10 for more information about the synchronization command.

---

table-map

```
table-map route-map
no table-map route-map
```

Configures   Behavior of BGP routes

Default   None

Description

This command allows you to specify a route map that modifies metric and tag values when the routing table is updated with routes learned from BGP. The given *route-map* is called whenever the routing table is updated with BGP routes.

This command can also be used to filter routes from entering the routing table without preventing them from being maintained and propagated by BGP.

tacacs-server attempts

```
tacacs-server attempts count
no tacacs-server attempts count
```

Configures   Number of attempts to reach the TACACS server

Default   3

Description

This command sets the maximum number of times the router attempts to reach the TACACS, extended TACACS, or TACACS+ server before deciding that the server is unavailable.

tacacs-server authenticate

```
tacacs-server authenticate connection [always]
tacacs-server authenticate enable
tacacs-server authenticate slip [always] [access-lists]
no tacacs-server authenticate
```

Configures   User authentication with TACACS and extended TACACS

Default   Disabled

Description

This command causes the router to contact the TACACS server and authenticate the user under the following conditions:

connection
    When the user makes a TCP connection.

enable
    When the user enters the enable command.

```
slip
```
    When the user starts a SLIP or PPP connection.

For authenticating TCP or SLIP connections, the `always` keyword indicates that the router should always perform authentication even if the user is not logged in. Note that it is possible for a SLIP or PPP user to be connected, but not yet logged in. For authenticating SLIP connections, the `access-lists` keyword tells the router to check with the TACACS server to see if an access list needs to be installed for the user.

If you are using TACACS+, use the `aaa authorization` command instead of the `tacacs-server authenticate` command.

---

tacacs-server directed-request   global

```
tacacs-server directed-request
no tacacs-server directed-request
```

Configures   Which TACACS server is contacted

Default   Enabled

Description

This command causes the router to split each username into two parts, separated by the @ symbol. The first part is the actual username used for authentication; the second part is the name of the TACACS server to send the request to. Disabling this feature causes the TACACS servers to be queried in order; the entire username string is used for authentication.

---

tacacs-server extended   global

```
tacacs-server extended
no tacacs-server extended
```

Configures   Extended TACACS

Default   Disabled

Description

If you have an extended TACACS server, this command enables the extended TACACS protocol.

---

tacacs-server host   global

```
tacacs-server host hostname [single-connection] [port number] [timeout seconds
    [key string]
no tacacs-server host hostname
```

Configures   The hostname of a TACACS server

Default   None

Description

This command allows you to list the TACACS servers you have available. If you list more than one hostname, the router attempts to contact them in the order they are listed.

hostname

> The hostname of a TACACS, extended TACACS, or TACACS+ server.

single-connection

> Optional. This keyword specifies that the router maintains a single connection to the TACACS server. In other words, after making a request, the router waits on the same connection for the server to respond. This feature works only with the TACACS+ protocol and CiscoSecure.

port number

> Optional. Use this option to run your TACACS server on a different port than the default (port 49).

timeout seconds

> Optional. This option allows you to specify a timeout value for this server in *seconds*. It overrides the default or the global setting configured by the tacacs-server timeout command.

key string

> Optional. This option allows you to specify an encryption key for this server. It overrides the global setting configured by the tacacs-server key command.

---

tacacs-server key   global

```
tacacs-server key key-string
no tacacs-server key
```

Configures   TACACS encryption key

Default   None

Description

This command sets the encryption key for the TACACS server.

---

tacacs-server last-resort   global

```
tacacs-server last-resort {password | succeed}
no tacacs-server last-resort {password | succeed}
```

Configures   Behavior if the TACACS server doesn't respond

Default   The request is denied

Description

This command sets the router's behavior when the TACACS servers you have configured don't respond to a request. For security reasons, the default behavior is

---

to deny the request. The `password` keyword challenges the user for the enable password before authorizing the action. The `succeed` keyword simply allows the action, and is discouraged because it blindly allows the user to do what they want without authorization.

tacacs-server notify global

```
tacacs-server notify {connection [always] | enable | logout [always] |
    slip [always]}
no tacacs-server notify
```

Configures   Sends messages to the TACACS server

Default   None

Description

This command tells the router to send messages to the TACACS server for accounting. It does not work with TACACS+; for that protocol, use the `aaa accounting` command. The following keywords specify when messages are sent:

connection
> When a connection is made by a user.

always
> Optional. A message is sent even if the user is not logged in. Note that it is possible for a SLIP or PPP user to be connected but not yet logged in.

enable
> When a user uses the enable command.

logout
> When a user logs out.

slip
> When a user starts a SLIP or PPP connection.

tacacs-server optional-passwords global

```
tacacs-server optional-passwords
no tacacs-server optional-passwords
```

Configures   Password authentication

Default   Disabled

Description

This command makes the user's password optional, depending on the TACACS server's configuration. When this feature is enabled, the router tries to authenticate the user with the username only. If that fails, the router tries again with both the username and password.

This command is for TACACS and extended TACACS only; it does not work with TACACS+.

tacacs-server retransmit

```
tacacs-server retransmit number-of-times
no tacacs-server retransmit
```

Configures   Number of times to try a TACACS server before giving up

Default   2

Description

This command sets the number of times the router should try to contact a TACACS, extended TACACS, or TACACS+ server before giving up and moving on to the next server.

tacacs-server timeout

```
tacacs-server timeout seconds
no tacacs-server timeout
```

Configures   The amount of time to wait for a response from a TACACS server

Default   5 seconds

Description

This command sets the maximum amount of time that the router should wait to receive a response from a TACACS, extended TACACS, or TACACS+ server. If the router doesn't receive a response within this time, it retries the connection attempt. The number of retries is set by the `tacacs-server retransmit` command.

terminal editing

```
terminal editing
terminal no editing
```

Configures   Advanced editing keys for the terminal session

Default   Enabled

Description

This command is enabled by default, allowing you to use control keys for advanced editing capabilities. These key sequences are listed in Chapter 1. Use the no form of the command to disable the advanced editing keys.

terminal escape-character

```
terminal escape-character ASCII-value
```

Configures   The escape character for the terminal line

Default   Ctrl-^ (Control+Shift-6)

Description

This command sets the value for the escape terminal character to *ASCII-value*, which is the ASCII value for the desired character. The escape character is used to escape certain processes in a router. For example, if you are pinging a device that isn't responding, you can cancel the ping by typing the escape character.

---

terminal history   command

```
terminal history [size number]
terminal no history
```

Configures   Terminal history for the current session

Default   Enabled; 10 lines

Description

This command enables history logging for the current session; it can also be used to change the size of the history buffer for that session. To enable history logging, use the `terminal history` command, which takes the last-used size as the buffer size. To change the size of the current history buffer, use the `size` keyword followed by the *number* of lines you want to save in the buffer. The buffer's size can be from 1 to 256 lines.

Use Ctrl-P or the up arrow to go up in the history list; use Ctrl-N or the down arrow to return to more recent commands in the list. To see the entire list, use `show history`.

Example

This example changes the history size to 100:

```
router# terminal history size 100
```

---

terminal length   command

```
terminal length number-of-lines
```

Configures   Window page size

Default   24 lines

Description

This command sets the size of the window for the current user session to *number-of-lines*. If output from any command exceeds your window size, the router suspends output and prompts you for a keystroke (—More—). This command is useful if you are using a terminal or terminal emulator with a viewing area that is not 24 lines long. Set *number-of-lines* to 0 to disable the —More— prompt.

Warning: Setting the length to 0, which disables paging, can be useful, but it can present a problem on long output.

Example

To set the window size to 10:

```
Router#terminal length 10
```

To disable the —more— prompt:

```
Router#terminal length 0
```

---

terminal monitor

command

```
terminal monitor
terminal no monitor
```

Configures

Debug and system error messages for the current terminal and session

Default   Disabled

Description

This command enables the display of debugging messages and system error messages for the current terminal (i.e., VTY or asynchronous line) session. It does not apply to the console itself; to disable console logging, use the command no logging console.

---

tftp-server

global

```
tftp-server flash [flash-partition-number:]filename [alias filename]
    [access-list]
tftp-server rom alias filename [access-list]
no tftp-server {flash | rom}
```

Configures   TFTP server

Default   Disabled

Description

The tftp-server flash command allows the router to act as a TFTP server that serves files from its flash filesystem. The *flash-partition-number* is the number of the specified partition number within the flash filesystem. If no partition is specified, the first partition is used. The *filename* is the name of the file that the TFTP service uses in answering read requests. The alias keyword allows you to provide an alternate name for the file.

The tftp-server rom command configures the router to serve the contents of its ROM using TFTP. The alias keyword, which is required for this form of the command, provides a name to be used to access the ROM contents.

Either form of the command allows you to specify an *access-list* that limits the hosts allowed to make incoming TFTP requests.

timers basic

```
timers basic update-value invalid-value holddown-value flush-value
[sleeptime-value]
no timers basic
```

Configures   Routing protocol timers

Default   The default timer values are shown in Table 15-21

Table 15-21: Default timer values

Timer	IGRP	RIP default
Update	90 seconds	30 seconds
Invalid	270 seconds	180 seconds
Holddown	280 seconds	180 seconds
Flush	630 seconds	240 seconds
Sleeptime	0 milliseconds	N/A

Description

This command allows you to adjust the routing timers. All values expect for *sleeptime* are in seconds.

update-value
> The interval at which routing updates are sent.

invalid-value
> The interval after which a route is considered invalid if an update does not arrive.

holddown-value
> The time that the router waits after deciding that a route is invalid before accepting further information about it. For example, if a router decides that a certain route has become invalid, it waits for the hold-down period to pass before believing any other information stating that the route is valid. This procedure helps to maintain routing stability.

flush-value
> The interval after which invalid routes are purged from the routing table.

sleeptime-value
> Optional. This timer's value is the interval in milliseconds to wait after a flash update. This value should be less than the update value. Sleeptime is not applicable to RIP.

timers bgp

```
timers bgp keepalive holdtime
no timers bgp
```

Configures   BGP timers

Default   *keepalive,* 60 seconds; *holdtime,* 180 seconds

Description

This command allows you to configure the keepalive and holdtime timers for BGP. *keepalive* specifies the interval in seconds between the keepalive message that a router sends to its peer routers. *holdtime* is the time in seconds after which a peer is considered unreachable because a keepalive message wasn't received.

timers spf   router

```
timers spf delay-time hold-time
no timers spf delay-time hold-time
```

Configures   OSPF timers

Default   Delay time, 5 seconds; hold time, 10 seconds

Description

This command sets the two types of timers that are important to the OSPF protocol. *delay-time* is the interval in seconds between the arrival of a topology change and the time BGP starts the shortest path first (SPF) calculation. *hold-time* is the minimum interval between two consecutive SPF calculations. Both timers must be in the range 0 to 65535. Reducing these values may cause the router to switch to a different path more quickly, but this may be a detriment to performance; the SPF calculation is CPU-intensive.

trace   command

```
trace [host]
```

Description

This command allows you to determine the most likely path to a specified *host*. It is often useful in troubleshooting, and is similar to the `traceroute` command on Unix systems or the `tracert` command on Windows systems. If you omit the hostname, you'll be prompted for the necessary information. As with the `ping` command, the prompts differ depending on the mode you are in. The output from the `trace` command uses the special characters shown in Table 15-22.

Table 15-22: Special characters for trace output

Character	Meaning
xx msec	Round-trip time in milliseconds
*	Packet timeout
?	Unknown packet received
A	Administratively unreachable; possibly means that an access list or equivalent function on another router is blocking the packets
H	Host is unreachable
N	Network is unreachable
P	Protocol is unreachable

Table 15-22: Special characters for trace output (continued)

Character	Meaning
Q	Source quench
U	Port unreachable

Example

This example shows what happens when you use the trace command without supplying a hostname. Note that you're prompted for many values that can't be specified on the command line. Omitting the hostname therefore gives you more control over the command's behavior than you would otherwise have.

```
Router#trace
    Protocol [ip]:                    Protocol
    Target IP address: 10.10.1.2      Can be hostname or network address
    Source address:                   The IP address of the interface to use
    Numeric display [n]: y            Numeric display is not the default
    Timeout in seconds [3]:           Seconds to wait for each probe
    Probe count [3]:                  Number of probes to execute at each TTL.
    Minimum Time to Live [1]:         The first TTL level to begin the trace
    Maximum Time to Live [30]:        The TTL level to stop the trace
    Port Number [33434]:              The UDP port number to probe
    Loose, Strict, Record, Timestamp, Verbose[none]:    Header Options

    Type escape sequence to abort.
    Tracing the route to 10.10.1.2
      1 10.10.1.2 0 msec 4 msec 0 msec
```

traffic-shape adaptive   interface

```
traffic-shape adaptive [bit-rate]
no traffic-shape adaptive
```

Configures   Traffic shaping on a Frame Relay subinterface

Default   Disabled

Description

This command enables traffic shaping on a Frame Relay subinterface. Traffic shaping means that the interface estimates the available bandwidth on the link when it receives BECNs (backwards explicit congestion notifications). The *bit-rate* parameter is optional and specifies the lowest bit rate (in kbps) at which traffic is shaped.

traffic-shape group   interface

```
traffic-shape group access-list bit-rate [burst-size [excess-burst-size]]
no traffic-shape group access-list
```

Configures   Traffic shaping for general outbound traffic

Default   Disabled

Description

This command allows you to specify an access list that selects the packets to which traffic shaping applies.

access-list

Traffic shaping is applied to packets that match this access list.

bit-rate

The access bit rate in your service contract with your Frame Relay service provider.

burst-size

Optional. The sustained number of bits that can be transmitted per interval, defined in your service contract with your Frame Relay service provider. Default is the *bit-rate* divided by 8.

excess-burst-size

Optional. The maximum number of bits that can exceed the burst size during a congestion event. The default is the *burst-size*.

---

traffic-shape rate   interface

```
traffic-shape rate bit-rate [burst-size [excess-burst-size]]
no traffic-shape rate
```

Configures   Traffic shaping for all outbound traffic

Default   Disabled

Description

This command applies the traffic shaping to all outbound traffic. It is similar to traffic-shape group, but does not use an access list to select traffic.

bit-rate

The access bit rate in your service contract with your Frame Relay service provider.

burst-size

Optional. The sustained number of bits that can be transmitted per interval, as defined in your service contract with your Frame Relay service provider. Default is the *bit-rate* divided by 8.

excess-burst-size

Optional. The maximum number of bits that can exceed the burst size during a congestion event. The default is the *burst-size*.

---

traffic-share   router, IGRP, EIGRP

```
traffic-share {balanced | min}
no traffic-share {balanced | min}
```

Configures

How traffic is distributed when multiple routes exist for the same destination

---

Default   balanced

Description

This command defines the way multiple routes are handled when they have different costs.

balanced
> Traffic is distributed based on the metric ratios.

min
> All traffic is sent using the route with the minimum cost.

---

transport   line

```
transport input protocol
transport output protocol
transport preferred protocol
```

Configures   The transport protocol

Default   Output and preferred, telnet; input, none

Description

This command specifies the transport protocol the router should use. input specifies the protocol to use for incoming connections on a line; output is for output connections on a line; and preferred is the transport protocol to use when the user does not specify one.

Using the command transport preferred none helps to prevent typos at the command line from causing a bogus DNS lookup. (With the default output setting, a mistyped command is frequently interpreted as a hostname for the telnet, initializing a DNS lookup.)

The protocol parameter specifies which protocol to use; possible values are given in Table 15-23.

Table 15-23: Transport protocols

Protocol	Meaning
lat	DEC LAT protocol, when connecting to DEC hosts
mop	Maintenance operation protocol
nasi	Netware asynchronous services interface protocol
none	No protocol selection is to be made on this line
rlogin	The Unix rlogin protocol
telnet	TCP/IP telnet protocol
all	All in the list
v120	ISDN asynchronous protocols

Example

Routers do not allow incoming network connections to a TTY by default, so you must use the `transport input` command to enable this feature:

```
line tty 2
  transport input all
```

---

tunnel checksum   interface

```
tunnel checksum
no tunnel checksum
```

Configures   The checksumming of packets on a tunnel interface

Default   Disabled

Description

This command enables packet checksumming on a tunnel interface. It applies to GRE tunnels only. When enabled, the router drops packets that fail the checksum test.

---

tunnel destination   interface

```
tunnel destination destination
no tunnel destination destination
```

Configures   The IP address or hostname of the tunnel's destination

Default   None

Description

This command specifies the tunnel's destination IP address or hostname.

Example

The following commands set up a tunnel interface called `tunnel0`. The source address for the tunnel is the address of the `serial0` interface; the destination of the tunnel is 172.25.1.1. The tunnel uses the GRE protocol.

```
interface tunnel0
  tunnel source serial0
  tunnel destination 172.25.1.1
  tunnel mode gre ip
```

---

tunnel key   interface

```
tunnel key key
no tunnel key key
```

Configures   A key identifier for a tunnel

Default   None

Description

This command assigns a key to a tunnel. In this case, the *key* is just an integer that serves as a tunnel ID; it is not a cryptographic key. As such, it provides at best very weak security. The range for *key* is 0 to 4294967295.

---

tunnel mode

interface

```
tunnel mode type
no tunnel mode type
```

Configures   The type of tunnel

Default   General Routing Encapsulation (GRE)

Description

This command sets the encapsulation mode for a tunnel. Values for *type* are given in Table 15-24. Both ends of the tunnel must use the same encapsulation type.

Table 15-24: Tunnel types

Tunnel type	Meaning
aurp	AppleTalk Update Routing Protocol
cayman	Cayman TunnelTalk with AppleTalk encapsulation
dvmrp	Distance Vectory Multicast Routing Protocol
eon	EON-compatible CLNS tunnel
gre ip	General Route Encapsulation (GRE) protocol over IP
nos	KA9Q/NOS-compatible over IP

---

tunnel sequence-datagrams

interface

```
tunnel sequence-datagrams
no tunnel sequence-datagrams
```

Configures   The tunnel interface

Default   Disabled

Description

This command tells the tunnel interface to drop any tunnel packets that arrive out of sequence.

---

tunnel source

interface

```
tunnel source source
no tunnel source source
```

Configures   The source IP address of the tunnel

Default   None

Description

This command specifies the tunnel's source IP address.

Example

The following commands set up a tunnel that uses the address of the serial0 interface as its source address. The destination of the tunnel is 172.25.1.1.

```
interface tunnel0
  tunnel source serial0
  tunnel destination 172.25.1.1
  tunnel mode gre ip
```

---

txspeed   line

```
txspeed bits-per-second
no txspeed
```

Configures   Transmit speed

Default   9600 baud

Description

This command sets the transmit speed. Use the no form to remove the command from the configuration.

Example

The following example sets the transmit speed on line 1 to 1200:

```
line 1
  txspeed 1200
```

---

undebug   command

```
undebug {debug-level | all}
```

Description

This command turns off debugging at the selected *debug-level*. Use the all keyword to turn off all currently active debugging.

Example

If you enabled debug with:

```
#debug ip eigrp
```

You can disable it with:

```
#undebug ip eigrp
or
#undebug all
```

undelete

undelete *file-number* [*device:*]

Description

This command allows you to recover deleted files on Class A and B filesystems. The *file-number* is the index of the file in the directory. The *device* field is optional and specifies the flash device you wish to undelete from: bootflash, slot0, or slot1. This command cannot recover files after they have been purged by the squeeze command.

username

username *name* [nopassword | password *password*] [access-class *access-list-number*] [autocommand *command*] [callback-dialstring *phone-number*] [callback-rotary *rotary-group-number*] [callback-line [tty] *line-number* [*ending-line-number*]] [nocallback-verify] [noescape] [nohangup]

Configures   Username information for authentication

Default   None

Description

The username command provides authentication information for a user. It is used to build a username database on the router itself (as opposed to on an external server, like a RADIUS server). Many different types of information can be provided, using the following options:

nopassword
> No password is required for the user; this option is useful when combined with autocommand.

password *password*
> Specifies a password for the user.

access-class *access-list-number*
> Specifies an outgoing access list for the user, overriding the access list specified in the access-class command in the line configuration.

autocommand *command*
> Causes the specified command to be issued automatically when the user connects. This is commonly used to start PPP sessions.

callback-dialstring *phone-number*
> Specifies the phone number to pass to the modem for asynchronous callback.

callback-rotary *rotary-group-number*
> Specifies the rotary group to use for asynchronous callback.

callback-line tty *line-number ending-line-number*
> Specifies which lines can be used for asynchronous callback. The optional tty keyword restricts the callback to TTY lines.

`nocallback-verify`

Callback not required for this user.

`noescape`

Prevents the user from using an escape character.

`nohangup`

Prevents the communication server from disconnecting. The user gets another login prompt when he attempts to disconnect.

Example

The following commands create two users. An access list is applied to the user Bob for the duration of his sessions. The router automatically starts PPP when the user Jane logs in.

```
username bob password letmein access-class 10
username jane password thisisme autocommand ppp
```

---

vacant-message   line

`vacant-message delimiter message text delimiter`
`no vacant-message`

Configures   A message displayed to an idle line

Default   None

Description

This command sets the message that is displayed when a terminal is idle and waiting to begin a session. It is often used at terminals that are connected to routers or access servers for generic network access. The message is specific to a particular line; you must specify the message explicitly for every line. `delimiter` marks the beginning and end of the message; it can be any single character that is not used in the message itself. To disable this message, use the no form of this command.

Example

```
Router(config)#line 2
Router(config-line)#vacant-message # Welcome to the Network,
    Press return to begin! #
```

---

validate-update-source   router

`validate-update-source`
`no validate-update-source`

Configures   Validation of routing sources

Default   Enabled

Description

The `validate-update-source` command checks to make sure that the source IP address of incoming routing updates is on the same network as the interface receiving the update. This feature gives some protection against spoofing attacks.

Example

To disable this feature, use the no form of this command:

```
router rip
  network 10.10.0.0
  no validate-update-source
```

---

variance   EIGRP, IGRP

```
variance multipler-value
no variance multipler-value
```

Configures   Multiplier value for load balancing

Default   1 (equal-cost load balancing)

Description

This command lets you specify a *multiplier-value* for use in load balancing with IGRP and EIGRP. The *multiplier-value* can be from 1 to 128. Routes within a factor of *multiplier-value* of the best routes are used to carry traffic. Normally, all traffic is sent over the route with the best metric; if two or more routes share the same metric, load balancing takes place between those routes.

Example

Assume that your router has three routes to the same destination. The routes have metrics of 10, 30, and 50. With the default variance of 1 (equal-cost load balancing), all traffic is sent using the route with the metric of 10. For load balancing to take place, another route with a metric of 10 must appear in the routing table.

To force the router to use multiple paths in this situation, you can change the variance (unequal-cost load balancing). If you increase the variance to 3, routes with a metric within a factor of 3 of the best route are used. In this situation, the routes with metrics of 10 and 30 will be used to carry traffic, and the route with a metric of 50 will not.

```
router eigrp 100
  variance 5
```

---

verify   command

```
verify {flash | bootflash}
```

Description

This command verifies the *flash* checksum value with the stored flash image.

Example

```
Router#verify flash

System flash directory:
File  Length   Name/status
```

```
    1   6070088  igs-j-1.110-3
[6070152 bytes used, 2318456 available, 8388608 total]

Name of file to verify? igs-j-1.110-3
Verifying checksum for 'igs-j-1.110-3' (file # 1)...  OK
```

---

version router (RIP)

```
version {1 | 2}
no version
```

Configures   Version of RIP protocol to use

Default   Accepts both versions but transmits only Version 1

Description

This command specifies which version of the RIP protocol to use. The `ip rip` command can also be used to select the RIP protocol version.

Example

The following commands configure the router to communicate only with RIPv2.

```
router rip
    network 10.10.0.0
    version 2
```

---

vty-async global

```
vty-async
no vty-async
```

Configures   VTY line features

Default   Disabled

Description

This command configures all virtual terminal lines to support asynchronous protocol features.

---

vty-async dynamic-routing global

```
vty-async dynamic-routing
no vty-async dynamic-routing
```

Configures   VTY line features

Default   Disabled

Description

This command enables dynamic routing on all VTY asynchronous lines.

vty-async header-compression

global

```
vty-async header-compression [passive]
no vty-async header-compression
```

Configures   VTY line features

Default   Disabled

Description

This command enables header compression on all VTY asynchronous lines. The
passive keyword is optional. It tells the router to compress headers only if
headers on the incoming packets on the same line are compressed as well.

vty-async keepalive

global

```
vty-async keepalive seconds
no vty-async keepalive seconds
```

Configures   VTY line features

Default   10 seconds

Description

This command specifies the keepalive frequency on VTY asynchronous lines. The
value can be from 1 to 32767.

vty-async mtu

global

```
vty-async mtu bytes
no vty-async mtu
```

Configures   VTY line features

Default   1500 bytes

Description

This command specifies the MTU of IP packets sent over this line. The value can
be from 64 to 1000000 bytes.

vty-async ppp authentication

global

```
vty-async ppp authentication {chap | pap}
no vty-async ppp authentication {chap | pap}
```

Configures   VTY line features

Default   Disabled

Description

This command enables PPP authentication on the VTY asynchronous lines.

Reference
T-W

vty-async ppp use-tacacs   global

```
vty-async ppp use-tacacs
no vty-async ppp use-tacacs
```

Configures   VTY line features

Default   Disabled

Description

This command tells PPP sessions using VTY lines to use TACACS for authentication.

---

width   line

```
width characters
no width
```

Configures   The terminal width for a line

Default   80 characters

Description

This command sets the width, in *characters*, of a terminal line. Setting this value correctly helps deal with lines that are too long to be displayed on your terminal window or screen.

---

write   command

```
write erase
write memory
write network
write terminal
```

Description

The write commands are used to work with the current configuration. They are obsolete and have been replaced by the copy, show, and erase commands. Table 15-25 shows the correspondence between the two sets of commands.

Table 15-25: Write commands and their equivalents

Write command	Equivalent
write erase	erase startup-config
write memory	copy running-config startup-config
write network	copy running-config tftp
write terminal	show running-config

Index

We'd like to hear your suggestions for improving our indexes. Send email to *index@oreilly.com*.

editing
  access lists, 85
    named, 91
    TFTP or RCP, using, 100
  command line, keyboard shortcuts, 6
  terminal editing command, 544
editing command, 327
EIGRP (Enhanced IGRP), 139–150
  administrative distance for, 324
  authentication, 145
  auto-summary for subnet routes,
    disabling, 272
  bandwidth percent allowed, 367
  configuration, route
    summarization, 141–145
  enabling on network, 139–141
  features, summary of, 110
  hello interval, 379
  hold time for networks, 380
  IGRP network, converting to, 148
  metrics, 145
  passive interface command and, 112
  redistributing into RIP, 115, 119
  redistributing other protocols into, 147
  redistributing RIP into, using route
    maps, 121
  redistributing routes into OSPF, 497
  show commands, 146
  summarizing routes, 417
  tuning, 145
eigrp log-neighbor-changes
    command, 327
ELAN (Emulated LAN), 78, 295
  LECS database, name and id, 462
  setting default name, 307
enable command, 15, 327
  configuring IOS image download, 14
  entering privileged mode, 2
enable last-resort command, 328
enable password command, 26, 328
enable password, privilege levels, 231
enable secret command, 328
enable use-tacacs command, 329
encapsulation
  ARP packets, specifying type for, 262
  ATM, types used for, 73
  automatic detection of, 271
  Ethernet interfaces, types of, 51
  GRE, 553
  ISDN links, 52

PPP (see PPP)
  serial interfaces, 55
encapsulation command, 329
encryption
  enable mode passwords, 328
  key for TACACS server, 542
  key, radius server communications, 495
  passwords, 26, 230
  SNMP user authentication key and
    password, 531
  tunnels, 222–229
    configuring, 223–226
    DSS and DES, 222
    IPSec, 226–229
end command, 330
end station ID (ESI), 266
engine ID (SNMP)
  encryption of user password and
    authentication key, 532
  setting, 527
Enhanced IGRP (see EIGRP)
equal-cost load balancing, 137
erase command, 21, 330
erase commands, replacing write
    commands, 560
erase startup-config command, 23
erasing counters for statistics, 293
error messages
  current terminal session, 546
  receiving or blocking, 90
escape characters, terminal line, 544
escape codes for chat scripts, 292
escape sequences, prompt command, 25
escape-character command, 330
ESI (end station ID), 266
established connections, access lists, 89,
    92
Ethernet interfaces, 51
  bridging, 207–211
  configuring for router, 14
  encapsulation, 51
  ethernet0, IP address of, 57
  Fast Ethernet, 292
  outgoing frames, bridge group access
    list, 285
exception core-file command, 331
exception dump command, 331
exception memory command, 331
exception protocol command, 332
exception spurious-interrupt
    command, 332

hanging up automatically after closing
session, 271
hardware
ATM, 72
configuration, asynchronous lines, 57
flow control, 38
hardware addresses (see MAC addresses)
hardware flow control, 42
hash algorithms, 227
HDLC encapsulation, 55
compression, 299
headers
multicast packets, caching, 389
RTP and TCP, compressing, 348
RTP, compressing, 345
TCP/IP, compressing, 345
TCP/IP, compressing on Frame Relay
DLCI to IP address map, 349
hello interval
bridge-group, setting for, 286
EIGRP, 379
HSRP, changing, 537
IS-IS routing, 431
OSPF, 401
help command, 355
help (full), enabling on line
configuration, 354
hexadecimal numbers, NSAP
addresses, 75
history command, 356
history log, router commands used, 8
history, terminal, 545
hold time
BGP, 547
CDP packets, 290
EIGRP networks, 380
HSRP, 537
IS-IS, 431
NHRP, 396
hold-character command, 43, 356
hold-queue command, 357
hop counts, IGRP, 136
host broadcasts
secondary IP addresses, problems
with, 48
hostname command, 24, 357
hostnames
deleting, 27
mapping IP addresses to
enabling DNS, 27
mapping to IP addresses, 26

hosts
bridge, 280
determining most likely path to, 548
ICMP unceachable messages, 421
receiving SNMP traps, defining, 529
SNMP access, restricting, 30
static hostname, defining IP address
for, 380
Hot Standby Routing Protocol (see HSRP)
HSRP (Hot Standby Routing
Protocol), 206, 211–215, 536–538
load sharing, using for, 214
multiple group, 213
show standby command, 214
hssi external-loop-request command, 357
hssi internal-clock command, 357
HTTP server, enabling on router, 381
hub command, 358

I

iBGP, 167
implementing, checklist for, 172
ICMP
access list entries, 90
redirects, 412
unreachable messages, 49, 421
ICMP Router Discovery Protocol
(IRDP), 384
IEEE 802.2 packets, access lists for, 283
IGMP, 382–384, 404–409
ignore-dcd command, 358
IGP protocol, synchronizing with
BGP, 539
IGRP (Interior Gateway Routing
Protocol), 132–139
configuration, basic, 133–135
converting network to EIGRP, 148
Enhanced (see EIGRP)
features, summary of, 110
load balancing, 137
metric, calculating, 135
packet size (MTU), 136
range of network, modifying, 136
redistributing other protocols into, 139
IKE policy, configuring, 227
images, IOS, 10–23
backing up current to network
server, 15
execution location, 13
feature set, 12
filenames, 10

About the Author

James Boney has worked at Chesapeake Computer Consultants, Inc. for the last eight years as a consultant specializing in a wide variety of subjects: network design, network management, Unix administration, and programming in various languages (Perl, Java, Tcl/Tk, and C/C++).

For the last three years, he has been working on the vLab project, which allows complete access to Cisco routers over the Internet.

Jim lives in Pasadena, Maryland with his wife, Peggy.

Colophon

Our look is the result of reader comments, our own experimentation, and feedback from distribution channels. Distinctive covers complement our distinctive approach to technical topics, breathing personality and life into potentially dry subjects.

The animal on the cover of *Cisco IOS in a Nutshell* is a donkey, *Equus asinus*, also known as a domesticated ass. Today's donkeys are probably descendants of the African wild ass, and they were domesticated by the Egyptians in around 4000 B.C. They're about four feet tall, and they're known for their long ears, the short mane that looks a bit like a push broom, and the braying noise they make. The big ears and braying enabled wild asses to keep in touch across the distances that often separated them as they searched for sparse food sources in the African desert. Donkeys are relatives of the horse; though they are considerably smaller in stature than their cousins, they live longer, up to 25–30 years. They can also run as fast as 30 miles per hour.

Emily Quill was the production editor and Rachel Wheeler was the copyeditor for *Cisco IOS in a Nutshell*. Ann Schirmer and Sada Preisch provided quality control; Derek DiMatteo and Philip Dangler provided production assistance. Ellen Troutman wrote the index.

Hanna Dyer designed the cover of this book, based on a series design by Edie Freedman. The cover image is a 19th-century engraving from the Dover Pictorial Archive. Emma Colby produced the cover layout with QuarkXPress 4.1 using Adobe's ITC Garamond font.

Melanie Wang designed the interior layout, based on a series design by Nancy Priest. Mihaela Maier converted the files from Microsoft Word to FrameMaker 5.5.6 using tools created by Mike Sierra. The text and heading fonts are ITC Garamond Light and Garamond Book. The illustrations that appear in the book were produced by Robert Romano and Jessamyn Read using Macromedia FreeHand 9 and Adobe Photoshop 6. This colophon was written by Leanne Soylemez.

Whenever possible, our books use a durable and flexible lay-flat binding. If the page count exceeds this binding's limit, perfect binding is used.

How to stay in touch with O'Reilly

1. Visit Our Award-Winning Web Site

http://www.oreilly.com/

★ "Top 100 Sites on the Web" —PC Magazine
★ "Top 5% Web sites" —Point Communications
★ "3-Star site" —The McKinley Group

Our web site contains a library of comprehensive product information (including book excerpts and tables of contents), downloadable software, background articles, interviews with technology leaders, links to relevant sites, book cover art, and more. File us in your Bookmarks or Hotlist!

2. Join Our Email Mailing Lists

New Product Releases

To receive automatic email with brief descriptions of all new O'Reilly products as they are released, send email to:
ora-news-subscribe@lists.oreilly.com
Put the following information in the first line of your message (not in the Subject field):
subscribe ora-news

O'Reilly Events

If you'd also like us to send information about trade show events, special promotions, and other O'Reilly events, send email to:
ora-news-subscribe@lists.oreilly.com
Put the following information in the first line of your message (not in the Subject field):
subscribe ora-events

3. Get Examples from Our Books via FTP

There are two ways to access an archive of example files from our books:

Regular FTP

• ftp to:
  ftp.oreilly.com
  (login: anonymous
  password: your email address)
• Point your web browser to:
  ftp://ftp.oreilly.com/

FTPMAIL

• Send an email message to:
  ftpmail@online.oreilly.com
  (Write "help" in the message body)

4. Contact Us via Email

order@oreilly.com
To place a book or software order online. Good for North American and international customers.

subscriptions@oreilly.com
To place an order for any of our newsletters or periodicals.

books@oreilly.com
General questions about any of our books.

cs@oreilly.com
For answers to problems regarding your order or our products.

booktech@oreilly.com
For book content technical questions or corrections.

proposals@oreilly.com
To submit new book or software proposals to our editors and product managers.

international@oreilly.com
For information about our international distributors or translation queries. For a list of our distributors outside of North America check out:
http://www.oreilly.com/distributors.html

5. Work with Us

Check out our website for current employment opportunites:
http://jobs.oreilly.com/

O'Reilly & Associates, Inc.
1005 Gravenstein Hwy North
Sebastopol, CA 95472 USA
TEL 707-829-0515 or 800-998-9938
    (6am to 5pm PST)
FAX 707-829-0104

O'REILLY®

TO ORDER: **800-998-9938** • order@oreilly.com • www.oreilly.com
ONLINE EDITIONS OF MOST O'REILLY TITLES ARE AVAILABLE BY SUBSCRIPTION AT **safari.oreilly.com**
ALSO AVAILABLE AT MOST RETAIL AND ONLINE BOOKSTORES

International Distributors

http://international.oreilly.com/distributors.html • international@oreilly.com

UK, EUROPE, MIDDLE EAST, AND AFRICA (EXCEPT FRANCE, GERMANY, AUSTRIA, SWITZERLAND, LUXEMBOURG, AND LIECHTENSTEIN)

INQUIRIES
O'Reilly UK Limited
4 Castle Street
Farnham
Surrey, GU9 7HS
United Kingdom
Telephone: 44-1252-711776
Fax: 44-1252-734211
Email: information@oreilly.co.uk

ORDERS
Wiley Distribution Services Ltd.
1 Oldlands Way
Bognor Regis
West Sussex PO22 9SA
United Kingdom
Telephone: 44-1243-843294
UK Freephone: 0800-243207
Fax: 44-1243-843302 (Europe/EU orders)
or 44-1243-843274 (Middle East/Africa)
Email: cs-books@wiley.co.uk

FRANCE

INQUIRIES & ORDERS
Éditions O'Reilly
18 rue Séguier
75006 Paris, France
Tel: 33-1-40-51-71-89
Fax: 33-1-40-51-72-26
Email: france@oreilly.fr

GERMANY, SWITZERLAND, AUSTRIA, LUXEMBOURG, AND LIECHTENSTEIN

INQUIRIES & ORDERS
O'Reilly Verlag
Balthasarstr. 81
D-50670 Köln, Germany
Telephone: 49-221-973160-91
Fax: 49-221-973160-8
Email: anfragen@oreilly.de (inquiries)
Email: order@oreilly.de (orders)

CANADA

(FRENCH LANGUAGE BOOKS)
Les Éditions Flammarion ltée
375, Avenue Laurier Ouest
Montréal (Québec) H2V 2K3
Tel: 1-514-277-8807
Fax: 1-514-278-2085
Email: info@flammarion.qc.ca

HONG KONG
City Discount Subscription Service, Ltd.
Unit A, 6th Floor, Yan's Tower
27 Wong Chuk Hang Road
Aberdeen, Hong Kong
Tel: 852-2580-3539
Fax: 852-2580-6463
Email: citydis@ppn.com.hk

KOREA
Hanbit Media, Inc.
Chungmu Bldg. 210
Yonnam-dong 568-33
Mapo-gu
Seoul, Korea
Tel: 822-325-0397
Fax: 822-325-9697
Email: hant93@chollian.dacom.co.kr

PHILIPPINES
Global Publishing
G/F Benavides Garden
1186 Benavides Street
Manila, Philippines
Tel: 632-254-8949/632-252-2582
Fax: 632-734-5060/632-252-2733
Email: globalp@pacific.net.ph

TAIWAN
O'Reilly Taiwan
1st Floor, No. 21, Lane 295
Section 1, Fu-Shing South Road
Taipei, 106 Taiwan
Tel: 886-2-27099669
Fax: 886-2-27038802
Email: mori@oreilly.com

INDIA
Shroff Publishers & Distributors Pvt. Ltd.
12, "Roseland", 2nd Floor
180, Waterfield Road, Bandra (West)
Mumbai 400 050
Tel: 91-22-641-1800/643-9910
Fax: 91-22-643-2422
Email: spd@vsnl.com

CHINA
O'Reilly Beijing
SIGMA Building, Suite B809
No. 49 Zhichun Road
Haidian District
Beijing, China PR 100080
Tel: 86-10-8809-7475
Fax: 86-10-8809-7463
Email: beijing@oreilly.com

JAPAN
O'Reilly Japan, Inc.
Yotsuya Y's Building
7 Banch 6, Honshio-cho
Shinjuku-ku
Tokyo 160-0003 Japan
Tel: 81-3-3356-5227
Fax: 81-3-3356-5261
Email: japan@oreilly.com

SINGAPORE, INDONESIA, MALAYSIA, AND THAILAND
TransQuest Publishers Pte Ltd
30 Old Toh Tuck Road #05-02
Sembawang Kimtrans Logistics Centre
Singapore 597654
Tel: 65-4623112
Fax: 65-4625761
Email: wendiw@transquest.com.sg

AUSTRALIA
Woodslane Pty., Ltd.
7/5 Vuko Place
Warriewood NSW 2102
Australia
Tel: 61-2-9970-5111
Fax: 61-2-9970-5002
Email: info@woodslane.com.au

NEW ZEALAND
Woodslane New Zealand, Ltd.
21 Cooks Street (P.O. Box 575)
Waganui, New Zealand
Tel: 64-6-347-6543
Fax: 64-6-345-4840
Email: info@woodslane.com.au

ARGENTINA
Distribuidora Cuspide
Suipacha 764
1008 Buenos Aires
Argentina
Phone: 54-11-4322-8868
Fax: 54-11-4322-3456
Email: libros@cuspide.com

ALL OTHER COUNTRIES
O'Reilly & Associates, Inc.
1005 Gravenstein Hwy North,
Sebastopol, CA 95472 USA
Tel: 707-829-0515
Fax: 707-829-0104
Email: order@oreilly.com

O'REILLY®

TO ORDER: **800-998-9938** • **order@oreilly.com** • **www.oreilly.com**
ONLINE EDITIONS OF MOST O'REILLY TITLES ARE AVAILABLE BY SUBSCRIPTION AT **safari.oreilly.com**
ALSO AVAILABLE AT MOST RETAIL AND ONLINE BOOKSTORES